ROUTLEDGE HANDBOOK OF GLOBAL ECONOMIC HISTORY

The *Routledge Handbook of Global Economic History* documents and interprets the development of economic history as a global discipline from the later nineteenth century to the present day. Exploring the normative and relativistic nature of different schools and traditions of thought, this volume not only examines current paradigmatic western approaches, but also those conceived in less open societies and in varied economic, political and cultural contexts. In doing so, it clears the way for greater critical understanding and a more genuinely global approach to economic history.

This handbook brings together leading international contributors in order to systematically address cultural and intellectual traditions around the globe. Many of these are exposed for consideration for the first time in English. The chapters explore dominant ideas and historiographical trends, and open them up to critical transnational perspectives.

The volume is essential reading for academics and students in economic and social history. As this field of study is very much a bridge between the social sciences and humanities, the issues examined will also have relevance for those seeking to understand the evolution of other academic disciplines under the pressures of varied economic, political and cultural circumstances, on both national and global scales.

Francesco Boldizzoni is Research Professor in Economic History at the University of Turin and a life member of Clare Hall, Cambridge.

Pat Hudson is Emeritus Professor of Economic History at Cardiff University and recently completed a four year term as Visiting Professor in Economic History at the London School of Economics.

'Of all the subjects representing higher education in the humanities and social sciences, economic history has experienced almost no difficulties or resistance to taking the global turn. The distinguished editors of this collection of essays have recruited an impressive group of scholars from many national traditions to tell us how the field has evolved into the universal discipline for our times.' — Patrick K. O'Brien, Centennial Professor of Global Economic History, London School of Economics and Political Science.

'This Handbook is a splendid introduction to the way economic development and capitalism has been imagined and researched. Even more important, it's a powerful contribution to understanding modern societies everywhere from a world perspective, not just a European/American perspective. Researchers and students from all the social sciences, as well as specialists in economic history, will learn important lessons here.' — Raewyn Connell, Professor Emerita at the University of Sydney, and author of *Southern Theory: The Global Dynamics of Knowledge in Social Science.*

'To understand contemporary globalization, there is no question that comparative economic history provides an unparalleled vantage point for readers from any discipline. In this volume Boldizzoni and Hudson bring together a superb group of specialists in the field from around the globe.' — Carlos Marichal, Professor of Latin American Economic History, El Colegio de México.

'Boldizzoni and Hudson call to action a number of world experts to debate the contours of economic history for a global age. Whilst economic history has become a global field of research, they claim that it should not be a simple extension of the tools, narratives and methodologies adopted in the West. This book pioneers a new age for economic history.' — Giorgio Riello, Professor of Global History, University of Warwick.

'At last a book that explores the diverse approaches to economic history adopted across the world. A dominant Anglo-American account of the "Rise of the West" or "Great Divergence" is diluted and a new approach to world economic history comes to the fore. This is an important book for academics and university students who are genuinely interested in understanding, researching and publishing on this important subject.' — William J. Ashworth, University of Liverpool.

'This book will become required reading for economic historians who are interested in the historiography of their own field. Global economic history has so often been viewed from a particular national perspective. This book shows how different regions had different academic labour markets and political agendas, and these shaped how economic history was written.' — Helen Paul, University of Southampton.

ROUTLEDGE HANDBOOK OF GLOBAL ECONOMIC HISTORY

Edited by Francesco Boldizzoni and Pat Hudson

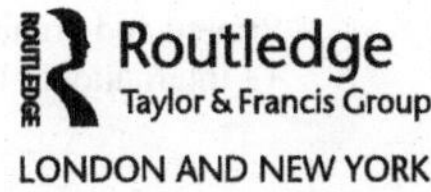
LONDON AND NEW YORK

First published 2016
by Routledge
2 Park Square, Milton Park, Abingdon, Oxon OX14 4RN

and by Routledge
711 Third Avenue, New York, NY 10017

Routledge is an imprint of the Taylor & Francis Group, an informa business

British Library Cataloguing in Publication Data
A catalogue record for this book is available from the British Library

Library of Congress Cataloging in Publication Data
Names: Boldizzoni, Francesco, 1979– editor. Hudson, Pat, 1948– editor.
Title: Routledge handbook of global economic history/edited by Francesco Boldizzoni and Pat Hudson.Other titles: Handbook of global economic history Description: New York: Routledge, 2016.
Includes index. Identifiers: LCCN 2015027151
ISBN 9781138838031 (hardback)
ISBN 9781315734736 (ebook) Subjects: LCSH: Economic history.
Classification: LCC HC21 .R68 2016 DDC 330.9—dc23LC record available at http://lccn.loc.gov/2015027151

ISBN: 978-1-138-83803-1 (hbk)
ISBN: 978-1-315-73473-6 (ebk)

Typeset in Bembo
by RefineCatch Limited, Bungay, Suffolk

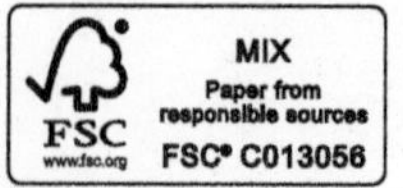

Printed and bound in Great Britain by
TJ International Ltd, Padstow, Cornwall

In memory of Jacek Kochanowicz, 1946–2014

CONTENTS

FIGURES

TABLES

CONTRIBUTORS

Erik Aerts, KU Leuven, Belgium.

Luiz Felipe de Alencastro, Escola de Economia de São Paulo, Brazil.

Luis Bértola, Universidad de la República, Montevideo, Uruguay.

Francesco Boldizzoni, University of Turin, Italy.

Leonid Borodkin, Lomonosov Moscow State University, Russia.

Ulbe Bosma, Vrije Universiteit Amsterdam and IISG, the Netherlands.

Li Bozhong, Hong Kong University of Science and Technology, China.

Antonie Doležalová, Charles University, Prague, Czech Republic.

Bill Freund, University of KwaZulu-Natal, South Africa.

Jean-Yves Grenier, Ecole des Hautes Etudes en Sciences Sociales, Paris, France.

Ylva Hasselberg, University of Uppsala, Sweden.

Jan-Otmar Hesse, University of Bayreuth, Germany.

Roman Holec, Comenius University, Bratislava, Slovakia.

Pat Hudson, Cardiff University, UK.

Iñaki Iriarte-Goñi, University of Zaragoza, Spain.

Huri Islamoglu, Boğaziçi University, Istanbul, Turkey.

Jacek Kochanowicz, University of Warsaw, Poland.

György Kövér, Eötvös Loránd University, Budapest, Hungary.

Sandra Kuntz Ficker, El Colegio de México, Mexico.

Naomi R. Lamoreaux, Yale University and the NBER, USA.

Patrick Manning, University of Pittsburgh, USA.

Douglas McCalla, University of Guelph, Canada.

David Meredith, Oxford University, UK.

Ayodeji Olukoju, University of Lagos, Nigeria.

Deborah Oxley, All Souls College, Oxford, UK.

Prasannan Parthasarathi, Boston College, USA.

Javier Rodríguez Weber, Universidad de la República, Montevideo, Uruguay.

Kaoru Sugihara, National Graduate Institute for Policy Studies, Tokyo, Japan.

ACKNOWLEDGEMENTS

Many colleagues from around the world have contributed to the production of this volume. From the outset, we have benefited from the advice and support of Peter Burke and Patrick O'Brien. We had further encouragement from Joseph Inikori, Jürgen Kocka, Chris Lloyd, Linda Grove, Janet Hunter, Simon Szreter and others, who attended our lively session at the IEHA Congress in Stellenbosch in 2012. For discussing the scope of the project, suggesting contributors and for commenting upon individual chapters, we owe thanks to Frank Ankersmit, Ivan Berend, Tine Bruland, Marco Cattini, Qian Chengdan, William Gervase Clarence-Smith, Kent Deng, Mark Elvin, Leigh Gardner, Peter Gatrell, Mark Harrison, Anthony Hopkins, Alejandra Irigoin, Even Lange, Beverly Lemire, Colin Lewis, Carlos Marichal, Philippe Minard, Laura Panza, Alessandro Stanziani, Alice Teichova, Marcel van der Linden and Herman van der Wee. Special thanks go to Keith Tribe for his support and for translating chapter 7, and to Joanna Wawrzyniak for dealing with the final processing of the Polish chapter (13) following the untimely death of her father Jacek Kochanowicz. The volume is dedicated to him as a tribute to Jacek's intellectual calibre and subtle understanding of our field.

It has been a privilege to work with our large international group of contributors some of whom have maintained their commitment to the project over several years. All have shown great flexibility and fortitude in responding to our ideas and suggestions, and have remained patient through the many delays that have occurred, as might be expected, with a transnational, multi-authored volume of this kind. Some members of the team have read several contributions and assisted with comments and suggestions for improvements. Only the editors know fully how much several of our authors have sacrificed to ensure the timely delivery of their contributions and in cutting substantial pieces of work down to size. Only we can thank them fully for this, and we do, most sincerely.

Elements of the project have been exposed and debated in lectures and seminars at the University of Glasgow, the Graduate Institute in Geneva, the University of Warwick, El Colegio de México, Central European University and the University of Reading, and we thank audiences for their suggestions and ideas. Anonymous referees have been very supportive and have made useful suggestions except for one who thought that the story of economic history was universal: evolving in the same way in all places, though at different speeds, and improving with the accumulated knowledge and application of theories and tools with universal applicability! The many and varied stories included in this volume prove that this is not the case. Our editorial team at Routledge, particularly Emily Kindleysides and Laura Johnson, have been enthusiastic about the project and gently guided it throughout the publication process. We thank them for encouraging additional chapters to ensure that our story of the international development of economic history is relatively comprehensive.

All faults remaining are our own. If the volume enlightens our colleagues, as much as it has ourselves, and repays, even in part, the great effort and labour of love involved in producing it, we will be delighted.

1

GLOBAL ECONOMIC HISTORY

Towards an interpretive turn[1]

Francesco Boldizzoni and Pat Hudson

This Handbook differs from a conventional set of essays on global history. Rather it aims collectively to document, evaluate, and hence to relativize, varied ideas, frameworks and methodologies that have characterized economic history as it has emerged in different parts of the world. By introducing an eclectic and rich repertoire of traditions past and present, and particularly by exposing insights that are ignored or sidelined in the English-speaking literature, it is hoped that the volume might encourage greater pluralism of approaches in the subject and promote an interpretive framework that is, above all, sensitive to time and place. The specific purpose of the Handbook, and the focus on economic and social history, makes it complementary to earlier and concurrent projects such as Iggers and Wang (2008), Sachsenmaier (2011), Woolf (2011), Barnett (2015) and the *Oxford History of Historical Writing* (2011–15).

Historians have a tendency to view global history merely as an extension of the *geographical range* of their studies. Employing a restricted toolbox of concepts and methods to various regions of the world, they see comparative and connective histories as global research, simply because they draw evidence from more than one world region.[2] But the frameworks and methodologies employed are often too ethnocentric or anachronistic to make one confident of the value of the endeavour. The approach favoured here, one we hope that the Handbook might promote, interrogates the historical experience of far-flung continents, nations and regions, together with their associated historiographies, in order to highlight the genesis and wealth of alternative, and often appropriate, tools of analysis that might be more widely employed. Varied ecological, economic, political and cultural contexts have given rise to fundamentally different challenges in the long-term quest for food security, material comforts and social development. These challenges have moulded the definitions and the parameters of social science and the humanities in the course of their evolution. An appreciation of the global history of a discipline, on the border between humanities and social science, highlights not only the shortcomings of certain frameworks and the dead-end nature of some approaches, but also the potential that lies hidden in literatures that are little accessed because of linguistic, cultural and ideological barriers and prejudices.

The contingent and contested nature of the emergence of dominant anglophone approaches, their potential and their weaknesses, are best revealed by considering their evolutionary context and by comparing them with contrasting ideas and methodologies conceived within, and in relation to, other very different world contexts. A first step in recognizing where a truly global approach to history might lead is to rediscover, and to be reflexive in our appreciation of, the ideas and literatures that have populated our global past.

Globalization and the historical imaginary

These are interesting times for history-writing. The end of the Cold War, the rise of new powers such as China, India and Brazil and the acceleration of the globalization process have followed one another rapidly during the last few decades. It is no longer easy to view the processes of industrialization and modernization as congruent, nor to view economic development as a unilinear phenomenon. Debates surrounding the socio-economic and political impact of contemporary globalization in different world contexts have stirred parallel interests about global economic dynamics in the past. Contemporary concerns, amongst other things, about growing intra- and inter-national inequality of wealth and income; about the problems of modern measures of comparative economic success or well-being; about free markets and the role of state intervention; and about the effects of consumerism upon the environment, demand a response from historians.

At the same time, an accelerated globalization of higher education and training, and of intellectual ideas, has also taken place, fostered by the revolution in international communication, the expansion of the internet and the wider availability of electronic resources. This has of course meant that widely accepted approaches are more readily exposed to critiques arising from different global political and cultural viewpoints than in the past. However, these critiques are often ignored, especially when they come from the periphery. The globalization of scholarship has in fact endorsed the power of North Atlantic academic orthodoxies through control of major journals, conferences, funding for research and global intellectual prestige. Some alternative traditions have been insulated more fully from leading paradigms than have others and western perspectives have not been passively received elsewhere, rather they have undergone processes of acceptance, modification and rejection. In addition, the 'western canon' has indeed incorporated valuable insights from other global predispositions, although these have often been radically changed in the process, in ways that are not always acknowledged (see chapter 26). Overall, as far as economic history is concerned, alongside a widening geographical range of work, the globalization of academia has, perhaps paradoxically, also brought a narrowing of the main focus of transnational scholarship. As in the past, but more so, the nature and timing of western 'primacy' and whether or not this was an inevitable outcome of precocious human proclivities in favourable environments, dominates the literature. The motivations and long-term goals of economic action, and the ecological penalties of energy-intensive and materially wasteful economic growth are seldom questioned by economic historians these days, although they have been a major concern for such historians in the past and figure prominently in several of the narratives in this volume. A number of scholars, sensitive to the attraction of other cultural perspectives, have attempted to challenge the canon from within.[3] But, despite the disagreements that characterize what is a deeply divided field, it remains the case that the main story in global economic history has thus far been, and is increasingly, constructed around the rise of the West.

A few years ago, Amartya Sen argued that western historians and social scientists these days generally write from the perspective of the 'end of history'.[4] In other words they think within the assumption that liberal 'capitalism' and associated traditions of 'freedom' and 'democracy' have so triumphed globally that alternative paths or patterns of economic, political and cultural change, and the insights that these may have generated, are generally inferior and have little to offer to current intellectual endeavour. In an era marked by the dominance and confidence of such perspectives, we have tended both to ignore alternative approaches and traditions and to lose sight of the idea that history (and other disciplines), as well as 'society' itself, will inevitably look different if observed from a diversity of cultural and political viewpoints, past and present.

The western canon in global history

A considerable portion of the 'rise of the West' literature has a Whig character and carries a triumphalist, teleological agenda. Strong claims are made about western exceptionalism, the origins of which are traced back to the Enlightenment, the Glorious Revolution and sometimes to the Middle Ages or even Antiquity. Whig accounts often rely on peculiarly West European if not British culture, institutions or rationality promoting improvements and inventions and/or the rise of bourgeois virtues, first in North-western Europe but spreading elsewhere thereafter (with leads and lags), changing the nature of society globally (Landes 1999; Jones 2003; Clark 2007; McCloskey 2010; Mokyr 2010; Jacob 2014). Although W. W. Rostow's 'non-communist' stage theory of growth, which was designed to be universally applicable, is now largely discredited as a legacy of the Cold War (at least in its detailed specifications), his underlying assumptions still frequently surface in the literature, if only implicitly. The master path remains one of market-driven capital-intensive growth in capitalist–liberal states, as pursued by the West over the past two or three centuries, and this is seen as the *natural* path towards development and modernization. Qualitative and quantitative differences in the structure and performance of other parts of the world are seen as resulting largely from institutional constraints and distortions that have prevented them from following the normal route of development (North 2005; Greif 2006; North et al. 2009; van Zanden 2009a; Acemoglu and Robinson 2012).

But the more we talk about the constraints on human behaviour the more we implicitly accept that there is some invariable human nature (across the world and across cultures, as well as over time) to be constrained. This is clearly an illusion (Sahlins 2004a and 2008; Halperin 1994; Archer 2000). Claims about 'superior' western values or rationality similarly betray an old essentialist belief at odds with what anthropologists have taught us about cultural diversity as an adaptive response to different environmental circumstances. Many forms of economic conduct deviate from the pursuit of utilitarian goals within individualistic societies dominated by materialist concerns. These forms of conduct correspond to an amazing historical variety of transactional modes and sorts of societal organization past and present (Polanyi 1957; Gudeman 2001; Granovetter 2005; Hann and Hart 2011) but they are too often dismissed by economists and historians as second-best solutions to the 'problem of scarcity' or a distraction from the pursuit of ever more rapid growth. The western fallacy of 'particular universalism' ascribes to societies far away in time and space the values of a rationalist, acquisitive individualism that is alien to them and at the same time lambastes them when they do not fulfil the expectations.[5]

In recent decades, rational choice theory, sophisticated and bolstered by the new institutional economics, has strengthened the authority of neoclassical analysis of markets and of endogenous growth theory, the assumptions of which are repeated as axiomatic in undergraduate and graduate teaching at most of the West's major academic institutions (Marglin 2008). Growing efficiency, the removal of constraints upon action and performance, and increasing incentives to profit-seeking and innovation can be appealing goals. But whilst they occupy the centre ground in research, assumptions about the culture and purposes of economic activity lie unquestioned. Little outside of the box of endogeneity gets considered and the highest prestige work earns its points for employing in formal models, in game-theoretical or in discursive forms, a limited number of tautological 'buzz' concepts surrounding variations in transaction costs – moral hazard, agency problems, asymmetric information – that are seen to distort what is accepted as natural market behaviour.

Alongside the preoccupation with modern economic growth, defined to replicate the western pattern of capital-, energy- and consumption-intensive development, there has developed a craze within the 'western canon' for measuring comparative rates of growth transnationally even though the pitfalls of such exercises are legion and their value, beyond very restrictive purposes, shaky. One of the drivers of this trend is the perceived need to identify the extent to which various parts of the globe were ahead or behind in terms of levels of per capita gross domestic product (GDP), or average real wages at particular points in time (e.g. Maddison 2007; van Zanden 2009b; Allen 2009; Broadberry et al. 2015). Leaving aside the contentious implication that comparative development is best viewed as some sort of race, the major measurements used in time series and comparative panel data have fundamental problems when applied retrospectively and comparatively. This is unsurprising given that they were originally conceived as a guide to economic planning by western governments in the interwar period and not as tools of cross-cultural or cross-temporal comparison. Neither were they originally intended as measurements of the success or failure of economies (Kuznets 1953; see Speich 2011). Inadequate evidence and lack of commensurability of data across time and space compromise comparative figures. Data is always drawn from the recorded economy which means that conventional yardsticks of growth are most seriously distorting for economies with a large informal or (inadequately recorded) self-employment sector (Jerven 2014; Coyle 2014: 106ff.). Information is likely to be fuller for economies where the state is strong and keeps good records for fiscal and other purposes. This leads to the problem of circularity in that measures such as GDP and real wages are sometimes a better indicator of the strength of the state than of real economic change.[6]

The impact of these approaches, concepts and measures on history-writing has proven irresistible especially in the United States where they largely originated and where they have been absorbed to the point of appearing as common sense on the part of a large proportion of academics in the discipline (Boldizzoni 2011; Lamoreaux, chapter 3 in this volume).[7] They have also had a considerable influence in parts of Western Europe, particularly in Britain and the Netherlands. Such frameworks and paradigms have not however been easily adopted by those wishing to demonstrate the progress of ideas and of the discipline in other parts of the globe. For example, as early as 1979, in a collection of abstracts and assessments of major works and schools of Japanese economic history, the original structure of the volume that had been suggested by Bert Hoselitz (possibly the most eclectic member of the Chicago economics department at the time), turned out to be unworkable: 'the concepts of development and of quantitative economic history as taught in U.S. colleges and universities [did] not provide a useful editorial framework for the organization and presentation of the . . . book'. Instead the emphasis had to be placed upon 'the structure and dynamics of the entire societal system': a 'system consciousness' in which the *raison d'être* of economic history lay in its contribution to a better understanding of politics and culture as well as the economy (Sumiya and Taira 1979: x).

Post-Californian approaches and their limits

The most prominent globally cited alternative to the 'rise of the West' accounts has grown out of the work of the California school which spread to Europe via the LSE-based Global Economic History Network (GEHN), its continental offspring, the European Network in

Universal and Global History (ENIUGH) and the more material- and trade-history oriented Warwick Centre for Global History.[8] The Californian and post-Californian response to Whig scholarship, since Kenneth Pomeranz's *The Great Divergence* (2000), has attempted to minimize the importance of precocious western cultural factors, emphasizing instead geographical elements or factor endowment constraints that prevented other economies from keeping pace with the West. Outright rejection of the institutional explanation, which at the beginning was a hallmark of this approach, has in time given way to a more ambivalent attitude on that front. The post-Californians have also downplayed the significance of the first industrial revolution and reconceptualized it as a transitory phase of primacy or just one of the many efflorescences experienced by the world's civilizations over the long term. The economies of China, India and Europe, it is argued, were comparably advanced in the seventeenth and eighteenth centuries and, after an interlude, the gap is now closing again. This perspective has the potential to dislodge the western breakthrough to modern economic growth from its determining place in the literature.

Central to the approach is the methodology of 'reciprocal comparison' proposed by R. Bin Wong, applied by Pomeranz and subsequently taken up by many others. The idea behind reciprocal comparison is that both sides of the comparison (for instance, the British and Chinese economic trajectories) should be viewed 'as "deviations" when seen through the expectations of the other, rather than leaving one as always the norm' (Pomeranz 2000: 8). The contribution of some scholars to opening up the field to new perspectives, based on this premise, has been substantial. Particularly inspiring has been Patrick O'Brien's (2010) invitation to treat British industrialization as a conjuncture (one of many) in global history. He joins Chakrabarty (2000) in suggesting that European thought on the subject of development must be deprovincialized by exploring the experience of regions well removed from the early industrializing core. In this perspective, 'delays' of decades or even centuries between national experiences of 'take-off', and the analogy of a competitive race, lose much of the importance traditionally attached to them. Differences in initial conditions as well as in the perceived nature of constraints upon development also lose some of their explanatory value. Moreover, by questioning East–West dichotomies such as state-led versus stateless growth (Vries 2015), or unfree versus free labour (van der Linden 2008; Stanziani 2014), the 'new global history' has exposed a number of weaknesses that undermine the foundations of Whig grand narratives.

This notwithstanding, post-Californian approaches have serious limits. Despite the best of intentions, some of these limits are inherent in the concept of reciprocal comparison. As Prasannan Parthasarathi has noted, while 'this procedure [of comparison] denaturalizes the European path of development . . ., it continues to operate within the framework of presences and absences, of things that Europe possessed but Asia did not'. Capital-intensive industrialization is still seen as the master path 'unless it is prevented from emerging', and 'the plural possibilities for change that existed in the eighteenth century' are not taken into account (2013: 76). Another issue is the casualness with which tools from western social science are advocated for and sometimes applied to the Global South in order to make the analysis of such regions more congruent with the theoretical mainstream. For example, Gareth Austin (2007) applauds the application of both public choice theory and the new institutional economics to the African past. By claiming that *homo oeconomicus* was indigenous to Africa, global historians wish to liberate the continent from 'condescending' colonial stereotypes but there is a danger that they also do a disservice to African history. Although adoption of these frameworks may increase the relevance of African history to broader global social science debates, the approach is in thrall to the 'western illusion of human nature' and other deterministic assumptions underlying the supposed universal applicability of tools and outlook.[9]

The main problem at the root of such shortcomings lies in the positivist understanding that Californians and post-Californians share with their predecessors about the comparative method. There are no clear criteria for determining whether or not a specific theoretical tool is suitable for application to a certain problem, area or epoch. The historian is supposed to be an external observer who is in the position to detect 'absences', 'accidents', 'obstacles' and 'blockages' precisely because of his or her third-party condition. But historians inevitably project onto the past their own values and categories *unless* they are committed to a *reflexive interpretation* of the social and cultural systems of which they are part as well as of those that form the object of their enquiry. (We return to this aspect in the following section.) A related problem lies in the fact that global history is still very much a western enterprise. It is written by western historians (mostly from Anglo-American universities), and published in journals whose editorial board is made up of the same scholars. Not surprisingly, debates tend to be self-referential. As Dominic Sachsenmaier (2011: 109) observes,

> most global historical scholarship published in other languages and countries is hardly even recognized by its peer group in the United States. Although the declared aim to 'let others speak' may have been applied to the study of the past, there are strong indications that our international academic communities remain as hierarchical, Western-centric, and imbalanced as they were a hundred years ago.

This situation has generated dissatisfaction in the West itself but, above all, in the developing world. As research and historical analysis in and of Latin America, Asia and Africa continues to grow, scholars from the Global South and East would like to see their contributions recognized more centrally by the profession, rather than finding their work confined to footnotes or used as a source of figures and information (Olukoju, chapter 23 in this volume). In a recent article, Erik Green and Pius Nyambara (2015) argued that, although valuable research in the field has been carried out at sub-Saharan universities, only a tiny fraction of this work gets published in western journals because of irreducible differences between the way the discipline is conceived in Africa and in the English-speaking world. African historians, as opposed to Anglo-American Africanists, are uninterested in applying theoretical insights from mainstream economics and their work is devalued partly as a result. The strength of indigenous research lies in its interdisciplinarity, the employment of unorthodox political economy, and the use of multiple local sources including non-documentary evidence (Olukoju, Freund, Manning, chapters 23, 24, 25, respectively, in this volume).[10] The counterargument that indigenous African research is less abundant and of a lower quality, if not merely descriptive, because of the poor financial circumstances and resources of local universities (Austin 2015), is unsatisfactory given the range and quality of research being produced, especially if one takes a broader and less ethnocentric definition of the field. This reaction in any case misses the point by implying that if indigenous scholars had better economic resources, they would be willing to embrace North Atlantic theory and enthusiastically reframe their own research within fashionable western templates. This has not inevitably happened in better resourced parts of the non-western world, nor even within large parts of Western Europe, as many chapters in this volume demonstrate. The Global South has its own lively and thought-provoking theoretical traditions (Connell 2007) but they receive limited recognition in the metropole.

The case for an interpretive turn

A thought experiment may be useful at this point. Suppose that two subjects, *A* and *B*, are observing the behaviour *x* of another subject *C*. Observer *A* characterizes *x* as wrongdoing and declares that *C* is 'corrupt' or 'deformed'. *B*, on the other hand, although viewing the behaviour as wrongdoing, rejects the moral judgement of *A* and endeavours to find some extenuating circumstances: for example, *C* was 'forced by someone or something', 'acted in self-defence', or again: 'it was not *C*'s fault that she received the wrong education'. What eludes both *A* and *B* is that *C* (and possibly also *D, E, F*, . . .) may not herself view behaviour *x* as wrong at all. She sees nothing strange about it. *A* and *B* have no way to find this out unless they respectfully interrogate *C*. However, they are reluctant to do this and uninterested in listening to the answers. *A* has fundamentalist views about how the world should work and the civilizing mission of her culture. *B*, for her part, is content to ensure that *C*, for whom she feels sympathy, is not labelled 'corrupt' or 'deformed'. *C* is too busy trying to get her own voice heard to challenge external ethnocentric impositions.

It is clear that, if *A* represents the Whig-type, *B* the post-Californian, *C* and *x* the actors and processes of global economic history, conspicuously absent from this picture is a concept of culture that allows one to evaluate the actors' behaviour, and its outcome or performance, against the actors' own ends. For Marc Bloch, historical comparisons require 'a certain similarity between observed phenomena' and 'a certain dissimilarity between the environments in which they occur' (1928: 17) but these superficial resemblances ('au premier coup d'œil', as he writes) cannot, per se, suggest explanations. Facts, which are the result of actions, do not contain information about 'causes', nor does the historian possess some form of intersubjective knowledge. If they are not to be baseless, arbitrary exercises, comparisons must be made, and conclusions drawn, only after a preliminary *interpretive act* aimed at grasping the *meaning* of actions to those on the ground (rather than to those sitting on the jury or the referees' bench). To Clifford Geertz we owe awareness that 'man is an animal suspended in webs of significance he himself has spun'; those webs form the culture in which human action is embedded. Hence the analysis of culture should not be 'an experimental science in search of law but an interpretive one in search of meaning' (1973: 5).

Max Weber first envisaged the idea of webs of significance but the concept of interpretation was rooted in German hermeneutics from at least the late nineteenth century and the work of Wilhelm Dilthey. The latter theorized the distinction between *Erklären* (causal explanation), as the guiding principle of natural sciences, and the *Verstehen* (interpretive understanding) at the basis of humanistic enquiry, with various degrees of combination between the two being necessary in different contexts (see Makkreel 1992). By the interwar period, the interpretive method had spread across the humanities and social sciences and was common, if debated, in political economy and in nascent economic history throughout Europe (see Parts II and III of this volume). When Werner Sombart published his *Drei Nationalökonomien* (1930), he described the knowledge based on *Verstehen* as the highest form of economic knowledge. In the postwar era this view was gradually, but fairly comprehensively, sidelined by the rise of American social science founded on pragmatism and logical empiricism (Steinmetz 2005: 3–25; Mirowski 2005). Yet, in the 1970s it started to re-emerge powerfully, in France, Italy as well as in the United States itself – hence the cultural turn, the rise of microhistory and the reaction against *histoire sérielle* within western historiographical traditions.[11]

Unfortunately, the revolution did not fulfil its promise. Quite apart from the excesses of postmodernism, the *fin de siècle* anti-positivist reaction too often went hand in hand with a rejection of the economy as an object of study. Keen to avoid the ideological taint of historical materialism, as well as disillusioned with neoliberal, present-centred economic discourse, historians often threw out the baby with the bath water. The cultural turn could have represented an opportunity to reflect on the motivational sphere underlying economic life and the limits of explanatory objectification in this field. But global economic history has been largely unaffected by these developments and thus remains shackled by an outdated idea of historical comparison. This can be traced back to the historical sociology of the 1960s and 1970s, exemplified by William Sewell's misinterpretation of Bloch's 'logic of comparative history' which he reduced to 'hypothesis testing' (Sewell 1967). In order to overcome the problem it is, in our view, advisable to return to Bloch's original formulation, keeping in mind his repeated warnings against anachronism and focusing, first of all, on decoding symbols. In any society, decisions involved in production, distribution and consumption, and acts of exchange and monetary practices, embody specific conventions and rules of behaviour that must be seen as symbolic acts loaded with meaning about the ways in which historical actors view the world.[12] This way, and once the societal value structure is accounted for, it will be clear that absence of sustained economic growth does not always indicate a 'failure'; that development, industrialization and modernization follow multiple paths; and that for some human groups, optimal adaptation to the ecosystem makes some of these transitions unnecessary.[13] In other words, although historical processes *do* have a logic, the overarching categories derived from standard economic and social analysis have no universal meaning.

Table 1.1 contrasts the three approaches to global economic history that are described in this chapter. Each of them assigns a specific role and weight to a set of factors that are commonly invoked to explain economic outcomes. Indeed no single practitioner perfectly fits any of these definitions; they should rather be regarded as ideal types. For example, not all Whig historiography is equally judgemental about culture and not all post-Californians would subscribe to the utilitarian incentive-response view of human nature. But the table elucidates quite well the distinctive features of the interpretive approach. The 'rise of the West' literature sees culture (b) as 'positive' or 'negative' depending on its supposed effects on economic performance. Post-Californian accounts, on the other hand, reject the concept in order to avoid these value judgements. The interpretive approach takes the opposite stance: it accepts cultural differences as foundational and considers economic outcomes to be a function of culturally determined societal preferences. It also acknowledges the pervasive influence of

Table 1.1 Modes of explanation

Approach	*(a) Human nature*	*(b) Culture*	*(c) Institutions*	*(d) Physical environment*	*(e) Power*
Whig/New institutional	Utilitarian, incentive-response model	Defined as positive or negative; constrains (a)	Defined as positive or negative; constrain (a)	Not relevant	Absent
Post-Californian	Substantially utilitarian, incentive-response model	Not relevant	May constrain (a)	Constrains (a)	No consensus
Interpretive	Humans mostly a product of nurture	Not subject to value judgements	Result from (b), (d), (e)	Interacts with (b)	Pervades economic life

physical environment (d) and power relations (e) on economic life. Unlike the new institutional economics, which takes institutions (c) as given and endorsed by path dependency, the approach to economic history we are advocating here sees them as shaped by all of the other forces. They are thus mutable but not subject to a unilinear trajectory.

The Handbook: structure and central questions

The international team of contributors assembled for the Handbook are specialists familiar with the economic history and the historiography of their respective world regions. Whenever possible historians who were trained and/or had based their career within their indigenous culture were favoured. A distinctive contribution of the chapters therefore comes from their privileged access to sources. This is an aspect often overlooked by global historians who have got accustomed to interpretations based upon cherry-picked secondary materials and upon inadequate, partial and delayed translations. We are not suggesting that indigenous scholars are inevitably more qualified than others to interpret their native cultures although we do accept, other things being equal, that they have the opportunity to be better informed and that indigenous and external perspectives are likely to differ.

Contributors were tasked to examine the evolution of economic historiographies in each part of the world in relation to concerns dictated by local, national and international contexts, from the inception of the discipline (and its precursors) to the present. A common agenda of questions (see below) was devised in order to facilitate a better comparative analysis of the findings overall, which we attempt, in a preliminary way, in chapter 26. Authors, however, decided to interpret our agenda in a multitude of unforeseen ways. Some of the essays are built around a clear-cut thesis and the analytical focus prevails over the aim of documenting the wealth of intellectual accomplishments. Others appear to be more concerned with preserving the detail of national and institutional traditions. As editors, we have deliberately avoided superimposing an artificial uniformity over the collection. Differences in emphasis and style offer important clues about how individual historians and societies wish to represent and to understand themselves.

The agenda encouraged contributors to relate their narratives to influences derived from the trajectory of economic development in each region, the dominant sectors of the economy, the position of the society within the power relations of world trade, the nature of the polity and shifts in these factors over time. Specific questions for the project overall included: how and why do approaches and methodologies within a discipline vary between nations and cultures, as well as over time? What has been the impact of specific cultural, economic and political concerns on the definition and boundaries of economic history, as well as upon the approaches and methods of study employed? To what degree have politically and economically powerful nations, cultures and ideologies influenced the emergence and evolution of the field internationally? What impact have alternative or counter-approaches had, and upon what foundations have these been built? Why is economic history in some contexts defined largely by topic or subject matter, and in others defined largely by methodology? Are there lesser known approaches to the subject hidden away in work which is not defined as economic history in the eyes of the dominant canon? Why are these approaches marginalized and do they become more salient if one takes the sort of trans-cultural approach to the global history of the discipline that this volume has in mind?

Contributors were asked to consider the following specific factors that may have influenced the emergence and nature of the field of economic history in their location. These have obviously been relevant to very different degrees and in different combinations.

1 The context of the emergence of social science and statistical movements.
2 State formation: national and nationalistic histories, ideology, instrumentalism and associated policy imperatives.
3 Openness to cross-national and cross-political influences; and, conversely, the degree of internal political and intellectual repression.
4 State support and state policy regarding intellectual and academic development (past and present), together with funding imperatives.
5 Institutional factors in relation to education, science and intellectual enquiry.
6 The impact of past and contemporary globalization.

The volume's structure has been designed to suggest a reading itinerary that proceeds from what has been the 'core' of the late twentieth-century world system towards the 'periphery'. Our point of departure is the broad cultural area of the Anglosphere (including its accommodation in settler contexts). We then go through the hundred nuances of the continental West. Thence we turn to East European historiographies: their valuable contribution has been almost completely neglected since the dissolution of the Soviet bloc. The journey then continues towards Asia (taking the reader from the Middle East, through India, to China and Japan), Central and South America (in its Spanish- and Portuguese-speaking components) and sub-Saharan Africa (particularly Western and Southern). Much space is devoted to 'marginal Europe' and to regions of the globe often far removed from the commonly accepted intellectual core of the field. This is because we are convinced, as much as was Sidney Pollard (with respect to Europe), that 'the margin, generally pitied or despised, could be, at times, ahead of the rest, at the cutting edge of economic and social advance' (1997: 1). We are also of the view, following Chakrabarty, that global history will be best served by exploring how it may be renewed both 'from and for the margins' (2000: 16).

The chapters in the Handbook are of value in and of themselves as narratives of the national and regional development of economic history, exposing much work that is little known to anglophone readers. Together the chapters constitute the first attempt at a global history of our field of study. As attempts at self-understanding, the historiographies in the volume offer precious clues to the interpretation of past economic cultures and practices making us aware of the power of contemporary western intellectual templates and filters. The point of this exercise is not to explore regional details just for their own sake. The purpose is rather to conceive a history of the whole in and from its details – a *Detailgeschichte des Ganzen* (Medick 1996: 23–4). Hopefully our project will form a first step away from an old global history seen as standing above national and regional histories and towards a new one that rebuilds our knowledge from understandings found on the ground and, to an important extent, reflected in the rich writings of our forebears.

Notes

1 Some of the concepts we introduce here have been elaborated more thoroughly on two recent occasions: Pat Hudson's Tawney lecture on 'Industrialisation, Global History and the Ghost of Rostow', University of Warwick, 30 March 2014; Francesco Boldizzoni's AMHE lecture 'Do Nations Really Fail? Reconceptualizing the History of Development', El Colegio de México, 17 February 2015. A recording of the former, and the text of the latter, are available respectively at http://www.ehs.org.uk/multimedia/tawney-lecture-2014-industrialisation-global-history-and-the-ghost-of-rostow and http://www.amhe.mx/jornadas/docs/Colmex_lecture.pdf. (Sites accessed 29 May 2015.)

2 This approach is well summarized in Bayly's (2004) textbook. For his own critical take on global economic history, see Washbrook (2013).

3 For example, Fernández-Armesto (1995), Frank (1998), Hobson (2004), Goody (2004).
4 Michael Portillo's series on Democracy, BBC Radio 4, 18 May 2010. The original statement regarding the end of history in this sense is Fukuyama (1992).
5 The concept of 'particular universalism' was introduced by Bruno Latour (1991: 105).
6 GDP in many economies is also less appropriate for growth measurement than gross national product (GNP) which is net of the earnings of foreign direct investment. Difficulties also arise in applying a transnationally acceptable deflator. For GDP the 1990 Geary–Khamis dollar is generally used and, for real wages, a silver standard: both add further and unequal distortion to the appearance of temporal and spatial differences.
7 On 'rationalist individualism', and its embeddedness in American culture, see Wagner (2000).
8 Their main journal is the *Journal of Global History* (founded 2005) which adds to the *Journal of World History* (founded in 1990, restructured in 2003).
9 On this anxiety about being relevant to social science debates, see Hopkins (2009), who also introduced his fellow Africanists to the approaches of mainstream economics – with a word of warning. The rather frustrating outcome of the attempted conversation is testified by the economists' contemptuous reaction (e.g. Fenske 2010).
10 The use of non-written sources was pioneered by the Nigerian sociologist Akinsola Akiwowo. West African scholars have often drawn on radical political economy syncretically merged, in French-speaking countries, with the critical philosophy of Paulin Hountondji.
11 See Hudson (2010); Boldizzoni (chapter 8); Grenier (chapter 7) in this volume.
12 Symbols and meanings were introduced into western anthropology by Marcel Mauss (1914, 1923–24) who overcame Durkheimian functionalism. They entered historical research with Bloch's (1924) study of the 'royal touch'.
13 Classic examples are given by Boserup (1965) and Sahlins (2004b) in their studies of pre-agricultural societies.

References

Acemoglu, Daron and James A. Robinson. 2012. *Why Nations Fail: The Origins of Power, Prosperity, and Poverty*. New York: Crown Publishers.

Allen, Robert C. 2009. *The British Industrial Revolution in Global Perspective*. Oxford: Oxford University Press.

Archer, Margaret S. 2000. 'Homo Oeconomicus, Homo Sociologicus *and* Homo Sentiens', in Archer and Tritter (2000), 36–56.

Archer, Margaret S. and Jonathan Q. Tritter, eds. 2000. *Rational Choice Theory: Resisting Colonization*. London: Routledge.

Austin, Gareth. 2007. 'Reciprocal Comparison and African History: Tackling Conceptual Eurocentrism in the Study of Africa's Economic Past' *African Studies Review* 50.3, 1–28.

Austin, Gareth. 2015. 'African Economic History in Africa' *Economic History of Developing Regions*, DOI: 10.1080/20780389.2015.1033686.

Barnett, Vincent, ed. 2015. *Routledge Handbook of the History of Global Economic Thought*. London: Routledge.

Bayly, C. A. 2004. *The Birth of the Modern World, 1780–1914: Global Connections and Comparisons*. Oxford: Blackwell.

Berg, Maxine, ed. 2013. *Writing the History of the Global: Challenges for the 21st Century*. Oxford: Oxford University Press.

Bloch, Marc. 1924. *The Royal Touch: Sacred Monarchy and Scrofula in England and France*. London: Routledge and Kegan Paul, 1973.

Bloch, Marc. 1928. 'Pour une histoire comparée des sociétés européennes' *Revue de synthèse historique* 46, 15–50.

Boldizzoni, Francesco. 2011. *The Poverty of Clio: Resurrecting Economic History*. Princeton, NJ: Princeton University Press.

Boserup, Ester. 1965. *The Conditions of Agricultural Growth: The Economics of Agrarian Change under Population Pressure*. London: Allen & Unwin.

Broadberry, Stephen, Johann Custodis and Bishnupriya Gupta. 2015. 'India and the Great Divergence: An Anglo-Indian Comparison of GDP Per Capita, 1600–1871' *Explorations in Economic History* 55.1–2, 58–75.

Chakrabarty, Dipesh. 2000. *Provincializing Europe: Postcolonial Thought and Historical Difference.* Princeton, NJ: Princeton University Press.

Clark, Gregory. 2007. *A Farewell to Alms: A Brief Economic History of the World.* Princeton, NJ: Princeton University Press.

Connell, Raewyn. 2007. *Southern Theory: The Global Dynamics of Knowledge in Social Science.* Cambridge: Polity.

Coyle, Diane. 2014. *GDP: A Brief but Affectionate History.* Princeton, NJ: Princeton University Press.

Fenske, James. 2010. 'The Causal History of Africa: A Response to Hopkins' *Economic History of Developing Regions* 25.2, 177–212.

Fernández-Armesto, Felipe. 1995. *Millennium: A History of the Last Thousand Years.* New York: Touchstone.

Frank, Andre Gunder. 1998. *ReOrient: Global Economy in the Asian Age.* Berkeley: University of California Press.

Fukuyama, Francis. 1992. *The End of History and the Last Man.* New York: Free Press.

Geertz, Clifford. 1973. *The Interpretation of Cultures.* New York: Basic Books.

Goody, Jack. 2004. *Capitalism and Modernity: The Great Debate.* Cambridge: Polity.

Granovetter, Mark S. 2005. 'The Impact of Social Structure on Economic Outcomes' *Journal of Economic Perspectives* 19.1, 33–50.

Green, Erik and Pius Nyambara. 2015. 'The Internationalization of Economic History: Perspectives from the African Frontier' *Economic History of Developing Regions,* DOI: 10.1080/20780389.2015.1025744.

Greif, Avner. 2006. *Institutions and the Path to the Modern Economy: Lessons from Medieval Trade.* Cambridge: Cambridge University Press.

Gudeman, Stephen. 2001. *The Anthropology of Economy: Community, Market, and Culture.* Oxford: Blackwell.

Halperin, Rhoda H. 1994. *Cultural Economies: Past and Present.* Austin: University of Texas Press.

Hann, Chris and Keith Hart. 2011. *Economic Anthropology: History, Ethnography, Critique.* Cambridge: Polity.

Hobson, John M. 2004. *The Eastern Origins of Western Civilisation.* Cambridge: Cambridge University Press.

Hopkins, A. G. 2009. 'The New Economic History of Africa' *Journal of African History* 50.2, 155–77.

Hudson, Pat. 2010. 'Closeness and Distance: A Response to Brewer' *Cultural and Social History* 7.3, 375–85.

Iggers, Georg G. and Q. Edward Wang. 2008. *A Global History of Modern Historiography.* London. Pearson.

Jacob, Margaret C. 2014. *The First Knowledge Economy: Human Capital and the European Economy, 1750–1850.* Cambridge: Cambridge University Press.

Jerven, Morten. 2014. *Economic Growth and Measurement Reconsidered in Botswana, Kenya, Tanzania, and Zambia, 1965–1995.* Oxford: Oxford University Press.

Jones, Eric. 2003. *The European Miracle: Environments, Economies and Geopolitics in the History of Europe and Asia.* 3rd edn. Cambridge: Cambridge University Press.

Kuznets, Simon. 1953. 'International Differences in Income Levels: Reflections on Their Causes' *Economic Development and Cultural Change* 2.1, 3–26.

Landes, David S. 1999. *The Wealth and Poverty of Nations.* New York: Norton.

Latour, Bruno. 1991. *We Have Never Been Modern.* Cambridge, MA: Harvard University Press, 1993.

McCloskey, Deirdre N. 2010. *Bourgeois Dignity: Why Economics Can't Explain the Modern World.* Chicago, IL: University of Chicago Press.

Maddison, Angus. 2007. *Contours of the World Economy, 1–2030 AD.* Oxford: Oxford University Press.

Makkreel, Rudolf A. 1992. *Dilthey: Philosopher of the Human Studies.* Princeton, NJ: Princeton University Press.

Marglin, Stephen. 2008. *The Dismal Science: How Thinking Like an Economist Undermines Community.* Cambridge, MA: Harvard University Press.

Mauss, Marcel. 1914. 'Les origines de la notion de monnaie', in *Œuvres,* vol. 2: *Représentations collectives et diversité des civilisations.* Paris: Editions de Minuit, 1969, 106–12.

Mauss, Marcel. 1923–24. 'Essai sur le don. Forme et raison de l'échange dans les sociétés archaïques' *Année sociologique* (n.s.) 1, 30–186.

Medick, Hans. 1996. *Weben und Überleben in Laichingen, 1650–1900.* Göttingen: Vandenhoeck und Ruprecht.

Mirowski, Philip. 2005. 'How Positivism Made a Pact with the Postwar Social Sciences in the United States', in Steinmetz (2005), 142–72.

Mokyr, Joel. 2010. *The Enlightened Economy: An Economic History of Britain, 1700–1850*. New Haven, CT: Yale University Press.

North, Douglass C. 2005. *Understanding the Process of Economic Change*. Princeton, NJ: Princeton University Press.

North, Douglass C., John J. Wallis and Barry R. Weingast. 2009. *Violence and Social Orders: A Conceptual Framework for Interpreting Recorded Human History*. Cambridge: Cambridge University Press.

O'Brien, Patrick. 2010. 'Deconstructing the British Industrial Revolution as a Conjuncture and Paradigm for Global Economic History', in *Reconceptualizing the Industrial Revolution*, ed. by Jeff Horn, Leonard N. Rosenband and Merritt Roe Smith. Cambridge, MA: MIT Press, 21–46.

Oxford History of Historical Writing, 5 vols. Oxford: Oxford University Press, 2011–15.

Parthasarathi, Prasannan. 2013. 'Comparison in Global History', in Berg (2013), 69–82.

Polanyi, Karl. 1957. 'The Economy as Instituted Process', in *Trade and Market in the Early Empires: Economies in History and Theory*, ed. by Karl Polanyi, Conrad M. Arensberg and Harry W. Pearson. Glencoe, IL: Free Press, 243–70.

Pollard, Sidney. 1997. *Marginal Europe: The Contribution of Marginal Lands since the Middle Ages*. Oxford: Clarendon Press.

Pomeranz, Kenneth. 2000. *The Great Divergence: China, Europe, and the Making of the Modern World Economy*. Princeton, NJ: Princeton University Press.

Sachsenmaier, Dominic. 2011. *Global Perspectives on Global History: Theories and Approaches in a Connected World*. Cambridge: Cambridge University Press.

Sahlins, Marshall. 2004a. 'Preface to New Edition', in Sahlins (2004b).

Sahlins, Marshall. 2004b. *Stone Age Economics*, 2nd edn. London: Routledge.

Sahlins, Marshall. 2008. *The Western Illusion of Human Nature*. Chicago, IL: Prickly Paradigm.

Sewell, William H., Jr. 1967. 'Marc Bloch and the Logic of Comparative History' *History and Theory* 6.2, 208–18.

Sombart, Werner. 1930. *Die drei Nationalökonomien. Geschichte und System der Lehre von der Wirtschaft*. Munich and Leipzig: Duncker & Humblot.

Speich, Daniel. 2011. 'The Use of Global Abstractions: National Income Accounting in the Period of Global Decline' *Journal of Global History*, 6.1, 7–28.

Stanziani, Alessandro. 2014. *Bondage: Labor and Rights in Eurasia from the Sixteenth to the Early Twentieth Centuries*. New York: Berghahn.

Steinmetz, George, ed. 2005. *The Politics of Method in the Human Sciences: Positivism and Its Epistemological Others*. Durham, NC: Duke University Press.

Sumiya, Mikio and Koji Taira, eds. 1979. *An Outline of Japanese Economic History, 1603–1940*. Tokyo: University of Tokyo Press.

Van der Linden, Marcel. 2008. *Workers of the World: Essays Toward a Global Labor History*. Leiden: Brill.

Van Zanden, Jan Luiten. 2009a. *The Long Road to the Industrial Revolution: The European Economy in a Global Perspective, 1000–1800*. Leiden: Brill.

Van Zanden, Jan Luiten 2009b. 'The Skill Premium and the "Great Divergence"' *European Review of Economic History* 13.1, 121–53.

Vries, Peer. 2015. *State, Economy and the Great Divergence: Great Britain and China, 1680s–1850s*. London: Bloomsbury.

Wagner, Peter. 2000. 'The Bird in Hand: Rational Choice – the Default Mode of Social Theorizing', in Archer and Tritter (2000), 19–35.

Washbrook, David. 2013. 'Problems in Global History' in Berg (2013), 21–31.

Woolf, Daniel. 2011. *A Global History of History*. Cambridge: Cambridge University Press.

PART I

Anglo-American traditions

2
ECONOMIC HISTORY IN BRITAIN
The 'first industrial nation'

Pat Hudson

This chapter considers how and why particular sorts of knowledge, and methods of enquiry, have come to the fore in economic history in Britain. There are some detailed studies already of the evolution of the subject, especially up to the 1980s (Harte 1971; Coleman 1987; Kadish 1989; Hudson 2001, 2003). Here, we bring the story up to date and provide an analysis of the political, social, cultural and economic forces that have made economic history in Britain different from that practised elsewhere. Some of these forces relate to Britain's peculiar historical trajectory: the early rise of a centralised fiscal–military nation state; the impact of Scottish enlightenment writers; the response to early and drawn-out processes of industrialisation and urbanisation; the position and needs of the nation in global industry, trade and finance; the imperatives and attitudes of a major imperial power in rise and decline; and the influence of changing British political and economic policy priorities. To these one must add the distinctive intellectual position of economic history in Britain: how it arose from parent disciplines that have travelled different methodological roads. The degree of exposure and openness of the subject to approaches and ideas from outside Britain is also important. The geographical, imperial and political position of Britain in the past century and a half has made the country particularly accessible to intellectual exchanges. However, as we shall see, external ideas can be rejected or misunderstood and their reception is affected by the absence of translation, or translation bias. They are also adapted to and moulded by, as well as combined with, existing traditions to produce particular hybrids. Finally, our analysis includes more serendipitous factors such as the zeal, career development, rivalries and early deaths of particular individuals.

The influence of early statistical thinking

Britain was early in establishing a quantitatively oriented approach to understanding and to attempting to control the economy and society. This was provoked by the evolution of the nation state and by Britain's rise to economic pre-eminence during the two centuries following the Restoration of the Monarchy (1660–88). Her manufacturing development, demographic growth, urbanisation, international trading rivalries, and the need to support, control and exploit imperial expansion were important in placing Britain, alongside France, at the forefront of the development of economic and social data collection and of statistical thinking during the eighteenth and nineteenth centuries (Cullen 1975; Porter 1988; Cook and O'Hara 2011). The growth of state power internally as well as externally, and the expanding state bureaucracy, increased the need for accurate estimates of wealth and taxable revenues. This not only influenced the nature of early work in what was later to be defined as economic history, but also bequeathed a plethora of early data (of mixed reliability) for later historians to use.

One can identify influential antecedents of economic history in the writings of John Graunt and William Petty in the 1660s and 1670s. Petty saw the collection of statistical data and its analysis as an indispensable preliminary to a scientific understanding of the functioning of society and to the achievement of social and political control and reform (Petty 1664, 1676). Graunt worked on some of the earliest historical demography. He analysed the London Bills of Mortality to consider urban and rural death rates, infant mortality rates, the excess of female births over deaths and the formation of life tables (Graunt 1662).[1] Petty and Graunt were not alone amongst eighteenth-century writers in extolling the virtues of 'statistics' (meaning at this point ordered facts about the state, non-numerical as well as numerical), not just actuarially but also in areas of public finance, including war finance, customs and excise, imports and exports (Hoppit 1996; Ashworth 2003). There were fifteen different estimates of national income between Petty's research and that of Patrick Colquhoun in the 1790s and the estimations did not stop with the United Kingdom. The Board of Trade surveyed the population and trade of the Empire as early as 1721 and Ireland was a particular focus, as well as Scotland (Petty 1687; Sinclair 1791–8; Hoppit 1996, 2002, 2006). All of these developments and the data generated can be seen to have influenced the nature and approaches of a central strand of British economic history a century, and even two centuries, later.

The close link between economic history as an emerging academic discipline from the end of the nineteenth century and the culture of statistical thinking in Britain was sealed in the Victorian period which saw the grip of quantitative investigation tighten across many aspects of society and policy, largely as a result of the economic and social problems created by industrialisation. Statistics of health, crime, education and factory employment were gathered from the 1810s but the most important developments in the use of social statistics were the establishment of the census (from 1801) and Civil Registration (from 1837) (Cullen 1975; Porter 1988; Cook and O'Hara 2011). John Rickman who was in charge of the first census collected returns from the clergy of decennial baptism and burial figures 1700–80 and yearly figures thereafter, forming the basis for much subsequent research in historical demography. Measures of demographic change and of the social, political and moral determinants of population growth had been a key focus of political economy long before Thomas Malthus's *Essay on the Principle of Population* in 1798 but his ideas further provoked debate about the relationship between population growth, social class and poor relief in particular. This not only lay behind attitudes and changes in Victorian social policy but his influence has continued amongst British economic historians to the present day, generating a preoccupation with the ending of the 'Malthusian threat' for example (Wrigley and Souden 1986; Glass 1973; Wrigley and Schofield 1981; Wrigley, 2004; Broadberry et al. 2015).

The General Register Office was joined by the Home Office, the War Office, the Board of Trade, the Admiralty and the Poor Law Commission in generating masses of data during the nineteenth century. In addition, there developed a large number of private and voluntary reform associations such as the Statistical Society of London, the Central Society of Education, the Health of Towns Association and the Society for the Diffusion of Useful Knowledge. Many provincial improvers promoted local investigations as a counterweight to what was seen as central government interference and attendant high taxation (Cullen 1975). Such institutions and individuals, and the data they gathered, had a strong impact upon the emergence and nature of economic history.

The evolution of the British Census, especially under William Farr at the General Registry Office from the mid-nineteenth century, had an impact upon the preoccupations and the available data for economic history in Britain from its early years, along with the centrally collected information from Parliamentary investigations of the state of trade, the health of towns and factory conditions. Farr's preoccupation with mortality and diseases, sanitary reform and improvements in occupational health determined the structure and nature of the questions framed in the census schedules and the priorities absorbed by the enumerators, as well as driving much of the broader statistical analysis undertaken by the Office. Farr's work from the 1840s anticipated later developments in economic history as it included 'statistically controlled experiments' designed to enable him to separate out the influences of sex, location, climate and occupation upon epidemics and mortality rates. He was also interested in the age of marriage and rate of remarriage and in the production of new life tables. Because of this the late nineteenth-century British censuses have been generally of more use and interest to demographic and medical historians than to historians interested in the family economy or the nature of work and employment of men and women as the information on these is patchy and unreliable, especially for women (Cullen 1975 chapter 2; Higgs 1987; Cook and O'Hara 2011; campop.geog.cam.ac.uk/research/occupations).

Farr represented a much wider nineteenth-century obsession with health leading to major collections of statistical information, from the heights and weights of members of the armed forces and transported convicts to local and large-scale surveys of urban disease and living conditions. These subsequently informed the history of medicine as well as demographic research. In recent years they have furnished raw data for a number of pioneering anthropometric analyses concerning health, nutrition and living standards. A close relationship exists between some of the foundational methodological approaches of British economic history, and economics, and late nineteenth-century developments in actuarial statistics, probability theory and Eugenics. These approaches emerged as a direct result of demographic change, the need for more accurate predictability of risk in insurance and business dealings, and from the hierarchical and racialised imperatives of a bourgeois society and an imperial elite (Hacking 1990; Porter 2010). Thus economic history in Britain from its inception, in its ideology and purposes, as well as its sources, has been closely connected with the peculiarities of British socio-political and economic development, and with state formation and state policy.

The Scottish enlightenment and what followed

Other writings of a more philosophical nature were vital in providing foundational ideas for the development of economic history. The Act of Union (1707) brought the four universities of Scotland into the UK. These were geared to teaching for the professions rather than the Church. The writings of their alumni, especially David Hume, William Robertson, Sir James Steuart, Adam Ferguson, John Millar and Adam Smith, were most important in an evolving tradition of historical and political commentary that incorporated economic and business matters within a broad analysis of social development (Coleman 1987).[2] Short, ephemeral, uncertain and contradictory as many publications on the economy were at this time, the major Scottish writers ensured that a nascent political economy was emerging (Hoppit 2006). The work of John Millar in particular anticipated many central issues in economic history in the twentieth century: stages of economic development; the impact of commerce and manufactures on social and political transformation; the role of technology, trade and the protection of private property; the influence of economic subsistence upon the position of women and parental authority, social hierarchies of wealth and power, social and political behaviour and how these vary across societies and at different points in time. There is more than a hint of economic determinism in Millar and some of his contemporaries; certainly there was a desire to identify trends and even general laws. In considering the social, cultural and moral consequences of economic development, Millar in his later work drew upon and complemented Adam Smith's *Theory of Moral Sentiments*, emphasising the social and cultural factors in economic relationships and the drawbacks as well as the riches of progress in the economy.

This inductive and socially oriented Scottish enlightenment tradition of writing about the economy declined for almost a hundred years after Millar and Smith, before being rediscovered by economic historians of the late nineteenth and early twentieth centuries (Backhouse and Tribe 2014). In the climate of nineteenth-century economic growth and Britain's global domination of trade and empire, history and economic analysis went separate ways. History largely focused upon political, dynastic and diplomatic developments reflecting Britain's dominant contemporary position and actions. At the same time Adam Smith's *Wealth of Nations* was reinterpreted in the mid-nineteenth century for a new laissez-faire age, a reinterpretation that largely ignored the historical element in his political economy and that involved collective amnesia about the *Theory of Moral Sentiments* (Hodgson 2001). The economic writings of the nineteenth century, of James Mill and J. R. McCulloch, for example, had little engagement with the historic past (Coleman 1987). Orchestrated by the analytical framework of David Ricardo, the trajectory of classical economics has been described as being 'set on a dead end track' for the following two centuries: preoccupied by discussion of key concepts rather than change over time and tied to immediate policy issues (Backhouse and Tribe 2014). The liberal free-trade model of the new political economy promising scientific answers to economic problems, such as the reform of finance and banking and the repeal of the corn laws, endorsed belief in the merits of the Ricardian approach. The marginalist or neoclassical revolution of the 1870s to 1890s, overturned classical value theory, potentially opening the way to more dynamic theories of economic activity. However, it also made economics more formal (mechanical, mathematical and graphical) in its methods and more deductive (depending upon the testing of theoretical hypotheses, the predictive ability of generalisations and statistical inference). The introduction of marginal utility theory by W. S. Jevons and further developed by Alfred Marshall and others gave primacy to comparative statics and this has been the keystone of economics, and of some economic history in Britain, ever since.

Economic history, allied to historical economics, when it started formally to emerge at the end of the nineteenth century was viewed and pursued, by figures such as William Cunningham, W. J. Ashley, H. S. Foxwell, W. A. S. Hewins and L. L. Price, as an attempt to find an alternative methodology to the growing mainstream in economics, one which would better take account of different time periods and cultures (Koot 1987; Kadish 1989: 76–102). T. E. Cliffe Leslie, Professor of Economics at Queen's College, Belfast, made a major contribution by calling for a rehabilitation of Smith's historical work as well as incorporating ideas from the German Historical School (Cliffe Leslie 1870, 1875, 1879). In other writers the call to revisit ideas from the Scottish enlightenment was more muted but the challenge to neoclassical orthodoxy was strong. Cunningham, who wrote the first English economic history text, objected to the idea of 'economic man' as a rational calculating and maximising individual whose behaviour could be seen as deriving from an immutable human nature, present in all societies. He, along with Ashley in particular, favoured the study of societies in their own time and with their own social and cultural attitudes and motivations (Cunningham 1882; Ashley 1888, 1893). As has been well documented, their views came out in debates with Marshall. Although Marshall himself saw economics as 'the study of man in the ordinary business of life' and he was much concerned with innovation in industrial districts (both of which subjects have subsequently engaged economic historians in Britain), the method, which he helped to establish, encouraged economists to specialise in abstract generalised theorising (Maloney 1976; Hodgson 2001; Raffaelli 2004). Similar debates between the historical school and formal, neoclassical economists were going on in Europe and particularly in Germany where the *Methodenstreit* (debates upon method) in economics was most vociferous, partly because of the strength and particularism of the Historical School there (Kadish 1989). Much German economic history arose from challenges, in turn, to the Historical School because of the latter's desire to elicit universal or general laws of social development, through observation and induction (Hesse, chapter 6 in this volume). A similar severe disinclination to apply theory and to search for any general laws or grand narratives affected a large swathe of economic history in Britain, as it developed out of these debates.

The democratisation of history and the commitment to social reform

The emergence of a distinct discipline of economic history in Britain at the end of the nineteenth century arose from developments in history, as an academic subject, as well as from the challenge to economic orthodoxy. There was a growing concern to write histories of the mass of the population, of agriculture, industry and trading and not just the history of elites, diplomacy and wars. This democratisation of history was related to the process of industrialisation and the social dislocations created by economic change. It was not unique to Britian. The precursor of this shift in academic orientation can be seen in popular scientific writers and journalists earlier in the century, in the proliferation of encyclopedias and dictionaries of invention and industry and in local historical analyses of particular industries. Abraham Rees's *Cyclopedia of Arts, Sciences and Literature* (1819), Andrew Ure's volumes between 1835 and the 1870s, and Edward Baines's *History of the Cotton Manufacture of Great Britain* (1835) or John James's *History of Worsted Manufacture* (1857) can be seen in this light as can G. R. Porter's *Progress of the Nation* (1836). The merchant and financier Thomas Tooke's collaboration with William Newmarch in producing their *History of Prices 1793–1856* (six volumes 1838–57) and Samuel Smiles's works, including *The Lives of the Engineers* (1861–62) are other examples of this trend which was complemented in the provinces by a mass of papers and journals published by a plethora of local antiquarian and topographical societies.[3]

The approach within universities was exemplified by the work of Sidney and Beatrice Webb, founders of the London School of Economics (LSE), by Arnold Toynbee, Barbara and John Hammond, Charles Beard and many of the first generation of academic writers in the field. William Ashley, who held the first chair in Economic History in the world (at Harvard, from 1892) and who later founded the College of Commerce at the University of Birmingham, was the first British historian to adopt a periodisation not derived from political history. By the time of publication of the new *Cambridge Modern History of Britain*, from 1902, economic history was seen as sufficiently important to require chapters in each volume. Contributors included Cunningham and John Clapham, the latter recommended by Marshall. Volume XII, published in 1910, included a chapter on social movements by Sidney Webb. All of the economic and social history chapters were isolated contributions however, and there was as yet little attempt to integrate economic, political, social and intellectual history, in the way earlier attempted by Millar and Smith, and advocated by Cliffe Leslie (who had died in 1882, at the age of 55, his major work unfinished) (Coleman 1987: 43–4). With some notable exceptions, this lack of integration has continued to mark economic history in Britain.

Both Oxford and Cambridge universities included lectures in economic history from the 1880s, the LSE soon followed. Emerging research in the subject used hitherto untouched historical documents such as the censuses of population and production, overseas trade figures, local municipal records, parliamentary reports and commissions, business archives. This broke new ground because the sources and concerns that economic and social historians tackled had not traditionally been regarded as a priority for historians or even a legitimate sphere of their interests. A strong impulse, as with the statistical movement, came from social commentators and historians looking to provide evidence of the need for government regulation of the impact of industrialism or to support tariff reform in opposition to the dominant free-trade strain in orthodox economics. The slackening pace of industrial growth in the last decades of the nineteenth century helped to motivate these historians as did surveys of the conditions of the working poor by Charles Booth and Seebohm Rowntree. The work with most lasting impact upon economic history from this period, Arnold Toynbee's *Lectures on the Industrial Revolution* (1884), has been described by one historian as *the* classic, of several examples at this time, of 'bourgeois social contrition' (Coleman 1987: 59). But Toynbee's great influence as a teacher was not merely emotional. He advocated a strong connection between history and political economy and had a formative influence on Ashley (and many others) who attended his lectures at Oxford and wrote them up for publication following Toynbee's early death.[4]

One might expect to find a strong link between the reformist impulse in economic history at this time, and early socialist writings. Ashley, Cunningham and Unwin all refer to Marx, as part of their rejection of orthodox economics, and approved of his integrative approach to history and society, even if they were critical of historical materialism (for example, Ashley 1888, 1893). Although many economic historians in Britain at this time were influenced by forms of Fabian and Christian socialism, their commitment to reform and even to a collectivist stance, appears to have been driven more by social compassion, than by socialism. Religious conviction was also prominent: it is not accidental that several early figures in economic history also held clerical positions.[5] The roots of the national accounting approach to the economy (a pillar of economic history in Britain thereafter) grew from the same outlook. It was pioneered initially by historians who wished to expose market failures and to highlight where collective action or the state might step in (Clark 1940; Offer 2008).

Britain's powerful imperial position during the early decades of the emergence of economic history as a discipline had many ramifications not least in the ways in which assumptions were made about the universality of tools for global economic investigation but also in generalising models of development and economic growth that crystallised from the 1940s onwards. Even earlier there had developed a direct influence: Malthus, Richard Jones and later Toynbee lectured on political economy at Haileybury College, to many cohorts of young men training for the imperial civil service (Coleman 1987: 42–3). The central importance of the British higher education system, more generally, in training imperial and commonwealth administrators and scholars, and international students, continued to have a significant impact on the spread of dominant Western ideas globally from the late nineteenth century to the present. In other cases international scholars training in Britain brought challenges to home-grown ideas and initiated major debates in the field, as with Eric Williams's thesis, *Capitalism and Slavery* (1944).

Methodological issues and bifurcation in the early twentieth century

To understand the particular antagonism of most economic historians towards orthodox economics in Britain it is important to recognise the degree to which Cunningham, Ashley and, in a different manner, George Unwin (first holder of the Edinburgh Chair in the subject from 1908), were influenced by the German Historical School, especially by the writings of Wilhelm Roscher and Gustav Schmoller. All three had studied for a time in Germany. Ashley's inaugural lecture was dedicated to Schmoller (Harte 2001: 1). But the challenge to Ricardian and, later, marginalist economics also had a native British perspective centred upon social morality and social improvement. This can be traced as early as the writings of T. R. Malthus (1776–1834), and his belief that political economy was much more about the science of morals and politics than about mathematics (Malthus 1836: 1). The commitment to economic history by socialists and reformers bent upon engineering society, as well as conservatives and liberals, made for keen debates within British economic history about purpose and method. The battle of ideas between free marketeers (associated with the deductive formalist approach) and those in favour of state intervention (generally relying upon induction and rhetoric) played a major role at the start of economic history (Kadish 1989; Hodgson 2001) and has continued to mark a bifurcation in the discipline in Britain ever since.

The political or moral tradition represented in the work of R. H. Tawney, Barbara and John Hammond, Sidney and Beatrice Webb and G. D. H. Cole sought connections with other developing fields of the social sciences and attempted to answer big questions of causality such as the causes of the English Revolution or of industrialisation (Coleman 1987). These historians also sought answers to contemporary moral and political questions through interrogating the past and were as engaged with social as much as with underlying economic changes. Tawney wrote that 'Too much time is spent today . . . by writers who pile up statistics and facts, but never get to the heart of the problem' (Winter and Joslin 1972: 56). Tawney held the first chair in Economic History at LSE (from 1931). His best known work *Religion and the Rise of Capitalism* (1926) challenged the thesis of Max Weber that the rise of capitalism in Western Europe was spurred by the social and economic values of Calvinism. Tawney argued that Calvinism provided a religious rationale for capitalism and that both puritanism and capitalism were perversions of those Christian values that favoured social obligation over individualism (Goldman 2013). Tawney's interpretation of the capitalist ethic and other subjects became the focus of intense debate within British economic history over many decades.

A second grouping within economic history at this time might be termed the empirical, conservative tradition, characterised by a more strictly economic focus, undeveloped cultural and political context, a neutral ethical stance, and a disinterest in formulating theories or laws about cause or effect (Coleman 1987). Distrust of theory was partly a reaction to the break from mainstream economics but also against the inductive search for general laws that came from the influence of the Historical School. The earlier neutral statistical or empirical tradition, such as that of Thorold Rogers, also played a part. Rogers (1823–90), cleric and Professor of Economics and Statistics at Kings College, London, and a free trader (unlike most others of the Historical School), had been the first to attempt the collection of comprehensive long-run data on the agricultural sector (six volumes from the 1860s) and on work and wages more broadly (Kadish 2006). This research remained influential amongst economic historians in Britain for the following century. The empirical approach by the 1920s and 1930s had a somewhat closer relationship with orthodox economics than in the past but did not adopt its methods. It was generally marked by the collection and interpretation of quantitative data, as exemplified in the work of Sir John Clapham, E. C. K. Gonner and W. R. Scott. The latter two were economists at Liverpool and Glasgow and produced work on enclosure and joint stock companies respectively. Clapham, the central figure, was a Cambridge economic historian and protégé of Marshall. His influential three-volume *Economic History of Modern Britain* (1926–38) used a range of evidence to study sectors of the economy in detail. He rejected the term industrial revolution because he uncovered how gradual and partial change was at the time. He also challenged the socialist and moral tradition by suggesting that, with the exception of a few dying trades, living conditions improved for the masses during industrialisation. His style provided a strong contrast with the emotionally charged accounts of the reformist economic historians. T. S. Ashton, who succeeded Tawney to the Chair of Economic History at LSE in 1944, was also in the Clapham tradition but his use of Marshallian economics (in the statistical analysis of economic fluctuations, for example) was much more apparent (Ashton 1959). Like Unwin, Ashton was sceptical about the efficacy of government economic policy and largely ignored it in his studies. In this respect he entirely overturned the sort of pro-interventionist economic history that had been common since Cunningham (Ashton 1948).[6]

Economic history as a popular, integrative social science

The 1920s was a key decade for the expansion of economic history in Britain. It saw the foundation of the Economic History Society and the *Economic History Review*. Many new university appointments were made in the field, particularly at the LSE but also at Manchester, Edinburgh and Belfast. In the decades before the Second World War economic history expanded to fill the void left by the increasingly present-centred nature of the other social sciences in Britain at this time. Despite internal differences, the work of the majority of economic historians, such as Tawney, Unwin, Eileen Power, Ephraim Lipson, Lillian Knowles, Herbert Heaton, A. P. Wadsworth and Julia Le Mann, defined the subject as a broadly based branch of historical enquiry with a wide definition of the economic sphere. Because of this it had a wide appeal, not just as a university subject, but amongst a lay readership. It had long been popular in university extension studies classes and in courses run by the Workers' Educational Association. The roots of this can be traced in the nineteenth century in links between several early economic historians and the University Settlement Movement (Coleman 1987, ch. 4).[7] Cunningham himself had launched his academic career by serving as an extra-mural lecturer in Leeds, Bradford and Liverpool, teaching as many as 600 students each term (Koot 2006). Most economic historians of the first half of the twentieth century wrote in an accessible, non-technical style, for a popular as well as an academic readership. Tawney's *Religion and the Rise of Capitalism* had total sales running into six figures and was translated into several languages. T. S. Ashton's best-seller *The Industrial Revolution* was written for a general readership in the Oxford Home Library of Knowledge series. Economic history before the mid-twentieth century also included many female academics who contributed to the accessibility of the subject and its internationalism (Berg 1992).

Recognition that economic history could act as a focus for popular and integrative social science grew in this period. Donald Coleman traced such impulses in the inaugural lectures and work of Tawney and Eileen Power but gave pride of place to M. M. Postan who succeeded Clapham as Professor of Economic History at Cambridge in 1938 (Coleman 1987: 90–1). Perhaps because of his Russian origins and European background, as well as his training at LSE, he broke new ground within economic history in concerning himself overtly with methodological issues. He believed that economic history needed to carve a path between the more dogmatic and generalised ideas of both economics and sociology whilst also availing itself of concepts from these subjects, where these were useful. He demonstrated that using first principles of economic theory to think through the impact of food shortages and population growth could be particularly useful for periods when evidence is patchy. His argument about the decline of feudal relations in England rested on detailed economic reasoning about the impact of the Black Death upon the prices of land, labour and agricultural produce (Postan 1972). His analysis of peasant economies was influenced by the Russian A. V. Chayanov (1888–1937) whose writings he exposed to a British readership and whose work has since remained important in medieval and proto-industrial studies. Postan's attack on the fact gathering of orthodox history gained him disdain from many Cambridge contemporaries but he helped to establish a distinctive place for economic history: methodologically aware if more politically neutral than much of its reformist past.

Economic instability, war, the Cold War and economic development

Economic history in Britain was changing in the 1930s to 1950s partly in reaction to interwar and post-war economic crises, the exigencies and the lessons of wartime state intervention and the new world political order. Historians started to incorporate more theoretical insight from contemporary economics, especially trade cycle theory, and ideas derived from Keynsian economic management that fitted well with the older state interventionist traditions. This resulted in some classic studies of trade cycles by Ashton (1959) amongst others (following a pattern set by N. D. Kondratieff and Joseph Schumpeter). It also stimulated work on the money supply, banking, government expenditure and consumption in influencing economic stability and growth (for example, King 1936; Gilboy 1938; Clapham 1944).

The tools of macro-economic management and analysis were developed in the 1930s and 1940s, tools that economic historians could (in theory at least) apply retrospectively and cross-culturally. The needs of the wartime state necessitated a revolution in the collection of official statistics. This information was geared not, as in the past, to fiscal requirements, but to the need to fulfil the demands of the war economy without inflation (by controlling domestic consumption) and, in the post-war years, to serve the development of the welfare state and an acceptance that the state should act to stabilise the economy, to maintain economic growth and to keep unemployment low. The development of national accounts was thus placed on a new footing.

It is no accident that the composition and growth of GNP in different phases of economic development became a central concern of economic history from the mid-twentieth century and that forms of retrospective national accounting were applied. This is seen most obviously in the work of Phyllis Deane and W. A. Cole in the 1960s, in the research of Charles Feinstein and N. F. R. Crafts in the 1970s and 1980s and in the estimates of Steve Broadberry and others in recent years (Deane and Cole 1962; Feinstein 1972; Crafts 1985; Broadberry et al. 2015). Deane was initially employed by Cambridge economist Austin Robinson in 1941 to collected national accounts data for parts of the empire with the idea that this might be useful in administering and developing the colonies. Deane collected all of the information available in wartime London for Northern Rhodesia, Nyasaland and Jamaica and after the war spent eighteen months in Central Africa but her conclusion was that the task was indelibly flawed for countries where the informal economy dominated (Deane 1953). The paucity of accurate statistical data for British national accounts earlier than 1945 was also highlighted. Output analysis for Britain was particularly dogged by the absence of transport, distribution and services from the Censuses of Production. This is one reason for the relative neglect of the importance and role of the tertiary sector in the process of industrialisation until relatively recently (Broadberry 2006; Tribe 2015).

Against the background of the needs and decline of the post-war British empire, and debates about economic growth in the dependencies and the commonwealth, in Asia, Latin America and Africa, there was a flowering of development economics in the decades after 1945 which economic historians were keen to share. There was a growing tendency within British (and more broadly within Western) economic history in these years to see the British economy and British industrialisation not just as the basis for the evolution of universal tools of analysis such as national accounts, but as a paradigmatic model or path of development that other areas of the globe should follow. Inequalities in imperial and global development might be erased by formalizing and applying the secrets of western advance. This is illustrated most clearly in the work of W. W. Rostow whose *Stages of Economic Growth* (1960) had a major impact upon British historiography. The Cold War alliance made British economic historians receptive to American ideas in which Rostow's model had pride of place. His work stimulated controversy which in the USA centred mainly upon his statistical estimates (Lamoreaux, chapter 3 in this volume). In Britain debate extended to the role of the cotton industry and the railways as leading sectors, the threshold of capital formation needed for a 'take off', the linear trajectory of his model and the end point of history in an age of high mass consumption.[8] As Rostow's model was also frequently posed (as he had intended) against models based upon historical materialism, the internal debates within economic history at this time took on an ideological biting edge.

Following the Second World War, British academics were engaged to 're-educate' the German academy and history was seen as a major tool. Eric Hobsbawm, for example, recounts his assignment in 1947 as a teacher in North Germany (Hobsbawm 2002). The Marshall Plan and various American educational initiatives supported by the Rockefeller Foundation had a strong bias in favour of teaching liberal economics in the cause of political freedom. This was seen in some of the early work of the International Economic History Association, founded in 1959, which considerably increased the scope for East–West European dialogue between economic historians during the Cold War years. Although the initiative arose from leading British and French economic historians (Postan and Braudel in particular), the organisation benefited from Rockefeller finance for various meetings, research support and conference planning (Berg 2015). Other chapters in this volume comment on the mixed influence this had in bringing Anglo-American ideas and methods, such as neoclassical analysis and cliometrics, to the Continent, including to Eastern Europe.

Economic history in Britain became more exposed to continental ideas through these exchanges. Various debates transcended national boundaries in the 1970s and 1980s, for example: the seventeenth-century crisis, the spread of industrialisation in Europe, the role of guilds, the influence of proto-industry. But the most remarkable thing is the relatively limited impact of transnational European dialogue on the practice of economic history in Britain. Partly for language reasons, there was very little take-up or even acknowledgement of the interdisciplinary innovations of the *Annales*, for example, and important works from Germany and Poland lay untranslated or were only selectively translated to suit Anglo-American tastes. For historians unable to access the literature in German, the work of Max Weber, for example (before the translations of Wilhelm Hennis, which were slow to spread from the late 1980s), was approached in Britain very largely through the partial and biased translations and analysis of the US sociologist and theorist of modernisation, Talcott Parsons. Parsons fashioned Weber as a founding father of sociology stressing the psychology and cultural anthropology in his writings at the expense of the politics and economics that made him a radical analyst of modernity (Weber 1930, 1947). The influence of his ideas in economic and social history was commensurately compromised, as in the influential work of Harold Perkins (1969). Fernand Braudel's *La Méditerranée et le monde méditerranéen à l'époque de Philippe II*, originally published in 1949, did not appear in English until 1972, despite its importance. Similarly the key works of Witold Kula, particularly his *An Economic Theory of the Feudal System*, took fourteen years to translate into English, whilst *The Problems and Methods of Economic History*, although available in Polish in 1963, was not published in English until 2001, depriving British historians of an important, and very different, methodological voice.[9]

In short, in Britain in the Cold War decades the dominant strand in economic history exhibited a strong Anglo-American free-market bias in which various forms of modernisation theory were at the forefront, with Britain's experience of industrialisation and economic growth being held as paradigmatic. In addition, the development of national accounting and the welfare state provoked studies of the movement of GNP and state intervention over time and saw the first attempts to apply the tools of national accounting transnationally, although inevitably with mixed results. The empirical, more neutral approach in economic history remained prominent, especially in business history which flourished in the 1960s and 1970s with the production of a string of commissioned monographs often centring on the story of a particular firm, such as Peter Mathias on brewing, Donald Coleman on textiles and paper, Charles Wilson on Unilever, Theo Barker on Pilkingtons. Because the firms themselves had often financed the research, this development was often less neutral than it seemed. It tended to encourage interpretations favourable to big business and was responsible for Coleman's comment that *economic* history was sometimes about 'writing as little history as possible for as much money as possible'(Coleman 1985).

British Marxist economic history

There was a parallel tradition alongside the enduring Cold War liberal model. The Marxist influence in economic history in Britain between the 1950s and the 1970s can be seen as part of the political polarisation of the post-war decades and also as a direct legacy of the reformist tradition. The flowering of Marxist ideas in the social sciences more generally supported this tendency. British Marxist economists and historians wrote varied, theoretically informed, socio-economic histories seen in the work of Maurice Dobb, Eric Hobsbawm, Christopher Hill, Rodney Hilton, Edward Thompson, Victor Kiernon and others. Exciting, often controversial, economic history was produced in the 1960s and 1970s, its popularity bolstered by the political climate and youth culture. Many of the Marxian works sold thousands of copies well outside the realm of academe and they were influential beyond Britain. A succession of volumes by Eric Hobsbawm on international themes have sold in their hundreds of thousands across the globe since the 1960s (Kaye 1995; Renton 2005). Stress upon the dynamic forces impelling change and upon the pivotal role of the economy, however strongly mediated by social and cultural factors and by human agency, made the work of Hilton, Hill, Hobsbawm and Thompson required reading on all undergraduate economic history courses. Political cleavages in the subject during these decades created acrimonious and lively debate in the pages of learned academic journals, including the Marxian-inspired, *Past & Present* (founded 1952), on topics such as the rise of the gentry and the rise of capitalism (debates carried over from Tawney's writings); the standard of living and the threat of political insurrection during the industrial revolution; the causes and impact of imperialism.

Partly because of the influence of Marxist social historians, particularly E. P. Thompson, but also because of the general expansion of social science in these years, much economic history, whether Marxian or not, incorporated a great deal of social history and some cultural history. This was evident in histories of social protest, labour and social conditions, trade unions and class. Much social history at this time was written 'from below', from the perspective of working people rather than the elites, an approach embodied in the History Workshop movement and the *History Workshop Journal* (founded 1976). But there was no significant presence in Britain in these years of serious study of the quotidian or 'everyday life' to parallel such trends on the Continent. One could argue that the strength of 'history from below', within a Marxian, politicised framework, with the emphasis upon class struggle and collective protest, took centre stage for those historians interested in the lives of ordinary people, leaving little room for histories of the poor, the unorganised and women, or for less stridently political studies that might focus upon habit or routine.

For the same reason the *Annales'* approach, developed in France from the 1920s, had surprisingly muted impact in Britain in the post-war years, certainly in terms of overt acknowledgement.[10] British nineteenth-century attempts at the production of long-term statistical series were not followed through until the work of Deane and Cole (1962) and Mitchell and Deane (1988). This and the national accounts approach were developed from different methodological roots to the *Annales'* serial studies. Similarly, in regional economic history there was no counterpart in Britain of the integrative regional studies of the *Annales' histoire totale* and little affinity with longer established German, Swiss or Norwegian regional historiographies that tackled history in the round, often including folklore, food, dress, family, community and daily living. Regional economic history in Britain had its own roots and trajectory based upon long-standing local antiquarian initiatives coupled with a focus upon industrial, sectoral and business history studies in the 1950s to 1970s, and an input from historical geography which increased from the 1960s. In 1981 Sidney Pollard made the region his unit of analysis in considering the industrialisation of Europe, but this was unusual in British historiography and, although *Peaceful Conquest* was a best-selling text, his ideas were taken up more by geographers than historians.

Econometric history and neo-institutionalism

The impact of 'New Economic History' spreading from the United States from the early 1970s was relatively weak if we equate it with analytical statistics in league with the formal deductive methods of neoclassical economics and applied to economic circumstances, data and choices in the past. Such was attempted only by a few, partly because most economic historians in Britain were not trained in economics or mathematics. The crude nature and technical limits of some of the early econometric research also limited take-up. There is however no doubt that economic history in Britain became more associated with quantification (largely descriptive statistics) during the last quarter of the twentieth century and that national income accounting also came to the fore at this time.[11] Disaffection in the face of increasing quantification was one reason why economic history declined in popularity for several decades, from the peak that it achieved in the early 1970s (Coleman 1995). Decline was aggravated because increasingly formalistic British economics departments in the late twentieth century ceased to include history. Although the technical limits of economics have been greatly extended since the 1970s allowing formal models to incorporate change over time and include many more variables and more complex interactions, it remains the case that very few economic historians practise econometric history. This is not only through lack of training but also because of a justified fear that the quality of the historical data is often insufficiently robust to bear the weight of sophisticated modelling (Crafts 1987). In addition there are widespread misgivings about the commitment to neoclassical models and assumptions that generally underpins econometric work (Hudson 2003).

Neo-institutionalism, deriving initially from the work of Douglass C. North, has been influential in economic history in Britain but the best work on institutions in the subject in Britain has tended to be done by socio-economic and cultural historians rather than by econometricians or economic historians, and in qualitative rather than formal or quantitative studies (for example, Muldrew 1998; Epstein and Praak 2010; Finn 2013). Whereas economists generally focus upon institutions as potential constraints upon, or facilitators of, utility-maximising activity, there is no such preconception with the approach to institutions from a cultural history perspective. Indeed, one of the problems of the American institutional turn in economic history, which has discouraged wider uptake in Britain, is the relatively limited departure from neoclassical orthodoxy and from a western-oriented modernisation teleology that it has created despite celebrations to the contrary (Rutherford 2001; Zamagni 2010). For similar reasons, and more obviously, the new economics of the household has failed to gain a significant purchase in economic history in Britain largely because of its adherence to a universalising rational choice, utility-maximising methodology. In British economic history, as in British social science more generally, rational choice theory features in only a small minority of studies.

Compartmentalisation and retreat

Between the 1960s and the 1980s, perhaps partly as a defensive move, specialised areas of research involving economic history emerged, or were consolidated, such as urban history, agricultural history, transport history, labour history, business history, medical history, demographic history. Many developed their own journals. Most of these specialisms were shaped by the major expansion of social history and of social sciences in universities at this time but also by the peaking of interest in debates within Marxism (about structure and agency or about class). The use of an anglicised Weberian analysis as an alternative to Marxism, and ideas deriving from various forms of modernisation theory were also important in the rise of social history. In addition, both sociology and anthropology in these years developed their own historical branches of study which fed into the expansion of research and writing of social history and influenced the nature and methods of socio-economic history. Many concepts were borrowed by historians from sociologists: family, community, race, gender, consumerism and the comparative approach. These, together with a more sophisticated use of descriptive statistics and the collection and interpretation of oral evidence, were areas pioneered by sociology but used more and more by historians. In economic history the expansion of social science and social history in the third quarter of the twentieth century prompted more studies of women in economic life, especially women's work, more on children, especially child labour, on ethnic minorities, migration and especially on consumption. Indeed the demand side of the economy, for the first time, began to attract almost as much attention as supply side changes, especially in studies of industrialisation.

Sub-disciplinary specialisation produced much useful research. In business history for example the subject broadened out to include work using insurance records, bankruptcy cases and other sources to look at smaller more typical firms. But specialisation was accompanied by a damaging compartmentalisation which generally hindered understanding of historical processes in the round (Wrightson 1993; Marshall 1997). The divorce of business history from labour history was an obstacle to understanding industrial relations, whilst urban history separate from agricultural history encouraged individual case studies rather than attempts to understand links between the two. In the field of demography, path-breaking work appeared using many new techniques but demography in Britain until the last decade or two was predominantly a technical subject, generally defined to exclude discussion of courtship, sexual behaviour or sexuality without which an understanding of changes in nuptiality and fertility can only be partial (Wrigley and Schofield 1981; Wrigley et al. 2005). Such concerns were left to cultural historians. With one or two key exceptions the need to understand long-term change in a holistic way slipped down the agenda.

Thus, in its older forms, economic history was in retreat in Britain in the 1980s and 1990s. Many independent departments of the subject that were opened in the 1970s were re-merged with history. The identification of economic history with increasingly formalised economics had weakened interest in the subject and fragmentation into specialised fields undermined both the rounded identity of economic history and its integrative role in social science. The counter-attraction of social and cultural history, the retreat from positivism and the decline of Marxism with its stress on the economy, also contributed to the diminishing role of economic history within the history establishment. Especially in the neo-liberal years of Thatcher and Reagan, concern to avoid any charge of economic or technological determinism or any association with what popular opinion now saw as a discredited body of theory contributed to a general and damaging disinterest in the relationship between the economy and the rest of society. Economic retrenchment since the 1980s and especially in recent years has also played a role in the fortunes of the discipline. It is more difficult to gain research funding or an academic position if one's subject is not vocational and if one's research topic does not have contemporary policy relevance or a discernible 'impact' in generating economic growth or social stability. Economic history of the recent past, attuned to contemporary problems and dominant economic philosophy, thus fares relatively well compared with medieval or pre-industrial studies. European and private research funding helps to fill the gaps but differentially. Thus whilst a number of major trans-European projects (in early modern textile history, for example) and medical research in all periods have been salient in the last decades, many other fields have been relatively discouraged.[12]

From imperial history to global history

There was a strong internationalist flavour to many early twentieth-century works in British economic history: a preoccupation with international trade and with the nature of economic development in various parts of the globe (Berg 1992). It might be argued that the early internationalist strand in the discipline was influenced by Britain's contemporary position in global trade and finance and by the powerful, but weakening, formal and informal empire over the course of the twentieth century. This helps to explain the link between social reform and imperialism that drove so many of the early practitioners in our field, making them adherents of tariff reform and imperial preference and influencing their research focus in particular ways (Semmel 1960). This also partly explains the preoccupation in economic history throughout the twentieth century with debates about the costs and benefits of empire and of slavery, research on particular colonies and ex-colonies and research on Britain's role in global shipping and finance. Similarly, relating directly to the close imperial bond between Britain and India, the work of British scholars has been important in the historiography of Indian economic development, contributing to lively debates about the positive as well as the negative impact of the imperial relationship upon Indian economic development (see Parthasarathi, chapter 17 in this volume) (Bayly 2004; Ferguson 2004).

Although the internationalism of economic history declined in relative terms in the middle decades of the twentieth century, a recent flowering of global economic history is provoking long-run comparative data projects and re-evaluations of the processes of industrialisation on a global scale. British historians have played a major role in the analysis of global relative factor prices, wage comparisons and comparative GDP, challenging the California School's conclusions about the timing and causes of the Great Divergence (Broadberry and Gupta 2006; Allen 2009; Allen et al. 2011; Broadberry et al. 2011). There is also growing interest in the economic histories of Africa and the Middle East and promising signs of a shift from Anglocentric and Eurocentric studies. But too often this literature applies western yardsticks and methodological assumptions to other parts of the globe, rather than using the knowledge of growth and development elsewhere to reflect and inform how we might differently view all paths and patterns of change, including western experiences.

From the history of consumption to the economics of material culture

Until the last three decades or so, economic history in Britain and elsewhere has privileged the study of production over consumption, supply over demand. But as this began to change it opened up the discipline to new sorts of insights from social and cultural history. Whilst the supply side remained the focus of the discipline, the input from social history was concentrated in the area of labour relations and social conditions affecting the supply and quality of the workforce, or on the determinants of entrepreneurial quality. Once demand was in the ascendant in the discipline, the way was open for insights from museum studies, cultural anthropology, fashion, design and art history to join with economic history in providing new insights into the processes of economic growth as driven by changes in consumption, in ideas and in culture. Thus the last decade has seen major studies of households and their contents, interpersonal relationships of material support and credit, textiles and dress, fashion and furnishings, reading and books, comestibles and the objects and rituals surrounding their consumption, lifestyles, nutrition, health, leisure and sociability. But these cannot be studied in isolation from internal and international trading patterns and logistics, including the translation of changes in taste, incomes and demand into changes in supply, through global routes and global relationships. Thus a significant segment of economic history is, in many corners of academe, and in alliance with other social science, arts and science disciplines, currently reinventing itself in Britain. A number of historians have forged new alliances with the boom in cultural history in the past two decades and this has been fundamental in the growth of a global orientation that interrogates cultural difference and examines the impact of cultural as well as economic exchange.[13]

Conclusion

Britain's economic and intellectual trajectory over many centuries, her changing position in the world economy, her various political and cultural alliances and antagonisms have fed into the social construction of all academic disciplines but perhaps most of all into economics and economic history, because of their strong association with ideological and policy imperatives. The current expansion of global history, and its ability to question assumptions and methodologies long accepted as universal, creates an opportunity for renewal of the subject. Whether or not the opportunity will be fully taken by economic historians depends upon their first accepting the normative nature of the subject in the past and the forces that made it so.

Notes

1 Whether Graunt or Petty wrote this work is a matter of some dispute: see Cullen 1975 p. 2.
2 Coleman (1987: 5–56) emphasises the importance of these writers in forming economic history in Britain.
3 All of the above-mentioned authors and their works can be further explored in the first instance via the online *Oxford Dictionary of National Biography*: http://www.oxforddnb.com
4 Toynbee died in 1883 at the age of 30.
5 William Cunningham and J. E. Thorold Rogers, for example.
6 All of the historians mentioned in this section are considered by Coleman and Kadish and have informative recently revised entries in the *Oxford Dictionary of National Biography* online http://www.oxforddnb.com
7 The first University Settlement was inspired by Arnold Toynbee.
8 Further provoked by Rostow (1949).
9 *The Problems and Methods of Economic History* was translated into Spanish and Italian in the early 1970s. *An Economic Theory of the Feudal System* (1962) was not translated into English until 1976.
10 The exception being acknowledgement of the *Annales* in the first paragraph of the first issue of *Past & Present*. The *Annales* movement was generally (wrongly) associated with Marxism and had too broad a cultural and geographical reference to appeal to most British economic historians of the time.
11 This is illustrated by the British individuals interviewed in Lyons et al. (2008). See review, Hudson (2009).
12 European Union funding has underpinned trans-national research within Europe whilst the Wellcome Trust ploughed much money into medical history in the 1980s and 1990s.
13 Seen most obviously but by no means exclusively in the work of the Centre for Global History, University of Warwick: warwick.ac.uk/fac/arts/history/ghcc

References

Allen, R. C. (2009) *The British Industrial Revolution in Global Perspective.* Cambridge.

Allen, R. C., J.-P. Bassino, D. Ma, C. Moll-Murata and J. L. van Zanden (2011) 'Wages, Prices and Living Standards in China, 1738–1925: In Comparison with Europe, Japan, and India' *Economic History Review* 64, February supplement, 8–38.

Ashley, W. J. (1888, 1893) *Introduction to Economic History and Theory* (vol. 1: 1888, vol. 2: 1893). London and New York.

Ashton, T. S. (1948) *The Industrial Revolution, 1760–1830.* Oxford.

Ashton, T. S. (1959) *Economic Fluctuations in England, 1700–1800.* Oxford.

Ashworth, W. (2003) *Customs and Excise: Trade, Production and Consumption in England, 1640–1845.* Oxford.

Backhouse, R. and K. Tribe (2014) 'Economic Thought and Ideology' in R. Floud and J. Humphries, eds., *The Cambridge History of Modern Britain*, vol. 2. Cambridge, 506–28.

Bayly, C. A. (2004) *The Birth of the Modern World: Global Connections and Comparisons, 1780–1914.* Oxford.

Berg, M. (1992) 'The First Women Economic Historians' *Economic History Review* 45.2, 308–29.

Berg, M. (2015) 'East–West Dialogues: Economic Historians, the Cold War and Détente' *Journal of Modern History* 87.1, 36–71.

Braudel, F. (1972) *The Mediterranean and the Mediterranean World in the Age of Philip II.* London.

Broadberry, S. N. (2006) *Market Services and the Productivity Race, 1850–2000: Britain in International Perspective.* Cambridge.

Broadberry, S. N. and B. Gupta (2006) 'The Early Modern Great Divergence: Wages, Prices and Economic Development in Europe and Asia, 1500–1800' *Economic History Review* 59.1, 2–31.

Broadberry, S. N., B. Campbell, A. Klein, M. Overton and B. van Leeuwen (2011) 'English Economic Growth, 1270–1700' www.lse.ac.uk/economicHistory/seminars/ModernAndComparative/papers2011-12/Papers/Broadberry.pdf

Broadberry, S. N., B. Campbell, A. Klein, M. Overton and B. van Leeuwen (2015) *British Economic Growth, 1270–1870.* Cambridge.

Clapham, J. H. (1926–38) *An Economic History of Modern Britain*, 3 vols. Cambridge.

Clapham, J. H. (1944) *The Bank of England: A History, 1694–1914*, 2 vols. Cambridge and New York.
Clark, C. (1940) *The Conditions of Economic Progress*. London.
Cliffe Leslie, T. E. (1870) 'The Political Economy of Adam Smith' *Fortnightly Review* (November 1).
Cliffe Leslie, T. E. (1875) 'The History of German Political Economy' *Fortnightly Review* (July 1).
Cliffe Leslie, T. E. (1879) *Essays in Political and Moral Philosophy*. Dublin and London.
Coleman, D. C. (1985) 'What is Economic History?' *History Today* 35, 2.
Coleman, D. C. (1987) *History and the Economic Past: The Rise and Decline of Economic History in Britain*. Oxford.
Coleman, D. C. (1995) 'History, Economic History and the Numbers Game' *Historical Journal* 38.3, 635–46.
Cook, T. and G. O'Hara (2011) *Statistics and the Public Sphere: Numbers and the People in Modern Britain, c. 1800–2000*. London.
Crafts, N. F. R. (1985) *British Economic Growth during the Industrial Revolution*. Oxford.
Crafts, N. F. R. (1987) 'Cliometrics 1971–86: A Survey' *Journal of Applied Economics* 2, 171–92.
Cullen, M. J. (1975) *The Statistical Movement in Early Victorian Britain: The Foundations of Empirical Social Science*. London.
Cunningham, W. (1882) *The Growth of English Industry and Commerce*. Cambridge.
Deane, P. (1953) *Colonial Social Accounting*. Cambridge.
Deane, P. and W. A. Cole (1962) *British Economic Growth, 1688–1959: Trends and Structure*. Cambridge.
Epstein, S. R. and M. Praak, eds. (2010) *Guilds, Innovation and the European Economy, 1400–1800*. Cambridge.
Feinstein, C. (1972) *National Income, Expenditure and Output of the United Kingdom, 1855–1965*. Cambridge.
Ferguson, N. (2004) *Empire: How Britain Made the Modern World*. London.
Finn, M. C. (2013) *The Character of Credit: Personal Debt in English Culture, 1740–1914*. Cambridge.
Gilboy, E. W. (1938) 'The Propensity to Consume' *Quarterly Journal of Economics* 53.1, 120–40.
Glass, D. V. (1973) *Numbering the People: The Eighteenth-century Population Controversy and the Development of Census and Vital Statistics in Britain*. Farnborough.
Goldman, L. (2013) *The Life of R. H. Tawney: Socialism and History*. London.
Graunt, J. (1662) 'Natural and Political Observations upon the Bills of Mortality' in Hull (1899), vol. 2.
Hacking, I. (1990) *The Taming of Chance*. Cambridge.
Harte, N. B., ed. (1971) *The Study of Economic History: Collected Inaugural Lectures 1893–1970*. London.
Harte, N. B. (2001) 'The Economic History Society' in Hudson (2001).
Higgs, E. (1987) 'Women, Occupations and Work in the Nineteenth-century Census' *History Workshop Journal* 23, 59–80.
Hobsbawm, E. (2002) *Interesting Times: A Twentieth-Century Life*. London.
Hodgson, G. M. (2001) *How Economics Forgot History: The Problem of Historical Specificity in Social Science*. London.
Hoppit, J. (1996) 'Political Arithmetic in Eighteenth-century England' *Economic History Review* 49.3, 516–40.
Hoppit, J. (2002) *A Land of Liberty? England, 1689–1727*. Oxford.
Hoppit, J. (2006) 'The Contexts and Contours of British Economic Literature, 1660–1760' *Historical Journal* 49.1, 79–110.
Hudson, P., ed. (2001) *Living Economic and Social History*. Glasgow.
Hudson, P. (2003) 'Economic History' in S. Berger, H. Feldner and K. Passmore, eds., *Writing History: Theory and Practice*. London, 252–70.
Hudson, P. (2009) Review of Lyons et al. (2008) *Economic History Review* 62.3, 779–81.
Hull, C. H., ed. (1899) *The Economic Writings of Sir William Petty*, 2 vols. Cambridge.
Kadish, A. (1989) *Historians, Economists, and Economic History*. London.
Kadish, A. (2006) 'James Edwin Thorold Rogers (1823–1890)' *Oxford Dictionary of National Biography* http://www.oxforddnb.com/view/article/23979 (accessed 6 March 2013).
Kaye, H. J. (1995) *The British Marxist Historians*. Basingstoke.
King, W. T. C. (1936) *History of the London Discount Market*. London.
Koot, G. M. (1987) *English Historical Economics, 1870–1926*. Cambridge.
Koot, G. M. (2006) 'Cunningham, William (1849–1919)' *Oxford Dictionary of National Biography* http://www.oxforddnb.com/view/article/32669 (accessed 6 March 2013).

Kula, W. (1976) *An Economic Theory of the Feudal System: Towards a Model of the Polish Economy, 1500–1800.* London.

Kula, W. (2002) *The Problems and Methods of Economic History.* Aldershot.

Lyons, J., L. P. Cain and S. H. Williamson, eds. (2008) *Reflections on the Cliometrics Revolution: Conversations with Economic Historians.* London.

Maloney, J. (1976) 'Marshall, Cunningham and the Emerging Economics Profession' *Economic History Review* 29.3, 440–51.

Malthus, T. R. (1836) *Principles of Political Economy*, 2nd edn., repr. Oxford 1951.

Marshall, J. D. (1997) *The Tyranny of the Discrete.* Aldershot.

Mitchell, B. R. and P. Deane (1988) *Abstract of British Historical Statistics.* Cambridge.

Muldrew, C. (1998) *The Economy of Obligation: The Culture of Credit and Social Relations in Early Modern England.* Basingstoke.

Offer, A. (2008) 'Charles Feinstein (1932–2004) and British Historical National Accounts', *Proceedings of the British Academy: Biographical Memoirs of Fellows*, vol. 7.

Perkins, H. (1969) *The Origins of Modern English Society.* London.

Petty, W. (1664) 'Verbum Sapienti' in Hull (1899), vol. 1.

Petty, W. (1676) 'Political Arithmetic' in Hull (1899), vol. 1.

Petty, W. (1687) 'A Treatise of Ireland' in Hull (1899) vol. 2.

Pollard, S. (1981) *Peaceful Conquest: The Industrialisation of Europe, 1760–1970.* Oxford.

Porter, T. M. (1988) *The Rise of Statistical Thinking, 1820–1900.* Princeton, NJ.

Porter, T. M. (2010) *Karl Pearson: The Scientific Life in a Statistical Age.* Princeton, NJ.

Postan, M. M. (1972) *The Medieval Economy and Society: An Economic History of Britain, 1100–1500.* Berkeley, CA.

Raffaelli, T. (2004) 'Whatever Happened to Marshall's Industrial Economics?' *European Journal of the History of Economic Thought* 11.2, 209–29.

Renton, D. (2005) 'Studying Their Own Nation without Insularity? The British Marxist Historians Reconsidered' *Science and Society*, 69.4, 559–79.

Rostow, W. W. (1949) *British Economy of the Nineteenth Century.* Oxford.

Rostow, W. W. (1960) *The Stages of Economic Growth: A Non-Communist Manifesto.* Cambridge.

Rutherford, M. (2001) 'Institutional Economics: Then and Now' *Journal of Economic Perspectives* 15.3, 185–90.

Semmel, B., ed. (1960) *Imperialism and Social Reform: English Social-Imperial Thought, 1895–1914.* London.

Sinclair, J. (1791–8) *The Statistical Account of Scotland.* Edinburgh.

Tribe, K. (2015) 'The Measurement of Economic Activity and the Growth Metric: Constructing National Income in Britain, 1907–41' in *The Economy of the Word: Language, History, and Economics.* Oxford, 89–107.

Weber, M. (1930) *The Protestant Ethic and the Spirit of Capitalism* (trans. T. Parsons). London.

Weber, M. (1947) *The Theory of Social and Economic Organization* (trans. A. M. Henderson and T. Parsons). New York.

Williams, E. (1944) *Capitalism and Slavery.* Chapel Hill, NC.

Winter, J. M. and D. M. Joslin, eds. (1972) *R. H. Tawney's Commonplace Book.* Cambridge.

Wrightson, K. (1993) 'The Enclosure of English Social History' in A. Wilson, ed., *Rethinking Social History.* Manchester.

Wrigley, E. A. (2004) *Poverty, Progress and Population.* Cambridge.

Wrigley, E. A. and D. Souden, eds. (1986) *The Works of Thomas Robert Malthus*, 8 vols. London.

Wrigley, E. A. and R. S. Schofield (1981) *The Population History of England and Wales, 1541–1871.* Cambridge.

Wrigley, E. A., R. S. Davies, J. E. Oeppen and R. S. Schofield (2005) *English Population History from Family Reconstitution.* Cambridge.

Zamagni, V. (2010) 'What is the Message of *Understanding the Process of Economic Change* for Historians?' *Structural Change and Economic Dynamics* 21.2, 157–63.

3

BEYOND THE OLD AND THE NEW

Economic history in the United States

Naomi R. Lamoreaux[1]

There have never been separate departments of economic history in the United States. Instead, economic historians have always been divided in varying proportions among economics and history departments, with the occasional appointment in sociology or political science. This lack of an independent disciplinary home has had both positive and negative consequences for the field. On the minus side, practitioners have invariably found themselves in the position of step-children in their parent disciplines, often losing out in the competition for attention and resources to their mainstream brethren. On the plus side, economic historians have never been isolated from intellectual developments in their home disciplines. As a result, the field has constantly been reinvigorated by borrowings from economics, history, and the other disciplines within which economic historians reside.

This reinvigoration has worked best when ideas stimulated by developments in one discipline were tested in a broader interdisciplinary context. After the so-called Cliometric Revolution of the 1960s, however, economists came to dominate the practice of economic history in the United States. Historians largely abandoned the field and interdisciplinary conversation for the most part came to a halt. This chapter tells the story of that transformation and its effect on the practice of economic history. In recent years there has been a resurgence of interest in the field among historians, and the essay ends with a discussion of the potential that this development brings for renewed cross-disciplinary fertilization.

Early (inter) disciplinary foundations

Economic history had its formal beginnings in the United States in the late nineteenth century at the very moment when the structure of the country's newly emerging universities was solidifying around formal academic departments (Rudolph 1965: 399–402; Veysey 1965: 320–4). Harvard's economics faculty awarded the nation's first chair in economic history to British scholar William J. Ashley in 1892, just a few years before its members formally constituted themselves a department (Cole 1968: 558–60; Mason and Lamont 1982: 396–9). Other chairs in the field were established around the same time by economics departments preoccupied with forming their professional identities and distinguishing what they did from other units of the university (Mitch 2011: 240–1). An important part of the process of department building was the differentiation of the various social sciences from history, the main subject around which teaching in old-style colleges had been organized, and so the new social sciences staked out claims to historical study by their practitioners, even though historians elsewhere might be engaged in very similar research (Ross 1991; Adcock 2003; Mitch 2011).

In economics, the role of history in the process of identity formation was more fraught than in the other social sciences because the dominance of classical economics was then under assault by scholars like Richard T. Ely who had been trained in the German school of historical economics. The latter deplored the classical theorists' deductive methods, arguing that economists could only generate useful knowledge if they proceeded inductively and inferred the laws and principles of economic life through careful study of the past.[2] The spread to the United States of marginalist ideas beginning in the late 1880s eased the strain between the old guard and their historicist challengers and paved the way for a productive division of labor between economic historians and economists more generally (Mason and Lamont 1982). Uniquely equipped to probe the stages through which economies had evolved over the centuries, economic historians were "expected to play an important part in that reconstruction of economic science which was then going on" (Callender 1913: 80). As Ashley announced upon his arrival at Harvard, economists now willingly acknowledged that "economic conclusions are *relative* to given conditions," that those conditions change over time, and that understanding such changes requires consideration of a range of factors besides purely economic ones (Ashley 1893: 118).

Although the first chairs in economic history were all in economics programs, research in the subject was simultaneously expanding within history departments. Like economics, the field of history was undergoing professionalization during the late nineteenth century. Many of the new breed of academic historians were trained in Germany, where they absorbed research techniques similar to those advocated by historical economists (Higham 1965). Comparing historical articles published in economics journals such as the *Journal of Political Economy* (*JPE*) or the *Quarterly Journal of Economics* (*QJE*) with those appearing in the *American Historical Review* (*AHR*) or other historical journals in the early twentieth century, one is struck by how little there was to differentiate the work methodologically. Searches of JSTOR show, moreover, that authors who published historical articles in economics journals often simultaneously disseminated their research in history and other social science publications, as well as by writing books. Even the assumptions about human behavior that historians made were generally the same as those made by economists. For example, the so-called "Progressive" historians who dominated the study of US history analyzed the economic underpinnings of major historical developments in ways that economists found appealing. One of the most famous products of this school, Charles A. Beard's 1913 book arguing that the Constitution was shaped by the economic interests of the founding fathers, received favorable reviews in leading economics journals (see Levermore 1914; Wright 1914).

Perhaps because so little writing in economic history was geared toward generating broad theoretical insights, the field's relationship to the larger discipline of economics soon became strained. Guy Callender complained in 1913 that economists had lost interest in history to such an extent that "topics in economic history found no place upon their programme" (Callender 1913: 81). Although the *QJE* and especially the *JPE* continued to publish historical pieces, articles on economic history were strikingly absent from the American Economic Association's new flagship journal, the *American Economic Review* (*AER*), which began publication in 1911. There were also few presentations on economic history at the association's annual meetings until economic historians began to assert themselves in 1926 by organizing what became a regular round table on the field.

The years following the First World War were a time of institution building in economic history. Most of the new organizations founded during the 1920s aimed to bolster the relationship between economic history and economics. Ashley's successor at Harvard, Edwin Gay, joined with Wesley Mitchell, a historically minded economist at Columbia, to found the National Bureau of Economic Research (NBER) on the principle that research in economic history, particularly the careful collection of long-term quantitative data sets, provided a vital foundation for economic policy making. Other new organizations created at this time, such as the Commission on Recent Economic Changes, the Commission on Recent Social Trends, and the Social Science Research Council, had similar motivations (Heaton 1952, 1965: 467–9; Cole 1968: 573–83).

Writing in 1931, British economic historian J. H. Clapham faulted earlier scholarship in the field for its tendency to generalize on the basis of scanty data or even worse the statements of self-interested participants. These criticisms fell on fertile ground in the United States, where economic historians in economics departments increasingly called upon their colleagues to make more systematic use of quantitative methods (see, for example, Usher 1932). As one economist later put it, "the outstanding characteristic" of economic history writing in the 1930s was scholars' attention to "such questions as How much? How many? How quickly? Or How representative?" (Heaton 1942). The result was the birth during the interwar period of a new style of economic history that intentionally put research in the field in service of the economics profession, or, as Chester Wright (1938) put it, in service of raising the standard of living. Using historical data, for example, Elizabeth Gilboy (1934) derived supply and demand curves for commodities such as tea and coffee, and scholars such as Mitchell (1927), Edwin Wilson (1934), and Clarence Long (1939) analyzed the structure of the business cycle.

In their zeal for quantification, some economists were already challenging the conventional wisdom of historians in ways that foreshadowed the later Cliometric Revolution. For example, C. M. Thompson (1927) criticized the idea that the antebellum South was overspecialized in cotton, anticipating findings by Albert Fishlow (1964) and Ralph Anderson and Robert Gallman (1977) by reporting that the southern United States produced more than enough food for the region's sustenance and that large cotton plantations were also large producers of foodstuffs. Similarly, Carter Goodrich and Sol Davison (1935 and 1936) contested Frederick Jackson Turner's famous thesis that the frontier functioned as a "safety valve" for urban workers by presenting evidence on the high costs of migration and on the small number of industrial laborers who actually moved west.

Economic historians in economics departments also began to call for more use of economic theory in historical research. According to Gay, for example, German historical economics had failed to generate a body of inductive theory that could replace the deductive insights of mainstream theorists, but in response to its challenge "economics ha[d] increased the range and depth of its contemporary observation; its use of the deductive method ha[d] become more guarded, its analysis more subtle." In Gay's opinion, these changes had made possible a new cooperative relationship between economic history and economics, characterized by "more community of training, interest and awareness of interdependence" between the two bodies of scholarship. For the relationship to work, however, Gay argued that economic history had to be informed by, as well as to inform, economic theory (Gay 1941: 14–15).

Although economic historians trained in economics departments were increasingly oriented toward their parent discipline by the 1930s, they maintained ties with practitioners in history and other disciplines. And more than ties: most contemporary writing by economists on historical topics continued to be qualitative and descriptive and to differ little in terms of sources and methods from writing on similar topics by historians.[3] When American economic historians determined to organize their own professional society in 1941, therefore, it was an interdisciplinary effort. A group of historians had proposed to form an Industrial History Society in 1939, but that organization never came to fruition. Instead, a small coterie of economists led by Anne Bezanson, Arthur Cole, Earl Hamilton, and Herbert Heaton swept the historians into a new Economic History Association (EHA), ratified at joint meetings with both the AHA and the AEA in 1940. At the outset, the EHA had 361 members and supported its own scholarly publication, the *Journal of Economic History* (*JEH*) (Heaton 1941: 107–9; 1965: 470–2).

The formation of the EHA was accompanied by a burst of related organization building led by many of the same individuals. An important result was the creation of the Committee for Research in Economic History (CREH) in the winter of 1940–41 with support from the Rockefeller Foundation (Cole 1970; Sass 1986: 54–9). The Committee sponsored a number of important studies and also became the locus of planning for a new Research Center in Entrepreneurial History, which was founded, again with Rockefeller seed money, at Harvard in 1948. Although the scholars who organized the EHA and the CREH were mainly economists, both organizations attracted an interdisciplinary mix of participants. The early issues of the *JEH* published an eclectic range of scholarship. For example, Volume 5's regular issues included one article by an economist, five by historians, one by a sociologist, and one by a geographer. The same volume's "Tasks" issue (papers presented at the EHA's annual meeting) contained two papers by economists, two by historians, and two by sociologists (including a paper by C. Wright Mills on "The American Business Elite"). One of the CREH's major accomplishments was to fund a series of studies of the role of government in the American economy before the Civil War. Commissioned in the wake of the New Deal, these studies aimed to show that government had played an active role in the US economy through much of its history.[4] This project produced classic works by historians Oscar Handlin and Mary Flug Handlin (1947) and political scientist Louis Hartz (1948), among others.

The group that assembled at the Research Center in Entrepreneurial History was even more interdisciplinary. The starting point for their thinking was Joseph Schumpeter's concept of entrepreneurship as a creative act that in discontinuous fashion shifted outward the economy's production possibility frontier (Schumpeter 1934). Entrepreneurship was important to study, they believed, because this kind of creativity was the key to greater economic well-being. Schumpeter himself was unable to explain why some societies at some times produced disproportionate numbers of entrepreneurs, and neoclassical price theory also appeared to lack answers to such questions. After an active search for a usable theory (traceable through the pages of the center's in-house organ, "Explorations in Entrepreneurial History"), they turned to Parsonian sociology. Some of the most important historians with the center, such as David Landes, Thomas Cochran, and Alfred D. Chandler, Jr., consistently employed concepts and addressed debates at the heart of this sociological literature, even when they did not make extensive use of its rather arcane vocabulary and categories of analysis (Galambos 1969; Sass 1986: 107–223).

As the star-studded list of scholars associated with these ventures suggests, the interdisciplinary collaboration sparked during this period of organization building was extraordinarily fruitful. But it would not last. The Rockefeller Foundation moved on to fund other activities, and the CREH and its spinoff Research Center in Entrepreneurial History faded out of existence when their initial grants expired (Cole 1970; Sass 1986: 243–9). For several decades the EHA continued to attract members from history as well as economics and to publish work by scholars trained in both disciplines (and occasionally other fields as well), but the Cliometric Revolution of the 1960s would disrupt the interdisciplinary mix, and economists would increasingly dominate both the association and its journal.

The Cliometric Revolution

Spurred by the Great Depression, the Second World War, and the Cold War that followed, the discipline of economics underwent major changes over the middle third of the twentieth century, including the invention of national income accounting, the development of econometrics, and the spread of new computer technology (Morgan 2003). Economists were also increasingly preoccupied during this period with understanding how newly independent nations might develop vibrant free-market economies (Easterly 2001), and as a result interest in the history of countries that had successfully negotiated the transition to sustained economic growth was on the rise. The Cliometric Revolution would emerge out of a combination of this renewed interest in history and the energetic iconoclasm of proponents of the new quantitative methods.

The basic elements of the revolution were already apparent in 1960 at a conference organized by the International Economic Association around W. W. Rostow's book, *The Stages of Economic Growth* (1960). At stake was Rostow's theory that the US and Western European economies had "taken off" by means of large-scale investments in leading sectors like the railroad. The most biting critiques were offered by two historically minded American economists who between them trained most of the leaders of the Cliometric Revolution: Simon Kuznets (1963), a development economist famous for his pioneering work in national income accounting,[5] and Alexander Gerschenkron (1963), a specialist in Soviet planning who was developing his own, more historically contingent theory of economic growth.[6] Although there was undoubtedly a political subtext to the debate (Rostow subtitled his book *A Non-Communist Manifesto*), the critique was fundamentally methodological. Rostow had provided only the most casual theoretical and empirical support for his stage theory of economic development, and his critics bore in on both weaknesses. Another attendee at the conference, Douglass North, himself one of the leaders of the Cliometric Revolution, put forward an alternative, export-led theory of economic development (North 1961 and 1963a). When North published his book the next year, it was subjected to similar critical scrutiny (see, for example, Fishlow 1964). Cliometrics' negative and reactive essence was on display in both episodes: practitioners used basic economic theory to subject scholarly works to quantitative tests of consistency with the evidence and generally found them wanting, regardless of their interpretative slant.[7]

During the post-Sputnik expansion of higher education, funds were suddenly available to support initiatives in the quantitative social sciences. The same year as the Rostow conference a group of entrepreneurial young economists at Purdue, including Lance Davis and Jonathan R. T. Hughes, secured backing for a series of conferences to promote this "new economic history" (Davis 1990: 9–10). The Purdue meetings became famous for their feisty criticism and camaraderie, and they helped to form participants into a cohesive group. According to Hughes, "the intellectual atmosphere was intense" but also fun (Hughes 1985: 3; 1991: 24). Robert Fogel, a Kuznets student who would later share the Nobel Prize in economics with North, was still writing his dissertation when he attended the 1960 meeting and got caught up in the "tremendous excitement and exhilaration" (Fogel 1990: 6). Robert Gallman went to the first Purdue meeting thinking of himself "as a development economist of a Kuznetsian variety." The conference converted him to economic history and transformed his career (Gallman 1992: 5–6).

Although the cliometricians made their mark by challenging existing scholarship, the older generations' response was initially positive. John Meyer recalled the reaction to his and Alfred Conrad's controversial paper (1958) critiquing the traditional view that slavery was unprofitable as "quite open-minded" (Meyer 1995: 4). Gallman agreed, noting that there was no general division between "cliometricians and traditionalists," and that several of the latter gave "thoughtful and friendly reviews" of cliometric papers (Gallman 1992: 4). Indeed, some senior economic historians saw the work as an extension of their own commitment to quantification, "welcomed the new departures with open arms, and minds," and rewarded the young cliometricians with leadership positions (Hughes 1985: 2). Cole offered the directorship of the Research Center in Entrepreneurial History to North in 1954 and three years later chose Meyer as acting editor of *Explorations in Entrepreneurial History* (the journal that grew out of the Center's in-house publication). Frederic Lane put North on the council that replaced the CREH in 1959, and the board of trustees of the EHA chose North and William Parker to be coeditors of the *JEH* in 1960 (Cole 1970; Sass 1986: 245; Williamson 1994: 116).

Over time, however, the reaction turned more negative. In part the problem was the increasingly pointed attacks that cliometricians mounted against earlier work. The "young turks," as Claudia Goldin (1995) called them, built interest in their achievements to a large extent by denigrating their predecessors. In a 1963 communication published in the *American Economic Review*, for example, North proclaimed that "a revolution is taking place in economic history in the United States" and went on to justify in sweeping terms the overthrow of the old regime. "Even a cursory examination of accepted 'truths' of U.S. economic history suggests," he asserted, "that many of them are inconsistent with elementary economic analysis and have never been subjected to – and would not survive – testing with statistical data" (North 1963b: 128–9) Two years later he expounded on the "deficiencies of economic history" as previously practiced. "Many writings in economic history are loaded with statements which have economic implications and imply causal relationships which . . . run counter to basic economic propositions" supported by only "a mishmash of quotations and oddly assorted statistics" (North 1965: 87).

There was, in fact, considerable "low hanging fruit" in the form of untested or inadequately documented quantitative statements in the literature. As Hughes recalled, "In those early years of Cliometrics it seemed like you could hardly miss. Pick any topic in Economic History. Did it make sense as theory? If not, why not? Were there data available? If so, BINGO" (Hughes 1985: 1–2). Fogel showed that Eugene Genovese's claim that plantation slavery hampered southern industrialization depended on a number of assumptions that Genovese never tested, for example that the relevant industries were characterized by economies of scale (Genovese 1962; Fogel 1967: 285–9). Peter Temin challenged historians' assertion that Andrew Jackson's destruction of the Second Bank of the United States was the root cause of the rapid inflation of the 1830s. He pointed out that such an argument implicitly assumed that bank reserves fell after Jackson's veto, but when he looked at banks' balance sheets (readily available in government publications), he found that historians had too readily taken the charges of Jackson's critics at face value (Schlesinger 1945; Hammond 1957; Temin 1969).

The older generation's antipathy to cliometrics focused in particular on Fogel's use of counterfactual analysis to dispute the notion that railroads were "indispensable" to American economic development. Fritz Redlich ranted to Gallman about "that madman Fogel" who "plans to build canals across the Appalachian Mountains" (Gallman 1992: 5), and after North and Parker published Fogel's article in the *JEH* in 1962, several EHA trustees moved to get them fired (North 1993: 11). The fuss about counterfactual history was itself, however, largely a proxy war for a more fundamental disagreement about the importance of entrepreneurial innovation to economic growth. Fogel promoted the neoclassical view that technological change was induced by movements in relative prices that signaled opportunities for profit. In the absence of the railroad, he argued, not only was it likely that the canal system would have expanded to meet the demand for low-cost transportation services in the USA, but the automobile could well have been developed earlier: "The axiom of indispensability proceeds on the implicit and unverified assumption that the success of railroads did not choke off the search for other solutions to the problem of overland transportation" (Fogel 1964: 14–15).

Other leading cliometricians shared Fogel's view that technological innovation was largely a response to demand-side stimuli. Meyer "tended to be very skeptical of the importance of any intangible, such as entrepreneurship" and committed "some of that skepticism to paper," despite his position as acting editor of *Explorations in Entrepreneurial History* (Meyer 1995: 22). North explicitly downgraded the role of the entrepreneur in his *Economic Growth of the United States*, arguing instead that technological innovations were "a nearly automatic response to successful expansion of industries in an acquisitive society under competitive market conditions." Although the cotton gin was "unquestionably the most significant invention during the years between 1790 and 1860," he thought there was little to be gained from studying Eli Whitney. The gin was the product of a "concerted search" for a solution to a pressing economic problem. If Whitney had not invented it, someone else would have (North 1961: 8, 52).

It was precisely this reliance on neoclassical price theory and the methodology of comparative statics that the economic historians who had been associated with the Harvard Center decried. Fogel's social savings calculation compared the cost of shipping various goods by railroad and the cheapest alternative means of transport at a given point in time. He later acknowledged that the calculation ignored possible dynamic consequences of the railroad, "such as the effect of transportation improvements on the spatial location of economic activity, induced changes in the industrial mix of products . . ., induced changes in the aggregate savings rate, and possible effects on either the rate of technological change in various industries or on the overall supply of inputs" (Fogel 1979: 5). Yet these were sorts of changes that the entrepreneurial historians thought should be the focus of attention. Chandler notably argued that Fogel's calculation underestimated the magnitude of the railroad's most important contribution to economic growth: the greater speed and regularity of transportation compared to canals, which made possible the integration of mass distribution and mass production in large, managerially directed enterprises (Chandler 1977).

What cliometricians like Fogel had done in effect was to move beyond Gay and completely upend the original division of labor between economics and economic history. At a time when economic theory was becoming more uniformly neoclassical (Morgan 2003), they pushed consciously and deliberately to expand its domain by emphasizing the explanatory value of the price signals and market processes that this type of theory was so well suited to analyze. For the most part, they used the neoclassical toolkit destructively – to critique the work of "traditional" economic historians, as well as to demolish each other's contributions. At the height of the Cliometric Revolution, however, some attempted to go further and formulate a positive theory of historical change. Thus Lance Davis and Douglass North co-authored a book-length study (1971) promoting the utility of a simple model in which rational actors organized to secure institutional change whenever the benefits of the change outweighed the costs of obtaining it.

Cliometricians succeeded in attracting the attention of the economics profession, advancing their own careers and bringing new practitioners into the field. As late as 1959, the EHA's individual members numbered 476, just 32 percent more than at the organization's inception.

By 1965, however, the rolls had swelled to more than 800 (Heaton 1965: 472). Most of the new members were economists, and the association took on an increasingly cliometric tone. Robert Whaples has analyzed trends in the content of the *JEH* and found a dramatic increase in the proportion of cliometric-type articles – up from about 10 percent in 1956–60 to more than 40 percent in 1966–70 to more than 70 percent in 1971–75 (Whaples 1991: 293). At the same time, cliometricians gained control of *Explorations in Entrepreneurial History* in 1969, renamed it *Explorations in Economic History*, and redefined the journal's target audience to be economic historians trained in economics (Rosenberg et al. 1970: 3; Neal 1999: 9–10).

The movement of economists into the EHA in turn induced many historians to switch their allegiance to a new organization called the Business History Conference (BHC). The BHC had its origin in a series of meetings that brought together economic and business historians critical of the atheoretical type of business history that N. S. B. Gras was promoting at the Harvard Business School. The group met sporadically between 1954 and 1958 and then yearly thereafter, and in 1971 transformed itself into a full-fledged professional association. Although many of the BHC's original members were economists, during the 1970s the organization increasingly provided an intellectual home to historians unhappy with cliometricians' dominance of the EHA (Lamoreaux et al. 1997: 61).

Bottom-up history and the cultural turn

Meanwhile, trends in the historical profession during the 1960s and 1970s, particularly the growth of "bottom-up" and "New Left" history, were fostering a basic distrust of cliometric work. Historians who wrote about the "underside" of history started from the premise that economic development had dire consequences for the bulk of the laboring population. They had little sympathy for the idea, espoused by many cliometricians, that market forces operated for the general good. Nonetheless, the view of human behavior that underpinned much of this scholarship was not fundamentally at odds with the cliometricians' assumption that human beings rationally pursued their economic self-interest (Sewell 2005: 22–80). New Left historians such as William Appleman Williams (1959 and 1969) and Gabriel Kolko (1963 and 1965) saw American foreign policy and government regulation as straightforward expressions of businesses' economic interests. Similarly, much of the bottom-up history of the period aimed to restore rational agency to those whom historians had ignored or treated as helpless victims (Thernstrom 1964; Dublin 1979; Prude 1983).

The growth of cultural history had a more profound effect on the relationship between the historical profession and economic history because it effectively redefined historical studies, in the words of one commentator, "as the investigation of the contextually situated production and transmission of meaning" (Toews 1987: 882). It is beyond the scope of this chapter to analyze the sources of this trend or survey its scope. Suffice it to say that some of the new cultural historians made sophisticated use of poststructural literary theory and the work of such thinkers as Michel Foucault, whereas others engaged in largely descriptive investigations of cultural practices. Virtually all, however, rejected the idea that human behavior could be reduced to the model of economic rationality at the heart of neoclassical theory. That model might apply to "capitalists," but not to most ordinary historical subjects. Thus, Michael Merrill, Christopher Clark, and James Henretta drew on ideas from the French *Annales* tradition to argue that the *mentalité* of early American farmers was not capitalist – that farmers put other values before profit maximization, such as insuring that their children would be able to earn a "competence" or maintaining an ethic of mutuality with members of their community (Merrill 1976; Henretta 1978; Clark 1979). Similarly, historians of American labor drew on E. P. Thompson and other British scholars to highlight the cultural traditions that bolstered resistance to industrialization (Montgomery 1968; Foner 1976; Sewell 2005: 22–80). Others rejected the simple model of homo economicus for everyone, claiming that capitalists too were imbedded in larger cultural systems that shaped their behavior, including their business decisions. Businessmen, for example, often discriminated in employment practices against women and minorities in ways that cannot be explained away as economically rational (Kessler-Harris 1990 and 1991; Kwolek-Folland 1994).

Within the larger historical profession, there was a general move in the 1980s and 1990s away from topics related to economic and business history, and, as a result, job opportunities in these subfields largely dried up. Many historians in the Business History Conference responded by embracing the shift to cultural history, eschewing not only economic history but also the types of business history, such as Chandler's studies of the managerial enterprise, that seemed to abstract business behavior from its larger cultural context. Indeed, critiquing "internalist" studies of the Chandlerian variety became a veritable industry (Rosen 2013). As an alternative, William Becker advised business historians to learn from what "those engaged in, broadly speaking, cultural studies" had to offer (Becker 1996: 4). Kenneth Lipartito rejected the "current practice" of explaining business behavior in "functional" terms and instead advocated an approach centered on the concept of business culture, which he defined as the "set of limiting and organizing concepts that determine what is real or rational for management, principles that are often tacit or unconscious" (Lipartito 1995: 2). Historian of technology Thomas J. Misa (1996: 55–6) likewise urged business historians to turn away from the "structural–functionalist approach pioneered by Alfred Chandler" and, following the lead of sociologists of knowledge, explore the tension-filled cultural systems that shaped business decision-making. There was simultaneously a concerted effort to move the study of gender and race into the center of business history. A search of the print archive of *Business and Economic History*, which published papers presented at the BHC's annual meeting, shows no papers with titles relating to women or gender before 1979, six from 1979 to 1989, and fifteen in the 1990s. Similarly, there was only one paper relating to African Americans or race before 1990 and then five in the 1990s.[8]

Contemporary developments in economic history

The movement of historians from the EHA into the BHC and the cultural turn accelerated at about the same time that controversy erupted over *Time on the Cross* (1974), the analysis of antebellum southern slavery offered by Fogel and his co-author Stanley Engerman. Fogel and Engerman began the book with a list of the conventional historical interpretations that their theoretically informed, quantitatively grounded research would overturn. In place of that received wisdom, they offered a relatively benign view of the institution of slavery in which rational, profit-maximizing plantation owners took care of their human property, understood that keeping families together was important for reproduction, used positive more than negative incentives to motivate their hands, and organized their workforces to capture economies of scale.

This kinder, gentler portrait of slavery rankled many historians, especially since Fogel and Engerman had reached beyond the kinds of questions that econometric techniques were most useful for resolving, such as whether the cultivation of cotton using slave labor was profitable or whether large plantations benefited from economies of scale, to consider the incentives that plantation owners used to drive their hands and whether enslaved workers internalized the Protestant work ethic. To address these more subtle issues of motivation required different kinds of sources and different sets of skills. Although historians hesitated to assess Fogel and Engerman's econometric work (they let other cliometricians do that), they felt no compunction about examining their handling of textual sources, and they found much to criticize in the way Fogel and Engerman read and analyzed plantation documents. For example, Herbert Gutman (1975) offered a devastating critique of Fogel and Engerman's claim that masters made relatively limited use of physical punishments such as whipping.

As cliometricans jumped into the debate and highlighted even more glaring faults, Gutman and others fretted that Fogel and Engerman's sloppiness would discourage historians from using quantitative techniques – that "the egregious errors" that critics had uncovered would provide "a perfect foil for those skeptical of efforts to employ techniques and methods of the social sciences in the reconstruction of the past" (Yetman 1976: 202). Whether it was indeed the errors that turned historians away is difficult to assess. Whatever push came from this debate may well have been swamped by the powerful pull of the cultural turn in the larger discipline. There is no doubt, however, that historians stopped following the criticism of Fogel and Engerman's work and stopped paying attention to research in economic history more generally. As a result, their views of the literature remained frozen in time, and most subsequent critics have written about the field as if there was little or no change in approach or method since the 1970s (see, for example, Adelman and Levy 2014). If they had not stopped paying attention, however, they would have seen that what was at stake in the debate over *Time on the Cross* was greater than tendentious research methods. At the heart of the controversy was a more fundamental argument over the appropriateness of the simple neoclassical models that Fogel and Engerman had used for studying the past.

Even before the debate over *Time on the Cross*, some leading economic historians had moved significantly away from basic neoclassical theory. North dismissively dubbed the earliest of these apostates the "Harvard Wing," because a number of them had studied with Gerschenkron at that institution (Sutch 1994: 77–9). By the mid-1970s, however, North himself had joined their ranks, declaring in his 1974 address as president of the Economic History Association: "Neo-classical economic theory has two major shortcomings for the economic historian. One, it was not designed to explain long-run economic change; and two, even within the context of the question it was designed to answer, it provides quite limited answers since it is immediately relevant to a world of perfect markets" (North 1974: 2). From the mid-1970s on, North worked to transcend these theoretical limits by developing his own, more general theory of institutional change (see North 1981, 1990, 2005; and North et al. 2009).

Parker had fretted in his own presidential address that economic historians, in their eagerness to showcase the explanatory power of market forces, were "in danger of producing simply a kind of hymn to what really happened" (Parker 1971: 6, 7). Not finding enough intellectual sustenance in neoclassical theory, he read more widely – in German historical economics, *Annales*-school history, sociology, and anthropology. As he later mused, "The response to opportunity is a problem of human organization – a political problem rather [than] an economic one. . . . It is about power and contrivance and how individuals control one another mutually." Parker strove to look "past the 'opportunity' part to this other element, where culture, society, and a collection of individual personalities all come into the structure of explanation, piled on top of one another in layers" (Parker 1991: 21).

The debate over *Time on the Cross* accelerated the move beyond basic neoclassical principles. At the simplest level, critics observed that the evidence on the brutal treatment of slaves was not consistent with the idea that rational, profit-maximizing slave owners took good care of their human property. However, a more profound revision emerged from scrutiny of Fogel and Engerman's claim that large slave plantations were more productive than small, slaveless farms. Plantations only appeared more efficient, the critics argued, because they grew relatively more cotton, which had a higher value in world markets than other crops (David and Temin 1976 and 1979; Wright 1976 and 1979). At existing market prices, it would have been profit maximizing for free farmers to grow as much cotton as could they pick, but instead they chose to grow relatively more corn. To explain this behavior Gavin Wright (1978) developed a "safety-first" model in which small farmers were primarily concerned with their ability to feed their families and preserve their status as independent landowners. If historians had been paying attention, they might have noticed that Wright's model was analogous in important ways to the concept of competency that historians were developing around the same time to explain the *mentalité* of early nineteenth-century northern farmers (Merrill 1976; Henretta 1978; Clark 1979).

By the 1970s mainstream economists were developing new fields of research such as information economics, game theory, and mechanism design that recognized that information was imperfect and costly, that human beings were only boundedly rational, that they behaved strategically, that they differed in their access to information, that models might yield multiple equilibria, and that the outcome of any economic process might therefore be a matter of history.[9] Stimulated by these developments many of the cliometricians who had criticized *Time on the Cross* pushed the field of economic history in new directions in the years that followed. Temin, for example, sought to understand why popular support for federal pharmaceutical regulation was so concentrated temporally and turned to anthropology for a model of how personality type might interact with change in the larger society to produce this pattern (Temin 1980). Collaborating with historian Louis Galambos (1987), he puzzled over the AT&T executives who settled the antitrust suit against the company by making what was (with hindsight) the wrongheaded choice to spin off Bell Labs and Western Electric (that is, the company's research and development capabilities) into a separate company. He joined with Daniel Raff and Naomi Lamoreaux to explore how some of the new theory might be useful for writing business history (see Temin 1991; Lamoreaux and Raff 1995; Lamoreaux et al. 1999 and 2003). He also, in his presidential address to the Economic History Association, called for economic historians to take up the study of culture (Temin 1997a).

David, pondering the awkward organization of the QWERTY typewriter keyboard, seized upon the concept of path dependence and argued that societies find it difficult to adopt alternative technologies or ways of organizing economic activity, even when it would clearly be more efficient to do so (David 1985). He and Gavin Wright challenged the simple notion that economic actors respond in a straightforward neoclassical way to factor endowments. The US rise to industrial leadership in the early twentieth century may have been resource-based, they showed, but the USA was not particularly well-endowed with mineral resources. At the heart of the country's economic success, in their view, was a set of institutions and cultural beliefs that encouraged individuals and companies to search for minerals, provided them with the necessary expertise, and supported and even subsidized their efforts (David and Wright 1997). Wright went on to devote much of his career to documenting the role that racism played in maintaining apartheid-like institutions in the South, making the case that change had to be imposed by the federal government even though whites as well as blacks stood to benefit from an end to segregation (Wright 1986 and 2013).

This is not to say that economic historians abandoned neoclassical theory or their cliometric roots. Most economic historians draw eclectically on a mix of theoretical traditions and still consider the standard model of perfect competition to be a valuable part of their toolkit. Thus Temin used a clever one-factor (so-called Ricardian) trade model to defend the idea that there was an industrial revolution in Britain (Temin 1997b), and Engerman and Kenneth

Sokoloff (a Fogel student) traced present-day variation in levels of economic development in the Americas to the factor endowments that Europeans encountered at the time of settlement (2012). Although these contributions underscore the continued power of simple theoretical concepts in economic history, they also show how far the field has moved since the Cliometric Revolution. Temin used his model to challenge the essentially neoclassical arguments of N. F. R. Crafts and C. Knick Harley (Harley1982; Crafts 1985; Crafts and Harley 1992) that there was no significant break that could be called an industrial revolution in Britain in the late eighteenth century, and his critique has provided reinforcement to economic historians, such as Joel Mokyr (a student of Parker's), who has argued that enlightenment culture was an important driver of the industrial revolution (Mokyr 2009). Moreover, Engerman and Sokoloff did not consider their factor-endowments story to be alternative to an explanation based on institutions. Rather their goal was to propose a mechanism for understanding why institutions in some parts of the Americas were much less conducive to economic development than those elsewhere. Where initial factor endowments produced high levels of inequality, Engerman and Sokoloff hypothesized, they enabled the wealthy to establish institutions that perpetuated their advantages – institutions that insured that the bulk of the population would remain poor and uneducated and thus inhibit technological change and productivity growth.

Promising signs and ongoing concerns

Over the last couple of decades there have been scattered but promising signs of renewed interdisciplinary conversation. Some of this rapprochement has been a byproduct of continued institution building. In California, for example, several prominent economic historians took advantage of an effort by the University of California to foster intellectual exchange among the system's various campuses to organize the All-UC Group in Economic History. Formed originally in 1972, the group is still going strong. It has attracted participants from other schools in the region and made California the center of economic history in the United States. Although its initial leadership came mainly from economists, the group's successful navigation of the politics of the UC system required that its composition be interdisciplinary as well as inter-campus, and the group has provided funds and a supportive intellectual environment for training graduate students in history, as well as in economics.[10] Other exemplary interdisciplinary initiatives include the Early Modern Group in Social Science History founded by Jean-Laurent Rosenthal at Caltech[11] and the Joint Centre for History and Economics founded by Emma Rothschild at Harvard and Cambridge.[12]

Interdisciplinary conversation is difficult to sustain under any circumstances, but it is especially difficult when practitioners from the different disciplines have not been talking to each other for decades. Lack of interaction makes it easier to stereotype the "other" and react with hostility to those who dare to cross disciplinary boundaries. The attack on Kenneth Pomeranz's *Great Divergence* (2000) by Philip Huang and others is a good example. Although Pomeranz is a historian by training who has done substantial archival work in Chinese sources, the historians who slammed his study cast him as overly influenced by neoclassical (and even classical) theory and, like the stereotypical economist, dependent on secondary sources for information about Chinese history (Huang 2002). Historian R. Bin Wong, Pomeranz's intellectual partner in developing a new view of Chinese economic history, was subjected to similar treatment for his book *China Transformed* (1997). Both scholars, however, benefited from the serious and supportive reception their ideas received from the economic historians in the All-UC group and from economic historians more generally.[13] Their claim that the wealthiest parts of China had levels of economic development similar to those of the wealthiest parts of Europe in the eighteenth century has revolutionized the study of both Chinese history and world economic development. It has stimulated new empirical challenges (see, for example, Broadberry and Gupta 2006 and Allen 2009). It has also called attention to complementary work by scholars such as historian Madeleine Zelin, whose studies of salt producers in Zigong and business organizational forms are characterized by deep archival research and the creative use of economic theory (Zelin 2005 and 2009).

Beyond encouraging unproductive stereotyping, the lack of interdisciplinary conversation can adversely affect the quality of scholarship of both historians and economists. Historians in the USA are now flocking to study topics in the history of capitalism that are closely related to work in economic history. The phenomenon began during the early to mid-2000s, when a number of scholars started dissertations that became the books that ultimately staked out the field (Mihm 2007; Hamilton 2008; Moreton 2009; Hyman 2011; Ott 2011), and when Sven Beckert inaugurated his conferences at Harvard on the history of capitalism. But it took on the trappings of a movement once the financial crisis of 2008 rekindled historians' interest in the economy. The scholars in the forefront of this movement are trained in cultural history and make little use of quantitative sources. To the extent, therefore, that they focus on what people were saying was happening, rather than what we can see occurring from the sources, they are likely to repeat the errors of the past. A good example is Edward Baptist's *The Half Has Never Been Told* (2014), an important effort to place the violence of slavery squarely at the center of the history of American capitalism. Baptist makes much of the growth of productivity in cotton picking that cliometricians Alan Olmstead and Paul Rhode (2008) have documented for the first half of the nineteenth century, but he dismisses their contention that the increase owed much to the development of new varieties of cotton that were easy to pick and instead attributes it primarily to coercion. Undoubtedly, both biological innovation and violence were behind the rise in productivity, but the relative contributions matter and cannot be established, as Baptist tries to do, by a few quotations deprecating the new seed types. Another lapse is Baptist's claim – and also Beckert's in *Empire of Cotton* (2014) – that slave-based cotton cultivation drove US economic development and the world economy in the antebellum period, a claim that ignores the abundant evidence to the contrary amassed by economic historians since the 1930s.

Economists also stand to benefit from renewed interdisciplinary conversation. There has been a resurgence of interest in history among mainstream economists as a byproduct of the search for novel "instrumental" variables. Economists have been preoccupied in recent years with the technical problem of how to establish a causal relationship between one variable and another. One way of making the case for causation is to find a third variable (an instrument) that is plausibly not a function of either of the variables of interest and only affects outcomes through the posited causal channel. Variables from the distant past are obvious candidates for instruments and their successful use (see Acemoglu et al. 2001) has stimulated a number of such studies. Perhaps inevitably, economists came to see the instruments themselves as explanations, and the channels they were supposed to help identify faded into the background (Rodrik et al. 2004). The result has been a flurry of "historical" studies in which history itself plays little role. Instead, economists emphasize the persistent effects of bygone institutional or cultural patterns and implicitly treat everything that happened in the interim as if it were of little consequence (see, for examples, Nunn 2008; Nunn and Wantchekon 2011; Alesina et al. 2013).

Although some economic historians have jumped on the persistence-studies bandwagon, others have checked to see if the observed statistical relationships are stable over time, as the method implies they must be, and have uncovered considerable evidence that they are not (see, for examples, Musacchio 2008; and Frankema and Van Waijenburg 2012). These findings in turn have resulted in increased interest in the study of cultural change, long the domain of historians, and in political economy, a subject increasingly attracting the attention of the new historians of capitalism. It would therefore seem to be a propitious time to bridge the gulf that has opened up between economists and historians and encourage not only interdisciplinary conversation but collaboration. Historians generally do not have the theoretical or quantitative skills to tackle many of the questions of political economy in which they are interested or to move beyond hermeneutics and develop a systematic understanding of cultural change. Economists, in turn, are often handicapped by an overly stylized view of cultural practices and the workings of social and political institutions and could benefit not only from historians' deeper understandings but also from consideration of models developed in the other social sciences.

Interdisciplinary exchange, though obviously valuable, will not be easy to accomplish and undoubtedly will be accompanied by intellectual fireworks. But that should not be a reason to avoid it. I have already mentioned the important contributions that the debate over Pomeranz's and Wong's books stimulated. Economist Avner Greif's work on medieval commerce sparked a similarly acrimonious response (Greif 1989; Edwards and Ogilvie 2012; Greif 2012). Although the debate has been contentious, it has brought to the fore important new studies of medieval and early modern trade by Francesca Trivellato (2009) and Jessica Goldberg (2012). Marrying cultural and economic analysis in a sophisticated way, these books provide tangible evidence of the gains to be derived from renewed interdisciplinary conversation.[14]

Notes

1 This chapter draws on, but substantially revises and updates, Lamoreaux (1998). I have benefited from comments from the editors Francesco Boldizzoni and Pat Hudson, as well as from Timothy Guinnane, Paul Rhode, Ariel Ron, and Francesca Trivellato.

2 See chapters 2 and 6 by Pat Hudson and Jan-Otmar Hesse respectively in this volume.

3 There were substantial differences across economics journals, however: 60 percent of the 38 regular articles on historical topics published in the *JPE* during the 1930s did not include any tables or figures, whereas almost all of the 17 articles in the *QJE* did. The *AER* still published very little economic history.

4 See the Preface to the 1969 Revised Edition of Handlin and Handlin 1947. See also Cole 1970: 729.

5 See "Simon Kuznets, The Sveriges Riksbank Prize in Economic Sciences in Memory of Alfred Nobel, 1971," http://www.nobelprize.org/nobel_prizes/economic-sciences/laureates/1971/kuznets-facts.html (accessed 15 December 2014).

6 See Albert Fishlow's restrospective review of Gerschenkron's *Economic Backwardness in Historical Perspective*, http://eh.net/book_reviews/economic-backwardness-in-historical-perspective-a-book-of-essays/ (accessed 15 December 2014).

7 Most of the first generation of cliometricians were trained by Kuznets, Gerschenkron, and North (Williamson 1994: 115).

8 Not all papers presented at the annual meetings appeared in *Business and Economic History*. Publication was voluntary, and there was in some years an element of selection.

9 The change is apparent in the list of recipients of the Nobel Prize in Economic Sciences (http://www.nobelprize.org/nobel_prizes/economic-sciences/laureates/), but see especially the work of George Akerlof, Joseph Stiglitz, Eric Maskin, Oliver Williamson, Peter Diamond, and Jean Tirole.

10 For lists of participants and past conferences, see the group's website: http://allucgroup.iga.ucdavis.edu

11 http://people.hss.caltech.edu/~jlr/jlr_files/ECHIEV.htm

12 http://www.fas.harvard.edu/~histecon/index.html; http://www.histproj.org

13 See, for example, Pomeranz's CV for the list of presentations he made of this work at All-UC conferences and at economic history workshops at UC campuses and elsewhere. https://history.uchicago.edu/sites/history.uchicago.edu/files/uploads/PomeranzCV.pdf (accessed 26 April 2015).

14 Both Trivellato and Goldberg participate in the interdisciplinary early modern group that Rosenthal convenes at Caltech.

References

Acemoglu, D., S. Johnson, and J. A. Robinson. (2001) 'The Colonial Origins of Comparative Development: An Empirical Investigation', *American Economic Review*, 95 (1): 1369–1401.

Adcock, R. (2003) 'The Emergence of Political Science as a Discipline: History and the Study of Politics in America, 1875–1910', *History of Political Thought*, 24 (3): 481–508.

Adelman, J., and J. Levy. (2014) 'The Fall and Rise of Economic History', *Chronicle of Higher Education*, http://chronicle.com/article/The-FallRise-of-Economic/150247/ (accessed 17 January 2015).

Alesina, A., P. Giuliano, and N. Nunn. (2013) 'On the Origins of Gender Roles: Women and the Plough', *Quarterly Journal of Economics*, 128 (2): 469–530.

Allen, R. C. (2009) 'Agricultural Productivity and Rural Incomes in England and the Yangtze Delta, c.1620–c. 1820', *Economic History Review*, 62 (3): 525–50.

Anderson, R. V., and R. E. Gallman. (1977) 'Slaves as Fixed Capital: Slave Labor and Southern Economic Development', *Journal of American History*, 64 (1): 24–46.

Ashley, W. J. (1893) 'On the Study of Economic History', *Quarterly Journal of Economics*, 7 (2): 115–36.

Baptist, E. E. (2014) *The Half Has Never Been Told: Slavery and the Making of American Capitalism*, New York: Basic Books.

Becker, W. H. (1996) 'Presidential Address: Managerial Culture and the American Political Economy', *Business and Economic History*, 25 (1): 1–7.

Beckert, S. (2014) *Empire of Cotton: A Global History*, New York: Alfred A. Knopf.

Broadberry, S., and B. Gupta. (2006) 'The Early Modern Great Divergence: Wages, Prices and Economic Development in Europe and Asia, 1500–1800', *Economic History Review*, 59 (1): 2–31.

Callender, G. S. (1913) 'The Position of American Economic History', *American Historical Review*, 19 (1): 80–97.

Chandler, A. D., Jr. (1977) *The Visible Hand: The Managerial Revolution in American Business*, Cambridge, MA: Harvard University Press.

Clapham, J. H. (1931) 'Economic History as a Discipline', *Encyclopaedia of the Social Sciences*, New York: Macmillan, 1931, Vol. 5, pp. 327–30.

Clark, C. (1979) 'Household Economy, Market Exchange, and the Rise of Capitalism in the Connecticut Valley, 1800–1860', *Journal of Social History*, 13 (2): 169–89.

Cole, A. H. (1968) 'Economic History in the United States: Formative Years of a Discipline', *Journal of Economic History*, 28 (4): 556–89.

Cole, A. H. (1970) 'The Committee on Research in Economic History: An Historical Sketch', *Journal of Economic History*, 30 (4): 723–41.

Conrad, A. H., and J. R. Meyer. (1958) 'The Economics of Slavery in the Ante Bellum South', *Journal of Political Economy*, 66 (2): 95–130.

Crafts, N. F. R. (1985) *British Economic Growth during the Industrial Revolution*, Oxford: Clarendon Press.

Crafts, N. F. R., and C. K. Harley. (1992) 'Output Growth and the Industrial Revolution: A Restatement of the Crafts–Harley View', *Economic History Review*, 45 (4): 703–30.

David, P. A. (1985) 'Clio and the Economics of QWERTY', *American Economic Review*, 75 (2): 332–7.

David, P. A., and P. Temin. (1976) 'Slavery: The Progressive Institution?', in P. David, H. G. Gutman, R. Sutch, P. Temin, and G. Wright. (eds.) *Reckoning with Slavery: A Critical Study in the Quantitative History of American Negro Slavery*, New York: Oxford University Press.

David, P. A., and P. Temin. (1979) 'Explaining the Relative Efficiency of Slave Agriculture in the Antebellum South: Comment', *American Economic Review* 69 (1): 213–18.

David, P. A., and G. Wright. (1997) 'Increasing Returns and the Genesis of American Resource Abundance', *Industrial and Corporate Change*, 6 (2): 203–45.

Davis, L. E. (1990) 'An Interview with Lance Davis', *Newsletter of the Cliometric Society*, 5 (2): 3–10.

Davis, L. E., and D. C. North. (1971) *Institutional Change and American Economic Growth*, Cambridge: Cambridge University Press.

Dublin, T. (1979) *Women at Work: The Transformation of Work and Community in Lowell, Massachusetts, 1826–1860*, New York: Columbia University Press.

Easterly, W. (2001) *The Elusive Quest for Growth: Economists' Misadventures in the Tropics*, Cambridge, MA: MIT Press.

Edwards, J., and S. Ogilvie. (2012) 'Contract Enforcement, Institutions, and Social Capital: The Maghribi Traders Reappraised', *Economic History Review*, 65 (2): 421–44.

Engerman, S. L., and K. L. Sokoloff. (2012) *Economic Development in the Americas since 1500: Endowments and Institutions*, New York: Cambridge University Press.

Fishlow, A. (1964) 'Antebellum Interregional Trade Reconsidered', *American Economic Review*, 54 (3, Proceedings): 352–64.

Fogel, R. W. (1962) 'A Quantitative Approach to the Study of Railroads in American Economic Growth: A Report of Some Preliminary Findings', *Journal of Economic History*, 22 (2): 163–97.

Fogel, R. W. (1964) *Railroads and American Economic Growth: Essays in Econometric History*, Baltimore, MD: Johns Hopkins Press.

Fogel, R. W. (1967) 'The Specification Problem in Economic History', *Journal of Economic History*, 27 (3): 283–308.

Fogel, R. W. (1979) 'Notes on the Social Saving Controversy', *Journal of Economic History*, 39 (1): 1–54.

Fogel, R. W. (1990) 'An Interview with Robert W. Fogel', *Newsletter of the Cliometric Society*, 5 (3): 3–8, 20–9.

Fogel, R. W., and S. L. Engerman. (1974) *Time on the Cross: The Economics of American Negro Slavery*, Boston, MA: Little, Brown.

Foner, E. (1976) *Tom Paine and Revolutionary America*, New York: Oxford University Press.

Frankema, E., and M. Van Waijenburg. (2012) 'Structural Impediments to African Growth? New Evidence from Real Wages in British Africa, 1880–1965', *Journal of Economic History* 72 (4): 895–926.

Galambos, L. 1969. 'Parsonian Sociology and Post-Progressive History', *Social Science Quarterly*, 50 (1): 25–45.

Gallman, R. E. (1992) 'An "Interview" with Robert E. Gallman', *Newsletter of the Cliometric Society*, 7 (1): 3–10.

Gay, E. F. (1941) 'The Tasks of Economic History', *Journal of Economic History*, 1 (supplement): 9–16.

Genovese, E. D. (1962) 'The Significance of the Slave Plantation for Southern Economic Development', *Journal of Southern History*, 28 (4): 422–37.

Gerschenkron, A. (1963) 'The Early Phases of Industrialization in Russia: Afterthoughts and Counterthoughts', in W. W. Rostow (ed.) *The Economics of Take-Off into Sustained Growth: Proceedings of a Conference Held by the International Economic Association*, New York: St. Martin's Press.

Gilboy, E. W. (1934) 'Time Series and the Derivation of Demand and Supply Curves: A Study of Coffee and Tea, 1850–1930', *Quarterly Journal of Economics*, 48 (4): 667–85.

Goldberg, J. (2012) *Trade and Institutions in the Medieval Mediterranean: The Geniza Merchants and their Business World*, New York: Cambridge University Press.

Goldin, C. (1995) 'Cliometrics and the Nobel', *Journal of Economic Perspectives*, 9 (2): 191–208.

Goodrich, C., and S. Davison. (1935) 'The Wage-Earner in the Westward Movement I', *Political Science Quarterly*, 50 (2): 161–85.

Goodrich, C., and S. Davison. (1936) 'The Wage-Earner in the Westward Movement II', *Political Science Quarterly*, 51 (1): 61–116.

Greif, A. (1989) 'Reputation and Coalitions in Medieval Trade: Evidence on the Maghribi Traders', *Journal of Economic History*, 49 (4): 857–82.

Greif, A. (2012) 'The Maghribi Traders: A Reappraisal?', *Economic History Review*, 65 (2): 445–69.

Gutman, H. G. (1975) *Slavery and the Numbers Game: A Critique of Time on the Cross*, Urban: University of Illinois Press.

Hamilton, S. (2008) *Trucking Country: The Road to America's Wal-Mart Economy*, Princeton, NJ: Princeton University Press.

Hammond, B. (1957) *Banks and Politics in America: From the Revolution to the Civil War*, Princeton, NJ: Princeton University Press.

Handlin, O., and M. F. Handlin. (1947) *Commonwealth: A Study of the Role of Government in the American Economy: Massachusetts, 1774–1861*, New York: New York University Press.

Handlin, O., and M. F. Handlin. (1969) *Commonwealth: A Study of the Role of Government in the American Economy: Massachusetts, 1774–1861*, rev. edn; Cambridge, MA: Harvard University Press.

Harley, C. K. (1982) 'British Industrialization before 1841: Evidence of Slower Growth during the Industrial Revolution', *Journal of Economic History*, 42 (2): 267–89.

Hartz, L. (1948) *Economic Policy and Democratic Thought: Pennsylvania, 1776–1860*, Cambridge, MA: Harvard University Press.

Heaton, H. (1941) 'The Early History of the Economic History Association', *Journal of Economic History*, 1 (supplement): 107–9.

Heaton, H. (1942) 'Recent Developments in Economic History', *American Historical Review*, 47 (4): 727–46.

Heaton, H. (1952) *A Scholar in Action, Edwin F. Gay*, Cambridge, MA: Harvard University Press.

Heaton, H. (1965) 'Twenty-Five Years of the Economic History Association: A Reflective Evaluation', *Journal of Economic History*, 25 (4): 465–79.

Henretta, J. A. (1978) 'Families and Farms: Mentalité in Pre-Industrial America', *William and Mary Quarterly*, 35 (1): 3–32.

Higham, J. (1965) *History: Professional Scholarship in America*, Baltimore, MD: Johns Hopkins University Press.

Huang, P. C. C. (2002) 'Development or Involution in Eighteenth-Century Britain and China? A Review of Kenneth Pomeranz's *The Great Divergence: China, Europe, and the Making of the Modern World Economy*', *Journal of Asian Studies*, 61 (2): 501–38.

Hughes, J. (1985) 'Cliometrics: Memories and Predictions', *Newsletter of the Cliometric Society*, 1 (1): insert.

Hughes, J. R. T. (1991) 'An Interview with Jonathan R. T. Hughes', *Newsletter of the Cliometric Society*, 6 (3), 3–6, 18–26.

Hyman, L. (2011) *Debtor Nation: The History of America in Red Ink*, Princeton, NJ: Princeton University Press.

Kessler-Harris, A. (1990), *A Woman's Wage: Historical Meanings and Social Consequences*, Lexington: University of Kentucky Press.

Kessler-Harris, A. (1991) 'Ideologies and Innovation: Gender Dimensions of Business History', *Business and Economic History*, 20: 45–51.

Kolko, G. (1963) *The Triumph of Conservatism: A Re-Interpretation of American History, 1900–1916*, New York: Free Press of Glencoe.

Kolko, G. (1965) *Railroads and Regulation, 1877–1916*, Princeton, NJ: Princeton University Press.

Kwolek-Folland, A. (1994) *Engendering Business: Men and Women in the Corporate Office, 1870–1930*, Baltimore, MD: Johns Hopkins University Press.

Kuznets, S. (1963) 'Notes on the Take-Off', in W. W. Rostow (ed.) *The Economics of Take-Off into Sustained Growth: Proceedings of a Conference Held by the International Economic Association*, New York: St. Martin's Press.

Lamoreaux, N. R. (1998) 'Economic History and the Cliometric Revolution', in A. Molho and G. S. Wood (eds.) *Imagined Histories: American Historians Interpret the Past*, Princeton, NJ: Princeton University Press.

Lamoreaux, N. R., and D. M. G. Raff. (eds.) (1995) *Coordination and Information: Historical Perspectives on the Organization of Enterprise*, Chicago, IL: University of Chicago Press.

Lamoreaux, N. R., D. M. G. Raff, and P. Temin. (1997) 'New Approaches to the Study of Business History', *Business and Economic History*, 26 (1): 57–79.

Lamoreaux, N. R., D. M. G. Raff, and P. Temin. (eds.) (1999) *Learning by Doing in Firms, Markets, and Countries*, Chicago, IL: University of Chicago Press.

Lamoreaux, N. R., D. M. G. Raff, and P. Temin. (2003) 'Beyond Markets and Hierarchies: Towards a New Synthesis of American Business History', *American Historical Review*, 108 (2): 404–33.

Levermore, C. H. (1914) '*An Economic Interpretation of the Constitution of the United States*. By Charles A. Beard', *American Economic Review*, 4 (1): 117–19.

Lipartito, K. (1995) 'Culture and the Practice of Business History', *Business and Economic History*, 24 (2), 1–41.

Long, C. D. Jr. (1939) 'Long Cycles in the Building Industry', *Quarterly Journal of Economics*, 53 (3): 371–403.

Mason, E. S., and T. S. Lamont. (1982) 'The Harvard Department of Economics from the Beginning to World War II', *Quarterly Journal of Economics*, 97 (3): 383–433.

Merrill, M. (1976) 'Cash is Good to Eat: Self-Sufficiency and Exchange in the Rural Economy of the United States', *Radical History Review*, 4 (1): 42–71.

Meyer, J. R. (1995) 'An Interview with John Meyer', *Newsletter of the Cliometric Society*, 10 (1): 3–6, 20–4.

Meyer, J. R., and A. H. Conrad. (1957) 'Economic Theory, Statistical Inference, and Economic History', *Journal of Economic History*, 17 (4): 524–44.
Mihm, S. (2007). *A Nation of Counterfeiters: Capitalists, Con Men, and the Making of the United States*, Cambridge, MA: Harvard University Press.
Misa, T. J. (1996) 'Toward an Historical Sociology of Business Culture', *Business and Economic History*, 25 (1): 55–64.
Mitch, D. (2011) 'Economic History in Departments of Economics: The Case of the University of Chicago, 1892 to the Present', *Social Science History* 35 (2): 237–71.
Mitchell, W. C. (1927) *Business Cycles: The Problem and its Setting*, New York: National Bureau of Economic Research.
Mokyr, J. (2009) *The Enlightened Economy: An Economic History of Britain, 1700–1850*, New Haven, CT: Yale University Press.
Montgomery, D. (1968) 'The Working Classes of the Pre-Industrial American City, 1780–1830', *Labor History* 9 (1): 3–22.
Moreton, B. (2009) *To Serve God and Wal-Mart: The Making of Christian Free Enterprise*, Cambridge, MA: Harvard University Press.
Morgan, M. S. (2003) 'Economics', in T. M. Porter and D. Ross (eds.) *The Cambridge History of Science, Volume 7: The Modern Social Sciences*, Cambridge: Cambridge University Press.
Musacchio, A. (2008) 'Can Civil Law Countries Get Good Institutions? Lessons from the History of Creditor Rights and Bond Markets in Brazil', *Journal of Economic History*, 68 (1): 80–108.
Neal, L. (1999) 'Larry Neal Retires after Seventeen Years of Explorations', *Newsletter of the Cliometric Society*, 4 (1): 1, 9–13.
North, D. C. (1961) *The Economic Growth of the United States, 1790–1860*, Englewood Cliffs, NJ: Prentice-Hall.
North, D. C. (1963a) 'Industrialization in the United States (1815–1860)', in W. W. Rostow (ed.) *The Economics of Take-Off into Sustained Growth: Proceedings of a Conference Held by the International Economic Association*, New York: St. Martin's Press.
North, D. C. (1963b) 'Quantitative Research in American Economic History', *American Economic Review*, 53 (1/1): 128–30.
North, D. C. (1965) 'The State of Economic History', *American Economic Review*, 55 (1/2): 86–91.
North, D. C. (1974) 'Beyond the New Economic History', *Journal of Economic History*, 34 (1): 1–7.
North, D. C. (1981) *Structure and Change in Economic History*, New York: W. W. Norton.
North, D. C. (1990) *Institutions, Institutional Change, and Economic Performance*, New York: Cambridge University Press.
North, D. C. (1993) 'An Interview with Douglass C. North', *Newsletter of the Cliometric Society*, 8 (3): 7–12, 24–8.
North, D. C. (2005) *Understanding the Process of Economic Change*, Princeton, NJ: Princeton University Press.
North, D. C., J. J. Wallis, and B. R. Weingast. (2009) *Violence and Social Orders A Conceptual Framework for Interpreting Recorded Human History*, New York: Cambridge University Press.
Nunn, N. (2008) 'The Long-Term Effects of Africa's Slave Trades', *Quarterly Journal of Economics*, 123 (1): 139–76.
Nunn, N., and L. Wantchekon. (2011) 'The Slave Trade and the Origins of Mistrust in Africa', *American Economic Review*, 101 (7): 3221–52.
Olmstead, A. L., and P. W. Rhode. (2008) 'Biological Innovation and Productivity Growth in the Antebellum Cotton Economy', *Journal of Economic History*, 68 (4): 1123–71.
Ott, J. C. (2011) *When Wall Street Met Main Street: The Quest for an Investors' Democracy*, Cambridge, MA: Harvard University Press.
Parker, W. N. (1971) 'From Old to New to Old in Economic History', *Journal of Economic History*, 31 (1): 3–14.
Parker, W. N. (1991) 'An Interview with William N. Parker', *Newsletter of the Cliometric Society*, 6 (2): 3–8, 19–25.
Pomeranz, K. (2000) *The Great Divergence: China, Europe, and the Making of the Modern World Economy*, Princeton, NJ: Princeton University Press.
Prude, J. (1983) *The Coming of Industrial Order: Town and Factory Life in Rural Massachusetts, 1810–1860*, New York: Cambridge University Press.

Rodrik, D., A. Subramanian, and F. Trebbi. (2004) 'Institutions Rule: The Primacy of Institutions over Geography and Integration in Economic Development', *Journal of Economic Growth*, 9 (2): 131–65.

Rosen, C. M. (2013) 'What is Business History?', *Enterprise & Society*, 14 (3): 475–85.

Rosenberg, N., J. G. Williamson, and M. Rothstein (1970) 'Editors' Note', *Explorations in Economic History*, 8 (1): 3.

Ross, D. (1991) *The Origins of American Social Science*, New York: Cambridge University Press.

Rostow, W. W. (1960) *The Stages of Economic Growth: A Non-Communist Manifesto*, Cambridge: Cambridge University Press.

Rudolph, F. (1965) *The American College and University: A History*, New York: Vintage.

Sass, S. A. (1986) *Entrepreneurial Historians and History: Leadership and Rationality in American Economic Historiography, 1940–1960*, New York: Garland.

Schlesinger, A. M. Jr., (1945) *The Age of Jackson*, Boston, MA: Little Brown & Co.

Schumpeter, J. A. (1934) *The Theory of Economic Development: An Inquiry into Profits, Capital, Credit, Interest, and the Business Cycle*, trans. R. Opie, Cambridge, MA: Harvard University Press.

Sewell, W. H. Jr., (2005) *Logics of History: Social Theory and Social Transformation*, Chicago, IL: University of Chicago Press.

Sutch, R. C. (1994) 'Douglass North and the New Economic History', in *Two Pioneers of Cliometrics: Robert W. Fogel and Douglass C. North*, Oxford, OH: The Cliometric Society.

Temin, P. (1969) *The Jacksonian Economy*, New York: W. W. Norton.

Temin, P. (1980) *Taking Your Medicine: Drug Regulation in the United States*, Cambridge, MA: Harvard University Press.

Temin, P. (ed.) (1991) *Inside the Business Enterprise: Historical Perspectives on the Use of Information*, Chicago, IL: University of Chicago Press.

Temin, P. (1997a) 'Two Views of the British Industrial Revolution', *Journal of Economic History*, 57 (1): 63–82.

Temin, P. (1997b) 'Is it Kosher to Talk about Culture?', *Journal of Economic History*, 21 (3): 371–89.

Temin, P., with L. Galambos. (1987) *The Fall of the Bell System: A Study in Prices and Politics*, New York: Cambridge University Press.

Thernstrom, S. (1964). *Poverty and Progress: Social Mobility in a Nineteenth Century City*, Cambridge, MA: Harvard University Press.

Thompson, C. M. (1927) 'Economic History', *American Economic Review*, 17 (1, Supplement): 11–12.

Toews, J. E. (1987) 'Intellectual History after the Linguistic Turn: The Autonomy of Meaning and the Irreducibility of Experience', *American Historical Review*, 92 (4): 879–907.

Trivellato, F. (2009) *The Familiarity of Strangers: The Sephardic Diaspora, Livorno, and Cross-Cultural Trade in the Early Modern Period*, New Haven, CT: Yale University Press.

Usher, A. P. (1932) 'The Application of the Quantitative Method to Economic History', *Journal of Political Economy*, 40 (2): 186–209.

Veysey, L. R. (1965) *The Emergence of the American University*, Chicago, IL: University of Chicago Press.

Whaples, R. (1991) 'A Quantitative History of the *Journal of Economic History* and the Cliometric Revolution', *Journal of Economic History*, 51 (2): 289–301.

Williams, W. A. (1959) *The Tragedy of American Diplomacy*, Cleveland, OH: World Publishing Co.

Williams, W. A. (1969) *The Roots of the Modern American Empire: A Study of the Growth and Shaping of Social Consciousness in a Marketplace Society*, New York: Random House.

Williamson, S. H. (1994) 'The History of Cliometrics', in *Two Pioneers of Cliometrics: Robert W. Fogel and Douglass C. North*, Oxford, OH: The Cliometric Society.

Wilson, E. B. (1934) 'The Periodogram of American Business Activity', *Quarterly Journal of Economics*, 48 (3): 375–417.

Wong, R. B. (1997) *China Transformed: Historical Change and the Limits of European Experience*, Ithaca, NY: Cornell University Press.

Wright, C. W. (1914) '*An Economic Interpretation of the Constitution of the United States*. By Charles A. Beard', *Journal of Political Economy*, 22 (5): 492–5.

Wright, C. W. (1938) 'The Nature and Objectives of Economic History', *Journal of Political Economy*, 46 (5): 688–701.

Wright, G. (1976) 'Prosperity, Progress, and American Slavery', in P. David, H. G. Gutman, R. Sutch, P. Temin, and G. Wright (eds.) *Reckoning with Slavery: A Critical Study in the Quantitative History of American Negro Slavery*, New York: Oxford University Press.

Wright, G. (1978) *Political Economy of the Cotton South: Households, Markets, and Wealth in the Nineteenth Century*, New York: W. W. Norton.

Wright, G. (1979) 'The Efficiency of Slavery: Another Interpretation', *American Economic Review* 69 (1): 219–26.

Wright, G. (1986) *Old South, New South: Revolutions in the Southern Economy since the Civil War*, New York: Basic Books.

Wright, G. (2013) *Sharing the Prize: The Economics of the Civil Rights Revolution in the American South*, Cambridge, MA: Harvard University Press.

Yetman, N. R. (1976) 'The Rise and Fall of Time on the Cross', *Reviews in American History*, 4 (2): 195–202.

Zelin, M. (2005) *The Merchants of Zigong: Industrial Entrepreneurship in Early Modern China*, New York: Columbia University Press.

Zelin, M. (2009) 'The Firm in Early Modern China', *Journal of Economic Behavior & Organization*, 71 (3): 623–37.

4
MAKING A COUNTRY (AND AN ECONOMY)

Economic history in Canada

Douglas McCalla

Following the American Revolution, Britain's remaining colonies on the northern half of the American continent were tiny. In 1800, there were not quite 100,000 people in five colonies on the Atlantic; more than 200,000 along the St Lawrence River in Lower Canada; and fewer than 40,000 upriver and along the lower Great Lakes, in Upper Canada (Harris 1987: plates 32, 68). A majority of the entire population was French-speaking. Through the Hudson's Bay Company, Britain also claimed the remaining lands to the west and north. Between 1867 and 1873, this territory (except for Newfoundland, population 170,000) was united in the Dominion of Canada, an independent country within the British Empire. Over three-quarters of the Canadian population of about 3.7 million lived in what now were the provinces of Quebec and Ontario. Upper Canada/Ontario alone represented over 40 percent of the Canadian total, and its per capita income was the highest in Canada by a substantial margin (Inwood and Irwin 2002: 161–2). In the next century, settlement expanded across the continent, central Canada industrialized, and the Canadian population grew to 22 million. That was still little more than 10 percent of the population of the United States. Although the two western provinces, British Columbia and Alberta, were becoming more important by 1971, economic power still was concentrated in the Montreal area and in southern Ontario.[1]

This summary suggests a number of Canadian issues for economic historians, including the transformation of marginal colonies into a highly developed national economy; the character of pre- and post-contact aboriginal economies; the relationship of the colonial and Canadian economies to France, Britain, and the United States; and variation among regions and cultures. Understanding that economy also requires consideration of growth, migration, demography, technology, industrialization, and inequality – standard themes that have locally specific elements.

Of course, the entire world is open to economic historians working in Canada, and they have made important contributions to the study of every region and period (for examples from medieval history, see Munro 1994; Squatriti 2014). In the recent *Oxford Encyclopedia of Economic History* (Mokyr 2003), for example, there are three articles on exclusively Canadian subjects; that at least forty contributors have Canadian affiliations speaks eloquently to the practice of economic history in Canada. But work on the history of other places tends to fall within frameworks appropriate to them, and it is difficult to identify particularly Canadian dimensions in this scholarship (Neill 1991: ix–x).[2] Hence the decision to focus this chapter essentially on studies of Canada.

Political economy and the staples approach

The beginning of academic study of economic history in Canada reflected both Canadian recognition that industry and urbanization were transforming a primarily agricultural economy and wider trends in the study of western society (Ferguson 1993: xv, 5–6). At the University of Toronto, a youthful W.J. Ashley was recruited from Oxford as its first professor of political economy (McKillop 1994: 193–5).[3] As Ian Drummond writes (1983: 21), Ashley's inaugural lecture on 9 November 1888 'nailed his standard firmly to the German Historical flagpole. Classical economic doctrines . . . have "only a relative truth." Fruitful work was to be done not in "the abstract deductive method . . . but in the following new fields of investigations – historical, statistical, inductive." Laissez faire was no longer acceptable "as a general principle. Each case must be decided on its merits."' This was the spirit in which economic history developed in Canada, although Ashley himself soon left, lured to Harvard in 1892 as its first professor of economic history.[4] His immediate legacy at Toronto was his recommendation for a successor, James Mavor, whom he described as 'among the top ten or twelve most distinguished English economists' (Drummond 1983: 26). Later, the College of Commerce at the University of Birmingham, founded by Ashley, would influence Canadian curricular development, with its integration of economics, politics, commerce, and history.

Mavor was actually a Scot, whose many interests included deep concern at the impact of industrialization and urbanization on the poor in Glasgow. Active in socialist circles in the 1880s, with a wide circle of friends that included William Morris, George Bernard Shaw, and Patrick Geddes, he was moving by the end of the decade towards a more liberal perspective. In the thirty years he held the Toronto chair, he recruited faculty, shaped the curriculum, and laid the foundations of one of the university's and Canada's most important intellectual centres (Shortt 1976: 119–35; Drummond 1983: 26–52; McKillop 1994: 485).[5] Much of his writing was on current subjects, in reports commissioned by governments and business interests (e.g. Mavor 1905, 1925). Of his historical writings, the most enduring was a monumental *Economic History of Russia* (Mavor 1914).[6] An avid traveler, he understood economics to have strongly geographic dimensions, thinking that would be important at Toronto long after his retirement (Warkentin 2014).

At Queen's University, a Presbyterian institution in eastern Ontario, political economy was also introduced in 1888, taught by Adam Shortt, a Queen's graduate who had studied philosophy and science in Glasgow and Edinburgh (Shortt 1976: 95–116; Neatby 1978: 180). His research would focus on the history of Canada. A key theme was the history of money and banking from the French regime onwards, on which he published dozens of articles based on extensive documentary research (Canadian Bankers' Association 1986). But his work ranged far more widely, encompassing, Brian McKillop writes (1994: 197), 'the empirical study of the evolution of the country's economic, political, and financial institutions: tariff and transportation policy, war industries, currency, municipal government, taxation, trade, railways, industrial monopoly, and many other aspects of the "real" life of Canadian society.' After moving to Ottawa in 1908 to join Canada's new Civil Service Commission, he continued his historical work. Notably, with Arthur Doughty, the Dominion Archivist, he co-edited *Canada and Its Provinces*, a 23-volume history to which he contributed six chapters on economic history (Shortt and Doughty 1914–17). A seventh chapter, by O.D. Skelton, who now held Shortt's chair at Queen's, was an authoritative 180-page account of the Canadian economy since 1867 that laid out the main lines of a story that has continued to attract and challenge historians. Its final section, '1896–1912: The Coming of Prosperity,' begins with the settlement of the west; 'at last,' he writes, 'Canada's hour had struck,' as external forces turned favourable, a rising tide of prairie wheat found its way to world markets, and a rising tide of immigration peopled the prairies (Skelton 1914: 191). As an undergraduate, Skelton had studied classics at Queen's before obtaining a doctorate in political economy from the University of Chicago, where he had been much influenced by Thorstein Veblen. He was a prolific author on political and economic subjects; his prize-winning first book, for example, was a critique of socialism that drew wide praise, including a letter from Lenin, written from Zurich (Skelton 1911; Crowley 2007). In the early 1920s, Skelton too left for Ottawa, soon to become permanent undersecretary of Canada's new Department of External Affairs.

By then, he had recruited W.A. Mackintosh, a Queen's graduate teaching at Brandon College on the Canadian prairies, whose Harvard doctoral thesis focused on agricultural cooperation in the west, particularly the dramatic recent growth of farmer-owned grain-marketing cooperatives (Mackintosh 1924; Fay 1925).[7] Mackintosh quickly became a leading analyst of contemporary economic problems, especially when sharply falling grain prices and drought combined to devastate the prairies during the Depression.[8] After 1935, he also played a vital part in federal government policy making, including writing the 1945 white paper that laid out the government's postwar employment strategy (Granatstein 1982: 153–8). These activities were informed by his understanding of economic history, first spelled out in 1923. Citing Frederick Jackson Turner and especially Guy S. Callender, Mackintosh turned away from the industrial and urban developments that had initially motivated the establishment of economic history in Canada to argue the importance of rural products, the staples that, he said, had everywhere in North America been 'the prime requisite of colonial prosperity' (Mackintosh 1923: 14). Staples also underlay his study of post-Confederation economic history, a work that long outlived the circumstances of its writing, as a study for the Royal Commission on Dominion–Provincial Relations.[9] It argued that in an economy reliant on primary products whose prices were determined on world markets, 'variability of export income' was central to the regional fiscal imbalances on which the Royal Commission focused (Mackintosh 1964 [1939]: 180–1).

By then, staples had become the core of Canadian economic history, embodied in what remains its most fundamental work, Harold Adams Innis's *The Fur Trade in Canada* (Innis 1930; Berger 1986: 94–100).[10] A graduate of McMaster University who had been wounded on the western front, Innis pursued a doctorate in economics at the University of Chicago, writing a thesis on the history of the Canadian Pacific Railway [CPR] (Innis 1923). Appointed in Political Economy at the University of Toronto in 1920, he set out to construct an economic history and an economics that reflected the Canadian experience. 'A new country', he wrote in 1929 (in Innis 1956: 3), 'presents certain definite problems which appear to be more or less insoluble from the standpoint of the application of economic theory as worked out in the older highly industrialized countries.' Initially, he mainly taught economic geography – which he also practised. Thus, to understand a trade based on European taste in hats, aboriginal trappers and hunters, and the ecology of the beaver, Innis went beyond the archives, traveling widely in fur-trade country and to Britain and Europe (Watson 2006: 123–5, 166). Furs had drawn traders ever farther from the St Lawrence and Hudson Bay; eventually, a Montreal-based enterprise spanned the northern half of the continent. When the CPR was built in the 1880s, it represented a continuation of fur-trade canoe routes, with the latest technology. Contrary to a then-common cliché, that Canada was a country of regions created in spite of geography, Innis argued (1930: 392) that 'It is no mere accident that the present Dominion coincides roughly with the fur-trading areas of northern North America.'[11] In a period when Canadian intellectuals and artists were seeking to articulate a national identity, this idea had much appeal (Berger 1986: 91).

What made the book foundational was its twenty-page conclusion, which generalized beyond the fur trade. In a new land, settlement could succeed only if migrants found a way to buy goods that allowed them to retain a European culture and living standard. The possibilities for exports were limited to resource products. Although Canadians liked to think of their country as rich in natural resources, at any one time these had been few in number; and a resource economy was always vulnerable to forces beyond colonists' control: world prices, changes in metropolitan demand, and new technologies developed elsewhere. Thus, the economic history of Canada could be told as a sequence of staples whose properties, and what later would be called linkages, largely determined the location, character, timing, and limits of development: cod, beaver, pine timber, and wheat sold in and (in the case of cod) beyond Europe; and, later, sawn lumber, minerals, pulp and paper, and (in the era after he wrote) oil, natural gas, and even hydro-electric power, all more likely sold in the United States.[12]

Innis's argument was eloquently complemented by historian Donald Creighton, a colleague and friend, in *The Commercial Empire of the St. Lawrence* (1937), which embodied the vision of imperial officials in Canada, who prided themselves on having a larger perspective than most colonials, and of leading English-speaking merchants, who sought to maintain and later rebuild a Montreal-centred trans-Atlantic commerce linking the American Midwest and Britain. As the book closed, that dream – which took much of the actual economy of Canada in its period for granted – had failed. On the other hand, as Creighton's subsequent work argued, political and entrepreneurial visionaries would reorient it to build a new transcontinental nation, with the CPR as its essential link.

Innis wrote prolifically in the 1930s and was a key figure in encouraging others' writings. Besides a massive study of the original North American staple, the cod fishery (Innis 1940), he wrote many essays, both historical and current, the latter grounding their understanding of the problems of the Depression in Canada in an economy based on staples (Innis 1933, 1956). Universally recognized for his leadership in Canada, he was also by far Canada's best known social scientist internationally. He was the second president of the Economic History Association, turned down an attractive offer in 1945–46 to join the Economics Department at the University of Chicago (Mitch 2011: 245–7), and at the time of his death in 1952 was president of the American Economic Association. By 1940, his interests were shifting to the history of communications and cultural change in the very long term, extending the range of his work in ways that Canadian intellectuals continue to celebrate – and pore over (Acland and Buxton 1999; Bonnett 2013).

These discussions no longer engage, indeed entirely ignore, economic historians (Drummond 1987: 857–8), yet Innis's work remains fundamental in economic history. Having shaped the research agenda, staples framed the narrative of what became a classic textbook (Easterbrook and Aitken 1956).[13] From a description of how the Canadian economy came into being, this interpretation was extended into a theory of economic development (Watkins 1963; Caves 1965) and applied in the emerging field of development studies and subsequently in what practitioners called 'the new Canadian political economy', a comprehensive critique of capitalism, in Canada and beyond, that began in economic nationalism, soon to be combined with Marxism (Clement and Williams 1989; Watkins 2006). With its emphasis on unbalanced growth led by exports from one or more leading sectors, the staple approach fit well with other mid-century approaches and was taken up in settings beyond Canada, applied, for example, by Douglass North in his account of regional patterns in American economic history (1955: 247–8; 1961: 2, 19) and by McCusker and Menard in their rich study of the colonial American economy (1985: 10–13, 18–32).

If staples have provided Canadians with a compelling narrative, accepting it required ignoring important questions, raised long ago (Buckley 1958). As Stanley Engerman wrote (1977: 253), in a reflection on North's work that has more relevance to Canada than many have recognized, 'it would seem that the foreign and external demand sources must have been important to the explanation of what happened, yet the quantitative magnitudes always seem too small to make them necessary conditions for the growth that did occur . . . Any one sector is only a relatively small part of the economy.' Innis's emphasis on staples also had a deterministic quality, which obscured human agency and political decision making; and his writing style, particularly in his essays, sometimes drew conclusions about causes and relationships that did not fit actual sequences.[14] More generally, in making exports of primary products the main issue, the staple story ignored economic life in areas that did not have an obvious staple, assumed economic development in the heartland depended essentially on resource exports from the hinterland, and largely misrepresented agriculture in the Canadian heartland. Thus, Mackintosh (1923: 15) dismissed at least half the population of British North America in 1800 – and more than two centuries of French Canadian agriculture – for 'fail[ing] to rise beyond the stage of primitive diversified agriculture, a self-sufficient, conservative peasantry.'

Another language, a different space, alternative approaches

Anyone studying French Canadian society, as historians of Canada writing in French mainly did, had to confront this interpretation: was agriculture this backward; if it was, why; and did this explain the place of French Canadians in the twentieth-century economy? At Laval University in Quebec City, economic history began to be taught only in the post-Second World War era, by Albert Faucher. The leading graduate in Laval's first class in social sciences, he could not pursue further studies in France because of the war and instead worked with Innis in Toronto. A central theme of his research was to situate nineteenth-century Quebec in a North American context (Faucher 1973; Dupré 1992). In Laval's new history department, economic history was approached in the *Annales* tradition, that is, as an element within a comprehensive historical project. A pioneering work by Jean Hamelin (1960) began as a thesis on artisans during the French regime, supervised by Charles Morazé at l'École Pratique des Hautes Études in Paris. Setting its subjects within a larger view of the colony's social structure and economy, it sought to explain 'les faiblesses de l'économie de la Nouvelle-France en 1760.' One of these weaknesses, Hamelin concluded (1960: 123, 137), was that the principal wealth-generating elements were controlled from France, an argument that sharply challenged nationalist historians who argued that there had been a vibrant local bourgeoisie whose loss at the Conquest set the stage for French Canadians' subsequent economic difficulties.

Fernand Ouellet, a close colleague of Hamelin, continued this line of analysis for the post-Conquest period in a passionately argued 600-page work (Ouellet 1966). Greatly influenced by the approach of Ernest Labrousse, he used the movement of prices and international trade to identify conjunctures, combining these data with an interpretation of the *mentalité* of French Canadians to address the grand themes of society and politics (Poitras 2013: 350–1, 356 n.66). During the first forty years of British rule, with much unexploited land to develop, French Canadian farmers found no need to change attitudes and techniques. After 1802, Ouellet depicted a gathering crisis in the wheat economy that reflected and reinforced rural resistance to economic change. A backward agriculture that exhausted the soil, a rapidly growing population, a francophone commercial class that focused on merely local trades, and an inheritance system that led to the 'morcellement incessant des terres' (Ouellet 1966: 580) cut *habitants* off from the stimulating currents of the international economy and created deepening rural discontent that a growing class of liberal professionals turned against British authority. The outcome was a rebellion in 1837 and, by mid-century, the beginning of a massive exodus of French Canadians to the industrial towns of New England.

This interpretation was quickly accepted in English-language historical circles and remains prominent in national texts, in part, no doubt, because it was in the staples tradition and aligned with Creighton's account. In the 1960s, it also appealed to intellectuals celebrating Quebec's 'Quiet Revolution' as an escape from the constraints of the past. For us the more important point is the research it provoked on the Quebec economy, which, as selected examples indicate, questioned many elements of its interpretation. Thus, Gilles Paquet, an economist, and Jean-Pierre Wallot, a historian and later Canada's National Archivist, began to publish research that argued that it was precisely in this period that 'Un Québec moderne' began to take shape (Paquet and Wallot 2007). Their evidence included samples of probate inventories that documented increasing rural wealth and sophisticated rural strategies towards the accumulation and inter-generational transfer of land. Serge Courville, a historical geographer, and historians Jean-Claude Robert and Normand Séguin explored rural exchange, which Ouellet had downplayed; the rapid rise of villages in the period revealed dynamic and increasingly complex local economies (Courville 1990; Courville et al. 1995). There proved to be far more variation in rural society than Ouellet had allowed for, which called into question the basic idea that there was a singular rural *mentalité*. In fact, relating rural backwardness to the 1837 rebellion missed that support for the rebellion was strongest where French Canadian farmers had shown the greatest openness to change (Dechêne 1986: 199).

In relying on contemporary critics who lamented the subdivision of farms, Ouellet also missed the reality of rural practice; despite the legal formalities of equal inheritance, families consistently found ways to distribute estates that maintained farms at economic levels. Holdings too small to be viable farms were an element of the rural economy, not its essence, and even on them, many families proved to have been responding imaginatively, using land in strategic ways, such as to support migration (Ramirez 1991: 24–5, 44–5). Finally, many elements of French Canadian farm practice that nineteenth-century critics (and Ouellet) saw as backward were not unique to *habitants*; they were common among English-speaking farmers in Lower Canada, Upper Canada, and other North American regions too (McInnis 1982; Lewis and McInnis 1984). Ouellet was right that wheat growing diminished sharply in Lower Canada in the first third of the nineteenth century, but that cannot be explained by a common peasant *mentalité*. And because farmers were adaptable it did not constitute a long-term crisis.

The best indication of a crisis – although this too was not unique to French Canada (Gentilcore 1993: plate 31) – was large-scale emigration. Just 10,000 migrants (including about 2000 women) from France had settled and married in Canada during the French regime (Boleda 1990: 162, 168; Charbonneau et al. 1996: 33–5), but by 1850 their descendants were so numerous that they were pushing at the limits of potentially arable land in Quebec's St Lawrence valley.[15] The background to this nineteenth-century story was the subject of a long-term study launched in 1966 by demographers at the Université de Montréal. Much influenced by the work of Louis Henry, taking advantage of developing information technology, they set out to reconstitute the entire European population of New France, starting from a remarkable body of documents, the parish registers of births, marriages, and deaths that had been an essential element of the French regime (Charbonneau et al. 1987:

23–5). Some 690,000 records carried the PRDH [Programme de recherche en démographie historique] data base to the end of the eighteenth century.[16]

At exactly the same time, what would be the most powerful work on Quebec in the *Annales* tradition was in progress, Louise Dechêne's *doctorat d'état,* completed in 1973 under the direction of Robert Mandrou and much influenced by Fernand Braudel (Dechêne 1974; Rudin 1997: 178–81). It focused on the island of Montreal, a seigneurie well administered (and well documented) by the Sulpicien order with a population limited enough to study intensively (about 5000 at the end of her period). Notarial records took Dechêne beyond standard sources, such as official correspondence, to provide evidence on the strategies and practices of her subjects and on the structures that framed them. A key argument was that although the fur trade was vital to Montreal's merchants, there was a 'coupure' between it and the island's agriculture (Dechêne 1974: 484). The expansion of the latter, the principal sector of the economy, was driven not by the staple trade but essentially by demography, as a steadily growing rural population at once required and sustained the process of making new farms.

In subsequent work, Dechêne, her students, and other historians of New France extended and revised this analysis, finding, for example, more complexity in rural society and more links between agriculture and commerce, including the fur trade (Dépatie et al. 1998). Her work only grew in ambition, as she widened its frame to ask how an *Ancien Régime* state had functioned in a new world setting, with war and the ever-present possibility of war as the main theme (Dechêne 2008). Considering this particularly from the perspective of ordinary families, she made the rural economy central. Thus, to study government policy towards food supplies, a problem whenever war broke out, she closely analyzed the entire grain economy, beginning with the farmers themselves (Dechêne 1994).

Another former Laval student working in Paris in the late 1960s was Gérard Bouchard. His doctoral work at Nanterre, also directed by Mandrou, addressed demography and rural social structure in eighteenth-century France through a study of a village in the Loire region (Bouchard 1972).[17] On his return to Canada, he began a systematic study of the population and economy of the Saguenay-Lac St Jean region north-east of Quebec City, to which migrants from the eastern part of the province began to move in 1838. As he shaped a comprehensive body of data that integrated population, land, and other records, he produced a series of sophisticated conceptual and methodological studies and eventually a major book on families, land, and markets in the socio-economic history of the region that found parallels to rural strategies elsewhere in North America (Bouchard 1996).[18] He also set out to extend his population data base to cover all of Quebec, linking it to the PRDH and generating what is now known as BALSAC, a comprehensive register of at least the Catholic population that extends far into the twentieth century.[19]

The parish, notarial, and seigneurial records that supported much of this work on Quebec did not exist for other parts of Canada. There the decennial census, which began in 1851, provided the most direct documentation of the entire population, particularly for years when the census manuscripts survived and were accessible to researchers. The 1871 census, the first that fully met international statistical standards, was directed by Joseph-Charles Taché. Among his collaborators was abbé Cyprien Tanguay, whose comprehensive genealogical work was an antecedent for the PRDH and BALSAC projects. With concerns that closely matched those stressed by Ouellet, they aimed to situate the French Canadian population, historically as well as in their time (Curtis 2001: 238–51). An entire volume of the 1871 Census was devoted to summarizing every French and British census of the colonial era.

The quantitative turn: data and theory

As that volume indicated, governments had long sought information on population. Other areas of interest included public finance, international trade, banking, canals, and railways. After Confederation in 1867, such data began to appear annually in what became known as the *Canada Year Book*.[20] In 1918, many of the federal government's statistical efforts were drawn together in the Dominion Bureau of Statistics (now Statistics Canada). In addition to supporting public and private policy making, it provided abundant evidence for subsequent research in economic history, including many of the series incorporated in a comprehensive collection of historical statistics, produced by a large team (Urquhart and Buckley 1965). It included some series from before 1867, but mainly addressed the subsequent period, for which authoritative and consistent data were available, an emphasis even more pronounced in a second edition, which carried data into the 1970s (Leacy 1983).

Another dimension of the work of the Royal Commission on Dominion–Provincial Relations was to initiate efforts to create a system of national income accounts such as Simon Kuznets and colleagues had produced in the United States. This was a challenge government statisticians could not quickly respond to, but as the federal government's economic sophistication grew during the Second World War, the issue took on higher priority. The first systematic national income accounts appeared in 1946 (McDowall 2008). To supplement the official series, which ran only from 1926, O.J. Firestone, a senior economist with the federal government, used census data to extend it back to 1850 on a decennial basis (Firestone 1958, 1960). He found stronger economic growth in the final decades of the nineteenth century than had been generally understood. But the simplifying assumptions required to create his series, the ten-year gap between observations, and the loss of his underlying worksheets left many uncertainties. Hence M.C. Urquhart and several colleagues decided to revisit the period in an enormous project of research and synthesis that produced a new annual series for Canadian GDP and GNP from 1870 to 1926 (Urquhart 1986), accompanied by a meticulous presentation of their sources and procedures (Urquhart et al. 1993).[21] This was an absolutely fundamental resource for economic historians. Among other findings, it confirmed that there had been considerable growth in the later nineteenth century, although aggregate growth was substantially slower than in the United States and also slower than in Canada in the wheat boom era, between 1896 and 1913.[22]

As these projects demonstrate, Canadian economic historians were very much engaged in international discussions. Those working in economics departments had particularly close ties to American scholarship, their work frequently appeared in the principal American journals, and they regularly participated at the main American and international meetings. Firestone presented his work at the 1957 Conference on Income and Wealth, often seen as the foundational event in the cliometric movement, and Urquhart attended the famous Purdue Conference in 1960 where the movement declared itself. In Canada, economic historians soon began to organize regular conferences on the use of quantitative methods. Meetings featured work on both Canadian and non-Canadian subjects and included participants from the United States and elsewhere. At the third meeting, for example, Peter McClelland, a Canadian working in the United States, presented a paper that was among the most sophisticated of all the theoretical and empirical responses to Fogel and Fishlow's works on railroads and social savings (McClelland 1968).

At the first meeting, held in Toronto in 1965, a paper by E.J. Chambers and Donald Gordon, published soon after in an eminent American journal, fully captured the spirit of the new approach, posing an explicit counterfactual against which to test standard accounts of the wheat boom. 'Let us imagine', they wrote (1966: 317), 'what would have happened if all the land that was brought under cultivation [on the Canadian prairies] between 1901 and 1911 had been impenetrable rock.' This speculation was motivated by a contemporary concern, the role of primary products in economic development; their answer, which necessarily depended on the appropriateness of the theory drawn upon and on the applicability of available data, was that the wheat boom likely accounted for only about 5 percent of the increase in per capita incomes in Canada during the decade. That provoked an immediate reaction – and reinforced a research agenda that extended back to Mackintosh.[23] Conference presentations addressed a wide range of issues, but at almost every meeting for the next thirty years participants would discuss some aspect of prairie settlement and the wheat boom (e.g. Bertram [1973], presented at the fifth conference, and Norrie [1975], presented at the sixth).[24] Certainly aggregate and per capita growth accelerated after 1896, driven by migration and investment in which prairie settlement was vital. Yet that was not the only reason investment rose so sharply then; the new technologies of the second industrial revolution provided many attractive opportunities, for example, as did rapid urbanization.[25]

In Canada, as elsewhere, mainstream economics paid diminishing attention to history after the 1960s. At a growing majority of universities, including almost all the francophone institutions, there soon were no economist historians at all (Dupré and Huberman 2000: 166). In departments that continued to include history in their offerings, the number of historians scarcely increased despite the massive expansion in overall hiring. And a number of those historians did not pursue cliometric research.[26] Thus, the pool of economists identifying themselves with the new economic history in Canada was relatively modest. Working in a discipline that emphasized essays and journal articles, not book-length studies, they produced a substantial body of theoretically sophisticated research that sharpened understanding of many issues but rarely sought to problematize the larger staples narrative.[27] Their work was necessarily selective as well, as can be seen in the bibliographies of overviews by two leading quantitative historians: on many topics, older writings, often from before 1960, remained the authorities (McInnis 2000a: 871–5; Green 2000: 1066–71). Indeed, McInnis argued elsewhere (2000b: 427 n.68), 'We are a long way from being provided with a consistent story of the economic development of the Canadian segment of North America.'

An eclectic economic history

For more recent research, moreover, many of the principal authorities on subjects of economic importance are not economists. This can be seen, for example, in large collective projects, such as the three-volume *Historical Atlas of Canada*, shaped by historical geography, Innis's other early orientation. More than half of its plates address population and the economy (Harris 1987; Kerr and Holdsworth 1990; Gentilcore 1993).[28] A second example is the international effort to create an infrastructure of publically accessible population data sets from the manuscript census, in which the Canadian contribution is the work of historians, historical sociologists, demographers, and historical geographers (and just one economic historian, Kris Inwood).[29] A third example, a project based in the department of history at Memorial University in Newfoundland, was launched by Keith Matthews and David Alexander, both British trained, the latter in economic history. Using a massive collection of British records of crew agreements, the Maritime History Group transformed understanding of ships and shipping in and beyond Atlantic Canada; rather than a simple adjunct of the staple timber trade, the sector was shown to be complex, sophisticated, and global, carrying cargoes on the world's principal sailing routes, increasingly recruiting crews from throughout the

Atlantic world, and having diminishing links to the wider Canadian economy (Sager 1989; Sager with Panting 1990).[30]

If the latter complicated the staples narrative, other work deepened it. For the fur trade, modern research has enormously expanded understanding of economics, institutions, and culture. A pioneering work by historical geographer Arthur J. Ray used post accounts from one of the great resources for Canadian history, the records of the Hudson's Bay Company [HBC], to shift the emphasis from the European side of the exchange to its aboriginal participants, highlighting their agency and the place of the trade within their societies and economy (Ray 1974; Ray and Freeman 1978). Equally transformational were studies in history and historical anthropology that demonstrated the centrality of aboriginal women and of fur traders' families; from the latter, in the long term, an entire new people, the Métis, was born (Van Kirk 1980; Brown 1980; Ens 1996). In the exciting scholarship on aboriginal history that has followed, much more has been learned about the fur trade. In a notable recent book, for example, two leading economic historians use HBC records to model aboriginal peoples' responses to price changes; contrary to a common argument that higher prices produced smaller harvests because demand was relatively fixed, they show that increasing prices had the impact that might have been expected in other cultures, the application of additional effort to trapping and trading that led, eventually, to pressure on the stocks of beaver from overhunting (Carlos and Lewis 2010: 166).

In considering aboriginal peoples' consumption alongside their production, this literature is a reminder that the demand for European goods was basic to Innis's formulation of the staples approach. Yet this side of the exchange relationship was long taken largely for granted, with consumption understood as an essentially modern phenomenon (Parr 1999; Belisle 2011). Recently, historians and archaeologists addressing everyday patterns in the colonial era have begun to bring consumption into the foreground (Pope 2004; McCalla 2015). One result has been to complicate stories of a simple exchange of resource products for finished goods. Introducing a study that pays close attention to consumption in an area often imagined as one of the purest examples of a staples economy, the upper Saint John River valley in New Brunswick, Béatrice Craig notes the importance of this reorientation: historians now 'investigate concrete exchange networks, and participants' agency and choices. This shift in perspective on rural life has had several consequences: a new emphasis on regional and local markets as engines of growth and development in their own right; and a move away from the equating of "rural" with "farming" and of "market participant" with "men" or "producers"' (Craig 2009: 4).

Craig's work explicitly engages export-led growth models. In many cases, however, work on or pertinent to economic history by historians, geographers, and sociologists is less closely related to the staples narrative. Here it is possible only to suggest the value of an extensive literature through a few examples that illuminate how the economist's abstract variables, land, labour, and capital, actually functioned in Canadian settings. In contrast to the staples story, with its emphasis on only one or a few products, rural historians, as Craig argues, now aim to understand the entire rural economy, which until at least the end of the nineteenth century involved more than half of all Canadians. For these people, land was basic. In much of Lower Canada, it was held under seigneurial tenure until the 1850s; the implications for development and for the rural populace, then and later, already a main theme when Ouellet and Dechêne began writing, continue to be debated (Harris 2008: 82–7, 235–8). Elsewhere, land was held in freehold. For a long time, research focused on policy regarding the initial allocation of land, but historians and sociologists are at last exploring the actual market in land and farms (Darroch and Soltow 1994; Bouchard 1996; Wilson 2009).

Labour is central to historians of work and workers. The most powerful interpretive strand in Canadian historiography draws on Marx and E.P. Thompson, focusing on craftsmen and other working men and women, seeing them in contexts of workplace, family, neighbourhood, and class – as actors in the story rather than a factor of production (Kealey 1980; Palmer 1992).[31] Some of this research is set in resource towns and other sites of staple production, but often it addresses the growing towns and cities. In the latter settings, some of the most important works centre on gender and family (Parr 1990; Bradbury 1993; Sangster 1995).

Capital and its workings are at the heart of business history, whose foundations can be traced back to Adam Shortt and especially to the early work of Donald Creighton. It tends to a more positive view of economic change than working class history – or current Canadian political economy (Taylor and Baskerville 1994). As the thinking behind Ashley's original appointment reminds us, the principal central Canadian cities grew rapidly after the 1850s; in the west, the settlement boom fostered dramatic urban as well as rural expansion. Business history has offered one perspective on the implications. One approach was through the technologies and utilities of the modern city (Armstrong and Nelles 1986). Michael Bliss, like Nelles a student of Donald Creighton, captured many elements of this story in a brilliant biography of Joseph Flavelle (Bliss 1978). Flavelle began as a small town provisions merchant, moved to Toronto, and by 1900 was part of the city's leading circle of capitalists, whose activities touched almost every major segment of the swiftly emerging modern economy.[32]

'Traditional Canadian economic history', the authors of the current standard national textbook argue, 'appeals because it is eclectic' (Norrie et al. 2008: xi).[33] They draw on much of the new work in economic history, especially research by scholars identifying with the new economic history, but because cliometricians' coverage of the field has been selective and because the new is incorporated into a narrative whose periodization and emphases are traditional, their story to at least 1945 would be recognizable to O.D. Skelton, W.A. Mackintosh, and Harold Innis. A partial reason for that is the regional or local focus of so much modern historical research, which can make it difficult to integrate into a national account. But in framing issues differently, such work can reveal the importance of factors that the national story ignores or understates. For example, research on the economic history of Ontario suggests that a staples-led growth model does not fit the balanced pattern of the province's development (Drummond et al. 1987; McCalla 1993, 1998); and the leading modern overview of Canada's other central province takes a similar view, arguing 'the inadequacy of the staple theory in explaining the dynamics of economic activity in Quebec' (Dickinson and Young 2003: 139). So far, however, no one has taken up the challenge of scaling this research up to shape a new national story. Unless that happens, the main narrative of Canada's economic history is likely to continue to embody an interpretation that now is almost a century old.

Notes

1 In 2011, when Canada's population exceeded 33 million, Ontario still represented more than 38 percent of the total. By then the combined population of British Columbia and Alberta exceeded that of Quebec, a trend that has reinforced Canadian historians' attachment to the staples thesis.

2 As well, scholarly career trajectories sometimes carry those who worked in Canada to universities in the countries on which their work mainly focuses. For example, Robert Allen and C. Knick Harley, both American-born, had distinguished careers in Canada but then left for Oxford; and David Eltis, English-born, moved to Emory University after many years in Canada. Some who left, such as Michael Bordo and Ann Carlos, continue to work on Canadian as well as non-Canadian subjects.

3 Among the reasons for appointing someone from Oxford was a sense that Canadian candidates might draw the university into partisan politics. Ironically, he was interviewed in England by two leading Liberals, Oliver Mowat, the Premier of Ontario, and Edward Blake, Chancellor of the university and former leader of the federal Liberal Party. They were in England on legal business.

4 Lyons et al. (2008: 5) make Ashley's Harvard appointment the beginning of their story, at least 'in the English-speaking world.'

5 For example, Mavor persuaded the university to appoint the English economic historian, C.R. Fay, to a senior position in 1921. In the decade Fay spent at Toronto, his 'infectious zeal, broad knowledge, provocative ideas, and brilliant suggestions' mattered greatly to his younger colleague Harold Innis (Brady 1953: 91). Even after returning to Cambridge, Fay sometimes wrote on Canada. Newfoundland (after 1949 a Canadian province) was a particular interest (Ludlow 2010).

6 His links to Russia included his long-time friendship with the anarchist thinker Pyotr Kropotkin (who stayed with Mavor for some weeks during a visit to Toronto), and his very substantial role in facilitating Doukhobor settlement on the Canadian prairies.

7 When Skelton left for Ottawa, he considered Mackintosh, barely 30 years old, the best person to replace him as head of the department of economics and political science. Queen's instead offered the position to C.R. Fay, who declined; on Fay's recommendation, Herbert Heaton, unhappily situated in Adelaide, was appointed. In 1927 Heaton moved to the History Department at the University of Minnesota and Mackintosh became department head (Gibson 1983: 56–8; King 2006).

8 For example, he edited the nine-volume 'Canadian Frontiers of Settlement Series,' which was 'concerned chiefly with the agricultural settlement of the great central plain, the problems of which exceed in scope and significance those of any other Canadian region' (Mackintosh 1934: xiii). Funded by the American Social Science Research Council, this was one of the first systematic large-scale social science projects in Canada.

9 Two other classics of Canadian economic history were also written as studies for this Commission (Creighton 1963 [1939]; Saunders 1984 [1939]).

10 The book's impact was not evident in sales; it took 15 years to sell 1000 copies (Watson 2006: 128). Innis and Mackintosh each credited the other as the originator of the staple approach in Canada (e.g. Mackintosh 1953).

11 For a sharply worded critique of this idea, see Eccles 1979: 439–41.

12 For nationalists, the latter raised concerns both that Canada was becoming dependent on the United States and that its unity was being threatened because natural resources were provincially controlled and their development could be divisive.

13 Indeed, Alan Green contends that it remains 'probably the best survey on Canadian developments in the period up to Confederation' (Green 2000: 1067). The idea is also politically powerful, visible in the resource-oriented strategies of several provincial governments and of Canada's current federal government.

14 Thus, writing of the relationship between wheat and railways, he often made the latter a function of the former: in Upper Canada, for example, 'wheat . . . involved railways' (Innis 1956: 116). In fact, Upper Canada's wheat economy developed before railways (McInnis 1992: 17–48; McCalla 1993: 19–24, 71–6), and the strategy behind railways there had nothing to do with wheat, at least Canadian wheat.

15 One constraint was that expansion onto contiguous lands upriver, in Upper Canada, was impeded by Loyalist and later settlement there. A strong francophone presence was subsequently established in eastern and northern Ontario, but this outlet, like the Saguenay (discussed above), could only accommodate a small proportion of an exponentially growing rural population.

16 http://www.genealogie.umontreal.ca/fr/leprdh.htm (accessed 17 February 2015).

17 This was an important work, although questions have since been raised concerning the representative character of the village studied (Follain 2008: 22, 122–3).

18 Like Dechêne's *Habitants et marchands*, *Quelques arpents* was awarded the highest honour of the Canadian Historical Association, the Garneau Prize, which recognizes the best historical work published in a five-year period.

19 See http://balsac.uqac.ca (accessed 17 February 2015).

20 http://www66.statcan.gc.ca/acyb_000-eng.htm (accessed 17 February 2015).

21 See the 1995 interview of Urquhart by Marvin McInnis (Lyons et al. 2008: 64–76). Urquhart had worked closely with W.A. Mackintosh in Ottawa during the war and was involved in early work to

create the official series. He moved to Queen's afterwards, eventually succeeding to the chair that Shortt and Skelton had once occupied.

22 Although the significance of the issue is uncertain, the character of Canadian data on prices could have implications for interpreting real changes. To deflate his data for the nineteenth century, Urquhart had to rely heavily on a 1963 MA thesis on the cost of living in a small, slow-growing city in eastern Ontario (Urquhart 1986: 85–7; Dales 1986: 89).

23 And to economists at the time, such as the Canadian-born economist Jacob Viner (Viner 1924). Urquhart (1986: 32) emphasizes the degree to which his GNP series supports Mackintosh's understanding of the period.

24 For programs of all the conferences, see http://www.economichistory.ca/pastConferences.html (accessed 17 February 2015).

25 It is not that wheat was unimportant. But a narrow focus on wheat obscures that in a complex economy, a single product was not the sole determinant of economic performance (Vickery 1974: 52–4).

26 For example, they produced works in the staples tradition (e.g. McCallum 1980), major institutional histories (e.g. Neufeld 1972), and theoretically rigorous accounts of important policies (e.g. Dales 1966). Both Neufeld and McCallum later served as chief economist for Canada's largest bank, the Royal Bank of Canada. As well, some of those doing historical research taught and did research in contemporary fields, some (such as Angela Redish and Frank Lewis) published on both non-Canadian and Canadian topics, and a number worked only on non-Canadian subjects.

27 Some, indeed, reinforced the basic framework; for example, the only two papers on Canada in the *Journal of Economic History* in the decade after 2005 addressed migration to the prairies and the role of natural resources in the Canadian economy (Green et al. 2005; Keay 2007). The principal exception is McInnis (1992, 2000a, 2000b), who completely revised nineteenth-century agricultural history and substantially modified the standard story of forest products.

28 Historians also were substantial contributors, as was one economist, Marvin McInnis, whose work for the atlas informs his overviews of Canada's population history (McInnis 2000b, 2000c).

29 These include the Canadian Century Research Infrastructure initiative which, working in cooperation with Statistics Canada, has produced samples from the population schedules of the manuscript census for 1911 to 1951, and other projects that have created samples from preceding censuses back to 1852. For the former, see http://ccri.library.ualberta.ca/enindex.html; and for the latter, https://www.nappdata.org/napp/samples.shtml (both accessed 17 February 2015). The ambition and the possibilities of such projects are suggested by Baskerville and Inwood (2015).

30 Both founders died very young; the work was carried forward by colleagues and members of the team they had organized. These records are described at https://www.mun.ca/mha/mlc/ (accessed 17 February 2015). Several eminent economist historians, including Douglass North, were consulted on the project (Sager 1989: xvi).

31 The scope and variety of such work can be seen in the journal *Labour/le travail*, founded in 1976. Not surprisingly, given its perspective, its articles tend to take a pessimistic view of economic change. For example, it has rarely published material on workers whose skills were created by or adaptable to the industrial age. All but the most recent issues are now open online, at http://www.lltjournal.ca/index.php/llt (accessed 17 February 2015).

32 During the First World War, Flavelle headed the Imperial Munitions Board; with responsibility for the procurement of all Britain's war materials from Canada, it had a vital role in the wartime economy (and was, for a few years, much the largest enterprise in Canada).

33 That is, as written before the development of cliometrics. As this phrasing indicates, this is a positive comment.

References

Acland, Charles and William Buxton (eds.) (1999) *Harold Innis in the New Century: Reflections and Refractions*, Montreal: McGill-Queen's University Press.

Armstrong, Christopher and H.V. Nelles (1986) *Monopoly's Moment: The Organization and Regulation of Canadian Utilities, 1830–1930*, Philadelphia, PA: Temple University Press.

Baskerville, Peter and Kris Inwood (eds.) (2015) *Lives in Transition: Longitudinal Analysis from Historical Sources*, Montreal: McGill-Queen's University Press.

Belisle, Donica (2011) *Retail Nation: Department Stores and the Making of Modern Canada*, Vancouver: UBC Press.

Berger, Carl (1986) *The Writing of Canadian History: Aspects of English–Canadian Historical Writing since 1900*, 2nd ed., Toronto: University of Toronto Press.
Bertram, Gordon (1973) 'The Relevance of the Wheat Boom in Canadian Economic Growth', *Canadian Journal of Economics*, 6 (4): 545–66.
Bliss, Michael (1978) *A Canadian Millionaire: The Life and Business Times of Sir Joseph Flavelle, Bart., 1858–1939*, Toronto: Macmillan of Canada.
Boleda, Mario (1990) 'Trente mille Français à la conquète du Saint-Laurent', *Histoire sociale/Social History*, 23 (45): 153–77.
Bonnett, John (2013) *Emergence and Empire: Innis, Complexity and the Trajectory of History*, Montreal: McGill-Queen's University Press.
Bouchard, Gérard (1972) *Le Village immobile: Sennely-en-Sologne au XVIIIe siècle*, Paris: Plon.
Bouchard, Gérard (1996) *Quelques arpents d'Amérique: Population, économie, famille au Saguenay, 1838–1971*, Montreal: Boréal.
Bradbury, Bettina (1993) *Working Families: Age, Gender, and Daily Survival in Industrializing Montreal*, Toronto: Oxford University Press.
Brady, Alexander (1953) 'Harold Adams Innis, 1894–1952', *Canadian Journal of Economics and Political Science*, 19 (1): 87–96.
Brown, Jennifer S.H. (1980) *Strangers in Blood: Fur Trade Company Families in Indian Country*, Vancouver: University of British Columbia Press.
Buckley, Kenneth (1958) 'The Role of Staple Industries in Canada's Economic Development', *Journal of Economic History*, 18 (4): 439–50.
Canadian Bankers' Association (1986) *Adam Shortt's History of Canadian Currency and Banking, 1600–1880*, Toronto: Canadian Bankers' Association.
Carlos, Ann M. and Frank D. Lewis (2010) *Commerce by a Frozen Sea: Native Americans and the European Fur Trade*, Philadelphia: University of Pennsylvania Press.
Caves, Richard E. (1965) '"Vent for Surplus" Models of Trade and Growth', in R. E. Baldwin et al., *Trade, Growth and the Balance of Payments*, Chicago, IL: Rand McNally.
Chambers, E.J. and Donald Gordon (1966), 'Primary Products and Economic Growth: An Empirical Measurement', *Journal of Political Economy*, 74 (4): 315–32.
Charbonneau, Hubert, Bertrand Desjardins, André Guillemette, Yves Landry, Jacques Légaré et François Nault, avec la collaboration de Réal Bates et Mario Boleda (1987) *Naissance d'une population. Les Français établis au Canada au XVIIe siècle*, Paris: Les Presses Universitaires de France.
Charbonneau, Hubert, Bertrand Desjardins, Jacques Légaré et Hubert Denis (1996) 'La population française de la vallée du Saint-Laurent avant 1760', in Serge Courville (ed.), *Atlas historique du Québec: Population et territoire*, Sainte-Foy: les Presses de l'Université Laval.
Clement, Wallace and Glen Williams (eds.) (1989), *The New Canadian Political Economy*, Kingston: McGill-Queen's University Press.
Courville, Serge (1990) *Entre ville et campagne: L'essor du village dans les seigneuries du Bas-Canada*, Quebec: les Presses de l'Université Laval.
Courville, Serge, Jean-Claude Robert and Normand Séguin (1995) *Atlas historique du Québec: Le pays laurentien au XIXe siècle: les morphologies de base*, Ste Foy: les Presses de l'Université Laval.
Craig, Béatrice (2009) *Backwoods Consumers and Homespun Capitalists: The Rise of a Market Culture in Eastern Canada*, Toronto: University of Toronto Press.
Creighton, Donald (1937) *The Commercial Empire of the St. Lawrence*, Toronto: Ryerson Press.
Creighton, Donald (1963 [1939]) *British North America at Confederation*, Ottawa: Queen's Printer.
Crowley, Terry (2007) 'Oscar Douglas Skelton and Canada's Economic History', in Robert Whaples (ed.) *EH.NetEncyclopedia*: http://eh.net/encyclopedia/oscar-douglas-skelton-and-canadas-economic-history/ (consulted 6 December 2014).
Curtis, Bruce (2001) *The Politics of Population: State Formation, Statistics, and the Census of Canada, 1840–1875*, Toronto: University of Toronto Press.
Dales, J.H. (1966) *The Protective Tariff in Canada's Development*, Toronto: University of Toronto Press.
Dales, J.H. (1986) 'Comment [on Urquhart's paper]', in Stanley L. Engerman and Robert E. Gallman (eds.) *Long-Term Factors in American Economic Growth*, Chicago, IL: University of Chicago Press.
Darroch, Gordon and Lee Soltow (1994) *Property and Inequality in Victorian Ontario: Structural Patterns and Cultural Communities in the 1871 Census*, Toronto: University of Toronto Press.
Dechêne, Louise (1974) *Habitants et marchands de Montréal au XVIIe siècle*, Paris: Plon.

Dechêne, Louise (1986) 'Observations sur l'agriculture du Bas-Canada au début du XIXe siècle', in Joseph Goy et Jean-Pierre Wallot (eds.) *Évolution et éclatement du monde rural: Structures, fonctionnement et évolution des sociétés rurales françaises et québécoises XVIIe–XXe siècles*, Paris: Éditions de l'École des Hautes Études en Sciences Sociales.

Dechêne, Louise (1994) *Le partage des subsistances au Canada sous le régime français*, Montreal: Boréal.

Dechêne, Louise (2008) *Le peuple, l'état et la guerre au Canada sous le régime français*, Montreal: Boréal.

Dépatie, Sylvie, Catherine Desbarats, Danielle Gauvreau, Mario Lalancette and Thomas Wien (eds.) (1998) *Vingt ans après Habitants et marchands: lectures de l'histoire des XVIIe et XVIIIe siècles canadiens/ Twenty Years Later: Reading the History of Seventeenth- and Eighteenth-Century Canada*, Montreal: McGill-Queen's University Press.

Dickinson, John A. and Brian Young (2003) *A Short History of Quebec*, 3rd ed., Montreal: McGill-Queen's University Press.

Drummond, Ian M. (1983) with William Kaplan, *Political Economy at the University of Toronto: A History of the Department, 1888–1982*, Toronto: Faculty of Arts and Science, University of Toronto.

Drummond, Ian M. (1987) 'Innis, Harold Adams', in John Eatwell, Murray Milgate and Peter Newman (eds.) *The New Palgrave: A Dictionary of Economics, 2, E to J*, London: Macmillan.

Drummond, Ian M. with Peter George, Kris Inwood, P.W. Sinclair and Tom Traves (1987) *Progress without Planning: The Economic History of Ontario from Confederation to the Second World War*, Toronto: University of Toronto Press.

Dupré, Ruth (1992) 'Un historien chez les économistes: Albert Faucher [1915–1992]', *L'Actualité économique*, 68 (3): 409–14.

Dupré, Ruth and Michael Huberman (2000) 'L'influence de la science économique sur les historiens: une analyse de deux revues canadiennes d'histoire (1970–1996)', *L'Actualité économique*, 76 (1): 159–70.

Easterbook, W.T. and H.G.J. Aitken (1956) *Canadian Economic History*, Toronto: Macmillan.

Eccles, W.J. (1979), 'A Belated Review of Harold Adams Innis, *The Fur Trade in Canada*', *Canadian Historical Review*, 60 (4): 419–41.

Engerman, Stanley L. (1977) 'Douglass C. North's *The Economic Growth of the United States, 1790–1860* Revisited', *Social Science History*, 1 (2): 248–57.

Ens, Gerhard (1996) *Homeland to Hinterland: The Changing Worlds of the Red River Metis in the Nineteenth Century*, Toronto: University of Toronto Press.

Faucher, Albert (1973) *Québec en Amérique au XIXe siècle: Essai sur les caractères économiques de la Laurentie*, Montreal: Fides.

Fay, C.R. (1925) *Agricultural Co-operation in the Canadian West*, London: P.S. King

Ferguson, Barry (1993) *Remaking Liberalism: The Intellectual Legacy of Adam Shortt, O.D. Skelton, W.C. Clark, and W.A. Mackintosh, 1890–1925*, Montreal: McGill-Queen's University Press.

Firestone, O.J. (1958) *Canada's Economic Development 1867–1953*, London: Bowes and Bowes.

Firestone, O.J. (1960) 'Development of Canada's Economy, 1850–1900', in Conference on Research in Income and Wealth, *Trends in the American Economy in the Nineteenth Century*, Princeton, NJ: Princeton University Press.

Follain, Antoine (2008) *Le village sous l'Ancien Régime*, Paris: Fayard.

Gentilcore, R. Louis (ed.) (1993) *Historical Atlas of Canada, 2, The Land Transformed, 1800–1891*, Toronto: University of Toronto Press.

Gibson, Frederick W. (1983) *Queen's University, Volume II, 1917–1961: To Serve and Yet Be Free*, Kingston: McGill-Queen's University Press.

Granatstein, J.L. (1982) *The Ottawa Men: The Civil Service Mandarins, 1935–1957*, Toronto: Oxford University Press.

Green, Alan G. (2000) 'Twentieth Century Canadian Economic History', in Stanley L. Engerman and Robert Gallman (eds.) *The Cambridge Economic History of the United States, 3, The Twentieth Century*, Cambridge: Cambridge University Press.

Green, Alan, Mary MacKinnon and Chris Minns (2005) 'Conspicuous by Their Absence: French Canadians and the Settlement of the Canadian West', *Journal of Economic History*, 65 (3): 822–49.

Hamelin, Jean (1960) *Économie et société en Nouvelle-France*, Québec: Les presses de l'Université Laval.

Harris, Cole (2008) *The Reluctant Land: Society, Space, and Environment in Canada before Confederation*, Vancouver: UBC Press.

Harris, R. Cole (ed.) (1987) *Historical Atlas of Canada, 1, From the Beginning to 1800*, Toronto: University of Toronto Press.

Innis, Harold A. (1923) *A History of the Canadian Pacific Railway*, London: P.S. King.

Innis, Harold A. (1930) *The Fur Trade in Canada: An Introduction to Canadian Economic History*, New Haven, CT: Yale University Press.
Innis, Harold A. (1933) *Problems of Staple Production in Canada*, Toronto: Ryerson Press.
Innis, Harold A. (1940) *The Cod Fisheries: The History of an International Economy*, New Haven, CT: Yale University Press.
Innis, Harold A. (1956) *Essays in Canadian Economic History*, Toronto: University of Toronto Press.
Inwood, Kris and Jim Irwin (2002) 'Land, Income and Regional Inequality: New Estimates of Provincial Income and Growth in Canada, 1871–1891', *Acadiensis*, 31 (2): 157–84.
Kealey, Gregory S. (1980) *Toronto Workers Respond to Industrial Capitalism, 1867–1892*, Toronto: University of Toronto Press.
Keay, Ian (2007) 'The Engine or the Caboose? Resource Industries and Twentieth-Century Canadian Economic Performance', *Journal of Economic History*, 67 (1): 1–32.
Kerr, Donald and Deryck W. Holdsworth (eds.) (1990) *Historical Atlas of Canada*, 3, *Addressing the Twentieth Century*, Toronto: University of Toronto Press.
King, Jack (2006) 'Herbert Heaton: A Scholar "Exiled" from Australia', *History of Economics Review*, 43: 56–70.
Leacy, F.H. (ed.) (1983) *Historical Statistics of Canada*, 2nd ed., Ottawa: Statistics Canada.
Lewis, Frank D. and Marvin McInnis (1984) 'Agricultural Output and Efficiency in Lower Canada, 1851', *Research in Economic History*, 9: 45–87.
Ludlow, Peter (2010) 'Searching for the Past, Writing for the Present: Charles Ryle Fay and Newfoundland's Contested Past', *Acadiensis*, 39 (2): 89–108.
Lyons, John S., Louis P. Cain and Samuel H. Williamson (eds.) (2008) *Reflections on the Cliometrics Revolution: Conversations with Economic Historians*, London: Routledge.
Mackintosh, W.A. (1923) 'Economic Factors in Canadian History', *Canadian Historical Review*, 4 (1): 12–25.
Mackintosh, W.A. (1924) *Agricultural Cooperation in Western Canada*, Kingston: Queen's University.
Mackintosh, W.A. (1934) *Prairie Settlement: The Geographical Setting*, Toronto: Macmillan.
Mackintosh, W.A. (1953) 'Innis on Canadian Economic Development', *Journal of Political Economy*, 61 (3): 185–94.
Mackintosh, W.A. (1964 [1939]) *The Economic Background of Dominion–Provincial Relations*, Toronto: McClelland and Stewart.
Mavor, James (1905) *Report to the Board of Trade on the North West of Canada, with special reference to wheat production for export, 1904*, London: HMSO.
Mavor, James (1914) *An Economic History of Russia*, 2 vols., London: J.M. Dent.
Mavor, James (1925) *Niagara in Politics: A Critical Account of the Ontario Hydro Electric Power Commission*, New York: Dutton.
McCalla, Douglas (1993) *Planting the Province: The Economic History of Upper Canada, 1784–1870*, Toronto: University of Toronto Press.
McCalla, Douglas (1998) 'The Ontario Economy in the Long Run', *Ontario History*, 90 (2): 97–115.
McCalla, Douglas (2015) *Consumers in the Bush: Shopping in Rural Upper Canada*, Montreal: McGill-Queen's University Press.
McCallum, John (1980) *Unequal Beginnings: Agriculture and Economic Development in Quebec and Ontario until 1870*, Toronto: University of Toronto Press.
McClelland, Peter D. (1968) 'Railroads, American Growth and the New Economic History: A Critique', *Journal of Economic History*, 28 (1): 102–23.
McCusker, John J. and Russell R. Menard (1985) *The Economy of British America, 1607–1789*, Chapel Hill: University of North Carolina Press.
McDowall, Duncan (2008) *The Sum of the Satisfactions: Canada in the Age of National Accounting*, Montreal: McGill-Queen's University Press.
McInnis, R.M. (1982) 'A Reconsideration of the State of Agriculture in Lower Canada in the First Half of the Nineteenth Century', in Donald H. Akenson (ed.) *Canadian Papers in Rural History*, 3, Gananoque: Langdale Press.
McInnis, R.M. (1992) 'Perspectives on Ontario Agriculture, 1815–1930', in Donald H. Akenson (ed.) *Canadian Papers in Rural History*, 8, Gananoque: Langdale Press.
McInnis, Marvin (2000a) 'The Economy of Canada in the Nineteenth Century', in Stanley L. Engerman and Robert Gallman (eds.) *The Cambridge Economic History of the United States*, 2, *The Long Nineteenth Century*, Cambridge: Cambridge University Press.

McInnis, Marvin (2000b) 'The Population of Canada in the Nineteenth Century', in Michael R. Haines and Richard H. Steckel (eds.) *A Population History of North America*, Cambridge: Cambridge University Press.

McInnis, Marvin (2000c) 'Canada's Population in the Twentieth Century', in Michael R. Haines and Richard H. Steckel (eds.) *A Population History of North America*, Cambridge: Cambridge University Press.

McKillop, A.B. (1994) *Matters of Mind: The University in Ontario, 1791–1951*, Toronto: University of Toronto Press.

Mitch, David (2011) 'Economic History in Departments of Economics: The Case of the University of Chicago, 1892 to the Present', *Social Science History*, 35 (2): 237–71.

Mokyr, Joel (ed.) (2003) *The Oxford Encyclopedia of Economic History*, New York: Oxford University Press.

Munro, John (1994) *Textiles, Towns, and Trade: Essays in the Economic History of Late-Medieval England and the Low Countries*, Aldershot: Ashgate.

Neatby, Hilda (1978) *Queen's University, Volume I, 1841–1917: To Strive, to Seek, to Find, and Not to Yield*, Montreal: McGill-Queen's University Press.

Neill, Robin (1991) *A History of Canadian Economic Thought*, London: Routledge.

Neufeld, E.P. (1972) *The Financial System of Canada: Its Growth and Development*, Toronto: Macmillan of Canada.

Norrie, K.H. (1975) 'The Rate of Settlement of the Canadian Prairies, 1870–1911', *Journal of Economic History*, 35 (2): 410–27.

Norrie, Kenneth, Douglas Owram and Herbert Emery (2008) *A History of the Canadian Economy*, 4th ed., Toronto: Thomson Nelson.

North, Douglass C. (1955) 'Location Theory and Regional Economic Growth', *Journal of Political Economy*, 62 (3): 243–58.

North, Douglass C. (1961) *The Economic Growth of the United States 1790 to 1860*, Englewood Cliffs, NJ: Prentice-Hall.

Ouellet, Fernand (1966) *Histoire économique et sociale du Québec, 1760–1850*, Montreal: Fides.

Palmer, Bryan D. (1992) *Working Class Experience: Rethinking the History of Canadian Labour, 1800–1991*, 2nd ed., Toronto: McClelland and Stewart.

Paquet, Gilles and Jean-Pierre Wallot (2007) *Un Québec moderne, 1760–1840: Essai d'histoire économique et sociale*, Montréal: HMH.

Parr, Joy (1990) *The Gender of Breadwinners: Women, Men, and Change in Two Industrial Towns, 1880–1950*, Toronto: University of Toronto Press.

Parr, Joy (1999) *Domestic Goods: The Material, the Moral, and the Economic in the Postwar Years*, Toronto: University of Toronto Press.

Poitras, Daniel (2013) 'L'impossible oubli: Fernand Ouellet, la Révolution tranquille et la république contrefactuelle des Patriotes', *Revue d'histoire de l'Amérique française*, 66 (3–4): 339–64.

Pope, Peter E. (2004) *Fish into Wine: The Newfoundland Plantation in the Seventeenth Century*, Chapel Hill: University of North Carolina Press for the Omohundro Institute of Early American History and Culture.

Ramirez, Bruno (1991) *On the Move: French–Canadian and Italian Migrants in the North Atlantic Economy, 1860–1914*, Toronto: McClelland and Stewart.

Ray, Arthur J. (1974) *Indians in the Fur Trade: Their Role as Trappers, Hunters, and Middlemen in the Lands Southwest of Hudson Bay, 1660–1870*, Toronto: University of Toronto Press.

Ray, Arthur J. and Donald Freeman (1978) *'Give Us Good Measure': An Economic Analysis of Relations between the Indians and the Hudson's Bay Company before 1763*, Toronto: University of Toronto Press.

Rudin, Ronald (1997) *Making History in Twentieth-Century Quebec*, Toronto: University of Toronto Press.

Sager, Eric W. (1989) *Seafaring Labour: The Merchant Marine of Atlantic Canada, 1820–1914*, Kingston: McGill-Queen's University Press.

Sager, Eric W. with Gerald E. Panting (1990) *Maritime Capital: The Shipping Industry in Atlantic Canada, 1820–1914*, Montreal: McGill-Queen's University Press.

Sangster, Joan (1995) *Working Families: The Lives of Working Women in Small-Town Ontario, 1920–1960*, Toronto: University of Toronto Press.

Saunders, S.A. (1984 [1939]) *The Economic History of the Maritime Provinces*, Fredericton: Acadiensis Press.

Shortt, Adam and Arthur G. Doughty (eds.) (1914–17) *Canada and Its Provinces: A History of the Canadian People and Their Institutions, by One Hundred Associates*, 23 vols., Toronto: Glasgow, Brook.

Shortt, S.E.D. (1976) *The Search for an Ideal: Six Canadian Intellectuals and Their Convictions in an Age of Transition 1890–1930*, Toronto: University of Toronto Press.

Skelton, O.D. (1911) *Socialism: A Critical Analysis*, Boston, MA: Houghton Mifflin.

Skelton, O.D. (1914) 'General Economic History, 1867–1912', in Adam Shortt and Arthur G. Doughty (eds.) *Canada and Its Provinces: A History of the Canadian People and Their Institutions, by One Hundred Associates*, vol. 9, *The Dominion: Industrial Expansion, Part I*, Toronto: Glasgow, Brook.

Squatriti, Paolo (2014) 'Of Seeds, Seasons, and Seas: Andrew Watson's Medieval Agrarian Revolution Forty Years Later', *Journal of Economic History*, 74 (4): 1205–20.

Taylor, Graham D. and Peter A. Baskerville (1994) *A Concise History of Business in Canada*, Toronto: Oxford University Press.

Urquhart, M.C. (1986) 'New Estimates of Gross National Product, Canada, 1870–1926: Some Implications for Canadian Development', in Stanley L. Engerman and Robert E. Gallman (eds.) *Long-Term Factors in American Economic Growth*, Chicago, IL: University of Chicago Press.

Urquhart, M.C. and K.A.H. Buckley (eds.) (1965) *Historical Statistics of Canada*, Cambridge: Cambridge University Press.

Urquhart, M.C. et al. (1993) *Gross National Product, Canada, 1870–1926: The Derivation of the Estimates*, Kingston: McGill-Queen's University Press.

Van Kirk, Sylvia (1980) *'Many Tender Ties': Women in Fur-Trade Society, 1670–1870*, Winnipeg: Watson & Dwyer.

Vickery, Edward (1974) 'Exports and North American Economic Growth: "Structuralist" and "Staple" Models in Historical Perspective', *Canadian Journal of Economics* 7 (1): 32–58.

Viner, Jacob (1924) *Canada's Balance of International Indebtedness, 1900–1913: An Inductive Study in the Theory of International Trade*, Cambridge, MA: Harvard University Press.

Warkentin, John (2014) 'James Mavor: Forerunner in Canadian Geography', *Canadian Geographer*, 58 (3): 377–92.

Watkins, M.H. (1963) 'A Staple Theory of Economic Growth', *Canadian Journal of Economics and Political Science*, 29 (2): 141–58.

Watkins, M.H. (2006) *Staples and Beyond: Selected Writings of Mel Watkins*, Hugh Grant and David Wolfe eds., Montreal: McGill-Queen's University Press.

Watson, Alexander John (2006) *Marginal Man: The Dark Vision of Harold Innis*, Toronto: University of Toronto Press.

Wilson, Catharine Anne (2009) *Tenants in Time: Family Strategies, Land, and Liberalism in Upper Canada, 1799–1871*, Montreal: McGill-Queen's University Press.

5

THE RISE AND FALL OF AUSTRALIAN ECONOMIC HISTORY

David Meredith and Deborah Oxley[1]

Economies shape their own histories. Australia was a group of affluent British colonies, then a dominion, and finally an independent nation. It was rich in resources, a global supplier of raw materials and food, with large urban domestic markets. Around and through it flowed goods, capital, and people. There was no industrial revolution, no struggle for political independence, but there were first world living standards. How did these conditions mold the central concerns of Australian economic history? Did the Australian experience provide new insights into economic development, and if so, did these influence the practice of economic history internationally? We endeavor to tell the story of the rise and fall of Australian economic history from its foundation at the hands of the State Statistician, its take-off as an academic discipline situated firmly in economics, a period of global expansion and self-sustained growth, through to its current parlous state of decline. We examine its intellectual preoccupations and methodological approaches, and commit a heinous sin of simplification by imposing a coherent story on what is a particularly disparate set of scholarly works. The focus is on the economic history of Australia which was the principal, but not sole, area studied by those employed as economic historians. We conclude that Australia offers a strong tradition of empirical work supported by the state provision of official statistics; that Australian economic historians were early adopters of new approaches; and that the tyranny of distance – while protecting and nurturing an infant industry in economic history aimed at the domestic market – left the discipline largely marginal from the international mainstream. Now, when greater worldwide integration *might* have embraced an antipodean perspective, the discipline is a shadow of its former self.

Foundation

The first to attempt a comprehensive economic analysis of the nation was Timothy Coghlan who published *A statistical account of the seven colonies of Australasia* in 1893. Coghlan held the post of Government Statistician of New South Wales and drew heavily on the statistical records of each of the colonies. He is credited with compiling the 'first official series of modern national income estimates prepared and published anywhere in the world' along with parallel estimates of output and expenditure (Arndt 1949: 616; Studenski 1958: 135; Snooks 1991: 13 n.1; Haig 2006). Appropriately enough, Coghlan entitled these estimates *The Wealth and Progress of New South Wales* (Coghlan 1887–1902). Coghlan's notable achievements should be viewed in the context of other statists working in Australia in the late nineteenth and early twentieth centuries: William Archer, Henry Hayter, George Knibbs, Robert Johnston, James Sutcliffe, Stanley Carver and Colin Clark (see Groenewegen and McFarlane 1990, ch. 5; Haig 2001; Maddison 2004).

Coghlan's publications while Government Statistician may be regarded as 'trail-blazing' exercises in national accounting over the recent past, but in 1918, now retired from public duties, he moved away from national accounting and published the nation's first comprehensive economic history, *Labour and Industry in Australia* (Coghlan 1918). This was a substantial work: over 2300 pages (775,000 words) in four volumes. In it Coghlan adumbrated the phases of nineteenth-century Australian economic history in seven parts, following British invasion: crossing the Blue Mountains, abolition of the assignment system, discovery of gold, free selection of land, protection and public works, the financial crash of 1893 and the establishment of the Commonwealth in 1901. This provided economic historians with a periodization for the nineteenth century largely distinct from its political history or from the periodization of British economic history. Coghlan's approach could be summarized as 'real world economic history' – a close attention to detail, the importance of statistical framework and concentration upon the process of economic growth in the domestic economy. Coghlan also changed the way the census was taken, in 1890 replacing the Farr system with one that distinguished between 'breadwinners' and 'dependents', giving rise to considerable debate (Deacon 1985; Alford 1986, 1987; Endres 1987; Jones 1987; see Snooks 1994: 154–5). This had important ramifications in Britain, and eventually throughout the world.

Probably the first work to be published in Australia with the words 'economic history' in the title was Herbert Heaton's *Modern Economic History, with Special Reference to Australia* (1921).[2] In the 1930s major works of Australian economic history appeared. Edward Shann, professor of history and economics at the University of Western Australia, published *An Economic History of Australia* in 1930. Shann followed Coghlan's periodization – convicts, wool and gold, land settlement, 'protection all round', but took a more free trade and *laissez-faire* approach, concerned that Australia relied too heavily on foreign borrowing and artificially (and dangerously) supported living standards through protection. He placed more emphasis on the international economy – 'John Bull's Greater Woolsack' was the title of the chapter on the expansion of the wool industry – and on economic policy, particularly where it interfered with the free working of markets. In the same year W.K. Hancock expressed similar doubts concerning government intervention and pointed to the environmental impact of European settlement (Hancock 1930). In 1933 the Australian volume of the *Cambridge History of the British Empire* appeared and included chapters by Shann, Hancock and the economist D.B. Copeland (Scott 1933). Continuing in the Coghlan tradition, in 1935 the New Zealand economist Allan Fisher published *The Clash of Progress and Society*; in 1938 economists Colin Clark and J.G. Crawford produced *The National Income of Australia*; and then Fisher published a pioneering account of structural change from primary to secondary to tertiary production (Fisher 1939; Lloyd 2015: 57). At the end of the decade Brian Fitzpatrick wrote two important volumes on the British Empire in Australia. Like Shann, Fitzpatrick placed Australia in an international context. Unlike Shann, Fitzpatrick took a radical leftist approach to Australia's economic development and its relationship with Britain. In particular, he regarded much of what happened in the Australian economy as being directed by British capitalists in their own interests rather than those of the Australian people. He advocated collective action along socialist lines to support the Australian working class (Watson 1979).

While historians among the above offered nothing especially novel in the approach to writing economic history – their styles are similar to the likes of R.H. Tawney, J.H. Clapham, etc. – they made successful first attempts to map the economic development of Australia as a land of recent British settlement. Their interpretations differ but they each convey the opportunities and achievements of a small British population in a vast land of huge natural resources. Capital and migrants flowed in and exports of primary products flowed out. Australia prospered and even allowing for the excesses of the boom years and hardships of the depression, from the perspective of 1918 or 1930 or 1939, Australia's nineteenth-century economic history could plausibly be written as a success story.

Take-off, 1950–65

The works by Coghlan, Shann and Fitzpatrick formed the bedrock of Australian economic history at the end of the Second World War and the latter two in particular were used as texts in a growing number of university courses. It is at this point that Australia developed a particular institutional structure which shaped the practical and intellectual development of the discipline: economic history was conceived as a branch of applied economics. From this time, Australian economic history was firmly situated in faculties of economics and commerce. This would shape recruitment, areas of study and intellectual influences. The failure of economic history – or, indeed, any social science history – to gain a foothold within history faculties isolated the discipline from more social and cultural approaches. For example, while today the relevance of climate, biology and geography may be apparent to economists, back then this perspective of the *longue durée* brought by the *Annales* School largely passed Australian economic history by. The same might be said of 'history from below' and scholars like E.P. Thompson, of postmodernism, feminism and other major intellectual challenges. Economics was to exert by far the greatest influence over the development of the discipline.

The 1950s and early 1960s witnessed the publication of major works by Noel Butlin, Sydney Butlin, R.M. Hartwell and Geoffrey Blainey.

In the mid-1950s Noel Butlin produced a series of studies on economic growth in the second half of the nineteenth century, focused on public and private capital formation and the role of colonial governments (Butlin, N.G. and de Meel 1954; Butlin, N.G. 1955, 1958, 1959a, 1959b). Butlin was now following in the footsteps of Kuznets and the recently published United Nations' proposed system of national accounts but he was also building on an Australian tradition. That Butlin was strongly influenced by Coghlan is undoubted:

> Returning to *Labour and Industry* after working in detail over the period, one cannot fail to be struck by the greatness of this work, by the grandeur of Coghlan's mind, the keenness of his appreciation, his essential accuracy of both fact and judgement and his obvious fascination with his theme.
>
> *(Butlin, N.G. 1964: xv)*

His views on earlier contributions in national accounting by Mulhall, Coghlan, Benham, Sutcliffe and Clark and Crawford were set out at some length (Butlin, N.G. 1962: ch. 2; see also Haig 2001).

Meanwhile his older brother, Sydney Butlin, continued to publish his research findings on early financial history which culminated in 1953 with his monumental *Foundations of the Australian Monetary System 1788–1851*. The year after, Hartwell (1954) produced the first economic history treatment of Tasmania. He was interested in the business cycle as it played out in the colony, particularly the severe downturn in the depression of the 1840s. His book analyzed the distribution of land, the role of capitalists, convicts and workers, capital inflow, agriculture and pastoralism, sealing and whaling, manufacturing, internal and external trade and banking and insurance, in short the workings of the island economy in its formative years.

Blainey's history of the Mount Lyell Mining Company was both an economic and a business history of Tasmania in the later nineteenth century (1954). It ran through six editions, the sixth published in 2000. In *The Rush that Never Ended* (1963) he presented an overview of mining development in Australia and later described a theory of mineral discovery linked to the business cycle (Blainey 1970). Unusually for Australian economic historians he published this in a British journal. He became a household name with *The Tyranny of Distance* (1966), a study of the barriers to internal and external movements of goods and people, and how they were overcome. The book was reprinted numerous times and a second edition emerged in 1983. Although criticized for giving too much emphasis to the barriers of distance, and not enough to the ways in which they were overcome, it is an approach to economic history that is distinctly, and perhaps uniquely, Australasian. As such, it is as much part of the Australian canon as the work of the Butlins.

Noel Butlin's impressive two-volume reconstruction of Australian historical GDP, capital investment and borrowing (1962, 1964), was controversial: to many economic historians it represented a seismic shift of interpretation, or, as Schedvin put it, 'the decisive reorientation in the early 1960s towards uncovering the mechanism of economic growth and development' (1979: 542; see also Coleman 2015: 17–18). Economists were more critical of his methodology and findings (Clark 1963; Lydall 1963; Haig 2001). Butlin refocused Australian economic history from the international to the domestic economy in a correction to the orientation of both Shann and Fitzpatrick. Australians, not London bankers and wool brokers, were in charge of Australia's economic destiny and responsible for the successes and failures of the second half of the nineteenth century. In Butlin's view, 'Australian economic history was not a footnote to the Industrial Revolution nor was Australia a sheep-walk for the benefit of British imperialism' (Butlin, N.G. 1964: 5).

The publication of Australia's historical national accounts also invited international comparisons, some made by Butlin himself (1958: 12, 22; 1964: 5). The United States Bureau of the Census published historical GDP estimates in 1960 and Kuznets published his estimates between 1956 and 1964; Deane and Cole produced theirs for Britain in 1962, so the time was ripe for international comparisons of GDP, GDP per capita and economic growth. Placing Australia's real GDP per head in the second half of the nineteenth century against that of Britain seemed to confirm the Australian superiority that Mulhall had guessed at (1884). Butlin's estimates appeared in Kuznets's *Modern Economic Growth* in 1966 indicating that Australia was indeed a country that had shared in this phenomenon (Kuznets 1966).

The three early twentieth-century economic historians – Coghlan, Shann and Fitzpatrick – together with the post-war quartet of Sydney Butlin, Noel Butlin, Max Hartwell and Geoffrey Blainey – set the agenda for Australian economic history in the second half of the century. The main period for research was the nineteenth century, and thus the object of study was a group of separate colonies comprising 'Australia'. To what extent details pertaining to particular colonies could be aggregated into a pre-Federation 'Australian economy' remained an issue. The style was real world, empirical and detailed. In the hands of some, especially the Butlins but also Hartwell, Australian economic history was highly quantitative but statistics were basic and econometrics was avoided. Economic theory was usually to the forefront (Blainey least here) and post-war advances in growth theory and social accounting were prominent, especially in Noel Butlin's approach.

In their different ways these works stimulated further research, some familiar, some more novel. Fitzpatrick's concern about Australian economic sovereignty fostered a nationalist economic history, starting in 1957 when Ted Wheelwright drew attention to the degree of foreign ownership and control of Australian enterprise (Wheelwright 1957). But it was an emphasis on the domestic economy and economic growth led by physical capital investment that stimulated most work, on histories of the urban economy, manufacturing, utilities and transport. Indeed, Noel Butlin suggested that 'Australian economic development is mainly a story of urbanisation' (Butlin, N.G. 1958: 21). Business history became a major growth area. Banks and other financial institutions featured, as did firms in wool marketing, trading, shipping, mining and manufacturing. Colonial governments themselves were discussed as agents of economic change. Noel Butlin's term 'colonial socialism' became a shorthand for the varied ways in which the state intervened. Protection, the biggest area of political debate in Australia in the nineteenth and twentieth centuries, was probably the most significant single issue considered by economic historians (Butlin, N.G. 1959a; see also Ergas and Pincus 2015). Protection was one of three pillars designed to support the Australian economy. The other two were Arbitration (central wage fixing) and the White Australia Policy (race-based immigration controls). While not completely ignored by economic historians these were much more the focus of labor and general historians who engaged with the political arguments surrounding these institutions. When dealt with by economic historians, immigration tended to be treated separately from immigration policy (Pope and Withers 1994; Hatton and Withers 2015). Economic history in Australia was firmly established by 1965 and was set to expand at universities across the country. If Australian economic history was to have a golden age, surely it was now.

Self-sustained growth: 1965–95

By the later 1960s there was a need to write Australia's twentieth-century economic history. Little had been written (exceptions being Forster 1953; Butlin, S.J. 1955). Despite its subtitle, Fitzpatrick's *British Empire in Australia* (1941) devoted little space to the interwar years. The pioneers of Australia's twentieth-century economic history were Colin Forster, Ernst Boehm and Boris Schedvin. In 1964 Forster published a study of industrial development in Australia in the 1920s marking a shift to Australian industrialization in more recent times. Schedvin's 1970 tour de force tackled the 1920s and 1930s. Australian economic development in the twentieth century featured in an edited collection by Forster (1970); E.A. Boehm published two books (1971a, 1971b) followed by Sinclair (1976). Thanks to the efforts of Susan Bambrick (1970), Australia's long-run terms of trade were available. These works continued the tradition established by the Butlins: a focus on economic growth, the importance of the domestic urban economy, structural change, technology and institutions and a method securely anchored in macroeconomic theory, quantification and attention to detail.

The nature of the discipline after the mid-1960s can only be properly understood in relation to the institutional structure in which it operated. The fifteen years from 1965 to 1980 saw a massive expansion in the size of the discipline, a doubling from 37 permanent academics to 76. This level held steady for the following fifteen years, before contracting back again to 39 in 2005 en route to its current low number (see Figure 5.1).[3]

Much of this growth took place within departments of economic history, situated in economics faculties. The departmental structure was vital, increasing from two departments to eight between 1960 and 1975. With this expansion in the economic history labor force, buttressed by rising public investment in higher education, production of economic history, both Australian and non-Australian, increased strongly. The departmental structure fostered a fruitful research culture, attracted faculty funding that supported research and organized

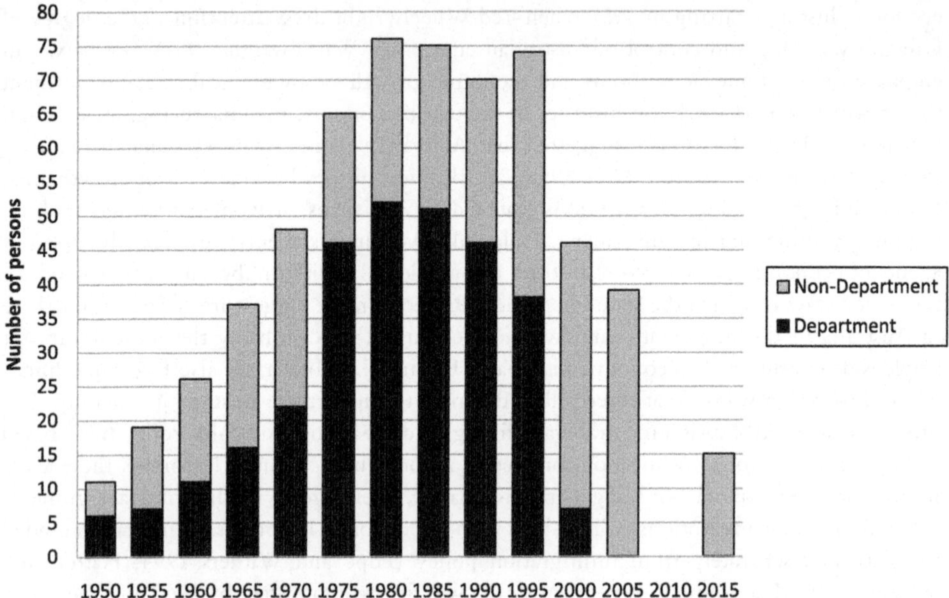

Figure 5.1 Number of economic historians at Australian universities 1950–2015 distinguishing those in departments of economic history.

Source: 1950–2005: *Commonwealth Universities Yearbook*; 2010 not available; 2015: university web pages.

teaching. University tuition fees were abolished in 1974 and student numbers drove the expansion in economic history as in all departments, underpinning its stability from 1980. Teaching economic history added to output directly as suitable texts were required (Sinclair 1976; Jackson 1977). Moreover, the expansion necessitated the recruitment of economic historians from across the spectrum, including history, and of foreign academics as Australian universities alone could not meet this level of rising demand (see Figure 5.2). The arrival of so many newcomers from overseas in a short space of time seemed like an invasion to some, though most of the 'new chums' researched non-Australian topics, at least to begin with. Undoubtedly their presence greatly expanded the geographical range of teaching and research: Drabble on Malaysia, Sigel on China, Inkster on Japan, Shlomowitz on India, later on van der Eng on Indonesia (even later Mariotti on South Africa, etc.). Australian economic historians increasingly contributed to non-Australian topics (for example, Snooks and McDonald 1986; Jackson 1994). Economic history in Australia thus developed much more of an international flavor. And with the ANU's superior budgetary power its Research School of Social Sciences was able to fund a stream of international visitors who generally spent some time in Canberra before fanning out to Melbourne, Sydney, Adelaide and Armidale. British and American economic historians took up chairs in Australian departments and introduced new approaches to economic and social history. All of this contributed to a definite broadening of economic history in Australia after 1970, which made the discipline more appealing and relevant.

The placing of Australian economic history in a more global context was evident in other ways. In 1964 John McCarty suggested that 'Australian historians particularly lack a suitable framework within which to analyse the growth of the Australian economy in the nineteenth century' and proposed that staple theory, developed with reference to Canadian economic development, could be used to explain the connection between the Australian export sector

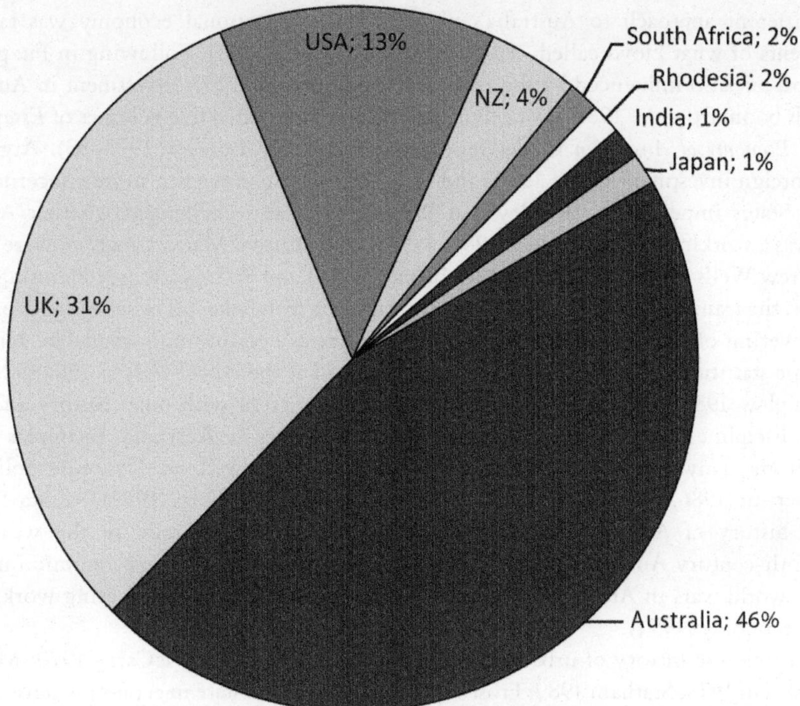

Figure 5.2 Seventy newcomers in economic history at Australian universities 1960–85 by place of first degree.

Source: Commonwealth Universities Yearbook.

and the domestic economy (McCarty 1964: 1). Comparative economic history was placed firmly on the menu. McCarty defined a 'pure type' of region of recent settlement as one possessing abundant natural resources, 'only sparsely inhabited by primitive peoples at the times of European occupation', having a capitalist economy, exporting cash crops and relying heavily on imports of capital and labor. Australia was the 'most pure' in this analysis. The United States, Canada, New Zealand, South Africa, Argentina, Colombia and Brazil 'complete a spectrum whose array of divergences from the "pure type" and from Australia, provide a comparative context that may inform our understanding of Australian history' (McCarty 1973: 149–51). Over the next forty years such comparisons would prove fruitful (McLean 2013). Dyster published on Argentina and Australia in 1979 and in 1985 a collection of essays examining the same comparator appeared (Dingle and Merrett 1985). In 1989 Boris Schedvin delivered the Tawney Memorial Lecture in Britain, 'Staples and regions of Pax Britannica', contrasting Argentina, Canada and New Zealand with Australia (1990). In Australia Donald Denoon's landmark *Settler Capitalism* (1983) compared Argentina, Chile, Uruguay, South Africa, Australia and New Zealand. He described the economic, social and political changes which occurred up to 1914, and argued that a 'settler mode of production' was a more useful concept than other deterministic theories such as staple theory. International growth accounting received a further boost in the 1980s when Angus Maddison converted real GDP in national currencies to US relative prices, thus allowing Australia to be compared with many countries (1982; Haig 1989).

A different approach to Australia's place in the international economy was taken by proponents of what Lloyd called 'radical nationalism' (2015: 61). Following in Fitzpatrick's footsteps, but also influenced by the massive foreign private direct investment in Australia's minerals boom from the 1960s, Wheelwright and Buckley edited five volumes of *Essays on the Political Economy of Australian Capitalism* (Wheelwright and Buckley 1975–83). Arguments about foreign investment in the 1960s and early 1970s were, however, more concerned with United States imperialism. Buckley and Wheelwright also challenged whether Australia really was a working man's paradise (1988, 1998). More formal Marxist analyses were offered by Andrew Wells (1989), and Philip McMichael (1984) and R.S. Neale (see Henning 1986).

Thus, the transition of economic history in Australia from take-off to sustained growth led to a flowering of lines of inquiry. In addition, statistics became more available. Historical economic statistics and working papers were produced at the ANU (ANU 1984–92, 1982–95; Vamplew 1987). This broadening and greater interaction with other history and social science disciplines marked a maturing of economic history in Australia. Examples of new work, from many that could be cited, include Greg Whitwell on economic policy and consumerism (1986, 1989), Brian Pinkstone on the history of exports (1992), Sandra Tweedie on the history of Australia–Asia trade (1994), William Rubinstein on the wealthy in nineteenth-century Australia (1979, 1980), Marnie Haig-Muir on the economic impact of the two world wars in Australia (1995, 1996), and John Williams's pioneering work on the convict economy (1994).

The economic history of urbanization was explored in depth (McCarty 1970; McCarty and Schedvin 1978; Statham 1989; Frost 1991). The role of the state in economic development in the nineteenth century came in for more attention (Butlin, N.G. et al. 1982; Jackson 1985; Boot 1998). Historical GDP estimates were pushed back to 1788 (Butlin, N.G. 1986; Butlin, N.G. and Sinclair 1986; Butlin, N.G. 1994). Further refinements of historical GDP were forthcoming (Haig 1967; Snooks 1972, 1979). Graeme Snooks, Butlin's successor as Timothy Coghlan Professor of Economic History at the ANU, produced three major works in quick succession, including an alternative set of GDP estimates that took into account non-market production (Snooks 1993a, 1993b, 1994). Combining labor force estimates with sectorial GDP gave Australian economic historians the opportunity to analyze factor productivity (Butlin, N.G. and Dowie 1969; Haig 1971). Above all, business history steamrollered on, involving commissioned histories as well as those based on public archives, continuing the tradition of an abiding interest in financial institutions, and contributing an impressive volume of studies to Australian economic history (Merrett 1985; Schedvin 1987, 1992; Salsbury and Sweeney 1988; Whitwell and Sydenham 1991). Why was business history so strong in Australia? Partly because business archives were readily available, partly because businesses commissioned them.

These works developed themes begun earlier in the twentieth century. A new departure was the quantification of human capital in the early years of white settlement, *Convict Workers* and *Convict Maids* (Nicholas 1988; Oxley 1996). As one contributor quipped, the former could have been titled *Time on the Southern Cross*, highlighting its indebtedness to the cliometric analysis of slavery (Fogel and Engerman 1974; see also Coleman 2015: 22–3). Not only did these works correct a widely held derogatory view of the economic worth of convicts, these large statistical compilations also described the social, economic and physical characteristics of ordinary people, propeling the early adoption of a new method: anthropometric history. The ramifications of these studies were not confined to Australia: they revealed much about the British and Irish working class in the early nineteenth century (Nicholas and Shergold 1987; Nicholas and Steckel 1991; Nicholas and Oxley 1993; Johnson and Nicholas 1995). Uncharacteristically for the discipline, this approach examined gender, for the first time tracing the biological fortunes of women compared with men.

Although this new methodology opened up questions of gender in Australian economic history there was a marked absence of this in other respects, the important exception to this being the work of Katrina Alford who described the tension between production and reproduction in colonial Australia to 1850 (1984, 1986). Alford's work highlighted the problem of measuring economic output solely by market transactions, a difficulty considered subsequently by Snooks, as mentioned. Most studies of women's work – paid or unpaid – came from outside, especially labor history, but had little impact on economic history (Ryan and Conlon 1975; Deacon 1985). The peculiar marginalization of women in Australian economic history perhaps derives from two factors: the near absence of parallel social science histories like demography (which barely existed outside the ANU); and the collapse of recruitment in economic history at the very time when women's history was making inroads elsewhere. New ideas tend to be brought in with new blood, and there was too little of either.

Even more obscured from view in Australian history was the Indigenous population. Only in the 1970s did this begin to change (Reynolds 1981). As had happened with other topics in Australian economic history, Geoffrey Blainey was the first Australian economic historian to tackle this issue (1975). Noel Butlin was the second (1983; see also Hunter 2015). Typically Butlin's contributions rested on quantification and economic theory. In Australia's bicentennial year Tony Dingle published *Aboriginal Economy, Patterns of Experience* (1988). In 1993 Noel Butlin estimated the economic cost of invasion and the size of the Indigenous economy.

Decline and fall: 1995 and beyond

In the early 1990s planning began for a prestigious publication in Australian economic history, *The Cambridge Economic History of Australia*, edited by R.V. Jackson. This was to be a two-volume work of twenty chapters written by eighteen authors. Collectively the chapters covered many of the topics that had dominated Australian economic history. Given its contents and line-up of authors it would have been a fitting memorial to Noel Butlin who died in 1991. It also meant that Australia was joining the group of countries for which Cambridge economic histories were produced. Writing was well underway by 1993 but in 1996 the project was unexpectedly cancelled.

This disappointing result came at a time when the discipline of economic history in Australian universities was coming under increasing pressure. This was the start of the decline. It is difficult to apply the argument that a neo-liberal shift in economics drove out economic history in Australia. There does not seem to be much evidence of such a sea-change in economics in Australia, whatever might be the case elsewhere (Millmow and Tuck 2013). The explanation seems far more pragmatic, tied to vocational needs and institutional aims in a shifting global environment.

In the first phases of post-war university expansion economic history had done well, establishing itself firmly in the five new universities founded between 1946 and 1958, joining the two 'ancient' seats of learning, the University of Sydney and the University of Melbourne. It also gained a presence when La Trobe and Flinders were founded. However, in the second wave of expansion, 1970–75, economic history failed to seed and there were no new departments. The third, and largest, wave of growth of the Australian university system, 1987 to 1994, witnessed the creation of nineteen new universities in a seven-year period. Economic history was not part of faculty at any of them.

There were probably several reasons for this failure, but a major one was the way in which the Australian economy was reformed and 'globalized' in the 1980s. The creation of new universities was part of this process of restructuring and they responded enthusiastically to rising demand for career-oriented higher education. The vocational orientation of these new universities set the pace and the older ones (and some that were not that much older) followed suit. Australian higher education had always been more attuned to the type of training favored by employers than in some other countries, a three-year pass degree being common, and this surge in courses in accounting, business law and taxation, management, business studies, marketing, information systems, hospitality and tourism was not confined to the newest institutions. All universities revamped to meet growing student demand for these subjects. University tuition fees were reintroduced in 1989 and graduates now emerged with long-term debts to be paid back through future earnings. This reform gave further impetus to courses that were perceived as having greater earning potential. The extent of expansion of these disciplines after 1990 at the eight universities where most economic historians worked is illustrated in Table 5.1.

The impact on economic history was dramatic. Compulsory first-year courses in economic history delivered in B.Com degrees underpinned expansion, providing thousands of students every year with flow through to later years. These were now squeezed out and eliminated. In faculty battles over resources in the face of pressure from other disciplines, economics looked after its own interests first rather than those of economic history, but this was driven by strategic rather than epistemological thinking. In less than ten years, all eight departments closed – two had been in existence for more than fifty years. The number of economic history academics employed fell swiftly – by more than half from 1995 to 2005 (Figure 5.1).[4] Typically the survivors were absorbed into economics or business and management – not history – and clustered disproportionately in the upper echelons of university (or national) administration.

Table 5.1 Number of staff in economic history, economics, history and accounting and commerce at eight universities, 1950–2005

Year	*Economic History*	*Economics*	*History*	*Commerce*		
				Accounting	*Other commerce*	*All commerce*
1950	10	31	28	1	10	11
1955	17	37	43	1	8	9
1960	26	55	51	14	8	22
1965	31	122	114	33	4	37
1970	39	151	129	49	10	59
1975	56	174	216	91	19	110
1980	66	217	228	103	8	111
1985	61	215	225	109	15	124
1990	46	202	169	104	56	160
1995	53	273	200	185	252	437
2000	34	287	171	173	547	720
2005	25	249	163	172	650	822

Source: Commonwealth Universities Year Book.

Notes: Universities: ANU, Flinders, La Trobe, Melbourne, Monash, New England, New South Wales, Sydney. Other commerce: Banking & Finance, Business, Business Law & Taxation, Commerce, Hospitality & Tourism, Information Systems/Studies, Management, Marketing.

Others fled the country. Recruitment largely stopped, and where it did occur had to mesh with needs of their new departments. All future appointments would need to be economists first, historians second. Even the economic history department in the RSSS at the ANU – flagship of the discipline since 1946 – succumbed to the new forces.

It is not possible to divorce the output of scholarly research in economic history from its institutional base for very long. Inevitably such a severe decline impacted on the ability of the discipline to maintain its output, let alone increase it. As the dire situation of the discipline began to dawn on its practitioners, towards the end of the 1990s, there was a phase of navel gazing and suggestions for how to stem, if not reverse, the tide (Lloyd 1997; Nicholas 1997; Whitwell 1997; van der Eng and Shanahan 2004; McLean and Shanahan 2007). Fortunately, the momentum of the boom was not immediately extinguished. Economic historians continued their impressive record of attracting research funding, and producing quality output. Between 1995 and 2014 nearly 150 articles on Australian economic history were published in the *Australian Economic History Review*. In contrast to the *Journal of Economic History*, judged increasingly technical and impenetrable to non-economists (Adelman and Levy 2014), there seems no dramatic change in the methodological basis of articles published in the *Australian Economic History Review* since 1970. Table 5.2 represents a somewhat crude attempt to quantify this, distinguishing papers containing descriptive statistics (tables and charts) from those containing analytic statistics (proofs, equations or regressions) and those containing neither. While there are fluctuations, there are no trends. What is evident is Australian economic history's strong empirical base and love of descriptive statistics.

Some familiar themes continued. Australian statistics received a fillip when Diane Hutchinson compiled an online resource (Hutchinson 2010). Further refinements were made to historical GDP (Haig 2001) and recently an important set of colonial/state annualized GDP figures have been produced by Gus Sinclair (available online: Sinclair 2009). International

Table 5.2 Articles in selected issues of the *Australian Economic History Review*, containing descriptive or analytic statistics

Years	*No. articles*	*Containing*					
		Tables or charts		*Equations, regressions, geometric proofs*		*None*	
1969–70	19	11	58%	2	11%	7	37%
1971–72	19	14	74%	6	32%	2	11%
1975–77	25	20	80%	7	28%	3	12%
1980–82	23	16	70%	10	43%	4	17%
1985–87	24	20	83%	7	29%	3	13%
1989–91	23	14	61%	6	26%	7	30%
1997–98	23	13	57%	3	13%	9	39%
2001–02	25	16	64%	1	4%	9	36%
2007–08	23	19	83%	5	22%	4	17%
2011–12	27	21	78%	9	33%	5	19%
1969–2012	**231**	**164**	**71%**	**56**	**24%**	**53**	**23%**
1969–1991	133	95	71%	38	29%	26	20%
1997–2012	98	69	70%	18	18%	27	28%

Source: Australian Economic History Review.

comparisons grew. North America was a focus: Bob Allen compared Sydney, Manchester, Chicago, San Francisco, Toronto and Vancouver (Allen 1994), and more was done on Canada by David Greasley and Les Oxley and the United States by Christopher Lloyd (Greasley and Oxley 1998; Lloyd 1998). Early in the new century, Ian McLean and Alan Taylor compared Australia with California (McLean and Taylor 2003). Eventually interest in the comparisons became part of a wider international concern with 'settler capitalism' (Lloyd et al. 2013). Further enhancement to global comparisons flowed from Maddison's later work in which Butlin's estimates were converted into 1990 international Geary–Khamis dollars to allow for more comprehensive comparison (Maddison 2006: 449–67). Although this put Australia more noticeably on the world stage, there was a possibility that Australian history would be trivialized. Butlin had warned against Australian economic history being a footnote to the British industrial revolution; now it was in danger of being relegated to the status of a 'neo-Britain' in the history of global capitalism (Austin 2014: 312). Still, perhaps better a footnote than no note at all.

Factor productivity continued to be a topic for debate (Broadberry and Irwin 2007; Irwin 2007; Haig 2008; Madsen 2015), as did urbanization (Frost 1998, 2015), and business history remained a lively field of study (Hutchinson 2001, 2015; Fleming et al. 2004; Merrett 2015; Schedvin 2008; Ville 2000, 2015). Work using anthropometrics extended into examining military recruits (Whitwell et al. 1997; Whitwell and Nicholas 2001; Cranfield and Inwood 2015) and the welfare of both Indigenous and White Australians (Nicholas et al. 1998), demonstrating that economic fortunes in Australia were not evenly shared. Economic historians continued to make a major contribution to research and interpretation of the Aboriginal economy, now a large area of scholarly activity (Lourandos 1997; Lloyd 2010, 2012; Hunter 2015; Altman and Biddle 2015), and this has secured recognition internationally.

Thus a decade and a half after the decline set in the corpse still twitches. From our distant purview in Oxford, we hear rumors of revival and something of a renaissance has been discerned (Ville and Withers 2015: 3). The ANU has restored a presence, with Tim Hatton, Martine Mariotti, John Tang and the recent appointment of Zach Ward to a new Centre for Economic History. Select economists are engaging with the past (e.g. Geoff Borland, Andrew Leigh, Richard Pomfret, William Coleman, Pauline Grosjean, Jakob Madsen). Melbourne has appointed Laura Panza, economic historian and development economist. Certainly the publication of the (one-volume) *Cambridge Economic History of Australia*, edited by Simon Ville and Glenn Withers in 2015, was a powerful indication that the discipline was not dead yet. The appearance of Ian McLean's *Why Australia Prospered* in 2013 also pointed to the same conclusion, and the new edition of Dyster and Meredith's *Australia in the Global Economy* (2012) marked more than twenty years in print. Fifty years after its first appearance, Cambridge University Press reprinted Butlin's 1964 book in paperback (Butlin, N.G. 1964, 2014).

Attention can be drawn as well to the continued publication of the *Australian Economic History Review* and its expansion to three issues per year from 1997. Its success is due to several interrelated factors: a deliberate reorientation towards Asian economic history, drawing authors (and editors) from beyond Australia and New Zealand; the digitization of its content (although frustratingly only from 1997); and a greater interest by international scholars in Australian economic history (Morgan and Shanahan 2010). One of the causes of Australian economic history's isolation was the failure to market the *AEHR* internationally. That the journal is now more 'global' is undoubted, but this does, of course, mean that it publishes a smaller proportion of Australian material, illustrated in Figure 5.3.[5]

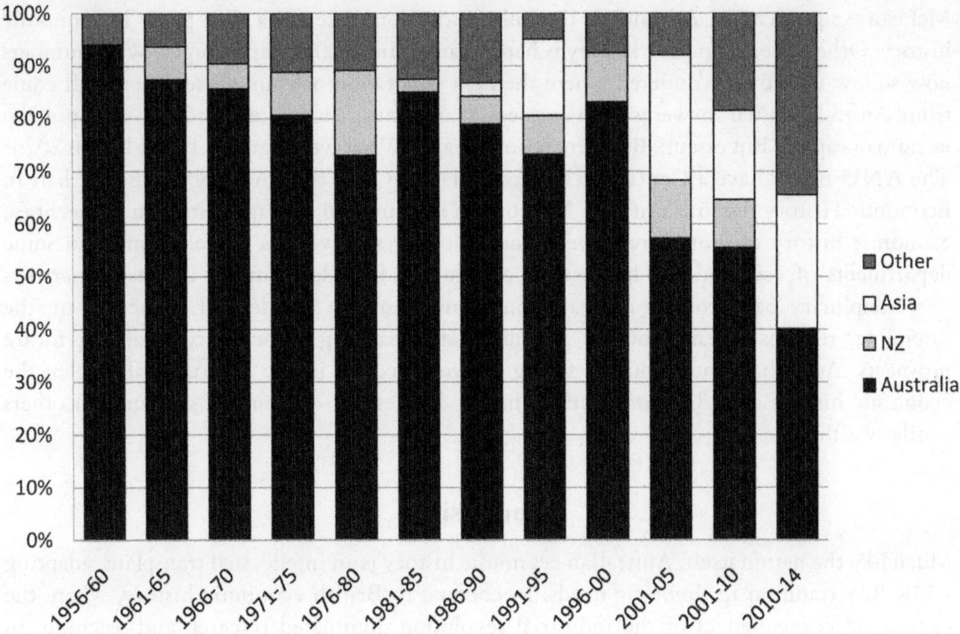

Figure 5.3 Articles published in the *Australian Economic History Review* arranged by region of subject (percent), 1956–2014.

Source: 1956–2010: calculated from database of Morgan and Shanahan 2010; 2010–14: *AEHR*.

Perhaps, also, Australian economic history's relationship with Australian history is undergoing rapprochement. As history's preoccupation with cultural theory has declined it is, possibly, looking with more interest at economic history. In 1967 Boris Schedvin commented, 'In their attempt to stay within reach of economic theory, Australian economic historians find themselves not only ignored by economists but also isolated from historians' (Schedvin 1967: 1). His observation regarding history retained much validity for the rest of the twentieth century, although the multi-volume *Australians: A Historical Library* (Fairfax et al. 1987) included contributions from a number of economic historians (Alan Barnard and Noel Butlin were editorial consultants) and one of its volumes – the first compendium of historical statistics to be published in Australia – was edited by economic historian Wray Vamplew (1987). Moreover, some prominent Australian historians maintained a closer interest in economic history (e.g. Abbott and Nairn 1969; Fletcher 1976; Macintyre 1983, 1986, 2015; Kingston 1988, 1994). The strong interest in urbanization among Australian economic historians also brought closer contact with historians with similar interests, such as Peter Spearritt, Max Kelly and Geoffrey Bolton. Most recently there have been signs of Australian history in general becoming more concerned with economic history: the *Cambridge History of Australia* included two chapters by economic historians, echoing the *Cambridge History of the British Empire* in 1933 (Frost 2013; Ville 2013).

Against the signs of renaissance must be put some less palatable aspects. The huge decline in the number of economic history academics employed full-time by Australian universities is obvious. Economic historians who moved on or retired were not replaced, a rare exception being the University of Adelaide which recently recruited Florian Ploeckl to replace Ian

McLean – significantly, Adelaide is the only institution to retain a core paper in economic history. Otherwise, economic history is hardly taught in Australia any longer. With numbers now so low it is to be wondered where the next generation of young researchers will come from. Australia's usual answer is from overseas, maintaining a long-held tradition of importing its human capital. But essentially, there is no demand. What will Figure 5.1 look like in 2025? The ANU might have a Centre for Economic History, but the Timothy Coghlan Chair in Economic History remains unfilled. Without an institutional base in Australian universities, economic history cannot thrive, even though it may survive as a minor element in some departments of economics. The absence of free-standing departments inevitably narrows the disciplinary backgrounds of practitioners and thus the intellectual influences on the discipline, reduces research output and decimates teaching capacity, constraining future prospects. Australia is not alone in facing a severe decline in the institutional base of the economic history discipline and, unfortunately, it does not offer much guidance to others similarly afflicted.

Conclusion

Much like the nation itself, Australian economic history is an intellectual transplant, adapting a UK/US tradition to domestic needs. In contrast to British economic history, where the causes and consequences of the industrial revolution dominated research and teaching, in Australia there was no single overriding question to be tackled and scholars worked on many areas. Thus the distinctiveness of economic history in Australia lies in its diversity. But if there was one large question, it was how Australia became, soon after 1788, a successful capitalist economy, with an average standard of living equal or superior to that in Britain, without undergoing an industrial revolution. Rostow's stages formula seemed inappropriate to Australia (Rostow 1960). So too did Malthus, Marx, Gerschenkron and the rest of the pantheon of growth theorists. Explaining Australian economic growth led to consideration of exports, the role of the state, the Indigenous economy, foreign capital, urbanization, import-substituting development, staple theory, settler capitalism, resource endowments, mining, business structure, the 'big end of town', to name but a few of the many areas covered. However, the discipline's institutional location within faculties of economics and commerce predisposed them to surrender key areas to other disciplines: unionism and arbitration to labor history, immigration to the historians, population increase to the demographers. Australian economic historians were quick to adopt new research methods where appropriate – GDP, cliometrics, anthropometrics, aided and abetted by sources generated through a powerful tradition of official statistics – and some contributed to the economic histories of other countries, in particular Britain and Ireland. However, even at its zenith there is little evidence that Australian economic history made a unique and indelible mark on the international scene. An Australian pioneered national accounting but it required an American to reinvent it before anyone took notice. The antipodean fringe remains far from integrated, and following its decline is perhaps unlikely ever to be, although nowadays it does add a parameter to many a panel data set.

Economic history in Australia has been a success story. Yet now it is somewhat imperiled. We hope the tale has a happy ending – not just for the discipline and its practitioners, or even the Australian university sector, but for Australian citizens who will (if this decline is not reversed) become increasingly ignorant of the historical genesis of the affluent existence of many, the poverty of some, and the critique offered by a rich and diverse economic history of the critical pathways that the nation traverses.

Notes

1 We wish to thank the editors for their very helpful comments and Christopher Lloyd for his on an earlier draft. All remaining errors are ours.
2 We are indebted to Christopher Lloyd for this information.
3 A sample of a single year at five-year intervals based on information supplied by each Australian university to the Commonwealth Universities Association 1950–2005. This method underestimates the true size of the discipline as it excludes those below lecturer level on fixed-term contracts. It also misses some individuals who moved institutions within the five-year period. Non-department is inflated by individuals outside the discipline who occasionally published in economic history.
4 In fact, the decline in staff was even steeper than this as full-time tutors on fixed-term contracts (the employment status of nearly all tutors) are not included and these members of economic history departments lost their jobs more rapidly than tenured faculty.
5 Our thanks are due to Stephen Morgan and Martin Shanahan for kindly providing us with a copy of their data on which their 2010 article is based.

References

Abbott, G.J. and N.B. Nairn (eds.) (1969) *Economic growth of Australia 1788–1821*, Melbourne: Melbourne University Press.

Adelman, Jeremy and Jonathan Levy (2014) 'The fall and rise of economic history', *Chronicle of Higher Education*, 1 December.

Alford, Katrina (1984) *Production or reproduction? An economic history of women in Australia, 1788–1850*, Melbourne: Oxford University Press.

Alford, Katrina (1986) 'Colonial women's employment as seen by nineteenth century statisticians and twentieth century economic historians', *Labour History*, 51: 1–10.

Alford, Katrina (1987) 'On polemics and patriarchy: a rejoinder', *Labour History*, 52: 93–5.

Allen, Robert C. (1994) 'Real incomes in the English-speaking world, 1879–1913', in George Grantham and Mary MacKinnon (eds.) *Labour market evolution: the economic history of market integration, wage flexibility and the employment relation*, London: Routledge.

Altman, Jon and Nicholas Biddle (2015) 'Refiguring Indigenous economies: a 21st century perspective', in Simon Ville and Glenn Withers (eds.) *The Cambridge economic history of Australia*, Cambridge: Cambridge University Press.

Arndt, H.W. (1949) 'A pioneer of national income estimates', *Economic Journal*, 59 (236): 616–25.

Austin, Gareth (2014) 'Capitalism and the colonies', in Larry Neal and Jeffrey G. Williamson (eds.) *The Cambridge history of capitalism, volume II*, Cambridge: Cambridge University Press.

Australian National University, RSSS, Department of Economic History, *Source Papers in Economic History 1–19* (1984–92).

Australian National University, RSSS, Department of Economic History, *Working Papers in Economic History* (1982–95).

Bambrick, S. (1970) 'Australia's long run terms of trade', *Economic Development and Cultural Change*, 19 (1): 1–5.

Blainey, G. (1954) *The peaks of Lyell*. Melbourne: Melbourne University Press.

Blainey, G. (1963) *The rush that never ended: a history of Australian mining*, Melbourne: Melbourne University Press.

Blainey, G. (1966) *The tyranny of distance: how distance shaped Australia's history*, Melbourne: Sun Books.

Blainey, G. (1970) 'A theory of mineral discovery: Australia in the nineteenth century', *Economic History Review*, 23 (2): 298–313.

Blainey, G. (1975) *Triumph of the nomads: a history of ancient Australia*, Melbourne: Sun Books.

Blainey, G. (2000) *The peaks of Lyell* (6th ed.). Hobart: St. David's Park.

Boehm, E.A. (1971a) *Prosperity and depression in Australia, 1887–1897*, Oxford: Clarendon Press.

Boehm, E.A. (1971b) *Twentieth century economic development in Australia*, Melbourne: Longman Cheshire.

Boot, H.M. (1998) 'Government and the colonial economies', *Australian Economic History Review*, 38 (1): 74–102.

Broadberry, S. and D.A. Irwin (2007) 'Lost exceptionalism? Comparative income and productivity in Australia and the UK 1861–1948', *Economic Record* 83: 262–74.

Buckley, K. and E.L. Wheelwright (1988) *No paradise for workers: capitalism and the common people in Australia 1788–1914*, Melbourne: Oxford University Press.

Buckley, K. and E.L. Wheelwright (1998) *False paradise: Australian capitalism revisited, 1915–1955*, Melbourne: Oxford University Press.

Butlin, N.G. (1955) *Private capital formation in Australia: estimates 1861–1900*, Canberra: Australian National University.

Butlin, N.G. (1958) 'The shape of the Australian economy, 1861–1900', *Economic Record*, 34: 10–29.

Butlin, N.G. (1959a) 'Colonial socialism in Australia, 1860–1900', in Hugh G.J. Aitken (ed.) *The state and economic growth*, New York: Social Science Research Council.

Butlin, N.G. (1959b) 'Some structural features of Australian capital formation, 1861–1939/39', *Economic Record*, 35: 389–415.

Butlin, N.G. (1962) *Australian domestic product, investment and foreign borrowing, 1861–1938/39*, Cambridge: Cambridge University Press.

Butlin, N.G. (1964, reprinted 2014) *Investment in Australian economic development, 1861–1900*, Cambridge: Cambridge University Press.

Butlin, N.G. (1983) *Our original aggression: Aboriginal populations of Southeastern Australia 1788–1850*, Sydney: Allen & Unwin.

Butlin, N.G. (1986) 'Contours of the Australian economy 1788–1860', *Australian Economic History Review*, 26 (2): 96–125.

Butlin, N.G. (1993) *Economics and the Dreamtime: a hypothetical history*, Cambridge: Cambridge University Press.

Butlin, N.G. (1994) *Forming a colonial economy, Australia 1810–1850*, Cambridge: Cambridge University Press.

Butlin, N.G. and H. de Meel (1954) *Public capital formation in Australia: estimates 1860–1900*, Canberra: Australian National University.

Butlin, N.G. and J.A. Dowie (1969) 'Estimates of Australian work force and employment, 1861–1961', *Australian Economic History Review*, 26 (2): 126–47.

Butlin, N.G. and W.A. Sinclair (1986) 'Australian gross domestic product 1788–1860: estimates, sources and methods', *Australian Economic History Review*, 26 (2): 126–47.

Butlin, N.G, A. Barnard and J.J. Pincus (1982) *Government and capitalism: public and private choice in twentieth century Australia*: Sydney: Allen & Unwin.

Butlin, S.J. (1953) *Foundations of the Australian monetary system 1788–1851*, Melbourne: Melbourne University Press.

Butlin, S.J. (1955) *War economy 1939–1942*, Canberra: Australian War Memorial.

Clark, Colin (1963) 'Review of N.G. Butlin, *Australian domestic product, investment and foreign borrowing, 1861–1938/39', Economic History Review*, 16 (1): 198–200.

Clark, Colin and J.G. Crawford (1938) *The national income of Australia*, Sydney: Angus and Robertson.

Coghlan, T.A. (1887–1902) *Wealth and progress of New South Wales*, Sydney: Government Printer.

Coghlan, T.A. (1918) *Labour and industry in Australia*, 4 vols., London: Oxford University Press.

Coleman, William (2015) 'The historiography of Australian economic history', in Simon Ville and Glenn Withers (eds.) *The Cambridge economic history of Australia*, Cambridge: Cambridge University Press.

Cranfield, J. and K. Inwood (2015) 'A tale of two armies: comparative growth in the mirror of WW1', *Australian Economic History Review* 55 (2): 212–33.

Deacon, D. (1985) 'Political arithmetic: the nineteenth-century Australian census and the construction of the dependent woman', *Signs* 11 (1): 27–47.

Denoon, Donald (1983) *Settler capitalism: the dynamics of dependent development in the Southern Hemisphere*, Oxford: Clarendon Press.

Dingle, A.E. (1988) *Aboriginal economy, patterns of experience*, Melbourne: McPhee Gribble.

Dingle, A.E. and David Merrett (eds.) (1985) *Argentina and Australia: essays in comparative economic development*, Clayton: Economic History Society of Australia and New Zealand.

Dyster, Barrie (1979) 'Argentine and Australian development compared', *Past & Present*, 84 (1): 91–110.

Dyster, Barrie and David Meredith (2012) *Australia in the global economy: continuity and change*, 2nd edn., Cambridge: Cambridge University Press.

Endres, A.M. (1987) 'A twentieth-century economic historian on colonial women's employment: comment on Alford', *Labour History*, 52: 88–92.

Ergas, Henry and Jonathan Pincus (2015) 'Infrastructure and colonial socialism', in Simon Ville and Glenn Withers (eds.) *The Cambridge economic history of Australia*, Cambridge: Cambridge University Press.

Fairfax, Syme and Weldon Associates (1987) *Australians: a historical library*, Sydney: Fairfax, Syme and Weldon.

Fisher, Allan G.B. (1935) *The clash of progress and society*, London: Macmillan.

Fisher, Allan G.B. (1939) 'Production, primary, secondary, and tertiary', *Economic Record*, 15 (1): 24–38.

Fitzpatrick, Brian (1939) *British imperialism and Australia, 1783–1833: an economic history of Australasia*, London: George Allen and Unwin.

Fitzpatrick, Brian (1941) *The British Empire in Australia: an economic history 1834–1939*, Melbourne: Melbourne University Press.

Fleming, Grant, David Merrett and Simon Ville (2004) *The big end of town: big business and corporate leadership in twentieth-century Australia*, Melbourne: Cambridge University Press.

Fletcher, Brian H. (1976) *Landed enterprise and penal society: a history of farming and grazing in New South Wales before 1821*, Sydney: Sydney University Press.

Fogel, Robert William and Stanley L. Engerman (1974) *Time on the cross: the economics of American Negro slavery*, New York: W.W. Norton.

Forster, Colin (1953) 'Australian manufacturing and the war of 1914–1918', *Economic Record*, 29: 211–30.

Forster, Colin (1964) *Industrial development in Australia, 1920–1930*, Canberra: Australian National University.

Forster, Colin (ed.) (1970) *Australian economic development in the twentieth century*, Sydney: Allen & Unwin.

Frost, L. (1991) *The new urban frontier: urbanisation and city-building in Australasia and the American West before 1910*, Sydney: UNSW Press.

Frost, L. (1998) 'The contribution of the urban sector to Australian economic development before 1914', *Australian Economic History Review*, 38 (1): 42–73.

Frost, L. (2013) 'The economy', in Alison Bashford and Stuart Macintyre (eds.) *The Cambridge history of Australia*, volume 1, Melbourne: Cambridge University Press.

Frost, L. (2015) 'Urbanisation', in Simon Ville and Glenn Withers (eds.) *The Cambridge economic history of Australia*, Cambridge: Cambridge University Press.

Greasley, David and Les Oxley (1998) 'A tale of two dominions: comparing the macroeconomic records of Australia and Canada since 1870', *Economic History Review*, 51 (2): 294–318.

Groenewegen, Peter and Bruce McFarlane (1990) *A history of Australian economic thought*, London: Routledge.

Haig, B. (1967) '1938/39 national income estimates', *Australian Economic History Review*, 7 (2): 172–86.

Haig, B. (1971) 'A comment on the Butlin–Dowie employment and workforce estimates', *Australian Economic History Review*, 11 (1): 59–62.

Haig, B. (1989) 'International comparisons of Australian GDP in the 19th century', *Review of Income and Wealth*, 35 (2): 847–62.

Haig, B. (2001) 'New estimates of Australian GDP: 1861–1948/49', *Australian Economic History Review*, 41 (1): 1–34.

Haig, B. (2006) 'Sir Timothy Coghlan and the development of national accounts', *History of Political Economy*, 38 (2): 339–75.

Haig, B. (2008) 'Real product and productivity of industries since the nineteenth century: a comment on "Lost Exceptionalism" by Broadberry and Irwin', *Economic Record*, 84: 511–14.

Haig-Muir, M. (1995) 'The economy at war', in Joan Beaumont (ed.) *Australia's war 1914–18*, Sydney: Allen & Unwin.

Haig-Muir, M. (1996) 'The economy at war', in Joan Beaumont (ed.) *Australia's war 1939–45*, Sydney: Allen & Unwin.

Hancock, W.K. (1930) *Australia*, London: Ernest Benn.

Hartwell, R.M. (1954) *The economic development of Van Diemen's Land 1820–1850*, Melbourne: Melbourne University Press.

Hatton, Tim and Glenn Withers (2015) 'The labour market', in Simon Ville and Glenn Withers (eds.) *The Cambridge economic history of Australia*, Cambridge: Cambridge University Press.

Heaton, Herbert (1921) *Modern economic history, with special reference to Australia*, Adelaide: Workers' Education Association.

Henning, G.R. (1986) 'R.S. Neale, 1927–1985', *Australian Economic History Review*, 26 (2): 91–5.
Hunter, B. (2015) 'The Aboriginal legacy', in Simon Ville and Glenn Withers (eds.) *The Cambridge economic history of Australia*, Cambridge: Cambridge University Press.
Hutchinson, D. (2001) 'Australian manufacturing business: entrepreneurship of missed opportunities', *Australian Economic History Review*, 41 (2): 103–35.
Hutchinson, D. (2010) *Measuring worth*, http://www.measuringworth.com
Hutchinson, D. (2015) 'Manufacturing', in Simon Ville and Glenn Withers (eds.) *The Cambridge economic history of Australia*, Cambridge: Cambridge University Press.
Irwin, D.A. (2007) 'The third Noel Butlin lecture: exceptionalism revisited', *Australian Economic History Review*, 47 (3): 217–37.
Jackson, R.V. (1977) *Australian economic development in the nineteenth century*, Canberra: Australian National University.
Jackson, R.V. (1985) 'Short-run interaction of public and private sectors in Australia, 1861–1890', *Australian Economic History Review*, 25 (1): 59–75.
Jackson, R.V. (1994) 'Inequality of incomes and lifespans in England since 1688', *Economic History Review*, 47 (3): 508–24.
Johnson, Paul and S. Nicholas (1995) 'Male and female living standards in England and Wales, 1812–1857: evidence from criminal height records', *Economic History Review*, 48 (3): 470–81.
Jones, F.L. (1987) 'Occupational statistics revisited: the female labour force in early British and Australian censuses', *Australian Economic History Review*, 27 (2): 56–77.
Kingston, Beverley (1988) *Oxford history of Australia, vol. 3: 1860–1900: glad, confident morning*, Melbourne: Oxford University Press.
Kingston, Beverly (1994) *Basket, bag and trolley: a history of shopping in Australia*, Melbourne: Oxford University Press.
Kuznets, Simon (1956) 'Quantitative aspects of the economic growth of nations: I. Levels of variability and rates of growth', *Economic Development and Cultural Change*, 5 (1): 1–94.
Kuznets, Simon (1966) *Modern economic growth: rate, structure and spread*, New Haven, CT: Yale University Press.
Lloyd, Christopher (1997) 'Can economic history be the core of social science? Why the discipline must open and integrate to ensure the survival of long-run economic analysis', *Australian Economic History Review*, 37 (3): 256–66.
Lloyd, Christopher (1998) 'Australia and American settler capitalism: the importance of a comparison and its curious neglect', *Australian Economic History Review*, 38 (3): 280–306.
Lloyd, Christopher (2010) 'The emergence of Australian settler capitalism in the nineteenth century and the disintegration/integration of Aboriginal societies: hybridization and local evolution within the world market', in I. Keen (ed.) *Indigenous participation in Australian economies: historical and anthropological perspectives*, Canberra: ANU Press.
Lloyd, Christopher (2012) 'Settler economies and Indigenous encounters: the dialectics of conquest, hybridization and production regimes', in N. Fijn, I. Keen, C. Lloyd and M. Pickering (eds.) *Indigenous participation in Indigenous economies II: historical engagements and current enterprises*, Canberra: ANU Press.
Lloyd, Christopher (2015) 'Analytical frameworks of Australia's economic history', in Simon Ville and Glenn Withers (eds.) *The Cambridge economic history of Australia*, Cambridge: Cambridge University Press.
Lloyd, Christopher, J. Metzer and R. Sutch (eds.) (2013) *Settler economics in world history*, Leiden: Brill.
Lourandos, H. (1997) *Continent of hunter gatherers: new perspectives in Australian prehistory*, Cambridge: Cambridge University Press.
Lydall, H.F. (1963) 'N.G. Butlin's anatomy of Australian economic growth: a review article', *Business Archives and History*, 3 (2): 204–10.
Macintyre, S. (1983) 'Labour, capital and Arbitration, 1890–1979', in B.W. Head (ed.) *State and economy in Australia*, Melbourne: Oxford University Press.
Macintyre, S. (1986) *The Oxford history of Australia, vol. 4, 1901–1942, The succeeding age*, Melbourne: Oxford University Press.
Macintyre, S. (2015) *Australia's boldest experiment: war and reconstruction in the 1940s*, Sydney: UNSW Press.
Maddison, Angus (1982) *Phases of capitalist development*, Oxford: Oxford University Press.
Maddison, Angus (2004) 'Quantifying and interpreting world development: macromeasurement before and after Colin Clark', *Australian Economic History Review*, 44 (1): 1–34.

Maddison, Angus (2006) *The world economy*, Paris: OECD.

Madsen, Jakob B. (2015) 'Australian economic growth and its drivers since European settlement', in Simon Ville and Glenn Withers (eds.) *The Cambridge economic history of Australia*, Cambridge: Cambridge University Press.

McCarty, J.W. (1964) 'The staple approach in Australian economic history', *Business Archives and History*, 4 (1): 1–22.

McCarty, J.W. (1970) 'Australian capital cities in the nineteenth century', *Australian Economic History Review*, 10 (2): 107–68.

McCarty, J.W. (1973) 'Australia as a region of recent settlement in the nineteenth century', *Australian Economic History Review*, 13 (2): 148–67.

McCarty, J.W. and C.B. Schedvin (eds.) (1978) *Australian capital cities: historical essays*, Sydney: Sydney University Press.

McLean, I.W. (2013) *Why Australia prospered. The shifting sources of economic growth*, Princeton, NJ: Princeton University Press.

McLean, I.W. and Martin P. Shanahan (2007) 'Australasian economic history: research challenges and big questions', *Australian Economic History*, 47 (3): 300–16.

McLean, I.W. and Alan Taylor (2003) 'Australian growth: a Californian perspective', in Dani Rodrik (ed.) *In search of prosperity: analytic narratives on economic growth*, Princeton, NJ: Princeton University Press.

McMichael, P. (1984) *Settlers and the agrarian question: capitalism in colonial Australia*, Cambridge: Cambridge University Press.

Merrett, David (1985) *ANZ Bank: an official history*, Sydney: Allen and Unwin.

Merrett, David (2015) 'Big business and foreign firms', in Simon Ville and Glenn Withers (eds.) *The Cambridge economic history of Australia*, Cambridge: Cambridge University Press.

Millmow, Alex and Jacqueline Tuck (2013) 'The audit we had to have: *The Economic Record*, 1960–2009', *Economic Record*, 89 (284): 112–28.

Morgan, Stephen and Martin Shanahan (2010) 'The supply of economic history in Australasia: the *Australian Economic History Review* at 50', *Australian Economic History Review*, 50 (3): 217–39.

Mulhall, M.G. (1884) *The dictionary of statistics*, London: George Routledge & Sons.

Nicholas, S. (1997) 'The future of economic history in Australia', *Australian Economic History Review*, 37 (3): 267–74.

Nicholas, S. (ed.) (1988) *Convict workers: reinterpreting Australia's past*, Cambridge: Cambridge University Press.

Nicholas, S. and D. Oxley (1993) 'The living standards of women during the industrial revolution, 1795–1820', *Economic History Review*, 46 (4): 723–49.

Nicholas, S. and Peter R. Shergold (1987) 'Human capital and the pre-famine Irish emigration to England', *Explorations in Economic History*, 24: 158–77.

Nicholas, S. and R.H. Steckel (1991) 'Heights and living standards of English workers during the early years of industrialisation, 1770–1815', *Journal of Economic History*, 51 (4): 937–57.

Nicholas, S., R. Gregory and S. Kimberley (1998) 'The welfare of Indigenous and White Australians 1890–1955', in J. Komlos and J. Baten (eds.) *The biological standard of living in comparative perspective*, Stuttgart: Franz Steiner Verlag.

Oxley, D. (1996) *Convict maids: the forced migration of women to Australia*, Cambridge: Cambridge University Press.

Pinkstone, B. (1992) *Global connections: a history of exports and the Australian economy*, Canberra: Australian Government Publishing Service.

Pope, David and Glenn Withers (1994) 'Wage effects of immigration in late-nineteenth century Australia', in Tim Hatton and Jeffrey G. Williamson (eds.) *Migration and the international labor market: 1850–1939*, New York: Routledge.

Reynolds, H. (1981) *The other side of the frontier: an interpretation of the Aboriginal response to the invasion and settlement of Australia*, Townsville: James Cook University.

Rostow, W.W. (1960) *The stages of economic growth: a non-communist manifesto*, Cambridge: Cambridge University Press.

Rubinstein, W.D. (1979) 'The distribution of personal wealth in Victoria 1860–1974', *Australian Economic History Review*, 19 (1): 26–41.

Rubinstein, W.D. (1980) 'The top wealth holders of New South Wales 1817–1939', *Australian Economic History Review*, 20 (2): 136–52.

Ryan, E. and A. Conlon (1975) *Gentle invaders: Australian women at work 1788–1974*, Melbourne: Nelson.

Salsbury, S. and K. Sweeney (1988) *The bull, the bear and the kangaroo: the history of the Sydney stock exchange*, Sydney: Allen and Unwin.

Schedvin, C.B. (1967) 'Economic history in Australian universities 1961–1966', *Australian Economic History Review*, 7 (1): 1–18.

Schedvin, C.B. (1970) *Australia and the Great Depression: a study of economic development and policy in the 1920s and 1930s*, Sydney: Sydney University Press.

Schedvin, C.B. (1979) 'Midas and the merino: a perspective on Australian economic historiography', *Economic History Review*, 32 (4): 542–56.

Schedvin, C.B. (1987) *Shaping science and industry: a history of Australia's Council for Scientific and Industrial Research, 1926–1949*, Sydney: Allen and Unwin.

Schedvin, C.B. (1990) 'Staples and regions of Pax Britannica', *Economic History Review*, 43 (4): 533–59.

Schedvin, C.B. (1992) *In reserve: central banking in Australia, 1945–1975*, Sydney: Allen and Unwin.

Schedvin, C.B. (2008) *Emissaries of trade: a history of the Australian Trade Commissioner Service*, Barton, ACT, Department of Foreign Affairs and Trade.

Scott, Ernest (ed.) (1933) *The Cambridge history of the British Empire, vol. VII, Part 1, Australia*, Cambridge: Cambridge University Press.

Shann, E.O.G. (1930) *An economic history of Australia*, Cambridge: Cambridge University Press.

Sinclair, W.A. (1976) *The process of economic development in Australia*, Melbourne: Cheshire.

Sinclair, W.A. (2009) *Annual estimates of gross domestic product: Australian colonies/states 1861–1976/7*, Monash University Research Repository, http://arrow.monash.edu.auy/hdl/1959.1/88855

Snooks, G.D. (1972) 'Regional estimates of gross domestic product and capital formation: Western Australia, 1923/24–1938/39', *Economic Record*, 48: 536–53.

Snooks, G.D. (1979) 'The arithmetic of regional growth: Western Australia, 1912/13 to 1957/58', *Australian Economic History Review*, 19 (1): 63–74.

Snooks, G.D. (1991) '"In my beginning is my end": the life and work of George Noel Butlin, 1921–1991', *Australian Economic History Review*, 31 (2): 3–27.

Snooks, G.D. (1993a) *Economics without time: a science blind to the forces of historical change*, Basingstoke: Macmillan.

Snooks, G.D. (1993b) *Historical analysis in economics*, London: Routledge.

Snooks, G.D. (1994) *Portrait of the family within the total economy: a study in long-run dynamics, Australia 1788–1990*, Cambridge: Cambridge University Press.

Snooks, G.D. and J. McDonald (1986) *Domesday economy: a new approach to Anglo-Norman history*, Oxford: Clarendon Press.

Statham, P. (ed.) (1989) *The origin of Australian capital cities*, Cambridge: Cambridge University Press.

Studenski, P. (1958) *The income of nations: theory, measurement and analysis*, New York: New York University Press.

Tweedie, S. (1994) *Trading partners: Australia and Asia 1790–1993*, Sydney: University of New South Wales Press.

United States, Bureau of the Census (1960) *Historical statistics of the United States: colonial times to 1957*, Washington, DC: US Department of Commerce.

Vamplew, W. (ed.) (1987) *Australians. Historical statistics*, Sydney: Fairfax, Syme and Weldon.

van der Eng, Pierre and Martin P. Shanahan (2004) 'The current and future role of AEHR: editorial reflections', *Australian Economic History Review*, 44 (2): 113–17.

Ville, S. (2000) *The rural entrepreneurs: a history of the stock and station agent industry in Australia and New Zealand*, Melbourne: Cambridge University Press.

Ville, S. (2013) 'The economy', in Alison Bashford and Stuart Macintyre (eds.) *The Cambridge history of Australia*, volume 2, Melbourne: Cambridge University Press.

Ville, S. (2015) 'Colonial enterprise', in Simon Ville and Glenn Withers (eds.) *The Cambridge economic history of Australia*, Cambridge: Cambridge University Press.

Ville, S. and G. Withers (eds.) (2015) *The Cambridge economic history of Australia*, Cambridge: Cambridge University Press.

Watson, D. (1979) *Brian Fitzpatrick, a radical life*, Sydney: Hale & Iremonger.

Wells, A. (1989) *Constructing capitalism: an economic history of Eastern Australia*, Sydney: Allen & Unwin.

Wheelwright, E.L. (1957) *Ownership and control of Australian companies: a study of 102 of the largest public companies incorporated in Australia*, Sydney: Law Book Co.

Wheelwright, E.L. and Ken Buckley (eds.) (1975–83) *Essays in the political economy of Australian capitalism*, vols. 1–5, Sydney: Australia and New Zealand Book Company.

Whitwell, G. (1986) *The Treasury line*, Sydney: Allen & Unwin.

Whitwell, G. (1989) *Making the market: the rise of the consumer society*, Melbourne: McPhee Gribble.

Whitwell, G. (1997) 'Future directions for the *Australian Economic History Review*', *Australian Economic History Review*, 37 (3): 275–81.

Whitwell, G. and S. Nicholas (2001) 'Weight and welfare of Australians, 1890–1940', *Australian Economic History Review*, 41 (2): 159–75.

Whitwell, G. and Diane Sydenham (1991) *A shared harvest: the Australian wheat industry 1939–1989*, Melbourne: Macmillan.

Whitwell, G., C. de Souza and S. Nicholas (1997) 'Height, health and economic growth in Australia, 1860–1940', in R.H. Steckel and R. Floud (eds.) *Health and welfare during industrialization*, Chicago, IL: University of Chicago Press.

Williams, J. (1994) *Ordered to the island: Irish convicts and Van Diemen's Land*, Sydney: Crossing Press.

PART II

West European roots and responses

6
THE LEGACY OF GERMAN ECONOMIC HISTORY
Archetypes and global diffusion

Jan-Otmar Hesse

The work of the German Historical School is usually considered the most prominent German contribution to the global literature in economic history. However, its main writings were originally intended as contributions to economics and social science rather than to economic history. Critique and adaptation of the School's teachings came from the academic disciplines nursing economic history in its early stages, that is, economics and history. The origins of German economic history cannot therefore be reduced to the approaches, albeit highly influential, of Gustav von Schmoller, Max Weber and Werner Sombart.

This said, the Historical School long remained influential in Germany, representing an academic standard and a constant benchmark. If we apply the notion of 'national academic cultures' that the French sociologist Marion Fourcade (2009) developed with respect to economics, references to the School can certainly be identified as an important aspect of the academic culture in German-speaking lands.[1] The notion does not imply that a particular style of reasoning or methodology will emerge from national characteristics, as might appear from stereotypes in past literature. By contrast, it acknowledges that the socio-economic context of intellectual enquiry, as well as the particular institutional setting and its contingent evolution, have a relevant influence on scholarly outcomes.

German historicism in economics developed a set of theories and concepts to deal with the transformations experienced by German economies and societies predominantly before the industrial revolution. Concepts such as 'structure' or 'economic order' as well as references to legal constitutions and social norms played a greater role in this approach than individual behaviour and decision making, which became a preferred object of consideration in the Anglo-Saxon countries. References to space, territory and 'region', to state intervention and economic policy, to the cooperation of powerful economic actors and not least to shared values or a common 'spirit' appear to be typical of this way of thinking. Such emphases can be found in German economic history far beyond the 'Historical School' paradigm and – as is argued here – to a greater extent than in other countries or 'academic cultures'. As a further element of distinction, it should be emphasised that, in contrast to Great Britain and France, Germany and Austria did not become colonial powers. Only for a very short period before the First World War did Germany succeed in exporting capital and being an essential part of global economic relations. This explains why German-speaking economic history remained largely focused, if not centred, on the nation or the *Volk*, as it was once termed.

Eventually, political history also drove the discipline's evolution. The Nazi era led to the expulsion of some open-minded and innovative scholars in the field from both Germany and Austria, while many of the remaining economic historians subscribed to the regime's racist convictions. After the division of Germany, a highly ideologically oriented school of thought evolved in East Germany with little connection to the major research questions in the Western world. All these factors explain some unquestionable peculiarities of German approaches. Certainly, this chapter is not meant to revive the *Sonderweg* hypothesis as an explanation of German economic history, which was justifiably criticised at the time that it was first suggested (Grebing 1986). The differences did not translate into more or less advanced research compared to other countries, nor did they ultimately lead to the discipline's global isolation. In contrast, as will be shown, there have been many examples of knowledge transfer in the course of the twentieth century as well as in more recent years.

The global impact of the German Historical School

The expression 'Historical School' is a common but highly controversial label for a great number of economists writing in Germany from the mid-nineteenth century until the First World War, when the 'School', in the sense of a compact paradigm organised around a common epistemic structure, dissolved (Köster 2011). The School addressed the conviction of many German social scientists that the economy cannot be explained by fundamental economic laws, valid for all times, but would change historically in character and structure. Its development culminated in the famous 1880s *Methodenstreit* between the German historicists and the Austrian marginalists. The 'battle' consisted of two debates between Gustav von Schmoller at the helm of the Germans and Carl Menger representing the Austrians, followed by a more general controversy on questions of value judgements at the meeting of the Verein für Socialpolitik in 1909, with Max Weber as the most prominent participant. Later on, the *Methodenstreit* was evoked to identify the bifurcation between the German and the Anglo-American neoclassical path to modern economics (Hodgson 2001). Whereas the historicists promoted research in economic history in order to detect and interpret context-specific regularities in the past, the Anglo-American tradition maintained the existence of general economic laws and sometimes acknowledged the usefulness of history for testing purposes.

It is common knowledge that this ideal-typical description of a geographical bifurcation does not entirely hold because historical schools also existed in the Anglo-American world whilst some neoclassical ideas actually originated in Germany (Tribe 2007). But instead of elaborating on the rather complex path and subtle differences in the evolution of economic thought, it has to be emphasised that the 'Historical School' and the contributions by Max Weber and Werner Sombart at that time had themselves not yet been conceptualised as economic history.

Earlier historicists contributed a number of stage theories of economic development. Karl Bücher (1893) saw economic development as a trajectory from the household economy of ancient times to the city-state economies of medieval Europe and the national economies of the nineteenth century. The framework was modified by Bernhard Harms (1914), the founder of the Kiel Institute of Economics, as an evolution from city-state economies to national economies and thence to the emerging global economy. The theory of economic stages, in which each one was described as a completely autonomous economic order, organised around specific economic principles, was in some respects influenced by Karl Marx's theory of the modes of production. However, it was an ostentatious non-Marxian approach since class struggle was not assumed as the driving force behind economic development, which was later identified in what Max Weber called the 'spirit of capitalism' (Weber 1904/5). Some stage theorists were more strongly influenced by German romanticism and perceived the evolution of races as the essential driving force behind history (Köster 2011). To some extent, Joseph A. Schumpeter's influential *Theory of Economic Development* (1912) can be considered a further elaboration of nineteenth-century evolutionary approaches, though in a direction that is neither fully German nor Austrian.

Although primarily intended as a contribution to economic and social theory, these ideas unquestionably encouraged a large amount of historical research. They triggered an 'age of monographs', as Harald Winkel once put it (1977), in economics as well as in history. Within economic history properly conceived, the *Vierteljahrschrift für Sozial- und Wirtschaftsgeschichte* ('Social and Economic History Quarterly'), arguably the first global journal in the field, was launched in 1903. However, most of the contributions by social scientists such as Weber and Sombart were debated and disputed by historians, with Weber's *The Protestant Ethic and the Spirit of Capitalism* (1904/5) being perhaps the preferred target of criticism. Weber's *Roman Agricultural History* (1909) was also criticised by some contemporary classicists for downplaying the efficiency and modernity of the ancient economy, though in the post-war period Weber's views, espoused by the American Moses Finley, would prevail among ancient historians. Among early critics of Schmoller's approach we should mention distinguished historian Georg von Below (Plumpe 2009: 242–8). Werner Sombart's *Der Moderne Kapitalismus* (1902–27) was questioned by medievalists and early modernists because of its supposedly selective use of archival sources in support of his idea of autonomous 'household economies' in pre-modern times (Hintze 1929). In the 1920s, a growing number of historians distanced themselves from what was now labelled 'the law school', especially in Viennese circles (Dopsch 1927). It was in this context of mixed feelings towards the German economists that economic history established itself as an autonomous discipline in the German-speaking countries. This can be traced back to the institution of the first university chairs in Cologne in 1919 (occupied by Bruno Kuske), in Munich (from 1921 occupied by the Fugger expert Jakob Strieder) and in Vienna, where Alfons Dopsch was appointed in 1922 (Henning 1988). But as early as 1910 Georg Brodnitz, who would later join the University of Halle, had written a manifesto for the new discipline.

Meanwhile, the ideas of the German Historical School continued to spread, at home as well as abroad, until the Second World War, being further developed and transformed by Arthur Spiethoff and others (see Häuser 1994). The paradigm perhaps exerted its deepest impact in the USA, where scholarly exchange with Germany had left its mark. The Old Institutionalism associated with Thorstein Veblen, John R. Commons and Wesley C. Mitchell had strong German roots (Reuter 1994; Rutherford 2007). In the interwar period, even the liberal economists in Chicago maintained their connections with the Historical School, as indicated for instance by the translation of Weber's *General Economic History* (1927) by Frank H. Knight (Füssel 2004). The first president of the Economic History Association Edwin F. Gay had a doctorate from the University of Berlin, where he had studied at the turn of the century under Schmoller. At Harvard he trained a lively group of influential disciples (De Rouvray 2004).

Economic history expelled and enclosed

In the interwar years, Germany showed a growing tendency to intellectual self-sufficiency and nationalism, and there was a progressive deterioration in German–American academic relations, accelerated by the Nazi takeover of power (Rausch 2007). The institutional development of the German economy oriented economic disciplines towards the study of institutions, legal constitutions and business collusion (Backhaus 1994). On the other hand, thanks also to the post-*Anschluss* diaspora, Austrian thought progressively extended its global reach in a number of fields in the arts and sciences. With regard to the global diffusion of, and international influences on, German-speaking economic history, three questions need to be addressed here. First, how did the Reich's expulsion of scholars influence the evolution of economic history abroad? Second, how did the ideological preoccupation of the authorities shape the evolution of the discipline in Germany and Austria? Finally, how, and to what degree, did this influence extend into the post-war period?

German-speaking science had traditionally been a magnet for Eastern European scholars. Russian economists such as Wassily Leontief and Jakob Marschak had migrated to Berlin and many more came to Vienna from the territories of the former Austro-Hungarian Empire. Karl Polanyi had also settled in Vienna, though he turned to academic life only after moving to England (thence to the USA) in the mid-1930s (Polanyi 1977). The Russian Alexander Gerschenkron worked at the Austrian Institute for Research on Business Cycles with Friedrich A. Hayek and Oskar Morgenstern, and eventually fled to the USA. Interestingly, there was apparently no relationship between the economists of the Austrian School's second generation and the lively centre of economic history that Alfons Dopsch had created at the University of Vienna (Hoffmann 1979). However, Dopsch's approach influenced post-war US economic history via Frederic C. Lane, who studied with him in the 1920s. Lane, who became a professor at Princeton University in the 1930s, acted as Rockefeller officer for Europe in the early 1950s. In an internal report he suggested that the Foundation should engage in 'reviewing what has happened during the war to the field of economic history in the countries of Western Europe, from which *we* have been cut off' (Lane 1944, cit. after Gemelli 2003, 122, emphasis mine).

Due to the 'Law for the restoration of the professional civil service', 1400 scholars in German social sciences were expelled for racial and political reasons after 1933 (Hagemann and Krohn 1999). Among expelled economic historians was the 41-year-old Fritz Redlich, who later joined the Centre for Entrepreneurial Research at Harvard University, where he collaborated with the young David Landes and Alfred D. Chandler. Though he had turned to a more empiricist approach, and published several intriguing contributions on American business history, Redlich's debt to the Historical School was durable and led him fiercely to oppose the 'new economic history' in the mid-1960s (Redlich 1965). Leo Liepmann might be taken as another example of the international impact of German economic history, though he never became influential in the field itself. After having taken his PhD from Freiburg University on questions of monetary history, Liepmann received a Rockefeller Fellowship dedicated to 'economic history' during the 1920s and spent two years in England. During the Nazi occupation he went back to England, where he worked with William Beveridge. Albert O. Hirschman had just started studying law and history at the University of Berlin in 1933, when anti-Jewish discrimination led him to an intellectual odyssey throughout several European countries (he would receive his doctorate from the University of Trieste in 1938). He then fled to the Americas where he worked in public administration before joining academia (Adelman 2013). His influence was certainly acknowledged much more by French and Italian political economists than by the Germans but he also served as an important interpreter between 'national cultures'.

In the 1930s German social sciences progressively reflected the ideological agenda of the Nazi party now driving academic politics. Research in economic history emerged within economic geography and anthropology, in particular in the so-called 'research on tribes'

(*Volkstumsforschung*) and, last but not least, the 'research on Eastern Europe' (*Ostforschung*). Economic historians remained scattered among a variety of disciplinary fields that were now increasingly subjected to the constraints of this agenda. The not-already-established scholars, in particular, had to attach themselves more firmly to research programmes that were supported by the government. Georg Brodnitz's beginnings at the University of Halle were suddenly interrupted when he was imprisoned and later died under Gestapo torture.

It is not easy to assess the value of this work carried out under the fabric of ideological language, which sometimes, but not always, was just rhetorical camouflage. However it continued to influence German economic history even after the Second World War. The contribution by a group of young scholars who met under the supervision of Hans Rothfels at the University of Königsberg (now Kaliningrad, Russia) proved especially important. Their research played against the background of the *Volkstumsforschung*, which also served as an academic justification for German military expansion in Eastern Europe. This group of medievalists was interested in understanding the 'racial' and economic characteristics of the local communities that had prevented Asian tribes from moving westwards. Their research also provided deep insights into the economic behaviour and productivity of small agricultural units in Eastern Germany from the twelfth to the seventeenth centuries, as well as into the legal framework. These were topics not dissimilar from those being independently investigated by French rural history, though the ideological underpinnings were different. What we today might call the 'institutional order' of economies and societies was named 'landscape' by Hermann Aubin (a professor at the University of Breslau) and 'agricultural constitution' by Werner Conze (then in Königsberg). Otto Brunner, one of the most prominent disciples of Dopsch, was also in touch with this group. His work on the tribal characteristics that he considered the backbone of institutional stability in this age became most influential in the long run (Burleigh 1988; Etzemüller 2001).

The post-war influence of the Königsberg group came via Conze and Erich Maschke, who in the 1950s were appointed professors of economic and social history at the University of Heidelberg. In 1957 the Arbeitskreis Moderne Sozialgeschichte ('modern social history workshop') was established by Conze, Brunner and Theodor Schieder as well as a younger generation of West German historians including Reinhard Koselleck and Wolfram Fischer. Despite his Nazi background, in 1946 Hermann Aubin also got a chair in economic history at the University of Hamburg (Mühle 2008; Beyrau 2012). Together with the Munich social historian Wolfgang Zorn he worked on a major synthesis of German economic and social history which was published after his death (Aubin and Zorn 1971–76). Brunner was dismissed by the University of Vienna at the end of the war, aged 47, for his collaboration with the Nazis during the occupation but was subsequently appointed at the University of Hamburg, where he succeeded Aubin in 1954. Though not connected to the other individuals, Hermann Kellenbenz has also to be mentioned in this context. He emerged from the Third Reich to become one of the most influential economic historians of post-war Germany as professor in Nuremberg and Cologne (Kellenbenz 1958). Wilhelm Abel started as an economist in Frankfurt and Königsberg during the Nazi period and established a leading group of agricultural historians at the University of Göttingen in the 1950s and 1960s (Abel 1966).

The Königsberg group undertook an astonishing modification of wording in the post-war years. The notions of 'landscape' and 'folklore' (*Volkstum*) were turned into 'structure'. When we speak of the 'history of structures' in Germany, we are generally aware of the semantic history of this expression. But the reasons for the lasting influence of this approach have to do with its partial confluence with the kind of structuralism advocated by the French *Annales* in the 1950s, with Fernand Braudel himself personifying the connection. Braudel had been captured by the German army at the beginning of the war and spent a long time as a prisoner in a military camp in Mainz. There he had the chance to read the works of the German Historical School that seem to have been a significant source of inspiration for his ground-breaking *Mediterranean* (Chun 2000).

The long-lasting impact of research carried out in the Nazi period can also be observed on the economic side of the profession. The main player was certainly Walther G. Hoffmann, who started his academic career as researcher at the Kiel Institute for the World Economy in the 1930s. Equipped with a Rockefeller Fellowship, in 1938 Hoffmann spent some time in England collecting material for his *Habilitation* thesis on British economic growth during the industrial revolution (published in 1940).[2] His time series received global attention and was still referred to as a benchmark in the 1980s, when Nicholas Crafts and Knick Harley worked on their revised estimates (e.g. Harley 1982). In the 1950s Hoffmann, by then a professor at the University of Münster, was one of the most influential economists in the country. In his subsequent work on Germany, he provided a complete reconstruction of national accounts since 1850 (Hoffmann 1965). Although the work has been criticised for mistakes and inappropriate assumptions it is still nonetheless a useful and often-used reference work. In Wolfram Fischer's (1984) view, Hoffmann represented the connection between the Historical School and modern economic theory.

Strands of post-war research

The division of Germany after the Second World War resulted in a bifurcation of economic history as well. In East Germany, the great expansion experienced by the discipline is inseparably connected to the name of Jürgen Kuczynski. Kuczynski was a member of the Communist Party who had left Germany in the 1930s and joined the American Forces, becoming a member of the Strategic Bombing Survey, where he met Paul Sweezy, John K. Galbraith and Barrington Moore (Parker 2005). Already collaborating with the KGB, he returned to Germany by the end of the war and took up a chair at the former Friedrich-Wilhelms-Universität in East Berlin, reopened as Humboldt University, where he was the key figure in the transformation of the faculty of economics into a strict Marxist–Leninist institution (Hesse and Rischbieter 2010). According to the Marxian theory of class struggle, economic history was perceived as an essential part of economics and Kuczynski was able to assemble a respectable group of economic historians within the faculty of economics. However, in the late 1950s he came under attack from the Party and had to give up his university position, but he managed to re-establish himself and his team at the Academy of Sciences.

Kuczynski left an immense oeuvre among which his 40-volume *History of the Working Class under Capitalism* has to be considered the most remarkable contribution. His disciples also contributed greatly to our knowledge of German economic evolution. Hans Mottek's *German Economic History* (1970–74) and the work by Dieter Baudis and Helga Nussbaum (1978) stand out for their non-orthodox Marxist approach which was well (but not uncritically) received even in West Germany in the context of debates on 'organised capitalism' in the 1970s (Winkler 1974). Furthermore, we should mention at least Hartmut Harnisch's (1989) contributions to agricultural history and the history of technology. However, the former strong tradition of East German economic historians started to lose ground as early as the late 1970s and, by the time of the reunification, only a few scholars of international reputation were left, despite hundreds of PhDs having been granted over the years.

In the Federal Republic, the evolution of economic history took a more decentralised path, institutionally as well as intellectually. At the beginning, the discipline found a home mainly in the faculties of economics. As the strong impact of Keynesian macroeconomics required formal expertise, the older generation of German economists tended to specialise in economic history. Friedrich Lütge in Munich, Wilhelm Abel in Göttingen and Horst Jecht in Münster reinvented themselves this way, while scholars originating from the *Ostforschung* (such as Carl Jantke and Erich Maschke) sought affiliation with sociology and history centres (Hesse and Rischbieter 2010). Although economic history still consisted of scholars from highly diverse academic backgrounds, a progressive shift in the discipline's focus favoured closer cooperation between approaches. Whereas economic and social history in the interwar period was mainly concerned with the Middle Ages and early modern times, after the war it increasingly focused on the industrial period.

In the 1960s and 1970s, the discipline received an important impulse from a parallel transformation within history departments. The 'history of society' paradigm of the Bielefeld School – as it was called abroad because important figures from that approach built a new centre at the University of Bielefeld in the early 1970s – started to push historical research towards an examination of societal structures, power allocation and socio-economic foundations. The Bielefeld historians borrowed the concept of structure from their conservative teachers Theodor Schieder, Werner Conze and Otto Brunner and combined these influences with a critical approach to bourgeois society informed by Karl Marx. The *Annales* School was a less important source of inspiration for Hans-Ulrich Wehler and Jürgen Kocka, who rather paid attention to British working-class historians such as E. P. Thompson and Eric Hobsbawn (Berghahn 2004). They focused on Imperial Germany, when economic policy was strongly influenced by business associations as well as agricultural pressure groups. Strong relations between industry and banking, increasing state intervention in the economy and the suppression of German trade unions, as well as an increasing social inequality, were identified as characteristics of German industrialisation, a path that was named 'organised capitalism' in contrast to the (liberal) British way to modernity (Wehler 1973). In this respect, the group took issue with the writings of the Hamburg historian Fritz Fischer, who had famously suggested that the Great War was triggered by the imperial ambitions of an influential elite of German capitalists and politicians (Geiss 2003).

Besides these key historiographical contributions to modern German industrial history, the Bielefeld School launched important debates on the methodology of social and economic history in Germany. The School was set up explicitly with the aim of improving historical methodology by systematically adopting modern social science. It was intended to rebuild history as 'historical social science' (*Historische Sozialwissenschaft*) in order to understand the complex structure of past societies better than the old philological approach of Leopold von Ranke had ever been able to do. If theory occupied a central place in the Bielefeld agenda, the School nevertheless privileged social history over economic history. Wehler developed his *Gesellschaftsgeschichte* approach along the lines of Max Weber's and Talcott Parsons's constructions intermingled with Walt W. Rostow's stage theory and Schumpeter's business cycle theory (Wehler 1987, introduction). Jürgen Kocka started from business history, initially drawing on Alfred D. Chandler and Fritz Redlich (Kocka 1969, 1975). The Bielefeld School of historians remained hypercritical of the 'new economic history'. The latter was seen as no more than the application of a purely 'mechanical' perspective on the economy, as determined by unchangeable 'economic laws'. They thus reinforced the position of the German Historical School to which frequent references were made and deliberately obstructed the evolution of German economic history towards American social science history models such as econometric history, monetary history and the new institutional economics, which appeared in Germany only in the 1990s.

While the Bielefeld School has to be considered the predominant approach for the integration of economic history within the historical profession, the economic side in this period showed greater connections with what was going on in the Anglo-American world. The group led by the American Richard H. Tilly, who became professor of economic history at the University of Münster in 1966, partly on the initiative of Hoffmann, proved most productive. Following the Hoffmann tradition of empirical–statistical description of economic growth, the group examined the development of the railway system, the iron and steel industry and the mining industry in the nineteenth century. Formal methods were later applied, especially by Tilly himself in his work on the credit markets (Tilly 1966), but also by disciples like Reiner Fremdling, who wrote a path-breaking study of the German railway system (Fremdling, 1975), and Carl-Ludwig Holtfrerich, who dealt with interwar hyperinflation (Holtfrerich 1980). The work of the Münster group, which also included Horst Dumke (1976) and Toni Pierenkemper (1979), resulted in macroeconomic quantification and debates on business cycles on the one hand, and renewed interest in German industrial history on the other.

The development of the 'regional industrialisation' paradigm and emphasis upon 'industrial districts' before the 1871 Unification, responded to the need to account for German regional divergence. The English economic historian Sidney Pollard, who became a professor at Bielefeld in 1980, strongly influenced and supported this line of research and tried to push for the methodological integration of economic history into the Bielefeld School paradigm (Pollard 1980, 1986). Within more recent scholarship on processes of globalisation and transnational history, the concepts of 'industrial district' and 'region' still remain influential. Three further approaches, inspired either by the Bielefeld School's accomplishments or the evolution of the 'new economic history' in the USA, were central to the development of the discipline in the 1970s. The most influential internationally was the protoindustrialisation approach of Peter Kriedte, Hans Medick and Jürgen Schlumbohm (Kriedte et al. 1977) at the Göttingen Max Planck Institute for History. The concept, though initially coined by Franklin Mendels, seemed to perfectly capture the particular decentralised, agricultural pre-history of German industrialisation and inspired a lot of research on German pre-industrial textile-producing regions. It also seemed to fulfil the aims of a socio-economic history in the sense of the Bielefeld School.

On the economic side, Knut Borchardt, himself a disciple of Friedrich Lütge, established an active centre at the University of Munich. Borchardt can be considered as the last economic historian of the 'old school' and arguably the most prominent in the post-war period. Despite his closer ties to economics, he was successful in inspiring, and engaging with, both economists and historians. He used descriptive quantitative methodologies in the tradition of Mitchell and Hoffmann, combined with a sound command of theory. His writings, especially his discussion of Brüning's deflation policy during the Great Depression (Borchardt 1982; see also Ritschl 2003), are based on a deep knowledge of Keynesian as well as monetarist economic theory and archival material. Prominent was his role in the debate over the effects of the Marshall Plan known as the 'Abelshauser controversy' (Abelshauser 1981; Borchardt and Buchheim 1986). Borchardt also left his mark as an editor by organising the translation of Carlo Cipolla's *Fontana Economic History of Europe* (Cipolla and Borchardt 1976–80).

At the Free University of Berlin another group of economic historians emerged under the chairmanship of Wolfram Fischer. Like Jürgen Kocka (who joined the university in the 1990s), Fischer had profited from a Rockefeller Fellowship that took him to the USA in

1961–62 and worked on south-west German small business and state policies during early industrialisation (Fischer 1968). Among his disciples, Reinhardt Spree was probably the most influential. Spree's work on nineteenth-century German business cycles (1977) represents a valuable contribution at the intersection of history and economics. The contemporaries of Fischer, Borchardt and Tilly were not school-spawning in a similar way but contributed more on an empirical level to the advancement of economic history. Wilhelm Abel's school of agricultural history at the University of Göttingen was continued by Friedrich-Wilhelm Henning and Karl-Heinrich Kaufhold, who worked on German craftsmen (Henning 1964; Abel 1966; Kaufhold 1968). During his time in Cologne, Henning (1973/74) also published on the industrial revolution. Karl Erich Born, who wrote on the history of German banking and the financial system, was especially productive (Born 1967, 1977).

The receptive age of German economic history

At the risk of being provocative, German economic history in the 1990s must be described as being predominantly receptive. Whereas in former periods German economic historians had been innovative in the sense that research in German economic and social history affected methodological debates abroad, the 1990s were characterised almost entirely by the transfer of foreign concepts to German debates. A number of factors may have contributed to this lack of innovative capacity. Focused as it was on the twentieth century, German economic history was a rather atypical case. Moreover, whereas economic historians in Britain and France were driven by their colonial histories to pay attention to international economic relations, global trade and economic diplomacy, Germany's economic development from 1914 to the 1950s had largely been a product of its international isolation and economic autarchy. The country's particular economic organisation that developed under these circumstances was hardly comparable with the liberal market economies in the Anglo-Saxon world, whose approaches to economic history were becoming increasingly influential. However, as an economically successful example it still attracted several scholars from Britain, the USA and France, who became respected international experts on questions of German economic history – among them, Gerald Feldman and Harold James certainly stand out. Overall, the receptive period in German economic history resulted in a paradoxical impoverishment of the debate. Albrecht Ritschl (2002) serves perhaps as a unique counter example since his research, focusing on the very exceptional economic situation of Weimar Germany, had an impact abroad, facilitated by his international career at Barcelona, Zurich and the LSE. By contrast, even important domestic contributions like Fritz Blaich's description of the cartel movement in Imperial Germany (Blaich 1973), Gerold Ambrosius's extensive consideration of the complex interrelationship between the economy and the state in the Weimar Republic (Ambrosius 1982) or the examination of the organisation of industrial relations in Germany (Welskopp 1994; Plumpe 1999; Lauschke 1999) did not receive comparable international attention. Finally, the country's reunification may have encouraged a certain self-centred attitude of the discipline, since it provided emerging scholars with unexpected job opportunities (made possible by the removal of East German economic historians, in many cases compromised by the GDR regime).

Research in modern German economic history since the 1990s can be grouped in five main areas.[3] A first variety, which reminds one of debates among economists in the 1950s (Erbe 1958), has dealt with the structure and performance of the Nazi economy. A controversy raged in the mid-1990s on the question of whether there was a German 'economic miracle' in the 1930s as Werner Abelshauser had suggested, downplaying at the same time the role of the Marshall Plan. While Abelshauser (1999) maintained that the application of proto-Keynesian economic policies led to the country's quick recovery from the Great Depression, his main opponent argued that signs of prosperity were already evident before the Nazis came to power (Buchheim 2001). Another debate arose around the question of whether the Nazi economy could be described as a market economy or if planning and state intervention rather dominated the scene (Buchheim and Scherner 2009). Most scholars today would probably speak of a highly regulated 'command economy' and recent research in this area tends to focus on the gold and currency management (Banken 2009) as well as on foreign trade (Boelcke 1994). Overall, this renewed interest in the Third Reich produced a vast and detailed body of knowledge with studies on economic sectors such as the chemical industry (Hayes 1987), the aircraft industry (Budraß 1998) and banking (Kopper 1995), but also on business statistics (Spoerer 1996).

Second, in connection with the Nazi economy, business history had a veritable boom in the 1990s, fuelled by commissioned company history projects on the history of forced labour on the one hand, and the use of confiscated gold reserves by the German big banks on the other. Although most company histories focused on the interwar period and widened our knowledge of business behaviour under a totalitarian regime (Gall et al. 1995; Grieger and Mommsen 1996; Bähr et al. 2006), business history research subsequently extended to nearly all periods of German history from the early modern merchant house to the modern big corporation (Pierenkemper 2000; Berghoff 2004), paying increasing attention to small and medium-sized enterprises, so significant for the German path to industrial modernity, which cannot be easily grasped within a Chandlerian framework. Furthermore, social history and network analysis have contributed to our understanding of entrepreneurship and entrepreneurial networks (Herrigel 1996).

Third, casting itself as an antithesis to the Bielefeld School, the new cultural history started to dominate history departments during the 1990s. The linguistic turn has not always proved hostile to economic history. Whenever cultural history merged with economic history (Berghoff and Vogel 2004), it produced a new interest in the history of advertising, marketing (Borscheid and Wischermann 1995) and, more generally, in perceptions and representations of economic life rather than economic life itself (Tooze 2001; Hesse et al. 2002).

Fourth, Germany's reunification and the unprecedented opportunities of access to archival material about the recent past generated another area of interest for economic historians: the economic history of the GDR, conveniently summarised in André Steiner's (2010) synthesis. The study of particular aspects of central planning and social policy (Boldorf 1996) has gone hand in hand with reassessment of East German macroeconomic performance and the eventual transition to the market.

Finally, as an increasingly sharp reaction against the historians' cultural turn, a new generation of economists emerged aiming to catch up with the methodological evolution of modern econometrics as it has been applied to economic history, especially in the USA, during the last four decades. Using Charles P. Kindleberger's (1990) terminology, we may call this approach 'historical economics' as opposed to 'economic history'.[4] Since the 'new economic history' was perceived rather critically in Germany in the 1970s (with the exception of Münster and Munich) and history departments seemed to have extended their interest in economic history much faster than the faculties of economics, the economists' approach to economic history was deficient in Germany at the end of the twentieth century. The only successful example in the 1990s was anthropometrics, introduced by the American John Komlos at the University of Munich and further spread by his pupil Jörg Baten (Komlos 1989; Baten 1996). Providing alternative measures for economic growth, the Munich school has generated several data sets during the last decade. As their American forerunners did 50 years ago, German historical economists who started their university careers after the turn of the twenty-first century insist upon clear-cut research questions, testable hypotheses of causality and the application of advanced methods like Bayesian statistics. The topics investigated so far have been patents and innovation in German industrialisation (Streb 2003; Streb et al. 2006), the existence of borders in Imperial Germany and Poland (Wolf 2003) and banking after the stock-market crash of 1873 (Burhop 2004). However, the future will show if this research really aims at pursuing dialogue with the older discipline rather than simply putting economic history under the powerful wing of economics. Some contributions seem to spend immense effort answering research questions that had in fact already been answered by the empirical work of twentieth-century economic historians. Further scepticism may arise from the fact that historical economics tends to concentrate on periods in German history for which data gathering is relatively easy and the institutional setting stable. Imperial Germany has therefore been examined extensively, in contrast to the time before 1870, the troubled interwar period, or post-war Germany with its oversupply of statistical information and direct competition from fully-fledged economists.

Conclusion

Given the territorial transformations and major changes in the economic organisation of Germany since the late nineteenth century, as well as its role in the integration and disintegration of the world economy, it is not surprising that structural change has been at the heart of economic history-writing.

The 'German Historical School' provided a methodological approach to cope with structural change. This interest and methodological core continued in the course of the twentieth century through different political and academic regimes. To economic historians, the effects of changing economic orders and the political regulation of markets were of greater interest than economic stability and growth. State intervention received more attention than spontaneous forces, regional diversity was emphasised over national uniformities and deviation from global development was stressed rather than conformity. In the long run, historical circumstances seem to have driven the discipline's evolution away from approaches that perceive the economy as operating in a stable way over time, implying regularity and predictability in individual behaviour and economic decision-making. In Kindleberger's terminology, 'economic history' dominated over 'historical economics' for most of the time.

However, in recent years both groups have experienced remarkable methodological as well as empirical advances. Neither camp has been satisfied with the historical generalisations of Reinhart and Rogoff, Acemoglu and Robinson, or Thomas Piketty, who treat historical transformations in too superficial a way and tend to neglect the bulk of past historical literature. These contributions did however bring economic history to the attention of a general public demanding deeper explanations for current economic issues and even policy advice. But this attention has not yet translated into new positions or major research programmes.

Over the last twenty years, German economic history shrank to no more than 35 permanent university positions, scattered all over the country and often maintained through painful negotiations with the local faculties. In this context, strategic alliances between 'historical economists' and 'economic historians' may prove important for the survival of the discipline. Providing historical economics can become not just 'applied economics, leaving most of the history out', and economic history can avoid description without explanation, cooperation will be easier and more productive.

Notes

1 I use the phrase 'German-speaking' to refer to German as well as Austrian economic historians but not to those working in the German-speaking parts of Switzerland.
2 Hoffmann (1940), translated into English by O.W. Henderson in 1955 as 'British Industry 1700–1950'. For a biographical note, see Hoffmann (1970).
3 Here I cannot elaborate on research in early modern economic history, which became an increasingly separate field.
4 The phrase 'historical economics' was already introduced in the USA in the 1880s, but only in the 1990s did it become a vehicle for ostentatious self-description of economists. See also Ziegler (1997).

References

Abel, Wilhlem (1966), *Agrarkrisen und Agrarkonjunkturen. Eine Geschichte der Land- und Ernährungswirtschaft Mitteleuropas seit dem hohen Mittelalter.* Hamburg and Berlin: Parey.

Abelshauser, Werner (1981), 'Wiederaufbau vor dem Marshall-Plan. Westeuropas Wachstumschancen und die Wirtschaftsordnungspolitik in der zweiten Hälfte der vierziger Jahre', *Vierteljahrshefte für Zeitgeschichte* 29, 545–78.

Abelshauser, Werner (1999), 'Kriegswirtschaft und Wirtschaftswunder. Deutschlands wirtschaftliche Mobilisierung für den Zweiten Weltkrieg und die Folgen für die Nachkriegszeit', *Vierteljahrshefte für Zeitgeschichte* 47, 503–38.

Adelman, Jeremy (2013), *The Worldly Philosopher: The Odyssey of Albert O. Hirschman.* Princeton, NJ: Princeton University Press.

Ambrosius, Gerold (1982), *Die öffentliche Wirtschaft in der Weimarer Republik. Kommunale Versorgungsunternehmen als Instrumente der Wirtschaftspolitik.* Habilitation thesis, FU Berlin.

Aubin, Hermann and Wolfgang Zorn (1971–76), *Handbuch der deutschen Wirtschafts- und Sozialgeschichte.* Stuttgart: Klett-Cotta.

Backhaus, Jürgen G. (1994), 'Wirtschaftsverfassung und Ordnungspolitische Grundvorstellungen im nationalökonomischen Denken der zwanziger Jahre. Ein endgültiger Zwischenbericht'. In Knut Wolfgang Nörr et al. (eds.), *Geisteswissenschaften zwischen Kaiserreich und Republik. Zur Entstehung der Nationalökonomie, Rechtswissenschaft und Sozialwissenschaft im 20 Jh.* Stuttgart: Franz Steiner Verlag: 403–21.

Bähr, Johannes, Klaus-Dietmar Henke, Harald Wixforth and Dieter Ziegler, eds. (2006), *Die Dresdner Bank im Dritten Reich.* Munich: Oldenbourg Wissenschaftsverlag.

Banken, Ralf (2009), *Edelmetallmangel und Großraubwirtschaft. Die Entwicklung des deutschen Edelmetallsektors im Dritten Reich 1933–1945.* Berlin: De Gruyter.

Baten, Jörg (1996), *Economic Development and the Distribution of Nutritional Resources in Bavaria.* Munich: Volkswirtschaftliche Fakultät of the University.

Baudis, Dieter and Helga Nussbaum (1978), *Staat und Wirtschaft im 19 Jahrhundert.* Vaduz: Topos-Verlag.

Berghahn, Volker (2004), 'Foreign Influences on German Social and Economic History'. In G. Schulz et al. (eds.), *Sozial- und Wirtschaftsgeschichte. Arbeitsgebiete – Probleme – Perspektiven.* Stuttgart: Franz Steiner Verlag, 447–68.

Berghoff, Hartmut (2004), *Moderne Unternehmensgeschichte. Eine themen- und theorieorientierte Einführung.* Paderborn: Schöningh.

Berghoff, Hartmut and Jakob Vogel (2004), 'Wirtschaftsgeschichte als Kulturgeschichte. Ansätze zur Bergung transdisziplinärer Synergiepotentiale'. In *Wirtschaftsgeschichte als Kulturgeschichte. Dimensionen eines Perspektivenwechsels.* Frankfurt a.M.: Campus: 9–41.

Beyrau, Dietrich (2012), 'Eastern Europe as a "Sub-Germanic Space": Scholarship on Eastern Europe under National Socialism', *Kritika: Explorations in Russian and Eurasian History*, 13.3, 685–723.

Blaich, Fritz (1973), *Kartell- und Monopolpolitik im kaiserlichen Deutschland: Das Problem der Marktmacht im deutschen Reichstag 1879–1914.* Düsseldorf: Droste.

Boelcke, Willi A. (1994), *Deutschland als Welthandelsmacht 1930–1945.* Stuttgart: Kohlhammer Verlag.

Boldorf, Marcel (1996), *Sozialfürsorge in der SBZ/DDR 1945–1953. Ursachen, Ausmaß und Bewältigung der Nachkriegsarmut.* Stuttgart: Steiner.

Borchardt, Knut (1982), *Wachstum, Krisen, Handlungsspielräume der Wirtschaftspolitik: Studien zur Wirtschaftsgeschichte des 19. und 20. Jh.* Göttingen: Vandenhoeck & Ruprecht.

Borchardt, Knut and Christoph Buchheim (1986), 'Die Wirkungen der Marshallplan-Hilfe in Schlüsselbranchen der deutschen Wirtschaft', *Vierteljahreshefte für Zeitgeschichte* 35, 317–47.

Born, Karl Erich (1967), *Die deutsche Bankenkrise 1931. Finanzen und Politik*. Munich: Piper.

Born, Karl Erich (1977), *Geld und Banken im 19. und 20. Jahrhundert*. Stuttgart: Kröner.

Borscheid, Peter and Clemens Wischermann, eds. (1995), *Bilderwelt des Alltags. Werbung in der Konsumgesellschaft des 19. und 20. Jahrhunderts*. Stuttgart: Franz Steiner Verlag.

Brodnitz, Georg (1910), 'Die Zukunft der Wirtschaftsgeschichte'. In Werner Plumpe (ed.), *Wirtschaftsgeschichte*. Stuttgart: Franz Steiner Verlag, 2008, 41–57.

Bücher, Karl (1893), *Die Entstehung der Volkswirtschaft: sechs Vorträge*. Tübingen: Laupp.

Buchheim, Christoph (2001), 'Die Wirtschaftsentwicklung im Dritten Reich – mehr Desaster als Wunder. Eine Erwiderung auf Werner Abelshauser', *Vierteljahrshefte für Zeitgeschichte* 49, 653–64.

Buchheim, Christoph and Jonas Scherner (2009), 'Corporate Freedom of Action: A Response to Peter Hayes', *Bulletin of the German Historical Institute* 45, Fall, 43–50.

Budraß, Lutz (1998), *Flugzeugindustrie und Luftrüstung in Deutschland 1918–1945*. Düsseldorf: Droste.

Burhop, Carsten (2004), *Die Kreditbanken in der Gründerzeit*. Stuttgart: Franz Steiner Verlag.

Burleigh, Michael (1988), *Germany Turns Eastwards: A Study of 'Ostforschung' in the Third Reich*. Cambridge: Cambridge University Press.

Chun, Jin-Sung (2000), *Das Bild der Moderne in der Nachkriegszeit. Die westdeutsche "Strukturgeschichte" im Spannungsfeld von Modernitätskritik und wissenschaftlicher Innovation 1948–1962*. Munich: Oldenbourg.

Cipolla, Carlo M. and K. Borchardt, eds. (1976–80), *Europäische Wirtschaftsgeschichte*. Stuttgart: Fischer.

De Rouvray, Christel (2004), '"Old" Economic History in the United States: 1939–1954', *Journal of the History of Economic Thought* 26.2, 221–39.

Dopsch, Alfrons (1927), 'Zur Methodologie der Wirtschaftsgeschichte'. In *Walter Goetz zu seinem 60. Geburtsage*. Leipzig: Teubner, 518–38.

Dumke, Rolf Horst (1976), *The Political Economy of German Economic Unification: Tariffs, Trade, and Politics of the Zollverein Era*. Madison: University of Wisconsin.

Erbe, René (1958), *Die Nationalsozialistische Wirtschaftspolitik 1933–1939 im Lichte der modernen Theorie*. Zürich: Polygraphischer Verlag.

Etzemüller, Thomas (2001), *Sozialgeschichte als politische Geschichte. Werner Conze und die Neuorientierung der westdeutschen Geschichtswissenschaft nach 1945*. Munich: Oldenbourg Wissenschaftsverlag.

Fischer, Wolfram (1968), *Wirtschafts- und sozialgeschichtliche Probleme der frühen Industrialisierung*. Berlin: Colloquium-Verlag.

Fischer, Wolfram (1984), *Walther G. Hoffmann als Wirtschaftshistoriker*. In Ernst Helmstädter (ed.), *Die Bedingungen des Wirtschaftswachstums in Vergangenheit und Zukunft. Gedenkschrift für Walther G. Hoffmann*. Tübingen: Mohr Siebeck, 18–30.

Fourcade, Marion (2009), *Economists and Societies: Discipline and Profession in the United States, Britain, and France, 1890s to 1990s*. Princeton, NJ: Princeton University Press.

Fremdling, Reiner (1975), *Eisenbahnen und Deutsches Wirtschaftswachstum 1840–1879*. Dortmund: Gesellschaft für Westfälische Wirtschaftsgeschichte.

Füssel, Karl-Heinz (2004), *Deutsch-amerikanischer Kulturaustausch im 20. Jahrhundert. Bildung – Wissenschaft – Politik*. Frankfurt: Campus-Verlag.

Gall, Lothar, Gerald D. Feldman, Harold James, Carl-Ludwig Holtfrerich and Hans E. Büschgen (1995), *Die Deutsche Bank 1870–1995*. Munich: Beck.

Geiss, Imanuel (2003), *Zur Fischer-Kontroverse. 40 Jahre danach*. In Martin Sabrow (ed.), *Zeitgeschichte als Streitgeschichte: Große Kontroversen seit 1945*. Munich: Beck, 21–57.

Gemelli, Giuliana (2003), '"Leadership and Mind": Frederic C. Lane as Cultural Entrepreneur and Diplomat', *Minerva* 41, 115–32.

Grebing, Helga (1986), *Der Deutsche Sonderweg in Europa 1806–1945. Eine Kritik*. Stuttgart: Kohlhammer.

Grieger, Manfred and Hans Mommsen (1996), *Das Volkswagenwerk und seine Arbeiter im Dritten Reich*. Düsseldorf: ECON.

Hagemann, Harald and Claus-Dieter Krohn, eds. (1999), *Biographisches Handbuch der deutsch- sprachigen wirtschaftswissenschaftlichen Emigration nach 1933*. Munich: Saur.

Harley, K. N. (1982), 'British Industrialisation before 1841: Evidence of Slower Growth during the Industrial Revolution', *Journal of Economic History* 42, 267–89.

Harms, Bernhard (1914), *Volkswirtschaft und Weltwirtschaft. Versuch einer Begründung einer Weltwirtschaftslehre*. Jena: Fischer.

Harnisch, Hartmut (1989), 'Die Agrarreformen in Preußen und ihr Einfluß auf das Wachstum der Wirtschaft'. In Toni Pierenkemper (ed.), *Landwirtschaft und industrielle Entwicklung*, Stuttgart: Franz Steiner Verlag, 27–44.

Häuser, Karl (1994), 'Das Ende der Historischen Schule und die Ambiguität der deutschen Nationalökonomie in den Zwanziger Jahren'. In Knut Wolfgang Nörr et al. (eds.), *Geisteswissenschaften zwischen Kaiserreich und Republik. Zur Entstehung der Nationalökonomie, Rechtswissenschaft und Sozialwissenschaft im 20 Jh.* Stuttgart: Franz Steiner Verlag, 47–74.

Hayes, Peter (1987), *Industry and Ideology: IG Farben in the Nazi Era.* Cambridge: Cambridge University Press.

Henning, Friedrich-Wilhlem (1964), *Herrschaft und Bauernuntertänigkeit.* Würzburg: Holzner.

Henning, Friedrich-Wilhelm (1973/74), *Wirtschafts- und Sozialgeschichte.* Paderborn: Scöningh.

Henning, Friedrich-Wilhelm (1988), *Bruno Kuske (1876–1964).* In *Kölner Volkswirte und Sozialwissenschaftler. Über den Beitrag Kölner Volkswirte und Sozialwissenschaftler zur Entwicklung der Wirtschafts- und Sozialwissenschaften.* Cologne: Böhlau, 69–95.

Herrigel, Gary (1996), *Industrial Constructions: The Sources of German Industrial Power.* Cambridge: Cambridge University Press.

Hesse, Jan-Otmar and J. Laura Rischbieter (2010), 'Die Wirtschaftswissenschaftliche Fakultät der Humboldt-Universität zu Berlin nach 1945'. In Rüdiger vom Bruch and Hansjörg Tenorth (eds.), *Geschichte der Universität Berlin.* Berlin: Akademie Verlag, 255–77.

Hesse, Jan-Otmar, Christian Kleinschmidt and Karl Lauschke (2002), *Kulturalismus, Neue Institutionenökonomie oder Theorienvielfalt. Eine Zwischenbilanz der Unternehmensgeschichte.* Essen: Klartext.

Hintze, Otto (1929), 'Der moderne Kapitalismus als historisches Individuum. Ein kritischer Bericht über Sombarts Werk', *Historische Zeitschrift* 139, 457–509.

Hodgson, Geoffrey M. (2001), *How Economics Forgot History. The Problem of Historical Specificity in Social Science.* London: Routledge.

Hoffmann, Alfred (1979), 'Alfons Dopsch und die Wiener Schule der Wirtschafts- und Sozialgeschichte'. In *Staat und Wirtschaft im Wandel der Zeit.* Munich: Oldenbourg, 56–61.

Hoffmann, Walther G. (1940), *Wachstum und Wachstumsformen der englischen Industriewirtschaft von 1700 bis zur Gegenwart.* Jena: Fischer.

Hoffmann, Walther G. (1965), *Das Wachstum der deutschen Wirtschaft seit der Mitte des 19. Jahrhunderts.* Berlin: Springer.

Hoffmann, Walther G. (1970), 'Mein Werdegang'. In Ernst Helmstädter (ed.), *Die Bedingungen des Wirtschaftswachstums in Vergangenheit und Zukunft. Gedenkschrift für Walther G. Hoffmann.* Tübingen: Mohr Siebeck, 1984, 1–9.

Holtfrerich, Carl-Ludwig (1980), *Die deutsche Inflation 1914–1923.* Berlin: de Gruyter.

Kaufhold, Karl Heinrich (1968), *Das Handwerk der Stadt Hildesheim im 18. Jahrhundert. Eine wirtschaftsgeschichtliche Studie.* Göttingen: Schwartz.

Kellenbenz, Hermann (1958), *Sephardim an der unteren Elbe. Ihre wirtschaftliche und politische Bedeutung vom Ende des 16. bis zum Beginn des 18. Jahrhunderts.* Wiesbaden: Steiner.

Kindleberger, Charles P. (1990), *Historical Economics: Art or Science?* Berkeley: University of California Press.

Kocka, Jürgen (1969), *Unternehmensverwaltung und Angestelltenschaft am Beispiel Siemens 1847–1914. Zum Verhältnis von Kapitalismus und Bürokratie in der deutschen Industrialisierung.* Stuttgart: Klett.

Kocka, Jürgen (1975), *Unternehmer in der Deutschen Industrialisierung.* Göttingen: Vandenhoeck & Ruprecht.

Komlos, John (1989), *Nutrition and Economic Development in the Eighteenth-Century Habsburg Monarchy: An Anthropometric History.* Princeton, NJ: Princeton University Press.

Kopper, Christopher (1995), *Zwischen Marktwirtschaft und Dirigismus. Bankenpolitik im Dritten Reich 1933–1939.* Bonn: Bouvier.

Köster, Roman (2011), *Die Wissenschaft der Außenseiter: die Krise der Nationalökonomie in der Weimarer Republik.* Göttingen: Vandenhoeck & Ruprecht.

Kriedte, Peter, Hans Medick and Jürgen Schlumbohm (1977), *Industrialisierung vor der Industrialisierung: gewerbliche Warenproduktion auf dem Land in der Formationsperiode des Kapitalismus.* Göttingen: Vandenhoeck & Ruprecht.

Lauschke, Karl (1999), *Die Hoesch-Arbeiter und ihr Werk. Sozialgeschichte der Westfalenhütte während des Wiederaufbaus 1945–1966.* Essen: Klartext.

Mottek, Hans (1970–74), *Wirtschaftsgeschichte Deutschlands.* Berlin: Deutscher Verlag der Wissenschaften.

Mühle, Eduard, ed. (2008), *Briefe des Ostforschers Hermann Aubin aus den Jahren 1910–1968*. Marburg: Verlag Herder-Institut.

Parker, Richard (2005), *John Kenneth Galbraith: His Life, His Politics, His Economics*. New York: Farrar, Straus and Giroux.

Pierenkemper, Toni (1979), *Die westfälischen Schwerindustriellen 1852–1913: soziale Strukturen und unternehmerischer Erfolg*. Göttingen: Vandenhoeck & Ruprecht.

Pierenkemper, Toni (2000), *Unternehmensgeschichte. Eine Einführung in ihre Methoden und Ergebnisse*. Stuttgart: Steiner.

Plumpe, Werner (1999), *Betriebliche Mitbestimmung in der Weimarer Republik. Fallstudien zum Ruhrbergbau und zur chemischen Industrie*. Munich: Oldenbourg.

Plumpe, Werner (2009), 'Die Wirtschaftsgeschichte in der Historischen Zeitschrift. Ein Überblick'. In *Historische Zeitschrift* 289, 223–51.

Polanyi, Ilona Ducyznska (1977), 'Karl Polanyi: Notes on His Life'. In Karl Polanyi, *The Livelihood of Man*, ed. by Harry W. Pearson. New York: Academic Press, xi–xx.

Pollard, Sidney (1980), *Region und Industrialisierung. Studien zur Rolle der Region in der Wirtschaftsgeschichte der letzten zwei Jahrhunderte*. Göttingen: Vandenhoeck & Ruprecht.

Pollard, Sidney (1986), *Peaceful Conquest: The Industrialization of Europe 1760–1970*. Oxford: Oxford University Press.

Rausch, Helke (2007), 'US-amerikanische "Scientific Philantropy" in Frankreich, Deutschland und Großbritannien zwischen den Weltkriegen', *Geschichte und Gesellschaft* 33, 73–98.

Redlich, Fritz (1965), 'New and Traditional Approaches to Economic History', *Journal of Economic History* 25, 480–95.

Reuter, Norbert (1994), *Der Institutionalismus. Geschichte und Theorie der evolutionären Ökonomie*. Marburg: Metropolis.

Ritschl, Albrecht (2002), *Deutschlands Krise und Konjunktur 1924–1934. Binnenkonjunktur, Auslandsverschuldung und Reparationsproblem zwischen Dawes-Plan und Transfersperre*. Berlin: Akademie Verlag.

Ritschl, Albrecht (2003), 'Knut Borchardts Interpretation der Weimarer Wirtschaft. Zur Geschichte und Wirkung einer wirtschaftsgeschichtlichen Kontroverse'. In Jürgen Elvert and Susanne Krauß (eds.), *Historische Debatten und Kontroversen im 19. und 20. Jahrhundert*. Stuttgart: Franz Steiner Verlag, 234–44.

Rutherford, Malcolm (2007), 'American Institutional Economics in the Interwar Period'. In Jeff Biddle et al. (eds.), *Companion to the History of Economic Thought*. Oxford: Blackwell, 360–76.

Schumpeter, Joseph Alois (1912), *Theorie der wirtschaftlichen Entwicklung*. Berlin: Duncker & Humblot, 2006.

Sombart, Werner (1902–27), *Der Moderne Kapitalismus*. Munich and Leipzig: Duncker & Humblot.

Spoerer, Mark (1996), *Vom Scheingewinn zum Rüstungsboom. Die Eigenkapitalrentabilität deutscher Industrieaktiengesellschaften 1925–1941*. Stuttgart: Steiner.

Spree, Reinhard (1977), *Die Wachstumszyklen der deutschen Wirtschaft von 1840 bis 1880*. Berlin: Duncker & Humbolt.

Steiner, André (2010), *The Plans that Failed: An Economic History of the GDR*. New York: Berghahn Books.

Streb, Jochen (2003), *Staatliche Technologiepolitik und branchenübergreifender Wissenstransfer. Über die Ursachen der internationalen Innovationserfolge der deutschen Kunststoffindustrie im 20. Jahrhundert*. Berlin: Akademie Verlag.

Streb, Jochen, Jörg Baten and Shuxi Yin (2006), 'Technological and Geographical Knowledge Spillover in the German Empire 1877–1918', *Economic History Review* 59, 347–73.

Tilly, Richard H. (1966), *Financial Institutions and Industrialization in the Rhineland 1815 –1870*. Madison: University of Wisconsin Press.

Tooze, J. Adam (2001), *Statistics and the German State, 1900–1945: The Making of Modern Economic Knowledge*. Cambridge: Cambridge University Press.

Tribe, Keith (2007), 'Historical Schools of Economics: German and English'. In Jeff Biddle (ed.), *Companion to the History of Economic Thought*. Oxford: Blackwell, 215–30.

Weber, Max (1904/5), 'Die protestantische Ethik und der Geist des Kapitalismus'. In Max Weber, *Gesammelte Aufsätze zur Religionssoziologie I*. Tübingen: Mohr, 1920, 17–206.

Weber, Max (1909), 'Agrarverhältnisse im Altertum'. In *Gesammelte Aufsätze zur Sozial- und Wirtschaftsgeschichte*, ed. by Marianne Weber. Tübingen: Mohr, 1924, 1–288.

Weber, Max (1927), *General Economic History*. Trans. Frank H. Knight. New York: Greenberg.

Wehler, Hans-Ulrich (1973), *Geschichte und Ökonomie*. Cologne: Kiepenheuer & Witsch.

Wehler, Hans-Ulrich (1987), *Deutsche Gesellschaftsgeschichte*. Munich: Beck.

Welskopp, Thomas (1994), *Arbeit und Macht im Hüttenwerk. Arbeits- und industrielle Beziehungen in der deutschen und amerikanischen Eisen- und Stahlindustrie von den 1860er bis zu den 1930er Jahren*. Bonn: Dietz.

Winkel, Harald (1977), *Die deutsche Nationalökonomie im 19. Jahrhundert*. Darmstadt: Wissenschaftliche Buchgesellschaft.

Winkler, Heinrich August, ed. (1974), *Organisierter Kapitalismus*. Göttingen: Vandenhoeck & Ruprecht.

Wolf, Nikolaus (2003), *Economic Integration in Historical Perspective: The Case of Interwar Poland, 1918–1939*. Berlin: Humboldt-University.

Ziegler, Dieter (1997), 'Die Zukunft der Wirtschaftsgeschichte. Versäumnisse und Chancen', *Geschichte und Gesellschaft* 23, 405–23.

7
ECONOMIC HISTORY IN FRANCE
A *Sonderweg*?

Jean-Yves Grenier[1]

The study of economic history in France goes back to the later nineteenth century, when history became an academic discipline. In France the new discipline was especially dominated by political history, the study of economic history playing only a subordinate role. Nevertheless, it would be wrong to think that the great masters of French historiography before the First World War, such as Ernest Lavisse or Charles Seignobos, overlooked the economic dimension of history; they did in fact lend it great emphasis, especially in their more popular works. The first publications of French economic history were primarily directed to the history of work and of employment (Emile Levasseur, Paul Mantoux, François Simiand), anticipating a lasting connection of economic and social history, an association that is by no means automatic, as shown by English work in economic history of that time. This emphasis upon the social led to the initial placement of economic history towards the left of the political spectrum. This perspective was lent support in 1903, when an initiative on the part of Jean Jaurès led to the foundation of a Commission charged with publishing archives reflecting economic life during the French Revolution, a documentary source that would become of great importance for twentieth-century historians of the French Revolution. Another important feature of French economic history in these first years was the way in which it took account of the geographical dimension, favouring a spatial appreciation of economic phenomena. This had an impact upon French historiography that lasted at least into the 1980s, in which the region or the *département* framed the historical perspective.

However, this influence was not that evident until the foundation in 1929 of the journal *Annales d'histoire économique et sociale.* The date coincides more or less exactly with the foundation of the *Economic History Review* (1927) and the *Journal of Economic and Business History* (1928); but the coincidence is doubly deceptive. In the first place, it was more the major German journal *Vierteljahrschrift für Sozial- und Wirtschaftsgeschichte* (founded 1903) on which Lucien Febvre and Marc Bloch modelled the *Annales*; additionally, the ambitions and programmes of these various initiatives differed. The two English-language journals represented a disciplinary field with a direct connection to the contemporary economics discipline; while *Annales* had from the beginning a much wider perspective (Boldizzoni 2011). Its ambition – the *Annales'* 'paradigm', if you like – was to transcend disciplinary barriers in order to map the contours of a global, or even total, history; and this ambition has itself been reflected in very varied ways by the research carried out under the influence of the *Annales* paradigm. Understood as such, economic history is only of interest or relevance when placed within the social and cultural history of men and women who are themselves placed in their natural environment.

What role for the economy?

Fundamental to the *Annales* paradigm is the principle that we cannot understand a historical fact of any kind if it is detached from its context – if it is not understood as a 'total social fact', as proposed by the anthropologist Marcel Mauss. It is this affirmation of the unity of the social that best characterises the *Annales* project during its entire history (Revel 1979). To realise this sense of totality, openings had to be created towards other disciplines, and to sociology and economics in particular. The model here is the *Année sociologique*, a journal founded by Emile Durkheim at the end of the nineteenth century, bringing together specialists from several disciplines. There was however an important difference between the *Annales* and the *Année sociologique*, since Bloch and Febvre thought that history, and not sociology, had to form the core of the social sciences; although there was not then any sense of hierarchy between disciplines, a state of affairs that opened the way to the interdisciplinarity of the 1970s.

Bloch and Febvre fully appreciated the need to integrate history into the new social sciences, whose appearance had transformed the understanding of society. However, from the beginning, the weight they gave to the economy remained ambiguous. Despite its importance, it was assigned no particular role, and the title of the periodical was expressive more of a wish to place it at the heart of a larger social reality. The economy was omnipresent though. The first years of the journal were those of the Great Depression, and these events fostered historical reflection upon contemporary economic phenomena, something that became a lasting obsession of the journal. We can find in the correspondence of Bloch and Febvre references to the work of Keynes at a time when his work was unknown to most historians. Their attempt to commission from Keynes an article for *Annales* demonstrates the interest they took in the development of contemporary economics, even if they were always critical of this discipline. Moreover, it was an economist who exerted the most influence on the founders of the *Annales*. François Simiand, a student of Durkheim, had proposed an epistemology specific to the requirements of an economic history: through sequencing historical data it would be possible, he argued, to transform the individual facts of traditional history into constructs that could be used in providing answers to questions formulated by the economic historian, moving beyond a traditional historical approach which imagined that the sources could be the source both of questions and answers. The unity of the social sciences was therefore above all a unity of method, and history could claim no special originality in respect of other disciplines. Simiand put his method to the test in two studies, both of which appeared in 1932; these rested upon the reconstitution of lengthy data series from which were then derived statistical regularities that could be used in causal explanations.

The *Annales* historians were fascinated by this use of statistics in historical work, especially in relation to the history of prices – the first issue of the journal even included an article on the price of papyrus in ancient Greece! They saw this as genuinely experimental work, the temporal dimension being the sole means of conducting an experiment in the social sciences which, by definition, study facts that are not reproducible. They were however somewhat suspicious of Simiand's causal determinism, and especially the manner in which he assimilated history to the other social sciences. Simiand's vigorous criticism of neoclassical theory, focusing upon its abstraction and hypothetico-deductive approach, did not prevent him exploring historical facts for 'relations of a general form' to render 'a genuine sense of the complexity of the real'. This set him at odds with the historical approach defended by the founders of the *Annales* and their successors, who thought the real to be too complex and fluid to be reduced to economists' general principles. They advocated a form of history that would not seek to forcibly eliminate breaks and discontinuities, but instead make such breaks and discontinuities the object of study. In this refusal to accept the idea of economic laws detached from their historical and institutional context we can detect an echo of the work of the German Historical School, of arguments put forward by Wilhelm Roscher and Gustav Schmoller for example; but this is a very faint echo, and it cannot be said that the German Historical School had very much influence on French historiography. Nor did either Bloch or Febvre study the writings of Max Weber and Werner Sombart very closely, even if the first issue of *Annales* did carry an article on Max Weber written by Maurice Halbwachs. As for Marx and the place of Marxism in history, they had little interest in this, occasionally expressing reservations, or even frank criticism. Besides their refusal to accept a pre-established model, they were interested in the economy because social relations were more dense and visible there than elsewhere, and not because it was the determining instance of the ensemble of social relations in Marx's sense. Marc Bloch emphasised this in this amusing observation on a Marxist English medievalist: 'Mr. Thompson, whose historical materialism is not always without a degree of intemperance, strives to discover economic motives in the religious movements of the Middle Ages. For myself, I am more struck by the economic outcomes of religious movements' (*Annales HES*, 1929, 2).

Quantitative history and causal explanation

The first major work of quantitative economic history was that of Ernest Labrousse on the causes of the French Revolution: was the Revolution the outcome of the poverty of the population (Michelet) or, on the contrary, of their increasing wealth (Jaurès)? An economist by training, Labrousse became in time more of a historian, and his university career was that of a historian. Of his two major works (1933, 1944), the first is a thesis in economics, and the other one in history, an uncommon duality that explains his ambition to write a history concerned with the social and political consequences of economic phenomena, an aspiration that distinguished his approach from that of Simiand. Both books are on the face of it massive compilations of official market price quotations. He reviews in detail their statistical validity before generating series in which cycles are revealed through the employment of moving averages, a technique new at the time. His interest in the statistical distribution of historical phenomena sharply distinguished him from contemporary historians, who were more interested in the uniqueness of phenomena. This use of quantitative methods in history did however coincide with the initial developments of cliometrics in the United States, with Wesley Mitchell's work on business cycles (Grantham 1997). Yet the methodology employed is quite different: following Simiand, Labrousse utilises an experimental history based upon the identification of recurring identical facts which suggest causalities. Hence in the case of agricultural under-production brought about by poor weather, he observes a recurring contradiction between the path of rising grain prices and that of falling real incomes aggravated by unemployment in manufacturing, a pattern that Labrousse took from French and British economists writing at the time of the Enlightenment. These recurring contradictions produce 'old-style crises' which repeat themselves in the course of the eighteenth century, becoming more acute under the influence of population growth and a secular fall in real wages. The French Revolution was both the unavoidable consequence of this progressive aggravation of social contradictions during these crises, and the culminating point of the time series: 'when the long-term trend in prices reaches its maximum following the beginning of the secular increase [in 1726], when at the same time the cycle reaches its maximum and, within a few weeks, seasonal movements trigger the Revolution' (Labrousse 1933). This temporal perspective, as powerful as it is determinist, is based on a causal succession that leads from the economic to the social, and then to the political. However, in no respect can Labrousse be called a Marxist, for, apart from anything else, he rarely refers to Marx, and his work is marked chiefly by its eclecticism.

The regulation of pre-industrial economies

After the Second World War economic history, building upon what Denis Richet calls the 'revolution of the 1930s', laid claim to being at the centre of the discipline of history in France. This was reflected institutionally in the creation of several university posts following the inauguration of the Sorbonne chair in economic and social history in 1927 for Henri Hauser; in 1936 Marc Bloch succeeded Hauser, and the chair was then assumed by Ernest Labrousse in 1944. From 1946 the subtitle of the *Annales* became 'Economies, Sociétés, Civilisations', beginning with economy and heading towards culture by way of society – and this neatly expresses the new hierarchy legitimating historical knowledge. The subsequent period of sustained growth that promoted the rapid modernisation of French society, despite a number of political setbacks (especially in the form of colonial wars), lent weight to the widely shared idea that the economy is the prime mover in the development of societies.

Nonetheless, it was difficult to build upon the legacy of Labrousse, since his socio-economic model is a simplified and conceptualised description of the real that cannot easily be elaborated or extended, nor does it take much account of variation; in this, Labrousse's approach differs from the Weberian ideal-type which, by contrast, grasps the real through difference. Instead of treating the obstacles presented by each new case (whether from different periods or regions) as an opportunity to enrich the model, Labrousse applied a standard model. This feature accounts both for the rapid appearance during the post-war years of monographs devoted to the study of regions, cities and *départements* with, at first, quite original findings (Goubert, Deyon); but which then settled into a repetitive pattern broken only by rare instances where the search for a more total history led to an emphasis on complexity – such as, for example, Jean-Claude Perrot's immense monograph on the city of Caen in the eighteenth century (1975).

The analysis of crises of the older type was not elaborated in any way, and this was the object of much criticism. David Landes challenged the central argument that an increase in the price of grain led to a fall in the consumption of manufactures on the grounds that the latter would be compensated by an increase in demand from those who sold grain (Landes 1950; and more recently Cullen 2005). The big change has been the addition of a demographic dimension. The work of Jean Meuvret and Pierre Goubert showed, using parish records and family reconstitution (which allowed the calculation of some parameters, especially the fertility rate), why economic crisis was always accompanied by a significant rise in mortality and a fall in both the birth rate and the rate of marriage. This changed the meaning of crisis: what for Labrousse was a periodically recurring fluctuation that led eventually to collapse became the manner in which the relationship of population and subsistence was regulated, explaining how the system was sustained between the thirteenth century and the Revolution. Post-war historians were less concerned about understanding the disequilibrium inherent in the Ancien Régime than describing the persistence, without significant economic growth, of a system riven by famine and epidemics, but also with some agricultural and manufacturing successes. Following on from the work of Michael Postan, Emmanuel Le Roy Ladurie put forward the most developed form of this Malthusian–Ricardian mode of regulation in respect of the Languedoc region (1966), describing long agricultural cycles dominated by the absence of technical progress and the joint fluctuation of agricultural productivity and of population. The disturbing element here is the growth of the state which, while providing a better structure for the king's subjects, reduced their share of the wealth they produced, and slowed cultural development, at least for elites; leading in turn to a Tocquevillian vision of social development. This elimination of the social led to intensive debate with those adhering to a Marxist-style interpretation, such as Guy Bois; for these historians, the dynamic of the Ancien Régime was to be explained in terms of the long-term consequences of the crisis of social relationships within the seigneurial system after the Black Death (see the debate 'Malthus ou Marx?', *Annales ESC* 1978). Following this, the idea of Malthusian demographic regulation was revised in the work of Jacques Dupâquier (1979). Using demographic and fiscal data from the rural population of the Parisian Basin during the reign of Louis XIV, he showed that the role of crises and of the Malthusian scissors were less important in the dynamic of Ancien Régime society than the demographic self-regulation of populations owing to variations in the age of marriage.

This departure required the employment of all disposable sources in constructing new indicators (such as rent of land, yields, taxation, rate of interest), converging with the methods of a total serial history that was then at its peak (Richet 1968). By applying the Labroussian model to different geographical frameworks historians had come to understand that the complexity of economic and social processes exceeded the explanatory capacity of the model. The way in which these new studies questioned behaviour also opened the way to another kind of quantitative history with a cultural dimension (focusing, for instance, on literacy rates or the use of birth control) that was able to supplement economic analysis; as well as introducing work on economic behaviour and representations inspired by historical anthropology. Examples here can be found in Georges Duby's study of the gift in the medieval economy (1973), Yves Castan on the notion of social courtesy (1974), or Le Roy Ladurie on wealth in rural societies (1983). This represented a kind of return to the spirit of the *Annales* of the 1930s, for both Bloch and Febvre had made the study of mentalities a central element in understanding economic and social factors.

The privilege of the *longue durée*

Since the 1930s French economic historiography has been characterised by a dedication to the construction of the temporalities and cycles that lend a rhythm to history. Central here was the long run, the *longue durée* – in Fernand Braudel's words, 'around which everything revolves' – since the most essential features of societies only reveal themselves in the long run (Braudel 1958). The central role given to this approach explains the difficult relationship of the *Annales* school with contemporary history and with politics. The basic three-phase model was set out by Braudel in his book on the Mediterranean (1949): the *longue durée* (extending sometimes over several centuries); the timing of peaks and long cycles (especially those of urban economies and the rhythm of states); and the event. The stake was primarily a disciplinary one: at a time when structuralism was in the ascendant, with Claude Lévi-Strauss publishing his *Anthropologie structurale* in 1958, it had to be demonstrated that history was the only discipline capable of articulating structure and change. In addition, this temporal trilogy was above all a way of thinking about society in its totality, confronting the rhythms of the different social sciences. In contrast with the causal deterministic mechanism of Labrousse, Braudel lent emphasis to complex interactions and temporal discontinuity – biological time rather than mechanical time. We can see here again the aspiration for a total history articulated around relationships with the natural and the human worlds, within which the economy had no autonomous and independent role. The desire to extend the perspective of the historian to the limits of the historical explains the interest of *Annales* historians in uncharted areas, such as the history of climate since the Middle Ages, reconstituted from a wide range of sources (the dates of grape harvests, the morphology of glaciers, among others) (Le Roy Ladurie 1959); the history of illness; the history of the human body; or the history of the environment. *Annales* historiography would never again so completely remove the social in order to inscribe the human being in its natural environment.

The idea of the *longue durée* has recently undergone a revival in the United States in the work of David Armitage and Jo Guldi (2014). They advocate, for reasons both intellectual and political, the use of a rejuvenated *longue durée* integrated within a new quantitative history making use of a much wider set of historical data. But is there anything in common between the *longue durée* of Big Data and the temporal structure long advocated by *Annales* (2015, 2)?

Cultural geography: another total history

If a national framework has sometimes been paramount in the foregoing studies, they have nonetheless been open to other spaces and dimensions. As early as 1954 Febvre asked himself 'what it means to do world history' (*Annales ESC* 1954). Braudel's *Mediterranean* had a very important influence here. His idea of an *aire culturelle* opens up another form of total history of which economic history represents an essential but never autonomous dimension. This is initially a space (without well-defined natural or political borders), so a domain of uncertainty and many choices that stands in contrast to a clear economic causality. It is also a global reality created out of the dynamics offered by networks, exchange and borrowings, and not arising from the stability of structures based upon repetition. Hence it deals with the emergence of economic mentalities at once lasting and changing, collective and particular, and which contradict the idea that economic behaviour is uniformly universal. These diverse elements are articulated within the *longue durée*, an ecological framework imposed by the milieu that is the most enduring of economic constraints. There is an important distinction to be drawn here with respect to the American idea of 'area studies', since this accords less emphasis to the milieu than to presentist concerns. Moreover, Braudel argues that the conception of an *aire culturelle* allows economic analysis to be integrated within the human sciences as practised in France, something that could not happen in the United States, where the social sciences have increasingly focused upon technique and technical issues. Another essential aspect of the programme of *aires culturelles*, and around which Braudel organised the Ecole des Hautes Etudes en Sciences Sociales and the Maison des Sciences de l'Homme, questions the specificity of Europe as a relevant space for analysis, since an *aire culturelle* can extend over several continents (three in the case of the Mediterranean) without including them entirely. The Turkish historian Ömer Barkan has underlined the uniqueness of spaces like the Mediterranean, in which there are quite diverse populations (in this case, Jews, Christians and Muslims, each of which is itself a composite), all of which however face similar natural and economic constraints (Barkan 1954).

The legacy of Braudel's *Mediterranean* includes many aspects, but all have in common the idea of questioning the specificity of Europe. However, the most successful realisation of the Braudelian approach is Denys Lombard's work on Java, and this remains unique in the genre. His stated objective is to break with a Eurocentric perspective on the history of the world by studying the lengthy genealogy of the diverse elements that go to make up contemporary

Indonesia and the Javanese mentality. He demonstrates that, well before the arrival of the Europeans and their idea of globalisation, Islamisation was the driving force of geographical integration, making Southeast Asia the site for a massive circulation of people, goods and ideas, linking the Mediterranean area to China via India. The economy has a major role in this 'historical essay in global history', but it is not isolated from other domains of social life, nor conceived as a universalist perspective in the pages that Lombard devotes to minute descriptions of entrepreneurial strategies and the making of profits among the Chinese diaspora; nor in those devoted to showing how the Europeans did not impose their economic rules and norms, but merged them into existing Asiatic networks, sometimes forcefully (Lombard 1990). Many pioneering works in global history have been heavily influenced by Braudel's *Mediterranean*, such as Chaudhuri's work on the commercial structure of the Indian Ocean before the arrival of Europeans (1985, 1990), or that of Reid on material culture and commercial activity in Southeast Asia from the fifteenth to the seventeenth centuries (1988, 1993). Very prominent among such work is Bin Wong's use of Braudelian regions to understand Chinese history, leading to a twin questioning of the European schema: first, while the period from the Enlightenment to the crisis of the nation-state is sometimes supposed to be a European creation, he rejects the idea that the crisis of the nation-state is simply the final and successful outcome of a historical process; then adopting an economic as well as a cultural point of view, he minimises the influence of pre-modern Europe upon Asia, though the roles were reversed in the nineteenth century. Here again, what is taken from Braudel's *Mediterranean* is not an economic grid-reading, but rather a means of dispensing with Eurocentrism and the developmental paths associated with it (Bin Wong 2001).

Economic history and the colonial heritage

This interest in non-European spaces is also evident in the historical experience of the retreat from empire. Initially, this took the form of a critique of colonialism. A number of historians, whether or not they were closely associated with *Annales*, supported movements for independence and against colonial wars (the Indochina War of 1954–62, then the Algerian War of 1954–62), sometimes working within the Communist Party. They felt an intellectual responsibility towards populations living under an imposed political system. The strongest issue concerned the forms of colonial exploitation, especially the connection between colonialism and forced labour (Coquery-Vidrovitch 1972), and more recently the question of slavery in the older colonies (for the Antilles, Oudin-Bastide 2005; for colonial Africa, Boutang 1998), sometimes on the borders of economic anthropology and history (Meillassoux 1986). This genealogy, combining the Atlantic slave trade, African slavery and the invention of forced labour through colonisation opens up the question of the long-term effects of colonisation and of the possibly rather troubled relationship today of African populations to work. Another approach to colonisation seeks to assess its economic costs and benefits, and the macroeconomic effects upon the French economy. Was it an unalloyed blessing for the metropolis, and did colonies contribute to the rise of French capitalism? There are varied responses to this recurring question. It appears that from the eighteenth century to the First World War the colonial empire was a privileged domain of expansion for French capitalism (Marseille 1989). It was at the same time a protected market that offered little competition, a useful complement to a domestic market whose growth was restricted by the extreme inequality of wages and of wealth, and a zone in which the rate of profit was higher for private capitals invested there (Tarrade 1972; Bonin 2008). The diffusion of Fordism after 1945 brought about a shift since, with the strong internal growth of the metropolis and the onset of mass consumption, a protected export market was no longer necessary and the colonies became a burden upon public finances, which were themselves involved in a major process of modernisation.

The economic aspects of non-European regions were also the subject of more general study. Africa especially appeared to be unique in world economic history and had to be understood as such. Discussion began in the Soviet Union over the applicability of the idea of an Asiatic mode of production. In France this was taken up in the pages of *La Pensée*, a Marxist periodical, turning on the question of the applicability of the idea to Africa where there were neither classes in the Marxist sense nor private appropriation of the land. This led to study of a specific 'African mode of production' that could not be comprehended either by Western pre-capitalist modes or by the Asiatic mode of production, given the absence of despotic rule aimed at the exploitation of a peasant class. The characteristics of African economies had to be taken into account; the mobility of populations and the extent of long-distance trade gave rise to the conception of the surplus value created by warfare and commerce, and not by production (Coquery-Vidrovitch 1969).

The nature of capitalism if viewed in terms of a non-European space became an issue from the 1960s onwards. Maxime Rodinson asked, in a book with a marked anti-Weberian tone, how it was that capitalism had triumphed in Europe and not in Muslim lands, despite their possession of many assets: active, market-oriented commerce, the idea of profit, commercial law, or a technically advanced system of finance that was able to by-pass the prohibition of usury. In a line of argument that would later be taken by Pomeranz with regard to China (though the notion of capitalism has been quite marginal to the Great Divergence debate), Rodinson also wondered why the Muslim world had not anticipated Europe in the development of capitalism. Refuting explanations framed in terms of fatalism or the lack of rationality he showed, contrary to many of the prejudices of the 1960s, that Islam was a 'neutral factor' that had had neither a positive nor a negative impact on the economic destiny of the Muslim world (Rodinson 1966).

The crisis of numbers and of serial history

The power of quantitative history depends on the idea that numerical data, when deemed reliable by historians, provides access to complex phenomena that can be weighted and assigned margins of uncertainty, achieving in this way a reasonable degree of certainty. A good example was provided by the calculation of the French population in the eighteenth century, taking advantage of the automatic processing of masses of parish records.

In the later 1970s the quantitative approach was however questioned, and this was done more actively in France (where serial history was in good standing) than elsewhere; the more clear-headed historians detected signs of exhaustion, due in particular to the repetitive nature of the results produced by this kind of historical work. French economic history entered a period of great methodological and epistemological uncertainty, uncertainty that paralleled growing criticism of the French economic and social system in the wake of the cultural shock of 1968 and the crisis of the Fordist model in the 1970s.

This malaise was brutally expressed in 1979. Lawrence Stone denounced in the pages of *Past and Present* a history that was so abstract that it neglected events in favour of structures, and which favoured models over narrative. Carlo Ginzburg for his part denounced what he called the 'Galilean paradigm', the search by historians for laws or regularities that would enable the construction of a causal explanatory structure. Criticism was directed precisely to the way in which serial history concerned itself with the demonstration of regularities, and the generalisations of findings. This approach was, according to Ginzburg, inspired by the exact sciences, but historical material was not amenable to such deductive methods. In its place he proposed to put an 'evidential paradigm' that did not seek to establish regularities, but instead interpret clues that only rigorous contextualisation, and not the construction of series, could make comprehensible.

One of the effects upon French historiography of this questioning was a collapse of the somewhat naive confidence that historians placed in numbers. This was brought about by the realisation that in the social sciences numbers lacked the objectivity and stability that they had in the natural sciences. Especially in the social and economic domain, a number is the outcome of social convention previous to the work of a statistician, and its validity depends on the way in which this relationship is dealt with. One example is data on enterprise failures: Jean-Pierre Hirsch was the first of many to demonstrate that, far from being the kind of economic barometer that users of time series supposed, statistics on bankruptcies were the outcome of interaction between the state and business actors, resulting either in a rise in cases of bankruptcy to promote economic rationalisation or, by contrast, in a fall in order to lend protection to firms (Hirsch 1991).

Hence in the *longue durée* numbers are sometimes an unreliable indicator, the realities that are measured being subject to change, and the measure itself losing its significance. For example, data on the French working population from 1800 to 2000, working hours and productivity as presented by the statisticians of the Institut National de la Statistique et des Etudes Economiques (Marchand and Thélot 1991) have been subject to vigorous criticism from historians and statisticians on the grounds that estimating the working population and unemployment over such a long period ignores the fact that conceptions of work and employment altered during the nineteenth and twentieth centuries, the category of unemployment itself being an idea first articulated at the very end of the nineteenth century. Likewise, the category of the salaried employee is one that can easily be used anachronistically, since it developed only very slowly during this period and at no point entirely corresponded to modern conceptions. This demonstrates the ambiguity inherent in all work based upon time series. Creating a graph of the percentage of economically active persons from 1800 to 2000 is also quite misleading, since many different things are here pushed into one classification. But might such an aggregate be treated as a useful or satisfactory approximation? Alain Desrosières (1993) argues not, for the discontinuities between the forms of measurement used can be quite significant, and this itself undermines any calculation of probability which is itself fundamental to quantitative history.

The crisis of numbers and of time series data also placed in doubt the temporal model or, more precisely, the causal reasoning derived from the presence of regularly recurring events. Instead of regularity, there is a preference for the event and its singularity. The new epistemological function conferred upon the event involves a profound transformation in our relationship with history. Henceforth, for historians events count. Schematically, we could say that we have seen in the last few years a progressive shift from a determinist approach to historical time towards one that could be called 'stochastic', where chance once more has a place. In the first approach, individual events played little part since they did not influence the broad trajectory of the *longue durée*; whereas in the second, the resulting trajectory depends on their outcome. Each event presents the possibility of several future outcomes; the history that has come to be is just the realisation of one of these outcomes. The best example of this is in the explanations offered for the origin and course of the French Revolution. The causal economic explanation of Labrousse has been displaced by that of François Furet, who was himself an experienced quantitative historian. Furet does not view the Revolution as a phenomenon determined by a universalist causality with a rigorously temporal structure, but rather as the outcome of the autonomisation of political action and ideological movements during the pre-Revolutionary decades. Seen in this light, the outbreak and course of the Revolution is more or less entirely independent of any kind of economic causality (Furet 1978).

And so while it has hitherto been thought that our societies turn upon economic relationships, the accent is now more on the social and the institutional, whose understanding is essential to throw light on the operation of society. Following the logic of this, economic history has bit by bit turned its back upon the discipline of economics. It is striking that a prominent work of economic history devoted to an account of the formation of the institutions of capitalism in the northern regions of France between 1780 and 1860, one of the prime centres of French industrialisation, makes no reference at all to economic analysis, whether orthodox or heterodox, when dealing with firms, markets, competition and business regulation (Hirsch 1991). By contrast, it is significant that the study of French economic history most influenced by the work of Douglass North is written by an American (Rosenthal 1992). Hirsch's study implicitly suggests that the tools of economics are of little use for understanding the genesis of industrial capitalism. He lends emphasis to the ambiguity in liberal ideas circulating in France after the Revolution which failed to match the need of businesses for institutions capable of supporting them while leaving them scope for the free development of their activities. Economic history over the past few decades has increasingly turned to the study of major economic institutions, in particular, those of the state, studying for instance the financial and fiscal system (Dessert 1984; Hamon 1994; Béguin 2012); or studying Colbertism, guilds and manufacturing policy (Minard 1998). Here the object is to demonstrate, in contrast to neo-institutionalism, how economic systems with quite different institutional structures can achieve a comparative level of economic performance.

Capitalism and Eurocentrism

There has long been an interest in reflecting upon global economic history, and it is an interest that recurs. Braudel's book on the Mediterranean drew the concept of *économie-monde* or 'world-economy' from the German idea of *Weltwirtschaft*, and in turn Immanuel Wallerstein (1974, 1980 and 1989) borrowed from Braudel in a series of books that were widely read in France, elaborating a world system of the capitalist economy, contrasting a European centre where profits were accumulated to a periphery dominated by traditional forms of exploitation. The major defect of this approach, especially in the light of our current circumstances, is that it presumed the superiority of a Europe whose population was more free and productive than elsewhere, together with commercial and political elites favourable to economic development. This deficiency is less marked in the work of North and Braudel, who put forward the two interpretations of long-run economic history that are most relevant today. North sees economic growth as the outcome of the rise of markets which become increasingly competitive thanks to the development of institutions like property rights. Braudel's (1979a, 1979b) interpretation is antithetical to this largely dominant view stemming from American neo-institutionalism. For him, in any society that is more or less developed the economy is articulated around three levels: ordinary material life, market economy and capitalism, a form of distinction which is also quite distant from Polanyi's approach, whose major work was translated into French during the same period and had a great influence on the social sciences in France. This distinction, especially that between market economy and capitalism, is fundamental because it is universal. However, the reasons for the European specificity that

Braudel studied are located in the nature of the capitalism developed in Europe; for, as Bin Wong (2001) has noted, it is on this that Europe is most different from China.

What is capitalism? While, for North, the market economy is characterised by fair and efficient competition, according to Braudel this is only the case for small-scale activities. In fact, the rules of capitalism run counter to those of the neoclassical perfect market. It is characterised by privilege, the creation of legal or de facto monopolies and a constant effort to recruit the state in support, especially in the very remunerative areas of defence, taxation and the financing of public debt. The early modern long-distance trading companies that existed thanks only to royal privilege are a perfect example of this, since they rested upon privileges granted to a minority of large capitalists, the military support of the state and protected access to the domestic market. The role of the state is precisely defined by this, but the balance has to be right: it has to be strong enough to exercise its right to impose force in acquiring particular markets, but not so strong that it hampers the free initiative of merchants and limits the prospect of the richest to accumulate over the long term. Braudel argues that this subtle balance was only to be found in Europe, the Islamic polities and the Chinese empire according too much power to a prince or to the state. It was not superiority of rationality or skill that furthered economic development in Europe, but a particular economic and cultural framework that fostered a political economy in which capitalism could take root. There are many criticisms of this model, such as that of Chaudhuri (1990), who argues that Asian political regimes were in fact no more despotic and insecure for persons and property than those in Europe. Again, if Jack Goody (2006) accepts that Braudel's analysis is a step forward in recognising a degree of parity between Orient and Occident, he does rebuke Braudel for assigning too great a weight to European cultural specificity and, in particular, falling back on a conception of capitalism that 'always seems to push the analysis in a eurocentric direction'.

A return to numbers

The relationship between economists and historians has undergone a great deal of development since the 1930s. Before 1940 the relationship was a strong one, as can be seen in the pages of *Annales*, because at that time economics was not highly formalised. However, the two disciplines quickly moved a long way apart. French economists adopted mathematical techniques more enthusiastically than elsewhere; soon enough economic history was absent from economics departments in contrast to the situation in the United States. It became the domain of historians who for the most part lacked any economic training and who were very distrustful of algebra. In France there was nothing like the American New Economic History, and it would only be with the book by Bourguignon and Lévy-Leboyer (1985) that there was a retrospective econometric history of France in the nineteenth century. Up to the end of the twentieth century, a time when cliometrics transformed economic history in many countries, there was a complete divorce between economists and historians. One paradox was that heterodox tendencies arguing for a return to history no longer had any influence on the writing of economic history. Regulation theory therefore remained a matter for economists even while they claimed membership of the *Annales* school, calling for a 'new alliance' between the two disciplines so that the historic nature of the forms of regulation in capitalism, and especially competition, might be better understood (Boyer 1986 and 1989). No collaborative venture between historians and economists led to any deeper understanding of historical and contemporary varieties of capitalism, an issue that was however of great importance.

Since the early 2000s things have changed, with historians beginning to take an interest in the economy and, from the opposite direction, a new generation of economists being sensitive to the historical dimension of the phenomena that they study. Also evident is the return to the quantitative approach, with a more relaxed attitude to the use of number and numerical data. A good example is that of the rate of bankruptcy. Widely used and then abandoned, data on bankruptcies is once more regarded as a relevant indicator, as shown by the study initiated in 2008 on the mechanisms underlying nineteenth-century bankruptcies, using the huge quantitative database provided by the official judicial statistics.

Inequality and credit

This new economic history can be seen at work in several areas. The first relates to long-run inequality and criticism of the famous Kuznets Curve which depicts the development of inequality in capitalist countries as an inverted U, inequality peaking before the First World War and then declining continuously. There have been many attempts to deal with this idea, but the pioneering work is without doubt that of Thomas Piketty (2001), an economist close to the *Annales* group, who used tax records to trace the development of high incomes in twentieth-century France. He demonstrated in particular the dual movement of the reduction of inequality (both of income and inherited wealth) between the First World War and the 1980s, and its increase thereafter. How can this be explained? Piketty places emphasis here upon the tax system, whose redistributive effect in France depended on the introduction of an income tax in 1914 and the introduction of a progressive inheritance tax from 1901; the reverse effect being evident in the USA from the early 1980s with the growth of inequality and the measures for tax relief introduced by Reagan. Competing explanations were put forward in the pages of *Annales*. Gilles Postel-Vinay (2003) saw the destruction of wealth brought about by two world wars as the major cause of a reduction in the inequalities of inherited wealth, while François Bourguignon (2003), loyal to the spirit of Kuznets, considers that the rise of a financial capitalism at the end of the century, combined with new technologies, accounts for the growth in inequality. Piketty's second book (2013) expanded upon his account of dynamic inequalities, which he saw as being a permanent characteristic of capitalism, and identified a persistent tendency in the long run for the rate of return on capital to exceed the rate of growth of GDP. A recent collection has examined the prospects for historicising this economic model by identifying different types of capitalism both in time and in space (*Annales HSS* 2015, 1).

Another quantitative approach to inequality can be found in the TRA project, a massive survey launched at the beginning of the 1980s. All French families whose surname begins with the letters TRA have been reconstituted from 1800 onwards until the end of the twentieth century (some 3000 families in all so far). The reconstruction of these individual trajectories to which economic data can be attached (income, legacies, employment) make possible precise analysis of the formation of inequality and how it is reproduced, together with its social and demographic effects (migration, age at death and so on). These were especially important questions in the nineteenth century when forms of access to wealth changed dramatically, with a clear contrast between two paths to wealth: one through work, and the other through inheritance (Bourdieu et al. 2000). This work is today mostly done in the Ecole d'Economie de Paris, where Piketty began his studies of inequality and projected them on to a world scale.

French historiography is always concerned about France's relative backwardness, relative first to Britain, and then to Germany; and, more generally, about the uniqueness of national capitalism, whether France has followed a *Sonderweg* on the path of economic growth since the industrial revolution. Central here are questions about banking and credit, both public and private. Jean Bouvier's study of Crédit Lyonnais (1961), Maurice Lévy-Leboyer's on European banks and nineteenth-century industrialisation (1964), and that of Alain Plessis (1982) on the Bank of France belong to this perspective. Recent works by French and American historians on financial intermediation in the eighteenth and nineteenth centuries share the same idea. In Britain a network of country banks quickly developed, but not in France. How was the economy financed? Using massive collections of legal contracts, Hoffman and others (1994 and 2000) have shown that notaries were very economically efficient as intermediaries, with a strong focus upon Paris; on the eve of the Revolution Parisian notaries were trading half of France's gross private debt, thanks in part to capital drawn from the whole country. In terms of information, costs, availability of short- and long-term credit or the capacity to make use of public borrowing, the network of notaries functioned as effectively as any other financial system. This very success did however have a negative impact, since until the 1860s it impeded the emergence of credit practices linked to commercial and banking activity, which were by then more effective.

The same kind of research into national specificities, especially for the early modern era, has focused upon the nature of public credit, which has been the object of strong international interest since the end of the 1980s and the general rise of national indebtedness. How was an absolutist monarchy like France able to finance the enormous budget deficits caused by war when it had no system of national representation and the state was chronically mistrusted by lenders, unlike Britain after the Glorious Revolution? French historians have sought to understand how a specific way of financing public debt emerged as a synthesis of the practices of other European states such as Britain and Spain. There was a dual principle. On the one hand, wealthy institutions dependent on the monarch to acquire or renew privileges were called upon. Following the work of David Bien on craft guilds (lenders obliged to the king), it has been shown that the venality of public office played an essential role in the financing of public debt from the early seventeenth century (Descimon 2006). On the other hand, those institutions that were to some extent autonomous in relation to the monarchy, and so credible for individuals, were used as intermediaries to guarantee royal borrowing. Bonds issued against the Paris Hotel de Ville from 1522 onwards by the king, but bearing upon the City of Paris, were the most common form of public debt up to the Revolution, and provided a secure and profitable form of investment for the urban bourgeoisie (Béguin 2012).

Criticism of economic categories

Debate on the use in historical studies of the universal categories of economics and, in particular, the principle of a maximising rationality, goes back at least to arguments between substantivists and formalists; but with the rise of New Institutional Economic History and, in particular, its use of game theory, it has come round once more. Avner Greif (2006) claims to combine archival work with highly formalised theory, and his work has made an impact among American economists because he proposes a new way of approaching economic history (for an internal critique of Greif see Boldizzoni 2011). *Institutions and the Path to the Modern Economy* was little read and badly received in France. Apart from the fact that its technical features make it relatively inaccessible to historians, it is entirely contrary to the *Annales* tradition, which since Febvre has been concerned with the historicisation of economic behaviour and attitudes. Robert Boyer has observed that this line of work while 'very convincing for a game theorist, will make the medieval historian smile; for it is marked by the sin of anachronism, attributing to individuals in the Middle Ages the logic and cognitive tools typical of our modern era' (Boyer 2009).

One way of escaping this anachronism is to revert to pre-modern categories. This leads us back to the history of political economy, mostly written by economists, but privileging not their own disciplinary perspective, but the relativist perspective of the historian. It can be shown, working against all teleological temptations, that older economic categories are not simply premature or partial versions of modern economic categories, but rather the product of a particular historical conjuncture. The pioneering works of Jean-Claude Perrot (1992) on the historicity of economic categories were followed by studies that made use of his insights, but also of practical representations, in studying the economies of the eighteenth century. These works have shown, for example, how the idea of profit then prevailing did not involve the idea of maximisation, but of diverse processes in the valorisation of capital (Grenier 1996); or that the dominant economic representation for Enlightenment administration involved an original 'economy of quality', closer to mercantilism than to classic liberal theory (Minard 1998).

Conclusion

Economic history as developed in France has been shaped by the complex relationship of history and economics, varying between times of convergence as in the 1930s, and times of divergence, as at the end of the twentieth century. This was at times out of phase with international developments, and in particular the development of economic history in the USA, as shown for instance in the return to an emphasis on quantitative technique in France in the early years of the twenty-first century, a development not so clearly reflected on the other side of the Atlantic. As is generally known, the roots of this troubled dialogue can be found in major epistemological differences. This line of argument applies to all countries, but it could be said to be a greater problem in France, because there the sensitivity to methodological issues is perhaps greater than elsewhere. This is indicated by the debate between Simiand and positivist historians in the early twentieth century; by discussion of the epistemological significance of numerical data during the 1990s; and, again today, with the resumption of argument over the use of formal rationality in historical understanding.

The distancing of the two disciplines is reinforced by the fact that French economists, whose elite has been trained in the tradition of engineer economists, always struggle with the idea that other social sciences might be of interest, especially history. In return, the tradition of total history represented by *Annales* is one opposed to the presumptions of economics, beginning with the idea that the understanding of economic phenomena is reducible to purely economic terms. The individual is a whole, and none of his or her activities can be thought of in isolation from the others. Nothing is further from this tradition than the idea of *homo oeconomicus*, in spite of the precautions taken by contemporary economists when seeking to insert this idea into the heart of the social sciences. Likewise, at the macro-historical level, the same desire to grasp the totality is always there, whether in Febvre's notion of civilisation, Braudel's *aire culturelle*, or the *économie-monde*.

Paradoxically, there is no need to hope that these tensions will dissipate. Living economic history can be neither an empty compromise, nor a covert annexation of one discipline by another. On the contrary, it needs both disciplines to have their own strong identity; an identity which, at certain moments or in relation to particular individuals, can become conjoined with the other.

Note

1 Translated by Keith Tribe.

References

Annales HSS 2015, 1. *Lire Le capital de Thomas Piketty.*

Annales HSS 2015, 2. *La longue durée en débat.*

Armitage, David and Jo Guldi. 2014. *The History Manifesto.* Cambridge, Cambridge University Press.

Barkan, Ömer Lutfi. 1954. 'La Méditerranée vue d'Istamboul', *Annales ESC*, 4, 189–200.

Béguin, Katia. 2012. *Financer la guerre au XVIIe siècle. La dette publique et les rentiers de l'absolutisme.* Seyssel, Champ Vallon.

Bin Wong, R. 2001. 'Entre monde et nation: les régions braudéliennes en Asie', *Annales HSS*, 1, 5–41.

Boldizzoni, Francesco. 2011. *The Poverty of Clio: Resurrecting Economic History.* Princeton, NJ, Princeton University Press.

Bonin, Hubert et al. 2008. *L'esprit économique impérial (1830–1970): groupes de pression et réseaux du patronat colonial en France et dans l'empire.* Paris, Publications de la SFHOM.

Bourdieu, Jérôme, Gilles Postel-Vinay, Paul-André Rosental and Akiko Suwa. 2000. 'Migrations et transmissions inter-générationnelles dans la France du XIXe et du début du XXe siècle', *Annales HSS*, 4, 749–89.

Bourguignon, François. 2003. 'La chute des inégalités françaises au XXème siècle. Explications alternatives', *Annales HSS*, 58.3, 675–86.

Bourguignon, François and Maurice Lévy-Leboyer. 1985. *L'économie française au XIXe siècle: analyse macro-économique.* Paris, Economica.

Boutang, Yann Moulier. 1998. *De l'esclavage au salariat. Economie historique du salariat bridé.* Paris, Presses Universitaires de France.

Bouvier, Jean. 1961. *Le Crédit lyonnais de 1863 à 1882.* Paris, SEVPEN.

Boyer, Robert. 1986. *La théorie de la regulation: une analyse critique.* Paris, La Découverte.

Boyer, Robert. 1989. 'Economie et histoire: vers de nouvelles alliances?', *Annales ESC*, 6, 1397–1426.

Boyer, Robert. 2009. 'Historiens et économistes face à l'émergence des institutions du marché', *Annales HSS*, 3, 665–93.

Braudel, Fernand. 1949 (2nd edn. 1966). *La Méditerranée et le monde méditerranéen à l'époque de Philippe II.* Paris, Armand Colin (*The Mediterranean and the Mediterranean World in the Age of Philip II.* New York, Harper & Row, 1972).

Braudel, Fernand. 1958. 'Histoire et sciences sociales. La longue durée', *Annales ESC*, 4, 725–53.

Braudel, Fernand. 1979a. *Civilisation matérielle, économie et capitalisme, XVe–XVIIIe siècle.* Paris, Armand Colin (*Civilization and Capitalism: 15th–18th Century.* 3 vols. London, Collins, 1982–84).

Braudel, Fernand. 1979b. *Afterthoughts on Material Civilization and Capitalism.* Baltimore, MD, Johns Hopkins University Press.

Castan, Yves. 1974. *Honnêteté et relations sociales en Languedoc 1715–1780.* Paris, Plon.

Chaudhuri, K. N. 1985. *Trade and Civilisation in the Indian Ocean: An Economic History from the Rise of Islam to 1750.* Cambridge, Cambridge University Press.

Chaudhuri, K. N. 1990. *Asia before Europe: Economy and Civilisation of the Indian Ocean from the Rise of Islam to 1750.* Cambridge, Cambridge University Press.

Coquery-Vidrovitch, Catherine. 1969. 'Recherches sur un mode de production africain', *La Pensée*, 4, 61–78.

Coquery-Vidrovitch, Catherine. 1972. *Le Congo au temps des grandes compagnies concessionnaires, 1898–1930.* Paris, Mouton.

Cullen, Louis. 2005. 'Labrousse, the Annales School, and Histoire sans Frontières', *Journal of European Economic History*, 34–1, 319–50.

Descimon, Robert. 2006. 'La vénalité des offices comme dette publique sous l'Ancien Régime français. Le bien commun au pays des intérêts privés', in Andreau, Jean, Gérard Béaur and Jean-Yves Grenier (eds.) *La dette publique dans l'histoire.* Paris, Comité pour l'histoire économique et financière, 177–242.

Desrosières, Alain. 1993. *La politique des grands nombres: histoire de la raison statistique.* Paris, La Découverte (*The Politics of Large Numbers: A History of Statistical Reasoning.* Cambridge, MA, Harvard University Press, 1998).

Dessert, Daniel. 1984. *Argent, pouvoir et société au Grand siècle.* Paris, Fayard.

Duby, Georges. 1973. *Guerriers et paysans: premier essor de l'économie européenne.* Paris, Gallimard.

Dupâquier, Jacques. 1979. *La population rurale du Bassin parisien à l'époque de Louis XIV.* Paris, Editions de l'Ecole des Hautes Etudes en Sciences Sociales.

Furet, François. 1978. *Penser la Révolution française.* Paris, Gallimard (*Interpreting the French Revolution.* Cambridge, Cambridge University Press, 1981).

Goody, Jack. 2006. *The Theft of History.* Cambridge, Cambridge University Press.

Grantham, George. 1997. 'The French Cliometric Revolution: A Survey of Cliometric Contributions to French Economic History', *European Review of Economic History,* 1, 353–405.

Greif, Avner. 2006. *Institutions and the Path to the Modern Economy: Lessons from Medieval Trade.* Cambridge, Cambridge University Press.

Grenier, Jean-Yves. 1996. *L'économie d'Ancien Régime. Un monde de l'échange et de l'incertitude.* Paris, Albin Michel.

Hamon, Philippe. 1994. *L'argent du roi: les finances sous François Ier.* Paris, Comité pour l'histoire économique et financière de la France.

Hirsch, Jean-Pierre. 1991. *Les deux rêves du commerce. Entreprise et institution dans la région lilloise (1780–1860).* Paris, Editions de l'Ecole des Hautes Etudes en Sciences Sociales.

Hoffman, Philip, Gilles Postel-Vinay and Jean-Laurent Rosenthal. 1994. 'Economie et politique: les marchés du crédit à Paris, 1750–1840', *Annales HSS*, 49, 65–98.

Hoffman, Philip, Gilles Postel-Vinay and Jean-Laurent Rosenthal. 2000. *Priceless Markets: The Political Economy of Credit in Paris, 1660–1870.* Chicago, IL, University of Chicago Press.

Labrousse, C.-E. 1933. *Esquisse du mouvement des prix et des revenus en France au XVIIIe siècle.* Paris, Dalloz.

Labrousse, C.-E. 1944. *La crise de l'économie française à la fin de l'Ancien Régime et au début de la Révolution.* Paris, Presses Universitaires de France.

Landes, David. 1950. 'The statistical study of French crises', *Journal of Economic History,* 10, 195–211.

Le Roy Ladurie, Emmanuel. 1959. *Histoire du climat depuis l'an mil.* Paris, Flammarion.

Le Roy Ladurie, Emmanuel. 1966. *Les paysans de Languedoc.* Paris, SEVPEN.

Le Roy Ladurie, Emmanuel. 1983. *La sorcière de Jasmin.* Paris, Seuil.

Lévi-Strauss, Claude. 1958. *Anthropologie structurale.* Paris, Plon.

Lévy-Leboyer, Maurice. 1964. *Les banques européennes et l'industrialisation internationale dans la première moitié du XIXe siècle.* Paris, Presses Universitaires de France.

Lombard, Denys. 1990. *Le carrefour javanais. Essai d'histoire globale,* 3 vols. Paris, Editions de l'Ecole des Hautes Etudes en Sciences Sociales.

Marseille, Jacques. 1989. *Empire colonial et capitalisme français: histoire d'un divorce.* Paris, Albin Michel.

Marchand, Olivier and Claude Thélot. 1991. *Deux siècles de travail en France.* Paris, INSEE.

Meillassoux, Claude. 1986. *Anthropologie de l'esclavage. Le ventre de fer et d'argent.* Paris, Presses Universitaires de France (*The Anthropology of Slavery: The Womb of Iron and Gold.* London, Athlone Press, 1991).

Minard, Philippe. 1998. *La fortune du colbertisme. Etat et économie dans la France des Lumières.* Paris, Fayard.

Oudin-Bastide, Caroline. 2005. *Travail, capitalisme et société esclavagiste, XVIIe–XIXe siècle.* Paris, La Découverte.

Perrot, Jean-Claude. 1975. *Genèse d'une ville moderne: Caen au XVIIIe siècle.* Paris, Editions de l'Ecole des Hautes Etudes en Sciences Sociales.

Perrot, Jean-Claude. 1992. *Une histoire intellectuelle de l'économie politique, XVIIe–XVIIIe siècle.* Paris, Editions de l'Ecole des Hautes Etudes en Sciences Sociales.

Piketty, Thomas. 2001. *Les hauts revenus en France au XXe siècle. Inégalités et redistributions, 1901–1998.* Paris, Grasset.

Piketty, Thomas. 2013. *Le capital au XXIe siècle,* Paris, Seuil (*Capital in the Twenty-First Century.* Cambridge, MA, Harvard University Press, 2014).

Plessis, Alain. 1982. *La Banque de France et ses deux cents actionnaires sous le Second Empire.* Geneva, Droz.

Postel-Vinay, Gilles. 2003. 'La question des hauts revenus. Un programme? Des programmes', *Annales HSS*, 58.3, 687–97.

Reid, Anthony. 1988 and 1993. *Southeast Asia in the Age of Commerce, 1450–1680,* 2 vols. New Haven, CT, Yale University Press.

Revel, Jacques. 1979. 'Histoire et sciences sociales: le paradigme des Annales', *Annales ESC*, 6, 1360–76.

Richet, Denis. 1968. 'Croissance et blocages en France du XVe au XVIIIe siècle', *Annales ESC*, 4, 759–87.
Rodinson, Maxime. 1966. *Islam et capitalisme.* Paris, Seuil (*Islam and Capitalism.* London, Saqi, 2007).
Rosenthal, Jean-Laurent. 1992. *The Fruits of Revolution: Property Rights, Litigation and French Agriculture 1700–1860.* Cambridge, Cambridge University Press.
Simiand, François. 1932. *Recherches anciennes et nouvelles sur le mouvement général des prix du XVIe au XIXe siècle.* Paris, Domat-Montchrétien.
Simiand, François. 1932. *Le salaire, l'évolution sociale et la monnaie*, 3 vols. Paris, Félix Alcan.
Tarrade, Jean. 1972. *Le commerce colonial de la France à la fin de l'Ancien Régime.* Paris, Presses Universitaires de France.
Wallerstein, Immanuel. 1974, 1980 and 1989. *The Modern World System*, 3 vols. New York, Academic Press.

8

THE FLIGHT OF ICARUS

Economic history in the Italian mirror

Francesco Boldizzoni

Although systematic forms of economic thinking could already be found in the Renaissance states, and Italian political economy produced its classic works during the Enlightenment, the study of economic history emerged from the great transformations of the twentieth century. The reasons lie as much in the political as in the economic and intellectual spheres.

Around 1848, Italy was still no more than 'a geographical expression', as Prince Klemens von Metternich famously wrote. The state-building process set in motion by the unification under the House of Savoy (1860–70) was accomplished quickly and from above. More than control over its territory, what the new state really needed was legitimation, and the rhetoric of the Risorgimento offered a convenient political narrative. It is quite revealing that, while this process was underway, 'statistical histories' produced by local history societies proliferated and were instrumental in reinforcing municipal identities (Patriarca 1996: 222–3).

This is not to say that attempts at the construction of a national imaginary were not made before. The dream of unifying what was once the backbone of the Roman Empire was cherished by intellectuals since the age of Dante. But the economic past was generally not part of the narrative. One exception is the *Dissertazioni sopra le antichità italiane* which Lodovico Antonio Muratori wrote in the first half of the eighteenth century with the clear intent to present the Middle Ages as a formative period for modern Italian civilization. This work, along with chapters devoted to the most esoteric topics (from the evolution of language to the origin of surnames, from political and religious institutions to women's customs), indeed includes considerations on public finances, money, trade and markets. Historical digressions were otherwise made by almost all the classical economic thinkers, as illustrative examples of their theories of value or arguments on the division of labour. In Antonio Genovesi's *Lezioni di economia civile* (1765) or Pietro Verri's *Meditazioni sulla economia politica* (1771), both of which enjoyed wide international circulation at the time, history performed the same function it had for Richard Cantillon or Adam Smith. It was not, however, a subject in itself.

In the context of European industrialization, Italy was a late joiner. The sense of rupture and separation between the present and the past created by the industrial revolution, which in many cases explains the arousal of historiographical interests, was not felt until the age of avant-gardes. An indicative point in time is the year 1909, when Filippo Tommaso Marinetti published his 'Manifesto of Futurism'. However, when the first signs of industrial growth appeared, at the turn of the century, the intellectual scene was dominated by idealism, a current that would continue to blossom until the 1930s. Only after the definitive fall of Fascism (1945), did Marxism start to gain a foothold. From the beginning, the discipline of economic history developed polycentrically. Along with persistent differences between the North and the South, it is the very strong sense of local identities, whose origins can be traced back as far as to the institutional particularism of medieval communes, which explains the absence of a national school, like the German Historical School or the French *Annales*, and even of a dominant school.

The formative years

The idealist philosophies of Benedetto Croce and Giovanni Gentile were different in many respects (not the least, for their opposite political implications). Nevertheless, both of them started from the Hegelian equivalence between the 'real' and the 'rational' which, in their view, gave order to history. Gentile's influence on historiography did not extend beyond the history of ideas. Croce, who wrote a piece on 'the way to understand pure economic historiography' (1942), conceived of economic history as a technical history. The reference to a 'pure' economic history echoed early twentieth-century controversies about the foundations of economics and the existence of an invariable (utilitarian) 'economic nature' in which he had been involved along with economists such as Vilfredo Pareto and Maffeo Pantaleoni. In fact, Croce's position, and the terms of the debate itself, appear to be quite confused (as Antonio Gramsci did not fail to notice in the *Prison Notebooks*) and had little impact on actual economic-history writing. The long-lasting consequence of idealism was a more practical one. It kept economic history and other *storie speciali* ('special histories') away from the historiographical mainstream and its temples, the faculties of letters and philosophy, thus relegating them to a second-rate existence.

Economic history as a discipline entered Italian academia in the early 1920s when chairs in the new faculties of economics and commerce, recently elevated to full university status, were established. It replaced a subject known as 'history of trade', a branch of legal history mainly concerned with rules and contracts in the medieval and early modern period. This clearly represented the back door into a historical profession that was quite conservative and still largely dominated by high political history. The pioneers were men born in the 1870s. First of all was Gino Luzzatto. Influenced by German historicism, he received an eclectic education, emphasizing juridical and institutional aspects. It would not be entirely correct to say that he came to economic history from legal history, as his interest in socioeconomic problems dates back to his pre-university years, when he got in touch with an unconventional economist and sociologist, Achille Loria.[1] Luzzatto mainly wrote about trade and public finance, but touched on many more aspects, all of them having in common the unit of analysis of the regional state. In his maturity, he devoted himself almost completely to the history of Venice. He was the author of the first economic history textbook (Luzzatto 1932–48) which set the standard for the future development of the discipline.

In 1936 the first specialized journal, *Rivista di Storia Economica*, was founded by Luigi Einaudi. Einaudi was a liberal economist working on public finance. Like many economists of his generation, he was also a practitioner of what Joseph Schumpeter called the 'history of economic analysis'. He used to convey his policy ideas through *La Riforma Sociale*, but in the mid-1930s this periodical, which did not endorse the corporatist doctrine and protectionist policies of the Fascist regime, had to close down. Einaudi then sought refuge in history. The new journal, however, was not the first one that dealt with economic history. In 1917 Corrado

Barbagallo had founded the *Nuova Rivista Storica* to counter philologist approaches to history-writing and to promote a sociohistorical approach instead. Although not a field journal, it had, from its inception, regularly published economic history articles.

Einaudi wrote little about economic history strictly conceived, and his best work is probably 'The Theory of Imaginary Money from Charlemagne to the French Revolution' (1936). To make up for this, he made a number of interventions on methodology. In one of the first issues of the *Rivista*, he argued with the *Annales* about the proper way to write intellectual history. Lucien Febvre maintained that economic ideas had to be contextualized. Einaudi, on the contrary, argued for a 'rational reconstruction' and the primacy of internal history. There followed a debate with Luzzatto who, standing on Febvre's side, stressed how ideas can be used to throw light on contemporary economic and social life. Einaudi reasserted that ideas have a history of their own, and this is a history of progress from error to reason. The same distance separated the two scholars when it came to conceptualizing the history of facts. According to Einaudi, economic history was to be a history from the 'economic point of view', and deal with how men and women solved 'the economic problem' in past times. Luzzatto's purview was broader and more inclusive. Here we can see a rather typical example of early controversies between formalist and substantivist conceptions of economic history.[2]

If Luzzatto is often considered the founding father of Italian economic history, the role of Barbagallo, who established the discipline in the South, can hardly be overstated. More distant from German culture and, since his youth, a supporter of historical materialism, he was dubbed by Gentile an 'angry socialist' because of his polemical verve.[3] In fact, Barbagallo was a polymath who cultivated interests in the decline of civilizations no less ambitious than those of Edward Gibbon or Oswald Spengler. His encyclopedic, if unsystematic, erudition made him an heir of the great Southern intellectuals from Giambattista Vico on. In the interwar period, he extended his interests to the modern era. Before committing full-time to a five-volume 'universal history' of mankind (1931–38), he wrote an account of 'capital and labour throughout the centuries' (Barbagallo 1927), which was criticized by Gramsci for the 'author's inclination to see in antiquity what is quintessentially modern, such as capitalism and the related phenomena' (1975: 382). Barbagallo's most remarkable contribution to the field was *Le origini della grande industria contemporanea* (1929–30), a comparative history of the industrial revolution.

In the post-war years, with Barbagallo's and Luzzatto's disappearance from the scene, another trait faded that had characterized the beginnings of Italian economic history – the integration of ancient and modern, favoured by the sound classical training of nearly all academics of their generation. Ancient economic and social history, which has an outstanding tradition in the country, would henceforth develop along specific paths which will not be covered here.

The post-war boom, 1945–75

In the 1950s and 1960s the Italian economy grew steadily at rates of 5–6 per cent per annum. During this period, known as *il miracolo,* what was still a half-agricultural country became one of the world's major industrial powers. They were years marked by great optimism and unparalleled levels of intellectual and artistic creativity, which found expression in the renewal of entire fields, from political philosophy to chemistry, from literature to cinematography, from architecture to industrial design.

New themes inevitably came to the fore. Some wondered why an economy that had been so advanced in the Middle Ages and Renaissance could fall behind for centuries. Carlo

Cipolla inaugurated the topos of the economic decline of Italy in an article first published in 1952 in the *Economic History Review*. The essay revolved around a simple idea: the crisis of early modern Italian manufactures was due to to the growing competition from Northwestern Europe but also to internal causes. In line with the neoclassical interpretations of the time, he emphasized the loss of entrepreneurial drive and stickiness of the labour market, whose development was prevented by the guilds. Cipolla restated the same thesis, with little variation, in 1959 and 1970, in his collection on *The Economic Decline of Empires*. Yet in 1974, at a conference on 'failed transitions' to modernity, he added something important. He contested 'the (arbitrary) assumption that all proto-capitalistic economies could or should lead to an industrial revolution' (Cipolla 1975: 8) because 'they possessed "traits" that scholars construed as typical of the "industrial world"'. Indeed, as Jeff Horn and colleagues note, 'long before the concept appeared, Cipolla understood that there was no single, "great divergence"' (2010: 7).

If one excepts Renato Zangheri's (1969) Marxist counter-argument, which insisted on the incomplete transition to capitalism of the medieval economy, it was only in the late 1970s that the problem was revisited (Sella 1979; Malanima 1982). Domenico Sella, in particular, made clear in his *Crisis and Continuity* that the Lombard decline was only relative and he gave a more nuanced picture of the seventeenth century. Unhappy with the urban bias of the existing literature, he turned to the countryside and reinterpreted deindustrialization as proto-industrialization. He could rely on the vast body of research on agricultural history that had been accumulating since the post-war years. It may seem paradoxical but early modern rural history began to be taken seriously when Italy ceased to be an economy mainly based on agriculture.

The industrial dream of the early twentieth century had kept historians focused on manufacture, and nostalgia for the Italian golden age had long attracted them to trade and merchant capitalism. At best, they interpreted investment in land as an expression of the instrumental rationality of urban businessmen. The merit for overturning this view goes to Aldo De Maddalena, who gradually developed a sociocultural interpretation. He showed that the actors' psychology was pervaded by emotional elements, which explains why attachment to land was stronger in times of crisis and lack of confidence.[4] Lombard agriculture was also investigated by Mario Romani (1957), who covered the age of Austrian reforms up to the unification, stressing distributive and social aspects. Other studies of inequality include Zangheri (1961) and Beltrami (1961). The latter wrote on the Republic of Venice, where landownership was increasingly concentrated in the hands of aristocracy. He indicted the Venetian ruling class, once a dynamic mercantile elite, for turning into an elite of lazy rentiers.

Eclecticism took rural history in unexpected directions. This was the case of Emilio Sereni and his masterpiece, the *History of the Italian Agricultural Landscape*, first published in 1961. Sereni represents agrarian landscape as an artificial construction. This man-made environment is the result of the interplay of 'productive forces' and 'relations of production'. But, at the same time, its sedimentation over the centuries in the form of crystallized structures places a limit on the development of those relations, in a way that reminds one of Braudel's interpretation of geography. Another important work of synthesis was Giorgio Giorgetti's (1974). Through the analysis of agrarian contracts, he was able to write a history of the relations of production in Italian agriculture from the sixteenth to the twentieth centuries. The progressive transition to agrarian capitalism brought with it the pursuit of productivity which impacted on the juridical framework.

This approach called into question a hidden variable – labour, which occupied a central place in the intellectual life of Luigi Dal Pane. Dal Pane's interest in labour history dates back to the 1940s. Influenced in his youth by Darwin and Marx, well read in German historical economics and close to the ideas of Antonio Labriola, he embraced a non-dogmatic form of historical materialism, alien from determinism and paying attention to the reciprocal conditioning between material base and sociocultural superstructure (Cazzola 2014). His *La storia come storia del lavoro* (1968) may be considered the manifesto of the Bologna school. The title has a twofold meaning. On the one hand, it conveys the idea that history, to be a social science, needs to be written from the point of view of those who make it through their own toil. On the other, it warns that labour history cannot be separated from the other aspects of social life. Hence it is, at the same time, a part and the engine of 'total history'.

Last but not least came the history of prices, wages and money. Price history, which elsewhere rose to prominence in the interwar years, had a delayed start in Italy. Fascist Italy was excluded from the international data-mining project led by William Beveridge and Edwin F. Gay (financed by the Rockefeller Foundation) and those who wished to enter the field did it their own way (Parenti 1939; Fanfani 1940). In the post-war period this genre enjoyed a surprising surge of interest. There is no obvious explanation for such a revival, as the macroeconomic stability of those years would have suggested different historiographical concerns – it may well be that the boom reminded historians of the sixteenth-century 'price revolution'. Anyway, the pioneering work was De Maddalena's (1949) reconstruction of prices in Milan. It was innovative in the use of sophisticated quantitative techniques and the unconventional choice of not converting prices into grams of silver. De Maddalena believed that what matters to the historian of everyday life is the pattern of living standards, not that of the purchasing power of silver.[5] Only a few daring people, by contrast, ventured into the technicalities of monetary history. Here we find again Cipolla (1956), who later thought 'with horror at the kind of "specialist" [he] might have become' (1970b: 73), his younger colleague Giuseppe Felloni (1968), Roberto Lopez (1951) and Ugo Tucci (1981).

Not all post-war historiography was cutting-edge, nor were virtuous examples prevalent. A non-negligible proportion of what was produced in the 1950s and 1960s consisted in the tired repetition of interwar historiographical models. The old history of trade had by no means disappeared. It retained its heroes – above all, the merchant capitalist – and its original focus on the Middle Ages. While some of this work has interesting things to say about commodities and commodity chains – from salt and sugar to fustian and dyes (e.g. Borlandi 1949) – most of it is either descriptive or asks trivial questions. For instance, Federigo Melis, who was from Florence, set out to prove that Florentines had some priority in inventing double-entry bookkeeping and banking historians working on Genoa and Tuscany were lost in endless controversies as to whether banking originated from the former or the latter. They were mercilessly depicted as academic 'ghosts' in a biting pamphlet by Ruggiero Romano (1978: 38).

The Indian summer, 1975–95

By the early 1970s, the golden age of the Italian economy was over. The slowdown of growth put an end to social peace and the country was not spared the oil shocks that hit the Western economies. The government attempted to turn inflation to its own advantage and increasingly resorted to public debt creation. Unlike in other European countries, however, the conflict between capital and labour took violent forms, with subversive actions by the Red Brigades culminating in the kidnapping and murder of former prime minister Aldo Moro (1978). In the same years, the university system underwent radical transformations. With the baby boomers grown up, universities lost much of their elitist character and turned into mass higher education providers. This had serious consequences on faculty recruitment as it resulted in an unprecedented number of people entering the academic profession. Unfortunately not all of these newcomers were up to the standard of their predecessors. Nevertheless, in 1984, the growth of the scholarly community led to the founding of the Italian Economic History Society.

The main historiographical novelty of the period was the rise of microhistory, which was consolidated from the end of the 1970s through the 1980s. Although mainly interested in sociocultural aspects, microhistorians made relevant contributions to economic history. Carlo Poni is the key figure for us. He trained in Bologna under Dal Pane and this Marxist background is evident in an early work on the plough (1963), where technology is used as a key to grasp the 'mode of production' in an attempt to write a social history of production. Poni was the only full-fledged economic historian in the quadrumvirate with Carlo Ginzburg, Giovanni Levi and Edoardo Grendi, dating back to their common militancy in the journal *Quaderni Storici*, and somewhat set apart from the group (he was not involved in the 'Microstorie' book series). He spent most of his career studying the functioning of hydraulic silk mills, also known as 'Bolognese mills', which spread throughout Northern Italy in the seventeenth and eighteenth centuries and were the prototype for the English mills (Poni 2009). Of course, meticulous research on technology and technological transfer and an almost obsessive taste for detail stemmed from the need to answer big questions. Poni found that centralized production, whose scale was sometimes remarkable, required a new organizational model and work discipline. Among mill workers, he even found examples of active resistance similar to those described by E. P. Thompson. But he also insisted, in accordance with Paul Mantoux, that this proto-factory system did not lead to an industrial revolution in Italy as much as in England. Costly silk would not find a market nearly as large as cotton.

Giovanni Levi is best known for his *Inheriting Power* (1985), which is only apparently 'the story of an exorcist' in seventeenth-century Piedmont, as the book's subtitle says. Levi shows that in ancien régime societies the intergenerational transfer of power, prestige, offices and professions was as much if not more important as that of land and money. He also dealt with eighteenth-century political arithmetic and experimented with the reconstruction of preindustrial consumption patterns through household accounts (an example of 'small-scale' observation), arguing that they depended on more complex factors beyond mere necessity. Edoardo Grendi, who had trained as a labour historian under Ralph Miliband, was mainly attracted by sociopolitical issues. However, in an essay from 1987, he used his historical–ethnographic method to interpret money counterfeiting in early modern Genoa and unveiled how deviance and the social life of money were inextricably intertwined with monetary structures.

According to Peter Burke (2008), Cipolla predated microhistory with his little books on the history of public health in the Grand Duchy of Tuscany, the first of which was *Cristofano and the Plague* (1973). They are idiographic not only in the sense that social histories are mirrored in individual biographies, but above all because they emphasize human agency. Whatever the case, microhistorians were not alone in their enthusiasm for microanalysis. A more widespread trend towards the latter can be observed in the intellectual context of the 1970s. These approaches did not always share, and even openly rejected, some of the methodological hallmarks of microhistory, such as its reliance on 'clues' and 'traces' as opposed to statistical regularities, which so much contributed to the self-identification of the affiliates (Ginzburg 1989; 1993: 21–2). For instance, the early work of Paolo Malanima (1977) on the private wealth of the Riccardi, a Florentine banker family which accomplished its social ascent thanks to a privileged political relationship with the Medici, took a more conservative stance in this respect.

An example of microanalysis that cannot be classified as either microhistory or idiographic history is Marco Cattini's (1984) important book on the peasants of San Felice, a village on the eastern border of the Duchy of Modena. The title echoes Le Roy Ladurie (1966) and the work itself stands along with other studies of rural communities (e.g. Doria 1968; Assante 1999). What is distinctive about it is the attempt Cattini made to model preindustrial microeconomics. In the wake of Kula (1962), he demonstrated that the 'laws' of supply and demand did not apply to the early modern Po valley. A mix of cultural, technological and environmental elements prevented the actors from responding to price signals. Their behaviour was either non-strategic or oriented towards non-economic goals. When it was market-oriented, it was subject to the constraints posed by the substantial unpredictability of the agrarian cycle.

It is not difficult to recognize in this particular taste for the small scale one of the *caractères originaux* of Italian civilization. Another characteristic almost timeless is urban culture. In what has been, since antiquity, one of the most urbanized areas of Europe, it makes sense that the history of towns and cities should occupy a central place. Urban history has developed into a variety of subfields and produced original results especially in conjunction with the history of consumption and ecological history, as in the more recent case of histories of waste.[6] On the other hand, quite specific to the milieu of the 1970s was a marked interest in public finance. The growing public debt and concurrent debates on expenditure and taxation prompted historians to look back into the past, as in the case with Vigo's (1979) study of sixteenth-century Lombardy and Stumpo's (1979) work on seventeenth-century Piedmont. Meanwhile, economic maturity brought about the need to make sense of the industrialization process. Giorgio Mori's (1967) collection of essays on industrial history is an early example of history from below focusing on factories and workers. Franco Bonelli's (1975) work on steel pioneered the study of business history and that of Valerio Castronovo (1977) on the Turin car entrepreneurs shed light on the history of Italian industrial capitalism in its love–hate relationship with the state. Vera Zamagni (1978) also wrote about the early industrial days. The first comprehensive textbooks were published in the early 1990s (Toniolo 1988; Zamagni 1993; Castronovo 1995).

In this phase, too, only a few scholars wrote about the history of other countries, and they generally dealt with money: among them, Claudio Rotelli (1982) and Marcello De Cecco (1974) tackled the English bullionist controversy and the international gold standard respectively; Manuela Albertone (1992) explored monetary ideas and the crisis of public finance in pre-revolutionary France. The history of economic thought grew in the 1980s and 1990s, favoured by the massive presence of heterodox economists, particularly post-Keynesian and neo-Ricardian. Unfortunately, however, its privileged relationship with economics prevented it from integrating into the broader field of intellectual history. The heroic example of Franco Venturi (1969), who situated eighteenth-century economic ideas within the context of his monumental fresco of the Enlightenment, found no followers. Despite some positive exceptions (e.g. Bianchini 1982; Guidi 1991; Romani 2002), as a whole the field still seems to conform to Croce's ideal of a 'special history'.

Historiographical itineraries

The overall picture outlined thus far can be further refined by breaking down the intellectual history of the discipline into a limited number of significant dichotomies. I would like to suggest two possible templates for analysis. The first and more obvious dichotomy is *North and South*. The development of economic history in the South was dominated by two main figures, Luigi De Rosa and Domenico Demarco, both students of Barbagallo, to whom we should perhaps add Giuseppe Galasso, who was a pupil of Croce. Their rivalry is legendary and went so far as to involve their respective schools which fought each other for decades. Given the paramount interest in the early modern period that has characterized both North and South, there are not substantial differences in the themes covered. In fact, a first-rate scholar like De Rosa tackled in his career all the main aspects of preindustrial economic history with the sole exception of agriculture (see Barbato 2010). What is really specific to the South is the attention paid to the problem of Italian economic dualism also known as the 'Southern question'.

The post-war debate was sparked off by Sereni's work *Il capitalismo nelle campagne* (1947), in which he coined the phrase 'history from below'. Sereni claimed that nineteenth-century Southern peasants were unable to get rid of feudal constraints and evolve into a modern class of consumers. The resulting low demand for goods would hinder industrialization. For Rosario Romeo (1959), on the contrary, it was this chronic underconsumption in the South that made possible Italian economic development. Capital accumulation and the construction of infrastructures required savings and a high tax burden placed on Southern agriculture. This view was criticized by Alexander Gerschenkron (1962) who argued that the banking system, and not the state, was the engine of the country's take-off. Luciano Cafagna (1989) maintained that economic growth had been more gradual than assumed in big-spurt models and proposed a bottom-up interpretation based on entrepreneurial agency. By stressing the importance of the silk proto-industry, he showed that the advantage of Lombardy and Piedmont over the South was already substantial before the unification. Therefore the North had no responsibilities in the underdevelopment of the South.

Meanwhile American social scientists had got in. Edward Banfield and Robert Putnam chose Italy as a lab to test their hypotheses on modernization and social cohesion. Banfield (1958) explained Southern backwardness in terms of the culture of 'amoral familism' that prevented close-knit social groups from pursuing the public good. Putnam (1993) also blamed the lack of 'social capital' and contrasted the vicious South to the virtuous North, romantically depicted as the cradle of Western republican liberties. The debate on institutions and culture has recently been revisited by Felice (2014). Following Acemoglu and Robinson (2012), he ascribes the region's persistent backwardness to the 'extractive institutions' inherited from the Kingdom of Naples. By blaming local elites, as Gaetano Salvemini (1955) already had, he absolves 'culture'. However, once again economic stagnation is seen as a sin which has to be wiped away rather than, for instance, the result of a value structure that does not put economic growth first.[7] Of course, truth may be in the middle. In any case it is hard to ignore that neither Southern Spain nor Greece are as wealthy as Catalonia or Bavaria, and this indicates that geography must play some role after all.

The second way to interpret this story, and Italian intellectual history more generally, is in terms of the partisan allegiances of *Catholics and Marxists*. Although closely tied to the politics of the period 1945–90, the significance of such a distinction is deeper as it exposes the mixture of sacred and profane, religious culture and secular institutions, at the root of Italian identity. These ideological and methodological affiliations had a strong geographical correlation. Marxist approaches tended to prevail in left-wing regions such as Emilia-Romagna and Tuscany while Catholic schools concentrated in Lombardy and the Veneto, where the Christian democratic party enjoyed considerable support. Historians in the South were more agnostic. For public intellectuals like Sereni, the identification of scholarship with politics was almost complete. On the contrary, Dal Pane insisted that scientific activity and civic engagement should be kept separate. What many figures had in common was their active role in politics: Sereni, Fanfani and Galasso held government positions, Zangheri and others served in parliament, Romani in the unions.

Marxist history-writing owed less to Marx than to the original developments of Labriola and Gramsci. If, on the one hand, some of the concepts envisioned by Gramsci such as 'subaltern classes', 'popular culture' and 'cultural hegemony' were more influential abroad and in the Global South, on the other hand Italian historiography retained a distinctive structuralist character. On the methodological plane, the emphasis placed on structures rather than on agency represents one of the most significant differences between Marxists and Catholics.[8] In Catholic academic circles, faith in human agency was sometimes taken to the extreme. For example, Fanfani, who made a name for himself with the controversial book *Catholicism, Protestantism, and Capitalism* (1934), argued against historical determinism on the ground of a doctrine of free will and the unfolding of providence in human history, something that was stigmatized by Barbagallo as unscientific (De Rosa 1990: 101–7). As in the case of the Marxists, however, we should make a distinction between Catholic historians and historians who happened to be Catholic, the scholarship of whom was not driven by their own religious beliefs (Romano 1978: 65).

Openness, influences and impact

Other interpretive clues may be derived from the coexistence of insiders and expatriates, which is a common finding in the global history of the discipline but is so important in this case as to give Italian economic history a 'dual' nature. Cipolla's joint appointment at Berkeley in the late 1950s came as a breath of fresh air, as he wrote in an autobiographical essay. For the first time in his life, he 'felt' the reality of Asia (1970b: 75). This led to a broadening of his interests, which resulted in books like *Guns, Sails, and Empires* (1965) or *Clocks and Culture* (1967). Ruggiero Romano (1992) and Marcello Carmagnani (2011), from their headquarters in Paris and Mexico City respectively, investigated the *longue durée* interdependencies between Europe and Latin America, thus contributing to the field of world history.[9] It was in Eastern Africa that Giovanni Arrighi, who later taught historical sociology in the United States, had his first encounter with world-systems theory. For others such as Lopez (who left Italy in 1939 after the introduction of the racial laws) and Sella (who followed Cipolla across the Atlantic) relocation abroad does not seem to have been a factor in the development of new research interests.

With the exception of Romano, who fell in love with the *Annales* in his early twenties, expatriates in the post-war period were already established scholars. By contrast, historians of the younger generations have almost invariably joined foreign universities as graduate students. This is paradoxical and suggests that, in the present age of unprecedented globalization, academic communities are more closed to cross-fertilization than they used to be in the past. Alessandro Stanziani, Luca Molà, Francesca Trivellato, Maria Fusaro and Giorgio Riello – to give some examples – have gradually embraced global/transnational perspectives as a result of their training in France, the United States and Britain.[10] Another difference lies in the ties kept with the motherland, which used to be stronger in the earlier generations. Thanks to their role as cultural mediators, expatriates had contributed substantially to opening up Italian economic history to external influences.

At this point, we should try to take stock of these external influences vis-à-vis the international impact of the local historiographical production. Until the 1970s, translations were an important medium for the circulation of ideas. Luzzatto himself did many translations of German authors including Ludo M. Hartmann, Friedrich Naumann, Walther Rathenau, Alfred Doren and, above all, Werner Sombart. Under the supervision of Romano, the Einaudi publishing powerhouse built a strong history list. Starting with Braudel's *Mediterranean* (1953), all the main works of *Annales* historians and of their international allies such as Witold Kula and Paul Bairoch were speedily made available in Italian. Also inspired by the French model were the *Storia d'Italia* (a multi-volume series started in 1972) and the *Storia d'Europa* (1993–96). Eventually, an Italian edition of the *Cambridge Economic History of Europe* (1966–89) was produced between 1976 and 1992.

Without Braudel, it would be difficult to imagine how the Istituto Datini, established in Prato in 1967, could have taken off. For about 15 years it was really a major international hub for historians of preindustrial Europe. However, because of this symbiotic relationship, when the patron saint left the Datini began its irreversible decline. For Braudel, the period 1968–84 was not free of difficulties and he had to struggle against the most conservative factions and reactionary structures of Italian academia (Gemelli 1990: 145ff.). Among economic historians, he had few sincere admirers and collaborators – these certainly include Dal Pane, De Maddalena, Tucci and their pupils. Aside from the publishing firepower of Romano, the overall influence exerted by the *Annales* school on Italian historiography appears to be modest.

Influence from English-speaking history and economics has been even weaker. The most lasting impact so far has been that of the US-style business history introduced by Franco Amatori (1997), who went to the Harvard Business School in the late 1970s to study under Alfred D. Chandler. A mild form of cliometrics was introduced by Stefano Fenoaltea and Gianni Toniolo, who spent a few years in the United States in the late 1960s. It was mild because part of their efforts was actually devoted to the reconstruction of national accounts or the history of central banking, something that does not necessarily require strong theoretical assumptions.[11] More recently, Giovanni Federico and Paolo Malanima (e.g. 2004), coming from history, have embraced the international vogue for very long-run estimates of GDP and agricultural productivity. While these may be seen as examples of anachronistic quantification, again the neoclassical content is somewhat lower than in the Netherlands where this trend originated.

The international impact of Italian economic and social history has been hindered by the fragmentary nature of trends, methods and approaches. Certain individuals, groups or schools have been more influential than others. Cipolla enjoyed considerable personal prestige but never developed an 'approach' that could be passed on to others. De Rosa managed to build some critical mass around the *Journal of European Economic History*, which nevertheless dissolved after his death in 2004. In addition to Gramsci, who became a global icon, the influence of Italian Marxism on British historiography was significant: it is enough to take a look at the footnotes of Eric Hobsbawm's works to get a sense of this. Microhistory was possibly the most successful product that post-war Italian historiography managed to export, though it cannot claim its exclusive paternity.[12] Compared to hard-core structuralist approaches, it certainly proved to be more compatible with the methodological individualism of the Anglo-Saxon world, but its fortune was mostly relegated to the domains of social and cultural history.

In this context, mention should be made of the many foreigners who have populated the country's libraries and archives over the decades. Some of them spent time at Italian universities as either visiting or permanent faculty and got fellowships at institutions such as the British and French 'schools' in Rome, the German Historical Institute, Harvard's Villa I Tatti and the European University Institute. In general, these foreign historians have been attracted by the golden age of merchant capitalism. This is particularly true for Americans, perhaps because, as Edward Muir says, Renaissance city-states speak 'a message that Americans can best understand, a message about the ideological and institutional underpinnings of republics'

(Muir 1995: 1096). A few scholars, however, did research on socioeconomic aspects of modern Italy.[13] In geographical terms, Florence, Tuscany, Venice and its overseas empire take the lion's share of research.[14] Genoa has mainly attracted historians of banking and trade.[15] By contrast, the Kingdom of Naples has received little attention, and interest in the region can in most cases be traced back to the scholars' family background.[16] The islands have not been neglected and some authors have explored commercial relations with Eastern Europe and the Black Sea.[17]

Decadence, 1995–2015

In the 1980s, despite the problems already mentioned, some amount of optimism was still present in Italian society. The Northern middle classes were in a state of moderate affluence, and generous welfare benefits for the working classes disguised the end of the historic compromise. The mood changed in 1992–93 when investigations in Milan uncovered a vast network of political corruption involving civil servants, public managers and entrepreneurs. In less than two years, the political elite that had ruled the country since the Second World War was swept away and this vacuum was filled by populist parties. In the South, the Mafia, taking advantage of the general state of confusion, carried out a series of spectacular terrorist attacks to hit institutional targets. In the meantime, the country's public enterprise system broke up under the wave of wild privatizations and the private sector, which had been heavily subsidized, lost efficiency. By the mid-1990s, only industrial districts, combining small firms and family business, kept themselves relatively healthy.

This crisis of politics, which persists up to the present day, is the expression of a broader moral crisis affecting Italian elites who do not seem to be able to form ruling classes up to the challenges of late modernity. During the past two decades, there has been no industrial policy, no science policy, no cultural policy. The most worrisome symptom has been perhaps the disappearance of intellectuals, first from the public sphere and then from academia itself. Scholarly work no longer reflects high ideals or public engagement but often appears to be the product of repetitive, routine exercise. Academic reproduction is in the main responsible for the profession's self-defeat, as the quality of new faculty members has continued to decline over the years. However, as in Britain and elsewhere, scholars are also despised by narrow-minded politicians who keep universities in a state of severe underfunding. The austerity regime following the recent eurozone crisis has made things worse, impairing the functioning of research libraries and leading to the demise of doctoral programmes.

At first sight, it might seem that the situation of economic history is not so depressing: by cherry-picking examples it is indeed possible to find good works, even highly innovative works – on an array of topics wide enough to include Renaissance art markets (Guerzoni 2011), Venice and the Ottoman Empire (Costantini 2009) and post-war international development (Alacevich 2009) – along with the revisitation of classic problems such as the 'long sixteenth century' (Alfani 2013), early modern fiscal states (Pezzolo 2012; Piola Caselli 2012), and macro views of the Italian economy (Ciocca 2007). However proportions should be kept into account. As of today, after the higher education cuts, Italy is still home to over 150 tenured economic historians and 30 historians of economic thought. These are considerable figures, probably higher than those for any other European country, but a great deal of what is currently produced is descriptive in character, and very seldom has a comparative remit or challenges social science interpretations. We might say that what was once the 'triumph of the local' has degenerated into provincialism. The absence of a colonial past compared to that of Britain, France or the Netherlands explains the delay with which global history has been received but it can no longer be an excuse for what is substantially lack of interest and engagement with international debates. For instance, it is surprising that no serious study of Italian colonialism has been done yet. The available works consist of no more than commented lists of goods produced and traded. They show no attempt to represent the point of view of the colonized and even contain awkward references to the '*valorization* of African colonies'.[18] These evident shortcomings on the part of economic historians expose them to the risk of being cannibalized by the economists, in whose departments they find themselves stuck – a consequence of the original sin of the founding fathers. Young scholars struggle to emerge, and the best ones tend to go abroad, fuelling the brain drain.

What can be learned from the history of Italian economic history, aside from its present lamentable status, has to do with the advantages of not being self-sufficient. Whenever it has come into contact with other traditions, research centres, or historical fields, it has achieved its full potential. Although Italian scholarship has been deeply embedded in the country's historical experience, there are no methodological approaches that can be described as specifically Italian. More than anything else, intellectual creativity and a good humanistic education have allowed individual historians to excel. Their varied heuristic repertoire, treating evidence in the double register of recurrence and singularity, has proved flexible enough to identify pluralities of experience in the past. The Italian case represents an interesting example for the globalized world with its growing, almost limitless potential for transnational exchanges and hybridization. It shows that innovation across traditions is possible and fruitful.

Notes

1 See Cattini (2005). On Loria, a pioneer of institutional/evolutionary economics, Pearson (1997: 40–1).
2 See *Rivista di storia economica* 1.2 (1936) and 1.3 (1936). The debate is discussed in Chartier (1989) and De Rosa (1990: 93–8).
3 Barbagallo (1899); Gentile's letter to Croce, 13 January 1899, in Gentile (1972: 156–7).
4 His essays on agricultural history and proto-industrialization have been reprinted in De Maddalena (1982, 1992). Cf. Cattini (2011).
5 The point was made by Einaudi (1940) a few years before.
6 See, for instance, Grohmann (1981) on medieval and early modern Perugia; and Sori (2001) on the history of waste. The latter was already an established scholar in the 1980s.
7 For a critique of Acemoglu and Robinson see Boldizzoni (2015).
8 On Italian Marxist historians see Romano (1978: 66ff.) and Favilli (2006).
9 Cf. Bértola and Weber (chapter 20) and Kuntz Ficker (chapter 21) in this volume.
10 I only give details here of their most recent works: Stanziani (2014), Molà (2000), Trivellato (2009), Fusaro (2015), Riello (2013).
11 See Fenoaltea (2011), a synthesis of his work on Italy, and Toniolo (2005).
12 To set the Italian contribution in context, see Clark (2004: 75ff.) and Burke (2005: 38ff.).
13 For example, S. B. Clough, Stuart Wolf, John A. Davis and Brian A'Hearn.
14 On Florence and Tuscany: Raymond de Roover, Felipe Ruiz Martín, David Herlihy, Richard Goldthwaite, Anthony Molho, Stephan R. Epstein. On Venice: Frederic C. Lane, Maurice Aymard, Jean-Claude Hocquet, Jean Georgelin, Reinhold C. Mueller, Frank Spooner, Brian Pullan, Richard Mackenney, Michael Knapton, Robert C. Davis, Alan Stahl.
15 The list includes Ramon Carande, José da Silva and, more recently, Steven A. Epstein and Thomas Kirk.
16 Among them, John A. Marino, Antonio Calabria, Gérard Delille and John A. Davis.
17 On Sicily, Maurice Aymard and Stephan R. Epstein; on Sardinia, John Day. On Poland and the Black Sea, Adam Manikowski and Sergej Karpov respectively.
18 These are all elements that can be found in Podestà (2004).

References

Acemoglu, Daron and James A. Robinson. 2012. *Why Nations Fail: The Origins of Power, Prosperity, and Poverty*. New York: Crown Publishers.

Alacevich, Michele. 2009. *The Political Economy of the World Bank: The Early Years*. Stanford, CA: Stanford University Press.

Albertone, Manuela. 1992. *Moneta e politica in Francia: dalla Cassa di sconto agli assegnati (1776–1792)*. Bologna: Il Mulino.

Alfani, Guido. 2013. *Calamities and the Economy in Renaissance Italy: The Grand Tour of the Horsemen of the Apocalypse*. Basingstoke: Palgrave Macmillan.

Amatori, Franco. 1997. 'Reflections on Global Business and Modern Italian Enterprise by a Stubborn "Chandlerian"'. *Business History Review* 71.2, 309–18.

Assante, Franca. 1999. *Romagnano: famiglie feudali e società contadina in età moderna*. Naples: Giannini.

Banfield, Edward C. 1958. *The Moral Basis of a Backward Society*. Glencoe, IL: The Free Press.

Barbagallo, Corrado. 1899. *Pel materialismo storico*. Rome: Loescher.

Barbagallo, Corrado. 1927. *L'oro e il fuoco: capitale e lavoro attraverso i secoli*. Milan: Corbaccio.

Barbagallo, Corrado. 1929–30. *Le origini della grande industria contemporanea (1750–1850): saggio di storia economico-sociale*. Perugia and Venice: La Nuova Italia.

Barbagallo, Corrado. 1931–38. *Storia universale*, 2nd edn. Turin: Utet, 1950–54.

Barbato, Michele, ed. 2010. *Luigi De Rosa Economic Historian* (Proceedings of the International Conference, Naples, 27 May 2009). Soveria Mannelli: Rubbettino.

Beltrami, Daniele. 1961. *La penetrazione economica dei veneziani in terraferma: forze di lavoro e proprietà fondiaria nelle campagne venete dei secoli XVII e XVIII*. Venice and Rome.

Bianchini, Marco. 1982. *Bonheur public et méthode géométrique. Enquête sur les économistes italiens (1711–1803)*. Paris: INED, 2003.

Boldizzoni, Francesco. 2015. 'Politics and the Neutralization of History: A Reply'. *Journal of the Philosophy of History* 9.1, 41–50.

Bonelli, Franco. 1975. *Lo sviluppo di una grande impresa in Italia: la Terni dal 1884 al 1962*. Turin: Einaudi.

Borlandi, Franco. 1949. 'Note per la storia della produzione e del commercio di una materia prima: il guado nel Medio Evo', in *Studi in onore di Gino Luzzatto*, vol. I. Milan: Giuffrè, 297–324.

Braudel, Fernand. 1953. *Civiltà e imperi del Mediterraneo nell'età di Filippo II*. Turin: Einaudi.

Burke, Peter. 2005. *History and Social Theory*. 2nd edn. Cambridge: Polity.

Burke, Peter. 2008. 'The Invention of Micro-history'. *Rivista di storia economica*, 24.3, 259–74.

Cafagna, Luciano. 1989. *Dualismo e sviluppo nella storia d'Italia*. Venice: Marsilio.

Carmagnani, Marcello. 2011. *The Other West: Latin America from Invasion to Globalization*. Berkeley: University of California Press.

Castronovo, Valerio. 1977. *Giovanni Agnelli: la Fiat dal 1899 al 1945*. Turin: Einaudi.

Castronovo, Valerio. 1995. *Storia economica d'Italia: dall'Ottocento ai giorni nostri*. Turin: Einaudi.

Cattini, Marco. 1984. *I contadini di San Felice: metamorfosi di un mondo rurale nell'Emilia dell'età moderna*. Turin: Einaudi.

Cattini, Marco. 2005. 'Gino Luzzatto: dall'economia induttiva alla storia economica e sociale'. *Ateneo veneto*, 4.1, 35–48.

Cattini, Marco. 2011. 'Aldo De Maddalena storico di Milano e della Lombardia: temi d'indagine e linee interpretative'. *Rivista storica italiana* 123.3, 1030–54.

Cazzola, Franco. 2014. 'Luigi Dal Pane: tra storia sociale e storia economica'. *Storia economica* 17.2, 319–34.

Chartier, Roger. 1989. 'Qu'est-ce qu'une discipline? Luigi Einaudi et l'histoire de l'économie politique'. *Revue de synthèse* 110.2, 257–75.

Cipolla, Carlo M. 1952. 'The Decline of Italy: The Case of a Fully Matured Economy'. *Economic History Review* 5.2, 178–87.

Cipolla, Carlo M. 1956. *Money, Prices, and Civilization in the Mediterranean World: Fifth to Seventeenth Century*. Princeton, NJ: Princeton University Press.

Cipolla, Carlo M. 1965. *Guns, Sails, and Empires: Technological Innovation and the Early Phases of European Expansion, 1400–1700*. Manhattan, KS: Sunflower University Press.

Cipolla, Carlo M. 1967. *Clocks and Culture, 1300–1700*. New York: Norton.

Cipolla, Carlo M., ed. 1970a. *The Economic Decline of Empires*. London: Methuen.

Cipolla, Carlo. M. 1970b. 'Fortuna Plus Homini Quam Consilium Valet', in *The Historian's Workshop: Original Essays by Sixteen Historians*, ed. by L.P. Curtis. New York: Knopf, 65–76.

Cipolla, Carlo M. 1973. *Cristofano and the Plague: A Study in the History of Public Health in the Age of Galileo*. Berkeley: University of California Press.

Cipolla, Carlo M. 1975. 'The Italian Failure', in *Failed Transitions to Modern Industrial Society: Renaissance Italy and Seventeenth-century Holland*, ed. by Frederick Krantz and Paul M. Hohenberg. Montreal: Interuniversity Centre for European Studies, 8–10.

Ciocca, Pierluigi. 2007. *Ricchi per sempre? Una storia economica d'Italia (1796–2005)*. Turin: Bollati Boringhieri.

Clark, Elizabeth A. 2004. *History, Theory, Text: Historians and the Linguistic Turn*. Cambridge, MA: Harvard University Press.

Costantini, Vera. 2009. *Il sultano e l'isola contesa: Cipro tra eredità veneziana e potere ottomano*. Turin: Utet.

Croce, Benedetto. 1942. 'Come si debba concepire la pura storiografia economica'. *Rivista di storia economica* 7.3–4, 97–102.

Dal Pane, Luigi. 1968. *La storia come storia del lavoro: discorsi di concezione e di metodo*. Bologna: Patron.

De Cecco, Marcello. 1974. *Money and Empire: The International Gold Standard, 1890–1914*. Oxford: Blackwell.

De Maddalena, Aldo. 1949. *Prezzi e aspetti di mercato in Milano durante il secolo XVII*. Milan: Malfasi.

De Maddalena, Aldo. 1982. *Dalla città al borgo: avvio di una metamorfosi economica e sociale nella Lombardia spagnola*. Milan: Franco Angeli.

De Maddalena, Aldo. 1992. *La ricchezza dell'Europa: indagini sull'antico regime e sulla modernità*. Milan: Egea.

De Rosa, Luigi. 1990. *L'avventura della storia economica in Italia*. Rome and Bari: Laterza.

Doria, Giorgio. 1968. *Uomini e terre di un borgo collinare: dal XVI al XVIII secolo*. Milan: Giuffrè.

Einaudi, Luigi. 1936. 'The Theory of Imaginary Money from Charlemagne to the French Revolution', in *Enterprise and Secular Change: Readings in Economic History*, ed. by F.C. Lane and J.C. Riemersma. Homewood, IL: Irwin, 1953, 229–61.

Einaudi, Luigi. 1940. 'Dei criteri informatori della storia dei prezzi', in *I prezzi in Europa dal XIII secolo a oggi*, ed. by Ruggiero Romano. Turin: Einaudi, 1967, 505–17.

Fanfani, Amintore. 1934. *Catholicism, Protestantism and Capitalism*. London: Sheed & Ward, 1935.

Fanfani, Amintore. 1940. *Indagini sulla 'rivoluzione dei prezzi'*. Milan: Vita e Pensiero.

Favilli, Paolo. 2006. *Marxismo e storia: saggio sull'innovazione storiografica in Italia (1945–1970)*. Milan: Franco Angeli.

Federico, Giovanni and Paolo Malanima. 2004. 'Progress, Decline, Growth: Product and Productivity in Italian Agriculture, 1000–2000'. *Economic History Review* 57.3, 437–64.

Felice, Emanuele. 2014. *Perchè il Sud è rimasto indietro*. Bologna: Il Mulino.

Felloni, Giuseppe. 1968. *Il mercato monetario in Piemonte nel secolo XVIII*. Milan: Banca Commerciale Italiana.

Fenoaltea, Stefano. 2011. *The Reinterpretation of Italian Economic History: From Unification to the Great War*. Cambridge: Cambridge University Press.

Fusaro, Maria. 2015. *Political Economies of Empire in the Early Modern Mediterranean: The Decline of Venice and the Rise of England, 1450–1700*. Cambridge: Cambridge University Press.

Gemelli, Giuliana. 1990. *Fernand Braudel e l'Europa universale*. Venice: Marsilio.

Genovesi, Antonio. 1765. *Lezioni di commercio o sia d'economia civile*. Venice: Remondini, 1769.

Gentile, Giovanni. 1972. *Lettere a Benedetto Croce*, ed. by Simona Giannantoni. Florence: Sansoni, vol. I.

Gerschenkron, Alexander. 1962. 'Rosario Romeo and the Original Accumulation of Capital', in *Economic Backwardness in Historical Perspective: A Book of Essays*. Cambridge, MA: Belknap Press, 90–118.

Ginzburg, Carlo. 1989. 'Clues: Roots of an Evidential Paradigm', in *Clues, Myths, and the Historical Method*. Baltimore, MD: Johns Hopkins University Press, 96–125.

Ginzburg, Carlo. 1993. 'Microhistory: Two or Three Things That I Know about It', *Critical Inquiry* 20.1, 10–35.

Giorgetti, Giorgio. 1974. *Contadini e proprietari nell'Italia moderna: rapporti di produzione e contratti agrari dal secolo XVI a oggi*. Turin: Einaudi.

Gramsci, Antonio. 1975. *Quaderni del carcere*, ed. by Valentino Gerratana. Turin: Einaudi.

Grendi, Edoardo. 1987. 'Falsa monetazione e strutture monetarie degli scambi nella Repubblica di Genova fra Cinque e Seicento', *Quaderni storici* 22.3, 803–37.

Grohmann, Alberto. 1981. *Città e territorio tra medioevo ed età moderna: Perugia (secc. XIII–XVI)*. Perugia: Volumnia.

Guerzoni, Guido. 2011. *Apollo and Vulcan: The Art Markets in Italy, 1400–1700*. East Lansing: Michigan State University Press.

Guidi, Marco. 1991. *Il sovrano e l'imprenditore: utilitarismo ed economia politica in Jeremy Bentham*. Rome and Bari: Laterza.

Horn, Jeff, Leonard N. Rosenband and Merritt Roe Smith, eds. 2010. *Reconceptualizing the Industrial Revolution*, Cambridge, MA: MIT Press.

Kula, Witold. 1962. *An Economic Theory of the Feudal System: Towards a Model of the Polish Economy, 1500–1800*. London: New Left Books, 1976.

Le Roy Ladurie, Emmanuel. 1966. *Les paysans de Languedoc*. Paris: Sevpen.

Levi, Giovanni. 1985. *Inheriting Power: Story of an Exorcist*. Chicago, IL: University of Chicago Press, 1988.

Lopez, Robert S. 1951. 'The Dollar of the Middle Ages'. *Journal of Economic History* 11.3, 209–34.

Luzzatto, Gino. 1932–48. *Storia economica dell'età moderna e contemporanea*. Padua: Cedam.

Malanima, Paolo. 1977. *I Riccardi di Firenze: una famiglia e un patrimonio nella Toscana dei Medici*. Florence: Olschki.

Malanima, Paolo. 1982. *La decadenza di un'economia cittadina: l'industria di Firenze nei secoli XVI–XVII*. Bologna: Il Mulino.

Molà, Luca. 2000. *The Silk Industry of Renaissance Venice*. Baltimore, MD: Johns Hopkins University Press.

Mori, Giorgio. 1967. *Studi di storia dell'industria*. Rome: Editori Riuniti.

Muir, Edward. 1995. 'The Italian Renaissance in America'. *American Historical Review* 100.4: 1095–118.

Muratori, Lodovico Antonio. 1751. *Dissertazioni sopra le antichità italiane*. Milan: Pasquali.

O'Brien, Patrick K. and Bartolomé Yun-Casalilla, eds. 2012. *The Rise of the Fiscal States: A Global History, 1500–1914*. Cambridge: Cambridge University Press.

Parenti, Giuseppe. 1939. *Prime ricerche sulla rivoluzione dei prezzi in Firenze*. Florence: Cya.

Patriarca, Silvana. 1996. *Numbers and Nationhood: Writing Statistics in Nineteenth-century Italy*. Cambridge: Cambridge University Press.

Pearson, Heath. 1997. *Origins of Law and Economics: The Economists' New Science of Law, 1830–1930*. Cambridge: Cambridge University Press.

Pezzolo, Luciano. 2012. 'Republics and Principalities in Italy', in O'Brien and Yun-Casalilla (2012), 267–84.

Piola Caselli, Fausto. 2012. 'The Formation of Fiscal States in Italy: The Papal States', in O'Brien and Yun-Casalilla (2012), 285–303.

Podestà, Gian Luca. 2004. *Il mito dell'impero: economia, politica e lavoro nelle colonie italiane dell'Africa orientale, 1898–1941*. Turin: Giappichelli.

Poni, Carlo. 1963. *Gli aratri e l'economia agraria nel Bolognese dal XVII al XIX secolo*. Bologna.

Poni, Carlo. 2009. *La seta in Italia: una grande industria prima della rivoluzione industriale*. Bologna: Il Mulino.

Putnam, Robert D. 1993. *Making Democracy Work: Civic Traditions in Modern Italy*. Princeton, NJ: Princeton University Press.

Riello, Giorgio. 2013. *Cotton: The Fabric that Made the Modern World*. Cambridge: Cambridge University Press.

Romani, Mario. 1957. *L'agricoltura in Lombardia dal periodo delle riforme al 1859*. Milan: Vita e pensiero.

Romani, Roberto. 2002. *National Character and Public Spirit in Britain and France, 1750–1914*. Cambridge: Cambridge University Press.

Romano, Ruggiero. 1978. *La storiografia italiana oggi*. Rome: Espresso Strumenti.

Romano, Ruggiero. 1992. *Conjonctures opposées: la 'crise' du XVIIe siècle en Europe et en Amérique ibérique*. Geneva: Droz.

Romeo, Rosario. 1959. *Risorgimento e capitalismo*. Bari: Laterza.

Rotelli, Claudio. 1982. *Le origini della controversia monetaria (1797–1844)*. Bologna: Il Mulino.

Salvemini, Gaetano. 1955. *Scritti sulla questione meridionale*. Turin: Einaudi.

Sella, Domenico. 1979. *Crisis and Continuity: The Economy of Spanish Lombardy in the Seventeenth Century*. Cambridge, MA: Harvard University Press.

Sereni, Emilio. 1947. *Il capitalismo nelle campagne (1860–1900)*. Turin: Einaudi.

Sereni, Emilio. 1961. *History of the Italian Agricultural Landscape*. Princeton, NJ: Princeton University Press, 1997.

Sori, Ercole. 2001. *La città e i rifiuti: ecologia urbana dal medioevo al primo Novecento*. Bologna: Il Mulino.

Stanziani, Alessandro. 2014. *After Oriental Despotism: Eurasian Growth in a Global Perspective*. London: Bloomsbury.

Stumpo, Enrico. 1979. *Finanza e stato moderno nel Piemonte del Seicento*. Rome: Istituto Storico Italiano.

Toniolo, Gianni. 1988. *An Economic History of Liberal Italy, 1850–1918*. London: Routledge, 1990.

Toniolo, Gianni. 2005. *Central Bank Cooperation at the Bank for International Settlements, 1930–1973*. Cambridge: Cambridge University Press.

Trivellato, Francesca. 2009. *The Familiarity of Strangers: The Sephardic Diaspora, Livorno, and Cross-Cultural Trade in the Early Modern Period*. New Haven, CT: Yale University Press.

Tucci, Ugo. 1981. *Mercanti, navi, monete nel Cinquecento veneziano*. Bologna: Il Mulino.

Venturi, Franco. 1969. *Settecento riformatore*, vol. I, *Da Muratori a Beccaria*. Turin: Einaudi.

Verri, Pietro. 1771. *Meditazioni sulla economia politica*. Venice: Pasquali.

Vigo, Giovanni. 1979. *Fisco e società nella Lombardia del Cinquecento*. Bologna: Il Mulino.

Zamagni, Vera. 1978. *Industrializzazione e squilibri regionali in Italia: bilancio dell'età giolittiana*. Bologna: Il Mulino.

Zamagni, Vera. 1993. *The Economic History of Italy, 1860–1990*. Oxford: Clarendon Press.

Zangheri, Renato. 1961. *La proprietà terriera e le origini del Risorgimento nel Bolognese, 1789–1804*. Bologna: Zanichelli.

Zangheri, Renato. 1969. 'The Historical Relationship between Agricultural and Economic Development in Italy', in *Agrarian Change and Economic Development: The Historical Problems*, ed. by E.L. Jones and S.J. Woolf. London: Methuen, 23–40.

9

MANUFACTURING THE HISTORIC COMPROMISE

Swedish economic history and the triumph of the Swedish model

Ylva Hasselberg

Swedish economic history was born between 1927 and 1932. The exact date of birth is not known. My claim is connected with two events that were crucial for the emergence of the Swedish welfare state: the instigation of the 1927 Unemployment Commission and the ascent of social democracy to political power in 1932. It was then that the founding figure of Swedish economic history, economist Eli F. Heckscher, finally gave up his claim to being a prominent economist and began to identify himself as an economic historian. The reader will have to accept this claim for the moment; I shall come back to it, and certainly qualify it, in a moment. The new-born child was weak, and did not receive much attention, but started to gain strength as the end of the 1930s drew near. The great depression had hit Sweden in 1931, but already in 1934 the economy had recovered, and the mean growth rate during the 1930s was over 3 per cent (Schön 2000: 348). The generational structure was particularly beneficial for the hasty turnaround of the economy. At the beginning of the 1930s, the age cohort 20–29 years rose steeply, as a result of high birth rates around 1910. Around 1935, the share of the Swedish population that belonged to this cohort was higher than at any other point in time during the twentieth century. A large segment of the population were young adults, ready to work, consume and build new families – providing of course that there were work opportunities. Unemployment insurance was the prime policy target of the social democratic government (Schön 2000: 353). In 1938, the well-known Saltsjöbaden agreement was signed by the parties of the labour market, putting an end to labour market conflicts and setting up institutional preconditions instrumental in securing political and industrial stability (Magnusson 2010: 447–9). These economic and political conditions form the backdrop for the emergence and distinctive evolution of economic history in Sweden, as we shall see. The take-off of the new discipline took place in 1948, in the aftermath of the Second World War, when for the first time four stable positions (however not *chairs*) in economic history were set up, through a decision in Parliament. This was a period when a new research policy aimed to provide room for expansion for an emerging social science that was beginning to see the light of day. Economic history became a *social* science, as was economics, but unlike the discipline of history, which remained within arts faculties. The child was now beginning to walk on its own two feet.

As can easily be anticipated, this chapter argues that the institutionalization of Swedish economic history was shaped by the political and economic development of Sweden in the period 1920–50, and that this also goes for the contents and arguments regarding the economic history of Sweden that became the core narrative of the discipline. Swedish economic history was built around a core narrative that supported the identity of Sweden as an industrialized nation and a welfare society. The constructed narrative in itself became an argument for the existence of the discipline. Economic history was seen as a progressive, central and *important* discipline, the value of which for society in general could simply not be questioned. How this came to be and what history it resulted in are the first questions that I will try to answer. The third question is how the nationalist character of the core argument should be interpreted, from the perspective of global history, and how economic history as a nationalist project in Sweden has fared during recent decades. Is it possible to discern a change or even a violent overturn of the traditional interpretation of Sweden's economic development over time?

The genealogy of the historic compromise: analysing the master narrative of social peace

There is a particular type of historical narrative that has given rise to the concept of the *grand narrative* (Lyotard 1984). Allan Megill (1995) has chosen to make a distinction between Jean-François Lyotard's *metanarrative*, the *grand narrative* and what he calls the *master narrative*. By master narrative Megill means a more specific narrative which purports to say something central and fundamental regarding the society in which we live. One example of a master narrative of Swedish society is the story of the Swedish *snilleindustri* (meaning literally 'genial industry', referring to a number of successful enterprises founded on inventions) that had been built on a solid tradition of technical know-how and proficiency, embodied in exceptionally talented and resourceful inventors and industrialists (Bergwik et al. 2014). Master narratives are highly rhetorical and often very stylized, their role being to provide identity and ideological foundation. This is not to say that the components of a master narrative are necessarily untrue or suspect. The development of the Swedish export industry *is* a success story, it cannot be denied.

Swedish economist Arthur Montgomery, of Scottish descent, became one of the main protagonists of the evolving discipline of economic history in the late 1920s. He took this road for many reasons, but it can safely be said that he would not have become involved, had it not been for the workings of Eli Heckscher, then professor in economics at the Stockholm School of Economics. Heckscher became his protector and mentor. In Montgomery Heckscher found a loyal and honest friend and supporter. When Montgomery, who was primarily interested in ethical issues at the time, became engaged in writing about poor relief and social policy in history, Heckscher quickly realized that this research interest could be turned into something useful that would give rise to a broader interest in economic history. During the 1930s, Montgomery's niche in the project of writing economic history became the writing of synthesizing narratives regarding a period that was termed contemporary history, i.e. the late nineteenth and early twentieth centuries. In 1931 he published *Industrialismens genombrott* (The breakthrough of industrialism); in 1934 *Svensk socialpolitik under 1800–talet* (Swedish social politics during the nineteenth century); in 1939 *The rise of modern industry in Sweden*; in 1946 *Sveriges ekonomiska historia 1913–1939* (Sweden's economic history 1913–1939); in 1955 *Ekonomiska utvecklingslinjer i Sverige och Västeuropa 1929–1954* (Economic development trends in Sweden and Western Europe 1929–1954). Montgomery wrote about subjects that other

Swedish historians just did not take notice of: how the industrialization process had happened; its roots and the consequences of it for society and its organization.

Of particular interest in this context is *The Rise of Modern Industry in Sweden*, published by P. S. King & Son and aimed at an international audience. The motivation for publishing a synthesis of Swedish economic history in English speaks for itself:

> The economic and social conditions of present-day Sweden have in recent years attracted considerable interest abroad. This may, perhaps, serve as a justification for my book; those who have become interested in the Swedish economic and social organisation of to-day may also like to know how it has evolved into its present state, which carries the tale rather far back into the country's past.
>
> *(Montgomery 1939: introduction)*

Clearly, the aim of *The Rise . . .* was not only to teach Swedish economic history to an English-speaking audience, but also, and perhaps more importantly, to explain and illuminate a phenomenon that had begun to attract international attention: the Swedish welfare state.

The polish historian Kazimierz Musiał (2002) has, in a very penetrating study, discussed the rise of the presently widely accepted view of the Scandinavian countries as progressive and modern. This view is not, as one could imagine, a post-war phenomenon. He convincingly argues that Denmark was seen as a Scandinavian apostle of modernism in the 1910s and 1920s. Danish society with its industrialized and highly efficient agriculture, its successful cooperatives and its modern educational system, was seen as a leader on the road to modernity. Sweden, on the other hand, was seen as a backwater: a conservative, poor and less developed country. But then in the 1930s, something happened. Not least American writers on the subject of social reform began to use Sweden as a starting point for discussing developments at home. Sweden was becoming a model example through its way of handling the depression and, in comparison with Roosevelt's New Deal, the politics of Swedish social democracy seemed very effective (Musiał op. cit.: 42–71, 81, 165ff.).

There are many aspects of this sudden rise to attention that merit further thought. One that is worth some consideration is that the new image of Sweden was a scientific construction, and that it grew out the encounter of a generation of young Swedish social scientists with their American colleagues. American and British commentators were also impressed with the strong position of Swedish economists as expert advisers in the political sphere (Musiał op. cit.: 97ff.). Swedish economists Gösta Bagge, Gunnar Myrdal and Bertil Ohlin went to the USA to find inspiration (and funding) for promoting social science in Sweden. In return, they exported the insight that Sweden was a model country: Musiał (op. cit.: 105), writes: 'In this way an American view of a rationally founded and progressive Sweden was created thanks to the very attractive notion of the "laboratory" country presented by its eminent scholars.'

It is in this light that we must understand the decision to publish *The rise . . .* The 1930s saw the sharpening of an ideological *and* scientific clash between the younger generation of Swedish economists, such as Bertil Ohlin, Alf Johansson and Gunnar Myrdal (later to be known as the Stockholm School of Economics), who held interventionist views of the role of the state in the economy, and the older generation of laissez-faire proponents. Eli Heckscher belonged to the anti-interventionist group, and he derisively referred to interventionist economic policy as 'neomercantilism', cleverly using historical knowledge of the mercantilist state to promote his views on controversial issues such as the active social democratic labour market policy. In his great work *Mercantilism* (Sw. *Merkantilismen*), which still today is the most internationally read and cited of his works, Heckscher devotes the penultimate chapter to a comparison between mercantilism and economic liberalism, and it is followed by a critique of the return of protectionist and interventionist policies, where he tries to answer the question of why the golden age of laissez-faire did not last (Heckscher 1931/1953: 304–27). His conclusion, a truly original one, was that the central difference between mercantilism and liberalism was the respect of economic liberalism for human values, in contrast to the ruthlessness and lack of respect for humanity of mercantilism. Admittedly, he underlined that socialism as an idea was in this respect also fundamentally different from mercantilism. But, he also attributed a total lack of theoretical understanding of the economy to mercantilism, which it supposedly shared with socially motivated interventionist policies. Thus he concluded the second edition with an excursus on the topic of J. M. Keynes and mercantilism, clearly suggesting that Keynes had not only 'tried to rehabilitate' mercantilism but was indeed a mercantilist himself (Heckscher op. cit.: 340). Mercantilism was and remained a *muleta* for Heckscher, and sometimes the reader wonders to what extent his analysis of mercantilism as a historical reality was indeed affected by his analysis of economic policy in his own time.

Economic history could, according to the views of Heckscher and Montgomery, form the basis of a counter-move to the persuasive image of Sweden as a country where progressivity was clearly linked to its emerging welfare state, a state that certainly did not refrain from an active economic policy. This insight creates a certain anticipation regarding the historical narratives constructed by economic historians. What, for example, did Montgomery stress in his analysis of Swedish economic development? It does not seem likely that he would have stressed the impact of recent welfare policies such as the very generous unemployment insurance.

Let us deconstruct the historical narrative that Montgomery began to create in the 1930s in order to explain the present status of Swedish society. The text that will be deconstructed is a short essay published in *Svenska folket genom tiderna* from 1939 to 1940, a multi-volume popular summary of historical knowledge at that time, with contributions from a number of well-known Swedish historians. The title of Montgomery's piece was 'Levnadsstandard och ekonomisk utveckling under de senaste hundra åren' (Standard of living and economic development during the last hundred years). It was largely a summary of the two monographs *Industrialismens genombrott i Sverige* (The breakthrough of industrialism in Sweden) from 1931 and *Svensk Socialpolitik under 1800-talet* (Swedish nineteenth-century social policy) from 1934.

'Standard of living . . .' (Montgomery 1940) begins with an irrevocable fact of great weight: the decreasing mortality in Sweden after 1720, resulting in a population increase. The result was pauperization, which in its turn led to a fear of social unrest and an increased burden for society in the form of poor relief. This social crisis was overcome through two separate trends: emigration and industrialization, of which industrialization was the main road forward. Industrialization led to increasing wage levels for workers in the period 1860–1936. The Swedish working class was 'deproletarized'. This development was strengthened by the fact that nativity now also was beginning to decrease, so as to work in favour of the bargaining position of the working class on the labour market. In Sweden, nativity fell sharply in comparison with other, comparable, countries. As the supply of labour fell, wages increased, letting the working class out of the 'Malthusian trap'.

The 'deproletarization' (meaning the rise of the working class from a proletariat state) of the Swedish working class was also much furthered by another central circumstance: the shortening of working hours. This meant that the pay per hour rose even more steeply than the yearly income, giving workers time to engage in other activities – cultural, organizational, political and sporting. This contributed to the levelling of classes. The reader cannot but draw the conclusion that the late nineteenth and early twentieth centuries were very favourable to the Swedish working class.

Industrialization, according to Montgomery, was the prime factor behind the rising living standard. The productivity of workers increased, thanks to improved technology and capital investment. This was even truer for industry. The net value of industrial products had increased by 800 per cent from 1860 to 1913, although this figure did not include the putting-out industry. Industrial expansion was substantial. By the late nineteenth century, industrialization resulted in rising demand for labour. The agrarian proletariat diminished both through emigration and through moving to industry. Among industrial workers great change had occurred. Workers had increased in number, while craftsmen had decreased. The differences between the working class of 1939 and its equivalent a hundred years earlier were so large that it defied comparison. Not only had economic standards improved but personal freedom had expanded as well. The rights of the master of the house and the patriarchal conditions connected with these rights had been abolished. Workers had gained the right to organize. Montgomery states that this right would not have filled its purpose a hundred years earlier, because the great mass of workers had been unable to organize even if they had had the right to do so. The level of education and 'spiritual training' of workers had been too unsatisfactory for them to have been able to build up large and complex organizations: 'It must however be strongly stressed that the "deproletarization" of the working class was not only an economic issue. It was also a spiritual movement' (Montgomery op. cit.: 270–1). In this spiritual movement, mass education and the compulsory four-year primary school (introduced in 1842) had played a pivotal role, together with the mass movements of the late nineteenth century: the temperance movement and the labour movement. The temperance movement had set the scene for the labour movement, through education and schooling in organization.

Thanks to the labour movement, the operational independence of workers from employers had grown. This was of course something which sharpened the consciousness of class conflict. 'However, in the long run it has also worked to lessen the acidity of these conflicts, by creating a feeling of being the equal of your counterpart', Montgomery (op. cit.: 271) claims. Furthermore, the labour movement was changing character, since new groups of a different social composition than the old working class were incorporated. White collar employees were now joining the labour movement. The direct influence of trade unions on wage levels, stated Montgomery, had been more limited than previously assumed. On the other hand its indirect influence had been substantial, primarily through the intimate cooperation between the labour movement and the social democratic party. It was through influencing political development that the labour movement had been able to promote its aims for increased pay. The best example of such a line of politics was the unemployment policy of the 1930s. In return, trade unions had stabilized the power base of the social democratic party, and to achieve this they had had to refrain from activities of a monopolistic character.

Another area where a great influence from the labour movement had been assumed was the emergence of modern social policies. But Montgomery argued that the influence of social policy on income distribution was easily overrated. National income rose parallel to industrialization; the income level of workers also rose in line with it. Through weighing a number of indicators against each other, Montgomery came to the conclusion that the poorer strata of the population had possibly improved their social and economic position faster than the rest of the population during recent decades. It was however hard to know whether this had also resulted in any real income equalization. In any case Montgomery thinks it evident that the general economic upturn had been the decisive factor in improving the economic position of the working class. Social policies had been of secondary importance. And he concludes:

> It has often been said that class contradictions have been levelled in Sweden during the last decades and there is evidently much truth in this claim. However, it would certainly be rash to suppose for sure that these conditions will be permanent. Admittedly there is no cause to believe that the present social peace is only depending on favourable economic circumstances, but it would be unreasonable to deny, that these have played a very important role.
>
> (*Montgomery op. cit.: 276*)

When we reach this point, we have come to the end of the historical process Montgomery is describing, and also to the central conclusion. The peak of the process is the realization of 'social peace'. The conclusion that this had something to do with the Saltsjöbaden agreement that had been signed the previous year does not seem out of place. Social peace was the highest level of development that had been reached in Sweden in 1939 – and the irony is of course that this social peace enters the scene at the same as the rest of the world entered the Second World War.

Analysing Montgomery's narrative, it is evident that the prime driving force behind social peace is economic development. The causal chain certainly starts with population growth, leading to social and economic crisis, but the solution to this crisis is industrialization and the great success of Swedish exports. An improved standard of living is seen as a central factor behind the fostering of educated and responsible workers – a cultivation of spirit and a rise in intellectual standard took place. This process, in its turn, was behind the success of the social democratic party, and led to an elevation of workers to equality with their employers. The use of the term 'deproletarization' in this context is highly interesting. It describes the uplift of an entire social class – a social class that hardly existed a hundred years earlier – from a proletariat condition. For a Swedish reader, the association with a stanza in the social democratic song *Arbetets söner* (Sons of Work) lies close at hand: 'From the demeaning grave of serfdom, up to an honourable and noble accomplishment'.[1] Social peace was born out of the meeting between the economic efficiency of Swedish industry and the self-initiated journey of the Swedish working class from economic, social and mental poverty into the light. Social peace was a child of the enterprise and ability of industrialists, their proven competence in banking, and timber and iron exports, together with the ability of the working class to capture the gains created by industrialization. Montgomery's narrative acknowledges and respects the parties that signed the Saltsjöbaden agreement, and lends legitimacy to the roles they played in history.

The social peace narrative has a strong flavour of the Whig interpretation of history, telling a story that seems to lead straight to the present, almost by necessity. In his other works, Montgomery develops the different aspects of and stages in the process. It would take up too much space to elaborate and give justice to the complexity of the narrative. A few points that are not evident from what I have already said need to be made, though. First, it is important to note that the starting point of the narrative, early nineteenth-century Swedish society, is painted in very dark colours. This goes for almost all aspects of society, and it creates a very dramatic effect and a stark contrast to the industrialization process. Liberalization, deregulation and industrialization are all positive forces according to Montgomery. Social problems were thus *not* a child of industrialization but something its historical mission was to cure. Furthermore, the process is depicted as very harmonious and fairly even, with no reverses, crises or hesitations. Second, there were certain historical structures and institutions in Swedish history before industrialization that were important preconditions for the positive development. One was the Swedish iron industry with its disciplined and loyal workers, and engaged owners. Here lay the roots to technical proficiency and here started the education of the Swedish engineers. Also, and to this we shall return, the early modern iron industry existed in a context of self-owning peasants whose hard labour and economic modesty was the pillar of society in general, and also the root of democracy. Third, the lesson to be learned by the 1930s was that economic development and economic stability were essential to a harmonious and stable society and that, for the sake of this, it was vital that all groups and interests in society worked to preserve and strengthen the economy, especially the export industry, on the back of which the future of Sweden relied. There was no cause to believe that the harmonious development would continue without ongoing economic growth. Therefore, it was risky to meddle with the economy through state intervention. The current discussion of socialization or more economic planning was an invisible but real issue in the narrative. According to Montgomery, the role of the state was not to control or regulate the economy, neither to stimulate the economy through public consumption, but to ease the social effects of economic downturns on the population. He saw for example unemployment benefits in this light.

It is a source of wonder, the elegant mixture of historical analysis and analysis of current issues that Arthur Montgomery produced. His narrative seems to shed a revealing light on issues that were controversial at the time: the falling birth rates, the active social democratic unemployment policy and the socialization plans. None of these issues were bluntly treated as part of a political discourse. Neither was there a tendency to criticize the emerging welfare state. The voice of Arthur Montgomery is ever modulated, careful and balanced. It is the voice of historic compromise speaking. In the same breath, socialization is dismissed at the same time as the flourishing cooperative movement is praised as being the newest branch on the trunk of Swedish industry. No wonder that this voice, that could speak with such impeccable scientific balance of relevant and interesting issues in society, at the same time giving legitimacy and clarification to industrialism through its own history, would win public approval and also create a space for *economic history*.

History of the people's economy

> I am convinced that we, with heightened levels of popular education, deeper scientific insight and, we have to add, because of the demand from the great mass of people, in time will teach history from a perspective where the people's economy and the historic acting of the people are the centre. This is a natural thing in a culture that likes to call itself democratic.
>
> *(Member of Parliament Ture Nerman in the first chamber of the Swedish Parliament, 7 April 1937)*

The father of Swedish economic history is undoubtedly Eli Heckscher. Every event that occurred during the period that concerns economic history can in fact be traced to the doings of Heckscher. Heckscher was born in 1879 in a Jewish family: his father Isidor had immigrated from Denmark and was a Danish trade consul in Sweden. His mother was Rosa Meyer of a Stockholm merchant family. The Heckscher family were well off, but not rich; they were intellectuals, and Eli grew up in an environment where reading, discussion, debate were constantly going on. His parents were not politically liberal though. Isidor, who was a lawyer by schooling, can best be described as a moderately conservative civil servant and law man. Rosa, by far the more interesting of the two, held views that in many instances can be called chauvinist: she did not agree with the suffragette movement; she was more or less against women's rights and could also possibly be termed anti-semitic in her views.

Heckscher took an early interest in economic history. He started his career as a young conservative historian, studying for the famous historian Harald Hjärne in Uppsala. The message from Hjärne to his pupils was that historians must be active in society; they must *matter.* Being a historian was to be a member of the elite, with a mission to take responsibility for the development of society, and to guard the interests of the state. Historians wrote the history of the state, they worked as civil servants; they handled the affairs of the state (Hasselberg 2007: 100–5). Intellectually and emotionally, the years in Uppsala formed Heckscher. According to the wishes of Isidor, who wanted his son to walk in his own footsteps and acquire a 'more practical' education within the faculty of law, he also studied economics with David Davidson. In 1904 he wrote an article in the central journal of Swedish history *Historisk Tidskrift*, where he expressed the opinion that economic history was needed, and that it had an important task to fulfil vis-à-vis both history and economics. Above all, studying the economic aspects of history would lead to understanding and explaining economic development, something which historians and economists had hitherto failed to do (Heckscher 1904). Heckscher wrote a PhD thesis on the benefit of railroads to the state and then acquired a chair in economics in the newly founded private Stockholm School of Economics in 1909. In the late 1920s, events began to press Heckscher in the direction of engaging fully in the project of building a new discipline. His position as a solidly empirical economist was beginning to erode, as a new generation of economists entered the scene and brought with them a more theoretical stance, and ideas that lay close to those of Keynes. Another aspect of this development concerned power and influence over politics. The younger generation began to take over positions as experts and advisers to the government (Hasselberg 2007: 65–95). To his dismay, Heckscher noticed that the new prophets advocated the idea of increased public spending. In this situation, he began the process of redefining his scientific identity, and he also began the process of creating political support for a discipline that did not yet exist. He was given a personal chair in economic history in 1929, and established a tiny research institute with his own and Montgomery's work as the main assets. He published his great work on *Mercantilism* (Heckscher 1931) – perhaps his most important scientific contribution.

During the 1930s, Heckscher's work to establish economic history began to bear fruit. Interestingly enough, Heckscher had followed two paths in his networking efforts. The first, and perhaps more natural path, was to curry favour with the business establishment. From his personal chair, he had started to direct his attention to business history, and had started off with a huge project of mapping business archives in the entire country. He and Montgomery now started to act as representatives of a 'more realistic' perspective on the economy, a perspective that did not start out from a theoretical model, but from solid knowledge of the actual economy and its history. In this respect, economic history was what economics no longer was. The reward for this was the support of right-wing politicians such as his old friend Gösta Bagge, the leader of the conservative party, and Ernst Trygger, who was the university chancellor until 1937. The university commission of 1933, led by Trygger, suggested a new chair in economic history to the government, as a countermeasure to the 'radical economic theoreticians'. The other path led in the opposite direction. In 1936 the communist MP Ture Nerman, after five years of stubborn work in Parliament, managed to get the Swedish Trade Union Confederation to finance a huge research project on the *history of the working class*. His ulterior aim was to reform the teaching of history in schools; industrialization had begun to transform society to such an extent that the history taught in schools seemed, and not only to the radicals, more and more old fashioned. Writing the history of the working class was a first step in the project of creating a body of knowledge that could substitute for traditional history in schools. Heckscher took up a seat on the editorial committee, as did his colleague and friend the conservative historian Bertil Boëthius, together with leading trade union representative Sigfrid Hansson, the political scientist Herbert Tingsten and the art historian Andreas Lindblom. Heckscher was also elected to be a judge in a prize competition initiated by the social democratic publishing house of *Tiden* (Time) where the task was to produce a history schoolbook that would reflect the demands of modern Sweden. Heckscher flirted with two diametrically opposed interests in his attempts to promote economic history – and strangely enough the positive response of social democracy did not repel the conservatives, or the other way around.

In the following year, 1937, Nerman again tried to stimulate an interest in Parliament in the reform of history teaching. The debate that followed his suggestion again tells a story of a discipline that had started to take shape as a result of what Thomas Gieryn (1999) calls *boundary work*. Economic history slid smoothly into the cultural space left vacant on the map by history. History was the history of kings. Economic history was the history of people. History was the history of wars. Economic history was the history of peace. Economic history was thus depicted in terms of a peaceful strife by people in general to win the daily bread, while history, on the other hand, was even more suspect when seen in the light of the present European tendencies: armament, dictatorship and a barbarian worship of heroes and uniforms. The arguments brought forward in the debate of 1937 thus combine the openly nationalistic demands for a new identity and a new education, better suited to the needs of industrial society, with the refutation of Nazi Germany and fascist Italy and their ideologies. Needless to say, the positioning of economic history was also the positioning of a country that would stick to its neutrality during the war. Although the first permanent chairs in economic history had to wait for another decade – because of the war – it was during the late 1930s that the discipline gained the support it needed. The realization of Heckscher's dream was only a matter of time.

One could thus conclude that the evolution of Swedish economic history as a discipline is in itself a mirror of the historic compromise. Arthur Montgomery was a leftist liberal or possibly a social-democrat, while Heckscher was an inveterate spokesman of laissez-faire politics with a political view hovering between Manchester liberalism and moderate conservatism. Others who engaged in the project of writing economic history were Bertil Boëthius (whom I will return to below), Torsten Gårdlund, economist and social democrat, and the Marxist historian and social-democratic politician Per Nyström, with whom Heckscher battled over the legitimacy of materialistic interpretations of history. They did not agree entirely on what was the core of economic history, and even less on the lessons to be learnt from it. But they agreed on the importance of economic history as a counterbalance to both economics and history, and in this mission they gained economic and political support both from the Swedish Trade Union Confederation and from representatives of private business.

Let us again turn to what resulted, what economic history became in the decades that are generally referred to as the golden age of high industrialism. I have dedicated much space and energy to the deconstruction of the history of Sweden's progress told by Montgomery. It is in many instances a progressive, liberal, history and its prime mover is industrialization. Montgomery was an expert in nineteenth-century trade policy and became an expert in the pre-history of welfare arrangements. However, the first links in the narrative chain he constructed were not his own, but borrowed from another historian and friend of Heckscher's: the solidly conservative historian Bertil Boëthius. Together with Heckscher and Montgomery, Boëthius engaged himself in the writing of economic history, and the three of them were in essence Swedish economic history from 1920 to 1950. Boëthius, belonging to a family of conservative scholars and priests, saw himself as a historian in the tradition of the nineteenth-century historian E. G. Geijer, legendary universalist and actually the first advocate of cultural history in Swedish historiography. Among Geijer's many lasting contributions was a persistent claim about the centrality of the Crown and its alliance with a self-owning class of free peasants with political representation. This mythical coalition was seen as a precondition for stable and balanced development, and also for checking and controlling the aristocracy. The aristocracy stood for everything that was ideologically suspicious according to Geijer and his followers: regional interests in contrast to national interest, greed, wastage and lack of moral fibre (Sjödell 1965; Hasselberg 2007: 255). A node in this master narrative of Swedish history was *odalbonden*, the Swedish self-owning peasant, whose closeness to the land, political independence, loyal support for the King, and general inclination towards continuity, fitted very well in the construction of national identity of a former great power, that had had to surrender this position permanently when Finland was lost in 1809.[2]

Boëthius was a late follower of Geijer, and he was in many instances typical. The Swedish archaeologist David Loeffler (2005: 63–71) in his thesis has analysed the common values of a number of families belonging to the late nineteenth-century Swedish cultural elite, to which the Boëthius family belonged. He discerns five central metaphors: 1. the existence of a culture emanating from a healthy and virtuous peasant class; 2 and 3. this peasant class as a racial entity with a common language, that needed protection from harmful influences; 4. the belief in a golden age in Sweden's history, in which this peasant class had played a major role; and 5. a stern belief in the inherent goodness of Nature. These metaphors were, according to Loeffler, connected to a high appreciation of the virtues of collectivism, duty, obedience and loyalty. To Boëthius and some of his colleagues, these metaphors and the virtues connected with them were the cornerstones of Swedish society, and they were also the pillars of their version of state-centred conservatism. When Boëthius wrote economic history – and he did contribute some important works, such as a social history of the workforce in the early modern iron industry, which was published in the above-mentioned history of the working class – he did it from a perspective that stressed continuity, loyalty, hard labour and simple ways as virtues. He constantly stressed reproduction and collective values above production and individualism (Boëthius 1917, 1921, 1940, 1951; Hasselberg 2007: 243–57). He cannot on one single point be accused of being a liberal.

Dismantling the progressive narrative of social peace as an inevitable and positive consequence of industrialization thus means embracing the insight that this seemingly modernist argument had roots that were all but liberal, and that included a nationalism that was not necessarily either progressive or open to the rest of the world. Swedish economic history in the 1930s and 1940s was truly a chameleon that combined narrative elements as well as values that were in some instances contradictory. The one thing that can be said for this chameleon is that it evidently worked. It attracted enough support to found a new discipline, and it attracted support from all political camps and from people of all social classes. It provided identity and legitimacy for members of the old elite, for the rural population, for workers, industrialists and social democratic politicians, alike.

It may seem awkward to the reader that Heckscher's violent anti-interventionism, based on a type of economic history that was solidly based on the conviction that the price mechanism must be allowed to work without interference, should result in the master narrative of social peace. It is also understandable if the reader wonders what became of Heckscher's anti-interventionism, and how it is possible to reconcile his legacy with the growth and success of the Swedish welfare state. The first answer to this riddle lies, as I understand it, in historicization itself. The core of Montgomery's argument is the claim that industrialization was the prime mover in relation to social welfare. This was the central claim and the central lesson to be learned. Social policy and welfare were the natural consequences of economic development, whereas the opposite, as could be learned from *Mercantilism*, was not true.

Second, in the 1950s and 1960s, the discipline slowly grew through expansion and diversification, not through overturning its established truths. It has often been said that the first generation of professors in economic history after Heckscher (Karl-Gustaf Hildebrand, Ernst Söderlund, Artur Attman and Oscar Bjurling) were occupied with revising and overthrowing the results of Heckscher. Though this may be true, it was a process of questioning and qualifying parts of Heckscher's enormous legacy, on the basis of more thorough empirical studies, not of rewriting the master narrative. None of the first generation of Heckscher's followers wrote syntheses, general overviews or course books. Rather, they produced monographs within the field of business history, history of trade and history of organized labour and capital. Eli Heckscher's general course book in Swedish economic history, published in 1944, was still in use on the basic course in economic history in Uppsala University as late as 1989.

Furthermore it must be said that Söderlund, Hildebrand, Attman and Bjurling were all historians, and that only Oscar Bjurling, the first professor in economic history in Lund, had studied economics on a more advanced level. Thus, and I think this accounts for the invisibility of anti-interventionism and Heckscher's more general views in their work, they *did not make any theoretical claims on the level of general economy and they did not really engage themselves in what Heckscher would have called economic analysis*. The reconciliation of Heckscher's legacy with the Swedish welfare state was accomplished through historicization and facticity, in which what was in essence still tension and perhaps even conflict, was carefully embedded.

A globalized Swedish model?

How then has the narrative of social peace fared in the last decades? Has the master narrative of Swedish economic history been adapted to the political and economic development of more recent years? It would certainly be reasonable to assume so. Swedish corporatism has suffered many defeats during the period since 1980, and the days of Keynesian economic policy are a thing of the past. Unemployment figures are closer to the European average than they were ever allowed to be during the golden decades, and this has been a fact since the economic crisis of the early 1990s. And ought one not also to assume that new perspectives and global influences must have had an impact on the discipline?

My analysis so far has concerned the foundation of a scientific discipline and how it came to occupy a certain space in the disciplinary structure as an independent discipline with a definite contribution to a body of knowledge that was *in demand*; that was asked for and filled a purpose in society. The formative period of economic history was finished in the early 1970s, which is when there actually were individuals who had their scientific training within the discipline and who had written theses. Economic history did not, however, rise to a central position as a discipline, although it enjoyed a brief spell of popularity in the 1970s as the result of a radicalization of society in general. Economic history has never attracted so many students as then. Two of the more prominent representatives of economic history, professors Bo Gustafsson and Lars Herlitz, were outspoken political radicals. Economic history could again position itself as the history of the working people, and also as a more radical alternative to economics. Critical perspectives on economic theory entered economic history. It was not that Gustafsson and Herlitz wrote a politicized history. In the case of Gustafsson, it has even been explicitly argued that the solution to the problem of how to handle the boundary between science and politics was to draw a strict demarcation line between them (Magnusson 2012). Still, radical students were attracted to the discipline, at a time when student enrolment virtually exploded in Sweden. Furthermore, economic history could ride on the wave of interest in writing one's own history; the so-called *grävrörelse* ('digging movement'). The digging movement acquired its name from Sven Lindqvist's (1978) book *Gräv där du står* (Dig where you stand), which was a call for people to write the history of their own working place and their own social context, as a tool for furthering economic democracy and altering the balance of power between employers and employees (Alzén 2011).

The 1970s and 1980s brought with them an expansion of the body of knowledge of economic history, and also an expansion of the range of subjects that could be defined as belonging within it. Radicalization brought not only labour history but women's history and developmental studies within the widening umbrella of economic history. In many instances, economic history was quicker to respond to social change than the history discipline. The reasons for this are of course hard to pinpoint, but it is reasonable to believe that the fact that the discipline was young and consisted of a small number of actors, and had its place within social science and not arts, must have contributed. No matter how susceptible to change the discipline was and how broad and inclusive it became, the master narrative of Sweden's development into an industrial nation was however left untouched.

Two later developments in relation to the industrialization narrative deserve to be discussed separately. The first is the 1970s debate as to the causes and structures behind industrialization. A very influential work was *Industrialismens rötter*, by Merike Fridholm, Maths Isacson and Lars Magnusson (1976). In this book the authors dealt with Sweden's industrialization by tying it to the proto-industrialization debate. This meant first that the focus on the last quarter-century of the nineteenth century was abandoned and second that the industrialization process was now discussed from the perspective of an international debate that concerned industrialization in general and thus put in a wider frame. It did not, however, mean that the peculiarly Swedish and nationalist character of the industrialization narrative vanished. The reader is probably aware of the fact that a more thorough study of the putting-out system was the general pillar of proto-industrialization studies. The early textile industry had been the particular centre of attention. In Sweden, the concept of proto-industrialization has primarily been tied to the iron industry, which has never been a domestic industry. Admittedly the focus on iron had led to a number of studies on iron trade and the export industry during the 1950s and 1960s that undoubtedly placed the iron industry and trade in an international context (e.g. Attman 1944, 1973). However, we have already seen that the iron industry, together with the self-owning peasants, were central to the master narrative of social peace. The proto-industrialization debate thus rather led to a reinvention of the narrative, perhaps even a strengthening of it. Inter-regional markets became more interesting than international trade. The idea of the Swedish ironworks as the historical source of both welfare arrangements and a strong and technically competent working class is a powerful idea, which has continued to flourish up to the present, not least through Maths Isacson's (1991) explicit argument for seeing the ironworks as giving birth to the welfare state. The position of the iron industry in Swedish economic history is, I would not hesitate to say, sacrosanct. In 2007 came the first real critically oriented attempt to analyse the global contribution of the Swedish iron industry, when Göran Rydén together with the British historian Chris Evans published *Baltic Iron in the Atlantic World in the Eighteenth Century*. Evans and Rydén (2007) showed that the Swedish iron industry – like the Swedish engineering industry of today, famous for its successful global export of weapons – flourished not only in the context of self-owning Swedish peasants, but also in the greater context of an Atlantic economy that was dependent on slave labour. Evans and Rydén have been quite singular in setting Swedish iron in this context but their thought-provoking argument has not attracted many new students to this problem.

The second development in the industrialization narrative that I would like to discuss briefly is the Schumpeterian argument that has been launched by Lennart Schön, and that has now begun to take on the character of the standard analysis of Swedish economic development over time. The third edition of Schön's course book on Sweden's economic history (2000/2007/2012) was published in 2012. His picture of Sweden's economic development that is brought up until the present places it firmly in an international frame, relating it to global business cycles and global economic development. One could thus argue that the nationalist character of Swedish historiography has experienced a severe downfall, and, superficially, this seems to be the case. However, a full analysis of Schön's argument reveals something else. It relies heavily on the particular version of Joseph Schumpeter's thesis on the nature of business cycles presented by Swedish economist Erik Dahmén (1950). Dahmén invented the concept of *utvecklingsblock* ('development blocks') in order to bring out the centrality of state-industry cooperation that has given birth to so many successful Swedish export industries. Once again, the theme of peaceful cooperation comes to the surface as the prime mover of economic development in Sweden, resulting in the innovation capability necessary to cope with global economic challenge.

The Swedish model is and remains central to Swedish economic history. Even though its present health and status in Swedish society can be questioned, not least in relation to changes in the labour market and terms of labour conditioned by a globalized economy, the discipline of economic history cherishes it as a central part of its identity. From its invention during the interwar period, the narrative of social peace and historic compromise has travelled forward in time. It remains because it so eminently fulfils both the goal of giving legitimacy and meaning to an academic discipline and the goal of supplying a factual base to a conception of who we Swedes are, that can also be used to think about the future. The difference today is that Arthur Montgomery wrote the history of social peace, with a warning finger pointed towards all policy measures that were potentially detrimental to Swedish industry, whereas today Lars Magnusson (2006/2013) explicitly asks in the title of one of his books: 'Will the Swedish model last?'. But when he tries to answer this question, the solution is no longer a Swedish affair, but a question of the unemployment rate and the innovation power of the economy in relation to other countries. The Swedish model has gone global. What can we learn from that? For me personally, the contribution of Swedish economic history to global economic perspectives is perhaps best captured in the question mark. Will the Swedish model last? At least, as economic historians, we do not believe in the inherent necessity of its downfall. The attempt to teach students how the welfare state was constructed, the sheer presenting of the fact that it was once politically feasible and possible to have both growth and social welfare, is not a bad bequest to leave. And the question mark itself, if attributed with a meaning, must mean that whether or not this will be possible in the future and how to manage it, is something that can be both discussed and politically negotiated.

Notes

1 The text to *Arbetets söner* was written in 1885 by Henrik Menander, and according to legend it was ordered by the socialistic pioneer and founder of the social democratic party August Palm. The song has a central place in the musical treasures of the Swedish labour movement still today.

2 'Odalbonden' is actually the title of a poem written by the Swedish poet cum historian Erik Gustaf Geijer in 1811.

References

Alzén, A. (2011) *Kulturarv i rörelse: en studie av 'gräv där du står'-rörelsen*, Mölndal: Brutus Östlings bokförlag Symposion.

Attman, A. (1944) *Den ryska marknaden i 1500-talets baltiska politik 1558–1595*, Lund University.

Attman, A. (1973) *The Russian and Polish markets in international trade 1500–1650*, Meddelanden från Ekonomisk-historiska institutionen vid Göteborgs universitet 26.

Bergwik, S., Godhe, M., Houltz, A. and Rodell, M. (eds.) (2014) *Svensk snillrikhet? Nationella föreställningar om entreprenörer och teknisk begåvning 1800–2000*, Lund: Nya Doxa.

Boëthius, B. (1917) 'Staten som lifsform', *Svensk Tidskrift* 7.

Boëthius, B. (1921) *Robertsfors bruks historia*, Uppsala: Almquist & Wiksells boktryckeri-aktiebolag.

Boëthius, B. (1940) 'Den karolinska tiden', *Dagens Nyheter*, 12 February.

Boëthius, B. (1951) *Gruvornas, hyttornas och hamrarnas folk. Bergshanteringens arbetare från medeltiden till gustavianska tiden*, Stockholm: Tidens förlag.

Dahmén, E. (1950) *Svensk industriell företagarverksamhet*, vol. 1. Uppsala: Almqvist & Wiksell.

Evans, C. and Rydén, G. (2007) *Baltic iron in the Atlantic world in the eighteenth century*, Leiden: Brill.

Fridholm, M., Isacson, M. and Magnusson, L. (1976) *Industrialismens rötter: om förutsättningarna för den industriella revolutionen i Sverige*, Stockholm: Prisma.

Gieryn, T. (1999) *Cultural boundaries of science: credibility on the line*, Chicago, IL: University of Chicago Press.

Hasselberg, Y. (2007) *Industrisamhällets förkunnare. Eli Heckscher, Arthur Montgomery, Bertil Boëthius och svensk ekonomisk historia 1920–1950*, Hedemora/Möklinta: Gidlunds förlag.

Heckscher, E. (1904) 'Ekonomisk historia. Några anteckningar', *Historisk Tidskrift*.

Heckscher, E. (1931) *Merkantilismen: ett led i den ekonomiska politikens historia*, Stockholm: Norstedt.

Heckscher, E. (1931/1953) *Merkantilismen*, 2nd revised edition, Stockholm: Norstedt.

Isacson, M. (1991) 'Bruket och folkhemmet', *Häften för kritiska studier* 2.

Lindqvist, S. (1978) *Gräv där du står*, Arbetsliv: dokumentation av industri och människa. Årsbok för Bygd och natur.

Loeffler, D. (2005) *Contested landscapes/Contested heritage. History and heritage in Sweden and their archeological implications concerning the interpretation of the Norrlandian past*, Archeology and Environment 18, Umeå: University of Umeå, Department of archaeology and Sámi studies.

Lyotard, J-F. (1984) *The postmodern condition: a report on knowledge*, Theory and History of Literature 10, Manchester: Manchester University Press.

Magnusson, L. (2006/2013) *Håller den svenska modellen?: arbete och välfärd i en globaliserad värld*, Lund: Studentlitteratur.

Magnusson, L. (2010) *Sveriges ekonomiska historia*, Stockholm: Rabén Prisma.

Magnusson, L. (ed.) (2012) *Vetenskap och politik: Bo Gustafsson 1931–2000, en minnesskrift på 80-årsdagen av hans födelse*, Uppsala studies in economic history 95.

Megill, A. (1995) '"Grand narrative" and the discipline of history', in F. Ankersmit and H. Kellner (eds.) *A new philosophy of history*, Chicago, IL: Chicago University Press.

Montgomery, A. (1939) *The Rise of Modern Industry in Sweden*, London: P. S. King & Son.

Montgomery, A. (1940) 'Levnadsstandard och ekonomisk utveckling under de senaste hundra åren', *Svenska folket genom tiderna. Vårt lands kulturhistoria i skildringar och bilder*, Malmö: Allhem.

Musiał, K. (2002) *Roots of the Scandinavian model: images of progress in the era of modernization*, Baden-Baden: Nomos Verlagsgesellschaft.

Schön, L. (2000/2014) *En modern svensk ekonomisk historia: tillväxt och omvandling under två sekel*, Lund: Studentlitteratur.

Sjödell, U. (1965) 'Kungamakt och aristokrati I svensk 1900-talsdebatt', *Historisk Tidskrift* 1.

10

SPANISH ECONOMIC HISTORY

Lights and shadows in a process of convergence

Iñaki Iriarte-Goñi[1]

The few instances of research that have analysed the evolution of economic history as a discipline in Spain (Vázquez de Prada 1990; Fernández Clemente 1995a and 1995b) coincide in affirming that it was a late developer compared to other countries. Indeed, its consolidation tends to be dated in practical terms to the 1970s; in other words, way behind the leading countries in the production of economic history, such as the United Kingdom or the United States. If we take our indicator to be the appearance of specialist journals on the subject, the delay is more than evident: while the *Economic History Review* was first published in 1927, and the *Journal of Economic History* appeared in 1941, the *Revista de Historia Económica* did not see the light in Spain until 1983. In spite of this, the study of economic history has forged ahead in this country over the past decades, and has significantly reduced the gap as regards other western countries. Today, the area of knowledge referred to as 'economic history and institutions' is taught at almost all the country's public and private universities; the Spanish Association of Economic History has 445 members, and when this figure is compared to the data available for other countries, it puts Spain in eighth place in terms of the number of economic historians, or in twelfth place in terms of their number per million inhabitants (Baten and Muschallik 2011). Numerous domestic conferences and workshops dedicated to different facets of the subject (including its teaching) are held each year, along with the issue of many specialist publications; besides the aforementioned *Revista de Historia Económica – Journal of Iberian and Latin American Economic History* (RHE–JILAEH), there are a further three journals specializing in the subject, which in order of appearance are the following: *Historia Agraria* (HA, which appeared in 1991), *Revista de Historia Industrial* (RHI, appearing in 1992) and *Investigaciones de Historia Económica – Economic History Research* (IHE–EHR, first published in 2005). Beyond our frontiers, the publications by Spanish scholars in foreign journals on the subject, including the most prestigious ones, have increased significantly in recent times, as has attendance at international congresses. Spain (together with Portugal) was the country with the highest residual propensity to take part in the editions of the World Economic History Congress (WEHC) held in 2002 and 2009.[2] Although no data have been analysed on the matter, the impression gained from the 2012 WEHC held in South Africa is that the presence of Spanish researchers is continuing to grow, and the trend is likely to be confirmed in the 2015 congress to be held in Japan. One may conclude that the evolution of the study of economic history in Spain has certain similarities with the country's own relative level of development, in the sense that there has been a process of convergence with more advanced countries and, while admittedly not catching up with them, it has significantly narrowed the gap existing at our point of departure. It would be a mistake, nonetheless, to view this convergence process solely as a success story. The increase in research in the discipline, in the number of its dedicated publications and its growing internationalization all point to an improvement, but it is worth delving further into the matter in order to understand the keys that may explain this trend, while also seeking to appraise the problems that have accompanied it. These are this chapter's main aims, in which the discipline's evolution in Spain is analysed, contextualizing it within different historical periods and seeking to shed light on the main lines characterizing it. This is not a traditional historiographical analysis that provides a review of the leading authors and their main works, but instead a historical and thematic analysis of the discipline's trajectory more as an economic–social and intellectual phenomenon than as the mere sum of its individual works.

Based on these considerations, the chapter is organized as follows: section two traces the reasons for the delay in the consolidation of the discipline of economic history in Spain, as well as the causes that may explain its rapid development as of the 1970s, seeking to discover whether any advantage has been gained from the original state of backwardness. Section three covers the main research streams followed in recent decades, analysing them from a perspective that we might describe as group-based. Section four puts forward a number of ideas regarding the main traditional debates involving Spanish economic historians, exploring the extent to which they may be interpreted in terms of path dependency. This is followed by section five, which analyses the internationalization process in which Spanish economic history is currently immersed and its impact upon topics and methods. Section six provides a number of basic conclusions.

Advantages of backwardness?

The temporal evolution observed in the development of economic history in Spain prompts three questions. First, why did it take the discipline so long to find its feet compared to other countries? Second, what are the reasons behind its rapid development basically from the 1970s onwards? Finally, and in relation to the two preceding questions, should we apply the concept of 'advantages of backwardness' that Gerschenkron (1962) proposed for economic development in general to the interpretation of the discipline's trajectory in Spain?

The delay in the study of economic history in Spain when compared to other countries, and especially the UK, may be linked to the country's economic and social development. The slow and irregular process of modernization that Spain underwent during the nineteenth century blocked the emergence of a suitable institutional and intellectual climate for the advancement of science in general, and in particular for that involving such disciplines as history or economics. Indeed, the works that address the development of history as science (Ruiz Torres 2002), economics (Fuentes Quintana 2003) or statistics (Meredíz 2004) highlight the problems these subjects faced for their consolidation. Although the situation began to improve in the first third of the twentieth century, the Spanish Civil War (1936–39) and the policy of autarchy pursued during the early years of Franco's dictatorship, and which lasted through to the 1950s, continued to hinder any scientific development on a scale comparable to other countries (Otero Carvajal 2001). In spite of this pessimistic outlook, some individual researches were able to shine out. The work of Rafael Altamira at the end of the nineteenth century on the historical evolution of property rights in land, the economic analysis in historical perspective of Flores de Lemus at the beginning of the twentieth century or, in the 1940s, the work of Ramón Carande on the Spanish sixteenth century analysing the problems of Charles V and his bankers, are good examples of how some intellectual creativity can flourish even in unfavourable social contexts.

It was in the 1950s that the intellectual atmosphere began to change, coinciding with a timid relaxation of the Franco regime. The founding of a number of new universities, a rise in the number of students in higher education (albeit still a very small minority of young people) and, in general, the country's own modernization led to the appearance of major opportunities for change. In the specific case of economic history, certain outward-looking professors began to use and disseminate the methodologies propounded by the *Annales* School (especially that of Braudel) and by other fellow French historians such as Labrousse and Vilar. Two major exponents of these currents were Jaume Vicens Vives and Felipe Ruiz Martín, whose merits lay not only in their works on economic history, but also in their ability to attract a school of followers.[3] The appearance of new faculties of economic sciences that taught subjects in economic history helped to mainstream the teaching and instruction of students interested in the subject. Although it did not specialize in economic history, the journal *Moneda y Crédito* was a major vehicle for the disclosure of research (Pérez Moreda 1975). Overall, the 1960s witnessed the formation of what could be considered Spain's first generation of economic historians in the current sense of the term.[4] The majority took part in the '*Primer coloquio de historia económica de España*' [Spain's first symposium on economic history], whose proceedings were published in the early 1970s (Nadal and Tortella 1974). In that same decade, several of them also published seminal works that, as we shall see, became veritable reference works.

The growth process recorded from then on should be set within a triple context: the reintroduction of democracy following Franco's death in 1975; administrative devolution through the creation of regional governments in the country's seventeen autonomous regions; and Spain's membership of the European Union. These three major milestones entailed economic, social, cultural and institutional changes without which one could not explain the development in the country of many scientific disciplines, including economic history. Yet within this general framework, the reason that best explains the growth in the number of economic historians in Spain is the consolidation of economic history as a compulsory subject in economics and business courses, and the persistence of that compulsory nature (albeit somewhat tempered) in sundry curricula from the 1970s through to the present day.[5] In response to this compulsory nature, the growth in the number of lecturers in economic history was linked to the sharp increase in courses in higher education.[6] This increase has been accompanied by an allocation of funding to higher education by both the central and regional governments, which amongst other things led to the creation of nineteen new universities between the end of the 1980s and 2000. All of these, as well as those that already existed, taught courses in economics and business. At the same time, the central and regional governments, as well as certain public institutions, have played a significant role in funding research, both through bursaries for the training of young researchers, and through the mainstreaming and regularization of projects in aid of research.

A more detailed analysis is required to discover whether the amount of the funding provided for science in general or for economic history in particular has been appropriate at each specific moment in time, and whether the funds have been managed in a more or less efficient manner. Yet with the benefit of hindsight it is difficult to deny that since the end of the 1970s, and at least until the onset of the current recession, public funding has been essential in the increased interest in Spain's economic history. The discipline's development is in some way reminiscent of Gerschenkron's view on the role the state may play in development processes in cases of backwardness. Within this context, it is also pertinent to seek similarities with the advantages that this very backwardness has provided for Spain's economic historians. Through research sojourns largely financed with public funds, they have been able to access the working methods and innovative techniques applied at foreign universities with much more experience in research. This may have reduced the costs of incorporating new methodologies, saved time and resources in their selection and, in short, helped relatively quickly to narrow the gap in the study of economic history between Spain and other countries.

Groups, networks and topics

The glut in research on economic history in Spain complicates the search for certain common denominators of development. Initially, the thematic focus of the research may be considered closely related to the creation of schools instigated by one or more 'masters', as pioneers in the analysis of certain topics. In the case of Spanish economic history, however, the rapid increase in output has largely outgrown this structure. Although especially in the 1970s and early 1980s some scholars opened up pathways that were subsequently followed by their disciples, the research has developed through groups rather than in schools, with the former not necessarily having a clear hierarchical structure of masters and disciples. Moreover, these are increasingly more open groups whose members tend to interrelate ever more closely with their counterparts in other groups, creating a complex networking structure. Within this context, it may be affirmed that the main research groups and networks in Spain have been linked to one or other of the discipline's scientific journals, which have acted not only as channels for the disclosure of the research, but also as vehicles for informing the research itself. We are therefore going to use the three oldest specialized journals (RHE–JILAEH, HA and RHI) as guides for listing the main research streams. This approach has the benefit of introducing some order into the narrative, but it is worth noting that this also poses some problems. The main one is that it is centred on works addressing the modern age, which are in a majority throughout the discipline.[7] This option leaves out most of the works studying the Middle Ages and especially the early modern period, which are of interest but we have insufficient space to cover them in this work.[8]

The groups and networks related to RHE–JILAEH in the early days were very closely linked to Gabriel Tortella (1973), author of *Los orígenes del capitalismo en España,* which studied the issues surrounding the implementation of a capitalist economy in the country, analysing mainly the role of the banking sector and the railways. Tortella is just about the only member of the first generation of Spanish economic historians who completed his education in the USA and who, probably influenced by that, very soon became the foremost exponent in Spain of what was termed New Economic History (NEH).[9] As regards the groups and networks associated with the journal RHI, the initial influence undoubtedly fell upon Jordi Nadal, who had already collaborated with Vicens Vives back in the 1950s, and who in the 1970s published his seminal work *El fracaso de la revolución industrial en España* (Nadal 1975) which set out to explain the reasons that, in his opinion, impeded greater industrial development in the country throughout the nineteenth century. Taking a longer-term view, and introducing more social elements, the work by Fernández de Pinedo (1974) was also a major referent in studies on industrialization, focusing in this case on the Basque Country.

For their part, the research groups linked to HA appeared somewhat later and had a more diverse origin, on the one hand attracting the disciples of a pioneer in studies on agrarian history, Gonzalo Anes (1970), and, on the other, scholars close to Vicens Vives, such as Josep Fontana and Ramón Garrabou, as well as certain disciples of Felipe Ruiz, such as Ángel García

Sanz. Some of the groups that were formed against this background were also influenced by historical materialism, although, with the exception of Josep Fontana, it is difficult to find openly Marxist approaches.

In the case of these three groups, they all became consolidated from the mid-1980s, with the appearance of a series of reference works; all with a much more detailed quantitative discourse than that adopted by the first generation, and which would set the tone for future research. In some aspects the stream related to the NEH emulated for Spain some of the classic works of the Economic History of the United States. The clearest example is the work about the role of railroads in Spanish economic growth (Gómez Mendoza 1982), clearly inspired by Fogel's approach. The work of Prados de la Escosura (1988) on the loss of the Spanish Empire at the beginning of the nineteenth century and the development of the Spanish economy until the 1930s, followed the NHE pattern with some provocative proposals and the use of counterfactuals trying to prove them. The reconstruction of some figures of GDP and the analysis of Spanish international trade was essential in this view. Also following neoclassical theory, other works reconstructed the monetary aggregates and the problems of monetary policy at the beginning of the twentieth century (Martín Aceña 1985) or public finance and its relation to economic performance in historical perspective (Comín 1988). In general terms, the concept of the backwardness of Spain in the context of the development of capitalism was the overriding idea of these works.

Networks focusing upon industrial growth in Spain also took important steps in the 1980s. One of the most important was the estimate of the Spanish Industrial Production Index (IPIES) for the nineteenth and twentieth centuries (Carreras 1988), constructed with a standard international methodology that allows comparisons with other countries. Figures of the IPIES reinforce the idea of *fracaso* (failure), coined by Nadal for the nineteenth century, and also the convergence process for the twentieth century, except for the period of the civil war and the autarchy (1936–50). A first general view of the outcomes of the different periods of the twentieth century was outlined in Nadal et al. (1987). From then on, many studies of industrialization appeared, focusing upon different industrial sectors including those that were not leading sectors (Nadal and Catalán 1994), or analysing regional industrial growth experiences (Nadal and Carreras 1990).[10]

Finally, networks oriented to the study of the agricultural sector also achieved important results in several ways. In the mid-1980s a big volume representing the state of the art in modern Spanish agrarian history (from 1800 to 1960) was published by Garrabou and others (1985 and 1986).[11] The contributions included not only aspects related to agrarian production, but also important questions referring to institutions, for example the establishment of a different set of property rights from the beginning of the nineteenth century. The importance of technology and also of long-term agrarian policy was stressed in some works. The interest in those topics led to a spread of regional and local research combining social with economic aspects of the rural world. If, in general, works coming from NHE or from industrial history grew apart from advances in social history, agrarian history was the field where interest in social development associated – or not – with economic performance was maintained.

In sum, during the 1980s the way for further advances in Spanish economic history was solidly paved. The 1989 edition of *Estadísticas Históricas de la España Contemporánea*, compiling the series produced by the leading specialists in each sector, constituted a major milestone in the consolidation of the quantitative approach to Spanish economic history (Carreras 1989; Carreras and Tafunell 2005) but was accompanied also by qualitative analysis of the main economic changes in the country.

The path dependence of the traditional debates

Nevertheless, from then on controversies over numbers and also over their interpretation were quite common. If we analyse the main traditional debates related to content and interpretations, it needs to be stated that almost all of them appeared in the 1990s or just after 2000 and also all of them focused on the period falling between the middle of the nineteenth century and 1936 (the outbreak of the Spanish Civil War); in other words, on the period that witnessed the formation and consolidation of a capitalist economy in Spain. By contrast, a high level of consensus in interpretations pertained to the period of outright divergence that began with the civil war and early years of Francoism and lasted through to the 1950s, and the stage of relative convergence that began its consolidation from the 1960s onwards.[12]

The debates over the 1850–1936 period were highly influenced by hypotheses already formulated in certain pioneering works from the 1970s. The view of Spain as a backward country that did not manage to emulate the processes of growth of the first-comers during the nineteenth century has informed a very considerable part of the research. Although there has been agreement over the fact that Spain grew at a slower rate than the rest of the western world, most of the discussions have focused on the specific growth rates determining the degree of backwardness and on the causes for it. Regarding the former aspect, the bulk of the controversy has been informed mainly by technical aspects of the metrics used. The main disagreements flared up in the early 1990s between the industrial growth calculated respectively by Carreras and by Prados de la Escosura (see, Nadal and Sudria 1993). After that the reconstruction of Prados de la Escosura of the GDP series for the period 1850–2000 (Prados de la Escosura 2004) became almost hegemonic in the measurement of Spanish economic performance in the long run. The inclusion of this work in the Maddison Project had probably much to do with its success. Nevertheless, in 2009 Maluquer (2009a) provided different estimates of the GDP adjusting it to the new European accounting system. A technical discussion took place in that year between the two authors (Prados de la Escosura 2009; Maluquer 2009b), but the measurement problem remained open.

Insofar as the causes of backwardness are concerned, these have been posed usually in terms of disagreements about the effects of some economic actors or some economic policies. For instance, the role of liberalization policy in the mining industry in 1868 and the burst of mineral exports that followed it until the First World War have been interpreted as indicative of a quasi-colonial exporter economy or rather as a symbol of modernization and integration in the international markets. In similar terms, the construction of railroads in the middle of the nineteenth century with engines and material bought in foreign countries has been seen negatively as an example of policy against the national industrial interest or favourably as an example of steps forward for the integration of the domestic market.[13] But one of the most controversial questions has been the tariff policy application and its effects on trade and growth at the end of the nineteenth and beginning of the twentieth centuries.

This debate started with some maximalist ideas about an extreme, comprehensive and indiscriminate protection of the domestic market oriented towards the interests of the industrial and agrarian lobbies. Although in this approach the measurement of the tariffs was quite rough, the trade policy was signalled clearly as a cause of Spanish backwardness.[14] After that, a revision of those approaches was made with better data, a refinement of techniques and the addition of more complex theoretical methods. The problem was inserted in the context of the external restrictions and the actual possibilities of the Spanish economy. In the new view, tariffs were applied in a selective manner, depending on the advantages of the different economic sectors.[15] Some authors, however, were unconvinced by the new measurements and maintained the old position. The discussion became a very technical one of little interest beyond highly specialized researchers.[16] From all those perspectives, it seems reasonable to refer to a path dependency in the discipline's development that has been heavily influenced by the very concept of backwardness and by the difficulties encountered in seeking to emulate a successful development process.

Against this background, one approach that explicitly challenged this view was that of certain agrarian historians (Pujol et al. 2001). Faced with the recurring notion that agrarian backwardness was responsible for holding the rest of the economy back, their approach put the very concept of backwardness on hold and championed a more complex understanding of the development process. The aim was to consider a multifaceted approach (from environmental to productive, including technological change in its broadest sense and institutional analysis) that would reveal other dimensions of the process, over and above its correspondence, or not, with an ideal model of agrarian development. Although the book focused on agriculture, in essence it was a wake-up call regarding the modus operandi of the mainstream studying the country's economic history, and in that sense it was a source of controversy for some time.[17] Nevertheless, as noted by Naredo (2003), the argument of the controversy did not explore the heart of the matter. Most of the scholars who entered the fray over the book made interesting criticisms, although they once again focused on the extent to which it was right or wrong to consider institutional or geographical factors as the cause of backwardness in the countryside. The focal point, that was supposedly the discussion over the very concept of backwardness and the possibilities it provided for opening up alternative paths and for a renewed vision of the specifics of the Spanish economic path, was omitted from the debate and, to a certain extent, buried.

In sum, the general interpretations of this backwardness, seen as the series of problems encountered in consolidating capitalism in Spain in order to mirror the path followed in development by the most advanced countries, seems to have prevailed almost until recent times, in a process of path dependency that is not easy to avoid. The added problem is that the exponents of differing positions in the major debates were not capable of finding sufficiently sound arguments to sway their opponents, finally becoming bogged down in technical matters, without rekindling a new discourse.

Spanish economic history on the global stage

Since the beginning of the twenty-first century, Spanish economic history has been immersed in a clear process of internationalization that has had an impact upon it at several levels and changed almost in part the outlook aforementioned. On the one hand, there has been a considerable increase in the tendency to concentrate the dissemination of research through papers designed for publication in high-impact, indexed journals. The incentives introduced through the regulations of the central and regional governments for measuring output and winning projects and promotions have clearly marshalled researchers in that direction, which had already been marked out by the English-speaking world. In the Spanish case, this trend has been accepted in an almost uncritical manner, in detriment to other forms of dissemination, such as in monographs, which are increasingly becoming less relevant in the discipline.[18] Within this setting, Spanish journals have shown a clear tendency to align with 'quality' publishing systems, and are now being included in international databases. Their impact factors are still as yet low, and an analysis is required to discover whether this is due to the brevity of the time they have been included in the rankings, or whether it is because the papers published have not managed to attract the interest of other international researchers, which may be because a large number of the papers are not published in English. Nonetheless, the indexing of Spanish journals is attracting an ever greater number of foreign authors (especially from Latin America), who publish research on their own countries.

Internationalization has also had other components. On the one hand, the past decade has seen sharp growth in the number of papers that Spanish economic historians have published in indexed journals abroad. When we compare the periods 2002–7 and 2008–14 with a view to obtaining a yardstick for this evolution (Figure 10.1), we may affirm that the total number of such papers has increased more than twofold. Furthermore, the process reveals another important aspect: the Spanish authors that publish in foreign journals are increasingly focusing on geographical areas other than Spain. Overall, in the second period considered, the papers devoted to Europe, other countries in Latin America or to other territories (including a few global studies) have accounted for 40 per cent of the total.

In this new scenario one question can be asked. Has this internationalization process led to changes in methods and topics followed by Spanish researchers? Table 10.1 includes the papers published by Spanish economic historians in the four main Spanish economic history journals and in foreign journals related to economic history, both grouped by topics. Although data are not conclusive, these figures can be used as a guide to say something about recent changes.

Regarding topics in Spanish journals, the agricultural sector continues to be a priority topic and account for more than a third of all publications. One reason is undoubtedly the importance, until only fairly recently, of the sector itself within the Spanish economy as a whole. Industry in its broadest sense (here including mining and infrastructures) also attracts constant attention over this period. In third place, the studies on businesses and firms have generated an interest that is clearly in the ascendant. The possibilities of resorting to case studies and also humanizing decision-making processes through the analysis of individual entrepreneurs seem to attract an ever increasing number of scholars. Elsewhere, the other two topics that are also revealing a growing dynamism are those referring to the public sector and the trend in standards of living. Finally, certain topics, such as those related to banking and finance and trade, have remained fairly stable over time. Others, such as the history of economic thought or demography have recorded a sharp drop-off in Spanish journals on

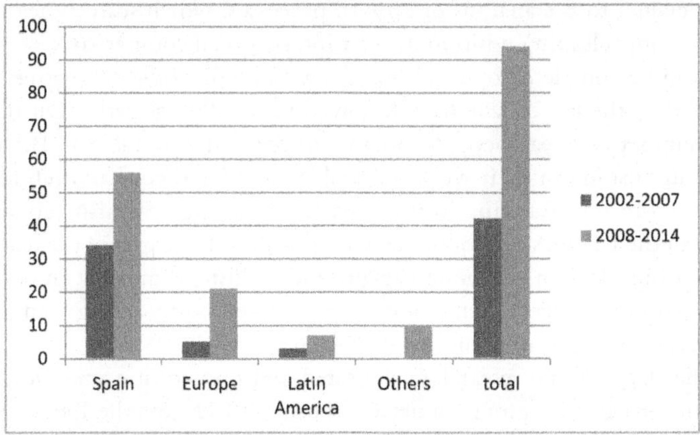

Figure 10.1 Papers by Spanish economic historians published in foreign indexed journals, sorted by area of study.

Source: EconLit and Spanish Economic History Association. Compiled by author.

Table 10.1 Topics in papers written by Spanish economic historians

	Spanish	*Foreign*	*Int Index*
Agricultural sector	36.3	17.0	0.15
Industry	18.9	12.1	0.20
Business and firms	11.9	25.5	0.67
Banking and finances	7.7	8.5	0.34
Public sector	7.0	9.9	0.44
Standards of living	4.0	9.2	0.72
Trade	5.5	3.5	0.20
Services	1.8	0	0
History of Economic Thought	2.4	0.7	0.09
Growth	1.8	11.3	2.00
Demography	1.8	2.1	0.38
Methods (and sources)	1.1	0	0
Total	100	100	0.31

Source: For Spanish journals: papers published in RHE–JILAEH, HA, RHI and IHE–HER. For foreign journals: EconLit and Spanish Economic History Association. Compiled by author.

Note: Int index = Number of papers in foreign journals divided by number of papers in Spanish journals, for each topic.

economic history, probably because they have remained on the margins of the discipline's structure in higher education, and because the research into those topics has been redirected towards foreign journals that specialize in these respective fields.

Topics in foreign journals show a different outlook. As is apparent, the two main topics in Spanish publications (agricultural sector and industry) record an internationalization index that is well below the average. By contrast, some of the topics that have increased in popularity over the past decade, such as business and firms, and standards of living, record a high internationalization index, which suggests that the expansion process these topics are involved in is also expanding beyond Spain's frontiers. A case worth mentioning involves those papers devoted to the analysis of growth processes, which scarcely feature in Spanish journals, but occupy a leading position in their international counterparts.

This state can be completed by combining it with methodological matters. In this sense, papers published in the last decade have followed very different paths. On the one hand, a considerable number of researchers (devoted to all the topics in Table 10.1) have not shown any particular disposition in their works to apply economic theory and refined quantitative methods. It is worth remembering in this sense that although Spanish economic history is taught mainly in the faculties of economics and business, a large part of the teaching staff that joined the profession had an academic background in history, and not in economics. Thus they have opted for traditional methods that, while mostly using and reconstructing quantitative variables, apply an inductive–statistical approach.

On the other hand, some researchers educated and trained in economics, most of them connected with departments, groups or networks using NEH from the 1980s, exhibit strength in a methodological stream based upon more and more sophisticated econometric tools. The organization from 2003 of the biennial *Iberometrics* conferences (along with Portuguese colleagues), has been the main debate forum for them. Topics have been varied. Although papers approaching general aspects of growth predominate, there are also papers about different topics, for example, agriculture or inequality. Some of these works follow neoclassical economic theory with an almost blind faith in the market mechanisms functioning throughout history, and on occasions undervaluing the social, political and ideological contexts. Nevertheless others try to incorporate more variables and recent developments in theory, for instance in economic geography, to explain problems of industrial concentration and migrations (Pons et al. 2007) or regional inequalities inside the country (Rosés et al. 2010). The econometric stream has never held a majority in the overall discipline in Spain. In 2006, a paper that sought to measure its real impact on publications over the previous decades, despite following very lax criteria that validated any work that used a smattering of economic theory and some quantification method, however unreliable it might be, concluded that one could confirm NEH's influence on the discipline but in no sense identify its dominance (Coll 2006). In recent years, the use of econometric models based on varied theoretical approaches is becoming more commonplace, although it is still a long way from being the prevailing methodology. It should be noted, furthermore, that sometimes the performance of econometric exercises is not always synonymous with the application of deductive methods based on economic laws, but rather that inductive–statistical methods are often applied seeking to contrast hypotheses based on the correlation of aggregate data.

Beyond the cliometrics other methodological postulates have been proposed. Mention could be made of the book *La historia cuenta* (Tello 2005), which is certainly a thorough review of the different theoretical streams in economics and their possible use for the study of history, highly critical of the orthodox economic approaches commonly used in economic history. On the other hand, Gallego (2007) in his work *Más allá de la economía de mercado* (Beyond the market economy) put forward some very interesting proposals, considering new ways of relating theory and history, based on empirical works and on theoretical streams close to the surplus–reproduction paradigm and to several institutional developments. Surrounding those critical streams at least four different matters have had a remarkable development in Spain in the last decade. The first has to do with institutions, an issue with a long tradition in Spanish economic history which has been addressed with changing approaches. Until the 1990s, interest in institutions focused mainly in formal political institutions and the greater or lesser success of the laws they passed. From then on, the interest has moved to a deeper concept of institutions including general norms and especially the role played by property rights. In this respect the ideas of North and the New Institutional Economics have had some followers, but recently approaches derived from Ostrom, and stressing rules for collective action, are being more used.[19]

The second matter relates to the standard of living question which has also developed different approaches. Given the difficulties of working with reliable series of Spanish wages, other indicators are used. Works based for instance on life expectancy, anthropometrics or in consumption baskets related to nutritional levels are offering appealing ideas.[20] The third matter is about the relations between economic development and the environment in the past which has also attracted the interest of some Spanish researchers. New methodologies related to social metabolisms based on material and energy flow accounting (MEFA), and socio-ecological transitions are starting to develop interesting environmental approaches which can be combined also with social and institutional variables (González de Molina and Toledo 2014). Finally works devoted to the analysis of business, firms and entrepreneurs are more and more present in Spanish economic history. An early subject of internationalization from the 1990s on, and of the use of a varied range of theories (new institutionalism, transaction costs, agency theories, gender in business debates or industrial organization theories), have clearly strengthened this stream in the last decade (Sudría and Fernández 2010).

To sum up, the internationalization process of Spanish economic history has brought about an increasing plurality affecting methodologies and matters. In spite of that, internal debates have almost disappeared in the last decade. In this context it should be stressed that not all the streams are equally open to international forums. In fact those Spanish economic historians who have published in journals abroad over the past decade account for around 20 per cent of the overall membership of the Spanish Economic History Association, and a large number of them (not all fortunately) are engaged with the cliometric stream. This suggests that a large proportion of Spanish economic historians appear to remain stuck in the domestic framework. Some of them also remain fixed in traditional paradigms, even practising some kinds of parochialism. However, others, probably a majority, are making interesting efforts towards a new understanding of development processes, stressing their economic, social and environmental implications. Sadly only a small group is showing its work in the international arena, but probably it is just a question of time.

Concluding remarks

Spanish economic history has undergone an undisputed transformation in recent decades, which has enabled it to narrow the gap with those countries in which the discipline has undergone greater development. Public support through regulations (compulsory nature of the subject on degree courses in economics and business), financing and incentives have played a key role in this convergence process. An overall assessment emphasizing its lights and shadows clearly shows that the former have prevailed over the latter. In these early years of the twenty-first century, the knowledge we have of our country's economic past and its international integration has considerably increased. From a quantitative perspective, beside the series of GDP and other macro metrics contained in statistical records, there has been a thorough reconstruction of series and indices of production, of domestic and foreign trade, and of agrarian and mining development, involving both infrastructures and industry, on a wide array of geographical levels.

From a qualitative perspective, we have a better understanding of the rural world and its transformations; of industrialization processes in different parts of the country, and of the sectors prevailing in each case; of monetary and budgetary issues and their ramifications; of working processes and technological change; of the workings of the institutions at different levels; and progress is being made in the analysis of standards of living, their metrics and the factors involved in their shaping; and also in the close relationships between economic growth and the environment. Although there is still a great deal of progress to be made, the overall assessment of the efforts expended so far must be a positive one.

Nevertheless, one should not be overly self-satisfied, and instead take a moment to note some of the shadows that have darkened the process. The scant interest that a considerable number of Spain's economic historians have shown for theory is one of them. The failure to embed research within a theoretical framework reduces the value-added of many papers by converting them into works that despite their interest do not fit into an articulated discourse. Another shadow cast over the study of Spanish economic history is that, for a long time, it has not managed to escape from a path dependency basically defined by a concept of 'backwardness' in which the most important aim was to explain why Spain did not get the same levels of growth as the richest western countries.

Recently an incipient process of internationalization is taking place at various levels. On the one hand, dedicated Spanish journals are following a process of alignment with top-tier international journals. This may be of importance for the disclosure of research, not only for

Spain but also for other countries in Southern Europe and Latin America. At the same time, certain Spanish scholars are increasingly featuring in greater numbers on the international stage, with publication abroad of papers not only on Spain, but also on other countries.

This internationalization process has brought about in Spain an increase in plurality affecting methodologies. There is no suggestion that Spanish economic historians have at any time been the champions of innovation in theory and methods of the discipline worldwide, but they are taking their cue and increasingly applying new approaches and techniques. Cliometric approaches engaged with the mainstream of the western canon of doing economic history have strengthened in recent years but it is far from being hegemonic inside Spain. Other theoretical approaches have also flourished, centred on institutions, the standard of living, the environment, or upon firms and businesses, with a complex understanding of the process of development and its implications beyond the realms of orthodox economic theory. The problem is that an important part of the Spanish researches on those matters is at the moment too poorly internationalized.

Regarding the new scenarios that appear to be opening up, everything seems to suggest that the importance of Spanish economic history in the future will depend upon its ability to further its international integration. An integration that far from following a single theoretical path should continue to involve different methodologies and questions, in order to contribute more broadly to global debates.

Notes

1 This work has been funded by grants (ECO2012-33286) from the Spanish Ministry of Economy and Competitiveness. I would like to thank for their comments the participants in the Seminar of Economic History in the University of Zaragoza as well as José Miguel Lana and Juan Antonio Rubio. Suggestions from the editors have also been very helpful.

2 The attendance propensity has been calculated by weighting the number attending from each country by the distance from the country of origin, by language difficulties, by income and by the size of the community of economic historians in each country (Baten and Muschallik 2011, table 6).

3 Ruiz Martín guided Braudel himself through several Spanish archives, and was subsequently a guest at *l'Ecole Pratique des Hautes Etudes* in Paris. Vicens Vives was very active not only as an author, but also as the editor of publications that despite appearing within Spain's Higher Research Institute (CSIC) avoided the strict intellectual control wielded by that institution in those days (Marín 2002).

4 Arranged in order of their date of birth, this first generation includes the following: Nicolás Sánchez Albornoz, 1926; Jordi Nadal, 1929; Josep Fontana, 1931; Gonzalo Anes, 1931; Francisco Bustelo, 1933; Pedro Schwartz, 1935; Gabriel Tortella, 1936, and Ramón Garrabou, 1937.

5 Resolution stipulating the guidelines to be followed by the curricula of the Faculties of Economic and Business Sciences, Spain's Official Gazette, BOE-A-1973-1142.

6 In absolute terms, the population with university studies increased fivefold from 1970 to 2012. In relative terms, higher education extended to 2 per cent of the adult population between the ages of 25 and 64 in 1970, and the figure has now risen to 31 per cent, which is slightly higher than the average for OECD countries. In 2012, 53 per cent of students were enrolled in social science and law faculties, where economic science is taught (MECD – Ministry of Education, Culture and Sport, 2012).

7 If we consider all the papers published in the four main Spanish economic history reviews in the last twenty years, around 75 per cent of them are centred in the nineteenth and twentieth centuries.

8 A large part of the analysis on the Spanish Empire and its effects were done from the 1930s by foreign hispanists, i.e. Hamilton (1934). On Hamilton and his works see López Losa (2013). The then state of the art on the Spanish Early Modern Age can be found in Llopis (2004).

9 Tortella himself does not use econometric models in his work, but he became the early main supporter in Spain of the application of standard neoclassical economic theory to historical analysis. Econometric exercises came later in the hands of some of his disciples.

10 More recent studies of Spanish economic history in regional perspective appear in German et al. (2001).

11 See the three volumes of contemporary agrarian history edited by Garrabou and García Sanz (1985); Garrabou and Sanz Fernández (1985); and Garrabou et al. (1986).

12 This consensus may end as research on the second half of the twentieth century matures, analysing changes in more detail.

13 Summaries of the debates may be found in Escudero (1996) for mining and in Herranz (2003) for the railways.

14 Palafox (1991), Tena (1992), Fraile (1993).

15 Two references to follow the debate are Gallego and Pinilla (1996), Tirado and Tena (1996).

16 See Sabaté and Pardos (2001).

17 In 2002, issue 28 of the journal *Historia Agraria* published several papers that challenged the book's findings.

18 The debate on the formats of research dissemination and on the problems arising from the way top-tier journals operate, such as those propounded by Macdonald and Kam (2007) for example, has yet to affect Spanish economic history.

19 An approach related to the New Institutional Economics is to be found in Carmona and Simpson (2010). Works associated with collective action problems are associated to the study of the Spanish common lands, cooperative movements and trade unions, or irrigation networks. See, for instance, Garrido (2011).

20 Most of the research involving these issues is enrolled in the NISAL Project (http://www.proyectonisal.org).

References

Anes, G. (1970) *Las crisis agrarias en la España moderna*, Taurus, Madrid.

Baten, J. and Muschallik, J. (2011) On the status and the future of economic history in the world, MPRA Paper 34704, Online at http://mpra.ub.uni muenchen.de/34704/

Carande, R. (1943 [2000]) *Carlos V y sus banqueros*, Crítica, Barcelona.

Carmona, J. and Simpson, J. (2010) El agricultor moral y la Nueva Economía Institucional, *Revista Española de Estudios Agrosociales y Pesqueros*.

Carreras, A. (1988) La industrialización española en el marco de la Historia Económica Europea: ritmos y caracteres comparados, in García Delgado, *España, Economía*, Espasa, Madrid.

Carreras, A. (coord.) (1989) *Estadísticas históricas de España. Siglo XIX–XX*, Fundación Banco Exterior, Madrid.

Carreras, A. and Tafunell, X. (coords.) (2005) *Estadísticas históricas de España siglos XIX y XX*, Fundación BBVA, Madrid.

Coll, S. (2006) La influencia de la revolución cliométrica en España. Las dos últimas décadas, in C. Barciela, G. Chastagnaret and A. Escudero (coords.), *La historia económica en España y Francia (siglos XIX y XX)*, Universidad de Alicante.

Comín, F. (1988) *Hacienda y economía en la España contemporánea (1800–1936)*, Instituto de Estudios Fiscales, Madrid.

Escudero, A. (1996) Pesimista y optimistas ante el 'boom' minero, *Revista de Historia Industrial*, 10, 69–92.

Fernández Clemente, E. (1995a) Doce años de la *Revista de Historia Económica* reflexión de aniversario, *Revista de Historia Económica – Journal of Iberian and Latin American Economic History*, 13, 611–28.

Fernández Clemente, E. (1995b) La historia económica de España en los últimos veinte años (1975–1995). Crónica de una escisión anunciada, *Revista de Historia Jerónimo Zurita*, 71, 59–94.

Fernández de Pinedo, Emiliano (1974) *Crecimiento económico y transformaciones sociales del País Vasco (1100–1850), siglo XXI*, Madrid.

Fraile, P. (1993) Una interpretación DISE del crecimiento económico en España, *Cuadernos de estudios empresariales*, 3, 283–8.

Fuentes Quintana, E. (dir.) (2003) Economía y economistas Españoles, Círculo de Lectores-Galaxia Gutenberg, Barcelona.

Gallego, D. (2007) *Más allá de la economía de mercado*, Marcial Pons, Madrid.

Gallego, D. and Pinilla, V. (1996) Del librecambio matizado al proteccionismo selectivo: el comercio exterior de productos agrarios y alimentos en España entre 1849 y 1935, *Revista de Historia Económica – Journal of Iberian and Latin American Economic History*, 14, 2, 371–420 and 14, 3, 619–39.

Garrabou, R. and García Sanz, A. (1985) *Cambio social y nuevas formas de propiedad (1800–1850)*, Crítica, Barcelona.

Garrabou, R. and Sanz Fernández, J. (1985) *Expansión y crisis (1850–1900)*, Crítica, Barcelona.

Garrabou, R., Barciela, C., Jiménez Blanco, J.I. and Sanz Fernández, J. (1986) *El fin de la agricultura tradicional (1900–1960)*, Crítica, Barcelona.

Garrido, S. (2011) Las Instituciones de Riego en la España del Este: una reflexión a la luz de la obra de Elinor Ostrom, *Historia agraria*, 53, 13–42.

German, L., Llopis, E., Maluquer de Motes, J. and Zapata, S. (2001) *Historia económica regional del España (Siglos XIX y XX)*, Crítica, Barcelona.

Gerschenkron, Alexander (1962) *Economic backwardness in historical perspective, a book of essays*, Belknap Press, Cambridge, MA.

Gómez Mendoza, Antonio (1982) *Ferrocarriles y cambio económico en España: (1855–1913): un enfoque de nueva historia económica*, Alianza Editorial, Madrid.

González de Molina, M. and Toledo, E. (2014) *The social metabolism. A socio-ecological theory of historical change*, Springer, Cham.

Hamilton, E. J. (1934) *American treasure and the price revolution in Spain, 1501–1650*, Harvard Economic Studies, 43, Harvard University Press, Cambridge, MA.

Herranz, A. (2003) Fracasó el sistema ferroviario en España? Reflexiones en torno a la 'paradoja del ferrocarril español', *Revista de Historia Industrial*, 23, 39–64.

Llopis, E. (ed.) (2004) *El legado económico del antiguo régimen*, Crítica, Barcelona.

López Losa, E. (2013) The legacy of Earl J. Hamilton's data for the study of prices in Spain, 1650–1800, *Investigaciones de historia económica – Economic History Research*, 9, 2, 75–87.

Macdonald, Stuart and Kam, Jacqueline (2007) 'Ring a Ring o'Roses': quality journals and gamesmanship in management studies, *Journal of Management Studies*, 44, 4, 640–55.

Maluquer de Motes, J. (2009a) Del caos al cosmos una nueva serie enlazada del Producto Interior Bruto de España entre 1850 y 2000, *Revista de Economía Aplicada*, 49, 5–46.

Maluquer de Motes, J. (2009b) Viajar a través del cosmos: la medida de la creación de riqueza y la serie histórica del producto interior bruto de España (1850–2008). Réplica a Prados, *Revista de Economía Aplicada*, 51, 25.

Marín, M.A. (2002) El fracaso de la normalización interior de la historiografía española en los años cincuenta, *Usos públicos de la historia*, VI Congreso de la Asociación de Historia Contemporánea, Universidad de Zaragoza, 425–7.

Martín Aceña, P. (1985) *La cantidad de dinero en España, 1900–1935*, Banco de España, Madrid.

MECD (Spain's Ministry of Education, Culture and Sport) (2012) Report on universities.

Merediz, A. (2004) *Historia de la estadística oficial como institución pública en España*, Instituto de Estadística de Andalucía, Seville.

Nadal, J. (1975) *El fracaso de la revolución industrial en España, 1814–1913*, Ariel, Barcelona.

Nadal, J. and Catalán, J. (eds.) (1994) *La cara oculta de la industrialización española. La modernización de los sectores no líderes*, Alianza, Madrid.

Nadal, J. and Tortella, G. (1974) *Agricultura, comercio colonial y crecimiento económico en la España contemporánea: actas del primer Coloquio de Historia Económica de España*, Ariel, Barcelona.

Nadal, J. and Carreras, A. (eds.) (1990) *Pautas regionales de la industrialización española (Siglos XIX y XX)*, Ariel, Barcelona.

Nadal, J. and Sudria, C. (1993) La controversia en torno al atraso económico español en la segunda mitad del siglo XIX (1860–1913), *Revista de Historia Industrial*, 3, 199–224.

Nadal, J., Carreras, A. and Sudria, C. (1987) *La economía española en el siglo XX. Una perspectiva histórica*, Ariel, Barcelona.

Naredo, J.M. (2003) Reflexiones metodológicas en torno al debate sobre el pozo y el atraso de la agricultura española, *Historia Agraria*, 33, 151–64.

Otero Carvajal, L. (2001) La destrucción de la ciencia en España. Las consecuencias del triunfo militar de la España franquista, *Historia y Comunicación Social*, 6, 149–86.

Palafox, J. (1991) *Atraso económico y democracia. La Segunda República y la economía española, 1892–1936*, Crítica, Barcelona.

Pérez Moreda, (1975) The journal 'Moneda y Crédito' and its contribution to Spanish historiography, 1942–1974, *Journal of European Economic History*, 4–3, 753–88.

Pons, J., Paluzie, E., Silvestre, J. and Tirado, D. (2007) Testing the new economic geography: migrations and industrial agglomerations in Spain, *Journal of Regional Science*, 47, 2, 289–313.

Prados de la Escosura, L. (1988) *De imperio a nación*, Alianza, Madrid.

Prados de la Escosura, L. (2004) *El progreso económico de España, 1850–2000*, Fundación BBVA, Bilbao.

Prados de la Escosura, L. (2009) Del cosmos al caos. La serie del PIB de Maluquer de Motes (REA, 49), *Revista de economía aplicada*, 51, 5–23.

Pujol, J., González de Molina, M., Fernández Prieto, L., Gallego, D. and Garrabou, R. (2001) *El pozo de todos los males. Sobre el atraso de la agricultura española contemporánea*, Crítica, Barcelona.

Rosés, J., Martínez-Galarraga, J. and Tirado, D. (2010) The upswing of regional income inequality in Spain (1860–1930), *Explorations in Economic History*, 47, 2, 244–57.

Ruiz Torres, P. (2002) La renovación de la historiografía española: antecedentes, desarrollo y límites, in M.C. Romeo and I. Saz, *El siglo XX. Historiografía e historia*, PUV, Valencia.

Sabaté, M. and Pardos, E. (2001) Una cuestión a debatir: el nuevo perfil del proteccionismo español durante la Restauración, *Revista de Historia Económica – Journal of Iberian and Latin American Economic History*, 19, 1, 155–66.

Sudría, C. and Fernández, P. (2010) Introduction: the evolution of business history as an academic field in Spain, *Business History*, 52, 3, 359–70.

Tello, E. (2005) *La historia cuenta*, El Viejo Topo, Barcelona.

Tena, A. (1992) *Las estadísticas históricas del comercio internacional: fiabilidad y comparabilidad (1890–1960)*, Banco de España, Madrid.

Tirado, A. and Tena, A. (1996) Protección arancelaria en la Restauración. Un debate, *Revista de economía aplicada*, 11, 4, 135–50.

Tortella, G. (1973) *Los orígenes del capitalismo en España. Banca, industria y ferrocarriles en el siglo XIX*, Tecnos, Madrid.

Vazquez de Prada, V. (1990) La historia económica en España (1940–1989): esbozo de su nacimiento y desarrollo, *Hispania*, 175, 473–87.

11

THE LOW COUNTRIES, INTELLECTUAL BORDERLANDS OF ECONOMIC HISTORY

Erik Aerts and Ulbe Bosma

Two small but economically precocious states on the western periphery of the European mainland have, for different reasons, punched above their weight as far as the global history of economic history is concerned. This is especially so in the case of the Netherlands in recent decades. Two authors here contribute their own interpretations of the emergence and trajectory of the field in their respective countries focusing upon their differing economic, political and intellectual contexts and their relationships with the outside world. The subject, as it has developed in both localities, has much to offer to the future of the discipline particularly because, in neither polity, has economic history been irrevocably divorced from social and cultural history. This is the case despite growing specialization of research tools and methods, and despite a concerning drift towards path-dependency arguments within the new institutional economics of recent years.

I BELGIUM

Erik Aerts

Economic history as an academic discipline in Belgium was a relatively late bloomer, but when it finally arrived it immediately gained a position in the forefront of historiography, both within Europe and further afield. In the following overview, we distinguish five phases. We explain why for the first half-century after the creation of the Kingdom of Belgium, economic history was unable to establish itself. During the last decade of the nineteenth century, the firm foundations were laid on which, after the Second World War, the study of economic history was truly able to flourish. This expansion came to a halt in the last decade of the last century. Finally, we consider the current situation. It should be emphasized that this is a first reconnaissance mission, a provisional picture pending an overview with more definitive and also quantitative support.

No economic history in the age of the archivists, 1830–85

In the autumn of 1830, revolutionaries proclaimed Belgium an independent state. The young nation was actively engaged at the time as the first country to introduce the industrial revolution to continental Europe. Large-scale industrialization was driven forward by mechanized coal, steel and textile industries in the provinces of Liège and Hainaut, a mechanized cotton industry in the city of Gent, an expanding world port in the city of Antwerp and an international banking system in the capital, Brussels. The young Belgium was also playing a pioneering role in another area. As early as 1841, the Belgian *Commission Centrale de Statistique* had been established to make government statistics more consistent and complete. This Commission was tasked with providing instruments for policy making and the organization of society. It was also hoped that a better understanding could be gained of the workings of the economy and demographic mechanisms (Bracke 2008: 399). The Commission primarily worked for the government and the administration, but it also served the scientific community. It soon acquired an international reputation thanks to its chairman, the Belgian mathematician, astronomer and sociologist Lambert Adolphe J. Quetelet (1796–1874). He was one of the first to apply statistical techniques in the social sciences.

Impressive industrial growth and the success of statistics in both science and government might have been expected to contribute to the flourishing of economic history. During the first half-century of the country's history, this did not prove to be the case. At this time, three institutions were important for the study of the past: the National or General State Archives, the Academy and the Royal Historical Commission. The historians who worked within these three institutions were cultivated autodidacts or scholars with a legal background; they had great conviction, but usually lacked method. The bulk of historical output was in the hands of archivists, under the powerful intellectual leadership of Louis Prosper Gachard (1800–85), National Archivist from 1831 until his death in 1885. So dominant was the group of archivists, not just in the three major institutions, but also in all kinds of societies and publication series, that Fernand Vercauteren described the half-century from around 1830 to 1880 in Belgian historiography as 'l'âge des archivistes' (Vercauteren 1959: 59). Hardworking archivists staffed the city and state archives as well as dominating the Royal Historical Commission. Among the historians, they were also the largest group within the Academy. At their frequent and well-attended sessions, they decided on projects, chose themes and allocated budgets. Their output was impressive, but the quality was very variable. The archivists were primarily busy with the transcription of sources (the 'véritable chasse aux documents' according to Arnould 1947: 68). However, haste and superficiality marred many editions of texts, which could not withstand comparison with what was being achieved by German historians at that time. In any case, the archivists were not interested in economic history, but in political events, artistic achievements, military actions and ecclesiastical conditions. National Archivist Gachard, who had a personal preference for the sixteenth century, did gradually introduce early modern history into a number of programmes, but he too remained mainly interested in political and religious history. Moreover, amid the nationalist euphoria of the young kingdom, the theme of external domination and foreign tyranny proved popular, while major individual figures were cherished as the forefathers of national history (Tollebeek 1992: 74). Both the economic context and the growing success of statistics went unnoticed by the archivists and romantic narrators (Peeters 2003: 167). It was necessary to wait for another institution, and above all for another generation of historians: the universities and the professors.

The emergence of economic history, 1885–1950

The start of economic history in Belgium can be dated to the last decade of the nineteenth century, and coincided with the concerted 'scientification' (or application of scientific standards) of the practice of history. Archivists and transcribers of texts were replaced by university-educated historians and professors. These also put economic history on the agenda. In 1874, Godefroid Kurth introduced seminars or '*travaux pratiques*' on the German model at the University of Liège, Léon Vanderkindere followed suit at the University of Brussels in 1877, Henri Pirenne imitated the example of his teacher Kurth at the University of Gent from 1886 and Paul Fredericq organized seminars in Liège in 1880. Before the turn of the century, Alfred Cauchie introduced the same innovation in Leuven. The seminar system gained formal recognition in the law of 10 April 1890, which at the same time made the doctoral dissertation a prerequisite for a university career (Schryver De 1997: 300–1; Tollebeek 1990: 8–9).

It was Henri Pirenne (1862–1935) who more than any other historian made an impressive contribution to the shaping of economic history in Belgium. In the young Pirenne, Belgium gained not just an ardent advocate of the new discipline, but an international reputation. Obviously Pirenne was not the first to study economic issues from Belgium's past. Before him, a number of archivists had devoted studies to urban craft associations, while keen amateurs had issued *mémoires* within the Academy about the economic history of Belgium. Numismatists had also done useful work.[1] Pirenne's work differed from that of these enthusiastic dilettantes through his compelling definitions of problems and working hypotheses, his attention to the context in Europe and even more widely, his ability to distil a powerful synthesis from a mass of facts, the rigorous source criticism that he had learned in Germany, and his clear and vivid style. Pirenne was born into a wealthy family of entrepreneurs in Verviers, a city with a thriving wool industry that played a major role in Belgian industrialization. Consequently, he was familiar with economic transformations and convinced of their great social importance from a young age (Sabbe 1936: 81; Pirenne 1938: 8–9). Moreover, while studying in Germany he had met Gustav von Schmoller, the spiritual leader of the young Historical School who was teaching economic history among other subjects in Berlin. Contact with Schmoller, and to a lesser extent with Karl Lamprecht in Bonn and later with Karl Bücher in Leipzig, proved decisive for Pirenne's interest after 1885 in what his teacher Godefroid Kurth called the '*école économiste*' (Rion 1986: 156, 184, 220; Lyon 1998: 508; Thoen and Vanhaute 2011: 325–7; Warland 2011: 435). We know that the liberal Pirenne was also influenced by Karl Marx's historical materialism (Thoen and Vanhaute 2011: 340–1; Dumolyn 2012: 127–8). Pirenne did not publish many individual or small studies on economic history. For the economic aspect of his work, it is necessary to turn instead to his great syntheses (Van Werveke 1938: 249). For example, the economy received extensive coverage in his monumental *Histoire de la Belgique*. Economic factors were also prominent in other key themes he studied during his career: the transition from the late Roman Empire to the early Middle Ages with the expansion of Islam, the rise of cities in the Middle Ages and the birth of commercial capitalism. A recent analysis points out that the development of capitalism in fact runs through Pirenne's œuvre as a *leitmotiv*. In the high Middle Ages, this capitalism was embodied in large cities with their rich merchants and powerful cloth guilds, and from the late Middle Ages by the central state which in the course of time was inevitably transmuted into the bourgeois, liberal and centralized nation-state of Pirenne's own day (Dumolyn 2012: 120–1).

Pirenne also helped ensure the emergence of new specializations such as historical demography. His influence on the emergence and promotion of economic history in Belgium was huge. This was not due purely to the scope and reputation of his own output. The numerous translations of Pirenne's work and his many lectures, his organizational skills and influence in Belgium's leading academic circles, and especially the many students he trained all played an important part. Many of these students themselves became influential professors or ended up occupying key positions in the archives: Guillaume Des Marez (urban land property), Georges Espinas (city finances and the cloth industry), François-Louis Ganshof (urban development and feudalism), Etienne Sabbe (the linen industry), Herman Vander Linden (overseas expansion), Hans Van Werveke (financial and monetary history), Fernand Vercauteren (urban history), Charles Verlinden (overseas expansion and maritime history) and others.

Outside the circle of Pirenne's pupils, historians within and outside the universities were also attracted by the new specialization of economic history. Two good examples are the Gent professor Hubert Van Houtte (1872–1948) and the Belgian National Archivist Joseph Cuvelier (1869–1947). The first of these was a pioneer in the recording of price series from the fourteenth to the eighteenth centuries and the author of a powerful synthesis on the economy of Belgium at the end of the Ancien Régime; the second worked under the influence of his friend Pirenne in the field of historical demography. In the first half of the twentieth century, these historians together laid a solid foundation on which the new discipline could flourish further after the most destructive global conflict the world had ever seen.

The great flowering, 1950–90

Various factors contributed to the flowering of economic history in post-war Belgium, and many of these factors were the same as elsewhere in Europe. The enormous material damage, the major problems experienced with economic reconstruction, but later also the prosperity of the 'silver fifties' and 'golden sixties', automatically brought economic factors to the fore. Further, with the development of neoclassical economic growth theory and of course Keynesianism, economic science had opened up powerful macroeconomic perspectives for historians in the first half of the twentieth century. In addition, like other historical specializations, economic history benefited from the expansion of the universities and from increasing subsidization. In 1949, the funding of the *Nationaal Fonds voor Wetenschappelijk Onderzoek* (NFWO)/*Fonds national de la Recherche Scientifique* (FNRS) was significantly improved by the government. Donations to the foundation were also exempted from tax. In 1965, this funding was further improved by the law on university expansion. While the old universities of Brussels, Gent and Leuven saw their student numbers and academic staff sizes increase due to population growth and the opening up of access to higher education, new initiatives also emerged. Some of these resulted from the linguistic conflict, which was particularly hard-fought in the 1960s. Often, a combination of political factors (e.g. the desire to strengthen the Flemish presence in Brussels) and educational factors (e.g. the desire to bring university education as close to young people as possible) also lay behind the emergence of new academic institutions. Apart from these new universities, economic university colleges or business schools were also created. In Brussels, the best-known were the Flemish Business School (Vlekho) from 1968 and the older Business School of St Aloysius (Ehsal), which became a university-level institution in 1970. In all these new or reformed institutions, economic history was taught and professors of economic history had a place to work.

Compared with the United States or Britain, the gap between economics and economic history remained quite large. Almost everywhere, economists and economic historians belonged to separate faculties at the universities and had little contact with one another. All the same, some change was noticeable, and tentative beachheads were established. Whereas in the publications of the pre-war generations of economic historians, economic theory had at best been vaguely implicit, some economic historians were now making a more explicit attempt to establish connections with the work of their colleagues in the economics faculties. Among other places, this occurred in the business schools, where economic historians were attached to economics departments (e.g. monetary history, taught by Valéry Janssens at Vlekho, or fiscal history and the epistemology of economic history, taught by Paul Janssens at Ehsal). At some universities, economic historians were working in economics departments, which were also booming during these years. Two examples are Pierre Lebrun at the University of Liège and Herman Van der Wee at the University of Leuven.

As early as 1948, Lebrun had already published a doctorate on the mechanization of the woollen industry in Verviers, and in the 1970s he went on to develop a *Centre d'Histoire quantitative* in Liège with the help of his teacher Paul Harsin. From 1979, this centre published a number of impressive doctorates on the origin and nature of the Belgian industrial revolution. The work of the Leuven economic historian Herman Van der Wee was more diversified and extensive. With his monumental doctoral dissertation, he can also be described as a pioneer of quantitative economic history in Belgium (Aerts 2014: 619–717). He deserves this title not just because he definitively introduced a number of techniques from statistics, but also and above all because he showed his students the way to quantitative and in some cases even econometric history. Although Van der Wee was influenced by the ideas of renowned British economic historians such as Eleanor Carus-Wilson, Jack Fisher, Thomas S. Ashton, Michael Postan and Richard Tawney as a result of his studies at the London School of Economics, in the field of historical statistics he drew inspiration mainly from the French tradition of the *Annales* and especially from Jean Meuvret. This underlines the fact that the famous 'new economic history' never gained much acceptance in Belgian economic history (Aerts 2007: 259). A small group of historians, less influential than in England, used Marxist-inspired economic theory. Examples include Catharina Lis and Hugo Soly (Brussels) with their analysis of the causes of poverty in pre-industrial Europe, and Erik Thoen (Gent) with his explanation of the relatively mild nature of the depression in late medieval Flanders. The Marxist analysis also attracted considerable interest from a number of economic historians of the contemporary period. A good example is Eric Vanhaute (Gent) with his numerous studies of family labour and income strategies in the Flemish countryside, labour relations and labour markets, and later with his explanation of the development of world systems as part of his approach to global history.

During this heyday of economic history, sources were also diligently published by specialist teams, long before electronic databases were created. The *Interuniversitaire Centrum voor de Geschiedenis van Prijzen en Lonen* (*Centre interuniversitaire pour l'histoire des prix et des salaires*) promoted research into prices and wages from the mid-1950s onwards, while at the University of Gent between 1959 and 1973 Charles Verlinden and in practice especially Jan Craeybeckx and Etienne Scholliers published five volumes of *Dokumenten voor de geschiedenis van prijzen en lonen*, amounting to some 3000 pages mainly on the late Middle Ages and early modern period. At the *Centrum voor Hedendaagse Sociale Geschiedenis* at the Vrije Universiteit Brussel from the mid-1970s onwards, research into these variables was continued in the nineteenth and twentieth centuries, under the leadership of Juul Hannes and Etienne Scholliers. At around the same time, the first computers made their appearance in Belgian economic history. For both the classification of data, calculations and descriptive statistical methods, use was made of 'mechanography'. Among other examples, this was done for the study of the finances of the royal demesne and central coinage (Eddy Van Cauwenberghe); mobility among the nobles (Paul Janssens); the reconstruction of traffic in the port of Antwerp (Karel Veraghtert) and of property and income as criteria for social stratification (Léon de Saint-Moulin); the analysis of population censuses (Claude Desama, Etienne Hélin); the analysis of overseas emigration and landownership (Ginette Kurgan-Van Hentenryk) and the study of certain types of serial documentation such as notarial protocols (Paulette Pieyns-Rigo).

The expansion of economic history led to new specializations that developed into fully fledged subdisciplines. Topics such as poverty, income, property, wealth, purchasing power, standard of living, social stratification, but also consumption, material culture, food and social mobility processes were now studied within a separate discipline, social history. This had developed in Belgium under the aegis of economic history (Noordegraaf 1990: 10) and in 1975 gained its own Belgian–Dutch journal (the *Tijdschrift voor Sociale Geschiedenis*). New auxiliary sciences were enthusiastically integrated into economic history and acquired the status of autonomous disciplines. Historical demography, which had already been accorded recognition by Pirenne, truly flourished, integrating the achievements of the French *Annales* school (Prevenier 1979: 558). Mention should also be made in particular of medieval archaeology (Van der Wee 1995: 173; Verhulst 1997: 95) as well as quantitative lexicology (specifically diachronic semantics) and more advanced historical statistics. During the golden years of economic history, there was not only a growing number of professors and projects and a further proliferation of themes, specializations and techniques: but the number of students opting for economic history at universities and the new business schools also grew faster than the total number of students. In the largest university in the country, which at that time also had the most history students, the University of Leuven, the average annual number of students opting for the discipline of economic history was five between 1970 and 1980, and twelve between 1980 and 1990. The total number of PhD students increased over these two decades by 48 per cent, but the number of PhD students in economic history rose by 83 per cent. In the other major Flemish university, the State University of Gent, the number of students with a Master's thesis in economic history grew during the decades 1972 to 1981 and 1982 to 1992 from an annual average of four to five.[2] During the years 1944 to 1960, the annual average had been just 1.6. The rise of social history, interpreted in the broadest sense, was already an established fact at the University of Gent by 1960.

Crisis and change after 1990

The publication of Laurence Stone's influential article in *Past & Present* in 1979 is often regarded as a pivotal moment at which the quantitative, generalizing approach to economic history was supplanted by 'the revival of narrative', the vivid account in which, under the influence of historical anthropology, attention began to be paid to the atypical element, to chance, to the specific and unpredictable event, to the small-scale *microstoria* (Soly 1992: 33–4, 37). This methodological shift coincided with a certain loss of prestige for economic history. However, there was no abrupt break in Belgium, or not around 1980 at any rate. In Leuven, Herman Van der Wee made a start in 1984 on a major project to reconstruct the national accounts of Belgium between 1795 and 1953 (Van der Wee and Dancet 1986: 145–68). The intention was to catch up with a number of European countries and the United States, where the first such studies had already appeared in the 1950s and especially in the 1960s, at the instigation of Simon Kuznets (Van der Wee and Klep 1975: 205–6). For reasons of consistency with the accounts published after 1953 Van der Wee preferred to apply the approach of the Belgian *Nationaal Instituut voor de Statistiek* (*Institut National de Statistique*), based on the methodology of the OECD. That project continued into the 1990s and led to a dozen monographs on the nineteenth and twentieth centuries and to several estimates for the Ancien Régime (Blomme and Van der Wee 1994: 77–96). In 1992, another major project was started on the reconstruction of time series on prices and wages, population, agriculture, industry, trade and money supply between the National State Archives of Belgium and the Universities of Gent, Leuven and Louvain-la-Neuve (Aerts 1995: 365–9).

Slowly, though, the changing *zeitgeist* and the pendulum of historical interest exerted their influence on economic historiography in Belgium as elsewhere. Influential economic historians did not of course abandon their specialist field, but fell under the spell of other aspects of historical reality. Social history was now fully emancipated and outshone economic history. Cultural history, which had been on the rise since the 1980s, also attracted much interest. The result was a shift in themes and in the methodological approach to certain themes, and the use of new sources such as diaries, literary texts, images and probate inventories. New consumption patterns were no longer accounted for exclusively by macroeconomic changes, but were also related to cultural and psychological variables such as identity, status, prestige, taste and fashion, self-perception and so on. Quantitative estimates of output of goods and services were supplemented by an analysis of the diffusion of new products across social groups. In food history, interest shifted from supply to consumers and their preferences. Statistical models of monetary circulation and a meticulous reconstruction of coin production gave way to analyses of the social role of credit relationships and the use of money by certain population groups. Demography was no longer confined to the calculation of a variety of ratios and coefficients: it now also took an interest in relations between husbands and wives and parents and children, health care, hygiene and sexuality. Economic historians discovered in Belgium, as elsewhere, that in addition to population, international trade, class relations and the money supply, nature could also be regarded as an explanatory variable in economic transformation processes. The interest in the environment and climate led in 1996 to the founding of the *Tijdschrift voor Ecologische Geschiedenis*, from which the *Jaarboek voor Ecologische Geschiedenis* originated in 1998.

In the late 1980s, the appearance of economic history in Belgium thus changed. The quantification of hard economic variables was replaced by or substantially supplemented with a qualitative approach that did not rely exclusively on economic theory, but made more explicit use of concepts and techniques from anthropology, communication theory, cultural studies, linguistics, literary studies, geography, ecology, psychology and sociology. Inevitably, economic historiography declined in popularity compared with social history, cultural history and the *histoire des mentalités*. Figures for the number of students at the history department of the University of Leuven who opted for a Master's thesis in economic history confirm this impression. During the decade 1970 to 1980, the percentage of Master's students opting for a topic in economic history was 13 per cent. That figure remained unchanged in the decade 1981 to 1990, but decreased to 8 per cent in the decade 1991 to 2000.

The reorientation within economic historiography did not put a stop to the ongoing process of specialization. Belgian economic historians were constantly tackling new themes: transport, retail, the knowledge economy (the importance of innovation and the transfer and circulation of knowledge for economic development), urban networks, urban mechanisms of inclusion and exclusion, the middle classes, perception of labour, the industrious revolution, the significance of the market. The 'return of the guilds' (a special issue of the *International Review of Social History* in 2008) was also greeted enthusiastically in Belgium, as was the renewed interest in institutions (the 'new institutional economics'). It was already being pointed out twenty years ago that this increasing specialization and segmentation was leading to an extraordinary fragmentation that was also characterized by the absence of a comprehensive paradigm or dominant theory. Instead, there was a variety of conceptual frameworks, with a lack of any coherent vision or summative metaphor. Belgium was no exception here to an international trend (Soly 1992: 27–8). Most Belgian historians also continued to write on the history of their own country. This last observation is of course related to Belgium's rich economic history and its abundant and extremely varied source material. Henri Pirenne already regarded his homeland as a kind of micro-Europe, a laboratory in which experiments were performed with the most fascinating institutions and economic organizational forms. For the same reason, the economic history of Belgium has always attracted numerous foreign scholars (Blockmans 1985: 602–3). Suffice it to recall here that in 1969 Franklin Mendels developed his concept of 'proto-industry' on the basis of eighteenth-century rural Flanders.

The current situation

On the eve of the First World War, some scholars still believed that there was a 'definite relationship between the size and power of a nation and the distinction of its historians' (Lyon 1981: 186). Such a mono-causal statement does injustice to other important variables such as the proportion of its income that the government wishes to invest in a particular discipline, the university structure (by the standards of other countries, Belgian professors endure a heavy teaching load), historiographical traditions and so on. But this is not to say that size and scale are unimportant. According to the figures of Baten and Muschallik, Belgium had about 60 economic historians in 2011. For a population of 11 million inhabitants, this represents 5.5 economic historians per million inhabitants. Belgium thus turns out to be an average performer in Europe in this respect, with a significantly lower rate than the neighbouring Netherlands (138 economic historians for a population of 16.7 million, i.e. a ratio of 8.3). The Scandinavian countries and the United Kingdom also score better, while countries such as France, Germany and Italy employ relatively fewer economic historians (Baten and Muschallik 2011: tables 2 and 3).

Today, economic history in Belgium is mainly studied at the universities; the federal scientific institutions (in particular the National State Archives and the Royal Library) and some financial institutions (such as the National Bank) also have a limited number of economic historians on their staff. There are no close-knit research clusters at individual universities and no division of labour between the universities, although a number of research focuses can be distinguished. At the University of Antwerp, the Centre for Urban History strives to investigate 'important aspects of urban culture, economy, religion, politics and institutions from the Middle Ages to the present' (according to the website). More or less the same objective is pursued by the research group HOST (Historical Research into Urban Transformation Processes) at the Vrije Universiteit Brussel, where the basic 'point of departure is how the interactions between diverse social groups shaped urban dynamics of change and stability within a long-term perspective' (again according to the website). At the same university, FOST (Social & Cultural Food Studies) conducts interdisciplinary research into the history of food. The Université libre de Bruxelles is internationally renowned for its research into the early medieval economy. In recent years, research has been conducted by a new generation of historians into urban geography, urban space, environmental challenges, and the relationship between natural resources and urban populations. At Gent there is a long tradition of urban history, agricultural history and demography, and these disciplines are still pursued actively there. Areas of focus include the social and financial aspects of the medieval and early modern city, rural and ecological history since the late Middle Ages and various aspects of the Belgian population in the late eighteenth and nineteenth centuries. At Leuven, research is conducted into late medieval and early modern monetary history at the department of history and into contemporary banking and business history at the department of economics, while at ICAG (or the Interfaculty Centre for Agrarian History) an interdisciplinary approach is taken to food, agriculture and the countryside after 1750, including in the former Belgian colony of Congo. At the universities of Liège, Louvain and Namur, economic historians are less numerous. Liège has a reputation for historical demography, while regional history and environmental history are high on the research agendas at Louvain and Namur.

Between universities there is tentative collaboration, sometimes for joint publications, formerly in the context of informal research groups and today within research projects or even more formally within institutes and associations. Between Flemish and Walloon universities, however, cooperation is rather limited. One exception to this is the Inter-university Attraction Poles Project 'City & Society in the Low Countries (ca.1200–ca.1850)', which brings together universities in Flanders, Wallonia and Brussels (as well as federal scientific institutions) and the universities of Leiden and Utrecht in the Netherlands.

It is appropriate to end this overview on a positive note. It has been suggested that Belgian historians in general adhered to their archival sources, excelled in the 'meagre and desiccated' reporting of facts about hyperspecialized topics, and showed a lack of vision, boldness and suggestiveness in grand and compelling syntheses (Soly 1992: 55; Pasture 2005: 421–2). This argument does not seem valid for economic history (see also Aerts 2000: 24). Indeed, there is no sense of crisis in Belgian economic historiography at present. Despite the difficult budgetary situation, there may never have been more economic historians active than today. Many of them publish, more than before, in the best general and specialized international journals. New and original syntheses on vast subjects are published regularly (e.g. Blockmans 2010; Blondé et al. 2015). While Belgium and the Southern Netherlands remain extremely important in economic historians' choice of topics, a global approach is becoming increasingly common. Examples of this international focus are found, for instance, in the Gent research group Communities–Comparisons–Connections which brings together historians and social scientists to analyse research topics in world history, world-systems analysis and globalization. Today global historiography also incorporates the colonial past of Belgium, including the controversial history of the Congo Free State under the Belgian king Leopold II. Research on the history of the Congo, Belgium's former colony, only started in the 1950s, meaning that for a long period British and American historians have been more active in imperial research than Belgian scholars (Vanthemsche 2012: 10). Apart from the economic colonial and postcolonial history of the Congo itself (see already ICAG above), its contribution to the economic development of Belgium and the long-term effects of colonial exploitation, a more global approach has developed. Recent research focuses on how parts of the Congo became integrated into complex world production systems, transnational division of labour and international capital movements. Much attention is given to the global strategy of multinationals (for example the *Union Minière*) in mining extraction which 'in terms of size and diversity was unique in colonial Africa' (Frankema and Buelens 2013: 4).

Even before the financial crisis of 2007–8 and the disappointing economic growth that followed, economic history in Belgium was enjoying a modest revival which has since grown further. Economic historians have learned to include social and cultural factors in their explanatory models and social and cultural historians are no longer averse to the economic context. This double realization means that the former twins have been drawing closer to one another again.

II THE NETHERLANDS

Ulbe Bosma

In the eighteenth century the Dutch Republic went through a period of institutional, technological and economic stagnation. While Britain introduced coal and iron, the Dutch continued with peat, wood, wind and water. While most states in Europe centralized, the Dutch elites were happy with their strongly federalist state. Seemingly devoid of entrepreneurial spirit the country was imbued with the mentality of the rentier who was content to have his abundant capital resting in public debt: a solid but low interest investment. Nevertheless, as Adam Smith rightfully pointed out, the Republic was the richest country in the world. This miraculous economic anachronism collapsed, however, during the French occupation, when Napoleon was siphoning off Dutch wealth on behalf of his ambition to conquer the world and the old federalist political system was abandoned in favour of a unitary state.

Under the dire economic circumstances of the French period a first attempt was made to reconstruct a balance of income and expenditure of the Dutch Republic that was based upon a division of agriculture, trade and manufacturing (van Zanden and van Riel 2004: 13). It would take yet another century before economic statistics became institutionalized. In 1892, the Central Committee for Statistics was established – provided with a Central Bureau for Statistics seven years later – to assemble material about the social question, the poor conditions of the working class.[3] From its very beginning economic and social history in the Netherlands has been developed in tandem with such welfare concerns as well as with regularly returning anxieties about the putative lack of scientific content of our profession. This combination of desires to catch up with the hard sciences and to become relevant to society marked the inaugural lecture of P. J. Blok, the first professor of social history in the Netherlands. He pleaded for history as a social science looking for universal laws in human society. The belief that the natural science approach could be equally successful in solving social questions as in clarifying the mysteries of the universe was not confined to universities. The ambition to apply scientific rigour to welfare concerns resonated among the authorities of the extensive colonial possessions of the Netherlands Indies with its 50 million or so inhabitants at the turn of the twentieth century. In 1910 the colonial government started the so-called Declining Welfare Investigation (*Mindere Welvaart Onderzoek*), a highly detailed multi-volume exercise on the economic development of Java and Madura, where the majority of Indonesians lived.

Despite Blok's clarion call, Dutch economic history in the early years of the twentieth century shunned any attempt at finding universal laws governing human economic behaviour let alone seeking societal relevance. Much of the best and most innovative work on economic history was conducted on the Middle Ages or early modern history. Dutch economic history was strongly influenced by the German Historical School with its strong empirical approach and its professed preference for studying economic trajectories in their historical specificity. Up until the 1930s, Dutch economic history continued its course of deeply empirical and quantitative work and, with the exception of some ideas of Werner Sombart, stayed aloof from international debates and from economic modelling in particular.

Although one can detect some familiarity between the Dutch emphasis on *longue durée* and data collection on the one hand and the *histoire sérielle* of the *Annales* School and the work of Werner Sombart on the other, one should not overstretch the similarities. In contrast to the *Annales* School, Dutch social-economic historians showed scant interest in the history of mentality. Although this approach was brilliantly represented by Johan Huizinga, in his work one will search in vain for any table or graph. Nevertheless, in the 1960s Dutch social-economic historians produced important work that could have fitted, in part at least, into the French mode of history writing. Bernard Slicher van Bath's research on demographic constraints and rural economic development serves as an outstanding example in this regard (e.g. Slicher van Bath 1963). The Wageningen School, which is the Agricultural University of the Netherlands, established a widely recognized reputation for its research on demography, occupational change and rural economics. Again, this 'sociographic' approach was deeply suspicious of theory, although at the same time permeated by a rather grim Malthusian perspective that brushed over the agency of the rural population.

Thanks to the absence of theoretical and methodological controversy, and thanks to the nation's proclivity for dialogue, social and economic history was able to develop as a single historical subdiscipline in the Netherlands. The unity of social and economic history was personified in N. W. Posthumus, generally considered to be the founder of Dutch economic and social history. According to Posthumus economic history should concern itself with business and bosses, whereas social history had to focus on the workers. The two complementary approaches were literally united under one roof. The two institutes created by Posthumus, the Netherlands Economic History Archive (NEHA) and the International Institute of Social History (IISH), are located in the same building in Amsterdam. Up to the present, history students are not trained as economic historians or social historians but as *economic–social* historians and their journal is the Dutch–Flemish *Low Countries Journal of Social and Economic History*.

Overcoming Dutch parochialism

In 1959, Z. M. Dittrich and A. M. Van der Woude – the latter would become a PhD student of Slicher van Bath one year later – threw a stone in the pond with their blistering attack on their colleagues' solipsistic indulgence in writing articles and books according to literary standards rather than collaborating to create, for example, one immense database of historical knowledge (Dittrich and van der Woude 1959). Nevertheless, Dittrich and Van der Woude must have noticed with satisfaction that in the 1970s chairs in social–economic history were established at every Dutch history department. It was not enough, however, because during these very years historians from abroad concluded that Dutch history was too important to be left to the historians of the Netherlands. Jan de Vries had begun to study the Dutch Republic as the first case of modern economic growth. Immanuel Wallerstein dealt with the Republic as the first hegemonic power possessing productive, commercial and financial superiority over all other core powers. Jonathan Israel wrote an entire volume about the Dutch Republic as the first global entrepôt. And last but not least there was Simon Schama's *The Embarrassment of Riches*, an immensely successful work on the Golden Age of the Dutch Republic. The message could not have been more painful to Dutch historians: they were assigned a seat on the backbenches.

Seeing that the Dutch historians were hardly participating in the burgeoning international field of their own history, the baby boomers who entered the profession in the 1970s and 1980s felt that there was an urgent need to elevate the status of history in the gaze of their colleagues abroad. In 1988 Karel Davids, Jan Lucassen and Jan Luiten van Zanden, all in their thirties and early forties, published a pamphlet, the title of which in English reads as 'Dutch history as the exception from the common pattern'.[4] By picking an approach that highlighted the singularity of Dutch history while firmly embedding it in European historiography they hoped to rally a group of historians from various disciplines both from the Netherlands and abroad around a common theme. The aim was a reappraisal of the Dutch Republic as part of Europe, by comparing the Dutch Republic with earlier city-states like Venice or Antwerp, with the only difference – and the sting is in the tail – that 'the Dutch Republic turns out time and again to have dwarfed all of its precursors' (Davids and Lucassen 1995: 440).

Another silver lining was less visible for most Dutch historians but nonetheless important for the international reputation of historical research in the Netherlands. This concerned the connections between history and scholarship in Asian cultures and societies, an academic interest that had been fostered in the context of the country's extensive colonial empire. Although on a smaller scale than Fernand Braudel, who succeeded in broadening the research agenda of his École des Hautes Études en Sciences Sociales by attracting specialists on histories beyond Europe, Posthumus and his successor at the helm of the IISH, A. J. C. Rüter, managed to widen the horizon of social and economic history beyond the European orbit in to late 1950s. Posthumus established the *Journal of Economic and Social History of the Orient* (JESHO) and Rüter inaugurated the *International Review of Social History*. Despite its orientalist name, JESHO did a highly commendable job in connecting the discipline of economic and social history with scholarship on the languages and cultures of a wide range of Asian societies. Dutch historians had an advantage in this respect through their immediate access to the immense collection of sources of the Dutch East India Company (VOC) with its unique documentation about Asian economies in the seventeenth and eighteenth centuries.

The *Review* encountered more obstacles than JESHO in overcoming methodological nationalism as it faced the dominant paradigm within labour history of the white industrial male wage worker. In the late 1990s the IISH decided to tackle this obstacle head on and launched the concept of global labour history. This was against the grain of the cultural turn, to which a generation of talented labour historians in the world, including those of the Subaltern Studies Group, felt attracted. The Dutch stayed within a classical framework of studying labour relations, which has been steadily widened to include gender, coerced labour, rural transformations and commodity chain approaches and this is now the international vanguard of labour history (e.g. van der Linden 2008).

The impact of the New Economic History in the Netherlands

While escaping from Dutch parochialism another danger was already looming, namely of a drifting apart of social–cultural history and economic history. This had definitely not been the intention of the initiators of the research agenda on the Dutch Republic as 'the exception from the common pattern', as they had aimed high at an integrated historical approach. Nonetheless, over the past decades concerns about increasing specialization and about a rift between qualitative and quantitative approaches have grown.

Many historians from all over the world believed in the 1970s that social and economic history had to become quantitative history or else it would be nothing. It was another rush hour in the secular drive towards scientific history and again the expectations of what the application of social sciences had in store were set high, some would say ridiculously high. One thing was serious this time, however. The work of the New Economic Historians Robert Fogel and Stanley Engerman made such an impression in Europe that Emmanual Le Roy Ladurie, historical demographer and eminent member of the *Annales* group, confessed in his in augural lecture in 1973: 'If we refuse to assimilate the most sophisticated elements of economic theory, our French school of research runs the risk of finding itself one day in possession of a slightly overvalued capital of historical knowledge' (Le Roy Ladurie 1977: 121). These most sophisticated elements were statistical in character and would not just change but redefine the field of social and economic history in the Netherlands. Cliometrics, including the econometric approach in history, became the engine of comparative study of economic growth as well as historical demography.

The quantitative turn in social–economic history inaugurated a long and arduous but eventually successful trajectory for the field in the Netherlands. It required millions of euros from the Dutch Science Foundation, but we can now clearly see the benefits of decades of investment. At the University of Groningen Angus Maddison developed his widely used data series on economic growth worldwide over the past thousand years. His project is continued and was widened in the current so-called CLIO-infra project, a joint programme of the IISH, the University of Groningen, Utrecht University and the Eberhard Karls University of Tübingen. The database presents a wide range of indicators of development (aside from output and GDP, including biological, institutional, environmental, human capital).[5] CLIO-infra comes close to facilitating the writing of integrated history in the spirit of the founders of *Annales* on a worldwide scale. In the field of historical demography, the Historical Sample of the Netherlands was developed as a multi-year project to follow the life courses of 80,000 Dutch citizens born between 1812 and 1922.[6]

The flip side of these successes is that it requires steady specialization in quantitative and digital humanities techniques to stay at the cutting edge of economic history. Just at the time that writing *histoire totale* seems to be technically within reach, social and economic history may succumb to overspecialization. The New Economic History, which so successfully bridged the gap between economics and history that had emerged since the late nineteenth century *Methodenstreit*, was now creating a new rift between the cliometricians and economic and social historians who were not part of statistics-based historical approaches. Meanwhile, the scope of economic history in the Netherlands narrowed towards the history of economic growth. Despite the fact that economic and social history is institutionally united at the Master's and PhD levels in the 'N. W. Posthumus inter-university research school of the Low Countries' (the Netherlands and Flanders), a rift is revealing itself. It is precisely within the setting of the Posthumus Institute that a pillarization of subdisciplines rather than cross-fertilization is taking place.

Some of these concerns were expressed at a symposium in 2007 on social and economic history in the Netherlands in the twenty-first century. The organizers were the same 'Young Turks' Karel Davids, Jan Lucassen and Jan Luiten van Zanden who twenty years before had launched the new research agenda and in the meantime had become leading and internationally acknowledged historians.[7] Satisfaction about the immense progress Dutch social–economic history had made since 1988, which had become visibly present in global academia, was coupled with concerns about the dominance of cliometrics and neoclassical economics. A telling detail was that social historians had not even bothered to send papers to the 2007 symposium. The consequence was, as Ewout Frankema and Jan-Pieter Smits observed in their contribution to this gathering, that while economic history had been attracting the attention of mainstream economists it had become utterly marginalized within the field of history (Frankema and Smits 2008).

The publications emanating from the New Institutional Economic History, fast becoming a subfield, were not however as inaccessible to historians of other persuasions as critics would like to think (North and Thomas 1973). Work of this school is often not only readable, and appealing to a wider audience, it is also daringly paints the big picture as is exemplified by the work of the most prominent of the Dutch economic historians Jan Luiten van Zanden (2009). His book on the nineteenth-century Dutch economy, in collaboration with Arthur van Riel, is a hallmark of New Institutional Economic History research, carefully intertwining the story of the modernization of an economy that was stagnant in the late eighteenth century, with another story of a state that was federalized in structure and developed into a unitary corporatist state in the course of the nineteenth century. I would argue that it is not cliometrics and lack of accessibility that deserve our scrutiny but the risk of an overemphasis on path dependency and the danger of adopting a unilinear perspective.

Beyond unilinear economic history?

To further illuminate the point about unilinearity, I make a brief detour to the economic history of Indonesia, once a Dutch colony. Here, we see debates, conducted mostly by Dutch historians, that are almost entirely focused on its late-colonial and postcolonial trajectories of economic growth: on how the colonial economic impediments impinged upon postcolonial economic growth. These are debates in which a variety of positions are taken (e.g. classical growth economics, institutional economic history, political economy, economic dualism, etc.), but still there is a striking imbalance in perspective.[8] The neoclassical growth model with its emphasis on institutional factors functions as the meta-narrative even though this may not be the approach that takes us closer to answering the classical question, why the former tropical colonies today are poor and Europe rich. Even if we move beyond the explanations that heavily focus on 'what went wrong in colonial times' and how it can account for current predicaments, it is still questionable whether involving pre-colonial times in our explanatory model will help.

A long-term perspective is illuminating but within New Institutional Economic History, as practised in Holland and elsewhere, economic growth is perceived as a linear process; growth may be slower and/or faster, may even be negative for a while but it has to follow some preordained path of sectoral change. Second, statistical methods cannot explain individual histories for the obvious reason that they can only take a limited number of factors into account. If path dependency could explain individual trajectories it could predict the future. But will we have developed a historical narrative to explain, for example, how the Philippines, an economic promise by 1950, ended up in dire straits economically thirty years later and did much worse than most other Southeast Asian countries? There is no way in which the neoclassical explanatory models with their focus on sectoral divisions and economic institutions can explain how the economies of Thailand and Korea that were a lot more agriculturally based than the Philippines in the 1950s could have surpassed the latter in the 1980s.

New Economic History runs the risk of aiming to explain too much with too little. It was precisely on this weak spot of New Institutional Economic History that the Dutch historian Peer Vries, professor at the University of Vienna, launched a blistering attack on Daron Acemoglu and James A. Robinson's *Why Nations Fail. The Origins of Power, Prosperity and Poverty* (2012). His article was entitled 'Does wealth really entirely depend on inclusive institutions and pluralist politics?' Referring to Jeffrey G. Williamson and Hekscher-Ohlin's observation that agricultural commodities suffer more from price volatility than industrial manufactures, he criticizes the endogenous bias in the path-dependency approach (Vries 2012: 81). Vries's diagnosis is that New Institutional Economic History might have explained why nations grew rich but not why others 'failed', as the latter usually happened because of factors beyond these nations' control. The rather disturbing conclusion one can attach to Vries's article is that if economic history cannot develop a single explanatory framework for the core and periphery, the New Institutional Economic History is in a blind alley.

Fortunately, there is a way out, one that accounts for the connectivity in history, that comparative historians have always recognized as posing particular methodological challenges. Most variables that econometricians want to correlate to explain trajectories of economic growth are seldom independent, particularly not if units of analysis are entire states. It is not something that can be solved by more sophisticated statistical analysis but requires different methodologies that address global entanglements. Such approaches would bring us closer to evolutionary economics, fathered by Thorstein Veblen and Joseph Schumpeter, with its emphasis on connectivity, creativity and destruction, than neoclassical growth economics

(Drukker 2003). Whereas in many respects economic historians have been considered as more successful than social historians in asking and answering global questions, with respect to the methodological implications of global connectivity and the absence of linearity I would not grant them that position. In this respect, reciprocal comparisons – suggested by Kenneth Pomeranz and elaborated by Gareth Austin – should guide us to avoid the mistake of applying the European experience as the Archimedean point in history (Austin 2007). Social historians have been more aware of these dangers, I would submit, and this is where one major strength of economic history in the Low Countries lies.

The consequence of accepting that history matters in economic history is that historical specificity has to be brought into the fold. The way to do that is by doing archival research, which is neither very popular among cliometric historians nor among poststructuralist social historians for that matter. I have already mentioned the rich archives of the Dutch East India Company, about 5 kilometres, which not only provide us with a detailed insight into the workings of the world's first multinational but also contain immensely valuable data on economic and social history in Asia. These archives – as archives of trading companies and colonial administrations of other European powers for that matter – are indispensable for making progress in the cluster of debates around the 'Great Divergence'. The problem in many countries of the Global South is that these archives are still underutilized in this respect not only with respect to real wages as Prasannan Parthasarathi (2011: 45–6) has emphasized for India, but also with respect to deindustrialization debates. As Tirthankar Roy has lamented, the 'sad state of economic history' still trailed the nationalist industrialization theme and ignored the specificities and ecological constraints of the Indian trajectory (Roy 2004). We can also read in Parthasarathi's and Roy's observations the need for keeping social and economic history as a single discipline.

Conclusion

Up until the 1970s Dutch social and economic history was solidly empirical, shunning theoretical reflections and the incorporation of economic theory. The fact that historians abroad made shining careers with the theme of the Dutch Republic served as a wake-up call. Thanks to economic historians like Angus Maddison and Jan Luiten van Zanden, and the historians they trained, the Netherlands economic historians became prominently visible in the international field. The number of Dutch historians publishing in economic history journals testifies to that. They are making good use of Dutch archives to participate in global debates on causes of growth, economic divergence, global migration and global commodity flows. While no one denies that choices in the past may restrict options for the future, a narrow focus on path dependency on the part of some economic historians runs the risk of being blind to exogenous factors and interactions. This is something outside of economic history: it involves perspectives on entanglements that are more popular among social historians. Fortunately social history and economic history are not yet separated in the Netherlands in the sense that social history has become cultural studies and economic history is only talking to economist–historians. We can thus look forward to the possibilities of reintegration before it is too late.

Notes

1 A general outline of such studies can be found in the detailed bibliographical overview of Belgian historical output up to 1914 (Pirenne 1931: 166–85).

2 For Leuven I have used my own calculations based on Verberckmoes (2008: 30–105). These figures disregard the economic history of antiquity. For Gent, the figures have been taken from François (1993: 21). The figures for Leuven and Gent are not directly comparable. In Gent, for example, François counted subjects such as the standard of living, prices and wages or the labour market under social history rather than economic history. Also the counting periods used are not exactly the same, and for Gent Master's theses about antiquity were included. The figures merely reflect trends *within* each institution.

3 To fill the gap of the absence of nineteenth-century data, Jan Luiten van Zanden would conduct a reconstruction of Dutch national accounts of this century in 1990, to be followed a few years later by a reconstruction of the national accounts of the Netherlands Indies.

4 The Dutch title of their pamphlet was 'De Nederlandse geschiedenis als afwijking van het algemeen menselijk patroon'.

5 https://www.clio-infra.eu/datasets/indicators

6 http://www.iisg.nl/hsn/

7 'Disscussiedossier', *Tijdschrift voor Sociale en Economische Geschiedenis,* 5 (2) 2008: 87–163.

8 The histories of the various phases of Dutch maritime and colonial history occupy a prominent place in the economic historiography of the Netherlands, too extensive to be discussed here. For an overview see Bosma (2014).

References

Aerts, E. (1995) 'The "Historical Statistics" Service Centre and Research Network within the General State Archives', *Nouvelles de la Science et des Technologies,* 13 (2–4): 365–9.

Aerts, E. (2000) 'Vlaamse historici tussen professionalisme en dilettantisme', *Hermes. Tijdschrift voor Geschiedenis,* 16 (4): 24–6.

Aerts, E. (2007) 'Statistiek in de mediëvistiek. Een balans van een halve eeuw onderzoek in België', *Jaarboek voor Middeleeuwse Geschiedenis,* 10: 254–94.

Aerts, E. (2014) 'De genese van de groei. *The Growth of the Antwerp Market* van Herman Van der Wee een halve eeuw (1963–2013)', *Belgisch Tijdschrift voor Filologie en Geschiedenis,* 92 (2): 699–717.

Arnould, M. A. (1947) *Historiographie de la Belgique des origines à 1830* (Collection nationale, 7me série, 80), Brussels.

Austin, Gareth (2007) 'Reciprocal Comparison and African History: Tackling Conceptual Eurocentrism in the Study of Africa's Economic Past', *African Studies Review* 50 (3): 1–28.

Baten, J. and Muschallik, J. (2011) 'On the Status and the Future of Economic History in the World' (unpublished paper, free downloadable from the 'Munich Personal RePEc Archive' as paper 34704).

Blockmans, W. P. (1985) 'Van buitenaf bekeken. Buitenlandse historici over staatsvorming in de Nederlanden van de veertiende tot de zestiende eeuw', *Bijdragen en Mededelingen betreffende de Geschiedenis der Nederlanden,* 100 (4): 588–605.

Blockmans, W. P. (2010) *Metropolen aan de Noordzee,* Amsterdam: Bert Bakker.

Blomme, J. and Van der Wee, H. (1994) 'The Belgian Economy in A Long-Term Historical Perspective: Economic Development in Flanders and Brabant, 1500–1812', in A. Maddison and H. Van der Wee (eds.) *Economic Growth and Structural Change. Comparative Approaches over the Long Run. Croissance économique et mutation structurelle. Comparaisons dans le long terme (session B13 – Proceedings Eleventh International Economic History Congress, Milan, September 1994),* Milan: Università Bocconi.

Blondé, B., Boone, M. and Van Bruaene, A.-L. (eds.) (2015) *Stad en samenleving in de Lage Landen (1100–1600),* forthcoming.

Bosma, Ulbe (2014) 'The Economic History of the Dutch Colonial Empire', in *Economic History of the Netherlands 1914–2014,* ed. Jacques van Gerwen, Co Seegers, Milja van Tielhof and Jan Luiten van Zanden, Amsterdam: Amsterdam University Press, 153–74.

Bracke, N. (2008) *Een monument voor het land: overheidsstatistiek in België, 1795–1870,* Gent: Academia Press.

Davids, Karel and Lucassen, Jan (1995) 'Conclusion', in *A Miracle Mirrored. The Dutch Republic in European Perspective,* ed. Karel Davids and Jan Lucassen, Cambridge: Cambridge University Press, 438–60.

Dittrich, Z. R. and van der Woude, A. M. (1959) 'De geschiedenis op de tweesprong', *Mens en Maatschappij* 34: 361–80, reprinted in *Ideeën en ideologieën. Studies over economische en sociale geschiedschrijving in Nederland 1894–1991*, ed. Leo Noordegraaf, Amsterdam: Historisch Seminarium, 1991, 240–57.

Drukker, Jan Willem (2003) *De revolutie die in haar eigen staart beet: hoe de economische geschiedenis onze ideeën over economische groei veranderde*, Utrecht: LEMMA.

Dumolyn, J. (2012) 'Henri Pirenne and Particularism in Late Medieval Flemish Cities: An Intellectual Genealogy', in D. Nicholas, B. S. Bachrach and J. M. Murray (eds.) *Comparative Perspectives on History and Historians*, Kalamazoo: Western Michigan University.

Frankema, E. and Smits, J.-P. (2008) 'De rol van cultuur en sociale cohesie in de economische geschiedenis', *Tijdschrift voor Sociale en Economische Geschiedenis*, 5(2): 93–116.

Frankema, E. and Buelens, F. (eds.) (2013) *Colonial Exploitation and Economic Development: The Belgian Congo and the Netherlands Indies Compared* (Routledge explorations in economic history, 64), Abingdon: Routledge.

François, L. (1993) *Een eeuw Gentse Historische School. Bibliografie van de licentiaats- en doctoraatsverhandelingen voorgelegd aan de Sectie Geschiedenis van de Universiteit Gent 1891–1992*, Gent: OSGG.

Le Roy Ladurie, Emmanuel (1977) 'Motionless History', *Social Science History*, 1(2): 115–36.

Lyon, B. (1981) 'Historical Research in Belgium and Its Meaning on An International Level', in G. Verbeke (ed.) *Belgium and Europe. Proceedings of the International Francqui-Colloquium, Brussels-Ghent, 12–14 November 1981*, Brussels: Paleis der Academiën.

Lyon, B. (1998) 'The War of 1914 and Henri Pirenne's Revision of his Methodology', in J. Tollebeek, G. Verbeeck and T. Verschaffel (eds.) *De lectuur van het verleden. Opstellen over de geschiedenis van de geschiedschrijving aangeboden aan Reginald de Schryver* (Symbolae Facultatis Litterarum Lovaniensis. Series A, 24), Leuven: Universitaire pers.

Noordegraaf, L. (1990) *Overmoed uit onbehagen: positivisme en hermeneutiek in de economische en sociale geschiedenis*, Hilversum: Verloren.

North, Douglass C. and Thomas, Robert P. (1973) *The Rise of the Western World: A New Economic History*, New York: Cambridge University Press.

Parthasarathi, Prasannan (2011) *Why Europe Grew Rich and Asia Did Not: Global Economic Divergence, 1600–1850*, Cambridge: Cambridge University Press.

Pasture, P. (2005) 'Views from Abroad. Foreign Historians on a Small State by the North Sea. With Reflections on Historical Writing in Belgium and Elsewhere', *Revue belge d'histoire contemporaine*, 35 (4): 413–31.

Peeters, E. (2003) *Het labyrint van het verleden: natie, vrijheid en geweld in de Belgische geschiedschrijving (1787–1850)* (Symbolae Facultatis litterarum Lovaniensis. Series B, 30), Leuven: Universitaire pers.

Pirenne, H. (1931) *Bibliographie de l'histoire de Belgique. Catalogue méthodique et chronologique des sources et des ouvrages principaux relatifs à l'histoire de tous les Pays-Bas jusqu'en 1598 et à l'histoire de Belgique jusqu'en 1914*, 3rd ed. by Nowé, H. and Obreen, H., Brussels: M. Lamertin.

Pirenne, J. (1938) 'Henri Pirenne', in *Henri Pirenne. Hommages et souvenirs*, vol. 1, Brussels: Nouvelle Société d'Éditions.

Prevenier, W. (1979) 'Hoofdtrekken en resultaten van de geschiedschrijving in België na Wereldoorlog II', *Ons Erfdeel*, 22 (4): 553–62.

Rion, P. (1986) 'La correspondance entre G. Kurth et H. Pirenne (1880–1913)', *Bulletin de la Commission Royale d'Histoire*, 152: 147–255.

Roy, Tirthankar (2004) 'Economic History: An Endangered Discipline', *Economic and Political Weekly*, 39(29): 3238–43.

Sabbe, E. (1936) 'Nécrologie Henri Pirenne', *Archives, Bibliothèques et Musées de Belgique*, 13 (1): 78–84.

Schryver, R. De (1997) *Historiografie. Vijfentwintig eeuwen geschiedschrijving van West-Europa* (Ancorae. Steunpunten voor Studie en Onderwijs, 8), Leuven: Universitaire pers.

Slicher van Bath, B. H (1963) *The Agrarian History of Western Europe, A.D. 500–1850*, London: Arnold.

Soly, H. (1992) 'Geschiedenis in de jaren tachtig: wetenschap of verhaal', in T. Venckeleer and G. Verbeke (eds.) *Cultuurwetenschappen in beweging*, Leuven-Antwerp: Vlaamse Vereniging voor Cultuurwetenschappen.

Thoen, E. and Vanhaute, E. (2011) 'Pirenne and Economic and Social Theory: Influences, Methods and Reception', *Revue belge d'histoire contemporaine*, 41 (3–4): 323–53.

Tollebeek, J. (1990) 'De uitbouw van een historische infrastructuur in Nederland en België (1870–1914)', *Theoretische Geschiedenis*, 17 (1): 3–21 (republished in Tollebeek, J. (1994) *De ijkmeesters. Opstellen over de geschiedschrijving in België en Nederland*, Amsterdam: Bert Bakker).

Tollebeek, J. (1992) 'Enthousiasme en evidentie in de negentiende-eeuwse Belgisch-nationale geschiedschrijving', *Leidschrift*, 8 (2): 61–81 (republished in Tollebeek, J. (1994) *De ijkmeesters. Opstellen over de geschiedschrijving in België en Nederland*, Amsterdam: Bert Bakker).
Van der Linden, Marcel (2008) *Workers of the World. Essays toward a Global Labor History*, Leiden: Brill.
Van der Wee, H. (1995) 'Postwar Research on the Social and Economic History of Medieval Europe: Some Remarks on its Results and on its Potential for the Future', in J. Hamesse (ed.) *Bilan et Perspectives des Etudes Médiévales en Europe* (Actes du premier congrès européen d'Etudes Médiévales, Spoleto, 27–29 Mai 1993), Louvain-la-Neuve: FIDEM.
Van der Wee, H. and Klep, P.M.M. (1975) 'Quantitative Economic History in Europe since the Second World War: Survey, Evaluation and Prospects', *Recherches Economiques de Louvain*, 41 (3): 195–218.
Van der Wee, H. and Dancet, G. (1986) 'De Belgische nationale boekhouding, 1920–1985: geschiedenis van haar berekenings- en reconstructiemethodologie', in V. Van Rompuy (ed.) *Actuele economische problemen. Theorie en politiek*, Leuven: Universitaire Pers.
Vanthemsche, G. (2012) *Belgium and the Congo, 1885–1980*, Cambridge: Cambridge University Press.
Van Werveke, H. (1938) 'Henri Pirenne et l'histoire économique', in *Henri Pirenne. Hommages et souvenirs*, vol. 1, Brussels: Nouvelle Société d'Éditions.
Van Zanden, Jan Luiten (2009) *The Long Road to the Industrial Revolution: The European Economy in a Global Perspective, 1000–1800*, Leiden: Brill.
Van Zanden, Jan Luiten and van Riel, Arthur (2004) *The Strictures of Inheritance. The Dutch Economy in the Nineteenth Century*, Princeton, NJ: Princeton University Press.
Verberckmoes, J. (2008) *De Leuvense historici betiteld. Titels van licentiaatsverhandelingen en doctoraten Geschiedenis 1934–2008*, Leuven: Vereniging Historici Lovanienses.
Vercauteren, F. (1959) *Cent ans d'histoire nationale en Belgique* (Collection: 'Notre Passé', 50), Brussels: La Renaissance du Livre.
Verhulst, A. (1997) 'Medieval Socio-economic Historiography in Western Europe: Towards an Integrated Approach', *Journal of Medieval History*, 23 (1): 89–101.
Vries, Peer (2012) 'Does Wealth Entirely Depend on Inclusive Institutions and Pluralist Politics? The Origins of Power, Prosperity and Poverty', *Tijdschrift voor Sociale en Economische Geschiedenis*, 9(3): 74–92.
Warland, G. (2011) 'Henri Pirenne and Karl Lamprecht's Kulturgeschichte. Intellectual Transfer or Théorie Fumeuse?', *Revue belge d'histoire contemporaine*, 41 (3–4): 427–55.

PART III

Turning to the East

12
ECONOMIC HISTORY FROM THE RUSSIAN EMPIRE TO THE RUSSIAN FEDERATION

Leonid Borodkin

Economic history as an academic discipline started in Russia at the end of the nineteenth century when Prof. M.I. Tugan-Baranovsky (1865–1919) published his fundamental works on business cycles in the economic development of England and other Western countries and on the evolution of Russian manufactures at the early stage of industrialization (Tugan-Baranovsky 1894, 1898, 1912). Being a prominent economist he belonged to the Legal Marxism school (and was criticized by V. Lenin for his views).[1] A further mark of the emergence of the field was the first course in Russia on the history of the economy. This was taught in 1885 by V.F. Levitsky (1854–1939) at the Demidov Law Lyceum in Yaroslavl city (Levitskij 1890; Majdachevskij 2011).

Several books were published in St. Petersburg and Moscow before 1917 on the economic history of Russia and Europe. An important contribution was that of M.M. Kovalevsky (1851–1916) who was the first prominent Russian sociologist. He developed social evolution ideas and believed in progress as one of the inevitable laws of history. According to Kovalevsky progress depended upon population growth as its main driving force. He supposed that the growth of international trade would bring world economic integration eliminating the causes of wars and leading to 'a world federation of democratic states'. After 1878, Kovalevsky read lectures in law at Moscow University and he published books on the economic growth of Europe, before the emergence of a capitalist economy, and on the evolution of the economic structure of the Russian Empire (Kovalevskij 1898–1903, 1900).

P.G. Vinogradoff's works on the social and economic conditions of early medieval England became very well known not only in Russia but in England and other European countries (Vinogradov 1887, 1911). Vinogradoff (1854–1925) was a famous Russian historian who represented liberal–positivist historiography. In 1884 he became professor of history at Moscow University but in 1902 after conflict with the minister of education he was obliged to leave Russia. Having settled in England, Vinogradoff became a professor at Oxford University in 1903, and a fellow of the British Academy. In 1908 he returned to Moscow University (keeping his position at Oxford and combining teaching at both universities). Vinogradoff studied the peasantry of the feudal age and the village community in England in detail showing that the typical Anglo-Saxon settlement was a free community and not a feudal manor.

I.M. Kulisher (1878–1933) was an economic historian of the next generation in pre-Revolutionary Russia.[2] He published his books on the history of customs policy, on the evolution of capital gains, in the context of development of European industry and trade, and on the history of economic life in Western Europe (Kulisher 1903, 1906, 1908, 1909, 1911). He did not follow a Marxist approach; he opposed the Marxist labor theory of value, the theory of surplus value. He denied the impoverishment of the proletariat under capitalism and considered advances in science and technology (and not the exploitation of workers) to be the main source of profit.

In this chapter we analyze distinctive features of economic history in Russia during the Soviet and post-Soviet periods. The focus is upon the impact of Russia's modernization process which covers one hundred years starting from the middle of the nineteenth century. Characterizing this historiography one should take into account the political context which changed dramatically during the twentieth-century development of Russia. As one of the leading Soviet economic historians, Yu. Rozaliev noted in 1992: 'Our economic history as a science has a nice pre-Revolutionary past to be proud of. After the Revolution (1917) it suffered the bitter fate of many areas of social science' (Rozaliev 1992).

Economic history in 1920s and 1930s: from 'soft' to 'hard' Marxism

In early Soviet Russia (in the 1920s, during the New Economic Policy [NEP] period) economic history developed quite actively. It was mostly undertaken by economists who belonged to the pre-Revolutionary generation of scholars. In that period state control was not yet too strong so publications on Russia's economic history were mainly based on solid statistical sources formed by Tsarist Russia's state institutions. Among authors of those works we should again mention I.M. Kulisher who continued his studies on Russian and European economic history, concentrating on the history of Russian industry and on the economy of Ancient Greece (Kulisher 1922, 1923, 1925a, 1925b, 1926). Most economic history published in the 1920s was clearly of Marxist orientation. K.A. Pazhitnov (1879–1964) published his first book in 1906 on the material conditions of Russian workers before the First Russian revolution (1905) (Pazhitnov 1906). In the 1920s he continued studying Russian workers during the serfdom period, the comparative history of workers' organizations in Russia and the West and, later, the history of the Russian oil industry (Pazhitnov 1924a, 1924b, 1940). S.G. Strumilin (1877–1974) who in the 1920s and 1930s was Head of the Department of Statistics of the People's Labor Commissariat, a Deputy Chairman of the USSR State Planning Committee and Professor of Moscow University, published his major works on the history of wages in Russia, on the quality of harvest statistics before 1917 and in the NEP period, and on the history of ferrous metallurgy in the USSR (Strumilin 1930, 1924, 1935).

In the 1920s the Russian/Soviet economist Nikolai Kondratiev (1892–1938) studied the dynamics of prices and interest rates in different countries from 1790 and revealed the long economic cycles (K-waves) which were considered to be phenomena of the world economy. He published his results in *The Major Economic Cycles* (1925) and in other works written in the second half of the 1920s (Kondratiev 1925, 1926, 1928). In May 1928 he was dismissed from his post as director of the Institute of Economic Conjuncture and in June 1930 he was arrested. At the beginning of 1932, Kondratiev, like a number of leading Soviet specialists, especially in agriculture (including A.V. Chayanov), was convicted as one of the leaders of the so-called Labor Peasants Party which never existed – and was imprisoned for eight years. In September 1938 Kondratiev was sentenced to death for 'anti-Soviet agitation in prison' but his work has remained influential to this day, well beyond as well as inside Russia.

Having studied the experience and history of the cooperative movement in Western Europe, Chayanov (1888–1937) became one of the most respected scholars in the field of agricultural cooperation and the organization of agriculture; he developed a methodology for determining the profitability of the peasant economy and its components (Chayanov 1925). Chayanov believed that agrarian development should be based on the cooperative structure of peasant households. He had no doubt about the benefits of large enterprises in industry but believed that a high degree of concentration of agricultural production is not profitable, and drew conclusions about the desirability of small- and middle-scale peasant households (Chayanov 1928). One of his conclusions concerned the traditional form of peasant activity which he considered to be the result of peasants' long-term adaptation to the natural economy, the non-market economy, which arose under feudalism but remained under capitalism. As Chayanov argued, this form of economy is much older than capitalism, it has a long tradition of survival in adverse conditions; it allows a flexible response to the economic downturns by reducing peasant requirements to a minimum. The views of Chayanov and his school were denounced as anti-Marxist in the USSR. In July 1930 Chayanov was arrested and in 1937 he was shot.

'The Great Break Through' of 1929 meant a transition to collectivization and forced industrialization, to strengthening of the 'class struggle' and to rigid Communist Party control over all social and political processes. As a result economic history became more ideologically sharpened, oriented to demonstrate the 'semi-colonial' nature of the Tsarist economy and its deep dependence on foreign capital. At the beginning of the 1930s the dominant Soviet school of historical studies headed by M.N. Pokrovsky (1868–1932) was subjected to rigid criticism because his Marxist approach was regarded as too moderate. Pokrovsky was a Soviet politician, one of the organizers of the Communist Academy (1924), and a member of the State Academic Council (1919), Institute of History, and Institute of Red Professors (1921). As Chairman of the Society of Marxist Historians (1925), Pokrovsky initiated 'purges' (*chistka*) of the Academy of Sciences when the OGPU[3] arrested a large group of historians.

Socialism – as Pokrovsky characterized it – meant the transfer of the land and all instruments of production, factories, and so on into the hands of working people. He argued that the best social arrangement for the development of technology is socialism. According to Pokrovsky capitalism, with its fierce competition between entrepreneurs striving towards monopoly, mainly in modern times, can inhibit the development of technology in a way little worse than the slave economy. The power of 'trade capital' reached its apogee in the nineteenth century, when it became the dominant force in Europe. In the Russian Empire – as Pokrovsky argued – the development of industrial production in the second half of the nineteenth century generated class struggle associated with 'industrial capital' which entered into competition with 'trade capital' and this resulted in the victory of the former by the beginning of the twentieth century.

Given the criticism from other Marxist historians, in his last years Pokrovsky acknowledged some of the shortcomings of historical views expressed in his earlier works and tried to improve them. In the book *On the Russian feudalism, the origin and nature of autocracy* (1931) he abandoned his original understanding of 'economic materialism', expressed in an underestimation of the production aspect and hyperbolization of the circulation of money. As a result, while continuing to emphasize the importance of 'trade capital' in the development of capitalism in Russia, Pokrovsky stopped using the term 'trade capitalism' and admitted that imperial absolutism was not just an instrument of trade capital. He urged that more attention be paid to the 'creative role of the masses' in the historical process.

Wide criticism of the so-called 'historical school of Pokrovsky' started in 1936. Pokrovsky's books were removed from libraries and history textbooks were rewritten in accordance with the new historical concept. Posthumous defeat of Pokrovsky was completed in the publication in 1939–40 of a two-volume edition titled 'Against Pokrovsky's historical concept' (Grekov et al. 1939–40). This campaign had a negative influence on research in economic history.

Rehabilitation of the Pokrovsky School started after the Twentieth Congress of CPSU (1956) and in the 1960s a four-volume edition of his collection of historical works was published. However even in the 1960s and 1970s Pokrovsky was criticized for 'eclectic attempts to connect Marxism with the bourgeois theories' and for misunderstanding historical laws identified by Marx.

Another discussion that continued for more than half a century started in the 1920s. It concentrated on the theory of the Asiatic mode of production (AMP). The first debate can be dated to the 1920s and 1930s when some Soviet historians working within the dichotomy of East–West tried to explain the uniqueness of the AMP which existed only in Eastern societies, in contrast to the mode of production established in Ancient Greece and Ancient classical Rome incorporating the slave system. This argument stressed the non-linearity of the historical process and its diversity (L.I. Magyar, V.V. Lominadze, E.S. Varga, and others). This discussion was caused mostly by the growing national liberation movements in Asia and Africa, and the desire of the Soviet leaders to export the proletarian revolution to the East (and – to some extent – by special interest in Marx in the East). The approach was opposed by supporters of the single line of the Marxist interpretation of history, which came to the conclusion that this mode of production existed not only in oriental societies, but also in humanity as a whole. In this case, the AMP was presented as an evolutionary link between primitive communism and the slave system. After the discussion, the supporters of the AMP were heavily criticized and the official Soviet historical methodology established the classic succession of five formations: the primitive communal, slave, feudal, capitalist, and communist (communism in this scheme was the initial stage of socialism). In this scheme, the concept of AMP was not used at all: all the ancient Eastern societies were assigned to the slave stage, and all the Middle Ages to feudalism.

A second debate on AMP (1957 to early 1970s) was caused by the rise of anti-colonial movements after the Second World War, publication of some early works of Marx, and revival of social and cultural life after the Twentieth CPSU Congress (the 'Khrushchev thaw'). Several rationales of the AMP concept were proposed. Ultimately, the debate turned into a discussion of current problems in the theory of the historical process including the concepts of Western authors which emphasized the similarity of AMP to the Soviet model of socialism (Karl Wittfogel, Roger Garaudy). The AMP problem was considered at the Moscow discussions (1965), attended by prominent historians of the Soviet Union, France, Hungary, and Germany. After the overthrow of Khrushchev (and especially after the 'Prague Spring' in 1968), the debate was gradually phased out. However, discussion of the issues raised did not stop and a final stage of this debate started in the early 1990s, with the weakening of censorship and of the Party ideological dictatorship. Many authors in the former Soviet Union began openly to speak of the importance of the AMP concept for understanding the nature of Soviet socialism and the history of Russia as a whole. It can be argued that the debate on the AMP in the Soviet Union led to a new interpretation of the history of primitive societies and of the formation of civilization.

It should be noted that in the middle of the 1930s an unexpected impulse was given to studies of labor history and the history of enterprises. It happened due to an initiative of the famous proletarian writer Maxim Gorki which was supported by the Party leaders who announced a program named the 'History of manufactures and plants'. This aimed to raise public interest in working-class history. Nowadays it could be interpreted in terms of business history and an early form of micro-history methodology.

Economic history in the period of late Stalinism

After the Second World War the development of economic history continued to be controversial. On the one hand in 1947 Prof. I.D. Udal'tsov (1885–1958) who was a founder of the Faculty of Economics at Moscow State University and its first dean (1941–54) established the Department of History of the National Economy and Economic Thought, the first in the country.[4] This institution had a significant impact on the improvement of education and the expansion of research in economic history. Similar departments were established in a number of universities in the USSR and economic history became an obligatory component of the curriculum at economics faculties.

At the end of the 1940s two volumes on the history of the Russian/Soviet economy were published in Moscow (Lyashchenko 1947, 1948). They were based on Marxist concepts of economic development but contained a lot of statistical data and interpretation and they were used in economics faculties as the basic textbooks for two generations of students. The author P.I. Lyashchenko (1875–1955) was awarded the Stalin Prize (1949) for this edition.[5] One of his main conclusions concerned the role of government in the modernization process: slowing the process of capitalist evolution of the agricultural system of Russia, the government at the same time contributed to the development of industry. Another book on the economic history of Russia was published in 1950 embracing the nineteenth and twentieth centuries (Hromov 1950). The author, P.A. Khromov (1907–87), followed the same Marxist methodology as Lyashchenko. During the 1950s and 1960s these books were in competition in their influence over economics departments.

At the same time the 1940s was marked by the campaign against 'objectivism' and 'cosmopolitanism' (1948–53) which was directed against a layer of the Soviet intelligentsia associated with pro-Western tendencies. It is often supposed that this campaign was anti-Semitic in nature. It was accompanied by accusations of 'rootless cosmopolitanism' and hostility to the patriotic feelings of Soviet citizens, on the part of Soviet Jews, as well as arrests and their dismissal from many posts. The campaign was oriented to emphasize Russian and Soviet priorities in the field of science and invention and to take administrative action against persons suspected of 'kowtowing to the West'.

The influence of those actions on economic historians was tangible. For instance at the History Faculty of Moscow University the campaign started in 1948 especially touching the Department of Medieval History. E.A. Kosminsky (1886–1959), the Head of Department, was accused of 'bourgeois objectivism'. He left his position. In his monograph on the agrarian history of England in the thirteenth century Kosminsky (as said by his critics) 'tried to replace Marxism–Leninism with economic materialism' (Kosminsky 1947, 1956). The charges were presumably based on the author's wide use of statistical calculations, his respect for historiographical traditions and his academic predecessors, as well as the absence of quotations from the writings by Stalin. Another charge addressed to Kosminsky and his colleagues was traditionalism ('denial of the fundamental significance of the Soviet science based on the only scientific methodology – Marxism–Leninism'). A.I. Neusykhin, Professor at the same Department and a prominent historian specializing in the economic and social history of early medieval Europe, was also accused of being a cosmopolitan and admiring Western bourgeois historiography.

S.B. Veselovsky (1876–1952) who worked at the Institute of History (Academy of Sciences of the USSR) in 1948 was accused of 'bourgeois objectivism'. After this, for several years, Veselovsky had very limited opportunities to publish his works on the agrarian history of medieval Russia.[6]

Economic history after Stalin: from 'Thaw' to 'Zastoy' and 'Perestroika'

During the Cold War period, one of the main tasks of Soviet economic historians was to demonstrate the achievements of the Soviet economy in competition with the West. As in the previous decades, studies of the economic history of pre-Revolutionary Russia were required to give arguments in support of the inevitability of the 1917 Great October Revolution. Most Soviet economic historians concentrated on studies of Russia's economic development in the post-Reform period 1861–1917 (the so-called *Great Reforms* were initiated by Alexander II in 1861); on the most important periods of Soviet economic reforms; and on the *take-off* period of Stalin's industrialization. The NEP period, collectivization, and Khrushchev's decentralization of Soviet economy also came under the spotlight but most publications had an apologetic character. Based on a Marxist–Leninist theoretical platform authors used statistical data and illustrative cases to prove the positive results of Soviet economic development and the inefficiency of the Tsarist economy. Studies of Russian agrarian history between the seventeenth and the nineteenth centuries were less controlled: they were coordinated by the Academic Council on agrarian history at the USSR Academy of Sciences which was established at the end of the 1950s.

It should be noted that since the 1960s economic historians in Moscow, Leningrad, and Novosibirsk started using quantitative methods. Most of them were engaged in studies of agrarian history. The most active group was formed in the 1970s at Lomonosov Moscow State University. Ivan D. Kovalchenko, the leader of this group, established a Laboratory for the application of quantitative methods and computers at the History Faculty of the University. In the late 1970s to the early 1980s this Laboratory developed cliometric-style research of the agrarian history of Russia. To some extent it was stimulated by contacts with distinguished American cliometrians. A bilateral cooperation program was established in the late 1970s by the USSR Academy of Sciences and IREX. Quantitative economic history was chosen as the field of cooperation due to its relative political neutrality. One more driver of introducing quantification in social sciences and humanities was enthusiasm for science and technological progress in the USSR in the 1960s and 1970s, especially in the area of computing. The Laboratory for the application of quantitative methods and computers in historical research was established at the Institute of Soviet History of the USSR Academy of Sciences in 1971 with twelve new research fellows. Year by year quantitative history research attracted more and more young scholars. They published papers on rural and urban history, agricultural history, historical demography, labor history, financial history, but most work remained descriptive owing to limited application of economic theory.

Although Soviet economic historians (as well as almost all historians in the USSR) were practically isolated from foreign historiographical influences, there were some channels for the transfer of ideas before and especially after the 1980s. First, the publication of books and articles positioned as criticism of Western bourgeois approaches was encouraged. This allowed Soviet historians to be more informed about global historiography. It included, for example, the critical book 'Historicism against eclecticism: French historical *Annales* School in contemporary bourgeois historiography' (1980) which gave Soviet historians an opportunity to be informed about the new methodological approaches developed by the *Annales* School in the 1970s (Afanas'yev 1980). *Annales* books were however available only for a limited circle of Soviet historians who usually did not mention those 'bourgeois' theories in their lectures and publications (or mentioned them only in a critical way). Some economic historians mentioned Max Weber's methodology although they generally tried to ally him to Marx (Afanas'yev 1980: 112). Overall, due to the dominating ideology and to isolation, the Soviet approach to economic history remained rather inflexible (and not only due to the dominating ideology). As one of the leading Soviet medievalists A.Ya. Gurevich noted, personal contacts with foreign colleagues were almost absent and those rare contacts were under close supervision (Gurevich 2004: 93). Gurevich himself was rather well informed on the methodological innovations in Western historiography of the 1960s to 1980s. He used them in his researches on the genesis of Scandinavian feudalism and medieval culture adopting a cultural anthropology approach. His articles compiled in the book *Problems in the genesis of feudalism* were sharply criticized by the Minister of Education A.I. Danilov and Gurevich was dismissed from the USSR Academy of Sciences (Gurevich 1967, 1970, 1972). The reason for that criticism was very clear: Gurevich had called into question part of the thesis of Marx and Engels – that feudalism was formed as a result of the enslavement of free peasants by barons who previously appropriated the peasants' land. According to Gurevich, under the weakness of supreme authority, free farmers seeking protection for themselves and their land voluntarily took the patronage of barons, changing freedom for security. Books by Gurevich, who used non-Marxist economic categories and concepts of cultural anthropology, were translated into several languages including English, French, Italian, Japanese, Spanish, Swedish, etc. (a rare case for historical books published in the USSR).

One more channel of international information exchange was the influence of the International Economic History Association (IEHA). Leading Soviet economic historians participated as members of the IEHA Executive Committee in its current activities (during the Cold War times two positions on this Committee were reserved for Soviet representatives and two for representatives of the USA). The Soviet delegation (usually about 40 scholars from almost all of the Soviet republics) took part in each IEHA Congress. Articles on the Congress sessions and papers were published in leading Soviet academic journals resulting in the accumulation of new information on the tendencies and achievements in the professional field in the West. A special role in this process belongs to the Fifth IEHA Congress held in Leningrad in 1970. Half of more than 1000 participants represented the USSR. It should be noted that most Soviet delegates presented their papers in Russian (which was one of the four official languages of the Congress) and the understanding of foreign papers was hampered by the language problem. However, the Congress definitely raised interest in economic history studies in the USSR, and contributed to the better understanding of the role of economic history as an interdisciplinary field bridging history and economics. A lot of Soviet scholars identified themselves now as economic historians (and not as just scholars involved in some concrete historical research).

Generalizing, one could say that in the periods of '*Thaw*' (Khrushchev's time), '*Zastoy*' (Brezhnev's time) and '*Perestroika*' (Gorbachev's time) economic history in the USSR developed breadth and depth. A number of books were published in the field of agrarian history which was the center of attention (Yatsunskij 1973; Koval'chenko and Milov 1974; Tihonov 1974; Druzhinin 1978; Anfimov 1980; Koval'chenko et al. 1982, 1988). New results appeared in financial and banking history (Gindin 1960; Anan'ich 1975; Bovykin 1991, 1967, 1984), industrial history (Livshits 1961; Pavlenko 1962; Bovykin 1983; Simonova 1987; Solov'eva 1990), history of the labor market (Rydzyunskij 1983; Kir'yanov and Volin 1983), history of internal trade and foreign trade (Semenov 1975; Kitanina 1978; Dvoretskij 1979; Rybachenok 1982). General works on Russian economic history were also published. In 1976–80 the Institute of Economic Studies of the Soviet Academy of Sciences published eight volumes under the title: 'History of the USSR Socialist Economy' (Gladkov et al. 1976–80). The domination of ideological pressure was evident but the volumes also contained a lot of factual material and statistical tables.

During the 1970s and 1980s discussions of Soviet economic historians were concentrated mostly on the character and nature of economic development in the Russian Empire in the second half of the nineteenth century and the beginning of twentieth century. One group of historians considered the Russian economy of that period as semi-feudal and backward, another group argued that both agriculture and industry demonstrated positive tendencies in the development of capitalism so that by the First World War Russian capitalism had entered a more mature phase. Interestingly, the second position was more acceptable for the Party authorities because it was more consistent with the Marxist thesis claiming that socialism must win in the country with the highest level of development of capitalism. The first group was highly criticized 'from above'.

The formation of economic history as a self-sufficient developing area was prevented in the period under consideration by the 'excommunication' of economists from economic history which happened in the early 1960s. Prior to this, many economists, including such prominent scholars as S.G. Strumilin, P.I. Lyaschenko, P.A. Khromov, and others, were actively engaged in economic history research. However, 'someone at the top' argued that the study of pre-Revolutionary history distracted economists from the solution of current problems, so they were quickly transferred into departments engaged in more contemporary and pragmatic research. Since that time the community of economic historians in Russia has lacked trained economists. Probably this is one reason for the growing tendency to study economic history in the wider context of political, social, and cultural circumstances and change, and mainly under the wing of history (a tendency that continued for a long time).

As one of the leading Soviet economic historians noted in 1995, 'Perhaps no other area of the social sciences has suffered so much from long-term "upper management" as economic history. The current state of knowledge in this area is a direct legacy of lengthy bans and persecutions' (Rozaliev 1996). This situation arose with the new developments in Soviet economics which was previously used to analyze large data sets and employ analytical tools to interpret them (and not just to give illustrations of orthodox approaches).

It is important to note that literature on Russian economic history written by émigrés of the revolutionary period (like S. Prokopovich, N. Jasny, B. Brutskus et al.), their approaches and results, were not available for Soviet scholars until the last years of *Perestroika.* Starting from the end of 1980s their works were translated and published as well as hundreds of Western works – both related to Russian economic history and more general historical and social science works. At the turn of the 1980s and 1990s personal contacts between Russian and Western colleagues became possible.

Economic history during post-Soviet times: decentralization and diversification of the research field

Economic history in post-Soviet Russia can be characterized first of all as a field that is not dominated by any unique theory/methodology. The Marxist approach is now just one of many others. The concepts of modernization, dependency, and the institutionalist approach are practiced in a number of research projects. Both in late Soviet and post-Soviet times most economic historians work at history departments or at the institutes of the Historical Branch of the Russian Academy of Sciences. They graduated from university history departments. However the number of economists contributing to economic history research has been growing slowly in recent years.

Cliometrics methodology is developing at several universities although it is definitely not in the mainstream in Russian economic history. Business history which was an underdeveloped research area in the Soviet period is now flourishing. However most publications in this area are of a descriptive nature; only some of them are methodologically based using A. Chandler's approach for example (Potkina 2004). More attention is now paid to the creation of large-scale data sets aimed at the study of the long-run tendencies of Russia's economic development in a comparative context. In recent years there has been substantial influence from Western approaches to global history research in Russia (including the establishment of the new specialized international journal).[7] At the same time a micro-history approach also became more attractive for Russian economic historians.

It is important to emphasize that starting from the early 1990s the influence of Western historians on Russian historiography became more and more substantial. Contacts between Russian and Western historians widened; they developed cooperation both in joint research and in the publication of declassified archival sources of the Stalinist period.[8] As a result the economic history of Russia during the last twenty-five years has been open to cross-fertilization. These two-way influences gave a lot of knowledge to both sides: more developed methodology for Russian historians, more historical context for Western colleagues. A number of Russian postgraduate students and post-doc fellows participated in economic history research and/or education programs in Western universities which gave them new methodological background. Since the 1990s economic history in Russia went global step by step but only a small minority of historians embraced Western contacts and thinking. During the last five years several all-Russian economic history conferences made it evident that there are numbers of Russian economists and economic historians who approved of Soviet economic experience and suggested going back to a command economy (Bakanov and Saukova 2013).

Since the beginning of the 1990s several issues have determined the main lines of discussion in economic history in Russia. The first one concerns the assessment of the results of two phases of industrialization in the Russian Empire and USSR (1880s–1914 and 1928–40 respectively). The discussion of pre-Revolutionary industrialization continues in principle the discussion on this issue among Soviet economic historians; however it develops on the basis of new methodology and data sources. An important impulse was given by the long delayed appearance in 1994 of Lev Kafengauz's book 'The Evolution of Russian Industrial Production (the last third of the nineteenth century to the 1930s)' (Kafengauz 1994). The book contains extended time series and a bulk of analytical material on Russian industrial production in the period 1887–1927. It was to have appeared by the beginning of the 1930s; however, it was only published half a century later. Kafengauz continued working on the monograph in prison after his arrest in 1930 but the authorities prohibited publication of his book. Data from the book made it possible to reevaluate the growth rate of Russian industrial production due to the extended set of products included by Kafengauz in numerous tables. Before publication of this book, which presented 29 products from industrial and mining branches qualifying as industries of Russia, historians had only limited time series data. The Kafenguaz tables have been used to verify the theory of Alexander Gerschenkron on the relative backwardness of the Russian Empire as a latecomer on the way to industrial development. All previous estimates of the industrial growth rate of the Russian Empire in the period 1887–1913 made by Gerschenkron and other Western economists on the one hand and by Soviet economists from the Kondratiev Institute of Conjuncture on the other, resulted in estimates of a 5.1 to 5.8 percent growth rate per annum. Calculation of the growth index based on Kafengauz's data gives an average of 6.65 percent. Such a rate of industrial growth in Russia for the last twenty-seven years before 1914 is comparable with that of the leading industrial countries.

However this conclusion has evoked a polemic among Russian economic historians in recent decades. Iu. P. Bokarev, one of the most authoritative practitioners, states that 'the motives of a number of researchers, who aspire to increase the rate of industrial growth in pre-Revolutionary Russia, are entirely clear. It is very flattering to think that had there been no revolution in 1917, the unusually fast economic growth of Russia would have allowed this country in the near future to eliminate economic backwardness' (Bokarev 2006). S.V. Il'in observed not long ago 'the enormous backwardness of the Russian Empire in comparison with leading countries of the West'. His conclusion reflects clearly the general evaluation of pre-Revolutionary Russia's economic development: 'In the Soviet era, the colossal industrial and cultural gap between our country and countries of the West was on the whole closed, which was a great achievement of our people, and, above all, that part of the people that was organized in the party' (Il'in 2004).

A different evaluation belongs to distinguished Russian economic historian V.I. Bovykin (1927–97) who published reliable data on the share of Russia, USA, Great Britain, Germany, and France in world industrial production at the end of the nineteenth and beginning of the twentieth centuries. He analyzed the dynamic indicators of comparative industrial development of leading world powers noting that Russia's relative backwardness, by comparison with Britain, fell by a third in 1885–1913 and by a quarter compared with Germany and USA (Bovykin 1996: 7).

The tradition of underestimating pre-Revolutionary Russia's economic potential is not new. V.I. Bovykin attributed it to the 1930s, when there appeared the 'notorious thesis of Stalin about the semi-colonial dependency of Russia'. In all books of that time indicators of gross industrial production of the country had to be substantially decreased along with Russia's share in world industrial production. These indicators are still widely used in historical literature. From those times, when characterizing the Russian economy, 'the accent fell on the technical-economic backwardness of the country and its dependence on foreign capital' (Bovykin 1996: 3).

Discussing the 'myth about the hopeless backwardness of pre-Revolutionary Russia, necessitating its path to socialism' (Bovykin 1996: 4), Bovykin observed that 'for our contemporaries, whose historical views were formed under the effect of this myth, it is difficult, understandably, to accept that Russia at the end of the nineteenth and beginning of the twentieth century was one of the most dynamically developing states of the world' (Bovykin 1996: 4).

Current discussion of estimates of Russia's growth rate concerns not only pre-Revolutionary industrialization but Soviet industrialization as well. Estimates given by Soviet and Western economists for the 1930s are radically different. The Soviet accounting methodology and statistical estimates of GNP and its components distinguish between productive and nonproductive labor, between material product and services. Gross Social Product (GSP) was calculated as the total of material values produced. Volume of output was estimated by gross turnover, gross production, and net production, at prevailing prices. Defense expenses were considered separately from material production. The value of foreign trade is estimated on the basis of domestic prices. During the Cold War period in the West, especially the USA, a number of works were published on the construction and analysis of Soviet national accounts. The pioneer of those works (coordinated and supported by the CIA), A. Bergson, and other prominent US economists, used standard Western methodology of national accounting. In 1991 just after the collapse of the USSR this work was discontinued by decision of the US Congress. Naturally, at the same time the number of serious historical and economic researches in Russia related to this problem increased significantly. Foremost in this work were Russian economists A. Ponomarenko, A. Poletaev, and V. Kudrov (Kudrov 1995; Ponomarenko 2002; Poletaev 2006).

Despite long-standing Soviet experience in national accounting it is clear today that official Soviet estimates of economic growth were substantially overstated. As Kudrov notes, a peculiar fact showing the internal inconsistency in the official national accounts of the USSR is that independent estimates of relative levels of Soviet Union and US national income and GNP comparisons suggested much lower growth rates (Kudrov 1995). Kudrov reviewed the history of the official national accounts in both the former Soviet Union and new Russia. From the end of the 1950s to the end of the 1980s the main source of comparative estimates of national accounts of the USSR and the USA were data published by the CIA (mostly in the yearbook *Handbook of Economic Statistics*). Official comparative assessment of the USSR Central Statistical Administration (ЦСУ) relied partly on the calculations of the CIA (usually the comparison was made in dollars) but overall this significantly overestimated the level of economic development of the USSR. In addition, the Soviet Union made informal comparison of the economies of the USSR and the United States, the results of which were close to CIA estimates (Poletaev 2006: 30).

Poletaev filled a gap between the study of the USSR economy prior to its collapse and studies of the Russian economy in 1990 to 2000s (Poletaev 2006: 30). The objective of his research was to analyze Russia's GDP and its main components in relation to the USA using a unified methodology on Soviet (1960–91) and post-Soviet (1992–2004) periods. As a starting point for comparisons he uses estimates of GDP and its components at purchasing power parities, the so-called international dollars method Elteto–Köves–Szulc (EKS$). Using this approach Poletaev addresses several fundamental conceptual questions. His discussion of these questions helps to understand the methodology of national accounting and the difficulties of applying it to very different economic regimes. First, is it possible to apply to a planned economy, with prices set by government, the concept of the national accounts, which to a large extent is based on the premise of market prices? Starting at least since Bergson, economists answer this question in the affirmative although this response, as Poletaev notes, seems not indisputable. The second question: is it possible in analyzing national accounts in the planned economy to use existing prices or, alternatively, to try to replace them with some other hypothetical (quasi-market) prices? Most economists inclined to the second option, but it is a difficult process and also arguable. In the economic literature there are two types of corrections of the actual prices in a planned economy. In the first version, which was proposed by Bergson, the so-called 'adjusted cost factor' is used. In the second version, which is not specific for planned economies, the assessment of purchasing power of national currencies is used. This latter approach, first proposed by C. Clark in 1940 but developed by Milton Gilbert and Irving Kravis in the 1950s, became firmly entrenched in the tools of economic analysis and it was used by Poletaev. The third of Poletaev's conceptual questions concerns the applicability of purchasing power parities (PPP): what are the limits of the use of point PPP estimates made at a given time for dynamic analysis, i.e. for interpolation, and most importantly for extrapolation of national indicators? The answer is again controversial. First, we are faced with a common problem of dynamic economic–statistical analysis: what is the duration of the period for which we can use the same weights (prices) for the calculation of time series? Second, more importantly, it is not clear whether we can basically connect estimates of purchasing power parities with estimates of rates of GNP/GDP change and its components, obtained on the basis of fundamentally different price structures.

Taking into account assumptions and difficulties mentioned above, Poletaev analyzed the trend of convergence/divergence of the economies of the USA and the USSR/Russia on the basis of data on their GDP per capita ratios. His model shows that from 1960 to the first half of the 1970s both countries were converging but in the 1990s the divergence of the economies of Russia and the United States became evident. However, when considering the convergence/ divergence of structural characteristics over the 1960s to the 1980s Poletaev's model shows that the differences between the economies of Russia and the United States were increasing; an apparent divergence of economic systems was the dominating trend (Poletaev 2006: 34).

The fact that the Soviet economy was characterized by an unusually high proportion of fixed capital formation and government military spending, and that these two related burdens to a large extent determined its decline, is well known. However, following Poletaev, it seems that the extent of structural imbalances in the Soviet economy remained undervalued by Western economists. In Soviet times price distortions did not allow recognition (even for Sovietologists) of the degree of perversity of GDP concepts when applied to a command economy (Poletaev 2006: 34–5).

The second current discussion concerns the roles of the State, foreign capital, and Russian entrepreneurs in Russia's pre-Revolutionary industrialization. According to A.S. Senyavsky, industrial modernization of the Russian Empire was not only controlled by government but was even driven by it so this process was generated 'from above' and definitely not 'from below' (Senyavskij 2009). In contrast to this point of view Yu.A. Petrov argues that the role of Russian entrepreneurs increased in the process of economic development after the Great Reforms so this force became 'the main player' in this process (Petrov 2011). He reconsidered the share of investments in Russian industry made by private Russian and foreign investors; following his estimations the share of Russian entrepreneurs was higher by 1913 (Petrov 2011: 15). At the same time Yu.A. Petrov acknowledges that to a large extent economic growth was supported by active government policy. The government promoted railroad construction, the growth of heavy industry and banks. It pursued a flexible customs policy aimed to develop domestic industrial production. Petrov does not however share Gerschenkron's concept of the decisive role of the government in developing pre-Revolution industrialization. He even suggests that Russia's industrialization could have been more dynamic and less costly to society if the government had played a less active role in its implementation and relied instead on private enterprise and free market forces (Petrov 2011: 14).

This discussion is closely connected with the issue of modernization. Updated versions of modernization theory are considered useful by a number of Russian economic historians (Borodkin 2013; Bespalov 2014). I.V. Poberezhnikov distinguishes two interpretations of Russian catch-up modernization – optimistic and pessimistic (Poberezhnikov 2006). According to the first one, which found its most vivid and clear expression in the works by B.N. Mironov, Russian history is interpreted as a peculiar repetition of the history of the West. In other words as a delayed evolution of the same nature, and in the same direction, that had already been experienced by Western Europe and North America (Mironov 2010). According to the pessimistic interpretation of Russian history, Russia's modernization is treated as unsuccessful or even disastrous in terms of the consequences of the attempt to get to the 'normal' Western path of development (the concept of pseudo-modernization has been applied). This interpretation implies a disharmony of economic and social development: inefficiency of political, legal and social institutions, a socio-cultural split in society, and the marginalization of a large part of the population (Bespalov 2014: 9).

The third discussion concerns the evaluation of the agrarian reforms conducted by the Russian government under the leadership of P.A. Stolypin. This started in 1906. The main goals were the transfer of land allotments to the peasants, the gradual abolition of the rural community as a collective owner of land, extensive lending to farmers and land management, including the elimination of strip farming. The attitude of Soviet historians to the Stolypin reforms initially depended upon Lenin's conclusion that the reforms failed completely. Soviet historians had no opportunity to express their disagreement with Lenin's estimates and were forced to adjust their findings even if this was in contradiction with their facts. Today Russian historians, with a wide range of opinions, on the whole view the Stolypin agrarian reforms quite positively. Two extensive special studies on the subject – by V.G. Tyukavkin and M.A. Davydov – published in the 2000s, unequivocally evaluate the reforms as useful and successful; they are based on big sets of statistical data (Tyukavkin 2001, Davydov 2003). At the same time the traditional Soviet assessment also persists in the current historiography. For instance A.Ya. Avrekh who expressed a very negative attitude to the Stolypin reforms in his works published in the 1980s and early 1990s still has followers today (Avrekh 1991; Senyavskij 2009).

In post-Soviet times much more attention is paid to financial history, banking history and the history of the stock market of the Russian Empire. Soviet historians practically ignored the stock market (it was not approved 'from above' because the stock exchange was viewed as an instrument of the capitalist economy and as an 'arena of speculation', a harmful object to be consigned to the past). In the last decade dozens of publications have touched on this topic (Lizunov 2003, 2004; Borodkin and Perel'man 2006; Perel'man 2009; Borodkin and Konovalova 2010). Borodkin and Perel'man constructed a stock index of leading industrial companies which traded on the St. Petersburg Exchange 1897–1914. The index correlates well with the business cycles which give evidence of the dominating influence of fundamental factors and not speculation as the driving force.

Banking history has also received a new impulse. On the one hand there has been a continuation of studies conducted in Soviet times by I.F. Gindin and V.I. Bovykin, on the other hand new questions have been placed on the agenda. Discussion about the differences between the St. Petersburg and Moscow models of banking has been going on for a long time. 'Cosmopolitan' St. Petersburg has been compared to 'traditionalist' Moscow since the days of the pre-Revolutionary financial press; however analysis of the differences was rare. S.A. Salomatina showed in her works that at the beginning of the twentieth century there was a gradual process of convergence of the structure of commercial banks' operations of different types, which led to the emergence of the universal type of bank (Salomatina 2004). S.A. Salomatina belongs to the new generation of Russian economic historians who apply contemporary methodological approaches accessed through participation in the international conferences and workshops and in networking activities. The relations between the Bank of Russia and commercial banks have been studied in works by Yu.A. Petrov, B.V. Anan'ich, S.G. Belyaev, S.K. Lebedev (Petrov 1998; Belyaev 2002; Lebedev 2003; Anan'ich 2006). They analyzed the process of widening networks of the regional branches of St. Petersburg and Moscow commercial banks in the early twentieth century. Another important aspect of their work related to the links between Russian banks and stock exchanges studied earlier by Salomatina.

Special attention should be paid to new studies of the economic history of the Soviet Union since the beginning of the 1990s. First of all, we should emphasize the important role of the 'archival revolution' which has radically changed and expanded the source base for researchers of the Soviet economy. Support from the Russian Foundation for the Humanities and other Russian and international foundations has resulted in hundreds of volumes of declassified archival documents being published. Removal of ideological control led to a revision of many assessments of the Soviet economy and the emergence of new research topics. As a result, a new interpretation was given to the experience of the mixed economy of the NEP period, the collectivization campaign, and the scale of demographic losses of the 1930s. The revision of Soviet data and statistics resulted in reevaluation of the industrial growth rate in the years of Stalin's industrialization and the dynamics of the standard of living of Soviet citizens (Popov 2000; Gajdar 2005; Senyavskij 2006; Kudrov 2007; Kondrashin 2008; Borodkin et al. 2010; Rakov 2012).

In the 1990s a completely new theme of forced labor throughout the Stalinist period emerged. Researchers gained access to declassified archival materials so they could study the scale and forms of forced labor in the USSR. Particular attention was paid to economic activity in the Gulag and its role in the industrialization of the USSR. The importance and novelty of this topic have wider implications for global scholarship pertaining to unfree labor regimes.

The share of the Gulag in the Soviet economy was surprisingly low: 2–3 percent (Borodkin et al. 2005). However, in some important sectors the Gulag contributed much more significantly (for instance in industrial construction, mining, timber). Unlike free workers who demanded material incentives to work in remote regions, penal labor could be dispatched by administrative decree. The use of punishment rather than material rewards was intended to save vital resources and 'surpluses' were to be extracted from camp workers. Was that intention realized in practice in the Gulag? Following P. Gregory (Houston University) and M. Harrison (Warwick University), Russian historians applied a principal–agent approach analyzing relations between NKVD/Gulag bosses and camp administrations; this approach helped to reveal conflicts of interests in this hierarchical system.

During the last two decades a number of papers and books on the Gulag economy were published on the basis of archival documentation of OGPU–NKVD–MVD.[9] One of the 'discoveries' relates to the question of inmates' labor stimulation. Archival holdings contain a lot of documents tracing the introduction of wages in the camp system at the end of the 1940s and its impact on the productivity of inmates' labor. However this measure did not result in an increase in the relatively low inmates' labor productivity so the Gulag could not exist on the basis of expected self-sufficiency (Borodkin et al. 2013).

Developing the infrastructure of economic history research

An important question for historians studying the economic development of the Russian Empire concerns the availability of statistical data related to different aspects of that development. During the last decade several projects in Russia have been carried out aimed at creating digital resources. Some of them have a regional scale; others are oriented to national data.

Studies of the dynamics of economic development of Russia/USSR in the twentieth century can today use a valuable resource presented in a book by V.M. Simchera (who was a director of the Research Statistical Institute at the Federal State Statistics Service). This contains much data covering the period 1900–2000 but the author did not create an electronic version (Simchera 2006). Unlike most developed countries, Russia did not initially have a sufficiently complete and detailed digital statistical resource describing economic development of the Russian Empire during the important period called the long nineteenth century (1800–1914). This made it difficult to study the economic history of the Russian Empire over the long term and to conduct comparative studies. The problem has now been resolved, in part at least because of a number of data digitization projects. The database 'Dynamics of Economic and Social Development of the Russian Empire in the 19th–early 20th centuries' produced by the History Faculty of Lomonosov Moscow State University in 2009–11 has been available online since 2012 and contains about 7000 time series divided into 15 sections.[10] Each indicator (time series) covers a different chronological period, depending on the data source used. Most of the indicators apply to the Russian Empire as a whole, but in those cases where there are systematic performance indicators related to the major regions of the country, they are also included in the resource.

Another resource supported by the 'Dynasty Foundation' was put on the Web in 2015: the Electronic Repository for Russian Historical Statistics. This focuses on Russian economic and social history of the eighteenth to twenty-first centuries. The repository provides regional level data for the territory of the current Russian Federation. Data are arranged along seven principal lines of inquiry (population, labor, industrial output, agricultural output, services, capital, land) and for five cross-sections of Russian history (1795, 1858, 1897, 1959, 2002).[11]

A few words should be said on the organizational side of economic history studies in the post-Soviet Russia. There are two lines of such activities. The first one is associated with the Academic Council on Economic History established by the Russian Academy of Sciences in 1989. The Council which includes 30 economic historians from different Russian universities and academic institutes initiates the organization of conferences and workshops and the publication of their proceedings and journals. The second line is associated with activities of regional centers for economic history. The first of such centers was established in 1994 at the History Faculty of Lomonosov Moscow State University, initially supported by the John and Catherine MacArthur Foundation (the project leader – Prof. C. Leonard, SUNY). During this period the center's activities were coordinated by the International Council (R. Fogel and I. Koval'chenko were co-chairmen). The establishment of the center was made possible by long-term cooperation in the field of economic history between the USSR Academy of Sciences, Moscow State University, and University of California System. Within this framework, in 1984–93 several bilateral conferences were organized and their proceedings published. Since 1994 the center has organized a seminar which attracts economic historians from all over Russia. By the end of 2014 the seminar had arranged 230 meetings. About 50 papers were given by foreign economic historians. The seminar became a permanent platform for exchange and discussion of methodological and theoretical approaches in the field of economic history. Research units of this type exist now at the Institute of Economics, Institute of Russian History, and Institute of World History of Russian Academy of Sciences. During the last decade several regional centers emerged at Russian universities in Siberia (Irkutsk, Barnaul), the Urals (Yekaterinburg, Chelyabinsk), and Middle Volga (Saransk). In the post-Soviet period three journals specializing in economic history were established (as well as the *Yearbook in Economic History*, the 14th volume of which was published in 2014). Unlike the case in many other countries, there is thus evidence of the strengthening of the institutional basis of economic history in Russia in recent decades.

Notes

1 In the beginning of the twentieth century Tugan-Baranovsky moved to the Neo-Kantianism that is reflected in his publications related to the cooperative movement.

2 Discussants at Kulisher's Master's degree defense at St. Petersburg University were M.M.Kovalevsky and M.I. Tugan-Baranovsky.

3 OGPU – the early security and political police of the Soviet Union (1923–34) and a forerunner of the NKVD.

4 I.D. Udal'tsov was 'Sovietizer' of social sciences at Moscow University from 1928 when he was appointed a rector of the University for the next three years.

5 P.I. Lyaschenko, a prominent expert on the agrarian history of Russia, began to publish his works before 1917 (Lyashchenko 1912). He continued this work after 1917 (Lyashchenko 1925, 1930).

6 For more details on this campaign, see Tihonov 2012.

7 *Journal of Globalization Studies.*

8 Prominent figures include A. Berelowitch, W. Berelowitch, R. Davies, S. Wheatcroft, A. Getty, L. Viola, M. Ellman. P. Gregory, M. Harrison, L. Conquest, L. Samuelson, T. Vihavainen, T. Emmons, C. Leonard, A. Graziozi, N. Werth.

9 Among other authors we could mention V.A. Berdinskikh, L.I. Borodkin, I.V. Gribanova, E.V. Kodin, G.M. Ivanova, O.V. Khlevniuk, A.I. Shirokov, A.V. Zakharchenko.

10 The resource is located on the website of the History Faculty of Lomonosov Moscow State University, http://www.hist.msu.ru/Dynamics/

11 Kessler, Gijs and Andrei Markevich (2014), Electronic Repository of Russian Historical Statistics, 18th–21st centuries, http://ristat.org/

References

Afanas'yev, Yu. N. (1980) *Istorizm protiv eklektiki: frantsuzskaya istoricheskaya shkola «Annalov» v sovremennoy burzhuaznoy istoriografii*, Moskva: Mysl'.

Anan'ich, B.V. (1975) *Rossijskoe samoderzhavie i vyvoz kapitala. 1895–1914*, Leningrad: Nauka, LO.

Anan'ich, B.V. (2006) *Bankirskie doma v Rossii 1860–1914 gg: Ocherki istorii chastnogo predprinimatel'stva*, Moskva: ROSSPEN.

Anfimov, A.M. (1980) *Krest'yanskoe hozyajstvo Evropejskoj Rossii 1881–1904 gg.*, Moskva: Nauka.

Avrekh, A. Ya. (1991) *P.A. Stolypin i sud'by reform v Rossii*, Moskva: Politizdat.

Bakanov, S.A. and E.S. Saukova (eds.) (2013) 'Kruglyj stol "Mobilizatsionnoye razvitiye i yego komponenty"', *Vestnik Chelyabinskogo gosudarstvennogo universiteta*, 297(6): 127–32.

Belyaev, S.G. (2002) *P.L.Bark i finansovaya politika Rossii. 1914–1917 gg.*, St. Petersburg: Izdatel'stvo St. Peterburgskogo universiteta.

Bespalov, S.V. (2014) *Ekonomicheskaya modernizatsiya Rossii v kontse XIX – nachale XX vv.: Sovremennaya istoriografiya*, Moskva: INION RAN.

Bokarev, Iu. P. (2006) 'Eshche raz o tempakh rosta promyshlennogo proizvodstava v Rossii v kontse XIX – nachale XX veka', *Otechestvennaia istoriia*, (1): 131–40.

Borodkin, L.I. (2013) 'Modernizatsionnye aspekty industrializatsii dorevolyutsionnoj Rossii', in S.P. Karpov and V.A. Tishkov (eds.) *Ot Drevnej Rusi k Rossijskoj Federatsii: istoriya rossijskoj gosudarstvennosti*, St. Petersburg: Aletejya.

Borodkin, L.I. and G.E. Perel'man (2006) Struktura i dinamika birzhevogo indeksa dorevolyutsionnoj Rossii: analiz rynka aktsij vedushchih promyshlennyh kompanij, in *Ekonomicheskaya istoriya: Ezhegodnik-2006*, Moskva: ROSSPEN, 145–73.

Borodkin, L.I. and A.V. Konovalova (2010) *Rossijskij fondovyj rynok v nachale XX veka: faktory kursovoj dinamiki*, St. Petersburg: Aletejya.

Borodkin, L.I., P. Gregori and O.V. Hlevnyuk (eds.) (2005) *GULAG: Ekonomika prinuditel'nogo truda*, Moskva: ROSSPEN.

Borodkin, L.I., T.Ya. Valetov, Yu.B. Smirnova and I.V. Shil'nikova (2010) *'Ne rublem edinym': trudovye stimuly rabochih-tekstil'shchikov dorevolyutsionnoj Rossii*, Moskva: ROSSPEN.

Borodkin, L.I., S.A. Krasil'nikov and O.V. Hlevnyuk (eds.) (2013) *Istoriya stalinizma: Prinuditel'nyj trud v SSSR. Ekonomika, politika*, Moskva: ROSSPEN.

Bovykin, V.I. (1967) *Zarozhdenie finansovogo kapitala v Rossii.* Moskva: Izdatel'stvo MGU.

Bovykin, V.I. (1983) Dinamika promyshlennogo proizvodstva v Rossii (1896–1910), *Istoriya SSSR*, (3): 20–52.

Bovykin, V.I. (1984) *Formirovanie finansovogo kapitala v Rossii. Konets XIX – 1908 g.*, Moskva: Nauka.

Bovykin, V.I. (1991) Frantsuzskij kapital v aktsionernyh predpriyatiyah v Rossii nakanune Oktyabrya, *Otechestvennaya istoriya*, (4): 159–81.

Bovykin, V.I. (1996) *Predislovie k knige: Rossia i mirovoi biznes: dela i sud'by*. Moskva: ROSSPEN.

Chayanov, A.V. (1925) *Organizatsiya krest'yanskogo khozyaystva*, Moskva: Kooperativnoe izdatel'stvo.

Chayanov, A.V. (1928) *Optimal'nyye razmery sel'skokhozyaystvennykh predpriyatiy*, Moskva: Novaya derevnya.

Davydov, M.A. (2003) *Ocherki agrarnoj istorii Rossii v kontse XIX – nachale XX vv.: (po materialam transportnoj statistiki i statistiki zemleustrojstva)*, Moskva: Izdatel'stvo RGGU.

Druzhinin, N.M. (1978) *Russkaya derevnya na perelome 1861–1880 gg.*, Moskva: Nauka.

Dvoretskij, E.B. (1979) Statistika vneshnej torgovli, in I.D. Koval'chenko (eds.) *Massovye istochniki po sotsial'no-ekonomicheskoj istorii Rossii perioda kapitalizma*, Moskva: Nauka.

Gajdar, E.T. (2005) *Dolgoe vremya. Rossiya v mire: ocherki ekonomicheskoj istorii*, Moskva: Delo.

Gindin, I.F. (1960) *Gosudarstvennyj bank i ekonomicheskaya politika tsarskogo pravitel'stva (1861–1892)*, Moskva: Gosfinizdat.

Gladkov, I.A., I.F. Suslov, A.S. Tolkachev et al. (1976–1980) *Istoriya sotsialisticheskoj ekonomiki SSSR. V 7 t. I. AN SSSR, Institut ekonomiki*, Moskva: Nauka.

Grekov, B., Em. Yaroslavskij and S. Bushuev (eds.) (1939–40) *Protiv istoricheskoj kontseptsii M. N. Pokrovskogo*, Moskva, Leningrad: Akademiya Nauk SSSR.

Gurevich, A. (2004) *Istoriia istorika*, Moskva: ROSSPEN.

Gurevich, A.Ya. (1967) *Svobodnoye krest'yanstvo feodal'noy Norvegii*, Moskva: Nauka.

Gurevich, A.Ya. (1970) *Problemy genezisa feodalizma v Zapadnoy Yevrope*, Moskva: Vysshaya shkola.

Gurevich, A.Ya. (1972) *Kategorii srednevekovoj kul'tury*, Moskva: Iskusstvo.

Hromov, P.A. (1950) *Ekonomicheskoe razvitie Rossii v XIX – XX vv.*, Moskva: Gospolitizdat.

Il'in, S.V. (2004) 'Promyshlennoe razvitie Rossii ot kontsa XIX v. do nachala stalinskogo "Velikogo pereloma"', *Konferentsii, diskussii, materialy 2004: Sbornik nauchnykh trudov kafedry istorii Rossii RUDN*, Moskva: Izdatel'stvo RUDN.

Kafengauz, L.B. (1994) *Evolyutsiya promyshlennogo proizvodstva Rossii (poslednyaya tret' XIX v. – 30-e gody XX v.)*, Moskva: Epifaniya.

Kir'yanov, Y.A. and M.S. Volin (eds.) (1983) *Rabochij klass ot zarozhdeniya do nachala XX v.*, Moskva: Nauka.

Kitanina, T.M. (1978) *Hlebnaya torgovlya Rossii v 1875–1914 gg. (Ocherki pravitel'stvennoj politiki)*, Leningrad: Akademiya nauk SSSR.

Kondrashin, V.V. (2008) *Golod 1932–1933 godov: tragediya rossijskoj derevni*, Moskva: ROSSPEN.

Kondratiev, N.D. (1925) Bol'shie tsikly kon'yunktury, *Voprosy kon'yunktury*,T.1 (Vyp.1).

Kondratiev, N.D. (1926) K voprosu o bol'shih tsiklah kon'yunktury, *Planovoe hozyajstvo*, (8).

Kondratiev, N.D. (1928) *Bol'shie tsikly kon'yunktury: Doklady i ih obsuzhdeniya v In-te ekonomiki*, Moskva: RANION, Institut economiki.

Kosminsky, E.A. (1947) *Issledovaniya po agrarnoj istorii Anglii XIII veka*, Moskva-Leningrad: Izdatel'stvo Academii Nauk SSSR.

Kosminsky, E.A. (1956) *Studies in the Agrarian History of England in the Thirteenth Century*, Oxford: Basil Blackwell.

Koval'chenko, I.D. and L.V. Milov (1974) *Vserossijskij agrarnyj rynok. XVIII – nachalo XX veka*, Moskva: Nauka.

Koval'chenko, I.D., N.B. Selunskaya N.B. and B.M. Litvakov (1982) *Sotsial'no-ekonomicheskij stroj pomeshchich'ego hozyajstva Evropejskoj Rossii v epohu kapitalizma*, Moskva: Nauka.

Koval'chenko, I.D., T.L. Moiseenko and N.B. Selunskaya (1988) *Sotsial'no-ekonomicheskij stroj krest'yanskogo hozyajstva Evropejskoj Rossii v epohu kapitalizma*, Moskva: MGU.

Kovalevskij M.M. (1898–1903) *'Ekonomicheskij rost Evropy do vozniknoveniya kapitalisticheskogo hozyajstva', t. 1–3*, Moskva: izd-vo «Lan'».

Kovalevskij, M.M. (1900) *Ekonomicheskij stroj Rossii / per. s frants.*, St. Petersburg: Izd. A.Ermolaevoj.

Kudrov, V. (1995) National accounts and international comparisons for the former Soviet Union, *Scandinavian Economic History Review*, 43(1): 147–66.

Kudrov, V.V. (2007) *Ekonomika Rossii v mirovom kontekste*, St. Petersburg: Aletejya.

Kulisher, I.M. (1903) *Ocherki po istorii tamozhennoj politiki*, St. Petersburg: Tipographiya V.Kirshbauma.

Kulisher, I.M. (1906, 1908) *Evolyutsiya pribyli s kapitala v svyazi s razvitiem promyshlennosti i torgovli v Zapadnoj Evrope, v 2 tt.*, St. Petersburg: Tipo-Litographiya Rosena.

Kulisher, I.M. (1909) *Istoriya ekonomicheskogo byta Zapadnoj Evropy: 1-e izd.*, St. Petersburg.

Kulisher, I.M. (1911) *Promyshlennost' i rabochij klass na Zapade v XVI–XVII stoletiyah 1-e izd.*, St. Petersburg: Brokgauz-Efron.

Kulisher, I.M. (1922) *Ocherk istorii russkoj promyshlennosti: 1-e izd.*, Petrograd: Izdatel'stvo K.-O. Petrogubprofsoveta.

Kulisher, I.M. (1923) *Ocherk istorii russkoj torgovli: 1-e izd.*, Petrograd: Atenej.

Kulisher, I.M. (1925a) *Ocherk ekonomicheskoj istorii drevnej Gretsii*, Leningrad: Knigoizdatel'stvo 'Seyatel' E.V.Vysotskogo.

Kulisher, I.M. (1925b, 1926) *Istoriya russkogo narodnogo hozyajstva, v 2 tt.: 1-e izd.*, Moskva: Mir.

Lebedev, S.K. (2003) *S. Peterburgskij mezhdunarodnyj kommercheskij bank vo vtoroj polovine XIX v.: evropejskie i russkie svyazi*, Moskva: ROSSPEN.

Levitskij, V.F. (1890) *Zadachi i metody nauki o narodnom hozyajstve*, Yaroslavl'.

Livshits Ya.I. (1961) *Monopolii v ekonomike Rossii*, Moskva: Mysl'.

Lizunov, P.V. (2003) *Birzhi v Rossii i ekonomicheskaya politika pravitel'stva (XVIII – nachalo XX vv.)*, Arhangel'sk: Izd-vo Solti.

Lizunov, P.V. (2004) *Sankt Peterburgskaya birzha i rossijskij rynok tsennyh bumag (1703–1917 gg.)*, St. Petersburg: Russko-Baltijskij informatsionnyj tsentr 'BLITs'.

Lyashchenko, P.I. (1912) *Hlebnaya torgovlya na vnutrennih rynkah Evropejskoj Rossii*, St. Petersburg: Izdatel'stvo Ministerstva torgovli i promyshlennosti.

Lyashchenko P.I (1925) *Ocherki agrarnoj evolyutsii Rossii, t. 1*, Leningrad: Priboj.

Lyashchenko, P.I. (1930) *Istoriya russkogo narodnogo hozyajstva, 2 izd.*, Mjskva-Leningrad: Gosizdat.

Lyashchenko, P.I. (1947) *Istoriya narodnogo hozyajstva* SSSR. *Tom 1. Dokapitalisticheskie formatsii*, Moskva: Politizdat.

Lyashchenko, P.I. (1948) *Istoriya narodnogo hozyajstva* SSSR. *Tom 2. Kapitalizm*, Moskva: Politizdat.

Majdachevskij, D.Ya. (2011) V.F. Levitskij: ekonomicheskaya istoriya v strukture nauk o narodnom hozyajstve, *Istoriko-ekonomicheskie issledovaniya*, (3).

Mironov, B.N. (2010) *Blagosostoyanie naseleniya i revolyutsii v imperskoj Rossii: XVIII – nachalo XX veka*, Moskva: Ves' mir.

Pavlenko, N.I. (1962) *Istoriya metallurgii v Rossii XVIII veka. Zavody i zavodovladel'tsy*, Moskva: Izd-vo Akademii nauk SSSR.

Pazhitnov, K.A. (1906) *Polozhenie rabochego klassa v Rossii*, St. Petersburg: Novyj mir.

Pazhitnov, K.A. (1924a) *Iz istorii rabochih artelej na Zapade i v Rossii. Ot utopistov do nashih dnej*, Petrograd.

Pazhitnov, K.A. (1924b) *Promyshlennyj trud v krepostnuyu epohu*, Leningrad: Put' k znaniyu.

Pazhitnov, K.A. (1940) *Ocherki po istorii bakinskoj neftedobyvayushchej promyshlennosti (ot kon. XVII v. do Vel. Okt. sotsialistich. revolyutsii)*, Moskva-Leningrad: Gostoptehisdat.

Perel'man, G.E. (2009) Sravnitel'noe issledovanie kursovoj dinamiki bumag promyshlennyh kompanij na Londonskoj i S. Peterburgskoj birzhah v kontse XIX – nachale XX vv., *Ekonomicheskaya istoriya: Ezhegodnik. 2009*, Moskva: ROSSPEN.

Petrov, Yu.A. (1998) *Kommercheskie banki Moskvy. Konets XIX v. – 1914 g.*, Moskva: ROSSPEN.

Petrov, Yu.A. (2011) Svoboda kak faktor ekonomicheskogo rosta (Razmyshleniya po povodu 150-letiya otmeny krepostnogo prava), *Ekonomicheskaya istoriya: Obozrenie*, (16).

Poberezhnikov, I.V. (2006) *Perekhod ot traditsionnogo k industrial'nomu obshchestvu: teoretiko-metodologicheskie problemy modernizatsii*, Moskva: ROSSPEN.

Poletaev, A.V. (2006) Valovoy vnutrenniy produkt Rossiyskoy Federatsii v sopostavlenii s Soyedinennymi Shtatami Ameriki, 1960–2004 gg., *Gumanitarnye issledovaniya (IGITI GU–VShE)*, 2 (21).

Ponomarenko, A.N. (2002) *Retrospektivnyye natsional'nyye scheta Rossii, 1961–1990*, Moskva: Finansy i statistika.

Popov, V.P. (2000) *Ekonomicheskaya politika Sovetskogo gosudarstva. 1945–1953*, Tambov: Izdatel'stvo Tambovskogo gosudarstvennogo universiteta.

Potkina, I.V. (2004) *Na Olimpe devogo uspeha: Nikol'skaia manufactura Morozovyh, 1797–1917*, Moskva: Izdatel'stvo Glavarhiva Moskvy.

Rakov, A.A. (2012) *Sotsial'no-ekonomicheskie aspekty «raskulachivaniya» krest'yan Yuzhnogo Urala (1930–1934)*, Moskva: ROSSPEN.

Rozaliev, Yu.N. (1992) Vokrug ekonomicheskoj istorii, *Byloe*, (6).

Rozaliev, Yu.N. (1996) Vystuplenie na "Kruglom stole" po itogam XI Mezhdunarodnogo kongressa po ekonomicheskoj istorii, 5 yanvarya 1995 g., *Ekonomicheskaya istoriya: Obozrenie*, (1).

Rybachenok, I.S. (1982) Vneshnyaya torgovlya Rossii i russko–frantsuzskie torgovye otnosheniya v 1891–1905 gg., *Istoriya SSSR*, (1).

Rydzyunskij, P.G. (1983) *Krest'yane i gorod v kapitalisticheskoj Rossii vtoroj poloviny 19 veka (vzaimootnosheniya goroda i derevni v sotsial'no-ekonomicheskom stroe Rossii)*, Moskva: Nauka.

Salomatina, S.A. (2004) *Kommercheskie banki v Rossii: dinamika i struktura operatsij, 1864–1917 gg.*, Moskva: ROSSPEN.

Semenov, L.E. (1975) *Rossiya i Angliya. Ekonomicheskie otnosheniya v seredine XIX v.*, Leningrad: Izdatel'stvo Leningradskogo universiteta.

Senyavskij, A.S. (eds.) (2006) *NEP: ekonomicheskie i politicheskie aspekty*, Moskva: ROSSPEN.

Senyavskij, A.S. (2009) Rol' ekonomicheskih faktorov v revolyutsionnom protsesse Rossii nachala XX veka, in *Mirovoe ekonomicheskoe razvitie i Rossiya (19 i 20 vv.)*, Moskva: Izdatel'skij tsentr IVI RAN: 94–7.

Simchera, V.M. (2006) *Razvitie ekonomiki Rossii za 100 let: 1900–2000. Istoricheskie ryady, vekovye trendy, institutsional'nye tsikly*, Moskva: Nauka.

Simonova, M.S. (1987) *Krizis agrarnoj politiki tsarizma nakanune pervoj russkoj revolyutsii*, Moskva: Nauka.

Solov'eva, A.M. (1990) *Promyshlennaya revolyutsiya v Rossii v pervoj polovine XIX veka*, Moskva: Nauka.

Strumilin, S.G. (1924) K reforme urozhajnoj statistiki, *Planovoe hozyajstvo. Byulleteni Gosplana. Ezhemesyachnyj zhurnal*, (4–5).

Strumilin, S.G. (1930) Oplata truda v Rossii (Istoricheskij ocherk), *Planovoe hozyajstvo*, (4, 7, 8).

Strumilin, S.G. (1935) *Chernaya metallurgiya v Rossii i SSSR*, Moskva-Leningrad: Izdatel'stvo Akademii Nauk SSSR.

Tihonov, V.V. (2012) Arhiv RAN: dokumenty lichnyh fondov istorikov o kampaniyah bor'by s «ob"ektivizmom» i «kosmopolitizmom». 1948–1950 gg., *Vestnik arhivista*, (3).

Tihonov, Yu.A. (1974) *Pomeshchich'i krest'yane v Rossii. Feodal'naya renta v XVII – nachale XVIII v.*, Moskva: Nauka.

Tugan-Baranovskij, M.I. (1894) *Promyshlennye krizisy v sovremennoj Anglii, ih prichiny i vliyanie na narodnuyu zhizn': 1-e izd*, St. Petersburg: Tip. I. N. Skorohodova.

Tugan-Baranovskij, M.I. (1898) *Russkaya fabrika v proshlom i nastoyashchem*, St. Petersburg: Izdanie L.F. Panteleeva.

Tugan-Baranovskij, M.I. (1912) *Ocherki razvitiya manufakturnoj promyshlennosti v Rossii*, Moskva.

Tyukavkin, V.G. (2001) *Velikorusskoe krest'yanstvo i stolypinskaya agrarnaya reforma*, Moskva: Pamyatniki istoricheskoj mysli.

Vinogradov, P.G. (1887) *Issledovaniya po sotsial'noj istorii Anglii v srednie veka*, St. Petersburg: Tipografiya V.S.Balasheva.

Vinogradov, P.G. (1911) *Srednevekovoe pomest'e v Anglii*, St. Petersburg.

Yatsunskij, V.K. (1973) *Sotsial'no-ekonomicheskaya istoriya Rossii XVIII–XIX vekov*, Moskva: Nauka.

13

A PERIPHERY AT THE CENTRE OF ATTENTION

Economic history in Poland

Jacek Kochanowicz

Poland's history in the nineteenth and twentieth centuries is marked by discontinuities – partitions, wars, rule of foreign powers, shifting borders, mass migrations, and far-reaching changes of economic regimes. Polish economic historians throughout the twentieth century not only had to solve the problem of what constituted the subject matter of their studies, but also had to react and accommodate to the challenges and pressures of the social and political environment in which they had to work. The beginnings of economic history as a discipline are traceable to the last quarter of the nineteenth century, its institutionalization to the interwar period, and its flourishing to the 1950s to 1970s – each of these periods radically different from the preceding one. As with other fields of historical studies, economic history has been closely related to nation-building, a complex process in the Polish case because of the nineteenth-century partitions, the troubled years of the interwar independence, the Second World War, the over forty years of a limited sovereignty under state socialism, and the changes after 1989. Despite the provincial location and the overall pressure to develop historical studies conforming to the nation-centred model, there were economic historians able to go beyond the local preoccupations, and – even if focusing on economic history of Poland – to put it into a broad, European and global framework, thus making it relevant for understanding geographically much wider processes of change. The following, while broadly sketching the development of the discipline over a century, focuses on personalities and works that made their mark due to their originality and broader significance.

A recognizable discipline

History in its modern shape formed in Poland in the second half of the nineteenth century, combined a scholarly approach with a participation in the nation-building project, interpreting the past in terms of the 'history of Poland'. The memory of the Polish state – founded in the tenth century, stretching to 900,000 sq. kilometres in the seventeenth century, and collapsing at the end of the eighteenth century – was a frame of reference. The degrees of cultural and political autonomy varied between the three partitions, the largest being the Austrian, where two Polish language universities existed, one in Kraków, the second in Lwów. In the German and Russian partitions, there was much less space for Polish-language institutions of higher learning and research, although publications in Polish were possible. After gaining independence in 1918, the new state engaged intensively in the (belated) nation-building process. Establishment of institutions of higher education was part of the process. This was the context in which the discipline of economic history was developing.

While a number of historians ventured into matters of the economic past of Poland in the nineteenth century, the institutionalization of economic history dates from the beginnings of the next century, with chairs and institutes devoted to the discipline, sessions on economic history at the congresses of Polish historians (1925, 1930, 1935), and one journal devoted specifically to the field of social and economic history. Two personalities stand out as programmatic leaders of the discipline and the founders of distinct schools of thought. These were Franciszek Bujak (1875–1953) and Jan Rutkowski (1886–1949).

Bujak, after finishing high school and with five zlotys in his pocket given to him by his peasant father, set out in 1894 for Kraków's Jagiellonian University (Bujak 1927). He obtained his doctorate in 1899, and his *Habilitationsschrift* on the medieval settlement of Małopolska, defended in 1905, is considered the first Polish work in economic history, a discipline in which he then started to lecture at the Jagiellonian University (Madurowicz-Urbańska 1976). In independent Poland, he transferred to the University of Lwów, where he established an institute devoted to economic history. In 1931 he and Rutkowski founded a journal, *Roczniki Dziejów Społecznych i Gospodarczych* (Social and Economic History Annales), which is still published today.

Throughout his writings and organizational efforts, Bujak worked to make economic history a discipline in its own right, in terms of a subject matter, research methods, and university curricula. His approach – as that of his Kraków university teachers – was positivist and empirical, with a stress on the use of statistics. He understood the discipline as history which is both economic and social and which should take into account demography, settlement and colonization, money, credit, and prices, but also the impact of such exogenous factors as weather, fires, epidemics, and wars. At the core of his proposed approach were systematically researched, multi-aspect monographs of basic units of social and economic life, such as households, villages, towns, landed estates, and industrial enterprises. Bujak was an institution-builder, creating what is known as 'the Bujak school'. Under his tutelage, his followers produced several volumes of price history, as well as various monographs employing his methods.

Rutkowski, coming from a well-to-do bourgeois family, was for most of his career a professor of economic history at the newly established University of Poznań (Topolski 1986). Having independent means, he travelled a lot. His contacts included Marc Bloch and Henri Seé. His own research, primarily on the agrarian history of the sixteenth to eighteenth centuries, combined empirical studies with attempts to develop a comprehensive, original programme of reformulation of economic history (Rutkowski 1956). He capped his work by a large comprehensive synthesis of Polish economic history, in its structure a model for the later publications of this sort (Rutkowski 1953).

Rutkowski wanted – in a way similar to the Annales School – to see economic history as not simply descriptive, but as problem-oriented and theory-informed. About standard economic theory's claim to universality he had his doubts and suggested that a specific theory might be necessary for each economic system (Rutkowski 1934a). His somewhat dry style of writing and his methodology were closer to social sciences than to traditional history – personalities do not show in his narrative; instead he employed a rigid comparative framework when explaining historical processes. What he labelled the problem of synthesis was a search for a theoretical axis that would integrate various sub-fields of economic history (Rutkowski 1925). He thought that such integration would be possible if the distribution of social (national) income between various social groups and institutions was treated as a key question of economic history. To this issue he devoted several works, one of book length, which developed a classification of incomes of landed estates and a methodology for their statistical reconstruction (Rutkowski 1938).

The perspective of distribution of income served Rutkowski as an analytical tool to address the key questions about modern Polish history: about the specific route of the Polish economy, since the sixteenth century onward, particularly the emergence of demesne farming, and the collapse of the Polish state at the end of the eighteenth century (Rutkowski 1925, 1934b). Why did the late medieval system of peasant tenancy based on money rents and similar to that of the West evolve into demesne farming, based on corvée? He answered this question through a comparative analysis of agrarian regimes in various countries and explained this process by the parallel occurrence, in the Polish case, of two factors: urban demand for grain and a possibility of reinforcing peasant serfdom. The latter gave the lords a possibility of controlling peasants more thoroughly and thus of increasing their share of incomes at the expense of the peasantry. In a book comparing serfdom in France, Germany, and Poland, he explained the diverse evolution of agrarian regimes by differences in the relations between the nobility and the state, both competing for the revenues that could be obtained from the peasantry (Rutkowski 1921: 108–9). Where the state was stronger, it could limit the nobility's power over the peasantry, thus weakening serfdom.[1] The weak Polish state, in turn, could not raise revenues necessary to sustain an adequate military force, which led to its eventual collapse (Rutkowski 1921, 1930). These sorts of ideas came to have great influence in international debates, and from the 1960s, were applied to 'feudal structures' on a broader geographical canvas (Wallerstein 1974; Aston and Philpin 1985).

The importance of Bujak's and Rutkowski's contributions went beyond their own research, as through their seminars and the work of their doctoral students they established schools of younger researchers following their tracks. Both scholars collaborated closely as editors of *Roczniki . . .*, but differed in their approaches to the discipline. While both were putting stress on statistics, and both considered the discipline as history which is economic and social, for Bujak the detailed multi-aspect monographs were a key tool, while Rutkowski stressed a problem-oriented approach. The former was closer to ethnography, giving weight also to psychological factors; the latter tended to see economic history as an objectivist social science. Both, and in particular Rutkowski, attempted to dissociate ideology from scholarly activity and to pursue a value-free type of research to the degree that it was possible.

Flourishing in hard times

The Second World War and its aftermath were a shock for Polish society. The material and human losses were immense; the state territory was moved over two hundred kilometres to the West, followed by mass migrations. The pre-war social structures were destroyed, with the middle and the landed classes eliminated either socially or physically, the Jews exterminated, and the intellectuals who survived put into poverty. Both the Nazis and the Soviets targeted the elite, making its human losses disproportionally high compared with other social groups. The discipline of history suffered additionally due to the destruction of many archives.

The process of post-war reconstruction involved academic life, with new universities established in Toruń, Łódź, and Wrocław. Reconstruction unfolded under new political conditions. The expansion of the Soviet sphere of influence over East Central Europe meant the imposition of state socialism and communist ideology. Remnants of pluralism remained until 1948/9; after that, the political system entered its totalitarian/Stalinist phase. Political life was liberalized only in 1956, the change being triggered by the famous Khrushchev secret speech during the twentieth congress of the CPSU.

Intellectuals accommodated to the new conditions partly out of necessity, partly out of the urge to participate in the reconstruction of the country, and partly out of conviction (Miłosz 1953). Witold Kula, a non-communist but leftist economic historian, wrote during the early 1950s an essay (published only in 1958) in the form of letters of two fictional Romans of the time when Christianity had been imposed upon the empire (Kula 1958). The protagonists were torn between a hope that the new faith would bring new promises and a fear that it would destroy the values of an established civilization. That was the inner dialogue of many intellectuals at the time.

History was meant to be rewritten. A 'grand narrative' of pre-war history was the story of the Polish nation and nation-state, with its ascent in the Middle Ages, the glory in the sixteenth century, the crisis of the seventeenth and early eighteenth, the partial revival in the late eighteenth, the collapse in 1795, the fight for independence in the nineteenth century, culminating with its revival in 1918. This vision was now to be replaced by the Marxist narrative, conceptualizing the past in terms of consecutive 'modes of production' or 'socio-economic formations' – feudalism, capitalism, and socialism – the change being fuelled by the rise of productive forces and class warfare. One of the tasks of the newly established Institute of History of the Polish Academy of Sciences (IH PAN) was to produce a multi-volume *History of Poland*, written according to these new prescriptions.

However, the Sovietization of intellectual life in Poland was far from complete; academics trained before the war – even if attacked by young party zealots – maintained high prestige and in most cases were allowed to keep at least research positions. The strength of the intelligentsia and academic *milieu*, hardened by the war experience (clandestine research and teaching included) made the imposition of Soviet-imported solutions far from easy, and made Poland different from other countries of East Central Europe (Connelly 2000; Górny 2007: 151). The authorities tried to remake academic institutions upon the Soviet model, one of the ideas being the establishment of the research institutes of the Polish Academy of Sciences, separated from teaching. However, looking for a degree of legitimization among the historical profession they accepted the internationally acclaimed medievalist Tadeusz Manteuffel (1902–70) as Head of IH PAN. He was not a communist. During the Nazi occupation he had served, together with many other historians (including Witold Kula), in the information and propaganda section of the clandestine Home Army, a military arm of the Polish government in exile in London.[2] Thus the above-mentioned *History of Poland*, of which Manteuffel and Kula were among the editors, while organized according to the Marxist interpretation, offered in fact a broad-minded picture of the past, duly reporting academic controversies and debates.

Ascertaining the real role of Marxism in Polish intellectual life in general and historical studies in particular is not an easy matter (Górny 2007; Pleskot 2010: 574–80; Stobiecki 1993). In the introductions to the historical works published in the first half of the 1950s, one finds mandatory ritualistic references to Marx, Engels, Lenin, and Stalin (Siewierski 2011: 157). They are usually followed by good practices of the 'historian's craft' – the discussion of literature (even if dubbed 'a bourgeois science'), and the criticism of sources. After 1956, Stalinist rituals vanished and scholarly language took more standard forms. Marxism, however, was present before and after 1956 not solely as an ornament or a camouflage, but also in some deeper sense. Many members of the Polish intelligentsia tended to be left-oriented (but rarely communist) before and, in particular, during and after the war (Miłosz 1953; Shore 2006). No doubt, the Great Depression was a formative experience for many who grew to maturity in the 1930s (Kula 1976: 455; 1994; Małowist 1988). They thought that capitalism brought little to Poland in terms of economic development and social fairness and were looking towards some form of socialist solution. Many treated Marxism seriously before it became mandatory, as opening new vistas for philosophy, social research, and the study of the past. Some of the younger people embraced communism, attracted by its Promethean promise. However, to take Marxism just as a faith was intellectually not easy. At its most abstract level, the Polish Marxist philosophers had to relate themselves to logical positivism, the most important philosophical current before the war, represented by the Lwów–Warsaw school (one of the members of which was the world-renowned logician and mathematician Alfred Tarski). As many of its representatives survived the war, it was influential even under the communist system. This tradition formed one of the checks against accepting Marxism in its primitive, Stalinist version, and also contributed to an empiricist current in the Marxist-inspired interpretations (Malewski 1956). Jerzy Topolski (1928–98), an economic historian turned methodologist, and initially an avowed Marxist, developed from the 1960s onwards his ideas of historical explanation which closely followed a Popperian–Hempelian approach (Topolski 1968: 368–499; 1983: 361–433).[3]

Paradoxically, economic history gained quite a lot of freedom in the otherwise difficult circumstances of the early 1950s. It was considered to be somewhat in tune with the official ideology, stressing so much the role of the 'forces of production'. As Topolski (1983: 96–7) observed, Marxism served the historians at that time as a tool of selection of the subject matter of research, privileging economic history. With this came opportunities in terms of positions and research funds, however meagre they were in the post-war conditions. Young, gifted historians became attracted to the field, feeling that it offered more elbow room than political history. At the same time, as teachers and role-models they had outstanding academics, trained before the war (Siewierski 2011). Research and publication of sources and monographs mushroomed, making the period between the early 1950s and the late 1970s the most prolific for the discipline. Not surprisingly, much attention was devoted to agrarian matters – manorial and peasant farming, peasant obligations, trade in agricultural products, and the like. Economic history was closely linked on the one hand with the history of material culture, on the other hand with social history. The latter initially focused on class warfare, in the 1960s and the 1970s, increasingly on social stratification, and also on family history. The 1960s brought rising interest in historical demography, which is active to this day (Kuklo 2009). While the bulk of the work done in the 1950s to 1970s was on the medieval and particularly the early modern period, nineteenth-century industrialization also attracted attention, as well as the short interwar period.

In terms of 'genre', the majority of books and articles were traditional, solid monographs, based on archival sources. Many works, particularly those on the nineteenth century, relied heavily on quantitative data, usually in the form of simple, descriptive statistics. Few works extended beyond relatively short periods of time, thus this large bulk of works presents a series of snapshots rather than an interpretation of the process of change. With few exceptions, Polish economic historians specialized in the study of the Polish past.

Marxism played some role in the selection of topics, and, to a certain degree, as a source of terminology – as was the conceptualization of historical periods in terms of 'feudalism' and 'capitalism' with its stages of free competition and monopoly. At the same time, Polish historians were open and receptive to Western scholarship. Except for a relatively short period of Stalinism (1949–56), travel to the West was possible and the professional literature accessible, although in a limited way because of lack of funds. The most important of contacts were these with the *Annales* School. From 1956, Poles were invited for shorter and longer stays by the École des Hautes Études en Sciences Sociales and by Maison des Sciences de l'Homme, the stays usually spent on library studies, seminar participation, and contact building rather than primary research (Kula 2010: 616). Hundreds of scholars visited both institutions, and some maintained close ties with the *Annales* circle, as duly documented in a recent large monograph (Pleskot 2010). The overall impact on the research done in Poland, however, is a matter of a debate. Contrary to an early positive assessment by Pomian (1978), Mączak (Mączak and Tygielski 2000: 167) and Pleskot (2010: 699–725) argue that the methodological influence of the *Annales* School was limited. Indeed, it is true that it would be hard to find Polish equivalents of *longue durée* regional monographs, weaving together demography, prices, land tenure patterns, and mentality into *histoire totale*. A period-specific solid monograph of a town, a village, an estate, with not much of a theoretical underpinning, remained the typical Polish product.

Men of vision

Some names stand above the large body of works produced during the three post-war decades. These are the names of historians who managed to combine meticulous research with a vision, to produce an ambitious interpretation of historical change, and to link specific research with a broad context, reaching outside the history of one country.

No doubt, one of them was Marian Małowist (1909–88), one of the few Polish economic historians who in his research went beyond Poland. He followed neither Bujak nor Rutkowski, developing instead his own original approach (Mączak 1993: 5). His doctoral dissertation was on Stockholm's foreign trade in the fifteenth century (Małowist 1935). Just before the war he finished his Habilitation on Kaffa, the Genovese colony in the Crimea which fell to the Ottomans in 1475. Of the three existing manuscript copies only one was miraculously saved, to be published just after the war (Małowist 1947). In the preface to this book he mentioned that, when reading about the cruelty of invaders' behaviour in Kaffa, he had thought these observations must have been exaggerated. Now, after what he saw during the war – part of which he spent in the Warsaw ghetto, and he lost his wife in the Holocaust – he thought they were not. He became a professor at the University of Warsaw and quickly published a large study of the early modern Dutch cloth-making industry and of Dutch economic expansion along the Baltic coast, to be followed by a series of articles on the trade relations and economic inequalities between East and West Europe (Małowist 1958, 1966, 1974, 2010). Published in foreign languages and offering a synthesizing perspective, they gave Małowist broad recognition. He crowned this line of interests with a large book on the economic relations between the East and the West of Europe in the late Middle Ages and in the modern era (Małowist 1973). His interests in Western Europe's relations with less developed regions, extended to Africa, and also to Portuguese overseas expansion (Małowist 1964, 1969, 1976).

At first glance, Małowist's writings seem descriptive. He avoided terms such as 'theory' or 'model' (Mączak 1993: 9). But, as Sosnowska (2004: 85) convincingly argues, he produced an 'implicit model' explaining inequalities and differences across space by the role of commerce and the character of social structures. He might have gone too far in interpreting the importance of Dutch capital in what he called 'the Baltic sphere' as colonization, as it was not accompanied by political dominance. He offered, however, an interesting interpretation of the rising backwardness of Eastern Europe (Małowist 1973). The crisis of the fourteenth century, affecting Western but not Eastern Europe, opened export possibilities for the latter. These exports were initially furs, timber, then increasingly grains, thus leading to the strengthening of second serfdom. Linking the primary sector of the economy with foreign markets weakened the urban economy, thus hampering economic development. Małowist's 'interpretative associations, his interests extending beyond Europe, his perception of the global economic linkages should be considered as antecedents of the present tendencies in the social sciences' (Sosnowska 2004: 89). Wallerstein (1974: ix) singled him out alongside Braudel as the source of inspiration for his world-system theory. Małowist had disciples and followers who became renowned economic historians themselves. They moved forward research on Baltic trade, on the Polish urban economy, but also on areas outside of Europe, particularly Africa and India.

Witold Kula (1916–88) is another important personality. Similarly to Małowist, he taught in high school before the war, while preparing his dissertation on the demography of the Congress Kingdom of Poland.[4] During the war, he taught in the clandestine university, served in the underground Home Army, and took part in the Warsaw Uprising (August–September 1944). After coming back from a German POW camp, he became a professor first at the University of Łódź and then at the University of Warsaw and simultaneously at the IH PAN. A serious illness forced him gradually to decrease his activities from the early 1970s.

Kula had a keen interest in the methodology of economic history and tried to grasp the totality of the discipline as it stood in his times. His book on problems and methods of economic history reviews a vast body of literature published in several languages, analysing the relations between economic history and other fields of historical study as well as with various social sciences (Kula 1963). It also offers a programme, according to which economic history should develop in close dialogue with economic theory; take into regard social and particularly class relations; and rely on quantification.

Like Małowist, Kula was close to the left and can be considered a Marxist, although – also like Małowist – he never belonged to the communist party. His early interest in economic history he explained by his disappointment with the history he was taught in school, solidaristic and nationalist. 'I was looking for the history of peasants and workers, of agriculture and industry; I was looking for the history of modest and unknown people, whose collective work, sacrifices, and suffering made our country as it is' (Kula 1976: 455). Inspired by a debate on whether the second half of the eighteenth century witnessed an economic revival of Poland after decades of stagnation, he set out to study early industrialization. In a Marxist vein, this was accompanied by a question about Poland's 'transition from feudalism to capitalism' (Kula 1955). Over two decades, he completed monographic studies of about twenty industrial enterprises, established in the late eighteenth century (Kula 1956). The results were contrary to initial expectations. What he found were not the beginnings of capitalism, but rather a dead end of feudalism. In particular the manufactures established by the king or by the magnates served mostly to supply luxury goods for their courts and had only a partly market character, as they relied on servile labour and raw materials coming from the landed estate with no money costs. The next wave of industrialization that occurred in the first half of the nineteenth century – as Kula's collaborators in a research team he created at the IH PAN had shown – was *not* a continuation of the earlier efforts, but a completely new process. However, this was hardly capitalist either – its main driver was the state (Jedlicki 1964).

The observations of early manufacturing undertaken in the context of the manorial economy prompted Kula (1962) to write a short book with a title clearly inspired by Rutkowski's 1934 paper – *An Economic Theory of the Feudal System.* It presents a model of the Polish economy from the sixteenth to the eighteenth centuries, and – in its broader implications – a way to analyse non-capitalist systems (Kochanowicz 1990). The model postulates two types of 'enterprises': demesne and peasant farms. The peasants' economic aim is survival and they rely on their own labour. The demesne farms produce grains for exports, but have no monetary costs of production, as they exploit the servile work of peasants. Cash revenues from selling the grains are spent upon the importation of luxury goods. The type of economic calculation and rationality in each kind of enterprise is system-specific and different from that of capitalism, mainly because both types of enterprise do not have to use money to acquire factors of production and are not motivated by profits in a capitalist sense. As a consequence, the book questions the validity of a universalist claim of one type of economic theory, in a manner that has wider lessons for economic historians (Boldizzoni 2011: 87). The model explains the short- and long-term dynamics of the system, in particular the strengthening of the manorial sector relative to the peasant one, and the self-destructive processes at work, such as the weakening of the urban economy.

While the material came from the Polish past, the methodology of the book refers to diverse theoretical legacies from beyond Polish borders. Apart from Marxism, visible in the way Kula treated the relations between lords and peasants, he draws on Alexander Chayanov's (1923, 1924) theory of peasant economy and on early theories of economic development, particularly that of Arthur Lewis (1954).[5] In this respect, *Theory...* reflected the lively interests of Polish economists of that time in the economic development of the Third World. Kula remained in close contact with Michał Kalecki and Ignacy Sachs, who established a research and training centre, visited by many young economists from the developing countries. The book was translated into several languages and triggered wide-ranging debate, amongst specialists in as diverse fields as Byzantine history and contemporary Indian economy.[6] Among others, it attracted the attention of Zygmunt Bauman (1963), then a rising star of Polish sociology, Douglass North (1977), Michael Postan (1977), and Fernand Braudel, who prefaced the French edition. It is characteristic, however, that – except for North – neither Kula's, nor Małowist's work was of interest to American neoclassical economic historians. Despite the wider applicability of the ideas and their lessons for an exclusively Anglocentric approach neither of these authors were mentioned in *The Oxford Encyclopedia of Economic History*, for instance, which pays only scant attention to the problem of the relative backwardness of Eastern Europe (Mokyr 2003).

The interpretations offered by both Małowist and Kula are pessimistic; they picture Poland and Eastern Europe as backward, stagnating, and locked in a position of dependency (the term, however, was not used by any of them) upon the West since the sixteenth century at least, and perhaps even earlier. Sosnowska (2004), in her important study of the economic historiography of the post-war period, points to 'backwardness' as a key idea organizing the thinking of Polish economic historians. Apart from Kula and Małowist, she singles out also Jerzy Topolski and Andrzej Wyczański (1924–2008) as those who offered important interpretations of Eastern Europe's and Poland's specific routes of development. Topolski, in a series of works, explained the rise of capitalism in Western Europe and the parallel strengthening of demesne farming in the East in terms of specific forms of economic activities of the gentry, attempting to increase incomes in the face of rising aspirations (Topolski 1964, 1994). Wyczański (1987) put forward an interpretation according to which Poland was, in the late Middle Ages and in the first half of the sixteenth century, 'catching up' with Europe, the later developmental divergence stemming from the incompleteness of this imitative process. Małowist, Kula, Topolski, Wyczański, and some of their colleagues and followers offered interpretations of Poland, and more generally Eastern Europe as linked to the West, but backward, or peripheral. These interpretations preceded and influenced those Western scholars working on the European and global economy, such as Perry Anderson, Fernand Braudel, and Immanuel Wallerstein (Sosnowska 2004).

Modernization

One is justified to ask: and what about the nineteenth and twentieth centuries, the period of industrialization and modernization of not only the West, but also Eastern Europe? The Hungarian historians Ivan Berend and György Ránki (1987) developed their thinking on this issue in a debate with the World-System approach proposed by Wallerstein. What about the Poles? What lines of argument did the researchers of the industrialization period develop?

The 'core–periphery' perspective (but without using these particular terms) is certainly present in a few excellent works on the history of ideas (Górski 1963; Janowski 1998; Jedlicki 1988; Kizwalter 1991; Kofman 1992). They reconstruct the views of the Polish intelligentsia, for whom the gap between their country and the West became, from the end of the eighteenth century, one of the most acute issues. While looking for solutions, many writers doubted whether backwardness could be overcome by market forces alone, and were thus looking for some mobilizing role for the state. Much work has been done in this respect on the intellectual history of the nineteenth century, some on the interwar period. Less has been done on state socialism, but no doubt there were hopes that 'socialist industrialization', together with other state policies – education first and foremost – would modernize the country (Koryś 2007).

However, in the abundant and valuable research on industrialization, based on very solid analysis of archival primary sources,[7] the 'core–periphery' perspective is less visible, as is the theory of modernization. With the exception of a few outstanding scholars, there are also hardly any attempts at interdisciplinary cross-readings. The theorizing is mostly reduced to Marxist terminology (the bulk of these works dating from the 1950s and 1960s), as for instance 'free competition' and 'monopoly' stages of capitalism. Needless to say, the neoclassical approach is absent as well, and there is little of the approach of a business history kind. Most of these works, often abundant in statistics, have a descriptive character. There are few, if any, attempts to produce long-term quantitative assessments of economic development in terms of output of various industries, factor productivity, and GDP. The task is not easy, if at all possible, taking in consideration historical discontinuities mentioned in this chapter. Lacking such assessment makes it difficult to place Polish developments in a comparative perspective.

Still, this research allows one to draw a general outline of the process of industrialization of the Polish lands in the nineteenth and twentieth centuries. This was quite intensive particularly in the second half of the nineteenth century, although belated and on a smaller scale in comparison with the West, with the considerable role of the state in the early nineteenth century and in the interwar period, and mostly stimulated by market forces in the period now dubbed 'the first globalization', i.e. 1870–1914 (Kula 1960). The interwar period had also been under intensive study, in large measure due to the pioneering efforts of Zbigniew Landau and Jerzy Tomaszewski. They themselves studied various aspects of the economic development of this period, particularly banking and finance, and synthesized the existing research in a multi-volume publication, available in a shortened version also in English (Landau and Tomaszewski 1967–89, 1985). The role of the state in industrialization, so important in the Polish case, was scrutinized by Drozdowski (1963), Gołębiowski (1985), and Kofman (1992). Andrzej Jezierski, initially a specialist on the nineteenth century, extended his interests into contemporary history and produced a valuable textbook on the economic history of Poland under state socialism (Jezierski and Petz 1988).

It is worth noting that the most interesting works of economic historians were conceived and discussed in a very particular intellectual climate of the period between 1956 and 1968, the beginnings of the post-Stalinist thaw and the anti-intellectual and anti-Semitic campaign, a reaction to students' and intellectuals' protests of March 1968.[8] After 1956, the lid of ideological suppression was partly opened, and intellectual and artistic life flourished, resulting in perhaps the best period of Polish cultural life after the Second World War. In that time Witold Lutosławski composed his highly acclaimed Second Symphony, the Polish Film School was at its best, posters created by Polish artists were influencing international graphic design, Leszek Kołakowski and Bronisław Baczko published works on Spinoza and Rousseau, Jerzy Grotowski and Tadeusz Kantor revolutionized theatre performance. Marxism in some ways was still treated seriously, but it was the Marxism of Gramsci rather than that of Lenin. However, one could also easily end up in jail for expressing certain views too loudly, as was the case with historian and activist Karol Modzelewski (born 1937). He was put in prison for three and half years in 1965 for writing, together with a prominent activist of the democratic opposition, Jacek Kuroń (1934–2004), a political pamphlet against the party (Kuroń and Modzelewski 1970). After his release, he focused on research, producing a doctorate which turned out to be one of the finest works on the economic history of the early Middle Ages, combining a detailed analysis of primary sources with a comprehensive synthesis of the economic bases of early-medieval monarchy (Modzelewski 1975).

The twilight

Topics other than economy increasingly drew the attention of those who started their careers as economic historians. Jerzy Topolski went his own way, towards researching the methodology of history. For other economic historians, the twin discipline of social history was the most important of these new fields. Małowist's disciples Maria Bogucka and Henryk Samsonowicz turned from studying the economy of medieval and early modern towns towards their social life. Bogucka later engaged in women's history. Wyczański and his followers researched social stratification of the early modern period, and some specialized in historical demography. Kula's collaborators, who in the 1950s focused on industrialization, later switched to a major project attempting to reconstruct social change in the Congress Kingdom of Poland in the nineteenth century. They were looking at the same processes as before, but from a different angle, studying the dissolution of the old order based on status and the emergence of a new one, with its specific patterns of social stratification. This was labelled by Kula – perhaps influenced by Gerschenkron, whose work he admired – as 'the development in the conditions of rising backwardness' (Kula 1979). Three books of Jerzy Jedlicki, one of the most talented among Kula's students of the 1950s, show vividly this broader trajectory of interests. The first was on the state-induced industrialization in the Congress Kingdom of Poland, the second about the changing place of the nobility under rising capitalism (Jedlicki 1964, 1968). The third – most known and discussed and which has much wider transnational application – is on ideas, on reactions of the Polish intellectuals of the nineteenth century to the modernity coming from the West (Jedlicki 1988). Jedlicki is also the editor-in-chief of the recent three-volume history of the Polish intelligentsia (Janowski 2008; Jedlicki 2008; Micińska 2008). Jacek Kochanowicz is one of the few of Kula's disciples who stayed with economic history, specializing in the peasant economy of the eighteenth to twentieth centuries (1981, 1992) and the processes of modernization of Polish lands (2006).

Witold Kula's own last large and perhaps most original work is devoted to traditional weights and measures and their replacement in continental Europe by the metric system (Kula 1970). It is clearly the work of an economic historian, but one who is even more a social and cultural historian, and an anthropologist at the same time (Piasek 2004). In this sense, it is well ahead of its time. The traditional systems of measures are treated as functionally related to a society's way of life and its vision of the world. Kula the Marxist shows how clashes of interests between lords and peasants, or town and country reflect in the conflict over what is a 'just and fair' measure. The introduction of the metric system in France and elsewhere he analyses as a part of a revolutionary attempt to impose upon various peoples a rationalistic social project.

Yet another was the route taken by Antoni Mączak (1928–2003), Małowist's disciple specializing in the sixteenth and seventeenth centuries. His early interests and important contributions were in the field of economic history; he studied the cloth-making industry, peasant economy, and the Polish–Dutch grain trade (Mączak 1955, 1962, 1972). In a small book targeted at a broader audience he presented an excellent synthesis of the beginning of modern economy in Europe (Mączak 1967). His book on sixteenth-century travellers is much closer to the cultural history of a few decades later in Western Europe and elsewhere, but the Małowist School's interest in economic divisions of Europe is still there, this time observed through the eyes of the travelling gentlemen (Mączak 1978). Once again he comes back to these differences from a perspective of political history, or perhaps historical sociology, comparing types of political structures across the continent (Mączak 1986). His last major study is on clientage, treated as an important social as much as a political institution (Mączak 2003).

The twilight of economic history, particularly of the pre-industrial period, was thus visible already in the 1970s; comparatively little has been produced since then (Kochanowicz and Sosnowska 2011). One may justly ask about the turning point of 1989 and its impact upon the discipline. After all, this was a profound change, ending the authoritarian regime, shifting Poland's position in the world geopolitically, and changing radically its economic system. Never before was the country so open and so exposed to the West, never before – with the exception of the last quarter of the nineteenth century perhaps – was it so capitalist. Moreover, the majority of the intellectual elite embraced the changes, including the turn towards neoliberal models of capitalism, with enthusiasm. Mainstream neoclassical economics, in a few years, had been imported by economics departments of leading universities and by think-tanks. But the impact of all this on the discipline of economic history has been minimal. First, overall relatively little is done as far as research on the economic past is considered. There are groups of scholars in Warsaw, Wrocław, Poznań, and Łódź, focused mostly on the twentieth century, but the bulk of this work is much smaller than was the case three or four decades ago. Second, most of it is descriptive and not engaging in dialogue with what is being done internationally, neither are Polish economic historians much visible on the international scene.

One of the reasons may be that those young historians who specialize in the earlier epochs, often fascinated by the 'literary turn' and postmodernism, focus rather on cultural history or the history of ideas. Those who are contemporary historians explore the new possibilities of studying the period of state socialism. Broadly speaking, these latter interests embrace two fields: the political history of repression and opposition, and the social history of everyday life. However, in the hundreds of historical publications on the communist period that came out during the last twenty years, very few touch on economic history (for example Chumiński 2010; Grala 2005; Tymiński 2001).

The striking paradox is that in the study of the economic past Marxism – vanishing already in the 1970s – has not been replaced by the neoclassical approach, despite the fact that Anglo-Saxon countries otherwise serve as a model in both the economic transformation and in the academic paradigms. The reason may be twofold: first, historians are not trained in the use of modern economic and econometric tools, and second, for economists, studying the past is not regarded as a way of promoting one's academic career. Additionally, the quantitative data necessary for this type of research are dispersed and not converted into electronic databases, increasingly the standard tool for neoclassically minded economic historians. Thus Polish economic history has been side-lined by the global neoclassical mainstream.

Concluding remarks

Polish economic historiography has been built upon the solid ground of a long-standing tradition of serious primary source research. It flourished, paradoxically, in the hard times of the early stages of state socialism. Talented scholars proved able to think creatively even under adverse circumstances of ideological and political pressure. Some of them were Marxists, but they treated Marxism in an open way, and were looking for other inspirations as well. This led them to pose new questions and to seek new answers in exploring the Polish economic past, particularly of the pre-industrial period. Simultaneously, the best Polish economic historians have not locked themselves in the study of the local past in isolation from the external world. Quite the contrary, the Polish economy was for them part of much broader systems.

In this sense, in the 1950s and 1960s they had already explored issues which became the focus of attention of the practitioners of world history and transnational history much later. While they differed in many respects among themselves, the overall picture they painted was that of an economy which, while staying in close contact with the West, took its own path, making it – mostly due to the development and strengthening of a specific system of demesne farming based on serf labour – increasingly backward in relation to the Western parts of Europe. Thus, they were talking about a 'periphery' before the concept gained its popularity, and their contribution had been noticed and reacted to. Still, these ambitious attempts were rather an exception than a rule. The lion's share of works by Polish economic historians are solid but narrow monographs; useful but less inspiring. They provide, however, a rich empirical background, a base upon which the works of the masters stand.

The importance and visibility of Polish economic historiography during the last three to four decades have declined. It stays out of touch with the recent methodological and theoretical approaches in the West, both those that stem from introducing a globalizing, transnational perspective, as well as those that come from neoclassical economics and econometrics. Neither following nor directly challenging the dominant Anglo-American methodologies means that, contrary to what it was four decades ago, Polish economic history is currently in the doldrums, despite a rich intellectual tradition that demands closer transnational re-examination.

This older intellectual tradition – despite the lapse of time – has a clear relevance to the debates of today, conceptualized in terms of transnational, global, or world history. First, on the most elementary level, it provides ample empirical material (unfortunately, hardly accessible to non-specialists because of the language barrier) upon the still under-researched (in the West) region of East Central Europe. This region, after all, has been an important component of the European and global economy, geographically and culturally very close to the 'core', but never capable of escaping its peripheral or semi-peripheral position. Understanding why this has been the case and what were the patterns of its development is relevant for better grasping global processes. Second, this older historiography is interesting because of its interpretations, not only of the visionaries such as Kula and Małowist – both in many ways precursors of approaches taken later in the West – but also of the authors of more modest descriptive monographs, because they dealt with an economy that was connected with the broader world and had to deal with those connections. Third, methodologically, the somewhat heterodox approach of Polish economic history – linking and mixing economic, social, cultural, and intellectual history – contributed to producing a multifaceted picture of the past, a picture in which economic processes are portrayed not in a sterilized way, but in the broader social context.

Notes

1 For the follow-up of this debate, see Kochanowicz (1989).
2 On the political background to this decision see Górny (2007: 147ff.).
3 Cf. Topolski (1977) for his views on Marxist theoretical and methodological inspirations.
4 For Kula's biography, see Kochanowicz (1985).
5 For the review of the debate, see Kochanowicz (1987). For the most recent appraisal of *Economic Theory*, see Boldizzoni (2011: 87–112).
6 Translations into Catalan, English, French, Italian, Portuguese, and Spanish.
7 Ihnatowicz (1965), Pietrzak-Pawłowska (1967, 1970), Puś (1997) are just examples.
8 On the political context, see Kemp-Welch (2008).

References

Aston, T.H. and C.H.E. Philpin (1985) *The Brenner Debate: Agrarian Class Structure and Economic Development in Pre-Industrial Europe*, Cambridge: Cambridge University Press.

Bauman, Z. (1963) Review of Witold Kula, *An Economic Theory of the Feudal System, Studia Socjologiczne*, 3 (3): 219–28.

Berend, I.T. and G. Ránki (1982) *The European Periphery and Industrialization*, Budapest, Akadémiai Kiadó.

Boldizzoni, F. (2011) *The Poverty of Clio: Resurrecting Economic History*, Princeton, NJ: Princeton University Press

Bujak, F. (1927) 'Drogi mojego rozwoju umysłowego', in F. Bujak (1976) *Wybór pism*, vol. I, ed. by Helena Madurowicz-Urbańska, Warsaw: PWN.

Chayanov, A.V. (1923) 'On the Theory of Non-Capitalist Economic System', trans. Christel Lane, in A.V. Chayanov (1966) *On the Theory of Peasant Economy*, ed. by D. Thorner, B. Kerblay, and R.E.F. Smith, Homewood, IL: Irwin & Co.

Chayanov, A.V. (1924) 'Peasant Farm Organization', trans. R.E.F. Smith, in A.V. Chayanov (1966) *On the Theory of Peasant Economy*, ed. by D. Thorner, B. Kerblay, and R.E.F. Smith, Homewood, IL: Irwin & Co.

Chumiński, J. (ed.) (2010) *Modernizacja czy pozorna modernizacja : społeczno-ekonomiczny bilans PRL 1944–1989*, Wrocław: Gajt Wydawnictwo.

Connelly, J. (2000) *Captive University: The Sovietization of East German, Czech, and Polish Higher Education, 1945–1956*, Chapel Hill: University of North Carolina Press.

Drozdowski, M.M. (1963) *Polityka gospodarcza rządu polskiego 1936–1939*, Warsaw: PWN.

Gołębiowski, J. (1985) *Sektor państwowy w gospodarce Polski międzywojennej*, Warsaw: PWN.

Górny, M. (2007) *Przede wszystkim ma być naród: marksistowska historiografia w Europie środkowo-Wschodniej*, Warsaw: TRIO.

Górski, J. (1963) *Polska myśl ekonomiczna a rozwój gospodarczy 1807–1830: studia nad początkami teorii zacofania gospodarczego*, Warsaw: PWN.

Grala, D.T. (2005) *Reformy gospodarcze w PRL (1982–1989): próba uratowania socjalizmu*, Warsaw: TRIO.

Ihnatowicz, I. (1965) *Przemysł łódzki w latach 1860–1900*, Wrocław: Ossolineum.

Janowski, M. (1998; English edition 2002) *Polish Liberal Thought up to 1918*, trans. Danuta Przekop, Budapest: CEU Press.

Janowski, M. (2008) *Narodziny inteligencji 1750–1831*,Warsaw: Instytut Historii PAN and Wydawnictwo Neriton.

Jedlicki, J. (1964) *Nieudana próba kapitalistycznej industrializacji*, Warszawa: KiW.

Jedlicki, J. (1968) *Klejnot i bariery społeczne: przeobrażenia szlachectwa polskiego w schyłkowym okresie feudalizmu*, Warsaw: PWN.

Jedlicki, J. (1988; English edition 1999) *A Suburb of Europe: Nineteenth-century Polish Approaches to Western Civilization*, Budapest: CEU Press.

Jedlicki, J. (2008) *Błędne koło 1832–1864*, Warsaw: Instytut Historii PAN and Wydawnictwo Neriton.

Jezierski, A. and B. Petz (1988, third edition) *Historia gospodarcza Polski Ludowej 1944*–1985, Warsaw: PWN.

Kemp-Welch, A. (2008) *Poland under Communism: A Cold War History*, Cambridge: Cambridge University Press.

Kizwalter, T. (1991) *'Nowatorstwo i rutyny': społeczeństwo Królestwa Polskiego wobec procesów modernizacji (1840–1863)*, Warsaw: PWN.

Kochanowicz, J. (1981) *Pańszczyźniane gospodarstwo chłopskie w Królestwie Polskim w I połowie XIX w*, Warsaw: Wydawnictwa Uniwersytetu Warszawskiego.

Kochanowicz, J. (1985) 'Czy tylko historia gospodarcza? Jubileusz Witolda Kuli', *Kronika Warszawy*, 1–2: 129–46.

Kochanowicz, J. (1987) 'La "Théorie économique . . ." après vingt ans', *Acta Poloniae Historica*, 56: 187–211.

Kochanowicz, J. (1989) 'The Polish Economy and the Evolution of Dependency', in *The Origins of Backwardness in Eastern Europe: Economics and Politics from the Middle Ages until the Early Twentieth Century*, ed. by Daniel Chirot, Berkeley: University of California Press.

Kochanowicz, J. (1990) 'Witold Kula i badania przedkapitalistycznych systemów gospodarczych', in *Dziedzictwo Witolda Kuli*, Warsaw: WNE UW and PTH.

Kochanowicz, J. (1992) *Spór o teorię gospodarki chłopskiej: gospodarstwo chłopskie w teorii ekonomii i w historii gospodarczej*, Warsaw: Wydawnictwa Uniwersytetu Warszawskiego.

Kochanowicz, J. (2006) *Backwardness and Modernization: Poland and Eastern Europe in the 16th–20th Centuries*, Aldershot: Ashgate Variorum.

Kochanowicz, J. and A. Sosnowska (2011) 'Economic History of Pre-Industrial Poland: An Obsolete Subject?' in F. Ammannati (ed.) *Where is Economic History Going? Methods and Prospects from the 13th to the 18th Centuries. Atti della 'Quarantaduesima Settimana di Studi'. 18–22 aprile 2010*, Firenze University Press.

Kofman, J. (1992; English edition 1997) *Economic Nationalism and Development: Central and Eastern Europe between the Two World Wars*, Boulder, CO: Westview Press.

Koryś, P. (2007) 'Idea nowoczesności w działaniach i planach partii komunistycznej w Polsce 1945–1980: przegląd problematyki', in E. Kościk and T. Głowiński (eds.) *Gospodarka i społeczeństwo w czasach PRL-u (1944–1989)*, Wrocław: GAJT.

Kuklo, C. (2009) *Demografia Rzeczypospolitej przedrozbiorowej*, Warsaw: DIG.

Kula, M. (2010) *Mimo wszystko bliżej do Paryża niż Moskwy*, Warsaw: WUW.

Kula, W. (1955) *Kształtowanie się kapitalizmu w Polsce*, Warsaw: PWN.

Kula, W. (1956). *Szkice o manufakturach w Polsce w XVIII wieku*, Warsaw: PWN.

Kula, W. (1958) 'Gusła', in W. Kula, *Rozważania o historii*, Warsaw: PWN.

Kula, W. (1960) 'Les débuts du capitalisme en Pologne dans la perspective de l'histoire comparée', in *Academia Polacca di Scienze e Lettere. Biblioteca di Roma. Conferenze 10*, Roma: Angello Signorelli Editore.

Kula, W. (1962; English edition 1976) *An Economic Theory of the Feudal System: Towards a Model of the Polish Economy, 1500–1800*, trans. Lawrence Garner, London: NLB.

Kula, W. (1963; English edition 2001) *The Problems and Methods of Economic History, translated by Richard Szreter from Problemy i metody historii gospodarczej, an original work by Witold Kula*, ed. with an introduction by Simon Szreter, Aldershot: Ashgate.

Kula, W. (1970; English edition 1986) *Measures and Men*, trans. R. Szreter, Princeton, NJ: Princeton University Press.

Kula, W. (1976) 'Moja edukacja sentymentalna', in W. Kula, *Wokół historii*, Warsaw: PWN.

Kula, W. (1979) 'Rozwój gospodarczy w warunkach rosnącego zacofania', in W. Kula and J. Leskiewiczowa (eds.) *Przemiany społeczne w Królestwie Polskim 1815–1864*, Wrocław: Ossolineum.

Kula, W. (1994) *Dziennik czasu okupacji*, ed. by N. Assorodobraj-Kula and M. Kula, preface and notes Marcin Kula, Warsaw: PIW.

Kuroń, J. and K. Modzelewski (1970) *An Open Letter to the Party*, London: Pluto Press.

Landau, Z. and J. Tomaszewski (1967–89) *Gospodarka Polski miedzywojennej 1918–1939*, vols 1–4, Warsaw: Książka i Wiedza.

Landau, Z. and J. Tomaszewski (1985) *The Polish Economy in the Twentieth Century*, trans. W. Roszkowski, New York: St. Martin's Press.

Mączak, A. (1955) *Sukiennictwo wielkopolskie XIV–XVI wiek*, Warsaw: PWN.

Mączak, A. (1962) *Gospodarstwo chłopskie na żuławach Malborskich w początkach XVII wieku*, Warsaw: PWN.

Mączak, A. (1967) *U źródeł nowoczesnej gospodarki europejskiej*, Warsaw: PWN.

Mączak, A. (1972) *Między Gdańskiem a Sundem: studia nad handlem bałtyckim od połowy XVI do połowy XVII w.*, Warsaw: PWN.

Mączak, A. (1978; English edition 1985) *Travel in Early Modern Europe*, trans. Ursula Phillips, Cambridge: Polity Press.

Mączak, A. (1986) *Rządzący i rządzeni: władza i społeczeństwo w Europie wczesnonowożytnej*, Warsaw: PIW.

Mączak, A. (1993) 'Marian Małowist (1909–1988)', in M. Małowist, *Europa i jej ekspansja, XIV–XVI w.*, selection of articles and introduction by Antoni Mączak, ed. by H. Zaremska, Warsaw: PWN.

Mączak, A. (2003) *Nierówne przyjaźnie; układy klientalne w perspektywie historycznej*, Wrocław: Fundacja na Rzecz Nauki Polskiej.

Mączak, A. and W. Tygielski (2000) *Latem w Tocznabieli*, Warsaw: Więź.

Madurowicz-Urbańska, H. (1976) 'Franciszek Bujak – o nowy kształt historii', in F. Bujak, *Wybór pism*, vol. I, ed. by H. Madurowicz-Urbańska, Warsaw: PWN.

Malewski, A. (1956) 'Empiryczny sens teorii materializmu historycznego', *Studia Filozoficzne*, 2: 58–81.

Małowist, M. (1935) *Handel zagraniczny Sztokholmu i polityka zewnętrzna Szwecji w latach 1471–1503*, Warsaw: Towarzystwo Naukowe Warszawskie.

Małowist, M. (1947) *Kaffa – kolonia genueńska na Krymie i problem wschodni w latach 1453–1475*, Warsaw: Towarzystwo Miłośników Historii.

Małowist, M. (1954) *Studia z dziejów rzemiosła w okresie kryzysu feudalizmu w zachodniej Europie w XIV i XV wieku*, Warsaw: PWN.

Małowist, M. (1958) 'Poland, Russia and Western Trade in Fifteenth and Sixteenth Centuries', in M. Małowist (2010) *Western Europe, Eastern Europe and World Development, 13th–18th Centuries: Collection of Essays of Marian Małowist*, ed. by J. Batou and H. Szlajfer, Leiden: Brill.

Malowist, M. (1964) *Wielkie państwa Sudanu Zachodniego w późnym średnioiwieczu*, Warsaw: PWN.

Małowist, M. (1966) 'The Problem of Inequality of Economic Development in Europe in the Later Middle Ages', in M. Małowist (2010) *Western Europe, Eastern Europe and World Development, 13th–18th Centuries: Collection of Essays of Marian Małowist*, ed. by J. Batou and H. Szlajfer, Leiden: Brill.

Małowist, M. (1969) *Europa a Afryka zachodnia w dobie wczesnej ekspansji kolonialnej*, Warsaw: PWN.

Małowist, M. (1973) *Wschód a Zachód Europy w XIII–XVI wieku*, Warsaw: PWN.

Małowist, M. (1974) 'Problems of the Growth of the National Economy of Central Eastern Europe in the Late Middle Ages', in M. Małowist (2010) *Western Europe, Eastern Europe and World Development, 13th–18th Centuries: Collection of Essays of Marian Małowist*, ed. by J. Batou and H. Szlajfer, Leiden: Brill.

Małowist, M. (1976) *Konkwistadorzy portugalscy*, Warsaw: PIW.

Małowist, M. (2000) 'Marian Małowist on history and historians: interview', *Polin*, 13: 331–43.

Małowist, M. (2010) *Western Europe, Eastern Europe and World Development, 13th–18th Centuries: Collection of Essays of Marian Małowist*, ed. by J. Batou and H. Szlajfer, Leiden, Brill.

Micińska, M. (2008) *Inteligencja na rozdrożach 1864–1918*, Warsaw: Instytut Historii PAN and Wydawnictwo Neriton.

Miłosz, C. (1953) *The Captive Mind*, trans. J. Zielonka, New York: Alfred A. Knopf.

Modzelewski, K. (1975) *Organizacja gospodarcza państwa piastowskiego: X–XIII wiek*, Wrocław: Ossolineum.

Mokyr, J. (ed.) (2003) *The Oxford Encyclopedia of Economic History*, Oxford: Oxford University Press, 5 vols.

North, D.C. (1977) Review of Witold Kula, *An Economic Theory of the Feudal System*, *Journal of European Economic History*, 6 (2): 508–10.

Piasek, W. (2004) *Antropologizowanie historii: Studium metodologiczne twórczości Witolda Kuli*, Poznań: Wydawnictwo Poznańskie.

Pietrzak-Pawłowska, I.(ed.) (1967) *Zakłady przemysłowe w Polsce w XIX i XX wieku: studia i materiały*, Wrocław: Ossolineum.

Pietrzak-Pawłowska, I.(ed.) (1970) *Uprzemysłowienie ziem polskich w XIX i XX wieku: studia i materiały*, Wrocław: Ossolineum.

Pleskot, P. (2010) *Intelektualni sąsiedzi: Kontakty historyków polskich ze środowiskiem 'Annales' 1945–1989*, Warsaw: IPN.

Pomian, K. (1978) 'Impact of the Annales School in Eastern Europe', *Review*, I (3–4): 101–18.
Postan M. (1977) 'The Feudal Economy', *New Left Review*, 103, May–June: 72–8.
Puś, W. (1997) *Rozwój przemysłu w Królestwie Polskim 1870–1914*, Łódź: Wydawnictwo Uniwersytetu Łódzkiego.
Rutkowski, J. (1921) 'Poddaństwo włościan w XVIII wieku w Polsce i w niektórych innych krajach Europy', in J. Rutkowski (1986) *Wieś europejska późnego feudalizmu*, ed. by J. Topolski, Warsaw: PIW.
Rutkowski, J. (1925) 'Zagadnienie syntezy w historii gospodarczej', in J. Rutkowski (1982) *Wokół teorii ustroju feudalnego: Prace historyczne*, ed. by Jerzy Topolski, Warsaw: PIW.
Rutkowski, J. (1930a) 'Gospodarcze podłoże rozbiorów Polski', in J. Rutkowski (1986) *Wieś europejska późnego feudalizmu*, ed. by J. Topolski, Warsaw: PIW.
Rutkowski, J. (1930b) 'La genèse du régime de la corvée dans l'Europe Centrale depuis la fin du Moyen Age', in *La Pologne Au VIe Congrès Internationale des Sciences Historiques, Oslo 1928*, Warsaw.
Rutkowski, J. (1934a) 'Czy jest potrzebna teoria ekonomiczna ustroju feudalnego?' in J. Rutkowski (1982) *Wokół teorii ustroju feudalnego: Prace historyczne*, ed. by J. Topolski, Warsaw: PIW.
Rutkowski, J. (1934b) 'Co to były folwarki w dawnej Polsce?' in J. Rutkowski (1986) *Wieś europejska późnego feudalizmu*, ed. by Jerzy Topolski, Warsaw: PIW.
Rutkowski, J. (1938) 'Badania nad podziałem dochodów w Polsce nowożytnej', in J. Rutkowski (1982) *Wokół teorii ustroju feudalnego: Prace historyczne*, ed. by J. Topolski, Warsaw: PIW.
Rutkowski, J. (1953) *Historia gospodarcza Polski (do 1864 r.)*, Warszawa: KiW.
Rutkowski, J. (1956) *Studia z dziejów wsi polskiej XVI–XVIII w.* ed. by W. Kula, Warsaw: PWN.
Shore, M. (2006) *Caviar and Ashes: A Warsaw Generation's Life and Death in Marxism, 1918–1968*, New Haven, CT: Yale University Press.
Siewierski, T. (2011) 'Popularność badań na dziejami gospodarczymi jako fenomen polskie historiografii lat 1949–1956: Próba nakreślenia przyczyn zjawiska', in: *Letnia szkoła historii najnowszej 2010*, ed. N. Jarska and T. Kozłowski, Warsaw: IPN.
Sosnowska, A. (2004) *Zrozumieć zacofanie: spory historyków o Europę Wschodnią (1947–1994)*, Warsaw: TRIO.
Stobiecki, R. (1993) *Historia pod nadzorem: spory o nowy model historii w Polsce (II połowa lat czterdziestych – początek lat pięćdziesiątych*, Łodź: WUŁ.
Topolski, J. (1965) *Narodziny kapitalizmu w Europie w XIV–XVII wieku*, Warsaw: PWN.
Topolski, J. (1968) *Metodologia historii*, Warsaw: PWN.
Topolski, J. (1977) *Marksizm i historia*, Warsaw: PIW.
Topolski, J. (1983) *Teoria wiedzy historycznej*, Poznań: Wydawnictwo Poznańskie.
Topolski, J. (1986) *O nowy model historii: Jan Rutkowski (1886–1949)*, Warsaw: PWN.
Topolski, J. (1994) *The Manorial Economy in Early-modern East–Central Europe: Origins, Development and Consequences*, Aldershot: Ashgate Variorum.
Tymiński, M. (2001) *PZPR i przedsiębiorstwo: nadzór partyjny nad zakładami przemysłowymi 1956–1970*, Warsaw: TRIO.
Wallerstein, I. (1974) *The Modern World System: Capitalist Agriculture and the Origins of Capitalist World Economy in the Sixteenth Century*, New York: Academic Press.
Wyczański, A. (1987) *Dogonić Europę, czyli Polska w czasach Zygmunta I (1506–1548)*, Cracow: KAW.

14

CONTINUITY AND DISCONTINUITY IN THE CZECH AND SLOVAK HISTORIOGRAPHIES

Antonie Doležalová and Roman Holec

This chapter highlights the main steps that have marked the development of Czech and Slovak economic history over the course of the twentieth century. Although there are quite a few works concerning the subject, this study is the first to look into the continuity of methodologies, topics and schools and also into the discontinuities produced by the totalitarian ideologies repeatedly interfering in the life of the field.

While it is not the aim of this chapter to provide an exhaustive overview, it is necessary to clarify several interpretive difficulties in advance. First, the prevailing view of Czechoslovak economic history in the twentieth century has tended to identify the field with history itself. Economic history was understood as an interpretive key to historical phenomena. At the same time, there was little institutional continuity. Thus, if we focused on just a limited number of academic institutions, we would exclude many individuals and research topics.

Second, economic history has traditionally been defined in thematic rather than methodological terms. Moreover, with respect to methodology, there is no consensus as to what belongs to the realm of history, what to economics and what is essential to economic history. This problem is further complicated by the fact that economic history, during the communist period, represented an example of a historiography that was quite isolated and minimally exposed to external methodological influences.

Third, due to the dramatic transformation of the conditions in science and education after 1948, some of the ways we ask and answer questions nowadays exceed the horizons of what was possible in the context of previous research. Teachers and scholars were only able to work at universities and academic institutions if they accepted state-approved curricula, followed the decisions made by the Communist Party and adhered to the Plan for Scientific Research. Twentieth-century scholars experienced, on multiple occasions, situations where not just their professional careers but even their very ability to retain a teaching or research job depended not on skills or knowledge but upon subservience and clientelism. Universities went from being places of education and science to being nurseries for raising the cadres that would serve the state–socialist economy and the bureaucratic apparatus of the Communist Party of Czechoslovakia (Connelly 2000). When assessing the relevance, and even the lasting value, of historical work, it is therefore necessary to distinguish between a scholar's own ideas and the way in which the work was received and developed (which, to a lesser or greater degree, may be dependent on the prevailing ideology at the given time).

This chapter is divided into two sections. The first observes the key stages of institutional development in the field. The second focuses on particular figures and topics that determined the direction of research in Czech and Slovak economic history and the methodological challenges that were faced.

Institutional foundations of economic history

Like other social sciences, economic history was established later in the Czech lands and Slovakia than in West European countries and also later than in Poland, for example. However, its remote origins can be traced back to the late eighteenth century, prompted by the socio-economic changes taking place at the time, by the Enlightenment and the development of statistics. By responding to the needs of state administration, research became dominated by statistics and topography and tended to focus on the current state of affairs alone. Since economic history failed to find support within universities, it became the domain of regional archivists, teachers and lawyers, who regarded it as a form of 'cultural' history broadly conceived. When the state engaged in the area of research, it aimed to support agricultural research in accordance with the agricultural character of the country. *The Peasants' Archive* was the first periodical to focus on economic history; it was first published in 1902 and renamed *The Agrarian Archive* in 1914. German historians in the Czech lands who were interested in economic history grouped themselves around *Verein für die Geschichte der Deutschen in Böhmen,* which was founded in 1862.

In the Czech lands, economic history began to change in the wake of the rise of the German Historical School and the spread of Marx's historical materialism. The University of Prague introduced German-style economics courses and young scholars were sent to pursue their own research in Germany. When they returned home, they usually taught the method to their students. Jan Peisker (1851–1933), a historian of Czech origin, was the first person to be awarded the *venia legendi* in social and economic history at the University of Graz (Austria) in 1901. He focused on agrarian history, especially the social conditions of peasants, being influenced by Karl Lamprecht and his approach. After the creation of Czechoslovakia, he lectured in economic history at the Charles University in Prague. However, when the German University in Prague established its first post in economic history in 1911, it was given to the economist and associate professor at the University of Berlin, Paul Sander. A pupil of Gustav von Schmoller, Sander focused on the history of cities from the perspective of their economic conditions.

Slovak researchers found some institutional support in the Hungarian Historical Society, though a much more important role was played by specialized Hungarian historical journals. The founding and existence of the national organization *Slovak Matica* (1863–75) made it possible, for the first time, to give direction to historical papers and set their priorities within the amateur settings of the journal *Letopis Matice slovenskej.* After the institution and its journal were abolished, the Slovak Museology Society became the next forum where *fin de siècle* Slovak intellectual elites could cultivate historiography. Until 1918, Slovak history writing was built upon unscientific foundations. It still overlapped with myth and was instrumental in the creation of a national narrative; as such it fulfilled an important function. Historical research was neither professionalized nor institutionalized. These were logical consequences of the problem of nationalities within the Austro-Hungarian Empire and the backwardness of the Slovak educational system, which lacked not only universities but also secondary schools.

In 1918 the Empire disintegrated and the state of Czechoslovakia was created, which brought about entirely new conditions for scientific research and history writing, especially at a national level. From the point of view of the institutional development of economic history, in the period that followed, the subject was pursued in two different contexts, that is, within and outside the university setting, with the latter initially taking the lead. In 1930, the Committee for Agricultural History was founded within the Czech Agricultural Academy, which not only researched the most recent historical periods (from the eighteenth century onwards) but also conducted archival investigations and promoted publications in the area of agrarian historiography. A separate sub-committee dealt with the history of prices and wages. Research in agrarian history was subsidized mostly by the Agrarian Party, the strongest political party in the First Republic, and by the Ministry of Agriculture. In addition, The Archive for the History of Industry, Trade and Technical Work was committed to research on Czech entrepreneurship. It had been established in 1913 thanks to the benefaction of Jaroslav Preiss, director of the Živnostenská bank, the main financial institution in the interwar years. Research in economic history was also carried out by the newly founded Historical Committee for the History of Nineteenth-Century Social Movements at the Institute for Social Research. While left-wing historians formed the so-called *Historical Group,* the Society for the History of the Jews in the Czechoslovak Republic was established in 1928 and their research interests included economic topics. The Czechoslovak Agricultural State Archive (founded in Prague in 1919) specialized in archival collections related to forestry and agriculture, and until 1938 Slovakia fell within its administrative purview. In 1928 the Regional Archive opened in Bratislava, whose role was to facilitate access to different archival collections relating to Slovak territory. Šafárik's Scholarly Society (1926–39) and, to a lesser extent, also the Slovak Museology Society (1893–1960) and the revived *Slovak Matica* played an important role in the development of the social sciences in Slovakia. *The Scientific Synthesis*, a circle of left-wing scholars, gained prominence especially in the study of post-1848 developments. After the creation of Czechoslovakia, a new centre of German historiography formed around the association *Gesellschaft zur Förderung deutscher Wissenschaft, Kunst und Literatur in Böhmen*, within which a historical committee was set up in 1918.

The importance of agrarian history was also reflected in its new role as a university subject. In 1922 Josef Kazimour (1881–1933) started lecturing as an associate professor at the University of Agriculture. A few years later, Bedřich Mendl (1892–1940) was awarded *venia legendi* by the Faculty of Arts at Charles University (1927) where he established a Department of Medieval and Early Modern Economic and Social History (1934). Comenius University, founded in Bratislava in 1919 with the contribution of Czech university professors relocated to Slovakia, played a key role in shaping Slovak historiography. Although economic history was among the subjects taught, it continued to be overshadowed by political history.

The interwar period also witnessed the establishment of publishing platforms for economic history. *Časopis pro dějiny venkova* ('*Journal for the History of the Countryside*') published widely in agrarian history. *Český časopis historický* ('*The Czech Historical Journal*') provided historians with information about new trends in European social history in the form of review articles. The growing interest in economic history is evident from the fact that, while in the 1920s research on the subject was indexed under the label of legal history, by the 1930s it had its own category, which was further subdivided into 'general economic and social history', 'agricultural history' and the histories of 'estates', 'handicrafts and industry', 'commerce', 'communications', 'social issues', 'finances and taxes'. Most of the papers were, admittedly, contributed by foreign authors and written in German, French or English. However, a number of Czech historians had the opportunity to publish their work in the French *Annales d'histoire économique at sociale*, and this raised international awareness of Czechoslovak historiography. In 1937–38 Marxist historians created their own journal, *Dějiny a přítomnost* (*'History and Present'*). Economists interested in the various aspects of past economic life took part in debate through the 'Papers of the Czechoslovak Economic Society'. In Slovakia, occasional articles on economic history could also be found in regional periodicals. They were authored by historians as well as by economists, sociologists and legal scholars.

The Second World War affected Czech and Slovak historiographies in different ways. The Nazi occupation of Bohemia and Moravia and the formation of an independent Slovak state brought about fundamental changes in both Czech and Slovak history writing. The Slovak Republic created conditions in which historical sciences could develop further, though it came at the price of the Czech scholars being forced to leave the country. The foundation of the Slovak Academy of Arts and Sciences in 1943 contributed greatly to the institutionalization of the historical profession. A small historical unit was set up within the Academy, which did not intensify its scientific activities until 1945 but which was to become the backbone of the future Historical Institute. Despite this, economic history continued to be of marginal interest. The Czech historical community gradually fell silent under the threat of repression and many were silenced because of their Jewish origin or political background. The survival of Czech historical sciences was endangered when universities and other academic institutions were suppressed on 17 November 1939, although the German University in Prague kept functioning and German historians thus ensured the scholarly and institutional continuity of economic history.

Overall, the Second World War had a devastating effect on the slowly progressing discipline of economic history. Mendl was driven to suicide by racial persecution and his department at the Faculty of Arts in Prague was never reopened. The communist takeover in 1948 brought with it the first wave of purges, which also meant that new professors were selected among those who enjoyed the full support of the Communist Party. For an academic career, being a member of the party often proved to be a more important qualification than expertise.

The year 1951 witnessed the creation of the Institute of Economic Geography and Economic History at the re-established University of Economics in Bratislava. In 1958 a Department of Economic History was opened at the University of Economics in Prague. The research team was led by Václav Průcha (b. 1931), who served as an investigator in various state projects conducted as part of the State Plan for Scientific Research. Projects other than those addressing the history of the workers' movements and the history of communist parties only received minimal subsidy (Myška 2010: 33–4). These two subjects became compulsory at all universities, and research institutes entirely devoted to the history of the Czechoslovak Communist Parties were also set up. The Slovak Academy of Arts and Sciences adapted to the new situation and founded its own Historical Institute in 1950. In 1953 a new Silesian Institute was created in Opava, which moved away from the history of Silesia and refocused on industrial history more generally. A small group of economic historians was based at the Institute of Czechoslovak and World History at the Academy of Sciences in Prague. In the 1960s, such professional associations as the Committee for Historical Demography and the Committee for Economic History came into existence, and the latter was affiliated with the International Economic History Association.

The Soviet occupation in 1968 was followed by a further wave of purges and some institutions being closed down. In the Czech lands, the continuity of research activities was ensured by the Silesian Institute, by the Committee for the History of Prices and Wages, and by researchers at the Museum of Agriculture. Consequently, a variety of research centres outside the academic context once again came to the fore. In keeping with its earlier tradition, post-war economic history had continued to entertain a privileged relationship with regional and company archives, often under the umbrella of labour history or the 'history of class struggles'. In 1972 an Institute of Social Sciences was established at the Slovak Academy of Sciences in Košice; its main focus was on the socio-economic development of Eastern Slovakia and its minorities after 1945. A dedicated economic history department was also established at the *Economic Institute* of the Slovak Academy of Arts and Sciences.

It was difficult for economic history to find a publishing platform during this period. *Ročenka hospodářských a sociálních dějin* ('*Yearbook of Economic and Social History*') followed in the tradition of the interwar *History and Present* and made room for the emergence of Marxist historiography, but lasted for only a short period (1946–47). Papers on economic history continued to be published by the above-mentioned *Československý časopis historický* and by *Politická ekonomie* ('*Political Economy*'), both based in Prague, and by the *Historický časopis* ('*Historical Journal*') in Bratislava. Paradoxically, the foundation of the stand-alone journal *Hospodářské dějiny* ('*Economic History*') in 1978 led to the isolation of economic historians and made it more difficult for the results of their work to reach the wider community of historians.

The year 1989 ushered in fundamental political and economic changes which also affected the social sciences. In Slovakia, the Department of Economic History at the University of Economics in Bratislava ceased to exist and the subject was in evident decline. Conversely, interest in economic history seemed to grow in the Czech lands and the discipline consolidated its position within the historical sciences. In 1992 the founding of the Institute of Economic and Social History at the Faculty of Arts of Charles University in Prague was regarded as a positive sign. Unfortunately, the post-1989 privatization euphoria led to the disappearance of almost all the company archives that had been part of former state enterprises. On the other hand, the increased interest in the study of the humanities, which had been brushed aside under communism to make way for technical subjects, resulted in a rush to set up regional universities, each with a history department. That said, not many historians embraced economic history as the main focus of their research, with the exception of those working at the University of Economics and the Faculties of Arts in Prague and in Ostrava.

The tasks of the Committee for Economic History were passed on to the Society for Economic History, founded in 1990 and later renamed as the Society for Economic and Social History. The journal *Hospodářské dějiny* remained the key publication platform, joined in 1994 by the *Prager wirtschafts- und sozialhistorische Mitteilungen* ('*Prague Economic and Social History Papers*'). To an extent, economic history was also covered by other historical journals in both the Czech and Slovak lands, while the coverage of the field in economics journals was very limited. After 1989, the arts and sciences in Czechoslovakia began to be financed by grant agencies. Unfortunately, economic historians found themselves outside the mainstream of grant recipients, and economic history turned out to be the most underfunded historical subfield with the only exception being historiography.[1] A number of private foundations emerged that sought to support science and research, but only the Hlávka Foundation covers economic history. While Czechs and Slovaks went their separate ways on 1 January 1993, the same cannot be said of their economic histories. Multilateral committees of historians provided a platform for cooperation, notably the Czecho–Slovak and Czecho–Slovak–German committees, occasionally addressing economic history topics.

A concise account of the Czech and Slovak traditions

Like other Central European traditions, both Czech and Slovak historiographies were in their early stages shaped mostly by the influence of the German Historical School. While other schools of economics were either deductively oriented or used statistical trends to formulate economic laws, the German Historical School was founded on the idea that approaching historical sources by means of empirical and inductive methods helps explain the origins of phenomena. History not only allows one to understand contemporary economic practices but also to formulate solutions to economic problems.

In late nineteenth- and early twentieth-century Slovakia, economic history was still mainly researched by archivists, teachers and priests. By contrast, in the Czech lands, alongside these amateur approaches, from the mid-nineteenth century some professional historians developed an interest in incorporating stylized economic facts into their interpretations of political history. However, until at least the First World War, economic history was taught as part of the economics curriculum and hence teaching was in the hands of professional economists. This is well documented by the fact that the term *Wirtschaftsgeschichte* (economic history), which emerged in the context of the German Historical School, was introduced into the Czech lands by Albín Bráf (1851–1912) who is regarded as the forefather of Czech economics. Bráf taught economic history at the Faculty of Law of Charles University in Prague.

As an economist, Bráf was a follower of the German historical approach. He was thoroughly familiar with, and appreciative of, the work of Adam Smith, but British liberalism struck him as one-sided. He was convinced of the need to contextualize economic activity within 'the specific features of a given time and place, the character of each nation and its prevailing customs' (Bráf 1904: 137). This formed the basis for his call to situate economic behaviour historically and develop an organic understanding of reality by means of a combination of statistical description and interpretation. While in later years he became influenced by the Austrian subjectivist school, he remained firm in his belief that economic activity had a greater purpose than just satisfying material needs, and that it was impossibile to disentangle the latter from the 'spiritual' needs also underlying human development. As Bráf understood it, economic history was a source of knowledge, lessons and even inspiration; the stage of economic analysis was always preceded by some historical interpretation. These two steps were for him preliminary to the search for policy solutions.

Bráf's research in economic history encompassed several thematic areas. He dealt with a broad range of agrarian issues, including agricultural production and agricultural credit, and worked extensively on social welfare – particularly on the relation between social security and self-help, which was very topical in his day. In any in-depth analysis of a particular phenomenon, however, he never lost sight of the larger whole. Bráf thought historically; he situated economic phenomena in their relevant temporal contexts and never blankly transposed the ideas of an earlier tradition or engaged in naive ahistorical criticism.

Bedřich Mendl (1892–1940) was the first Czechoslovak historian trained in economic history. In addition to statistics, he relied upon historical methods such as classification, typology-construction, comparison and hierarchization. Compared to Bráf, Mendl's work exhibits a more cautious and critical approach to sources. A close study of source materials was necessary, in his view, to test and complement the theoretical formulations of economists. By means of his typologies and comparisons, he was able to construct *longue durée* syntheses. His pioneering economic history of Europe (Mendl 1931) attempted to situate Czech economic development within a European and international context. Mendl spoke at several international historical conferences (e.g. Warsaw 1934, Zurich 1938) and published papers in foreign journals. He also welcomed methodological innovations from abroad, introducing them to the professional community in Czechoslovakia through his book reviews and by incorporating them creatively into his own research. Like his Belgian friend Henri Pirenne, whose work he translated into Czech, he was a medievalist by vocation but one who fully grasped the significance of modern history – the late-nineteenth century for him contained the seeds of the Czech transition to capitalism.

Mendl studied early modern social stratification and the effects of price trends on social conditions from the sixteenth to the eighteenth centuries, drawing on Werner Sombart and the German Historical School more generally. His research on the early stages of industrial production in the Czech lands and the development of medieval towns owed much to Max Weber. Drawing on his work, he distinguished between the economic and the political–administrative definitions of a town (Kutnar and Marek 1997: 758). He identified economic and social contradictions in the structure of medieval society, but stressed that economic factors represented only a part of the picture and that the rest had to be filled in with knowledge about the conditions of particular population groups and by studying the economic perceptions of different social groups. In this respect, his research had something in common with the early history of mentalities that was being developed by the French *Annales* School.

Mendl's approach, however, stemmed from his conviction that multi-causal interpretations of historical phenomena were needed without giving up the quest for general features. In his opinion, and in agreement with Henri Berr, history should seek to understand and identify the causes of phenomena. Although he rejected the Marxist idea of general stages of (historical) development, he looked for evidence of causality and tried to capture whatever period he was focusing on in its totality. His work would consequently trace a historical phenomenon over the long term and comparatively within a European context, which reminds one of the Weberian structural approach. The emphasis on structures and comparisons is especially apparent in his research on towns, where he would begin by enquiring into the causes of discontent in a particular city (Prague) and would then proceed to wonder about the triggers of social conflict in general. He would simultaneously examine what the effects of economic changes were on other aspects of urban life and how they were perceived by the population.

Like Weber, Mendl regarded terminology as the key to sorting and classifying facts and creating typologies of economic facts. Under the same influence, he altered his original distrust of sociology and emphasized the psychological aspects of development and structural change. This was in fact a response to Marxism and its emphasis on the economic base and, in such an endeavour, Johan Huizinga and José Ortega y Gasset were also sources of inspiration. However, his rejection of Marxism did not prevent Mendl from acknowledging the merits of historical materialism in identifying inequality in the distribution of property and income as a source of social conflicts.

Ahead of his time, at the newly established Archive for the History of Industry, Trade and Technical Work he initiated the debate on the transition from feudalism to capitalism. He did not subscribe to the anachronistic concept of 'mediaeval capitalism' and maintained that 'proto-capitalist' elements were instead responsible for weakening feudal structures. In the post-war period, Marxist historiography drew heavily on these ideas. Mendl's work on the whole underscored the key significance of economic changes for the life of societies and thus introduced Czechoslovak historiography to the question of how economic conditions influenced particular periods – from revolutionary movements to the mentalities of rural and urban populations. When historiography came to be dominated by Marxist–Leninist ideology and was used to legitimize communist rule, this question re-emerged in the form of an enquiry into the sources of social conflicts, particularly in connection with the history of labour movements and of the revolutionary traditions of the Czech and Slovak nations.

After 1948, the Marxist postulate of the primacy of the economic base over the superstructure necessitated that every research question be conceived from the angle of socio-economic conditions and effects. Every researcher – even if he or she was studying the reform movements of the Church in the Middle Ages – was confronted with economic history. However, economic history was now supposed to provide evidence of the revolutionary tradition of the Czechoslovak people, the existence of class conflict deep in the Middle Ages, and the inevitable transition from capitalism to socialism. That, however, was not a free intellectual exercise but rather the fulfilment of a task assigned by the Central Committee of the Communist Party of Czechoslovakia. Post-war historiography thus only devoted attention to economic history on a level that can be described as a 'search' for materialism in its reductionist Marxist–Leninist form. The scope of critically scrutinized sources expanded to include financial ledgers, polyptychs, tax and customs records, cadastres and statistics. In this pursuit, the prevalence of medieval and early modern studies was largely a consequence of the impossibility of approaching late modern, interwar and contemporary sources. These were under the control of the Party apparatus and only accessible to a selected circle of Party historians, in whose hands the history of the twentieth century was put to serve the ideological and propagandistic needs of the regime.

The works that sought theoretical, and therefore Marxist–Leninist, explanations of historical phenomena, and those that were based on description and quantification, both concentrated on economic aspects. Beyond declarations of principles, the ambition to analyse society gradually faded. It was nevertheless possible to maintain a surprisingly strong level of continuity with respect to the subject matters previously investigated, albeit at the price of incorporating into the new scholarship the essential Marxist–Leninist clichés. The most productive research areas remained feudalism (its crisis, the transition to capitalism, the economic development of towns and rural areas, serfdom and manorialism) and the early stage of the development of capitalism (urbanization, industrial branches and sectors, and issues relating to class struggle). Debates on these topics continued until 1989.

Two related issues deserve a more detailed discussion here – namely the study of prices, as indicators of the living standards of a particular epoch, and research on the industrial revolution which was seen as a key factor in the transition from feudalism to capitalism. Price history can be said to have begun with the work of Bráf and his contemporaries at the turn of the twentieth century and with their attempts to describe the material conditions of workers in different areas of Bohemia and Moravia. Mendl breathed new life into these efforts, and in this context mention is most often made of a pioneering study he published in the *Bulletin of the International Committee of Historical Sciences* (vol. 7, 1935) devoted to the impact of overseas discoveries on the economy of the Czech lands and in particular on the price of silver. In this study, Mendl examined the effects of the flow of the 'American treasure' to Europe on prices and the economy of the Czech lands in the sixteenth and seventeenth centuries. Although he certainly overestimated its impact, in common with many of his contemporaries, and overlooked the Euro-Asian trade in spices and luxury goods, the significance of this work is demonstrated by the fact that as late as 1960 Arnošt Klíma (1916–2000) mentioned it at the World Economic History Congress in Stockholm.

In the post-war period, an inspiring discussion about prices emerged within the Committee for the History of Prices and Wages (established in 1958). It focused on tracing long-term price trends for various commodities, their contextualization and the extent to which markets operated. A number of historians took part in the debate (among them, Miroslav Hroch, Jaroslav Petráň, Eduard Maur, Anton Špiesz and Štefan Kazimír) and the 'transition' theme was always in the background (see Petráň, 1977) but, in conformity with Marxist assumptions, the transition was twofold, as the ultimate goal was to understand the prerequisites for the advent of socialism. The market was seen not just as a space for the exchange of goods but also as a multi-causal environment that influences, and is influenced by, the laws of economic development – a dynamic and, above all, structured phenomenon. While scholars involved in this debate professed inspiration from Soviet, Hungarian and Polish historiography, individual studies showed clear signs of being influenced by the *Annales* School and its research on consumption and the standard of living. Following the model of the *Annales* School, Czechoslovak historians also created long-run time series of prices for different commodities and periods. Reference to Soviet and socialist historiography and frequent citation of classic Marxist–Leninist authors was sometimes a mere coping strategy and in most cases did not substantially alter the content of the works.

A sign of continuity in Czechoslovak historiography was that research on prices, wages, consumption habits and the living standards of different social classes in the past was regarded as a field in which it seemed to make sense to try to create a comprehensive picture of society, and to do so by combining synthetic and structural perspectives. Thus when studying a specific indicator the wider economic, social and political context around it was also examined, taking into account such factors as prevailing attitudes and worldviews, traditional and scientific knowledge, social psychology and all parts of the history of mentalities. Even in the more open period of the 1960s, however, this tendency never managed to culminate in a historical synthesis that really encompassed political, social, cultural and economic history. A direction took root, however, in which one particular historical–economic phenomenon was indeed studied comprehensively, within the totality of its developments, the factors that influenced it and the effects it itself gave rise to – and that phenomenon was the industrial revolution.

Industrialization became the subject of a dispute in the middle of the 1950s, when the Slovak economic historian Anton Špiesz (1930–93) disagreed with his Czech colleague Jaroslav Purš (1922–97) about the beginnings of the local industrial revolution, its timing and stages. According to Špiesz, Purš failed to fully draw on the ideas expounded in the classic Marxist writings on the industrial revolution in England and to apply those ideas to conditions in the Czech lands. Špiesz set the start of the industrial revolution in Slovakia as far back as the late eighteenth century, when the first spinning machines made their appearance, the workshop system went into decline, and most workers were already beginning to engage in wage labour, which was drawing them away from agriculture. Purš, by contrast, dated the beginning of the industrial revolution in the Czech lands to the early 1890s. Most of the participants in this debate were inclined to support his view. While initially this debate had unfolded under the influence of the latest research conducted in Soviet and Hungarian historiographies, Purš began to turn more and more towards non-Marxist historiography in his research; as a prominent Party historian, he enjoyed the opportunity to study abroad and take part in international conferences. Thanks to him the historical community was able to obtain information about international developments, though of course such information was couched in Marxist commentary (Myška 2010: 38). He was also, however, in the position to write that historical development cannot be confined to simplified schemes, and that the analysis by Soviet historians was incorrect. This discussion then continued primarily at an international level, with Jürgen Kuczynski, Eric Hobsbawm, Witold Kula and others joining in. Purš's debate with East German historian Jürgen Kuczynski went on for years and in time even became personal. Kuczynski emphasized the role of light industry and even theorized a 'Prussian way' to capitalism.

In 1973 Purš published his key, monumental work, *The Industrial Revolution: The Evolution of a Term and a Concept*, in which he devised and applied a complex approach to studying the industrial revolution. He placed it within the context of a more comprehensive revolution and revolutionary changes simultaneously occurring in other areas of society and the economy, primarily science and technology. While criticizing W. W. Rostow's stage theory of economic growth, he proposed alternative stages of development. Purš, however, overestimated the significance of the steam engine as a source of energy and his search for a connection between the industrial revolution and the social and revolutionary development of the working-class movement was a dead end, pursued in the service of the Marxist interpretation of historical development. After Purš, this line of research was mainly taken over by Slovak historiography – for instance, by Pavel Hapák and Ladislav Tajták. Conversely, Czech historians increasingly devoted themselves to the study of proto-industrialization, which Purš regarded as an inherently non-Marxist concept, though he did not entirely dismiss it, as his interventions at the 1982 World Economic History Congress in Budapest confirm.

The well-known work by Kriedte et al. (1981) on proto-industrialization caused heated discussions among Czech historians that lasted until the 1990s. The main contributors to this discussion were Arnošt Klíma, who had approached the issue independently since the 1950s (Klíma 1957, 1974), and Milan Myška (b. 1933), who extended Klíma's analysis of the 'manufactory period' to the early modern iron-making sector (Myška 1979). Klíma (1985) reached international prominence through his interventions in the Brenner Debate. Myška's (1991) concept of proto-industrialization was however left 'hanging in the air'. Only 'indigenous' scholars paid attention to it, despite its importance, for example, Ákoš Pauliny (b. 1929), a German historian of Slovakian descent. He had emigrated in 1969 so his contribution was itself marginal to the Slovakian and Czech discourse. Ostracized by the regime, Klíma and Myška were nonetheless assisted in their research by intermittent access to foreign literature, conference participation and visits abroad (in Göttingen, Vienna and elsewhere), which in the case of Myška only became possible in the early 1990s, though he managed to keep his contacts with the more open and independent Polish historiography.[2]

On the other hand, the contribution of Alice Teichová (1920–2015) was of fundamental importance for both Czechoslovakian and worldwide economic history. Along with her husband Mikuláš Teich (b. 1918), a renowned historian of science, she permanently left the country in August 1968, straight after the Soviet invasion. After spending a year in the USA, she was offered fellowships and later academic positions at Cambridge and the University of East Anglia in the UK. Thanks to correspondence with former colleagues, the Teichs were constantly informed about developments in Czechoslovak historiography such as debates and new publications and, in turn, they sent specialized literature back home. They also facilitated English language publications by Klíma and Myška in prestigious journals such as *Past and Present*, the *Economic History Review* and the *Journal of European Economic History*. They invited Czechoslovak colleagues to attend conferences abroad and to join international projects.

In 1970, the Academia publishing house removed Teichová's habilitation thesis on international investments in interwar Czechoslovakia from their editorial plans. Her book *An Economic Background to Munich* was however published by Cambridge University Press in 1974. This key book about Czechoslovak economic history was reviewed only abroad and it was from these reviews that some of her Czech colleagues learned about its existence. However, there are no citations from this or other books by Teichová to be found in the national historiography prior to 1989 and her domestic influence in this period was minimal. This was the effect of both censorship and autocensorship, as her works were available in academic libraries. After 1989, Teichová played a fundamental role in opening up Czech and Slovak historiographies to influences from the rest of the world. The fact that historiography became open to international influences did not immediately result in a methodological shift. More substantial changes have affected the hot areas of political history but economic historians began to engage again with a whole range of problems that had previously been abandoned. In comparison with earlier times, the scope of economic history has expanded considerably and productivity has increased. Numerous works, whose publication had been previously banned, were published in the first years after 1989, including some by historians based abroad.

In this new context, the traditional focus on medieval and early modern times (until 1848) has progressively weakened, while the history of the second half of the 'long' nineteenth century has received increasing attention. Many efforts have been dedicated to the period of the First Republic (1918–38). Economic conditions (Lacina 1990; Hallon 1995), policies (Doležalová 2007), banking (Novotný and Šouša 1996; Vencovský et al. 1999) and transport (Jakubec 1997) have all been investigated. On the other hand, industrial history (Holec 2011) and the histories of labour relations and foreign trade have been somewhat neglected. The Protectorate (1939–45) and the wartime Slovak State have grown in popularity (Jančík and Kubů 2005; Mičko 2010) and, in recent years, researchers have also turned to the post-war period. New syntheses intended to serve primarily as textbooks have been compiled (Průcha at al. 2004, 2009). However, they generally use political events as watersheds even when crucial economic issues such as monetary or agrarian reforms are at stake.

Conclusion

Individually and even combined, the Czech and Slovak contributions represent only a small fraction of the historiographical production of Europe as a whole. These traditions have been affected by geopolitical shocks, intellectual repression and ideological imperatives as well as by changes in the economic environment. During these troubled times, economic historians were kept under surveillance, ostracized, prevented from active research and sometimes even eliminated. The development of the discipline was also hindered by wartime occupation and numerous waves of emigration.

The field, initially an integral part of economics, later repositioned itself as a branch of history. Throughout the twentieth century, university departments, academies, museums and regional institutions coexisted as centres of intellectual enquiry. Company archives played a crucial role during the communist period because they provided historians expelled from academic institutions with the means to continue their work. Despite the imperatives of historical materialism, economic history never occupied a central place within the socialist organization of knowledge, and it is presently not regarded as a major historical field; its academic status remains rather weak. In the wake of 1989, economic history and social history merged for pragmatic reasons but did so without offering any deeper theoretical justification for this union. Social historians have increasingly focused on cultural history and disregarded their connection with economic history. On both sides, methodological debates have been kept at a minimum.

Even though some 150 historians in the Czech Republic today describe themselves as specializing in economic history, the discipline still lacks institutionalization as well as experts. Both Czech and Slovak practitioners are gradually integrating into the international community, but it must be said that at home they remain mostly marginalized individuals.

Notes

1 Most grants were allocated to projects about political history, followed by those addressing social and religious issues.
2 On intellectual exchanges in the Cold War era, see Berg (2015).

References

Berg, M. (2015) 'East–West dialogues: Economic historians, the Cold War, and Détente' *Journal of Modern History* 87.1: 36–71.

Bráf, A. (1904) 'Boj proti liberalismu', in *Život a dílo*, ed. by J. Gruber and C. Horáček, vol. 2, Prague.

Connelly, J. (2000) *Captive university: The Sovietization of East German, Czech, and Polish higher education, 1945–1956*. Chapel Hill: University of North Carolina Press.

Doležalová, A. (2007) *Rašín, Engliš a ti druzí*. Prague: Oeconomica.

Hallon, L. (1995) *Industrializácia Slovenska 1918–1938*. Bratislava: Veda.

Holec, R. (2011) *Dejiny plné dynamitu. Bratislavský chemický koncern Dynamit Nobel*. Bratislava: Kaligram.

Jakubec, I. (1997) *Železnice a Labská plavba 1918–1938*. Prague: Karolinum.

Jančík, D. and E. Kubů (2005) *'Arizace' a arizátoři*. Prague: Karolinum.

Klíma, A. (1957) 'Industrial development in Bohemia, 1648–1781' *Past and Present* 11: 87–99.

Klíma, A. (1974) 'The role of rural domestic industry in Bohemia in the eighteenth century' *Economic History Review* 27.1: 48–56.

Klíma, A. (1985) 'Agrarian class structure and economic development in pre-industrial Bohemia', in *The Brenner debate: Agrarian class structure and economic development in pre-industrial Europe*, ed. by T.H. Aston and C.H.E. Philpin. Cambridge: Cambridge University Press, 192–212.

Kriedte, P., H. Medick and J. Schlumbohm (1981) *Industrialization before industrialization: Rural industry in the genesis of capitalism*. Cambridge: Cambridge University Press.

Kutnar, F. and J. Marek (1997) *Přehledné dějiny českého a slovenského dějepisectví*. Prague: Nakladatelství Lidové noviny.

Lacina, V. (1990) *Formováni československé ekonomiky 1918–1923*. Prague: Academia.

Mendl, B. (1931) *Hospodářský vývoj Evropy*. Prague: Academia.

Mičko, P. (2010) *Hospodárska politika Slovenského štátu*. Cracow: Spolok Slovákov.

Myška, M. (1979) 'Pre-industrial iron-making in the Czech lands: The labour force and production relations circa 1350–circa 1840' *Past and Present* 82: 44–72.

Myška, M. (1991) 'Průmyslová revoluce z perspektívy historiografie 70. a 80. let' *Český časopis historický* 89.4: 533–46.

Myška, M. (2010) *Problémy a metody hospodářských dějin*. Ostrava: Ostravská univerzita.

Novotný, J. and J. Šouša (1996) *Banka ve znamení zeleného čtyřlístku. Agrární banka 1911–1938 (1948)*. Prague: Karolinum.

Petráň, J. (1977) *Problémy cen, mezd a materiálních podmínek života lidu v Čechách v 17.–19. století*. (Acta Universitatis Carolinae. Philosophica et Historica. Studia Historica.) Prague: Univerzita Karlova.

Průcha, V. et al. (2004 and 2009) *Hospodářské a sociální dějiny Česksolovenska 1918–1992*. Brno: Doplněk.

Purš, J. (1973) *Průmyslová revoluce*. Prague: Academia.

Teichová, A. (1974) *An economic background to Munich: International business and Czechoslovakia, 1918–1938*. Cambridge: Cambridge University Press.

Vencovský, F. et al. (1999) *Dějiny bankovnictví v českých zemích*. Prague: Bankovní institut.

15
CROSSROADS AND TURNS IN HUNGARIAN ECONOMIC HISTORY

György Kövér

From the Austro-Hungarian Monarchy to the Treaty of Trianon (1920), thence through the German and Soviet occupations to the current post-communist climate, Hungarian economic history has remained embedded in political upheavals and economic problems peculiar to Eastern Europe. This continuity/discontinuity has determined the approaches and topics that have dominated the field and the accessibility and reception of ideas from outside.

The term 'economic history' first appeared in 1878 in the title of a Hungarian monograph by Béla Weisz (1848–1945).[1] As a student in Vienna, Weisz had participated in Lorenz von Stein's lessons and he later attended those of Wilhelm Roscher in Leipzig. At the University of Pest, during his juridical studies, his master was Gyula Kautz, the founding father of the Hungarian national political economy school. Lajos Thallóczy's (1854–1916) dissertation on the early medieval royal tax 'lucrum camerae' (published in 1879) might be considered as another starting point for Hungarian economic history.[2] This double genealogy, with roots in the historical school of national political economy as well as in empirical historicism, characterizes the circumstances of the birth of the discipline fairly well.

Early professionalization: the *Hungarian Economic History Review* workshop

At the end of the nineteenth century, economic history was not yet institutionalized in university teaching. However, if the publication of a specialist journal can be taken as a sign of professionalization, then Hungarian economic history might be regarded as precocious. The first issue of the *Magyar Gazdaságtörténelmi Szemle* ('Hungarian Economic History Review') appeared in 1894, only one year after the publication of the German *Zeitschrift für Social- und Wirtschaftsgeschichte* (ZSWG).[3] In the journal title the word 'economic' originally had the meaning 'agricultural' and, in its establishment, an agricultural lobby, OMGE, had a decisive role (Izsépy 1969). The founding and managing editor of the journal, Alajos Paikert (1866–1948), was not an economic historian, but an ambitious young jurist and agronomist. Thanks to his networking skills, he secured funding from the Ministry of Agriculture.

While Paikert found the money, the co-editor Károly Tagányi (1858–1924) shaped the journal intellectually. Tagányi belonged to the first professionally educated generation of Hungarian historians, who had been influenced by positivism (R. Várkonyi 1973: I. 165–7;

Vardy 1976: 40–1; Csíki 2003: 20–3; Bognár 2013). His knowledge of both foreign literature and archival material was impressive.[4] His arguments, which incorporated international comparisons, convinced the agricultural ministry that a synthesis of Hungarian agricultural history could not be written without the necessary preparatory research.[5] Among those who worked on the early economic history agenda, mention should also be made of Ignác Acsády (1845–1906) (Acsády 1895). According to his view, the main reason for the underdevelopment of economic history in Hungary was the 'lack of interest' in the relationship between the state and society. While in Europe the adoption of the historical method fertilized contemporary political economy as well as national policies, in Hungary policy-makers tended to rely on foreign ideas and looked at the Hungarian past with 'sovereign indifference'.[6] In his overtly nationalistic rhetoric, the 'mission of economic history' was to put in a proper light the 'mission of the Hungarian nation, and the everlasting remarkable work it had done over a thousand years on the soil of the fatherland, what constitutes the main content of its history, the most stable right to rule'.[7]

The *Hungarian Economic History Review* regularly followed the specialist literature published in Hungary and abroad. References to the content of the brother periodical *Zeitschrift*, were common but only the articles 'having special interest' from a Hungarian point of view were reported (MGtSz 1898: 604.v). There were reviews also of the third volume of Inama-Sternegg's *Deutsche Wirtschaftsgeschichte* and of work on the history of the English milling industry. When Paikert left the *Review* in 1900, it was obvious that he had to offer the full editorship to Tagányi.[8] However Tagányi, after developing neurasthenia, had to hand over the post to someone else. Sándor Takáts (1860–1932), a trained historian and an ex-priest, was the preferred candidate, but he lived in Vienna, which seemed to be too far away. Finally the post was inherited by a young economic historian, Ferenc Kováts (1873–1956) from Pozsony (Bratislava). After studying law, he had spent a year in Breslau (Wrocław) and attended the lessons of Werner Sombart with whom he maintained frequent contact after returning home.[9] His first book was on foreign trade in the later Middle Ages. As editor of the *Review*, Kováts tried to develop the journal at an international level and contributed to the dissemination of Hungarian economic history in German-speaking countries through the *Vierteljahrschrift für Sozial- und Wirtschaftsgeschichte* (VSWG) (Kováts 1903: 605–17). The relatively high honorarium paid to the *Review*'s contributors brought back the offended Sándor Takáts who offered his work again: 'If you have not enough useful articles', he told the new editor, 'you have to write me – *the essence of the Viennese archives* can be found in my room.'[10] Despite these efforts, the number of subscribers did not increase, the financial deficit became greater and in 1906 the *Review* was forced to cease (Kövér 2013: 201–24). As Berlász (2010: 245) notes, 'whatever important role the . . . *Review* played in the formation of Hungarian economic and social history, it was not able to ensure the reproduction of writers for the new discipline'.

To close the story of the *Hungarian Economic History Review* and its editors: after the Treaty of Trianon, Ferenc Kováts moved from Pozsony to Szeged, and in the 1930s he became Professor of Economic History at the Budapest Polytechnic. According to Berlász, Kováts was 'our only genuine [*katexochen*] economic historian' (Berlász 2010: 246). It is questionable to what degree someone could be exclusively an economic historian in Hungary, but it is a fact that no school of economic history developed around Kováts. During the last decades of the Dual Monarchy and after its dissolution, the disclosure of sources about the former Habsburg Empire gave considerable impulse to research and source publication, though the newly established Hungarian Historical Institute in Vienna concentrated its energies outside economic and social history.[11]

The Institute for the History of Civilization and the Domanovszky school

The first Hungarian economic historians came from history seminars. Sándor Domanovszky (1877–1955) had been originally a specialist of medieval chronicles, but his interest turned towards economic history while he was teaching history at the Commercial Academy in Budapest. After 1914 he became the first non-ecclesiastical (moreover Lutheran) Professor of Cultural History in the Pázmány Péter University, and he drove a lot of students in that direction.[12] Bálint Hóman (1885–1951) started his career as a historian of money, public finance and economic policy. However, in the interwar period he turned to politics and administration, became Minister of Culture and, condemned as a war criminal, finished his life in prison (he was rehabilitated *post mortem* in 2014). When, in 1928, Hóman received a letter from Marc Bloch inviting him to join the project for a new international economic history journal, he declined and instead recommended Domanovszky.[13] The plan for this journal never materialized, but thanks to Domanovszky several reviews of Hungarian economic historiography were published in the first issues of the *Annales*.[14]

Domanovszky's international position was certainly reinforced by his personal connections to Polish historians and to Hans Nabholz from Zürich but also by his close scientific ties to Alfons Dopsch and his school in Vienna.[15] Dopsch's activity as a founder of the Seminar for Economic and Cultural History at the University of Vienna in 1922 served as a model for liberating economic history from the cage of the old juridical history school, and opening it to neighbouring disciplines such as social and cultural history. His methodological slogan ('Door and gates open') exerted great influence at that time, not only in Eastern Europe, and inspired interesting methodological discussions. For the reception of Dopsch's views, it was important that he was elected to an associate fellowship of the Hungarian Academy of Sciences in 1927 (two years before, he had given a lecture in Budapest on the methodological questions of social and economic history).[16] Domanovszky regularly sent his students to the Viennese Collegium Hungaricum. Once there, while studying the extremely rich archival material of the Habsburg Monarchy, they diligently attended the lectures and seminars of Alfons Dopsch and his colleagues.[17] Ten years later, Domanovszky's contribution to the Dopsch *Festschrift* provided an occasion for discussing one of his central theses. According to Dopsch, the expansion of the manorial economy (*Gutsherrschaft*) was not an exclusive characteristic of Eastern Europe and not only of the period following the late Middle Ages. On the basis of several empirical studies inspired by his cultural history seminar at the Pázmány University in Budapest, Domanovszky came to the conclusion that the manorial economy in Hungary 'because of different circumstances could not develop into a dominant economic type for a long time . . . and, until the nineteenth century, it was no more than a tentative endeavour'.[18]

In 1928 Domanovszky started to supervise a series of dissertations which resulted in fifteen volumes which were published under the title *Studies in the history of Hungarian agriculture*.[19] These formed the basis of his school (Vardy 1976: 164–71). In the preface to the series, Domanovszky reformulated the old positivist slogan: 'It is impossible to construct history without data' (Domanovszky 1930: 4). One of the members of the school, Imre Wellmann (1909–94), argued that its novelty did not lie only in the 'organization of work' and systematic planning, but in the practice of presenting the subject of agricultural history 'in the light of all surviving sources and taking into account national and European development in the totality of its aspects' (Wellmann 1937: 672, 674). This explains why, although Hungary remained a rural country, agricultural history became a leading field within the discipline only in the 1930s. The history of money and trade also had an important place in the activity of the Domanovszky school.

The *Geistesgeschichte*, a new direction of German historiography inspired by the holistic and anti-positivist views of Wilhelm Dilthey, had its impact on Hungary as well (Vardy 1976: 62–94; Erős 2012: 319–30, 354–67). Bálint Hóman edited a programmatic volume, which was reviewed by Domanovszky in the leading Hungarian historical periodical, *Századok*. The latter found 'the book's leading essays to be directed too much against the school of positivism, against the preparatory work of data mining and the liberal concept of history' (Domanovszky 1931: 277). The economic and social history chapter of the book was written by István Dékány, who was a well-educated methodologist in social sciences, but had never written a word about social and economic history (Dékány 1931: 183–237). His main conclusion however was clear – in Hungary it was difficult to write exclusively economic history because the centre of gravity was political and military endeavour. He stated: 'Economic history constitutes only a chapter of social history; the latter describes the entirety of productive relations, the former only their economic function' (Dékány 1931: 207, 214).

In 1932, the challenge of the *Geistesgeschichte* was confronted in a methodological symposium organized by the Hungarian Society of Economists. Sándor Gyömrei (1892–1957), who had been trained at the University of Leipzig, was the main contender. As usual, the discussion was shadowed by ideological confrontation and Gyömrei defended the idea of liberalism and progress. He stated that Hungarian economic history writing 'had been out of step with the results of foreign researches. Because of a lack of economic knowledge they [historians] became victims of the rather different "languages" of the sources. Our historians did not examine the substance of economic life, but its regulation.' The tragedy of Hungarian economic history was that *Geistesgeschichte*, 'as much as the old political history . . . had expelled the principles of economics' (Gyömrei 1932: 663, 678–9).

Gyömrei's position triggered a wave of harsh criticism. Béla Iványi-Grünwald jr. (1902–65), a young specialist of the history of credit, openly attacked him: 'with all respect, to the historian of economics we must put the question: whether economics has defined its notions with such a lack of ambiguity, that excludes those possibilities of errors, which can be pointed out if a historian looks at the past through its own ideas and ideals and not through the economic concepts of the present'. Similarly, according to Iványi-Grünwald, 'the historical segment distinguished by Gyömrei as economic history . . . believes to constitute itself exclusively in pure economic terms. But *we do not believe in this kind of limited economic history, we believe in history – and when we are speaking about economic history, it is only a temporary limitation of our material*, applied to the circumstances' (Iványi-Grünwald 1933: 362, 364, italics mine).

One of the students of Domanovszky, Emma Lederer (1897–1977) referred to the recently founded *Economic History Review* as representing the latest international trends and suggested that one should integrate the more developed German methodological ideas with practical English [i.e. positivist] spirit. In her opinion economic history means always research of particularities, the 'economic' factor is only a part of the 'total' as well as the 'spiritual' history. According to her, Gyömrei had overemphasized the dangers of *Geistesgeschichte* in the Hungarian context (Lederer 1933: 31, 37).

Due to these methodological differences, the leading Hungarian historians of the 1930s produced two distinct historical syntheses: one, by Hóman and Szekfű (1928–34), was written from the standpoint of *Geistesgeschichte*; the other one, written by young scholars under the direction of Domanovszky (1939–43), was in the tradition of the history of civilization and more open, though not uncritically, to positivist influences. One of the authors of the first synthesis, summarizing his views on the sources of economic history, declared that 'in the depiction of economic and social developments [he] refrained from referring to the abundant statistical material, because it by no means enlightens the essential questions.'[20] The editor in chief of the rival synthesis concluded in the preface of the first volume:

> Both material and mental factors will be covered, including transformations in the nature of landed property, the composition of the national population, society and economy, the genesis of several aspects of the spiritual life and finally the lifestyles of different groups . . . The place of the hero in this narration is occupied by the ways of life, the world of thought and the productive activities of the great mass of the nation.[21]

After the shock of the Treaty of Trianon, the so-called 'ethnic history' or *Volkstumsgeschichte* ('népiségtörténet' means 'ethnic' and 'people's history' at the same time) primarily associated with Elemér Mályusz (1898–1989) was regarded as an exciting endeavour, which was originally intended to be a social history of the local (something between the German *Ortsgeschichte* and *Territorialgeschichte*). During the late 1930s, Mályusz and his school actively participated in the 'history of civilization' enterprise. Geographically, this ethnic history school focused on the territories of Upper Hungary (now Slovakia) and Transylvania (today part of Romania) for both historical and political reasons. The influence of Mályusz – combined with the fascination for the rural sociology of Dimitrie Gusti (1880–1955) and the Bucharest school – gave impetus to the formation of a new generation of economic and social historians in Transylvania: among them Zsigmond Jakó (1916–2008), István Imreh (1919–2003), Elek Csetri (1924–2010) and Ákos Egyed (b. 1929) (Imreh 1979; Egyed 1981).

Continuity and change under the hegemony of Soviet-style Marxism

After 1945, the channels of continuity in the institutional development of economic history were gradually closed. Ferenc Kováts retired in 1945 and his department was inherited by Jenő Berlász (b. 1911). Among other applicants we have to mention the name Oszkár Paulinyi (1899–1982) and Imre Wellmann (the first was Dopsch's student in Vienna, the other a pupil of Domanovszky), all of whom were first-rate young economic historians of that time (Paulinyi 2005). However, Berlász could not enjoy his professorship for long because in 1948 he was dismissed from the newly established Karl Marx University of Economics. In 1948 Domanovszky was also forced to retire (his Department of History of Civilization ceased to exist). Very soon he was also removed from the Academy of Sciences.[22]

The personal, institutional and ideological preconditions of Soviet-style Marxist historiography were built up during the preparations of the first five-year plan in 1949–50. A register of Hungarian historians was set up in order to understand which (loyal) cadres were available for the new tasks of the party state system.[23] In a command economy, all natural and social sciences also had their five-year plan and they were financed exclusively by the state (Kövér 2012). The key institution for the history plan was the Historical Institute of the Academy of Sciences. Soviet science constituted the theoretical background of new historical knowledge (in the form of Moscow-graduated party soldiers, delegated Soviet advisers and a periodical of the Institute which contained mostly translations of the latest Soviet debates). Most of the old specialists were removed from the Institute, and only some of them kept to form 'working cooperatives' that concentrated on the newly defined directions of research. Half of the twelve 'priority areas' for history concentrated on economic history issues, though the Lenin slogan that 'economy is determining, but politics is the primary factor' was never forgotten. Some of the working cooperatives consisting of both old specialists and ideologically equipped young recruits produced collective volumes. However, a great deal of the projected research was never finished, because after the first year of the plan a new primary task was defined: to write a synthesis of Hungarian history in five or six volumes, which was called 'the university textbook'. Its mission was to replace the old comprehensive works of Hóman and Szekfű, and Domanovszky.[24] The original plan underwent revisions in 1951 and 1953 (under the administration of Prime Minister Imre Nagy). The second five-year plan was suspended just before its launch in 1955 and the unforeseen interference of the 1956 uprising did the rest.

A new workshop was founded for the discipline – the Department of Economic History at the Karl Marx University of Economics, chaired by a former student of Domanovszky, Pál Zsigmond Pach (1919–2001). A new generation of Marxist economic historians was educated in both economics and history: Iván Berend (b. 1930), György Ránki (1930–88) and Miklós Szuhay (b. 1928) and they became members of different 'working cooperatives'. The main emphasis was placed on the nineteenth and twentieth centuries – the period of the emergence of capitalism – partly because it had been neglected before the war, partly because the party–state ideologues believed that overcoming capitalism, and the liquidation of the interwar Horthy regime, would be more effective if they had a more elaborated image of the enemy.

Although, during the war, the first steps to produce a new industrial (and economic) history of modern Hungary had been taken (Eckhart 1941; Futo 1944), the elaboration of this topic was restarted during the 1950s from the point of view of Stalinist industrialization. A four-volume series on industrial history was published, aimed at representing this new strand of research, but the monographs were methodologically out of date in the very moment of their publication (Merei 1951; Lederer 1952; Sándor 1954; Berend and Ránki 1955).[25] Jenő Berlász's work on the history of the Ganz factory (written during the war yet left unpublished until after 1956) is still considered a remarkable experiment in the field of business history (Berlász 1957). Collections of articles on the agrarian history of capitalism must be mentioned as typical publications of the period produced by collective workshops (Pach and Sándor Pál 1956). Under Pach's editorship, in 1958 the Economic History Department started the book series *Gazdaságtörténeti értekezések* ('Treatises on Economic History'), which lasted until 1975 and produced seven volumes about agricultural, industrial, commercial and urban issues in the history of Hungarian capitalism, tackled from a post-Stalinist standpoint.

While the large-scale 'socialist factories' of economic history writing produced collective volumes and unfinished syntheses, in the shadow of these great enterprises some solid and comprehensive monographs were published as well. Their authors were young historians, who were better able to preserve their ideological independence and remained closer to the empirical sources (Makkai 1954; Szűcs 1955; Szabad 1957).

Reintegration into the international mainstreams (*Annales*, comparative studies, quantification)

The divorce from the Stalinist form of Marxism after 1956 was helped by a lot of factors. The Kádár regime itself proclaimed its intention to break with the 'faults of the past'. In this situation some tendencies, having been oppressed during the early 1950s, could revive. At the Kossuth Lajos University of Debrecen, István Szabó (1898–1969), who came from ethnic history (now turned into peasants' history), in spite of all the unfair attacks he received, was able to train a new generation of agrarian historians and collected their works in two comprehensive volumes in 1960 and 1965.[26] These projects were financed by special grants which were distributed by the Academy of Sciences outside of the official academic budget.

During the 1960s everybody had to make compromises with the official dominant Marxist ideology, but under formal loyalty there still remained some possibility of retaining the best of both the positivist and historicist traditions.

Researchers focused on the history of the peasantry within capitalism, which had been omitted from the mainstream of the old historiography. The issue was topical in a period when the new government attempted to liquidate the peasantry through collectivization. Subfield periodicals were founded (*Agricultural History Review* [1957–], *Studies in Historical Statistics*, *Review of the History of Technology*, *Contributions to Factory History*) and, in 1963, a research group was set up within the Agricultural Museum, which contributed not only to the publication of a *Yearbook* but also to an international bibliography (*Bibliographia historiae rerum rusticarum internationalis*). In the 1970s, a new wave of research on the history of crafts and guilds had been launched in the form of local and international conferences, the *Internationales Handwerksgeschichtliches Symposium* organized by István Éri (1929–2009). The papers were published in a series of more than twenty volumes (Szulovszky 2002).

Participation in international forums required special abilities, not only in a linguistic sense. In Eastern Europe, the system of party–state financed science demanded ideological reliability as well. It was true, after 1960, for those who wished to attend international history congresses and those of the Economic History Association, as well as the conferences on the history of the Austro-Hungarian Monarchy organized between 1955 and 1964 by the historical committees of the so-called 'friendly successor states' (Kövér 2009). But through these channels new intellectual challenges – first of all those which seemed to be compatible with Marxism – started to penetrate the Iron Curtain. The situation had paradoxical aspects: the 'take-off' of Rostow, for example, was compatible with Marxist historical theory when combined with the concept of 'industrial revolution', but the subtitle of his book, *A Non-Communist Manifesto*, made it inappropriate for 'mental' customs clearance. Moreover, it was not so easy to defend the innovations of international economic history against old-fashioned dogmatism. The head of the 'Scientific Socialism Department' at the Budapest Eötvös Loránd University, Aladár Mód (1908–73), an old representative of national communism, and his colleague, György Tolnai (1914–92), an old social democrat, took the ideological front in several discussions. These debates about optimism/pessimism, objectivity/subjectivity, peasant industry/industrialization, were disguised as scholarly disputes.

Some introduced quantitative arguments in the discussion, as indicated in a rather emphatic review article on 'The Triumph of Quantitative Economic History in Budapest' (Gross 1972) which referred to the study of László Katus (1927–2015), still a standard reference in the international literature, but never translated into Hungarian in its original form (Katus 1970). While, on the whole, the role played by quantitative economic history has been modest, the volume, nonetheless, can be interpreted as a sign of responsiveness to new trends in comparative historical studies.[27] The terminological setting of that time was rather flexible. Discussion of the notion 'Eastern' or 'East–Central' Europe, for example, always had a political meaning. After 1968 'East–Central Europe' fitted better with international discourse and the new identity-seeking process of the Habsburg successor states (Péter 1999). The polyglot Emil Niederhauser (1923–2010), speaking almost all East European languages, argued above all for the peculiarities of East European development (Niederhauser 1958). It was a long and winding way for Pach from the study of the industrial activity of the Orczy family estate in the late eighteenth century (Pach 1943), through the search for pecularities in the Hungarian 'previous accumulation' (Pach 1952), to the history of the *Abbiegung* ('deviation/diversion') of Hungarian (and East European) development from that of Western Europe in the period of 'late feudalism'. Later, he tried to determine the contours of the

East–Central European region in the context of early modern international trade (Pach 1960; Pach 1994; Nagy 2012). During the 1970s, medievalists joined the discussion extending the framework to the whole of Europe from early medieval times (Makkai 1970; Szűcs 1985).

From the 1960s, some younger Hungarian economic historians were offered opportunities not only to take part in international congresses, but also as visiting fellows abroad.[28] After Fernand Braudel's visit to Budapest in 1962, about three to five researchers from the Academy's Institute of History per year obtained fellowships at the Ecole. In the 1960s the active reception of the *Annales* paradigm started (Katus 2007: 162–3) and those years saw the development of long-run price history studies (Zimányi 1973). New chances were opened for world history research. After writing a monograph on the sixteenth-century price revolution, Tibor Wittman (1923–72) succeeded in forming a school at the University of Szeged that tried to set early modern East–Central European and Latin American history in a global context. Owing to his untimely death, Wittman's impressive oeuvre could not be completed (Wittman 1957, 1970–71). However, the studies of Makkai, Pach, Wittman, Zimányi and others managed to get into the international scientific debate about core–periphery relations (Wallerstein 1980)

Although in the original manuscript the authors had still used the term 'Eastern Europe', in the final version of their *Economic Development* from 1969 (the US translation appeared in 1974) Berend and Ránki pointed to 'East–Central Europe' as the basic unit of historical comparison. A further volume on the comparative economic history of European peripheries in the nineteenth century, which they produced in the context of intense international scientific cooperation, constituted the next important step on this road (Berend and Ránki 1982). During the late 1970s and early 1980s, there were several attempts at establishing closer contacts with West European historians through international workshops. The key figures of these (soon aborted) initiatives were I. Kostrowiczka, Z. Landau, J. Tomaszevsky, V. Prucha, J. Faltus and L. Barr. The process of reintegration of Hungarian historiography into the international mainstream made further progress in 1982 when the World Economic History Congress was held in Budapest. It represented a veritable meeting of generations, schools and cultures. The president of the IEHA Committee (Pál Zsigmond Pach), as always, represented the host country, but the main organizer was György Ránki. An 'A' theme was dedicated to the problem of large estates and smallholdings (particularly relevant looking from and at Eastern Europe), convened by László Makkai (1914–89), a member of the older generation in the Institute of History, a historian of technology and the most eminent follower of the *Annales* in Hungary. In the session 'From the Family Firm to Professional Management', which was also very timely from the point of view of Hungarian economic reform, the Hungarian speaker was Péter Hanák (1921–97), one of the young communist historians in the 1950s, author (with his wife) of the first modern business history study and a revisionist participant in the debates of the following decade on the Austro-Hungarian Monarchy (Hanák and Hanák 1964; Hanák 1982).

The 1980s at the Economic History Department of the University of Economics were years of thematic more than methodological innovation. This workshop produced, for example, the first critical work on the economic history of state socialism prior to the economic reform. The approach was positivistic, based on archival material and somewhat close to institutionalism (Berend 1983; Pető and Szakács 1985). New themes, such as the history of banking, started to emerge (Kövér 1991). The influence of international approaches cannot be identified in every direction in economic history. This is especially true for the Hungarian reception of cliometrics. It was Gyula Benda (1943–2005) who first introduced the Hungarian readership to the new economic history in 1975, but the first reaction of

György Ránki was rather negative (Ránki 1977: 93; cf. Ranki 1988). Some years later, John Komlos's book on the Austro-Hungarian customs union was translated into Hungarian but its publication should be contextualized in the new political climate (Komlos 1990) and, even then, the approach was generally received without enthusiasm. The first cliometrics university course was held by Scott M. Eddie at Eötvös Loránd University. The edited lectures were published in Hungarian and, since then, everybody who wants to get acquainted with those methods is able to do so (Eddie 1996). However, cliometrics has remained a non-indigenous international plant, which has not taken root on Hungarian soil, though many Hungarian students now get their PhDs from foreign universities and work in environments where cliometrics is stronger.

In the wake of political change

During the more recent decades of political change, political history came back to prominence. In the transition process, the government commissioned political histories and was also their main consumer. Economic history has declined from a combination of international and domestic factors such as the counter-reaction to the former hegemony of Marxist historical determinism, the temporary priority given to political history and the self-proclaimed autonomy of social history. As a consequence of Ránki's death (1988), and Berend's 1990 emigration to Los Angeles, at the UCLA, the position of the discipline became substantially weaker.[29] In recent years, the representatives of social science history have gathered under the flag of social history and in 1988 a new association with this logo (István Hajnal Circle – Social History Association) was established. Change has taken place in the institutional structure as well: during the transformation of the former Karl Marx (today Corvinus) University of Economics, the Economic History Department was dissolved and now only two economic historians work there, although this department has intensively participated in many international banking and business history research projects, organized by and around Alice Teichova, in cooperation with Austrian, Czech, Slovak, British, Norwegian, Swedish and of course Hungarian economic historians (Pogány 1999).

On the other hand, the creation of an Economic and Social History Department at the Faculty of Arts at Eötvös Loránd University (1991), with its own PhD programme (1993), was a promising development. The main profile of this department was originally urban history and, through the assistance of its founder, Vera Bácskai, intensive connections have been developed with the Urban History Group of Leicester University where many students have had an opportunity to study for one or two semesters in the framework of exchange programmes. But Hungarian students are showing little interest in economic history. Moreover, the current administration at the department does not seem to be inclined to support the further consolidation of this field. It is easy to interpret these difficulties as a manifestation of an international tendency, but it does not make us happy that this is the only area where our institutions are in step with world trends.

We can report some good news, though. My own research group at Eötvös Loránd has received funding from the Academy of Sciences to carry out research on nineteenth- and twentieth-century economic crises and, in the economics curriculum of the Social Science Faculty, economic history has gained a fairly important place. Two professors of economic history from the younger generation have been appointed at the universities of Szeged and Pécs. New textbooks have been published and reoriented research in directions such as comparative economic history, long-run agrarian change, and banking and industrial history (Tomka 2001, 2004 and 2013; Kaposi 2001 and 2007; Kover and Pogany 2002; Vári 2008;

Germuska 2010). In recent decades, entrepreneurial and business history has also developed in promising ways (Bácskai 1989; Halmos 2008; Klement 2012) and, for some time, regular joint workshops were held with the Business History Group of the University of Reading in the UK. New periodicals have been established, including the first Hungarian social history journal (*Korall*, 2000–), the *Yearbook of Historical Demography* (2000–) and *URBS*, the *Hungarian Urban History Yearbook* (2006–).

Retrospect and prospects

Looking back at twentieth-century Hungarian economic history, its early embeddedness in the national narrative is evident, as was the case with other European historiographies (Niederhauser 1989; Berger et al. 1999). The subsequent shifts in political history, from the Treaty of Trianon on, further encouraged the instrumentalization of this connection. Experiments to overcome historiographical nationalism took two directions: one in the 1920s and 1930s with the ethnic history of Mályusz and Szabó, which nevertheless never got rid of it completely or evolved into fully-fledged social history. The 'microhistory' of recent years has probably been more successful in this respect (Tóth 1989; Benda 2008). The other direction was that of comparative history which, after the antecedents of the Domanovszky school in the 1930s, produced internationally appreciated results in the 1970s and 1980s. However, the choice of the supranational scale (Central Europe, Eastern Europe, or the East/West axis) was always dictated by the political context.

As we have seen, the leading sector of the Hungarian economy, agriculture, and the institutional problems of the system of large estates were still in the foreground of research in the 1930s, and the golden age of modern peasant history only came during the shock of the 1960s. Neither can it be considered accidental that the great boom of industrial history took place in the 1940s and 1950s. A peculiar coexistence of modernization and dependency theories was characteristic of the mid-twentieth century. This was supported by the fact that the hegemonic Soviet-style Marxism could supply ideological arguments for both concepts.

Apart from Ferenc Kováts and Tibor Tóth, Hungarian historians have never shown an exclusive interest in 'pure' economic history but rather have combined it with other fields. For Tagányi, these were legal, social and cultural history; for Domanovszky, the history of medieval chronicles, of civilization and administration; for Hóman, the history of state formation and politics; for Eckhart, juridical history; for Berlász, the history of books and libraries; for Katus, ecclesiastical history; for Ránki, military and diplomatic history and so on. The causes of this phenomenon may be structural: in a small country, the division of labour is underdeveloped and there is no room for narrow specialization. Moreover, economic history has possibly been regarded as too narrow by the most versatile and influential personalities. On the other hand, these factors have had a positive impact in encouraging interdisciplinary ideas within the field (Kubinyi et al. 2008).

As far as economic history is concerned, it is hard to avoid the continuity/discontinuity question. The first professional generation of practitioners in the late nineteenth century was inspired by positivism. The new generation, tempted by *Geistesgeschichte* and cultural history, was mostly swept away after 1945, but some younger scholars turned to Soviet-style Marxism (Romsics 2011: 356–77). Pál Zsigmond Pach, Emma Lederer, Gyula Mérei and others became prominent in this period; many felt or at least showed loyalty to the new political system. All of them had to conform to it to some degree. The Marxist 'young garde' learned from them either at university or in the archive reading rooms. However, from the 1960s onwards, they were met with the challenge of international scientific life, mostly through periodicals and books but, for a small group, through participation in international conferences and fellowships abroad.

In this area of Europe, the state has always played an important role in financing historical research and publications. Without public funding, no major specialized periodical could have been established. After the nationalization of the research infrastructure and its transformation according to principles of the planned economy, state socialism was able to enforce ideological preferences in the conceptualization of research agendas (capitalism, industrialization, the 'Prussian way' and so on). Of course, the existence of a Marxist orthodoxy offered no legitimate possibility of free choice at the crossroads, but the way to revert to the good old historiography remained open for everybody. Those fortunate enough to experience the political transition at the end of the 1980s had a new chance to adapt themselves to these changed circumstances.

The discipline embraced the trends of international historiography to various degrees in different periods. Almost every contributor to the *Hungarian Economic History Review* spent some time as a student at German or Austrian universities and links with German-speaking historiography remained strong in the interwar period. On the other hand, the promising contacts with Strasbourg at the very beginning of the *Annales* school did not develop into closer collaboration until the age of Braudel. A gradual release from the grasp of the Soviet International started during the 1960s and 1970s. Bilateral academic cooperation, fellowships, participation in common international research projects and World Economic History congresses must be mentioned in this respect, along with the impact of foreign periodicals (e.g. *Annales, Geschichte und Gesellschaft, Journal of European Economic History*). Since the late 1990s, in addition to the free flow of the ideas due to the Internet revolution, the migration of university students has become more and more important. Today Hungarian economic history is definitely not threatened by the danger of straying into a specialist niche of the 'new economic history' (Boldizzoni 2011). Although statistical approaches and quantification have an indigenous tradition, this is alien from cliometrics. The discipline has remained equally unaffected by the more recent linguistic turn (Trencsényi and Apor 2007).

In sum, Hungarian economic history has striven to keep up with international trends and produced influential scholars as well. However, both organizational inertia and radical institutional changes hampered all but informal continuities among succeeding generations. In the midst of recurrent ideological and scientific paradigm shifts, economic history developed a special form of pragmatism. The discipline's strengths remain its links to other fields and its ability to survive and to reinvent itself over time, following paths not often congruent with the latest international fashions, in ways that address economic change and economic characteristics close to hand.

Notes

1 The main task of the work was to show 'how important economic history is for inductive problem-solving in national political economy' (Weisz 1878: 3). After 1881, Weisz took the name Földes. He later made an academic career as an economist and served in government during the war.

2 Thallóczy (1879). The idea that this was a pioneering work comes from Gunst (1961: 89).

3 Zorn (1985: 457–75). The *Zeitschrift* informed its readers about the launch of the Hungarian periodical: ZSWG 3 (1895): 533–4.

4 He was highly respected by the younger generation of historians, but he was seen as an 'odd person'. Cf. Lederer (1969: 76–7) and Glatz (1980: 113–19).

5 He referred to J. E. Thorold Rogers, Karl Lamprecht and Theodor Inama Sternegg. Report on the history of Hungarian agriculture for the committee meeting of 23 January [1894], OSzK Kt Fol. Hung. 1547.

6 Acsády (1890: 375–87). He quoted an economist with indignation: 'Hungarian economic history? It's a swindle; some old rubbish pieces of guild charters, that's all' (1890: 378).
7 Acsády (1895: 142–3.) It is worth noting that the main international authors cited by Acsády were not Germans, but Louis Bourdeau and James [Edwin Thorold] Rogers, in French translation.
8 Paikert became the director of the newly founded Agricultural Museum. The relation among the co-editors was not harmonious. Tagányi wrote in a personal letter: 'it was known by everybody that he hadn't helped me at all in editorial work' MTA KIK Kt Ms 2357/237, letter to Kováts Ferenc, 9 January 1901. In an earlier note in his diary, Paikert lamented the opposite: 'I have to keep Tagányi in check – he wants to use my services under the cover of friendship', OSzK Kt Quart. Hung. 3264/ 4 (12 February 1895).
9 See Sombart's letters to Ferenc Kováts, MTA KIK Kt Ms 2357/179–200.
10 Takáts to Kováts (29 April 1903), MTA KIK Kt Ms 2355/123, italics mine. An important article of his was on world trade (Takáts 1903). Takáts also carried out extensive research in the archives of Nuremberg on the early modern Hungarian cattle trade.
11 In the series of 'Fontes historiae hungaricae aevi recentioris', only one volume was published on economic and social history (Vardy 1976: 56–8). On changes in the original publication plan see Ujváry (1996: 76–83).
12 On the importance ofDomanovszky in Hungarian historiography see Glatz (1988); Granasztoi (1984).
13 Marc Bloch's letter to Hóman, OSzK Kt 15/327 (1928). Hóman's letter to Domanovszky, MTA KIK Kt Ms 4524/618 (20 July1928).
14 About the original project of the 'Revue internationale d'histoire économique' see Erdmann (2005: 92).
15 A review article on Hungarian economic historiography (Kring 1937) was written on the request of the Polish historians F. Bujak and J. Rutkowski (see correspondence of Bujak, Rutkowski and Kring with Domanovszky, 1936–37. MTA KIK Kt Ms 4523/337–338; Ms 4527/61–62; Ms 4525/635–638). On Dopsch and his school, see Dopsch (1968: 543–65), Hoffmann (1979: 57–61); Buchner (2008: 155–90).
16 On the reception see Eckhart (1928: 828–32).
17 See Letters to Sándor Domanovszky, MTA KIK Kt Ms 4523/19; 4526/645, 647.
18 Domanovszky (1938: 441–69). These views were certainly close to those of Jan Rutkowski and Polish historiography.
19 'Tanulmányok a magyar mezőgazdaság történetéhez', 15 vols. (1932–43).
20 Szekfű, in: Hóman and Szekfű (1933: VII, 445).
21 Domanovszky (1939: I, 16–17). The chapters on economic and social history were written by Imre Wellmann, Jenő Berlász, Oszkár Paulinyi, László Ungár and others.
22 On the Stalinist reorganization of the Academy, see Péteri (1998).
23 AL MTT Titk. Box 23/8.
24 The first and second volumes were published in 1954, the fifth and last in 1980, but the whole series was never completed.
25 Lederer was originally Domanovszky's student. Mérei's mentor was Gyula Szekfű, Vilmos Sándor came from the interwar workers' movement. Berend and Ránki, who had been Pach's students since Gymnasium years, represented the new generation.
26 Szabó (1960, 1965). On István Szabó as a historian Erős (2003) is an essential read.
27 A special variant of quantitative economic history was elaborated by Tibor Tóth (1941–2011) who attempted to unify micro and macro viewpoints in agrarian history (Tóth 1982).
28 In his memoirs, Berend emphasizes the importance of the Ford fellowship programme (Berend 1997: 153, 168).
29 Just before his death, Ránki was elected vice president of the International Committee of Historical Sciences, a position that was inherited by Berend, who finally became its president 1995–2000 (Erdmann 2005: 362). At UCLA, Berend continued the comparative programme started with Ránki (Berend 1996, 2003).

Archival sources and references

Acsády, Ignác (1890) 'Ipartörténetünk feladatai' *Nemzetgazdasági Szemle*, 14: 375–87.
Acsády, Ignác (1895) 'A magyar gazdaságtörténet feladatai' MGtSz, 2: 137–58.

AL MTT Titk: Akadémiai Levéltár Magyar Tudományos Tanács Titkársága [Archive of the Academy. Secretariat of the Hungarian Scientific Committee].
Bácskai, Vera (1989) *A vállalkozók előfutárai. Nagykereskedők a reformkori Pesten.* Budapest: Magvető.
Benda, Gyula (1975) 'New Economic History' *Történeti Statisztikai Tanulmányok*, 1: 261–76.
Benda, Gyula (2008) *Zsellérből polgár – Társadalmi változás egy dunántúli kisvárosban. Keszthely társadalma 1740–1849.* Budapest: L'Harmattan.
Berend, T. I. (1983) *Gazdasági útkeresés 1956–1965: A szocialista gazdaság magyarországi modelljének kérdéséhez.* Budapest: Magvető.
Berend, T. I. (1996) *Central and Eastern Europe 1944–1993: Detour from the Periphery to the Periphery*, Cambridge: Cambridge University Press [Hungarian edn. 1997].
Berend, T. I. (2003) *History Derailed: Central and Eastern Europe in the 'Long' Nineteenth Century.* Berkeley: University of California Press.
Berend, T. I. (2009) *History in My Life: A Memoir of Three Eras.* Budapest: CEU Press [Hungarian edn. 1997].
Berend, T. I. and Ránki, György (1955) *Magyarország gyáripara 1900–1914.* Budapest: Szikra.
Berend, T. I. and Ránki, György (1974) *Economic Development of East–Central Europe in the 19th & 20th Centuries.* New York: Columbia University Press [Hungarian edn. 1969].
Berend, T. I. and Ránki, György (1982) *Industrialization and the European Periphery 1780–1914.* Cambridge: Cambridge University Press [Hungarian edn. 1979].
Berger, Stefan, Donovan, Mark and Passmore, Kevin (1999) 'Apologias for the nation-state in Western Europe since 1800', in *Writing National Histories. Western Europe since 1800.* London: Routledge, 3–15.
Berlász, Jenő (1957) 'A Ganz-gyár első félszázada, 1845–1895' *Tanulmányok Budapest Múltjából*, 12: 349–459.
Berlász, Jenő (2010) 'A magyar gazdaság- és társadalomtörténet-írás kialakulása' in *Erdélyi jobbágyság – magyar gazdaság (Válogatott tanulmányok)*, ed. by János Búza and Dietmar Meyer. Budapest: Argumentum [Original edn. 1943].
Bognár, Szabina (2013) "'. . . a hazai gazdaságtörténet alapítójának és mesterének hálás ragaszkodással . . .": Tagányi Károly a Magyar Gazdaságtörténelmi Szemle élén (1894–1901)' *Ethnographia*, 124 (3): 273–97.
Boldizzoni, Francesco (2011) *The Poverty of Clio. Resurrecting Economic History*, Princeton, NJ: Princeton University Press.
Buchner, Thomas (2008) 'Alfons Dopsch (1868–1953). Die "Manningfältigkeit der Verhältnisse"', in *Österreichische Historiker 1900–1945. Lebensläufe und Karrieren in Österreich, Deutschland und der Tschechoslowakei in Wissenschaftsgeschichlichen Porträts*, ed. by Karel Hruza, vol. 1. Vienna: Böhlau, 155–90.
Csíki, Tamás (2003) *Társadalomábrázolások és értelmezések a magyar történeti irodalomban (1945–ig).* Debrecen: Debreceni Egyetem BTK.
Dékány, István (1931) 'Gazdaság- és társadalomtörténet', in *A magyar történetírás új útjai*, ed. by Hóman Bálint. Budapest: Magyar Szemle Társaság, 183–237.
Domanovszky, Sándor (1930) 'Előszó' [Preface] to Edit Jármay and István Bakács, *A regéci uradalom gazdálkodása a XVIII. században.* ('Tanulmányok a magyar mezőgazdaság történetéhez, vol. 1'). Budapest: 3–5.
Domanovszky, Sándor (1931) 'A magyar történetírás új útjai' *Századok*, 65 (7–8): 273–9.
Domanovszky, Sándor [Alexander] (1938) 'Zur Geschichte der Gutsherrschaft in Ungarn', in *Wirtschaft und Kultur. Festschrift zur 70. Geburtstag von Alfons Dopsch.* Baden b. Wien: 441–69.
Domanovszky, Sándor, ed. (1939–43) *Magyar Művelődéstörténet*, 5 vols. Budapest: Magyar Történelmi Társulat.
Domanovszky, Sándor (1939) 'Előszó' [Preface] in Domanovszky (1939–43), vol. 1, 16–17.
Dopsch, Alphons (1968) 'Zur Methodologie der Wirtschaftsgeschichte', in Id., *Gesammelte Aufsätze*, ed. by Erna Patzelt, vol. 1. Aalen: Scientia Verlag, 543–65 [Original edn. 1928].
Eckhart, Ferenc (1928) 'Alphons Dopsch: Verfassungs- und Wirtschaftsgeschichte des Mittelalters. Gesammelte Aufsätze. 1928' *Századok*, 62 (7–8): 828–32.
Eckhart, Ferenc (1941) *A magyar közgazdaság száz éve 1841–1941.* Budapest: Posner.
Eddie, Scott M. (1996) *Ami 'köztudott', az igaz is? Bevezetés a kliometrikus történetírás gondolkodásmódjába.* Debrecen: Csokonai.
Egyed, Ákos (1981) *Falu, város, civilizáció: tanulmányok a jobbágyfelszabadítás és a kapitalizmus történetéből Erdélyben 1848–1914.* Bucharest: Kriterion.

Erdmann, Karl Dietrich (2005) *Toward a Global Community of Historians: The International Historical Congress and the International Committee of Historical Science 1898–2000*, ed. by J. Kocka and W. J. Mommsen. Oxford: Berghahn.

Erős, Vilmos, ed. (2003) *A harmadik út felé. Szabó István történész cikkekben és dokumentumokban*. Budapest: Lucidus.

Erős, Vilmos (2012) *A szellemtörténettől a népiségtörténetig. Tanulmányok a két világháború közötti magyar történetírásról*. Debrecen: Debrecen University Press.

Futó, Mihály (1944) *A magyar gyáripar története*. Budapest: Magyar Gazdaságkutató Intézet.

Germuska, Pál (2010) *Vörös arzenál. Magyarország részvétele a nemzetközi hadiipari együttműködésben a KGST keretei között*. Budapest: Argumentum.

Glatz, Ferenc (1980) *Történetíró és politika. Szekfű, Steier, Thim és Miskolczy nemzetről és államról*. Budapest: Akadémiai.

Glatz, Ferenc (1988) 'Domanovszky Sándor. Történetíró és tudományszervező' in *Nemzeti kultúra – kulturált nemzet 1867–1987*. Budapest: Kossuth, 242–75.

Granasztói, György (1984) 'Egy történész időszerűsége – Domanovszky Sándor' *Történelmi Szemle*, 27 (1–2): 302–12.

Gross, Nachum T. (1972) 'The triumph of quantitative economic history in Budapest' *Journal of European Economic History*, 1: 153–61.

Gunst, Peter (1961) *Acsády Ignác történetírása*. Budapest: Akadémiai.

Gyömrei, Sándor (1932) 'A magyar gazdaságtörténet-írás új útja' *Közgazdasági Szemle*, 56: 661–9.

Halmos, Károly (2008) *Családi kapitalizmus*. Budapest: UMK.

Hanák, Péter (1982) 'The relationship between family enterprise and managerial enterprise (Hungary in the 19th and early 20th centuries)', in *From Family Firm to Professional Management: Structure and Performance of Business Enterprise*, ed. by Leslie Hannah. Budapest: 39–49.

Hanák, Péter and Hanák, Katalin (1964) *A Magyar Pamutipar története* 1887–1962. Budapest: PNyV.

Hoffmann, Alfred (1979) 'Alfons Dopsch und die Wiener Schule der Wirtschafts- und Sozialgeschichte' in Id., *Studien und Essays*, ed. by Alois Mosser, vol. 1. Vienna: 57–61.

Hóman, Bálint and Szekfű, Gyula (1928–34) *Magyar történet*, 8 vols. Budapest: Egyetemi nyomda.

Imreh, István (1979) *Erdélyi hétköznapok. Társadalom- és gazdaságtörténeti írások a bomló feudalizmus időszakából*. Bucharest: Kriterion.

Iványi-Grünwald, Béla ifj. (1933) 'Vita a gazdaságtörténet módszeréről' *Közgazdasági Szemle*, 57: 360–76.

Izsépy, Edit (1969) 'A Magyar Gazdaságtörténelmi Szemle történetéhez' *Századok*, 103 (5–6): 1077–104.

Kaposi, Zoltán (2001) 'A magyarországi uradalmi rendszer változásai a XVIII–XX. században' *Agrártörténelmi Szemle*, 43 (1–2): 239–61.

Kaposi, Zoltán (2007) *Die Entwicklung der Wirtschaft und Gesellschaft in Ungarn 1700–2000*. Passau: Schenk Verlag.

Katus, László (1970) 'Economic growth in Hungary during the Age of Dualism (1867–1913). A quantitative analysis', in *Socio-Economic Researches on the History of East–Central Europe*. Budapest: 35–129.

Katus, László (2007) '"Meghallani a sokszólamú zenét, az emberi történelmet": Bódy Zsombor és Cieger András beszélgetése Katus Lászlóval' *Századvég*, 45 (3): 123–72.

Klement, Judit (2012) *Hazai vállalkozók a hőskorban. A budapesti gőzmalomipar vállalkozói a 19. század második felében*. Budapest: ELTE Eötvös Kiadó.

Komlos, John (1990) *Az Osztrák-Magyar Monarchia mint közös piac*. Budapest: Maecenas [Hungarian transl. of *The Habsburg Monarchy as a Customs Union*. Princeton, NJ: Princeton University Press, 1983].

Kováts, Ferenc (1902) *Nyugatmagyarország áruforgalma a* XV. *században a pozsonyi harmincadkönyv alapján. Történet-statisztikai tanulmány*. Budapest: Politzer.

Kováts, Franz (1903) 'Ungarische Bibliographie 1900–1902' *VSWG*, 1: 605–17.

Kövér, György (1991) 'The Austro-Hungarian banking system', in *International Banking 1870–1914*, ed. by Rondo Cameron and V. I. Bovykin. Oxford: Oxford University Press, 319–45.

Kövér, György (2009) 'The economic achievements on the Austro-Hungarian Monarchy: scale and speed', in *The Austro-Hungarian Monarchy Revisited*, ed. by András Gerő. Boulder, CO: Social Science Monographs: 51–83.

Kövér, György (2012) 'A magyar történettudomány első ötéves terve és a gazdaságtörténet-írás', in *Tudomány és ideológia között*, ed. By Vilmos Erős and Ádám Takács. Budapest: Eötvös Kiadó, 22–43.

Kövér, György (2013) 'A Magyar Gazdaságtörténelmi Szemle (1894–1906) gazdaságtörténete. Intézményi megközelítés és historiográfia' *Történelmi Szemle,* 55 (2): 201–24.
Kövér, György and Pogány, Ágnes (2002) *Die binationale Bank einer multinationalen Monarchie. Die Österreichisch-Ungarische Bank (1878–1922).* (Beiträge zur Wirtschafts- und Sozialgeschichte 94.) Stuttgart: Franz Steiner Verlag.
Kring, Miklós (1937) 'Węgierska historiografia społeczno-gospodarcza w ostatnich 25 latach' *Roczniki dziejów spolecznych i gospodarczych* (Poznan), 6: 232–4.
Kubinyi, András, Laszlovszky, József and Szabó, Péter, eds. (2008) *Gazdaság és gazdálkodás a középkori Magyarországon: gazdaságtörténet, anyagi kultúra, régészet.* Budapest: Martin Opitz Kiadó.
Lederer, Emma (1933) 'A legújabb gazdaságtörténeti irodalom problémái' *Századok* 67 (1–3): 12–37.
Lederer, Emma (1952) *Az ipari kapitalizmus kezdetei Magyarországon.* Budapest: Közoktatásügyi Kiadó.
Lederer, Emma (1969) *A magyar polgári történetírás rövid története.* Budapest: Kossuth.
MGtSZ: *Magyar Gazdaságtörténelmi Szemle* (1894–1906).
Makkai, László (1954) *I. Rákóczi György birtokainak gazdasági iratai (1631–1648).* Budapest: Akadémiai kiadó.
Makkai, László (1970) 'Les caractères originaux de l'histoire économique et sociale de l'Europe orientale pendant le Moyen Age' *Acta Historica Academiae Scientarium Hungaricae,* 16 (3–4): 261–87.
Makkai, László (1982) 'Grand domaine et petites exploitations, seigneur et paysan en Europe au Moyen Age et aux temps modernes', *Eighth International Economic History Congress, (Budapest): 'A' Themes.* Budapest: Akadémiai Kiadó, 3–44.
MTA KIK Kt: Magyar Tudományos Akadémia Könyvtár és Információs Központ Kézirattára [Hungarian Academy of Sciences, Library and Information Centre, Manuscript Department].
Mérei Gyula (1951) *Magyar iparfejlődés 1790–1848.* Budapest: Közoktatásügyi Kiadó.
Nagy Balázs (2012) 'The study of medieval foreign trade in Hungary: a historiographical overview', in *Cities, Coins, Commerce.* (Essays presented to Jan Blanchard on the Occasion of his 70th Birthday), ed. by Philipp R. Rössner. Stuttgart: Franz Steiner Verlag, 65–77.
Niederhauser, Emil (1958) 'Zur Frage der Osteuropäischen Entwicklung' *Studia Slavica,* IV (3–4): 359–71.
Niederhauser, Emil (1989) 'A gazdaságtörténet-írás kialakulása Kelet-Európában', in *Gazdaság, társadalom, történetírás. Emlékkönyv Pach Zsigmond Pál 70. születésnapjára,* ed. by Ferenc Glatz. Budapest: MTA TTI, 181–95.
OMGE: Országos Magyar Gazdasági Egyesület [Hungarian National Economic Association].
OSzK Kt: Országos Széchényi Könyvtár Kézirattár [National Széchényi Library, Manuscript Department].
Pach, Zsigmond Pál (1943) Az Orczy birtokok ipari gazdálkodása a XVIII. sz.végén. A hagymási timsóház (1789–1825) [The industrial branch of the Orczy estates at the end of the XVIII century. The Alum factory of Hagymás] MTA KIK Kézirattár Ms 4538/11.
Pach, Zsigmond Pál (1952) *Az eredeti tőkefelhalmozás Magyarországon.* Budapest: Szikra.
Pach, Zsigmond Pál (1960) 'Die Abbiegung der Ungarischen Agrarentwicklung von der Westeuropäischen (Zur Frage der Eigentümlichkeiten des Überganges vom Feudalismus zum Kapitalismus in Ungarn)', in *XIe Congrès International des Sciences Historiques (Stockholm). Résumés des communications*: 154–6.
Pach, Zsigmond Pál (1994) *Hungary and the European Economy in Early Modern Times.* Aldershot: Ashgate.
Pach, Zsigmond Pál and Sándor, Pál, eds. (1956) *Tanulmányok a kapitalizmus történetéhez Magyarországon 1867–1918.* Budapest: Szikra.
Paulinyi, Oszkár (2005) *Gazdag föld – szegény ország. Tanulmányok a magyarországi bányaművelés múltjából,* ed. by János Buza and István Draskóczy. Budapest.
Péter, László (1999) 'Central Europe and its readings into the past' *European Review of History,* 6 (1): 101–11.
Péteri, György (1998) *Academia and State Socialism.* Boulder, CO: Social Science Monographs.
Pető, Iván and Szakács, Sándor (1985) *A hazai gazdaság négy évtizedének története 1945–1985,* vol. I: *Az újjáépítés és a tervutasításos irányítás időszaka 1945–1968.* Budapest: KJK.
Pogány, Ágnes (1999) 'Business history in Ungarn', in *Business History. Wissenschaftliche Entwicklungstrends und Studien aus Zentraleuropa,* ed. by Alice Teichova, Herbert Matis and Andreas Resch. Vienna: Manz. 77–87.
Ránki, György (1977) *Közgazdaság és történelem – a gazdaságtörténet válaszútjai.* Budapest: Akadémiai.
Ránki, György (1988) 'John Komlos: the Habsburg Monarchy as a customs union' *Századok,* 122 (3): 509–11.

Romsics, Ignác (2011) *Clio bűvöletében. Magyar történetírás a 19–20. században – nemzetközi kitekintéssel.* Budapest: Osiris.

Sándor, Vilmos (1954) *Nagyipari fejlődés Magyarországon 1867–1900.* Budapest: Szikra.

Szabad, György (1957) *A tatai és gesztesi Eszterházy-uradalom áttérése a robotrendszerről a tőkés gazdálkodásra.* Budapest: Akadémiai.

Szabó, István, ed. (1960) *Agrártörténeti tanulmányok.* Budapest: Tankönyvkiadó.

Szabó, István, ed. (1965) *A parasztság Magyarországon a kapitalizmus korában 1848–1914.* Budapest: Akadémiai.

Szulovszky, János (2002) 'Harminc év publikációi. Az MTA VEAB Kézművesipartörténeti Munkabizottsága kiadványainak tartalommutatója (1972–2002)', in *X. Kézművesipartörténeti Szimpozium.* Budapest: 171–99.

Szűcs, Jenő (1955) *Városok és kézművesség a XV. századi Magyarországon.* Budapest: Művelt Nép.

Szűcs, Jenő (1985) *Les trois Europes*, preface by Fernand Braudel. Paris: L'Harmattan.

Takáts, Sándor (1903) 'Két világkereskedelmi cikkünk a XVIII. században' *MGtSz,* 10: 97–153.

Thallóczy, Lajos (1879) *A kamara haszna (lucrum camerae) története – kapcsolatban a magyar adó- és pénzügy fejlődésével.* Budapest.

Tomka, Béla (2001) 'The development of Hungarian banking, 1880–1931: an international comparison' *Journal of European Economic History,* 30 (1): 125–62.

Tomka, Béla (2004) *Welfare in East and West: Hungarian Social Security in an International Comparison 1918–1990.* Berlin: Akademie Verlag.

Tomka, Béla (2013) *A Social History of Twentieth-Century Europe.* London: Routledge.

Tóth, Tibor (1982) 'Profitability and cost-efficiency in Hungarian agriculture in the 1930s' *Journal of European Economic History,* 11 (1): 157–64.

Tóth, Zoltán (1989) *Szekszárd társadalma a századfordulón. Történelmi rétegződés és társadalmi átrétegződés a polgári átalakulásban.* Budapest: Akadémiai Kiadó.

Trencsényi, Balázs and Apor, Péter (2007) 'Fine-tuning the polyphoning past: Hungarian history writing in the 1990s', in *Narratives Unbound: Historical Studies in Post Communist Eastern Europe*, ed. by Sorin Antohi, Balázs Trencsényi and Péter Apor. Budapest: CEU Press, 1–99.

Ujváry, Gábor (1996) *Tudományszervezés – történetkutatás – forráskritika. Klebelsberg Kuno és a Bécsi Magyar Történeti Intézet.* Győr: Győr-Moson-Sopron Megye Győri Levéltára.

Vardy, Steven Bela (1976) *Modern Hungarian Historiography.* Boulder, CO: East European Quarterly.

Vári, András (2008) *Herren und Landwirte. Ungarische Aristokraten und Agrarier auf dem Weg in die Moderne (1821–1910).* Wiesbaden: Harrassowitz Verlag.

R. Várkonyi, Ágnes (1973) *A pozitivista történetszemlélet a magyar történetírásban I–II.* Budapest: Akadémiai Kiadó.

Wallerstein, Immanuel (1980) *The Modern World-System* II. *Mercantilism and the Consolidation of the European World-Economy, 1600–1750.* New York: Academic Press.

Weisz, Béla (1878) *Bevezetés a gazdaságtörténetbe.* Budapest.

Wellmann, Imre (1937) 'Mezőgazdaságtörténetünk új útjai', in *Emlékkönyv Domanovszky Sándor születése hatvanadik fordulójának ünnepére. 1937. május 27.* Budapest: 664–714.

Wittman, Tibor (1957) *Az 'árforradalom' és a világpiaci kapcsolatok kezdeti mozzanatai (1566–1618).* Budapest: Akadémiai.

Wittman, Tibor (1970–71) 'Triángulo o cuadrángulo económico? Acerca del desenvolvimiento del mercado mundial visto desde Europa Central' *Anuario. Instituto de Antropología e Historia* (Caracas), 7–8: 457–72.

Zorn, Wolfgang (1985) '"Volkswirtschaft und Kulturgeschichte" und "Sozial- und Wirtschaftsgeschichte". Zwei Zeitschriften in der Vorgeschichte der VSWG 1863–1900' *VSWG,* 72 (4): 457–75.

Zimányi, Vera (1973) 'Mouvements des prix hongrois et l'évolution europeénne (XVIe–XVIIIe siècle)' *Acta Historica Academiae Scientiarum Hungaricae,* 19: 305–33.

PART IV

The wider world

16
ECONOMIC HISTORY IN MIDDLE EURASIA

Beyond histories of stagnation and deficiencies

Huri Islamoglu[1]

A central question of economic history since the nineteenth century has been why capitalist development (often identified with the transformations of modernity) took place in Western Europe and not elsewhere especially in China and Islamic lands which experienced early commercial expansion and the beginnings of industrial development. This question coincided with the establishment of European rule in non-European regions, particularly in Asia. Underlining the difference between the West and the others and acknowledging the superiority of one over the other became indispensable to the legitimation of the European presence in, and domination over, non-European regions. Accordingly, the writing of non-European histories was subjected to terms of comparison with Europe and trapped in a binary vision of world history, contrasting what Europe had with what others lacked. At issue were divergent institutional responses to changing conditions of trade and production. European responses were understood to have been conducive to economic growth and development resulting in Europe's prosperity and progress, while inappropriate responses by non-European societies were the reason for their poverty and lack of progress. The result was a dichotomous view of world history with cultural factors, religious or political, often serving to explain differences.

This chapter will address how economic historians of Middle Eurasia situated their histories in relation to world history, responding to changes in world historical contexts since the Second World War and to societal and political concerns in different areas of the region. With respect to the latter it is important to note that economic history spoke to immediate societal concerns at various points in time. These ranged from nation and state building, to critiques of free-tradism or of statist models of economic development, just as Eurocentric economic histories had spoken to concerns regarding the establishment of European domination. Eurocentric dichotomous visions of world history subordinating non-European histories to the European experience remained a reference point for Middle Eurasian economic historians, often delimiting or defining the questions they asked of history and their subject matter. Yet in the past few years changes in the world historical context, with the possibility of multipolar leadership in the global economy and the rising power of China, have served to demonstrate the limits of European world domination. Most importantly, they have pointed to the limits of understanding the world in terms of irreconcilable differences.

Middle Eurasia addressed here corresponds to what Marshal Hodgson called the 'Afro-Eurasian Oikoumene': the world extending from the Indian Ocean and northern India to

Afghanistan and Central Asia; and to Iran and Ottoman territories in Caucasia. It is a vast area encompassing the Anatolian plateau, Iraq, Syria, Palestine and the southeastern Mediterranean up to Egypt and North Africa. Islam was a common cultural input in the societal fabric which knitted together these different regions. Islam also provided explanations for their institutional deficiencies, their perceived divergence from a world historical course identified with Europe and its history. Max Weber (1978) in the nineteenth century attributed the stagnation of Islamic societies to the fact that Islam, unlike Protestantism, did not allow for a liberation of its law from ethical and religious concerns. This meant that Islamic law could not be 'rationalized' and put in the service of generating institutionally innovative responses to changing social conditions enabling market development. More recently, Timur Kuran (2011) once again evoked the specter of Islamic law impeding the formation of the key institutions of capitalist market societies, most notably corporations.[2] The vicissitudes of early modern Middle Eurasia, from the fifteenth century onwards, have often been identified with those of the Ottoman, Safavid and Mughal empires that shaped the histories of their regions. Therefore a political culture of authoritarian states, or 'Oriental despotism', was often called upon to explain Middle Eurasia's world historical failure or limited development (Islamoglu 1987).[3]

Since the 1990s Oriental despotism was given a facelift by liberal economic historians. In the rather defensive tone of post-colonial nativism, they sought to revise the despotic image by highlighting the benevolent-king traditions of ancient Iranian statecraft, somewhat re-fashioned to fit the role of night-watchman states with free-tradist understandings. For instance, Pamuk (2004) referred to a pragmatist disposition or culture of the Ottoman state as accounting for the Empire's longevity throughout the early modern period.[4] This state culture enabled multiple institutional responses to conditions of commercial expansion and inter-state competition, most importantly with respect to financial institutions. At the same time it accommodated multiple societal interests under changing conditions. Pamuk also pointed to the limits of the pragmatic culture as the state intensified its interventions in the economy and the society in the nineteenth century. In doing so it impeded capitalist market development in the Ottoman territories, leading to the Empire's subjection to European commercial imperatives and political collapse.[5] Pamuk's analysis, while pointing to early modern institutional innovativeness of the Ottoman government, in a commercial environment, did not escape the lure of blaming the autocratic nature of the government and its tendency to meddle in society. Pamuk's perspective provided a glimpse of vibrancy and responsiveness in Ottoman institutional history stemming from its pragmatic cultural disposition. But, in a dramatic act of reversal disturbingly reminiscent of orientalist cultural/essentialist images of the nineteenth century, where cultural essences became exhausted as they moved through history, he pointed to the limits of that culture and of Ottoman commercial development in the free-tradist liberal age of the nineteenth century which belonged to Europe.

Acemoglu and Robinson (2012) went further in casting those 'limits' in irrevocable flows of history and of historically grounded absences and presences of institutions in the East and the West. In addressing the issue of politics underlying state power in commercial contexts they drew attention to the nature of such politics and its institutions. They argued that whether or not politics, in the commercial environment, was premised on participatory/representative institutions affected the nature and sustainability of economic growth and its consequences. The presence of representative/participatory political institutions in past and present-day Europe (with an eye on the Anglo-Saxon world) accounted for sustainable economic growth while their supposed absence, and the prominence of autocratic institutions in non-European regions (including China and Turkey), pointed in the direction of unsustainable growth, notwithstanding the spectacular growth rates many of these areas are registering currently. In arguing this, Acemoglu and Robinson bring us back full circle to a dichotomous vision of world history, of irrevocable differences between the East and the West this time carved in a specter of autocratic/despotic non-Europe facing a democratic Europe. Unlike the situation in the nineteenth century, this dichotomous vision of world history did not so much legitimize Europe's singular economic/political superiority but claimed a difference for Europe in an increasingly multipolar global economy.

The dichotomous vision of world history, with its various explanations rooted in political or religious culture, are traceable to a nineteenth-century Orientalism or a body of knowledge about non-European regions. Orientalist knowledge originated in the environment of maritime ventures of European traders (Dutch and English) in open seas unimpeded by states or religion.[6] Steeped in the free-tradist *Weltanschauung* of the eighteenth and nineteenth centuries, Orientalist visions of world history embodied images of a civilized West, with its commercial economy enabled by the initiative of individuals enjoying representative governments and endowed with natural rights and liberties protected by the law. This faced an uncivilized East, agrarian and impoverished, where individual initiative was stifled by despotic governments and by lack of law protecting individual rights and liberties. Evoked at another moment of expansion of Western world trade in the late twentieth century, this vision became intimately linked to 'reformist' or civilizing discourse assigning the West the mission of introducing into non-European regions what they lacked historically and culturally and recreating those regions in the image of the West.[7] The promise of 'modernization'/ Westernization served to legitimize Europe's domination. Reforms sought to ensure the expansion of European trade including protection of the rights and liberties of European traders, investors and their representatives who, in the nineteenth century, had been chosen from among members of ethnic and religious minorities (Lewis 1968; Davison 1963).

With the development of national capitalist economies in the nineteenth century, 'the image of the West' no longer focused on the commercial activities of individuals unimpeded by states, or the Church. Following Weber, it focused on institutions, most importantly on rational bureaucratic states and on the role of law in enabling the institutions of industrial capitalist economies. It spoke to concerns of the commercial middle classes. In the case of Middle Eurasia (as elsewhere in Asia) the absence of rational institutions, attributed to their religious or political cultures, was understood to have held back their modernization. This perspective dominated the social sciences in the post-Second World War era with cultural features serving to explain the 'deficiencies' and 'underdevelopment' of Middle Eurasian regions in common with the rest of Asia and Africa (Lockman 2009).

Perspectives on modernization highlighting the role of institutions also prevailed in the economic history writing of Middle Eurasian regions. Historical research explored the institutions of Ottoman, Safavid, Mughal imperial states, most notably those of central administrations, military organizations and agrarian systems (Barkan 1943; Habib 1963; Lambton 1969; Inalcik 1973). These economic histories highlighted the secular character of early history pointing to the priority of a notion of justice, rooted in ancient Iranian traditions of statecraft. They embodied a conception of Middle Eurasian histories in terms of a 'golden age' and 'decline' similar to the Western civilizational perspectives of the nineteenth century. At the same time, these histories were responding to concerns arising from the making of secular modern states in India following the end of British rule, in Turkey, following the collapse of the Ottoman Empire, and in Iran, following the end of the Qajar dynasty. Secularist approaches often attributed the responsibility for the empires' decline to the resurgence of Islamic politics (Inalcik 1992).

Free-tradist Orientalism in the nineteenth and early twentieth centuries joined with a civilizational vision of world history (which enjoyed a revival in the wake of 9/11). In this vision, embroiled in the drama of the rise and fall of civilizations, Eastern civilizations, including the Islamic civilization, had their golden age in the past, but the nineteenth-century modern era was one in which Europe dominated the world from its civilizational heights (Gibb and Bowen 1969). The civilizational perspective also assumed an irreconcilability of the cultural essences of different civilizations. In the nineteenth century, that understanding of irreconcilability was not universally shared (as it came to be in the early twenty-first century). Universal histories of the late Ottoman era, while assessing Europe's place in modern history, also sought to determine the place of Ottoman history in that modernity, nowhere identifying that experience entirely with Europe (Toksoz 2012). This identification came later following the collapse of the Empire, when a generation of historians and elites looked at Europe as a benchmark for measuring the deficiency of their own histories.

The counter-reaction this time occurred at the beginning of the twenty-first century when a new generation of Islamist elites and historians took up the Western challenge of 'clash of civilizations' and highlighted the specificity and uniqueness of Islamic civilization. One dimension of this perspective overlapped with postmodernist trends of the 1990s and 2000s, with their decentering drive and their focus on the early modern era. It saw Islamic institutions as the mainstays of civil society: by establishing connections between society and the state, they ensured consensus over state authority (Akarli 2005). The decline of these Islamic institutions was blamed upon the development of Westernized, modern, secular states.[8] This understanding of the distinctiveness of Islamic civilization does not simply refer to the past but is extended to the present and into the future. Present-day Islamic states, as well as Islamic global organizations (seeking to build solidarity blocs in the global economy) look for institutional solutions in idealized Islamic institutions, most significantly those related to the regulation of financial markets as well as wealth distributive mechanisms (such as *waqfs* or pious endowments). Historical research engaged in uncovering these institutions, in order to examine the cultural distinctiveness of Islamic societies, has become instrumental in the building of that distinctiveness in the present and into the future (Cizakca 2013).

Looking beyond divided world histories: Braudel's vision of world history in Middle Eurasian mirrors

The Second World War signaled the twilight of Europe's world domination and crowned the rise of the US. Fernand Braudel's *Mediterranean*, written during the war, addressed the moment of Europe's dawn, looking beyond what divided world history to what united it. It posed a challenge to the dichotomous perceptions of world history with their ideological totalizing of Europe and non-Europe (Braudel 1966). Braudel's history captured the Mediterranean world at its zenith in the sixteenth century, united by geography and economic activity across the majestic sea and its coastal regions. This was a world flanked at both ends by two grand empires, Spanish Habsburg and the Ottoman, securing regional and interregional trade, linking towns to their hinterlands populated by peasant cultivators and nomadic pastoralists. The Mediterranean, with its trade routes, was the center of an economic system which, at the end of the sixteenth century, would shift towards the Atlantic signaling a dominance of the Dutch and the English. The depiction of that moment lent Braudel's history a bittersweet poignancy as he himself stood at the start of a new era, at the end of Europe's war, and of another shift of the center of the world economy to the Atlantic, this time to

North America. His vision of the unified history of the Mediterranean represented an aspiration for a united Europe and became an inspiration for the later European Union.

In the 1950s, for historians of the Ottoman Empire, Braudel's conception of a unified world history, beyond demarcation of East and West, Europe and non-Europe, offered a possibility of bringing the history of Ottoman territories back into the mainstream of world history. Nineteenth-century European Orientalism relegated (albeit awkwardly) Ottoman history to a defunct East, the domain of Islamic civilization. The Turkish republic, the main successor state to the Ottoman Empire, seeking to distance itself from the 'nightmare of the East' embraced a Westernist, secular identity. Braudel's view of Ottoman territories as part of a wider geographical/economic landscape, as part of a European (or global) historical drama of shifting world trade routes towards the Atlantic, served to confirm that distance. In other words, Ottoman economic historians of the 1950s did not draw on Braudel's work to question the Orientalist perspective on world history. For them, Braudel's view of the unity of the Mediterranean, by including the Ottomans among European Mediterrranean empires, simply pushed back the boundaries of the East which secular Westernist Ottoman histories presented as posing a cultural threat, most importantly in the form of Islam to which, in their view, the Empire had succumbed after the sixteenth century (Inalcik 1994). The implications of Braudel's work were addressed by historians of other Middle Eurasian regions in the 1980s and 1990s, a time of global economic expansion and the opening up of previously closed areas to world trade.

Braudel's world historical vision addressed the domain of economic activity, opening possibilities for comparative histories of different 'economies', beyond institutional aspects, while at the same time including the latter in a conception of total history. In the 1950s, a research group formed by O. L. Barkan, a leading Ottomanist inspired by Braudel and his team at the Ecole des Hautes Etudes en Sciences Sociales, set out to publish hundreds of Ottoman tax registers from which population and production data for the Ottoman Eastern Mediterranean could be gleaned (Barkan 1957). This was indeed research of world historical significance providing the economic history of the Ottoman Empire with a valuable quantitative dimension for the first time. This served to repatriate (if not legitimize) Ottoman history, much maligned since the Empire's defeat in the First World War. That history had represented a colonial past of backwardness and Islamic obscurantism in the Arab lands, the Balkans and Anatolia, now the backbone of the secular Turkish republic. Historians working on data on population and production turned to the sixteenth century as the golden age of the Empire, a time of economic prosperity based on agricultural and artisanal production in towns and of social peace secured and enabled by the efficiency of the Ottoman state and its institutions, committed to ensuring social justice (Barkan 1943; Inalcik 1973). State institutions and state power also enabled Ottoman territories to be an entrepôt not only for Mediterranean trade but also for the spice trade (as well as trade in dyes and textiles) from India via the Persian Gulf, and the silk trade connecting Iran to Ottoman towns (most notably Bursa) and the latter to Europe via Venice (Inalcik 1978 and 1994).

This economic history placed a strong emphasis on the state, mirroring economic concerns in the post-Depression interwar era. But Braudel himself was not averse to highlighting the state's role in the economy. He pointed to the role of imperial power in the making of the Ottoman as well as the Spanish empire (Braudel 1979, vol. III). Ottoman historians, on the other hand, traced the Ottoman state and its institutions back to ancient traditions of statecraft in Central Asia and Iran predating Islam (Inalcik 1994). This repatriated Ottoman history emphasized the secular and non-Islamic character of the state and its laws.[9] In fact, for Barkan (1943), and still for Inalcik (1992), 'Islamization' of law definitely contributed to Ottoman decline in terms of the deterioration of 'classical' institutions and the onset of Islamic ones. In this, they somewhat conceded to Weberian/Orientalist Islam-bashing for explanations of later Ottoman institutional depravation and degeneration. From the standpoint of these secular statist economic histories, Islamization of law encouraged the expansion of private ownership at the expense of state interests, posing a threat to the principles of distributive justice traditionally embodied in the Ottoman state (Inalcik 1992). In this perspective, Westernization was an evil only preferable to Islamization. At the same time, to demonstrate his distance from the West, Inalcik was careful not to credit Europe with the introduction of secularism. He viewed it as a pillar of Turkish republican ideology, grounding secular measures in pre-Islamic statecraft traditions adopted during the golden age of the Empire.

A second generation of Ottoman historians, Barkan's students at Istanbul University, still focusing on state institutions (and basing their research on state archival documents) extended their work beyond the sixteenth into the eighteenth century (Cezzar 1986; Guran 1998; Genc 2000) though increasingly with little impact as global trends in economic history were moving away from the accent on state building.

The world-systems perspective: a tradist Eurocentrism

In the 1960s the prevalence of culturalist explanations of the plight of post-colonial societies in Asia and Africa, represented by modernization theory, had obscured the world historical perspectives of the years immediately following the Second World War. In the 1970s Wallerstein's world-systems view rejected culturalist explanations of 'underdevelopment' in non-European post-colonial areas; it reverted to the world historical processes identified by Braudel in his account of the 'decline' of the late-sixteenth-century Mediterranean, to explain the modern subordination of non-European regions. For Wallerstein (1974), European domination in maritime trade began in the fifteenth century. First, the discovery of the Cape route resulted in a shift of the overland silk and spice trade to this route, and increased the control of India Ocean trade by European traders. Second, in the seventeenth century, the shift in world trade away from the Mediterranean to the Atlantic started a worldwide trend of subordination of non-European regions to the exigencies of European trade or their incorporation into the European sphere. The latter process spelled peripheralization of non-European regions involving the transformation of their production systems leading to a disappearance of their artisanal production in the face of competition from European industrial products. Peasant production gave way to estate economies producing raw materials and foodstuffs for the industrial European economies. It also involved the formation of 'weak' states which simply served to facilitate European trade in their regions. Peripheralization in Asian and African regions accounted for the lack of industrial development, the experience of famines and poverty, and government by military regimes, oppressive to their populations and subordinate to Western commercial interests. It also largely accounted for the 'development' of European areas as the destination for surpluses of the periphery and the ongoing divergence between a developed Europe and underdeveloped non-European regions. Most significantly, from a Wallersteinian perspective, the predicament of the non-European periphery was structural. It was condemned to a state of relative underdevelopment vis-à-vis a developed Europe: a modernization in reverse.

The world-systems perspective was embraced by historians based in Middle Eurasia (as it was by historians in other regions adversely affected by Western expansion, see for example chapter 20), and initially by Ottoman historians. This was a time of disillusionment with the West in post-colonial Third World areas. In the Cold War era, several Middle Eurasian countries experienced economic deprivation and oppressive military regimes supported by American governments. The Israeli aggression and occupation of Arab territories, too, prompted the rise of anti-colonial politics in the 1960s and 1970s of which the world-systems perspective was very much a part.

The world-systems approach provided historians of Middle Eurasia with an opening away from the emphasis upon institutional involutions and from torturous processes of internalizing perceived failures through reference to their own cultures (religious or political) and hence getting entrapped in a perpetual cycle of self-hatred followed by bouts of aggressive defensiveness. More specifically, in relation to Ottoman economic history, where it was first introduced (Islamoglu and Keyder 1977), the world-systems conceptualization had the effect of historicizing a unity of the different nation states in the Arab Middle East, North Africa and the Balkans. Previously, nationalist (as well as socialist) histories had dismissed the Ottoman past as corrupt, despotic and religiously obscurantist. What these histories perceived as Ottoman colonial rule was held responsible for the deprivation of the different imperial regions. The world-systems perspective simply shifted the responsibility for the deprivation of imperial territories to European commercial expansion since the seventeenth century. The history of the Empire's peripheralization provided a common world historical reference, unifying the histories of the different regions of the Empire (Islamoglu 1987; Owen 1993; Todorova 2009) and of other Middle Eurasian regions, including Iran – all unified in their subordination to European trade and power (Nashat 1981; Foran 1989). Research primarily focused on port-cities (Keyder et al. 1993); on European trade (Owen 1981); on structures of financial dependency, for example public debt administration; and on changing patterns of industrial production to meet European demand (Owen 1987; Quataert 1993). Transformations in the organization of agricultural production as well as the resilience of peasant production were also a preoccupation (Pamuk 1987).

Notwithstanding its anti-colonial politics, the world-systems vision of world history was one that was divided structurally and historically. It was also Eurocentric in privileging the history of Europe and European commercial development prior to the seventeenth century. And, by condemning non-European regions to trade subordination, it read their development through the terms of that subordination and through institutions enabling it. The world-systems perspective viewed the Ottoman Empire, prior to its peripheralization, as a world empire whereby the political logic of the state apparatus subordinated all economic activity (mostly reduced to the agrarian economy and peasant household production) to the dictates of its concern for tax collection. This conception conformed to a Marxian view of the Asiatic Mode of Production (AMP), with its mammoth state not allowing any intermediary structures (such as commercial classes) to develop and laying full claim to surpluses produced by peasant households in closed village communities. European commercial demand penetrated this essentially stagnant economy shaping it to its requirements (Abrahamian 1974; Keyder 1976).

This was, of course, a very different conception of the Ottoman Empire from that of Braudel who identified the Empire in the sixteenth century as a 'world-economy' (*économie monde*), an imperial power resting on the taxation of large agricultural producers, as well as traders but also promoting a significant level of economic prosperity. Braudel could imagine a state presence in the Ottoman Empire which from a Wallersteinian perspective was not admissible. For Wallerstein the 'strong' surplus-extracting imperial state was identified as the despot of the AMP, antithetical to commercial relations. The weak states of peripheral Asian development were seen as accommodative of European trade penetration (Wallerstein et al. 1987). By contrast, European states of the core were described as strong and 'enabling' the market activities of commercial actors. Braudel had emphasized the unity of the Mediterranean world, inclusive of different world economies (governed by imperial power in Ottoman and Spanish Habsburg lands); he did not envision a division in that world between world economies and world empires.

Recently, Faruk Tabak's important posthumous work has questioned the Wallersteinian vision of a historically divided world. In line with Braudel's understanding of a unity of the Mediterranean prior to its decline, Tabak's history shows that decline was a prolonged process, not solely due to shifts to Atlantic trade but also to a host of environmental factors lasting until the early nineteenth century. He insists that all Mediterranean regions, including the Ottoman, shared in that process (Tabak 2008). Hence, Tabak refers to the 'Mediterranean autumn' in the seventeenth and eighteenth centuries due to shifts in agrarian cycles occasioned by climatic changes and declining population, as well as shifts in cereal production to the Baltic regions, responding to demand from Northwestern Europe. It meant an end to large scale production of cereals and cotton, making way for peasant share-cropping economies producing olives and fruits, and for pastoral nomadism. For Tabak, this 'autumn' of the Mediterranean world economy, signaling its involution, was finally reversed with the growth of European demand, especially British demand, after 1815.

Notwithstanding its conceptual flaws, the world-systems perspective provided a generation of Middle Eurasian historians in the 1980s into the 1990s with an impetus to think about the histories of the Ottoman Empire (as well as other areas in Middle and Eastern Eurasia) in world historical terms and in relation to their economic structures. Braudel's world historical vision had had a similar effect on a previous generation. The world-systems perspective also led to an ongoing debate about the role of European trade in these histories. One aspect of that debate has been to counter the stagnationist view of the 'periphery' by focusing upon the analysis of internal dynamics (including economic organization, the nature of state power and government) (Islamoglu 1994; Faroqhi 1994; Toksoz 2010). This resulted in questioning the world-systems approach's emphasis on the impact of European trade in the region's transformation. It also led to attempts to qualify that influence in light of the internal dynamics of the region (economic as well as administrative) and as part of processes involving continual interactions and confrontations among different European and Middle Eurasian actors (Islamoglu 1987; Pamuk 1987; Kiyotaki 1997; Blumi 2005). Finally, objecting to the world-systems perspective's denial of agency to Middle Eurasian peripheries, indigenous historical research has pointed to societal resistance to European trade penetration on the part of workers, peasants, merchants and clerics; a resistance which, in the case of the Ottoman Empire, was often tacitly supported by the government (Quataert 1983; Kurmus 1987; Moaddel 1992; Foran 1994; Floor 2009).

Post-colonial free-tradist histories of the 1990s

In the 1990s and early 2000s globalized world economies, increased flows of goods, capital, peoples, information and ideas, and the rise of Asian competitors to the West in global markets, led to new perspectives in economic history both in the West and on the part of Middle Eurasian scholars. These questioned the Eurocentric thrust of earlier accounts with their focus on essential cultural differences accounting for absence or presence of commercial development. Wallersteinian visions of a structurally and historically divided world also lost appeal in a somewhat more optimistic era, keen to create utopias, albeit in the past, or idyllic images of global coexistence in the future. Employing the terminology of prevailing market discourse, A. G. Frank (1998) pointed to the competitive superiority of China as well as of

Ottoman and Mughal regions in world trade prior to the eighteenth century when Europe gained a competitive edge in achieving world domination.[10] Frank's history emphasized the historical, and therefore contingent, nature of Western development, showing that other regions had also known such development and world domination and would likely do so in the future.

Frank addressed a world history unified through trade flows evoking Braudel's vision. But as early as the 1960s, and in relation to the history of Middle Eurasian regions, Marshal Hodgson had rejected the Eurocentric dichotomous vision of world history in his neglected posthumous magnum opus.[11] He addressed the unity of the Islamicate world representing the areas where Islam spread as scattered with highly cosmopolitan commercial cities from Samarkand and Bukhara (in Central Asia) through Multan, Qandahar in Northern India, Herat, Isfahan in Iran, to Konya, Kayseri, Bursa in Anatolia, to Aleppo in the Eastern Mediterranean, to Cairo in North Africa and Granada in Spain.[12]

Hodgson's vision, like Braudel's, was marked by the experience of the war; it addressed commonalities in world history more than divisions. Starting with civilizational entities (albeit with numerous qualifications) as units of analysis, Hodgson's civilizations were unified through actions of individuals to achieve material success and to live a moral life in society (Islamoglu 2014). Hodgson saw this commonality among all civilizations, with the success and failure of any civilization depending on individual actions, responding to continually changing conditions and historical contingencies. For him, medieval Islamicate civilization (from the ninth to the thirteenth century and until the Mongol invasions) witnessed an unleashing of energies of individual Muslims resulting in a brilliant moment of commercial and cultural effervescence with merchants, scholars, lawyers, Sufis, artists, musicians, adventurers continuously traveling over the extent of Islamicate lands. They exchanged goods, money, ideas, information and innovations. They contributed to the creation of a string of cosmopolitan urban communities and to the economic and cultural integration of the Islamicate world. Though betraying a certain romanticism, Hodgson's analysis represented a masterful weaving together of strands of economic and cultural dynamism of Islamicate society, a far cry from Eurocentric Orientalist understandings of 'culture' obstructing economic activity and individual initiative.

Hodgson also talked about shared histories of civilizations; no civilizational success was possible without the rich cumulative history of institutional innovations in the Afro-Eurasian Oikoumene. At the same time, if a civilization lost its lead, it did not mean it was condemned to stagnation nor did it mean it would not have its moment again.

Hodgson's analysis attempted to do away with the cultural determinism of Orientalist civilizational discourse, assigning priority to history and historical contingency.[13] For a new generation of economic historians of Middle Eurasia, steeped in free-tradist liberal ideas and post-colonial understandings of the 1980s and 1990s, Hodgson's vision of the cosmopolitan, international Islamicate world resting on the actions of individuals unconstrained by state actions, had a certain appeal. They looked beyond the closures of national histories and of East/West, center/periphery divisions, envisioning a global history of 'connections' between different regions in Middle Eurasia as well as between Middle Eurasian regions and other world areas in Russia, China and Europe, via maritime and overland routes (Subrahmanyam 1997; Sood 2011, 2012).

Such new trade histories argued that the Middle Eurasian regions witnessed continued commercial vibrancy from the fifteenth until the nineteenth century, questioning interpretations of 'decline' following their glory in the sixteenth century (Faroqhi 1994; Dale 1994; Mathee 1999). Nor was this vibrancy solely an outcome of shifts and turns in overland trade primarily geared towards provisioning of the European market with silks and spices.[14] New trade histories drew attention to Middle Eurasia's commercial intensity and complexity, to the ways overland and maritime trades were intertwined with, and often embedded in, multiple regional and interregional trading networks within individual empires. Similarly, long distance trade was entangled in webs of power relations, of power struggles over its control between European and Middle Eurasian actors. This involved struggles between merchants and states (Mathee 1999), as well as struggles over access to goods among European actors.[15] In this highly intricate and complex commercial environment European trading companies backed by European states had to compete with multiple merchant networks extending over a hierarchy of markets ranging from long distance trade to interregional markets and down to urban–rural exchanges (Braudel 1979; Faroqhi 1994; Dale 1994; Islamoglu 1994). This may also have accounted for the existence of numerous towns, or centers of commerce, as well as artisanal production of all sizes throughout Middle Eurasian world economies.[16] The new economic histories also pointed to the backing given to Middle Eurasian merchant communities by Middle Eurasian governments, increasingly in the form of protection in their long distance ventures, a practice formerly thought to have been reserved for Europeans and granted by rulers either as a benevolent act or as a sign of their subordination to European power (Faroqhi 1994; Mathee 1999).[17]

Thus, new trade histories of the 1990s present a very different picture of overland and overseas trade than the one perpetuated by Eurocentric histories that had imagined overland trade through Middle Eurasian agrarian wastelands in terms of a corridor along which caravans carrying spices and silks flowed from the remote East to an equally mystified destination in Europe, barely touching the lives of people let alone being entangled in webs of regional and interregional markets, of merchants, communities and governmental actions. This view had assumed long distance traders to be European companies, forming isolated communities in coastal towns with their representatives chosen from indigenous religious and ethnic minorities.

Yet the vision of a global history of 'connections', lacking the world historical sweep of Hodgson's or Frank's works, was restricted in time to the early modern period between the fifteenth and the eighteenth centuries, abandoning the nineteenth century, the modern era, to European trade and domination, when those 'connections' were understood to have been disrupted or reconfigured to respond to European exigencies. This was tantamount to a withdrawal from modern history into an early modern free-tradist utopia. However, the integrated view of the commercial environment, and the blurring of lines between internal and external trades, provided the new economic histories with an opening for questioning Eurocentric (most notably Wallersteinian) perceptions of subordination of Middle Eurasian regions to the dictates of European trade. This questioning primarily focused on Middle Eurasian merchant communities and their activities, and on the issue of their competitiveness with European trading companies. Hence, histories told of Gujerati merchant communities, as well as Muslim, Indian and Armenian merchants, transporting silk, spices and cotton textiles from Indian Ocean coastal regions and Indonesian islands to the Mediterranean via the Persian Gulf, Basra and the Red Sea, supplying Ottoman and Venetian markets throughout the seventeenth and eighteenth centuries (Subrahmanyam 1997; Hanna 1998). Indian Ocean trade also linked the coastal regions of the Indian Ocean, inland to northern India, to Iran and via the sea to China. Along the vertical North–South route, in the same period, Hindki or Indian merchants from Multan in Northern India conducted a vibrant overland trade in Indian textiles and other goods linking that region to Isfahan and other cities in Northern Iran, up to Uzbek Turan and Astrakhan in Russia. Hindki merchants also branched out from Isfahan westward into Ottoman territories in Anatolia (Dale 1994; Faroqhi 1994). Similarly the overland silk trade from Safavid Iran, dominated by Armenian merchants of New Julfa in Isfahan, linked Safavid Iran to Ottoman territories and from there to Europe (Herzig 1991; Mathee 1999; Aslanian 2011). Furthermore, Ottoman Armenian communities in Amsterdam were a formidable presence in Dutch trade with Ottoman territories (Kadi 2012). Cairene merchants, on the other hand, controlled the Red Sea coffee trade from Yemen to Cairo. From there, coffee reached Ottoman regional markets via Ottoman merchants, thence European markets via Venetian, as well as Dutch and English merchants (Hanna 2011).

Eurocentric histories had described the Middle Eurasian merchants essentially as 'peddlers', unable to compete with European trading companies which were organized as joint-stock companies, with a worldwide organization, and backed by European states.[18] Countering the 'peddler thesis', new trade histories pointed to the versatility and flexibility advantages of small-scale enterprises based on networks, enabling them to move between different markets, trading in diverse products in regional and local markets as well as engaging in overland trade (Matthee 1999). These merchants also engaged in alternative activities, particularly financial transactions, and were thus able to weather trade fluctuations. Most significantly, historians pointed to a relationship between success in overland trade and the ability of traders to penetrate internal markets (Dale 1994; Faroqhi 1994 and forthcoming) pointing to a disadvantage of European trading companies with their limited reach in regional trading networks.[19] New economic histories suggested that this occurred especially in the regions which were not subjected to colonial administrations, such as the Ottoman Empire as well as Qajar Iran during the nineteenth century. In the Ottoman case the solution of employing members of ethnic and religious minority groups as representatives of companies did not seem to deliver optimal results for the European trading companies, limiting the volume of goods, especially cotton textiles, sold in Ottoman markets.[20]

Furthermore, an economic history literature on the nineteenth century, questioning the post-colonial and world-systems vision of the century as one of subordination for Middle Eurasian regions, showed continuities in both regional and inter-Middle Eurasian trade linking to long distance trade with Europe and Russia (Tabak 1988; Clarence-Smith 1989; Shields 1991; Quataert 1994; Gilbar 2003). There has also been a surge in works addressing indigenous economic dynamics. Continued prosperity of inland cities and industrial production largely artisanal (both rural and urban) mostly in textiles has been stressed, notwithstanding expectations of de-industrialization (Quatert 1993, 2003; Martin 2005). Upward trends in the agricultural economy, including a vibrancy of the nomadic/pastoral economy have also been uncovered (Guran 1998; Palairet 2003; Kasaba 2009; Toksoz 2010). With respect to Northern Indian/Central Asian trade, a revisionist perspective, while pointing to continuities in that trade, has highlighted how, under British rule, Indian merchants of Qandahar were marginalized. These merchants had previously played an important role in Central Asian trade but British administration sought to re-route that trade from Qandahar to Kabul, a city to be linked to the south and to the Indian Ocean via a main army route. Unfortunately that route secured the entry of the East India company in this regional trade (Hanifi 2011). This, in turn, points to a priority of governmental action and politics in determining which groups of merchants prevailed over others. In this perspective, governmental action in the nineteenth century, in the Ottoman context, largely accounted for the continued presence of Middle Eurasian merchants in major trade circuits as well as in regional markets.

A central issue for Middle Eurasian economic history, as we have seen, has been the economic role of the state. Braudel (1966), as part of a generation of historians (including Karl Polanyi) who had witnessed the 1930s Depression, understood well the importance of the institutional shaping of the economy by states.[21] Statist histories of the Ottoman Empire inspired by him focused on such institutional shaping of the economy, albeit reifying such institutions to represent an idealized image of the state vis-à-vis religion and its equally reified, idealized institutions (Inalcik 1994). Free-tradist historical perspectives downplayed the politics of government, most pertinently the state's role in shaping the Middle Eurasian commercial environment in the early modern period. Some histories completely ignored the state. So enthralled were they with merchant networks that one often got the impression that the environment was self-governing (Dale 1994; Sood 2012; cf. Subrahmanyan 1995). When their presence was acknowledged, early modern states were either assigned personal attributes of flexibility, tolerance (Barkey 2008) and pragmatism (Pamuk 2004) or they were identified with the actions of rulers described as benevolent, just or vigilant in protecting merchants, somewhat in conformity with the Smithian night-watchman state (Subrahmanyam 1997; Mathee 1999).

Personal attributes of states or state actions represented cultural dispositions.[22] States were shorn of their societal substance; politics was reduced to the personal politics of rulers (Mathee 1999) while institutions were instrumentalized to achieve the state's ends as defined by its cultural disposition (Pamuk 2004). The concept of 'negotiation' was resorted to for explaining the early modern state's positive dispositions and role (Scott 1998). Its flexible and accommodative character presented the state as a 'negotiated process', a favorite term in postmodernist histories of the 1990s (Barkey 2008; a critical view in Islamoglu and Perdue 2009), while modern states and their practices were understood to be non-negotiable. One popular focus of this discussion related to the ability of early modern states to manage 'difference' (religious and ethnic) contrasted with rigid, nationalistic, exclusionary practices of modern states (Barkey 2008).

Rethinking government: the politics in Middle Eurasian histories

In the past decade, a new trend has crystalized in writings on Middle Eurasian history. The new trend, concerned with government and politics in commercial environments, is situated closer to government studies and politics though rife with possibilities for economic history (Klein 2002; Ateş 2006). The new focus on government and politics resonates with similar concerns in present-day Middle Eurasia, most visibly in Iraq and Afghanistan, which since the 1980s have experienced global capitalism in the form of plunder of their resources enabled by military occupations leaving behind mayhem and civil strife (Mattei and Nader 2008). Most importantly, histories written from a governmental perspective have questioned the free-tradist underplaying of states or governments. These histories, primarily focusing on the nineteenth century, also question conceptions of world history in terms of an early modern/modern divide and the relegation of modern history to colonial history, to a history of modern states which were understood to stand outside of the societies concerned (Mitchell 1988). From the perspective of governmental histories, such conceptions deprive these regions of agency. Governmental histories question understandings (rooted in the post-colonial thinking of the 1980s and 1990s) of the 'absolute', non-negotiated character of the state's administrative power (Islamoglu 2004). Post-colonial perspectives vilified the Tanzimat or the reformed Ottoman state of the nineteenth century, which they identified as colonial, pointing to its oppressive practices vis-à-vis the local populations in the Arab lands as well as in the Balkans (Deringil 1998; Makdisi 2002).

Instead, the new governmental research (and some previous research recently revisited) points to continuities in the states' governmental practices and their institutional capacities from the earlier period into the nineteenth century (Islamoglu and Perdue 2009; Inalcik 1943). Also at issue are continuities between the practices of earlier imperial governments and nineteenth-century colonial governments (Mazumder 2009). For instance, Subrahmanyam (2009) argues that British administration in India assimilated the institutional capacities of Mughal government to manage regional diversity and religious denominational difference, independently of concerns for taxation capacities, which contributed to regional economic change.

At the same time, distancing itself from conceptions of the state or government as reservoir of institutions (North 1900; Pamuk 2004), the governmental perspective sees state government as reflecting political power relations (Islamoglu 2004). In this context, institutions or governmental regulations and rules which order social life (trade, provincial administration, landed property) are viewed as contested domains with different local as well as state actors confronting each other to negotiate their often conflicting claims (Islamoglu 2000). In the Ottoman Empire, such deliberations often resulted in the issuing of special provisions whereby governmental rulings addressed the demands of local elites, merchants and even peasants. These negotiations addressed property law, taxation and provincial administration. They took place in provincial councils, where different groups were represented, or in special commissions formed to respond to certain grievances with participation of all parties concerned (Thompson 1993; Rogan 1999; Islamoglu 2001, 2004; Ceylan 2006; Petrov 2006; Saracoglu 2007; Unlu and Rogan 2010). At issue here is a treatment of negotiation not as an explanatory principle in defining attributes but as an object of analysis which allows for evaluations of the different contexts in which negotiations took place and for tracing shifts in these contexts such as the development of modern states in the nineteenth century. The new context of the modern state signaled a new governmental politics where certain interests were given priority and others marginalized, according to the alliances forged and the outcomes of conflict mediation.

New governmental histories address, though in a preliminary way, the unity of the sovereign imperial state around a dominant group, with a political vision defining its goals. In the Middle Eurasian environments that vision focused on a certain understanding of societal justice aiming at a balance between moral/distributive concerns and those of economic growth and warfare. The claim to achieve that balance lay at the root of the legitimacy of Ottoman and Qajar states and of their general rulings in the nineteenth century. In fact, deliberations and contestation by peasants, workers, as well as local and central elites around specific governmental orderings continually held the governments to account, hence also representing the terrains for continually negotiating the legitimacy of the state (Inalcik 1943; Islamoglu 2001, 2004; Saracoglu 2007). Moreover, such claims provided a reference point for political resistance on the part of peasants and workers, both in Ottoman lands (Quataert 1983, 1987; Kurmus 1987) and in Qajar Iran (Burke and Yaghoubian 1993; Martin 2005), against European penetration, with tacit support on the part of these governments. This perspective on the sovereignty claims of Ottoman and Qajar governments in the nineteenth century, point to political possibilities in those imperial contexts. It represents a challenge for the Eurocentric image of the Middle Eurasian region as a patchwork of ethnic groups, religions, tribes, with no statehood or sovereign structures, let alone legitimate states. That image continues to plague Western perspectives on present-day Middle Eurasian regions that often dismiss their democratic movements as outbursts of religious fanaticism.

Conclusion

At the start of the twenty-first century global developments are attenuating differences between Western and non-Western regions in terms of material progress. The Western world hegemony is visibly waning, and non-Western regions (including those of Middle Eurasia), most notably China in the East, are recovering decisive positions in the new global order. Since the 1980s, Middle Eurasian histories have significantly distanced themselves from Eurocentric perceptions which designated the regions as economically stagnant and politically despotic, questioning the culturalist assumptions of those perceptions with historical research focusing on internal economic and governmental dynamics in different regions.

Yet, this new trend has led to a certain self-satisfied involution in history writing in Middle Eurasia which is often accompanied by attempts at ideologization of histories in defense of political and ideological positions. Conjoined with a trend of revisionist Islamist histories, economic histories of Middle Eurasia, especially those with an institutional focus, have taken a new 'culturalist' turn (Cizakca 1995, 1998; Pamuk 2004; Kuran 2011). They are inward-looking, continually and tirelessly seeking explanations for perceived past failures or successes. Institutionalist or not, the historical imagination of economic historians remains stuck at the point of free-tradist assumptions, reproducing the conceptual limits of those assumptions in dealing with the state as an economic actor. Incorporating politics and power relations in historical analysis, as well as a conception of institutions as part of political power fields, offers to be extremely important at a time when economic formulas resting on free-tradist themes are beginning to ring hollow amidst a serious crisis of employment and the unequal distribution of wealth and income worldwide. One central problem with current market development models is that they tend to subsume political power relations into their individualistic abstractions. The entire institutional framework is then put in the service of the individual which in the global context is identified with transnational corporations.

In the 1960s and 1970s, economic history addressed issues of social change in the 'underdeveloped' world, including Middle Eurasian regions, and debates (e.g. between substantivists and formalists; Marxist and world-systems scholars). In so doing it provided a point of departure for understanding the roots and possible solutions to underdevelopment. At that time, economic history was prominent in the economics departments of major Turkish universities. In the 1980s, throughout Middle Eurasia, politically repressive regimes hostile to 'progressive' subjects and sometimes favoring neoliberal policies (as in Turkey and Egypt) made the economy an act of faith, subtracted from public discussion, leading to the marginalization of economic history. Today, when economically inclined scholars address time series, for instance wage rates (Ozmucur and Pamuk 2002), they generally do so not to question present-day categories used in various fetishized aggregate measurements but in support of certain theoretical views. Similarly, from the perspective of 'qualitative' global history, the emphasis has moved away from comparative world histories addressing big questions towards tracing the global movements of goods and people. Yet, a problem-oriented perspective on global history as comparative world history could offer us a new chance to rethink the unity of history, emphasizing commonalities of historical experience worldwide rather than the differences that have earlier attracted so much attention.

Notes

1 The author would like to thank the Institute for Advanced Study, Nantes, for providing excellent research facilities and warm hospitality.

2 Kuran subscribes to the Northian institutionalist perspective on ideology as limiting or influencing an individual's ability to make rational decisions dictated by his/her self-interest.

3 K. Wittfogel (1957) employed the notion of Oriental despotism to study the Communist bureaucratic states in China and Russia during the Cold War. Oriental despotism, deployed to describe Asian

political power, acquired its negative connotation with Enlightenment thinkers and then with the Orientalists. By contrast, in the eighteenth century French kings caught in the midst of social crisis and losing their foothold in world trade saw in Oriental despotism an explanation for the long-lasting rule of the Ottomans (Kaiser 2000).

4 For an incisive critique of this culturalist perspective in relation to pragmatism as an attribute of the Ottoman state see Dağli (2013).

5 Pamuk (2004), in the wake of North (1990), emphasizes the role of the state as a reservoir of institutions enabling market activity. For accommodative capacities to respond to changing conditions in the Ottoman and Qing empires, cf. Islamoglu (2001).

6 Hugo Grotius, the seventeenth-century Dutch jurist, provided an antecedent for later Orientalist conceptions when he suggested that the activities of the Dutch East India Company in open seas – including appropriation of native lands and labor – had a civilizing effect on uncivilized natives (Tuck 2001).

7 Mattei and Nader (2008) critically address America's civilizing mission in Iraq promising to introduce free trade, human rights and democratic government, following the American invasion of Iraq in 2003 which ultimately sought to open the country to foreign investments.

8 In Turkey, Fatih University in Istanbul has programs on Islamic civilizational studies pursuing this line. Another program at George Mason University is funded by Islamic international organizations. The Global University of Islamic Finance in Kuala Lumpur, Malaysia, is a major center in this effort of operationalizing historical institutions in present-day global economies.

9 Repatriation of Ottoman history served to create a distance from nationalistic histories which sought to ground themselves in remote histories of Turkic peoples in Central Asia; cf. Islamoglu (2012).

10 Other world histories in the 1990s sought to relativize the European divergence by offering historical/environmental explanations (e.g. Pomeranz 2000).

11 Along with the binary vision, Hodgson also rejected a narrow concept of the Islamic civilization shared by the Orientalists, who confine it to the Arab period with its 'golden age' between the seventh and tenth centuries as attested by classical texts of high philological value (Hodgson 1974).

12 Hodgson's incisive critique of Eurocentric Orientalist thinking was ignored in the 1970s by an entire generation possibly because of its moral overtones mistaken for a religious Islamic orientation in the face of anti-colonial leftist perspectives (Wallerstein 1974) and of culturalist critiques of Orientalism (Said 1979).

13 Hodgson's thinking was wedded to the universal categories of the European Enlightenment; he would have felt uncomfortable with the particularistic culturalism of present-day postmodernists. The moral dimension was for him a universal category extending through all religions.

14 In the sixteenth century, Ottoman state policy succeeded in keeping the Portuguese from diverting the spice route away from the Mediterranean to the Indian Ocean following the discovery of the Cape route in the fifteenth century (Inalcik 1994; Findlay and O'Rourke 2007). This policy benefited both Ottoman and Venetian merchants.

15 Venetians (backed by the Ottoman government) confronted the Portuguese; Mediterranean merchants confronted the English and the Dutch. Cf. Subrahmanyam (1997); Inalcik (1994); Findlay and O'Rourke (2007).

16 A vibrant economy of urban artisans, with guilds fully integrated in merchant networks, is described by Faroqhi (2009), Genc (1994), Masters (2008) for the Ottoman Empire; by Hanna (2011) for Egypt. On Iran see (Ricks 1973; Floor 2009). On rural cottage industries, Faroqhi (1994); Shields (1991).

17 The practice of requesting Iranian merchants trading in Ottoman territories to submit a document of protection by the Iranian ruler was more strictly enforced beginning in the late seventeenth century (Faroqhi forthcoming).

18 Kuran (2011) attributes the peddler phenomenon to Islamic law preventing the establishment of corporations, and hence capitalist development in Islamic regions.

19 The Russian government's banning of Indian merchants from access to Russian internal trade had adverse effects on Hindki merchants' trade with Russia (Astrakhan) via Central Asia (Dale 1994).

20 British trade representatives in the Ottoman Empire complained about the sluggish demand for British exports of factory-made cotton cloths on Ottoman markets. British cloths could not compete with imports of fine Indian cotton textiles in urban middle-class markets, nor could they stand the competition from the rural cottage industry in mass markets (Inalcik 1987).

21 Braudel also highlighted the importance of imperial power in defining the boundaries of a world economy. Shah Abbas's intervention to secure the monopoly of Armenian merchants from New Julfa in overland silk trade, keeping the Dutch India company at bay, could also be seen as an act of consolidation of the Safavid world economy (Mathee 1999; Ricks 1973).

22 On the personalization of the state see again Dağli's (2013) critique.

References

Abrahamian, E. (1974) "Oriental Despotism: The Case of Qajar Iran," *International Journal of Middle East Studies* 5.1, 3–31.

Acemoglu, D. and J. A. Robinson (2012) *Why Nations Fail: The Origins of Power, Prosperity, and Poverty*. New York: Crown Business.

Akarli, E. (2005) "Law in the Marketplace: Istanbul 1730–1840," in M. Masud et al., eds., *Dispensing Justice in Islam: Kadis and Their Judgements*. Leiden: Brill, 245–70.

Aslanian, S. D. (2011) *From the Indian Ocean to the Mediterranean: The Global Trade Networks of Armenian Merchants from New Julfa*. Berkeley: University of California Press.

Ates, S. (2006) "Empires at the Margin: Toward a History of the Ottoman–Iranian Borderland Peoples, 1843–1881." Dissertation, New York University.

Barkan, O. L. (1943) *XV. ve XVI. Asirlarda Osmanli Imparatorlugunda Zirai Ekonominin Hukuki ve Mali Esaslari* (Fiscal and Legal Bases of the Agricultural Economy in the Ottoman Empire in the 15th and 16th Centuries), vol 1: *Kanunlar* (Codes). Istanbul: Istanbul Universitesi Yayinlari.

Barkan, O. L. (1957) "Essai sur les données statistiques des registres de recensement dans l'Empire Ottoman au XVe et XVIe siècles," *Journal of the Economic and Social History of the Orient* 1, 9–36.

Barkey, K. (2008) *Empire of Difference: The Ottomans in Comparative Perspective*. New York: Cambridge University Press.

Blumi, I. (2005) "The Consequences of Empire in the Balkans and Red Sea: Reading Possibilities in the Transformations of the Modern World." Dissertation, New York University.

Braudel, F. (1966) *La Méditerranée et le monde méditerranéen à l'époque de Philippe II*, 2nd edn. Paris: Colin.

Braudel, F. (1979) *Civilisation matérielle, économie et capitalisme, XVe–XVIIIe siècle*. Paris: Colin.

Burke, E. and N. Yaghoubian, eds. (1993) *Struggle and Survival in the Middle East*. Berkeley: University of California Press.

Ceylan, E. (2006) "Ottoman Centralization and Modernization in the Province of Baghdad 1831–1720." Dissertation, Bogazici University.

Cezzar, Y. (1986) *Osmanli Maliyesinde Bunalim ve Degisim: 18. yy' dan Tanzimat'a Mali Tarih* (Ottoman Fiscal Crisis and Change: A Fiscal History from the 18th Century to the Tanzimat). Istanbul: Alan Yayincilik.

Cizakca, M. (1995) "Cash Waqfs of Bursa, 1555–1823," *Journal of the Economic and Social History of the Orient* 38.3, 313–54.

Cizakca, M. (1996) *A Comparative Evolution of Business Partnerships: The Islamic World and Europe, with Specific Reference to the Ottoman Archives*. Leiden: Brill.

Cizakca, M. (1998) "Awkaf in History and its Implications for Modern Islamic Economies," *Islamic Economic Studies* 6.1, 43–70.

Cizakca, M. (2013) "Esham: A Shari'ah Based Yet Fixed Return Instrument for Investment," paper presented at the Third ISRA conference, Kuala Lumpur.

Clarence-Smith, W. G. (1989) *The Economics of the Indian Ocean Slave Trade in the Nineteenth Century*. Totowa, NJ: Frank Cass.

Dağli, Murat (2013) "The Limits of Ottoman Pragmatism," *History and Theory* 52.2, 194–213.

Dale, S. (1994) *Indian Merchants and Eurasian Trade, 1600–1750*. Cambridge: Cambridge University Press.

Davison, R. H. (1963) *Reform in the Ottoman Empire, 1856–76*. Princeton, NJ: Princeton University Press.

Deringil, S. (1998) *The Well-Protected Domains: Ideology and Legitimation in the Ottoman Empire*. London: I.B. Tauris.

Faroqhi, S. (1994) "Part II: Crisis and Change 1500–1699," in H. Inalcik and D. Quataert, eds., *An Economic and Social History of the Ottoman Empire*. New York: Cambridge University Press, 411–623.

Faroqhi, S. (2009) *Artisans of Empire: Crafts and Craftspeople under the Ottomans*. London: I.B. Tauris.

Faroqhi, S. (forthcoming) "Persian Traders (*Acem Tuccari*) in Ottoman Lands around 1700," in U. Devrim, ed., *Ottoman World: Foundational Coexistences*. Newcastle upon Tyne: Cambridge Scholars Publishing.

Findlay, R. and K. H. O'Rourke (2007) *Power and Plenty: Trade, War and the Economy in the Second Millennium*. Princeton, NJ: Princeton University Press.

Floor, W. M. (2009) *Guilds, Merchants, and Ulama in Nineteenth-century Iran*. Washington, DC: Mage.

Foran, J. (1989) "The Concept of Dependent Development as a Key to the Political Economy of Qajar Iran, 1800–1925," *Iranian Studies* 22.2–3, 5–56.

Foran, J. (1994) *A Century of Revolution: Social Movements in Iran (Social Movements, Protest and Contention)*. St. Paul: University of Minnesota Press.

Frank, A. G. (1998) *ReOrient: Global Economy in the Asian Age*. Berkeley: University of California Press.

Genc, M. (1994) "Ottoman Industry in the Eighteenth Century: General Framework, Characteristics and Main Trends," in D. Quataert, ed., *Manufacturing in the Ottoman Empire and Turkey, 1500–1950*. Albany: SUNY Press, 59–89.

Genc, M. (2000) *Osmanli Imparatorlugunda Devlet ve Ekonomi* (State and Economy in the Ottoman Empire). Istanbul: Otiken.

Gibb, H. A. R. and H. Bowen (1969) *Islamic Society and the West: A Study of the Impact of Western Civilization on Moslem Culture in the Near East*, vol. I. Oxford: Oxford University Press.

Gilbar, G. G. (2003) "The Muslim Big Merchant-Entrepreneurs of the Middle East, 1860–1914," *Welt des Islams* 43.1, 1–36.

Guran, T (1998) *19. yuzyilda Osmanli Tarimi* (Ottoman Agriculture in the 19th Century). Istanbul: Eren.

Habib, I. (1963) *The Agrarian System of Mughal India*. New Delhi: Asia Publishing House.

Hanifi, S. H. (2011) *Connecting Histories in Afghanistan: Market Relations and State Formation on a Colonial Frontier*. Stanford, CA: Stanford University Press.

Hanna, N. (1998) *Making Big Money in 1600: The Life and Times of Isma'il Abu Taqiyya, Egyptian Merchant*. New York: Cambridge University Press.

Hanna, N. (2011) *Artisan Entrepreneurs in Cairo and Early Modern Capitalism, 1600–1800*. Syracuse, NY: Syracuse University Press.

Herzig, E. M. (1991) *The Armenian Merchants of New Julfa, Isfahan: A Study in Pre-Modern Asian Trade*. Oxford: Oxford University Press.

Hodgson, M. G. S. (1974) *The Venture of Islam: Conscience and History in a World Civilization*. Chicago, IL: University of Chicago Press.

Huntington, S. (1993) "The Clash of Civilizations?" *Foreign Affairs* 72.3, 22–49.

Inalcik, H. (1943) *Tanzimat ve Bulgar Meselesi* (The Tanzimat and the Bulgarian Question). Istanbul: Eren.

Inalcik, H. (1973) *The Ottoman Empire: The Classical Age, 1300–1600*. New York: Praeger Publishers.

Inalcik, H. (1978) "Impact of the *Annales* School on Ottoman Studies and New Findings," *Review* 1.3–4, 69–96.

Inalcik, H. (1987) "When and How British Cotton Goods Invaded the Levant Markets," in H. Islamoglu, ed., *The Ottoman Empire and the World Economy*. New York: Cambridge University Press, 374–83.

Inalcik, H. (1992) "Islamization of Ottoman Laws on Land and Land Tax," in C. Fragner and K. Schwarz, eds., *Osmanistik-Turkologie-Diplomatik*. Berlin: Klaus Schwarz Verlag.

Inalcik, H. (1994) *An Economic and Social History of the Ottoman Empire*. New York: Cambridge University Press.

Islamoglu, H. (1987) "Introduction: 'Oriental Despotism' in World-System Perspective," in *The Ottoman Empire and the World Economy*. New York: Cambridge University Press, 1–26.

Islamoglu, H. (1994) *State and Peasant in the Ottoman Empire: Agrarian Power Relations and Regional Economic Development in Ottoman Anatolia during the Sixteenth Century*. Leiden: Brill.

Islamoglu, H. (2000) "Property as a Contested Domain: A Reevaluation of the Ottoman Land Code of 1858," in R. E. J. Owen, *New Perspectives on Property and Land in the Middle East*. Cambridge, MA: Harvard University Press, 3–63.

Islamoglu, H. (2001) "Modernities Compared: State Transformations and Constitutions of Property in the Qing and Ottoman Empires," *Journal of Early Modern History* 5.4, 353–86.

Islamoglu, H. (2004) "Towards a Political Economy of Legal and Administrative Constitutions of Individual Property" and "Politics of Administering Property: Law and Statistics in the Nineteenth

Century Ottoman Empire," in H. Islamoglu, ed., *Constituting Modernity: Private Property in the East and West*. London: I.B. Tauris, 3–34; 276–320.

Islamoglu, H. (2012) "Islamicate World Histories?" in D. Northrop, ed., *A Companion to World History*. Oxford: Wiley-Blackwell, 447–63.

Islamoglu, H. (2014) "World History as Fulfillment of Individual Moral Responsibility," paper presented at the workshop "Toward an Islamicate Cosmopolitan Imagination: The Moral Legacy of Marshall G. S. Hodgson," World Congress of Middle East Studies, Middle East Technical University, Ankara.

Islamoglu, H. and C. Keyder (1977) "Agenda for Ottoman History," *Review* 1.1, 31–55.

Islamoglu, H. and P. Perdue (2009) "Introduction," in H. Islamoglu and P. Perdue, eds., *Shared Histories of Modernity in China, India and the Ottoman Empire*. London: Routledge, 1–20.

Kadi, I. H. (2012) *Ottoman and Dutch Merchants in the Eighteenth Century: Competition and Cooperation in Ankara, Izmir and Amsterdam*. Leiden: Brill.

Kaiser, T. (2000) "The Evil Empire? The Debate on Turkish Despotism in Eighteenth-Century French Political Culture," *Journal of Modern History* 72.1, 6–34.

Kasaba, R. (2009) *Moveable Empire: Ottoman Nomads, Migrants, and Refugees*. Seattle: University of Washington Press.

Keyder, C. (1976) "The Dissolution of the Asiatic Mode of Production," *Economy and Society* 5.2, 178–96.

Keyder, Ç., Y. E. Özveren and D. Quataert (1993) "Port-Cities in the Ottoman Empire: Some Theoretical and Historical Perspectives," *Review* 16.4, 519–58.

Kiyotaki, Keiko (1997) "Ottoman Land Policies in the Province of Baghdad, 1831–1881." PhD Dissertation, University of Wisconsin–Madison.

Klein, J. (2002) "Power in the Periphery: The Hamidiye Light Cavalry and the Struggle over Ottoman Kurdistan, 1890–1914." Dissertation, Princeton University.

Kuran, T. (2011) *The Long Divergence: How Islamic Law Held Back the Middle East*. Princeton, NJ: Princeton University Press.

Kurmus, O. (1987) "The Cotton Famine and its Effects on the Ottoman Empire," in H. Islamoglu, ed., *The Ottoman Empire and the World Economy*. New York: Cambridge University Press, 160–9.

Lambton, A. (1969) *Landlord and Peasant in Persia*. Oxford: Oxford University Press.

Lewis, B. (1968) *The Emergence of Modern Turkey*. Oxford: Oxford University Press.

Lockman, Z. (2009) *Contending Visions of the Middle East: The History and Politics of Orientalism*. New York: Cambridge University Press.

Makdisi, U. (2002) "Ottoman Orientalism," *American Historical Review* 107.3, 768–96.

Martin, V. (2005) *The Qajar Pact: Bargaining, Protest and the State in Nineteenth-century Persia*. London: I.B. Tauris.

Masters, B. (2008) *The Origins of Western Economic Dominance in the Middle East: Mercantilism and the Islamic Economy in Aleppo, 1600–1750*. New York: NYU Press.

Mathee, R. P. (1999) *The Politics of Trade in Safavid Iran: Silk for Silver, 1600–1730*. Cambridge: Cambridge University Press.

Mattei, U. and L. Nader (2008) *Plunder: When the Rule of Law Is Illegal*. Oxford: Blackwell.

Mazumder, R. (2009) "When Strong Men Meet: Recruited Punjabis and Constrained Colonialism," in H. Islamoglu and P. Perdue, eds., *Shared Histories of Modernity in China, India and the Ottoman Empire*. London: Routledge, 147–204.

Mitchell, T. (1988) *Colonizing Egypt*. Berkeley: University of California Press.

Moaddel, M. (1992) "Shi'i Political Discourse and Class Mobilization in the Tobacco Movement of 1890–92," *Sociological Forum* 7.3, 447–68.

Nashat, G. (1981) "From Bazaar to Market: Foreign Trade and Economic Development in Nineteenth-century Iran," *Iranian Studies* 14.1–2, 53–85.

North, D. C. (1990) *Institutions, Institutional Change and Economic Performance*. Cambridge: Cambridge University Press.

Owen, R. (1987) "The Silk Reeling Industry of Mount Lebanon, 1840–1914: A Study of the Possibilities and Limitations of Factory Production in the Periphery," in H. Islamoglu-Inan, ed., *The Ottoman Empire and the World Economy*. New York: Cambridge University Press, 271–83.

Owen, R. (1993) *The Middle East in the World Economy, 1800–1914*. London: I.B. Tauris.

Ozmucur, S. and S. Pamuk (2002) "Real Wages and Standards of Living in the Ottoman Empire, 1489–1914," *Journal of Economic History* 62.1, 293–321.

Palairet, M. (2003) *The Balkan Economies, c.1800–1914: Evolution without Development*. Cambridge: Cambridge University Press.

Pamuk, S. (1987) *The Ottoman Empire and European Capitalism, 1820–1913: Trade, Investment and Production*. New York: Cambridge University Press.

Pamuk, S. (2004) "Institutional Change and the Longevity of the Ottoman Empire, 1500–1800," *Journal of Interdisciplinary History* 35.2, 225–47.

Petrov, Milen V. (2006) "Tanzimat for the Countryside: Midhat Paşa and the Vilayet of Danube, 1864–1868." Dissertation, Princeton University.

Pomeranz, K. (2000) *The Great Divergence: China, Europe and the Making of the Modern World Economy*. Princeton, NJ: Princeton University Press.

Quataert, D. (1983) *Social Disintegration and Popular Resistance in the Ottoman Empire, 1881–1908: Reactions to European Economic Penetration*. New York: NYU Press.

Quataert, D. (1987) "A Provisional Report Concerning the Impact of European Capital on Ottoman Port Workers, 1800–1909," in H. Islamoglu-Inan, ed., *The Ottoman Empire and the World Economy*, New York: Cambridge University Press, 300–10.

Quataert, D. (1993) *Ottoman Manufacturing in the Age of the Industrial Revolution*. Cambridge: Cambridge University Press.

Quataert, D. (1994) "The Age of Reforms, 1812–1914," in H. Inalcik and D. Quataert, eds., *An Economic and Social History of the Ottoman Empire*, vol. 2. Cambridge: Cambridge University Press, 759–944.

Quataert, D. (2003) "Recent Writings in Late Ottoman History," *International Journal of Middle East Studies* 35.1, 134–42.

Ricks, T. M. (1973) "Towards a Social and Economic History of Eighteenth-century Iran," *Iranian Studies* 6.2–3, 110–26.

Rogan, E. L. (1999) *Frontiers of the State in the Late Ottoman Empire: Transjordan, 1850–1921*. Cambridge: Cambridge University Press.

Said, E. (1979) *Orientalism*. New York: Vintage.

Saracoglu, M. S. (2007) "Letters from Vidin: A Study of Ottoman Governmentality and Politics of Local Administration, 1864–1877." Dissertation, Ohio State University.

Scott, J. C. (1998) *Seeing Like a State: How Certain Schemes to Improve the Human Condition Have Failed*. New Haven, CT: Yale University Press.

Shields, S. D. (1991) "Regional Trade and 19th Century Mosul: Revising the Role of Europe in the Middle East Economy," *International Journal of Middle East Studies* 23.1, 19–37.

Sood, G. S. D. (2011) "Circulation and Exchange in Islamicate Eurasia: A Regional Approach to the Early Modern World," *Past and Present* 212, 113–62.

Sood, G. S. D. (2012) "An Islamicate Eurasia: Vernacular Perspectives on the Early Modern World," in M. E. Bonine, A. Amanat, and M. E. Gasper, eds., *Is there a Middle East? Evolution of a Geopolitical Concept*. Stanford, CA: Stanford University Press, 152–69.

Subrahmanyam, S. (1995) "Of Imarat and Tijarat: Asian Merchants and State Power in the Western Indian Ocean, 1400 to 1750," *Comparative Studies in Society and History* 37.4, 750–80.

Subrahmanyam, S. (1997) "Connected Histories: Notes Towards a Reconfiguration of Early Modern Eurasia," *Modern Asian Studies* 31.3, 735–62.

Subrahmanyam, S. (2009) "The Fate of Empires: Rethinking Mughals, Ottomans and Habsburgs," in H. Islamoglu and P. Perdue, eds., *Shared Histories of Modernity in China, India and the Ottoman Empire*. London: Routledge, 74–108.

Tabak, F. (1988) "Local Merchants in Peripheral Areas of the Empire: The Fertile Crescent During the Long Nineteenth Century," *Review* 11.2, 179–214.

Tabak, F. (2008) *The Waning of the Mediterranean, 1550–1870: A Geohistorical Approach*. Baltimore, MD: Johns Hopkins University Press.

Thompson, E. (1993) "Ottoman Political Reform in the Provinces: The Damascus Advisory Council in 1844–45," *International Journal of Middle East Studies* 25.3, 457–75.

Todorova, M. (2009) *Imagining the Balkans*. Oxford: Oxford University Press.

Toksoz, M. (2010) *Nomads, Migrants and Cotton in the Eastern Mediterranean: The Making of the Adana-Mersin Region, 1850–1908*. Leiden: Brill.

Toksoz, M. (2012) "The World of Mehmed Murad: Writing *Histoires Universelles* in Ottoman Turkish," *Journal of Ottoman Studies* 40, 343–63.

Tuck, R. (2001) *The Rights of War and Peace: Political Thought and the International Order from Grotius to Kant*. Oxford: Oxford University Press.

Ünlü, U. C. and E. L. Rogan (2010) "A Snapshot of Historiography on the Nineteenth-century Ottoman Provinces," *New Perspectives on Turkey* 42, 237–53.

Wallerstein, I. (1974) *The Modern World-System*, vol. I. New York: Academic Press.

Wallerstein, I., H. Decdeli and R. Kasaba (1987) "The Incorporation of the Ottoman Empire into the World Economy," in H. Islamoglu, ed., *The Ottoman Empire and the World Economy*. New York: Cambridge University Press, 88–100.

Weber, M. (1978) *Economy and Society: An Outline of Interpretive Sociology*. Berkeley: University of California Press.

Wittfogel, K. A. (1957) *Oriental Despotism: A Comparative Study of Total Power*. New Haven, CT: Yale University Press.

17

THE HISTORY OF INDIAN ECONOMIC HISTORY

Prasannan Parthasarathi

Since the late nineteenth century India has been a major center for research and writing in economic history. Early pioneers included Mahadev Govind Ranade and Romesh Chunder Dutt, who turned to history in order to both critique British rule in India and to construct an economics that was appropriate for Indian conditions. In the early decades of the twentieth century a number of writers built upon the foundation established by these figures and combined a concern for contemporary problems of the Indian economy with an interest in historical issues. From the 1930s, however, economic history went into decline as the Keynesian revolution gave economists other sources of inspiration to create an Indian economics. In faculties of economics, the study and teaching of economic history was of secondary importance for a number of decades.

In the post-war period economic history revived. From the 1950s the growing influence of Marxism led economists to history and historians to the economy. Inspired by Marxian thought an impressive body of scholarship in economic history emerged, including D. D. Kosambi's writings on ancient India, Irfan Habib's studies of the Mughal Empire, and Amiya Bagchi's analyses of the colonial economy. Around the same time there was a revival of economic history at the great powerhouse of economics teaching and research in post-independence India, the Delhi School of Economics. This represented to some extent a resurgence of economic history within the ranks of economists, which was institutionalized with the founding of the *Indian Economic and Social History Review* and the establishment of a number of positions in economic history at the Delhi School.

The flourishing state of economic history in India in the 1960s and 1970s represented a confluence of different forces. Similarly, the decline of economic history from its highpoint of those years is due to multiple reasons, amongst them broad changes in both historical practice and economic thinking. The decline in Marxism and the linguistic and poststructural turns led to a shift from economic to cultural history. The rise of neoliberalism in economics faculties, including the Delhi School, led to a turning away from economic history, which came to be seen as neither relevant nor necessary for the contextualization of India's development problems.

Nationalism and economic history

Mahadev Govind Ranade is widely acknowledged to be the father of Indian nationalist economics, or Indian political economy. He was born in western India in 1842 and was an instructor in economics at Elphinstone College for a decade and a half where he taught the writings of Adam Smith and John Stuart Mill. Mill was the main figure on the syllabus, but to give his students a "wider perspective of political economy," he included Malthus, Bastiat, Ramsay, McCulloch, and Senior (Ganguli 1977: 164).

Indian nationalist economics had two goals. The first was the well-known critique of the economic impact of British rule in India. The second goal, less recognized but no less important, was to reject the universalism of economic theory and to construct a framework which captured the unique features of the Indian economy. As Ranade (1920: 2) put it in his seminal essay, "Indian Political Economy," delivered as a lecture at the Deccan College in Pune in 1892,

> The same teachers and statesmen, who warn us against certain tendencies in our political aspirations . . . seem to hold that the truths of economic science, as they have been expounded in our most popular English text-books, are absolutely and demonstrably true, and must be accepted as guides of conduct for all time and place whatever may be the stage of national advance. Ethnical, social, juristic, ethical, or economical differences in the environments are not regarded as having any influence in modifying the practical application of these truths.

Indian political economy was an economics rooted in the social, cultural, and political conditions of India. One inspiration for it was John Stuart Mill, who rejected the universal claims of political economy. Mill wrote in his autobiography that his teachers tried "to construct a *permanent* fabric out of transitory materials; that they took for granted the immutability of arrangements of society, many of which are in their nature *fluctuating or progressive*; and enunciate, with as little qualification as if they were universal and absolute truths" (cited in Ganguli 1977: 69). Such statements found an appreciative audience among Indians of the late nineteenth century.

The more important inspiration, however, was the German Historical School, which gave Indian economics a firm rooting in the study of the past. (Ranade [1920: 20] wrote, "The German school regards that universalism and perpetualism in economic doctrine are both unscientific and untrue.") Between these two influences, the Germans and Mill, B. N. Ganguli gives primacy to the German Historical School but reconciles them in the following terms: "Parts of the British economic theory, which had assimilated some of the contentions of the continental thinkers, were readily acclaimed by Indians. But where assimilation was doubtful and the resulting 'compromise' or rather 'balance,' uncertain, there was preference for the conclusions of the Historical School" (Ganguli 1977: 76).

Among the German economists, Friedrich List was to be the most influential. According to Ranade, "It was the writings of List, which gave the fullest expression to the rebellion against the orthodox creed . . . The function of the state is to help those influences which tend to secure national progress through the several states of growth and adopt free trade or protection, as circumstances may require" (cited in Ganguli 1977: 78–9). List was representative of a larger historical method in economic analysis. Again, to quote Ranade, "The method to be followed is not the deductive but the historical method, which takes account of the past in its forecast of the future; and relativity, and not absoluteness, characterizes the conclusions of economical science" (Ranade 1920: 20–1).

Romesh Chunder Dutt's two-volume *Economic History of India* was the most important historical work produced in this nationalist historical tradition. Dutt was a polymath, one of the first Indian entrants into the Indian Civil Service, the elite administrative cadre that governed British India. He resigned from the government after twenty-six years and devoted himself to politics and writing. He was active in the Indian National Congress and he produced novels, several historical works, translations from Sanskrit, as well as important political tracts. His two-volume study of the Indian economy under British rule established the contours of a nationalist economic history which endures even today. One commentator writes of the first volume, "In several respects this book would rank as the most valuable of books on India under the British rule" (Gopalakrishnan 1959: 147–8).

Agriculture is given pride of place in both volumes, perhaps not surprising given the importance of the land revenue for the British Indian state. Much attention is given to the formation of the land revenue systems in the different provinces of British India and their revisions. Industry, internal and external trade, finance, and railways and irrigation are all explored. The Listian influence is made explicit. After quoting a long passage from *The National System of Political Economy* in which List discussed the economic relationship between Britain and India, Dutt concludes, "While British Political Economists professed the principles of free trade from the latter end of the eighteenth century, the British Nation declined to adopt them till they had crushed the Manufacturing Power of India . . . [I]n India the Manufacturing Power of the people was stamped out by protection against her industries, and then free trade was forced on her so as to prevent a revival" (Dutt 1960: 215–16).

The commitment to a distinct Indian political economy continued into the early decades of the twentieth century, as did a commitment to a historical approach. As late as 1957 the economics department at the University of Madras was still called the "Department of Indian Economics." In the early twentieth century a number of the leading economists combined research in historical topics along with studies of contemporary Indian problems. P. J. Thomas, who became Professor of Economics at Madras University in 1927, wrote his Oxford doctoral thesis on British trade with India in the late seventeenth and eighteenth centuries, the now classic *Mercantilism and the East India Trade* (1926). He also produced, along with B. Nataraja Pillai (1933), a seminal study of the depression of the 1820s–1840s in South India. The rest of his oeuvre, however, was devoted to analyses of the Indian economy of the 1930s and 1940s and he served on the Provincial Banking Enquiry Committee and the Agricultural Economic Council, among other government bodies. Thomas took leave from the university in 1943 to take up a position in the Government of India, eventually resigning from his professorship three years later (Pillay 1957: 161–3).

Similarly, the publications of Radhakamal Mukerjee, who began his career as a lecturer in the department of economics at the University of Calcutta and then served as professor and head of the department of economics and sociology at Lucknow University, ranged from economic history to contemporary village studies. He published *The Economic History of India: 1600–1800* in 1939. Earlier in his career he was part of a sociological investigation in the Madras Presidency of Dravidian village communities and published several works on the foundations and postulates of Indian economics, housing and slums in urban India, comparative economics and demography (University of Calcutta 1920?: 65–6; Ghosh 1948: 44–5). Mukerjee is best remembered today as a founder of the Lucknow School of Sociology (Joshi 1986) and in his long scholarly career, he was committed to both history and serious fieldwork. In his autobiography, he wrote, "In the early years of my own teaching I deeply felt the necessity of relating economic theories and doctrines not only to economic history but also to the concrete social and economic environment" (Mukherjee 1997: 119).

Most famous of all these mid-twentieth-century figures is D. R. Gadgil, who was a major presence in Indian economics from the 1920s to the 1970s. His first book, *The Industrial Evolution of India in Recent Times* (1924), was submitted as a MLitt thesis at Cambridge University. Ostensibly, it was a study of industry from 1860 to 1914 (subsequent editions brought the story forward into the 1920s and 1930s), but it was in reality a broad economic history of the period. The work was a critique of British rule and in the later editions this critique, particularly of British laissez-faire, was made more explicit (Datta 1978: 51). (Gadgil provided an introduction to a Government of India reprint of Romesh Dutt's *Economic History of India*.) He later undertook important investigations on the impact of the Second World War on the Indian economy, industrial labor and wages, the urban economy of western India, and planning and development in post-independence India. Gadgil was also a staunch proponent of cooperatives for development and this, along with other positions sympathetic to the plight of laborers and peasants, led S. A. Dange, Chairman of the Communist Party of India, to produce a pamphlet in appreciation of Gadgil after the economist's death in 1971 (Dange 1971).[1]

The economic histories of India produced by Indian nationalism did not go unchallenged by the defenders of British rule. Among the most enduring defenses are the writings of W. H. Moreland (1920, 1923), the former civil servant turned historian, who concentrated his energies on the economics of the Mughal Empire. In Moreland's interpretation of Mughal rule and its economic impact, the problems of British India, including low standards of living and widespread poverty, were portrayed as long-standing features of Indian political economy. Others defended British rule along similar lines and attributed Indian economic problems to the deficiencies of culture and society, the most prominent being Vera Anstey, who was located not in India but at the London School of Economics.

From the 1930s the historical turn in Indian economics went into decline and a new generation of economists focused on the contemporary problems of India with little appeal to history and little interest in the past. The independence of India from British rule in 1947 reinforced these choices and the finest economic thinkers in the country turned their minds to the problems of development and planning, which preoccupied both academic and government experts in the 1950s. Perhaps no figure better symbolizes the new practices of Indian economists than V. K. R. V. Rao. Rao was born in South India in 1908. He was only seven years younger than D. R. Gadgil, but of a different generation in several important respects. Like Gadgil, he studied economics at Cambridge, where he was a student of John Maynard Keynes. Rao's early work was on the national income of India in the 1920s and 1930s. His subsequent research focused on macroeconomics, public finance, education, and development planning, as well as a variety of other topics. Unlike his predecessors, however, Rao did not venture into economic history (Rao 2002).

Why did Rao turn away from history, which had been a hallmark of Indian political economy since the late nineteenth century? In his "Rise and Decline of Development Economics," Albert Hirschman credits the Keynesian Revolution for creating the intellectual space to make development economics possible. He writes,

> Development economics took advantage of the unprecedented discredit orthodox economics had fallen into as a result of the depression of the thirties and of the equally unprecedented success of an attack on orthodoxy from within the economics 'establishment.' I am talking of course about the Keynesian Revolution of the thirties . . . The Keynesian step from one to two economics was crucial: the ice of monoeconomics had been broken and the idea that there might be yet another economics had instant credibility.
>
> *(Hirschman 1981: 6)*

Just as the Keynesian Revolution made possible an economics of development, it created the economic justification to develop an approach to the Indian economy, an Indian economics, which did not need recourse to history. On theoretical grounds alone, as Keynes showed, there were compelling arguments for multiple approaches to the study of economics. It was this door, which Keynes created, that Rao and his successors entered, leaving history behind. It would not be until the 1960s that Indian economists would seriously reckon with economic history again.

Marxism

While economists, especially those of a more mainstream persuasion, abandoned economic history in the 1940s and 1950s, the growing influence of Marxism, most strikingly among historians, infused economic history with new life and energy. Even in the early decades of the twentieth century, historians of India had dealt with economic questions, such as A. Appadorai's monumental two-volume study of economic conditions in medieval South India (Appadorai 1936). In the 1950s there were figures such as N. K. Sinha in Bengal, who wrote a path-breaking three-volume economic history of Bengal from the mid-eighteenth to the mid-nineteenth centuries (Sinha 1956–70). However, the bulk of historical research focused on political history and the state.

A Marxian interpretation of the Indian past emerged after Indian independence in 1947, displacing the high politics that had reigned supreme for several decades. According to Sumit Sarkar, the change in historical sensibilities emerged from the

> conjuncture of the 1950s and 1960s, marked by a strong and apparently growing Left presence in Indian political and intellectual life . . . It was not mainstream British or American historiography, not even writings on South Asian themes, but a journal like *Past and Present*, the "transition debate", and the work of historians like Hill, Hobsbawm and Thompson . . . that appeared most stimulating to Indian scholars exploring new ways of looking at history.
>
> *(Sarkar 1997: 37)*

The injection of Marxism into history writing in India opened up whole new worlds of possibilities. One of these was economic history, which flourished in major history departments of India from the 1960s. Many of the contributions to Indian economic history made in those decades were closely connected to research in social history, which too was energized by the Marxian turn.

The impact of Marxism and its contribution to a deeper engagement with economic life was felt across the long span of the Indian past. The study of ancient India was reinvigorated under the influence of D. D. Kosambi and his highly original use of Marxism as a starting point for historical inquiry. As Romila Thapar writes,

> The outstanding exponent of the Marxist interpretation of Indian history in all its complexity and the one, who ushered in a paradigm shift in the study of ancient Indian history, was D. D. Kosambi. The paradigm shift was the move away from colonial and nationalist frameworks and the centrality of dynastic history to a new framework integrating social and economic history and relating the cultural dimensions of the past to these investigations . . . For him history was the presentation in chronological order of successive developments in the means and relations of production.
>
> *(Thapar 2011: 553–4)*

Kosambi also influenced scholarship in medieval history with his arguments for the utility of the concept of feudalism in the study of India, which in his usage spanned the classical and medieval periods (Kosambi 2002). R. S. Sharma developed these ideas further (Sharma 1965). The debate on Indian feudalism sparked a major comparative exchange in the *Journal of Peasant Studies* on the appropriateness of the category for understanding societies outside Europe. Harbans Mukhia initiated the exchange with his essay, "Was There Feudalism in Indian History?" (Byres and Mukhia 1985).

The influence of Marxism was felt elsewhere in the study of medieval India, perhaps most strikingly in studies of the Mughal Empire where the focus shifted from the personalities of the ruling emperors to material conditions. Investigations were undertaken on the agrarian order, technology, commerce, banking, feudalism, and the potentialities of capitalism. Irfan Habib was the giant who loomed over the field of Mughal studies and his great work, the *Agrarian System of Mughal India*, was published in 1963. His structuralist interpretation of the empire and his articulation of lines of class conflict to explain the crisis of the empire and its decline took Mughal history by storm.[2]

Modern history also came under the Marxian rethink. While the study of the nationalist movement continued to be of great importance for historians of modern India, the rise of social history led to a greater emphasis on material conditions and, therefore, economic life. Sumit Sarkar sees the development of economic history as one of the major areas of advance in the study of the modern period in India. This was furthered by the fuller development of the nationalist paradigm, which "enriched through more sophisticated tools and empirical detail the basic critique of colonial policies and structures that had been initiated by the first generation of nationalist economists and developed by Marxists like R. P. Dutt" (Sarkar 1997: 39).

Modern economic and social historians tackled a broad range of issues, including demography, external as well as internal trade, finance, banking and currency, and national income estimation. However, the economic and social history of modern India centered on agriculture and industry, which is not surprising given that these sectors loomed large in policy discussions on economic development after independence. Nevertheless, it is somewhat surprising that important issues such as India's place in the global order, which had been a long-standing concern for nationalist economic historians of the late nineteenth and early twentieth centuries, received so little attention from these later historians. Dadhabai Naoroji, Romesh Chunder Dutt, and others were deeply concerned with the drain of wealth from India to Britain, which they saw as operating through the international payments and settlements system. G. Balachandran sees the neglect of this topic as due to the "canonical status of the 'nationalist economists' who wrote on the subject . . . the tightening of India's external economic controls since the 1950s; and the complicit evolution of disciplinary regimes in both mainstream economics and history" (Balachandran 2003: 1). The last point, on the divergent paths of history and economics, is one to which this chapter returns.

While the study of India's place in the world economy has been neglected for the modern period, it has flourished with respect to the period between 1500 and 1800. These centuries were traditionally considered to form part of the medieval history of India, but they are now increasingly considered to mark the flowering of an early modernity, manifest in economic, as well as political, social, and cultural life. In the 1960s and 1970s Indian economic historians, most notably Ashin Das Gupta, produced major studies of the subcontinent's maritime connections and laid the foundation for the new field of Indian Ocean studies (Das Gupta 2001).

Despite these exciting developments in pre-colonial trade history, when it came to the colonial period, agriculture and industry ruled the day. The agrarian turn was part of a larger "return of the peasant to South Asian history," in Eric Stokes's evocative language and from the 1960s enormous numbers of regional and local histories of agriculture were produced (Stokes 1978). These ranged from investigations of the British revenue settlements, a well-worn path of research, to the land market in colonial India, class relations in the countryside, to studies of famine. The richness of this scholarship defies easy summary and the continued value and wider applicability of many of these studies cannot be overstated.[3]

The most important Marxian debate in the agrarian history of India has come to be known as the "mode of production" debate. It took place in the 1960s and 1970s with many of the major contributions published in the *Economic and Political Weekly*, a remarkable publication which combined news, commentary, and scholarly articles, and has no counterpart outside India.[4] The debate began in the early 1960s between economists who were attempting to understand the nature of capitalist production relations in contemporary Indian agriculture. The debate widened quickly, however, to ask if the contemporary agrarian order could even be labeled capitalist, with feudalism and semi-feudalism proposed as alternatives. The debate also broadened its temporal remit and explored commercial relations in the countryside during the period of British rule as well as the extent to which the end of British rule represented a break in the development of agriculture. In terms of the historical dimension of the debate, the contributions of Jairus Banaji, especially his "Capitalist Domination and the Small Peasantry: Deccan Districts in the Late Nineteenth Century," were to be of the greatest importance.[5] Although the debate was at times highly technical, and occasionally appeared to be overly concerned with semantics, its impact was felt widely in the writing of Indian agrarian history.

The bulk of the participants in the mode of production debate focused on contemporary India, which reflected the larger disconnect – even within Marxian economics – between economics and history which, as we have seen, emerged in the 1930s. Nevertheless, the vigor with which economists embraced the historical dimensions is reminiscent of Indian economic thinking in the early decades of the twentieth century, at the time when the discipline was searching for an Indian political economy. This may be attributed to the historicism of Marxism, but, as we shall see, in the 1960s there was to some extent a rediscovery of history by Indian economists.

Industrialization and deindustrialization were the second major area of research within an economic and social history inspired by the Marxian turn. The deindustrialization of nineteenth-century Indian regions was a key plank of the nationalist critique of British rule and figured in Romesh Chunder Dutt's economic history of India. Amiya Bagchi's study of manufacturing employment in nineteenth-century Bihar may be the most important modern study of deindustrialization and sparked a renewed discussion and debate which drew participants from India as well as around the world.

Bagchi is also the author of what may be the most important study of industrialization in twentieth-century India, *Private Investment in India*. While the work is influenced by Keynesian macroeconomics, with its emphasis on demand as a crucial limit on private investment in the early decades of the twentieth century, its larger thesis is that "before the First World War, it was the governmental policy of free trade, and after the war it was the general depression in the capitalist system combined with the halting and piecemeal policy of tariff protection adopted by the Government of India, that limited the rate of investment in modern industry" (Bagchi 1972: 19). With this argument Bagchi took on a long line of thinkers who had argued that the problem of slow Indian growth and development was due to supply-side factors such as lack of capital, entrepreneurship or Indian values.

Bagchi combined his historical interests with research on contemporary issues. Both interests were brought together in his *Political Economy of Underdevelopment* (1982), which ranged beyond India to include discussions of Latin America, Indonesia, and China, as well as analyzing several problems in economic development, including land reform, labor, capital and the state, population growth, and planning. Bagchi's work investigated some of the classic themes in Indian economic history as inaugurated by the nationalists of the late nineteenth and early twentieth centuries, including deindustrialization, the constrained industrialization of British India, the extraction of resources through agricultural taxation, and the drain of colonial rule. Bagchi (1987, 1989, 1997) also produced seminal works on the financial history of British India.

The overlap between nationalist economic history and Marxian economic history illustrates what Sumit Sarkar has called a "Left nationalist–Marxist consensus." He wrote, "As the example of economic history indicates, there was considerable scope in modern Indian history for a kind of Left nationalist–Marxist consensus, a rough counterpart perhaps in historiography to the Nehruvian consensus which, at least in retrospect, seems to have characterized middle-class Indian intellectual life during those decades" (Sarkar 1997: 39). In this consensus the class struggle was subordinated to a critique of colonialism, which was seen as of greater consequence for understanding the evolution of the modern Indian economy.[6]

This consensus, along with its admixture of social and economic history, dominated major history departments in India from the 1960s. Even as late as 1997, a volume celebrating the seventy-fifth anniversary of Delhi University described the history department, which was one of the leading history departments in India, in the following terms: "Almost every member of the present Faculty has been constantly working on various aspects of socio-economic history cutting across chronological frontiers of Indian history . . . The Department has, over the years, set to achieve its objectives, viz. l'historire (*sic*) integrale: the study of 'total history' over the long (*sic*) duree" (Jain 2000: 165).

Economists re-engage with the past

While Marxism was reshaping the writing of history from the 1950s, economists at what had become the preeminent center for research and teaching of the discipline, the Delhi School of Economics, began to re-engage with the study of the past. In the closing years of the decade V. K. R. V. Rao, who established the Delhi School in 1949 and later became the Vice-Chancellor of Delhi University, invited Tapan Raychaudhuri to join the economics department, which he did in February 1959 (Raychaudhuri 2011: 274). In the early 1950s Raychaudhuri received a PhD in History from Calcutta University with a dissertation on the social history of Bengal in the Mughal period, after which he embarked upon a teaching career in Calcutta. Several years later he completed a DPhil in History at Oxford on the trade of the Dutch East India Company in South India. Upon returning to India he took up a post as the Deputy and then Acting Director of the National Archives of India.

It is not clear why Rao, who as previously noted showed little interest in history in his own career as an economist, asked a historian to join the economics department.[7] It is clearer, however, why Rao had to turn to someone trained as a historian and not as an economist: the decline of economic history within economics had meant that very few – if any – Indian economists had been trained in that field in recent decades. Raychaudhuri describes feeling lost in the midst of "very high-powered theoretical economics." This period was perhaps the heyday of the Delhi School as it boasted in its economics faculty K. N. Raj, Amartya Sen, Sukhamoy Chakravarty and Jagdish Bhagwati. Raychaudhuri writes in his memoir that he realized that he had made "a mistake in coming." At the same time, the colleagues were extremely accommodating. In 1964 a chair in economic history was created, to which he was appointed, and the department took a decision to specialize in economic history and economic development. This allowed for the addition of a reader in economic history, to which post Dharma Kumar was appointed, and the establishment of a visiting professorship in economic history, which drew top economic historians from the UK (including M. M. Postan, John Habakkuk and Peter Mathias), the United States, Japan, and the USSR. According to Raychaudhuri, "My colleagues were aware of my predicament, the professional isolation from which I suffered, and did their best to make me feel at home" (Raychaudhuri 2011: 278–9). With the growing presence of economic history at the school other members of the faculty were encouraged to venture into the field. Amartya Sen, for example, undertook studies of industrialization in India in the second half of the nineteenth century.[8]

In 1963 Tapan Raychaudhuri and Dharma Kumar launched the *Indian Economic and Social History Review*, which remains the leading journal of Indian economic history. The initial editorial committee included R. S. Sharma, Nurul Hasan, Ranajit Guha, K. N. Raj, M. N. Srinivas, Amartya Sen, Irfan Habib, and Dharma Kumar with Tapan Raychaudhuri as the managing editor. The journal, as suggested by the name and this group, had an interest in economic questions but was broadly defined to include the social and political dimensions. Over time cultural questions came increasingly under the purview of the journal as well. This broad approach also characterized the articles. The first issue of the journal contained essays on the nature of land rights in Mughal India, the pattern of public investment in early twentieth-century India, and two pieces on the nationalist movement and the agrarian economy.

Dharma Kumar and Tapan Raychaudhuri teamed up again to produce the *Cambridge Economic History of India*. The former (with the assistance of Meghnad Desai on the statistical parts), edited the second volume, which covered the period from the mid-eighteenth century to the present. The latter, along with Irfan Habib, edited the first volume, which ranged from 1200 to 1750. It was an unlikely editorial team. Tapan Raychaudhuri was a staunch nationalist, who had been jailed in 1942 during the Quit India movement, and Habib was a leading Marxist historian. Dharma Kumar, in the meantime, had made her name with an important critique of the nationalist narrative, arguing in her *Land and Caste in South India* (1965) that landless labor in South India was not a creation of British rule but predated it. The second volume of the *Cambridge Economic History* did not subscribe to the nationalist line and was criticized widely for this (Habib 1985).

In the 1970s economic history (along with econometrics) flourished at the Delhi School.[9] Economic history benefited from the fact that it made sense for students to remain at the school to pursue doctorates in the subject, as opposed to going to the UK or the USA (Kumar and Mookherjee 1995). From the 1960s the Delhi School produced a number of very fine economic historians, including Om Prakash, Omkar Goswami and Sanjay Subrahmanyam. Much of this work was not narrowly economic in its focus and included the social and political domains, as did the articles in the *Indian Economic and Social History Review*, and the interests and methods of the economic historians at the Delhi School shared much with historians in Delhi and elsewhere in India. While fine quantitative work emerged from the Delhi School, such as that of S. Sivasubramaniam (2000) on national income, cliometrics did not find a home, perhaps not least because of the poor quality of much Indian data.

Conclusion

In retrospect, the two-volume *Cambridge Economic History of India* marked the end of the heyday of economic history in India. While excellent work continued even after its publication in 1982, economic history slowly lost much of its glamour. At the moment, the Delhi School of Economics has no faculty in economic history. The leading history departments in India have shifted from social and economic history to social and cultural history. From the history recounted in this chapter, the decline of economic history may be seen as the outcome of two developments.

The first is the decline of Marxism, which had been the source of the economic turn in history departments from the 1950s. Of course, historians were not narrowly focused on only economic matters and they placed them in a broader context, but the economic came to be less central with the dwindling appeal of Marxism. For some, the shift from the economic was a reaction to crude reductionism, but for many it was a slow evolution as new concerns came to the fore. The career of Harbans Mukhia may be illustrative in which a shift from Marxism came from a deepening engagement with the *Annales* and the total history of that approach.[10] (This tension has already been seen in the Delhi University history department's commitment to social and economic history as well as total history.)

The second is the rise of a universal economics, or monoeconomics, within departments of economics. The search for an alternate paradigm drove the turn to history in Indian economics in the late nineteenth century. In the 1960s economic history flourished in tandem with development economics as they both sought to construct a framework that could help untangle the problems of the Indian economy. The growing influence of neoclassical economics and its universalization has eliminated the need for a historical approach in contemporary Indian economics.

Both of these developments – the decline of Marxism and the rise of neoclassical economics – are global in scope and are the latest chapter in the long interaction between Indian intellectuals and worldwide trends in thought. At the same time, domestic concerns have played a role as well. The rapid growth of the Indian economy after the late 1980s has come to be attributed to the liberalization and freeing of the economy from the command and control state system established by Jawaharlal Nehru. No matter the simple-mindedness of such an explanation, it has given sustenance to neoclassical orthodoxy.

A lesson of the history of economic history just recounted is that economic history thrives at times when heterodox thinking is given room to flourish. The decline of economic history in India may be seen as the product of the rise of orthodoxy. It remains to be seen if economic history may contribute to the emergence of new forms of heterodoxy in contemporary India or if we must await the rise of new heterodoxies in economics or in broader social science that can in turn reinvigorate economic historical inquiry.

Notes

1 For Gadgil's writings on cooperatives see his *Writings and Speeches of D. R. Gadgil on Cooperation* (1975).
2 This is how several years ago Harbans Mukhia described the impact of the book to me.
3 For a sense of the richness and range of agrarian history in recent decades see Chaudhuri 2008.
4 For a selection of key contributions to the debate see Patnaik 1990.
5 This essay has been reprinted in Patnaik 1990.
6 Amiya Bagchi confirmed this consensus in an interview, July 23, 2012.
7 According to Tapan Raychaudhuri, Rao had heard that he was not happy in his position at the National Archives and sought to help him with an appointment to the Delhi School. Interview with Raychaudhuri conducted on May 31, 2012.
8 See Sen 1965 and 1967.
9 Interview with Dilip Mookherjee, May 9, 2012.
10 See the intellectual biography of Mukhia by Rajat Datta (2008).

References

Appadorai, A. (1936) *Economic Conditions in Southern India (1000–1500 A.D.)*, 2 vols., Madras: University of Madras.

Bagchi, A. K. (1972) *Private Investment in India 1900–1939*, Cambridge: Cambridge University Press.

Bagchi, A. K. (1982) *The Political Economy of Underdevelopment*, Cambridge: Cambridge University Press.

Bagchi, A. K. (1987) *The Evolution of the State Bank of India: The Roots, 1806–1876*, 2 vols., Bombay: Oxford University Press.

Bagchi, A. K. (1989) *The Presidency Banks and the Indian Economy, 1876–1914*, Calcutta: Oxford University Press.

Bagchi, A. K. (1997) *The Evolution of the State Bank of India*, vol. 2, *The Era of the Presidency Banks, 1876–1920*, New Delhi: State Bank of India and Sage Publications.

Balachandran, G. (2003) 'Introduction', in G. Balachandran (ed.), *India and the World Economy 1850–1950*, Delhi: Oxford University Press, 1–45.

Byres, T. J. and H. Mukhia (eds.) (1985) *Feudalism and Non-European Societies*, London: Frank Cass.

Chaudhuri, B. B. (2008) *Peasant History of Late Pre-Colonial and Colonial India*, New Delhi: Pearson Longman.

Dange, S. A. (1971) *Gadgil and the Economics of Indian Democracy*, New Delhi: People's Publishing House.

Das Gupta, A. (2001) *The World of the Indian Ocean Merchant, 1500–1800: Collected Essays of Ashin Das Gupta*, New Delhi: Oxford University Press.

Datta, B. (1978) *Indian Economic Thought: Twentieth Century Perspectives 1900–1950*, New Delhi: Tata McGraw-Hill.

Datta, R. (2008) 'Harbans Mukhia: A Historian's Journey through a Millenium', in R. Datta (ed.), *Rethinking a Millenium: Perspectives on Indian History from the Eighth to the Eighteenth Century. Essays for Harbans Mukhia*, Delhi: Aakar Books, 361–79.

Dutt, R. (1960) *The Economic History of India*, vol. 1, *Under Early British Rule*, Delhi: Ministry of Information and Broadcasting, Government of India.

Gadgil, D. R. (1924) *The Industrial Evolution of India in Recent Times*, London: Oxford University Press.

Gadgil, D. R. (1975) *Writings and Speeches of D. R. Gadgil on Cooperation*, Poona: Gokhale Institute of Politics and Economics.

Ganguli, B. N. (1977) *Indian Economic Thought: Nineteenth Century Perspectives*, New Delhi: Tata McGraw-Hill.

Ghosh, S. C. (1948) *The Economic and Commercial Publications of the Post-Graduate Teachers of Calcutta University*, Calcutta: Calcutta University Press.

Gopalakrishnan, P. K. (1959) *Development of Economic Ideas in India (1880–1950)*, New Delhi: People's Publishing House.

Habib, I. (1963) *The Agrarian System of Mughal India*, Bombay: Asia Publishing House.

Habib, I. (1985) 'Studying a Colonial Economy without Perceiving Colonialism', *Modern Asian Studies*, 19 (3): 355–81.

Hirschman, A. O. (1981) 'The Rise and Decline of Development Economics', in his *Essays in Trespassing: Economics to Politics and Beyond*, Cambridge: Cambridge University Press, 1–24.

Jain, R. B. (ed.) (2000) *The University of Delhi: Faculties and Departments, A Profile*, Delhi: University of Delhi.

Joshi, P. C. (1986) 'Founders of the Lucknow School and their Legacy: Radhakamal Mukerjee and D. P. Mukerji: Some Reflections', *Economic and Political Weekly*, 21 (33): 1455–69.

Kosambi, D. D. (2002) 'Stages of Indian History', in his *Combined Methods in Indology and Other Writings*, Delhi: Oxford University Press.

Kumar, D. (1965) *Land and Caste in South India*, Cambridge: Cambridge University Press.

Kumar, D. and Dilip Mookherjee (eds.) (1995) *The D. School: Reflections on the Delhi School of Economics*, Delhi: Oxford University Press.

Moreland, W. H. (1920) *India at the Death of Akbar*, London: Macmillan.

Moreland, W. H. (1923) *From Akbar to Aurangzeb*, London: Macmillan.

Mukerjee, R. (1939) *The Economic History of India: 1600–1800*, London: Longmans, Green & Co.

Mukerjee, R. (1997) *India: The Dawn of New Era (An Autobiography)*, New Delhi: Radha Publications.

Patnaik, U. (ed.) (1990) *Agrarian Relations and Accumulation: The 'Mode of Production' Debate in India*, Delhi: Oxford University Press.

Pillay, K. P. K. (1957) *History of Higher Education in South India*, vol. 1, *University of Madras 1857–1957*, Madras: Associated Press.

Ranade, M. G. (1920) 'Indian Political Economy', in his *Essays on Indian Economics: A Collection of Essays and Speeches*, 3rd edn., Madras: G. A. Natesan.

Rao, S. L. (ed.) (2002) *The Partial Memoirs of V. K. R. V. Rao*, Delhi: Oxford University Press.

Raychaudhuri, T. (2011) *The World in Our Time: A Memoir*, Noida: Harper Collins Publishers India a joint venture with the India Today Group.

Sarkar, S. (1997) 'The Many Worlds of Indian History', in his *Writing Social History*, Delhi: Oxford University Press.

Sen, A. K. (1965) 'The Commodity Pattern of British Enterprise in Early Indian Industrialization 1854–1914', in the *Proceedings of the Second International Conference of Economic History Aix-en-Provence, 1962*, Paris: Mouton.

Sen, A. K. (1967) 'The Pattern of British Enterprise in India 1854–1914: A Causal Analysis', in B. Singh and V. B. Singh (eds.), *Social and Economic Change*, Bombay: Allied Publishers.

Sharma, R. S. (1965) *Indian Feudalism: c. 300–1200*, Calcutta: University of Calcutta.

Sinha, N. K. (1956–70) *The Economic History of Bengal*, 3 vols., Calcutta: Firma K. L. Mukhopadyay.

Sivasubramaniam, S. (2000) *The National Income of India in the Twentieth Century*, Delhi: Oxford University Press.

Stokes, E. (1978) 'The Return of the Peasant to South Asian History', in his *The Peasant and the Raj: Studies in Agrarian Society and Peasant Rebellion in Colonial India*, Cambridge: Cambridge University Press, 265–89.

Thapar, R. (2011) 'Early Indian History and the Legacy of DD Kosambi', *Resonance*, 16 (6): 551–73.

Thomas, P. J. (1926) *Mercantilism and the East India Trade*, London: P. S. King & Son.

Thomas, P. J. and B. Nataraja Pillai (1933) *Economic Depression in the Madras Presidency (1820–1854)*, Madras: Diocesan Press.

University of Calcutta (1920?) *Post-Graduate Teaching in the University of Calcutta 1919–1920*, Calcutta: University Press.

18

ECONOMIC HISTORY IN CHINA

Tradition, divergence and potential

Li Bozhong[1]

Economic history as a modern academic discipline arose in China in the early twentieth century, but as a field of study had a long indigenous tradition prior to 1900. Since then, the discipline has gone through periods of formation (1904–50), transformation (1950–78) and prosperity (1978–99), and now at the beginning of the twenty-first century, ironically, it faces unprecedented new challenges.

The *Shi-Huo* scholarship: the antecedents of economic history in China

Unlike many countries where economic history is a new academic discipline introduced by Western academe, Chinese economic history has its own local origins which can be traced back over two millennia. During the process of unification and centralization under imperial authority, political economy had already become a central topic of China's foundational schools of thought. The Spring and Autumn Period (770 BC–476 BC) and the Warring States Period (476 BC–221 BC) were characterized by "the contention of the hundred schools of thought" as statesmen and scholars debated how to rule over society and economy. There were animated and lively discussions not just of agriculture, handicrafts, commerce, "international" trade within the Chinese world of the time, tax and corvée systems, market management, consumption, profit, labor, but also of what wealth consisted, how market and money worked, what role price played in economic life, etc. The discussions were deep, comprehensive and far-reaching and produced systematic and complete classics and doctrines. From these classics and doctrines the basic concepts, principles and discourses of what Michel Cartier has called "Chinese classical political economy" were established (Qian Li and Da Tong 1994).

It is one of the major features of Chinese civilization that people seek for knowledge and wisdom, and for solutions to contemporary problems, not from God, but from the accumulated experiences of their predecessors, or history. This emphasis on past experience made economic history crucial to Chinese classical statesmanship. When China entered its early imperial period (221 BC–AD 589), economic history developed into a branch of historiography. In the Western Han Dynasty, Sima Qian (ca.145–ca.86 BC), the founding father of Chinese historiography, completed his writing of the first general history of China called *Shiji* (Historical Records of the Grand Historian) in 91 BC. In this voluminous masterpiece, he paid special attention to economic events and activities and included two special treatises, the *Pingzhun Shu* (Treatise of Equalizing Agronomical Matters) and the *Huozhi Liezhuan* (Collective Biography of Great Merchants), to describe these events and activities. The first one focuses on issues of national wealth and the state's policies on agriculture, handicrafts, commerce, currency and public finance, while the second one describes in detail commerce, trade and merchants of previous and contemporary times with a very insightful discussion of market mechanisms and the role of the market in national economic activities. These works laid the foundations for Chinese scholarship in economic history.

A century later, another great historian of the Eastern Han Dynasty, Ban Gu (AD 32–92), following Sima Qian's example, created the *Shi-Huo Zhi* (Treatise on Food and Money) in his great work, the *Han Shu* (History of the Western Han Dynasty). Since the words *shi* and *huo* in the *Han Shu* refer to the performances of agriculture and commerce, which constituted almost the entire Chinese economy at that time, the history of "food and money" is a general history of the economy of China from ancient times to the end of the Western Han Dynasty. Following the precedent of *Han Shu*, most *Zheng Shi* "Official Dynastic Histories" of China written by subsequent dynasties included their own *Shi-Huo Zhi*. The major sources for these *Shi-Huo Zhi* were government documents and archives.[2] Besides the *Shi-Huo Zhi*, similar "histories of food and money" also existed in other official compilations. In mid-imperial times, more and more scholars became interested in *Shi-Huo* scholarship. Three representative scholars were Du You (AD 735–812) of the Tang dynasty, Zheng Qiao (1108–66), of the Southern Song dynasty, and Ma Duanlin (1254–1323) of the Yuan dynasty. All three were first-class historians, each of whom compiled an encyclopedic documentary history of Chinese institutions from the earliest times to the present: the *Tongdian* (Comprehensive institutions) by Du, the *Tongzhi* (General Treatises) by Zheng and the *Wenxian tongkao* (General Study of the Literary Remains) by Ma. All three works were entitled *Tong* (general) and were collectively called the *Three Tongs*. Each is an enormous and original work covering such topics as military affairs, culture, religion, philology, phonetics, the development of families and descent groups, etc. but a good part of their works dealt with economic history. Quite different from the officially compiled *Shi-Huo Zhi,* these private histories are distinguished by strong personal observations and are richer in content and more informative. Moreover, the authors did not just collect huge amounts of original materials and classify the useful information from these materials carefully by subjects, but also did their research on many important issues of economic history from a long-term (trans- and multi-dynasty) perspective.

The continued compilation of similar works by later imperial dynasties, the *Shi-Tong* series (The Ten General Series), including the *Three Tongs*, contain over 2700 volumes, totaling more than 30,000,000 Chinese characters. Each work in the *Shi-Tong* series has volumes of *Shi-Huo*, which are much bigger than those in the "Official Dynastic Histories." The volumes contain more materials on economic history and the materials are better categorized, which is particularly important in systematically recording the systems, regulations and policies of state finance, taxation, disaster relief and other major fiscal institutions, and their changes. Other kinds of systematically organized collections of economic documents and records include the *Huidian* (Collected institutes and precedents) and *Huiyao* (Collected Statutes), which were compiled by the central government of each dynasty. Detailed records on economic practices of the government, at the central and provincial levels, were kept in *Zeli* (Regulations and precedents).[3] Local economic activities and events were recorded in gazetteers (or local histories) under the categories of "Local products," "Customs," "Water control activities," "Taxation," "Population registration," "Philanthropy," "Disaster relief" and so on.[4]

Though the state took over the compilation of economic documents and records, individual scholars did not stop their work of compilation of materials of economic history as well as of research of issues in society and economy from historical perspectives. A new intellectual movement of *Jingshi* (Statecraft), which aimed at "learning of practical use to society" (*jingshi zhiyong*), rose in China in the late twelfth and early thirteenth centuries and grew into a movement in the late sixteenth and early seventeenth centuries when China faced serious challenges. In the nineteenth century, when China was in crisis again, the school of statecraft was reactivated after a dormancy of more than a century. The emergence of revived interest led to the formation of the influential *Jingshi* School. The *Jingshi* scholars spent huge energy in collecting, compiling and analyzing historical materials, to try to find the solutions to the crisis. Their efforts resulted in the compilation and publication of the *Jingshi wenbian* (Collected Essays on Statecraft under the Reigning Dynasty) series which contain most important statecraft documents of the Ming and Qing dynasties, the majority of which are on social and economic issues. The *Jingshi* scholars also made their analysis of these issues from historical perspectives. The re-emergence of the statecraft school in the nineteenth century also benefited greatly from another important development of Chinese learning – the formation and growth of the *Qian-Jia* School. This school originated in the mid-seventeenth century, with two great scholars and enlightenment thinkers, Gu Yanwu and Huang Zongxi, being the representatives, both of whom strongly emphasized the importance of textual research, argumentation and composition, insisting that arguments should be based on reliable evidence.

In the first half of the Qing period, Chinese intellectual life was muted by the harsh cultural despotism of the Qing state. Scholars had to shift their interests from contemporary issues to "pure" academic issues, mainly the study of history. They inherited and developed the textual methods of interpreting classics and languages, and of proper presentation, which Gu and Huang applied to studying languages, textual criticism and philology. At first, they focused on interpreting the meanings of classical works. Later, they began to observe and study history, geography, astronomy, calendar, temperament (music), laws and regulations. As a result, bibliographical and textual criticism including the transmission of texts became a major focus of Qing scholarship. During the late eighteenth and early nineteenth centuries under the reigns of Emperors Qianlong and Jiaqing, the work of the *Qian-Jia* School reached its peak. Methodologically, this school shares many common principles with the Rankian Historical School which appeared in Europe in the late nineteenth century. According to Yu Yingshi (Yu Ying-shih), one of the leading historians in our times, it is no wonder that Rankianism was so easily accepted by the majority of Chinese historians when it was introduced into China in the early twentieth century (Yu Yingshi 1976: 248–51).

Thus by the twentieth century China had had a two millennia-long tradition of systematic and continual recording and describing of economic activities, events and institutions, as well as of analyzing and interpreting economic changes and performance. Chinese historians had also developed a methodology for dealing with historical documents which is quite similar to the Rankian one. But the *Shi-Huo* Studies are not economic history in the modern sense. The basic difference lies in the fact that they mainly focus on recording and describing economic activities, events and institutions. While some great scholars made original observations, analyses and interpretations of past economic phenomena and processes and had a few valuable insights in their studies some of which are very vital and striking even to us modern economic historians, they lacked a complete set of thematic and theoretical concerns, analytical methodologies and language which Chinese classical political economy could not provide.

The formation, 1904–50

In spite of the long Chinese antecedents of *Shi-Huo* Studies, the modern discipline of Chinese economic history is not indigenous; instead, it was introduced from the modern West. In the mid-nineteenth century, China was facing new and unprecedented challenges. Foreign invasions and internal rebellions shook the country. The most significant response by the Qing was the Self-Strengthening Movement which marks the beginning of China's modernization. The basic principles of the movement are "Chinese learning for the foundation, and Western learning for application." John Fairbank called this formulation a "halfway Westernization, in tools but not in values, which was apparent to a majority of the Chinese officials, who felt the necessity of learning from the foreigners but opposed all things Western" (Fairbank and Goldman 2006: 217). Western academic works were introduced to China on a large scale. The introduction of new ideas including, for example, those from Adam Smith's *Wealth of Nations* (translated by Yan Fu, a famous reformer), was extremely welcomed by the reform-minded Chinese. Partly because of the Chinese tradition of *Jingshi* thought, which shared some common features with early modern Western political economy, the *Wealth of Nations* immediately became a focus of the Chinese intelligentsia, after the translation was published in 1901.

While the end of the Qing dynasty, and the two thousand year-long imperial system, brought hope of creating a new and modern China to all the Chinese people, the Republican government was inept and could not control society as effectively as in imperial times. Partly for this reason, this period became one full of passions and excitements which had never been seen before in Chinese history. A feeling of freedom – free thinking, free speaking, free writing – spread over many Chinese cities, especially among educated young people. During the 1920s and 1930s, China saw an outpouring of Western thoughts. Many educated Chinese were eager to study every kind of political and social theory, examine the nature of their own social fabric, debate the values of new methods of social sciences, and explore the possibilities for progress that seemed to lie at the heart of Western learning. A core strategy of Chinese modernization was the self-conscious transformation and modernization of traditional Chinese scholarship. In the minds of many leading scholars, modernization, Westernization and scientification were virtually synonymous. Accordingly, the modernization of Chinese scholarship meant the creation of Western-style scholarship in China. One of the major tasks was to take Western academic research as the new standard and paradigm of disciplinary knowledge, and research methodologies for modern Chinese scholarship.

Economic history was one of the major products of this new intellectual movement. Since it is a Chinese tradition to study contemporary problems in a historical perspective, it was necessary to understand what was wrong with traditional Chinese society and economy and their failure to make China a "modern nation." It was clear that traditional Chinese scholarship could not complete this task, new scholarship was needed. The new scholarship could be available from the West (usually via Japan in the early stage). In his famous 1902 article titled "Xin Shixue" (New History), Liang Qichao (1873–1929), one of the founders of modern Chinese historiography, already called for a "revolution of history writing" and creating a "New History."[5] One of the major characteristic features of this "New History," according to Liang Qichao (1902), was to adopt "principles and laws of other disciplines," and use them in the study of history. The first achievement of the *New History* movement was Liang's *History of Chinese National Debt*, published in 1904, which marked the appearance of the discipline of Chinese economic history.

Liang's call for a New History began an inexorable trend. In the 1920s, Hu Shi and Fu Sinian, two leading historians as well as the leaders of the nationwide "New Culture" movement which was a development of the May Fourth movement, were at the vanguard of the push to study Western learning. Even those comparatively "conservative" historians who insisted that Chinese traditional scholarship should not be replaced by Western scholarship, were also indirectly influenced by the movement. The *New History* movement developed in different directions and evolved into two major schools of history in the 1920s and 1930s: the Historical Materialism School and the Textual Criticism School. The former focused on assembling a grand unified theory of historical evolution, while the latter emphasized the importance of dealing with the historical materials using more "scientific" methods. Both were highly influenced by late nineteenth century German scholarship which was overwhelmingly popular in Japan and China in this period. The Historical Materialism School derived basic ideas from Hegelian and Marxian philosophies of history, which argued that the historical development of human history follows a set of successive stages. Later, the school diverged further into two sub-schools: Marxist and non-Marxist schools. Both of the sub-schools put social and economic history at the core of their study of Chinese history.

The Textual Criticism School, also known as the "Scientific History," "Positivist History" or "New Textology" school, was influenced by the Rankian approach which focused on the empirical mode and positivist sciences, with great emphasis on facts. The leader of the Textual Criticism School, Fu Sinian (1896–1950), was labeled the "Chinese Ranke." According to Fu, the task of the historian exclusively consists of the verification and organization of historical material, allowing the bare facts contained in the sources to speak for themselves. Accordingly, they opposed the use of any kind of theory or view of history and fiercely condemned any involvement of the historian in politics. As Hu Shi (1891–1962), a leader of the school and of the modern Chinese intellectual movement, advocated, Chinese scholars should engage in "more study of problems, less talk of -isms." Deeply convinced of the feasibility of the experimentalist approach, with its reliance on coolness and reflective deliberation, Hu counseled the individual solution of individual problems with "bold hypothesis, but careful verification." Many of the scholars of this school used their skills in the study of social and economic history. The reorientation of historical studies on the basis of a combination of the methods and concepts developed by Western historical and social science and the Chinese *Qian-Jia* tradition is exemplified in the person of Zhang Yinlin (1905–42), who graduated from Stanford University.

In this intellectual climate, it is no wonder that economic history became the vanguard and the core of modern Chinese historical scholarship and experienced rapid growth.[6] According to an authoritative survey, 524 works on Chinese economic history were published in the first half of the twentieth century, mostly during the five years 1932–37 (Zeng Yeying 2000: 82–3). Moreover, a great improvement was achieved in the academic quality of the works. In the early 1930s two professional journals of economic history were published by two prestigious academic institutions. The first – *Zhongguo jindai jingjishi yanjiu jikan* (Journal of Modern Chinese Economic History), which was later renamed as *Zhongguo shehui jingjishi yanjiu jikan* (Journal of Chinese Socio-Economic History) – was published in 1932. The second, *Shi-Huo Bimonthly*, was published in 1934 with Tao Xisheng (T'ao Hsi-sheng) being the chief editor.[7] Both journals created a completely new approach, and laid a foundation in this field. Though the year of the creation of *Zhongguo shehui jingjishi yanjiu jikan* is seen as a watershed in the formation of the discipline, *Shi-Huo Bimonthly* may have been more influential and was considered the most famous journal of socio-economic history in China or even in East Asia with a circulation of 10,000.[8] The primary reason for the journals' success is that they initiated first-hand historical data gathering. They stressed that historians should find the issues and digest theories through data arrangement. Contributing to the new research atmosphere, they (in particular the *Shi-Huo Bimonthly*) introduced the theory and method of social science coming from Europe and America, and urged China's historical science to integrate into global trends. The two journals made great contributions to the development of fledgling Chinese economic history. Other journals such as *Yinhang Zhoubao* (Bank Weekly), *Zhonghang yuekan* (Bank of China Monthly) and *Nonghang yuekan* (Agricultural Bank Monthly) also published economic history subjects and became important to the discipline.

Professional academic societies of economic history appeared in this period. Behind *Zhongguo shehui jingjishi yanjiu jikan* was the Society of Historical Studies, while the Society of Shi-Huo took the *Shi-Huo Bimonthly* as the hub of their activities. Similar societies were established in other major Chinese universities, among which the best known may be the Society of Chinese Economic History of Sun Yat-sen University. As early as 1931 Peking University organized classes in Chinese Social History (in fact, it was Socio-Economic History) and Historical Materialism. Two years later the teaching and research section of Chinese economic history was founded in the Law School of the same university and a series of works on Chinese economic history was published. Outside campus, Marxist historians were quite active. Led by Guo Moruo (1892–1978), Fan Wenlan (1893–1969), Lu Zhenyu (1901–80), Li Jiannong (1880–1963) and Hou Wailu (1903–87), Marxist scholars translated major Marxist works into Chinese (including Karl Marx's massive *Das Kapital*, his *Zur Kritik der politischen Ökonomie* and others). Using Marxist discourses and frameworks of analysis, they produced a number of important works on Chinese social and economic history, which won increasing influence among the scholars of the younger generations, though some of them were criticized for being too dogmatic in their adherence to the Marxist model.[9]

All the changes listed above show that the discipline of economic history had grown rapidly and held an important position in modern Chinese history by the Japanese invasion in 1937. In spite of these achievements, major problems can be found in this period. First, though a few leading scholars emphasized the necessity of borrowing methods from social sciences and applying them in the study of Chinese economic history, only limited efforts were made. Second, though some historians began to focus on the characteristic features of Chinese economic history, Eurocentrism held the main position in the study. Third, many scholars believed that scholarship should serve to find the solutions of major contemporary Chinese problems. This is reflected in the continuous emphasis on presentist problems that marked the development of the discipline.[10] This "path dependency" had a mixed impact. On the one hand, it stimulated the interest of scholars in China's past social and economic conditions and thereby advanced historical knowledge; on the other hand, it made scholarship and politics intertwine which would harm academic developments.

The vigorous growth of Chinese economic history was interrupted by the Japanese invasion in 1937. During the extremely hard time of the war (1937–45) and the civil war (1946–49), however, Chinese scholars did not stop working and achieved considerable advancements. The most important one was the training of social and economic historians of the younger generations. Chinese elite universities (in particular the National Southwestern Associated University which was formed by a merger of three top universities – Peking University, Tsinghua University and Nankai University in 1937) did not stop their teaching of the subject. Almost all the best Chinese economic and social historians working in the second half of the twentieth century, whether in mainland China, Taiwan, Hong Kong or the USA, were trained in these universities during this period. It is these scholars who played a key role in the next phase of this story.

The transformation, 1950–78

In the West, after 1945 a sense of dissatisfaction with pre-war formulations gradually became apparent and from about 1955 the study of history entered a period of rapid change and reassessment (Barraclough 1978: 227, 229, 257). Such change also took place in China in the early 1950s, but followed a totally different path. For the majority of Chinese economic historians, the German influence remained strong throughout the interwar years. It was gradually superseded, from the 1920s onwards, by the influence of historical materialism, and a great controversy ensued which, in the case of China, was only resolved by the communist victory of 1949, though Marxism had been steadily gaining ground long before. The foundation of the People's Republic of China (PRC) in 1949 began a new era in the discipline of economic history. At first Soviet Marxist historiography was dominant, but beginning with the 1958 "Revolution of History," a new style of Marxist history writing – Maoist historiography – developed which by the 1960s and 1970s overwhelmed all other approaches.

In the early 1950s, Soviet Marxist historiography was imposed throughout China. As part of political indoctrination, all historians had to study the classics of Marxism and Soviet political education textbooks.[11] The Soviet version of Marxist theory of history was regarded as the supreme guide in the study of Chinese history. A good number of works of Russian and Soviet economic history were also introduced. The Stalinist theory of history was accepted as the official doctrine in the field and most Chinese historians aligned themselves with it. Because Marxism emphasizes the determinant of the "economic base," economic history held the central position in the new history. In the 1950s there were five nationwide debates which are called "five golden flowers of New China's history": the formation of the Han nation, the nature of landholding in feudal China, the interpretation of peasant uprisings, the transition from feudalism to capitalism and the origins of capitalism in China, and the periodization of modern Chinese history (1840–1949) with special reference to the impact and consequences of Western imperialism. Of the five debates, four belonged to, or were related to, social and economic history.[12] In these debates, a number of important works on Chinese economic history were produced. The establishment of Marxism as the "guiding theory" transformed the discipline. In contrast to the prejudice of pre-1949 mainstream scholarship which cherished the belief in "history is historical materials," the new scholarship raised a battle cry "the study of history must be guided with (Marxist) theory." Such high stress on the role of theories had never been seen before. Marxism provided a theoretic framework of analysis of economic history, which was missing in previous mainstream scholarship. The new scholarship also highlighted the activities of ordinary people and their roles in history, which were ignored in the earlier scholarship. All these changes were significant in the development of economic history.

During the 1950s and early 1960s some significant theoretical innovations were made by Chinese economic historians. Of them the theories of "Chinese capitalist sprouts" (or "Chinese capitalist embryo," "Chinese indigenous capitalism") and of "Chinese Feudal Society" are the most important. In the century before 1950, the view of "Unchanging China" or "stagnant China" had dominated the study of Chinese history. This view originated with Wilhelm Friedrich Hegel, who thought that China was outside modern development. His view had a profound influence on Western thinkers for generations, including Karl Marx. Marx placed China in his category of "Asiatic societies" which, he claimed, could not follow the Western way of evolution. He saw China as a mummy carefully preserved in a hermetically sealed coffin, which would dissolve whenever it was brought into contact with open air. According to this view, late imperial Chinese society and economy were hopelessly stagnant.[13] In contrast to this conventional wisdom, the theory of "Chinese Capitalist Spouts" held that late imperial Chinese society and economy were not stagnant but ever changing, and major changes that happened in China resembled the changes that happened in early modern Western Europe. The driving forces behind the changes of society and economy in both China and Western Europe were the same – capitalism, which was indigenous. However, many scholars found that the differences between imperial Chinese society and economy and the West European ones are so obvious that the concept of "feudal society" from the Marxist classics can hardly be applied intact to Chinese history. Compared with West European feudal society, Chinese "feudal society" seems both "precocious" as well as "immature."[14] Accordingly, it was argued that Chinese historians should find the characteristics of Chinese "feudal society," rather than forcing the Chinese reality into the West European model. Though these theories arose within the Marxist framework of analysis and discourse, they were important breakthroughs from the doctrines of Soviet historiography.

In the period 1955–65, the government organized and sponsored the work of collecting and cataloging economic historical materials. By 1966, several important collections and compilations of data had been published, which served as a basic source not only in this period, but also later.[15] However, serious problems were manifest in the subject at this time, of which the following two are most important. First, economic history became more and more politicized, and the mainstream of all pre-1950 Chinese scholarship was condemned as "bourgeois" and disregarded. In the 1950s Soviet scholarship was taken as the guide, while in the 1960s and 1970s with the Sino-Soviet rift the Chinese state imposed a sort of self-closure on the Chinese academe. Western scholarship was rejected totally. As a result, the study of Chinese economic history was isolated from the development of international scholarship. Second, dogmatism was prevailing and intensified. The pattern of evolution of West European history was seen as universal and Chinese reality had to conform to this universal pattern. In particular, Chinese historical development had to follow a "five modes of production" formula, going through the successive stages of primitive, slavery, feudal, capitalist and socialist modes of production. As the conclusion is predetermined, the approach was oversimplified.

Within this political climate, the room left to Chinese economic historians was very limited. Their major task was to justify the theory of class struggle and to interpret Chinese history via this theory. One of the main aims of the new historiography, in Jian Bozan's words, was to "reveal the laws of historical development and then respond and adjust to the laws," "not only interpret history, but change history" (Jian Bozan 1950). This led to concentration on a small number of key topics such as Chinese "feudalistic" economic systems (ownership, rent, taxation systems, etc.), the hardship of peasant life, the fragility and backwardness of peasant family economy, the cruelty and ruthlessness of the state, as well as the necessity and reasonableness of peasant uprisings.[16] During the Cultural Revolution (1966–76), the theory of "class struggle" was developed into an absurd theory of "line struggle," that is, the struggles between Confucianism and Legalism, or between the "anti-reactionary" and the "reactionary" lines in the ruling classes in Chinese history which was considered to be the dynamics behind all social and economic change. The politicization led to the political persecution of historians, Marxist and non-Marxist. Almost all economic historians were condemned as "bourgeois," some of whom, including such leading Marxist historians as Wu Han (1909–69) and Jian Bozan (1898–1968), were persecuted to death. Many famous non-Marxist historians such as Chen Yinke (1890–1969) and Liang Fanzhong (1908–70) also died in this atmosphere of terror. In this decade, the discipline of Chinese economic history was completely ruined. Courses of economic history were cancelled, professional journals were stopped, and libraries and archives were closed. No works of economic history were published and no foreign works of economic history were introduced during this decade.

The development of Chinese historiography between 1949 and the 1960s received a great deal of attention in the Soviet Union, where it has largely been assessed in ideological and political terms. No one is likely to deny that there are strong political overtones both in the choice of subject matter and in its handling; but we are concerned here with the positive results, and even unsympathetic critics are impressed with both the quantity of new work and its positive achievements. In economic history, in particular, many new research avenues were opened and the foundation laid for writing the economic history of modern China at a higher level of theoretical sophistication and with a more comprehensive control of the empirical data than was the case in the past. There is general agreement that much valuable new documentary material was made available, but it is recognized also that there were significant advances in methodology and that a real effort was made to create a new view of the Chinese past to replace the discarded Confucian version.

The prosperity, 1978–late 1990s

In December 1978, the CCP summoned the third plenum of the eleventh Central Committee. In this plenum, the political line of "taking class struggle as the key link" upheld in Mao's era was formally abandoned and replaced with a pragmatic line of modernization which is well known as "reform and opening up." This is a major landmark in modern Chinese history and inaugurated a new era of China's economic historiography.

With the passing of the fear generated by the Cultural Revolution, Chinese economic historians began to leave behind the conceptual straitjacket imposed for two decades by the theory of class struggle. In the 1980s, almost all economic historians who had been persecuted in political movements in the previous three decades were rehabilitated and given teaching or research jobs at academic institutions. Those who had received their professional training in the pre-1949 period became the backbone in the academic renaissance of Chinese economic history. They took this rare opportunity for disciplinary development and began anew their academic work. They concentrated on summarizing their work of the past decades and developing their research. This led to a massive resurgence of publication activities rarely seen ever in the history of the discipline. At the same time, these historians were eager to train a new generation of economic historians, deeply worried that the discipline would disappear since no scholars had been trained for more than a decade. Courses of economic history were offered and postgraduate training programs in social and economic history were created in many universities which were open to bright young people who passed highly competitive admission exams. The academic contingent of economic history expanded in size and improved significantly in professionalism. In sum, the discipline witnessed an unprecedented prosperity in the 1980s and 1990s.

The institutions of economic history that had been destroyed in the "Cultural Revolution" were resumed and new ones were created. Two major journals – the *Journal of Chinese Social and Economic History* published by Xiamen University and *Investigations in Chinese Economic History* published by the Institute of Economics of Chinese Academy of Social Sciences – were started in 1982 and 1985 respectively. They play a very important role similar to what the *Journal of Chinese Socio-Economic History* and *Shi-Huo Bimonthly* did in the 1930s. A professional Internet portal was established in 2000 which provides a new forum for economic historians. Associations of economic historians were founded in most provinces and major cities in the early 1980s. Building upon them, the Chinese Economic History Society (CEHS) was inaugurated in 1986. Nearly 20,000 works on Chinese economic history were published in the decade 1986–95 alone, which outnumbered the total publications in the 83 years since 1904 when Liang Qichao published his *History of Chinese National Debt*.[17]

More important than the quantitative progress was the qualitative improvement which had taken place in the discipline. The field has been enlarged greatly; new issues have been brought under study and advances have been made in the fields related to economic history such as historical demography, ecology, environment, geography, natural disasters, technology, water control, transportation and so on. These advances were very helpful to economic historians. In the 1980s, the overriding problem for Chinese historians was still to relate the historical development of China to the categories of the Marxist periodization of history, without doing violence to the unique features and special qualities of China's past. In 1978, a conference on "The Periodization of Chinese History" was held in Changchun which ushered in an unprecedented era of scholarly achievement. In the early 1980s four nationwide conferences were held on "Chinese capitalist sprouts," as well as other nationwide conferences on the "Economic Structure of Chinese Feudal Society" (1982, Guangzhou), the "Chinese Feudal Landlord Class" (1984, Kunming) and the like, which can be seen as the last glory of Chinese economic history as an academic discipline, arresting the nation's attention.

After three decades of self-isolation, with opening to the outside world, the decades after 1978 saw an upsurge of foreign scholarship. More works of economic history as well as of economics, sociology and other social sciences have been translated into Chinese. New theories and methods rushed into China at an unprecedented speed and scale and the old simplified approaches have given place to the new multi-analysis approaches. At the same time, many pre-1950 works of economic history were re-published, as well as a few important not-yet-published works which had been written in the 1950s and early 1960s.[18] Through these works the previous academic achievements made by Chinese economic historians became available to younger scholars. In particular, the empirical approach which dominated in the first half of the twentieth century but was disgraced in the three decades before 1980, was rehabilitated and once again became the foundational methodology of economic history.

Significant advances were achieved in the 1980s and 1990s. First, inspired by Deng Xiaoping's call to "Seek truth from facts" and to "Emancipate the mind," Chinese economic historians gradually broke through the shackles of dogmatism. Marxism was still the guiding theory of economic history, but there was a gradual relaxation of Marxist interpretation. With the abandonment of the ironclad rule to "take class struggle as the key link," the highly politicized and ideologized study of peasant uprisings which had dominated Chinese economic history in Mao's era gradually stepped down from the center stage. The Chinese Society of Peasant Wars which was founded in 1978 and became overwhelmingly influential, languished in the late 1990s and became almost completely defunct by the end of 1990s. With the shift of official ideological emphasis from "relations of production" to the "forces of production" (i.e. technology, resource use, productivity and the like) in the 1980s, the central concern of Chinese economic historians focused on a vital historical question: what were the economic origins of China's modernization? The new focus tends to be on specifics of civilization in traditional China, and the general paradigm of how China has responded to the dual challenges of interactions with the outside world and modernization in the post-1700 era. A new generation of scholars turned to address directly the question of economic development. Although the issue related chiefly to new policy, nonetheless the new studies were more and more depoliticized.

Second, a new focus spotlighted the developmental effects of the market. There were major efforts in the 1980s and 1990s to bring the concerns and methods of microeconomics to bear on Chinese history. Earlier studies had been mainly macroeconomic; the later approaches laudably turned the spotlight from gross national output to the neglected subjects of markets, prices, enterprise/household choice, etc. Third, in the previous period, the pattern of evolution of society and economy derived from West European experience was venerated as the universal law that Chinese history had to follow. This deeply seated Eurocentric paradigm is concerned mainly with counterfactuals and tends to ignore China's past reality. Although this sort of Eurocentrism has received increasing criticism in the West in the past decades, it remained the basic workhorse for most Chinese historians until the mid-1990s. Since then however, the universality of the pattern has been challenged. The theory of "Chinese Capitalist Sprouts" has been questioned, and then abandoned by many scholars.[19] The same is the case with the theory of the "Chinese Feudal Society."[20] Meanwhile, new theories and models have been proposed, aiming at finding better explanations for the evolution of early modern Chinese society and economy.[21] This change shows that to study Chinese history on the basis of Chinese facts has become the shared belief of a new generation of scholars and China's economic history must be looked at from a new perspective.

Fourth, a significant divergence has taken place in the discipline. Based on their different approaches, three major schools have emerged. They are (1) the School of Socio-Economic History, which has been the mainstream of China's economic historiography in most of the post-1950 period, but has changed greatly since 1978; (2) the School of Economic History led by Wu Chengming, which pays more attention to economic performance and to the use of theories and methods from economics; and (3) the School of Social History represented by Fu Yiling, which concentrates more on social changes from the perspective of sociology and anthropology. The emergence of these three schools changed the landscape of the discipline and ushered in a new period of "a hundred flowers blooming, and a hundred schools of thought contending."

Challenges and responses in the new century

China has witnessed a rapid and large-scale transformation in the past decades which has rarely been seen in world history. It is impossible to understand China's current economic miracle and predict its future if one does not know China's long-term social and economic experience. This gives China's historians an opportunity to look afresh at the past and evaluate its significance and that is why more and more first-class scholars in other fields are shifting to Chinese social and economic history.[22] By the way, as early as the late 1980s, some people warned that an intellectual crisis was coming.[23] And, by the late 1990s, everyone working in this field experienced the specter of impending crisis, whether "theoretical," "methodological," or "paradigmatic." Some scholars have pointed out that the "crisis" was not unique to China. Rather, it was a reflection of the global theoretical crisis of history (Huang 1991). After three decades of opening to the outside world, Chinese economic history was becoming part of international scholarship and hence could not avoid the global crisis in history. Moreover, for decades Chinese economic historians had been working within the analytical framework of Marxism, but now the dominant position of Marxism in the discipline was challenged leading to a generation gap in Chinese academe. Further challenges came from the postmodernist attacks, the need for new skills in big data processing and so on. All these brought serious problems to many scholars and made them feel at the end of their resources. It is understandable that they felt that the discipline was in dire straits.

But this is not the whole story. If we consider what has happened in the field of economic history in its entirety, we must say that, although the challenges are real, new and significant advances have been made in the first decade of the twenty-first century. In the twentieth century, Chinese economic historians were working in the theoretical system of classical political economy of Adam Smith, David Ricardo and Karl Marx. But in the last decades many other economic theories became important in China, though classical political economy still occupies a key place in the tools used in Chinese economic history. China has seen a wholesale introduction of current Western social science scholarship. New approaches in international scholarship of economic history, such as neo-institutional economics, quantitative economics, social classification theory, environmental science, demography and so forth, have been accepted by many Chinese economic historians. New scholarship has brought new topics and approaches to economic history, and the excessive concentration of attention in previous studies on a limited range of topical problems has gone forever. Such major paradigms of Western Chinese studies (mainly in the USA), as "Impact and Response Paradigm," "China-Centered Paradigm," "Global Oriented Paradigm," "Revolution Paradigm," "Modernization Paradigm" and so on, are welcomed by many younger scholars and animate lively discussions about the fitness and applicability of these paradigms in Chinese economic history.

The openness toward and awareness of the new theories and paradigms are significant to Chinese economic historians. Many of them reshape their approaches and make a more precise and deliberate application of well-defined theories. As a result, a few previously received theories in Chinese history are questioned or, more often, ignored by the majority of scholars of younger generations. For example, in the second half of the twentieth century, the overriding problem for Chinese historians was to relate the historical development of China to the categories of the Marxist periodization of history, without doing violence to the unique features and special qualities of China's past. All the main controversies among Chinese economic historians of the day centered round this basic question, and their preoccupation with periodization to a large extent determined the choice of topics upon which they were engaged. But most of the scholars have lost interest in such questions and accordingly no nationwide debates on such big topics have been held since the late 1990s. Philip Huang (1991) argued that "the theoretical impasse between the feudalism and incipient capitalism schools has bred pervasive skepticism among younger Chinese scholars, so much so that few bother even to address the operating analytical constructs of their seniors." The fact is that many Chinese scholars are not sure to what extent either the so far dominant Marxist scholarship or the newly introduced Western categories, concepts and tools can deal with Chinese experience.

Unlike the mainstream scholarship in previous decades which looks more like "philosophy of history," Chinese economic history in the new century is concerned more with the question "what did happen," than with the question "what should happen." Many economic historians now evade the grand narrative tradition and concern themselves more with the detailed analysis of specific issues. This situation has led to "a free-for-all" among Chinese economic historians, since few of them share common interests, so that some worry that the field today is "rudderless." For example, the Yangzi Delta, the richest area of China economically and culturally in the past millennium, has been under the most intensive study in the past century. Thanks to the great efforts made by scholars of several generations, we now have much better knowledge of the economy of this area than of any other parts of China. Yet though we know much about agriculture, rural industry, commerce, trade, land tenancy, taxation, etc., it is little discussed how all these aspects were connected with each other and integrated into a single entity. As a result, we don't really know what the economy looks like as a whole (Li 2013).

Although one of the results of the diversification of approaches in the past three decades is that the discipline is getting "atomized," it is no bad thing in some senses, because it means that scholars have more freedom both in the choice of subject matter and in its handling and bigger space for their academic explorations. With the introduction of more approaches from abroad, Chinese scholars have been made aware of the major shortcomings of previous scholarship and tried to overcome them. For example, the quantitative approach had been undervalued in Chinese economic history. The "quantitative revolution" which happened in the field of economic history in the West had little influence in China. But recently, realizing the strengths and weaknesses of the approach, younger scholars have paid more attention to it, though they also are very careful not to go too far.

Second, with the greater "internationalization" of the discipline, Chinese economic historians have got more deeply involved in international academic activities and Chinese economic history is studied in the perspective of comparative and global history. It is thus easy to understand why Chinese scholars are active in major international debates such as "Global Crisis of Economic History," "Involutionary Growth," "Great Divergence" and so on. The CEHS was affiliated to the International Economic History Association in 2002, which also confirms the eagerness of Chinese scholarship to take part in international conversation. Since the generation of scholars who have been educated in the post-1978 period, and who are open to Western scholarship, are playing a more important role in the discipline, this process has been less and less questioned.

Third, the importance of historical sources is now highly rated. The collection of primary materials has been carried out at an unprecedented scale and speed. The use of the "new" materials has led to more new explanations of the past and empirical studies which were despised in the 1950s to 1970s are now appreciated. Moreover, examination of the reliability of the materials is combining with new skills of data processing which make the information from the materials usable for the study. The empirical mode itself with its emphasis on facts is ascendant again, and historians, driven by the desire to use sources objectively and impartially, seek to appear neutral and unbiased. To overcome the weakness in data processing which is one of the major shortcomings of previous scholarship, new efforts have been made.[24]

In the open and more tolerant climate of the past decades, new generations of economic historians has grown up. Compared with their predecessors, they have received better education and more complete professional training. Many of them have spent some time abroad and have better knowledge of Western scholarship. Some younger scholars seek to satisfy their desire for something new by adopting approaches from the West, and few of them bother even to address those operating analytical constructs of their seniors. It leads to some kind of "generation gap" between the comparatively more "conservative" seniors and more "liberal" juniors but the gap has never turned into a "generation war."[25] Some scholars of older generations have questioned, or even opposed in some cases, the Western methodologies, but most of the best scholars of the generation who received their training before 1949 have no antipathy toward Western scholarship and this attitude has a profound effect on the scholars of younger generations, in particular the generations who were trained after 1978. For the even younger generations, they tend to accept Western scholarship as much as possible.[26]

Internally, the key to the future development of the subject is to deal more rationally with the traditions of the discipline of Chinese economic history. As is seen above, there are three main traditions: (a) the empirical tradition, which was the mainstream of China's scholarship of economic history in the 1930s and 1940s; (b) the Marxist tradition, which has been the mainstream since the 1950s; and (c) the comprehensive tradition, which has been rising since the mid-1990s. All of these are valuable elements of the discipline. Only based on these traditions together, is further development of the discipline likely. Though there are obvious differences in approach and orientation of research, these traditions share some basic essences. The traditions combined constitute the specifically Chinese character of the discipline which makes it not a simple copy of Western economic history. It is an "economic history with

Chinese characteristics." It is my opinion that such characteristics are deeply rooted in tradition.

Traditional Chinese historiography is based on a comprehensive worldview – the "heaven–man" thought, including the unity and integration of Heaven (Nature) and Man (Mankind). Since mankind is one integral part of nature, all the human activities, political, economic, social and other, can be conducted only within a certain natural environment. It is inevitable for the activities to be influenced, or even determined, by Nature, while Nature is changed more or less by the activities. Moreover, the interactions between Nature and mankind are enduring and can be studied only in a long-term perspective. According to this view, Sima Qian believed that the highest pursuit of the historian should be "to examine into all that concerns Heaven and Man, to penetrate the changes of the past and present, and then advance his own explanation of history."

These words can be understood in this way: by dialectically integrating "tradition" with "modernity" and exploring the laws of universe and human society, one can have a better understanding of the world. In some sense, this thought echoes the ideas of Comprehensive History (or "Total History") which appeared in the mid- and late twentieth century. In the field of economic history, Joseph A. Schumpeter made an excellent summary of the importance of comprehensive history:

> The social process is really one indivisible whole. Out of its great stream the classifying hand of the investigator artificially extracts economic facts. The designation of a fact as economic already involves an abstraction, the first of the many forced upon us by the technical conditions of mentally copying reality. A fact is never exclusively or purely economic; other – and often more important – aspects always exist. Nevertheless, we speak of economic facts in science just as in ordinary life, and with the same right; with the same right, too, with which we may write a history of literature even though the literature of a people is inseparably connected with all the other elements of its existence. [Therefore, economic history is] merely a part of universal history, only separated from the rest for purpose of exposition.
>
> *(Schumpeter 1934: 4, 58)*

Schumpeter's passage reminds one of Sima Qian's and the resemblance is no coincidence at all because great minds think alike.

For Chinese scholars, the job of creating economic history with Chinese characteristics is linked closely with another job: taking full account of trends in global scholarship. It is pretty clear that in this age of globalization, none can succeed academically whilst operating behind closed doors. Chinese economic history has been strongly influenced by scholarship in the West. In this sense, the discipline was a result of globalization from the beginning and since the globalization of economic history is an irresistible trend, the best way forward for economic history in China is critical engagement with Western scholarship. When such scholarship is applied to other parts of the world, there is a strong implication that it is universally valid and this should be questioned. China must break free of the Anglo-American and Eurocentric straightjacket, but we should also avoid throwing out the baby with the bath water: in a small world the destiny of the Chinese discipline is inevitably entwined with those of other countries in the search for resources, the exchange of ideas and the expansion of knowledge. It is in particular worth noting that Chinese economic history has always had strong orientation toward socio-economic history, while Western economic history has shown a trend to return to "economic and social history" after the disillusionment with the "revolution" of the "new economic history" (Hudson 2001). This common ground forms the basis for the integration of China's scholarship into the mainstream of international scholarship. This will benefit not only Chinese scholarship, but also international scholarship, not least because China has the longest tradition of economic history and one of the largest teams of economic historians in the present-day world.

Notes

1 This work is part of Project 643001, for which I acknowledge support from the RGC of Hong Kong. The chapter is partly based on my previous work "Retrospect and Prospect: The Rise of Chinese Economic History" which was published in *The Chinese Historical Review* in 2008. I thank the editor of the journal for generously giving me permission to draw on it.

2 Literally *Shi* means "food" and *Huo* means "commodities." But Nancy Lee Swan translated the *Shi-Huo Zhi* of *Han Shu* as *Food and Money in Ancient China* (Pan Ku 1972). Since Swan's annotated translation is widely accepted, here I follow her and use "food and money," not "food and commodities." The name of Ban Gu is spelled as Pan Ku in Swan's translation because she used the older Wade–Giles system to spell Chinese names, while I use the Pinyin system which has been adopted by the UN and other world agencies and is now widely used in scholarly works and newspapers alike.

3 The information includes the prices of major goods in official purchases, the standards of payment to hired labor in government services and the government-organized constructions, breakdowns of expenditure in state-run manufactures and so on.

4 According to an incomplete statistic, 8264 of pre-1949 gazetteers of different kinds have survived in mainland China, but the total is estimated to be much more than 10,000.

5 This article was written under the influence of the *General Introduction to History* of Ukita Kazutami (1860–1946), a well-known Japanese scholar and thinker.

6 Zhu Qianzhi (1899–1972), the founder of the *Journal of Modern Historiography* (est. in 1934), wrote: "The modern period is an age in which the economy is in the ascendancy. What we need is not political history or legal history, but economic history or social history, which describe the development of social phenomena, historical patterns of societies, and changes of these patterns. The new trend of modern historiography is definitely economic and social history" (Zhu Qianzhi 1936). For this reason, in 1935 the journal published a special issue on Chinese economic history. See also Chen Feng (2010).

7 Both of these journals predate the *Journal of Economic History* published by the American Economic History Association since 1942.

8 Circulation surpassed 10,000 copies on the eve of the Japanese invasion and there was a considerable number of Japanese subscribers.

9 Among these works, most important are Guo Moruo (1930) and Hou Wailu (1939 and 1947).

10 In the first two decades of the twentieth century, the central concern of Chinese economic historians, as well as of most Chinese intellectuals, was how to save China from exploitation under domestic "feudalism" and the aggression of foreign imperialism and transform it into a modern nation.

11 The two most important were (1) *The History of the Communist Party of the Soviet Union (Bolsheviks): Short Course,* which was edited by a Commission of the Central Committee of Soviet Communist Party and authorized by the Committee in 1937. Section 4 of Chapter 4, "Dialectical materialism and historical materialism," written by Joseph Stalin himself, was regarded as one of the Marxist classics in China; (2) *Political Economy: A Textbook*. This book was compiled by the Institute of Economics of the USSR Academy of Sciences under the supervision of Stalin and published in 1954.

12 These were: the periodization of Chinese history, the form of feudal landownership, the peasant war and the "capitalist sprouts." The fifth debate concerned the formation of the Han people.

13 Later in the twentieth century, this view evolved into new theories such as the "Impact–Response" model (the impact of the West and China's response to it), the "High-level Equilibrium Trap," the "Involutionary Growth" hypothesis and others. In short, all these theories share a common core – without an "impact" from outside, Chinese society and economy would be outside the path of modern development.

14 This is an expression by Fu Yilin (1911–88), a leading economic historian who fathered the theory of the "Chinese Feudal Society."

15 The datasets include Yan Zhongping et al., eds., *Zhongguo jindai jingjishi tongji ziliao xuanji* (modern economy); Li Wenzhi et al., eds., *Zhongguo jindai nongyeshi ziliao* (agricultural history); Sun Yutang et al., eds., *Zhongguo jindai gongyeshi ziliao* (industrial history); Peng Zeyi, ed., *Zhongguo jindai shougongyeshi ziliao* (handicraft history) and others.

16 According to incomplete statistics, from 1949 to 1989 over 4000 articles and more than 300 academic monographs, material collections and other books were published in mainland China on the history of peasant wars in imperial Chinese history. See Wang Xuedian (2004).

17 Feng Yuejian et al. (1996–97). See also Yu Heping (1999).

18 Among them the most important was Liang Fangzhong (1982). Liang (1908–70) was a historian who had studied economics in China, the USA and the UK before 1949. His long-unpublished masterpiece was finished in 1962.

19 They include Wu Chengming (1917–2011), the chief architect of the theory, who abandoned it in the late 1990s. In 1996 I published an essay on this issue which triggered a debate on whether the Chinese "capitalist sprouts" were a reality or just a scholarly construct devised by those who wished to see Chinese modernization follow the Western European path (Li Bozhong 1996). This was accompanied by a debate on the meaning of "capitalism" itself.

20 Before he passed away in 1988 Fu Yilin abandoned this theory which he had constructed, and argued that late imperial China was not a feudal society at all.

21 For example, the theories of the Chinese "traditional market" proposed by Wu Chengming and of the "middle-peasantization" (*zhongnonghua*) of Chinese peasantry by Fang Xing, the "Jiangnan pattern of economic growth" by Li Bozhong, and so on.

22 In this sense, Maddison (1998) started an international trend.

23 Early examples are Huang Liuzhu (1987) and Lu Fu (1989). For later and more balanced reappraisals, see, e.g., Wang Xuedian (2004) and Zhou Zhaochen et al. (2001: 36–52).

24 Recently, summer university courses on data processing skills in social and economic history have been offered in Shanghai, Taiyuan and other cities, to train young Chinese scholars.

25 For example, in my (Li Bozhong 2010) book I used HSNA (Historical System of National Accounts) method in the study of GDP of an area of China in the 1820s. Some senior scholars criticized the method as "utterly incomprehensible."

26 Philip Huang (1991) thought that "Most [of them] have sought to satisfy their desire for something new by adopting wholesale one or another fashionable approach from the West."

References

Chen, Feng (2010) "Cong shihuo zhixue dao shehui jingjishi" (From the *Shi-Huo* studies to social and economic history). *Journal of Nanjing University* (Philosophy, Humanities and Social Sciences), no. 3.

Barraclough, Geoffrey (1978) "History." In *Main trends of research in the social and human sciences*, Part II, vol. I, *Anthropological and historical sciences: Aesthetics and the sciences of art*, ed. by Jacques Havet. Paris, Mouton/UNESCO.

Fairbank, John King and Merle Goldman (2006) *China: A new history*. 2nd edn. Cambridge, MA: Belknap Press.

Feng, Yuejian et al. (1996–97) "1986 nian -1995 nian zhongguo jingjishi lunzhu suyin" (An index of the works on Chinese economic history). *Zhongguo jingjishi yanjiu* (Beijing), Supplements.

Guo, Moruo (1930) *Zhongguo gudai shehui yanjiu* (The study of ancient Chinese society). Shanghai: Shanghai lianhe shudian.

Hou, Wailu (1939) "Shehuishi daolun" (An introduction to social history). *Zongshu wenhua* (Chongqing), 4.2.

Hou, Wailu (1947) *Zhongguo gudian shehui shilun* (On Chinese ancient society). Shanghai: Xinzhi shudian.

Huang Liuzhu (1987) "'Shixue weiji' chuyi" (A discussion of 'Crisis in historiography'). *Zhongguoshi yanjiu dongtai* (Beijing), no. 4.

Huang, Philip C.C. (1991) "The paradigmatic crisis in Chinese studies: paradoxes in social and economic history." *Modern China* 17.3: 299–341.

Hudson, Pat, ed. (2001) *Living economic and social history*. Glasgow: Economic History Society.

Jian, Bozan (1950) "Zenyang yanjiu zhong lishi" (How to study Chinese history). *Xin Jianshe* (Beijing), vol. 3, no. 2 (Nov.).

Li, Bozhong (1996) "Zibenzhuyi mengya qingjie" (On the complex of 'Capitalist Sprouts'). *Dushu* (Beijing), no. 8.

Li, Bozhong (2010) *Zhongguo de zaoqi jindai jingji – 1820 niandai Huating-Louxian diqu GDP yanjiu.* Beijing: Zhonghua shuju. (Summarized in "An early modern economy in China: a study of the GDP of the Huating-Lou area, 1823–1829." In Billy K.L. So, ed., *The economy of lower Yangzi delta in late imperial China.* London: Routledge, 2013: 133–46.)

Li, Bozhong (2013) "An early modern economy in China: a study of the GDP of Huating-Lou area, 1823–1829." In Billy K.L. So, ed., *The economy of lower Yangzi delta in late imperial China.* London: Routledge.

Liang, Fangzhong (1982) *Zhongguo lidai hukou, tudi, tianfu tongji* (Statistics of residence registration, cultivated land and taxes under several dynasties). Shanghai: Shanghai renmin chubanshe.

Liang, Qichao (1902) "Xin shixue" (New history), originally published in *Xinmin Congbao*, vol. 19 (Yokohama, Japan); repr. in Liang Qichao, *Yinbingshi wenji.* Kunming: Yunnan renmin chubanshe, 2001: 1628–47.

Liang, Qichao (1904) *Zhongguo guozhai shi* (History of China's national debt). Shanghai: Guangzhi shuju.

Lu, Fu (1989) "Zhongguo dangdai de shixue weiji yu chulu" (The crisis of historiography in contemporary China). *Shehui kexuejia* (Guilin), no. 5.

Maddison, Angus (1998) *Chinese Economic Performance in the Long Run.* Paris: OECD.

Qian Li and Da Tong (1994) "Saina he ban liang shijia – Michel Cartier he Pierre-Etienne Will dui zhongguo shehui jingjishi yanjiu de gongxian" (Michel Cartier and Pierre-Etienne Will and their contributions to the study of Chinese social and economic history). *Zhongguo jingjishi yanjiu* (Beijing), no. 2: 106–13.

Pan, Ku (Ban Gu) (1972) *Food and money in Ancient China.* ed. Nancy L. Swann. New York: Hippocrene Books.

Schumpeter, Joseph A. (1934) *The theory of economic development.* Cambridge, MA: Harvard University Press.

Wang, Xuedian (2004) "Jin wushinian de zhongguo lishixue" (The Chinese historiography in the past fifty years). *Lishi yanjiu* (Beijing), no. 1.

Yu, Heping (1999) "50 nian lai de zhongguo jindai jingjishi yanjiu" (A review of the studies of Chinese modern economic history in the past 50 years). *Jindaishi yanjiu* (Beijing), no. 5.

Yu, Yingshi (Yu Ying-shih) (1976) *Shijia, shixue yu shidai* (The historian, history and time). Taipei: Lienching Press.

Zeng, Yeying (2000) *Wushinian lai de zhongguo jingdaishi yanjiu* (The study of modern Chinese history in the past 50 years). Shanghai: Shanghai shudian chubanshe.

Zhou, Zhaochen, Jiang Mei and Deng Jingli (2001) *Xin shiqi zhongguo shixue sichao* (Trends of Chinese historiography in the New Period). Beijing: Dangdai zhongguo chubanshe.

Zhu, Qianzhi (1936) "Chen Xiaojiang *Xihan shehui jingji yanjiu* xu" (Preface to Chen Xiaojiang's *A study of society and economy under the Western Han Dynasty*). Shanghai: Xinshengming shuju.

19

JAPANESE ECONOMIC HISTORY

Exploring diversity in development

Kaoru Sugihara[1]

Economic history has been an important subject for modern Japanese thought, because it discusses the nature of the rapid social change that the country has experienced since the mid-nineteenth century and its significance in relation to the rest of the world. The discipline was established in the 1930s and from then on to the 1960s economic (and social) history acted as a key discipline in the field of humanities and social sciences by providing a methodology for assessing the distance between the West and Japan in economic and social development and by offering an interpretation of indigenous sources of development. It made a vital contribution to the birth of social science in modern Japan.

This intellectual history has been carried out by enlightenment thinkers, political economists and academicians specialized in related fields such as history, economics and sociology, as well as by economic historians. The professionalization of the discipline began early: the Socio-economic History Society of Japan, the main association, was established in 1930 but, if we are to describe how the main themes and perspectives relating to economic history had been identified and debated since the late nineteenth century, we need to broaden our perspective and discuss the contributions of social scientists and historians at large to the development of economic history. On the other hand, the Society as a group of specialists has survived war, international attention to the 'Japanese miracle' and the subsequent rise of Asia, as well as the rise of Marxism and its decline and the impact of American economics, by producing scholarly works on economic history in a steady stream and by contributing to upgrading the quality of national, local, business and social histories.

By the 1970s the main topics of Japanese economic history were being professionally researched and debated within the discipline, with healthy interactions with both economists and historians. The academic community has grown to one of the largest in the world, with about two thousand members registered at one of the three main associations. The name of the main association implies its orientation towards economic and social history. The other two are the Business History Society and the Political Economy and Economic History Society. Today the majority of economic historians work for economics-related departments in universities, but they are not hostile to historians without knowledge of economics. Their inclination has been more towards history than economics, at least till relatively recently.

Why did economic history in Japan develop in this way? In what ways did methodologies, themes and main conclusions change over time and how were they related to changes in the nature of the domestic social and economic agenda and external influences? This chapter discusses these questions, and suggests that Japanese scholars have made persistent attempts, with varying degrees of success, to locate Japan in an international context by absorbing global economic changes and adapting to new intellectual trends, with an equally strong commitment to discovering indigenous sources of development with the use of primary (mostly Japanese-language) sources.

The next section offers a brief overview of Japanese modernization, economic thought and economic history. The following sections cover the introduction of Western economic thought and the early years of political economy and economic history under the influence of the German Historical School, the interwar Marxist debate on the nature of Japanese capitalism, and the diffusion of Euro-centred comparative economic history and its significance for the early postwar intellectual climate in Japan. Later sections discuss the nature and development of quantitative economic history, which emerged as a major force in the discipline by the 1980s, offering a coherent revision of the historiography for the period from the Tokugawa to high-speed growth. Finally, I discuss other research trends in the more recent period and Japanese contributions to Asian and global economic history, together with their connections to earlier scholarship. The conclusion summarizes the argument, with comments on the future.

Three phases in Japanese modernization

While no one disputes Japan's impressive record of economic development over the last century and a half, there is less agreement about the degree and ingenuity of the intellectual modernization that accompanied it.[2] Economic thought is no exception. Part of the assessment problem has to do with the difficulties inherent in any intellectual history. But it is particularly difficult in the Japanese case, as almost all the main figures concerned were Japanese who were primarily educated in Japan and expressed their ideas in Japanese. In other words, there was an accumulation of knowledge with relatively few face-to-face contacts with Western academia. On the face of it, Japan's history looks like a process of the absorption of, reaction to and articulation of Western thought. But, of course, this is not a straightforward story of the diffusion of Western ideas. A range of Japanese thought that had existed prior to the Western impact exerted a strong influence by adapting Western ideas to new circumstances and mixing with Western thought throughout the period of the modernization drive.

Although its origins can be traced back to the seventeenth century, Japan's modernization process gathered pace after the middle of the nineteenth century. Two major institutional changes were responsible for the acceleration. The first of these was the Meiji Restoration of 1868, which ended two hundred and sixty-five years of peace and stability enjoyed under the Tokugawa regime. The arrival of Commodore Perry in 1853 and the subsequent opening of Japanese ports to foreign trade exposed the regime's inability to deal with national crisis. The Tokugawa Shogunate thus accepted the restoration of imperial rule. After a short period of internal warfare, the new government carried out a series of institutional changes, abolishing the samurai class and the caste-like occupational division, monetizing the land tax and freeing the peasant farmers from the land, and introducing Western technology and organizations in government-sponsored model factories. Looking at the process leading to the enactment of the Constitution in 1889, scholars debated whether it should be understood as a revolution or a change with qualified acceptance of modern ideas, and placed varied emphases on elements of continuity and change (see the fifth section of this chapter).

The other major change came with the Japanese surrender at the end of the Second World War in August 1945. The occupation by allied forces lasted until 1951 when the peace treaty was signed. During this time, as with during the Meiji Restoration, a series of important institutional changes were carried out without causing severe political disruption. While democratization was attempted and largely realized, scholars also found room to argue, on the one hand, that part of the change was an extension of the institutional reform begun during the war and, on the other hand, that, due to the change in the occupation policy (the so-called 'reverse course' as a result of the socialist penetration in East Asia), some of the reforms were watered down and ended up as reorganization that lacked substance (Okazaki and Okuno-Fujiwara 1999; Teranishi and Kosai 1993). Nevertheless, surrender and occupation marked the start of Japan's recovery from the ashes, which eventually led to the 'Japanese miracle', a name coined to signify the first sustained high-speed growth experience the world had ever seen.

Yet there was another turning point in modem Japanese history, which chronologically separates these two changes, and it is this second turning point that makes the study of Japan's modernization truly important from a comparative perspective. While the two other changes were induced by pressures from Western Europe and the United States, this one occurred in the period from the latter half of the 1920s to the early 1930s, in response to interwar depression and the growing influence of Marxism. While advanced Western countries suffered from the Great Depression and the collapse of world trade, Asia, following the Bolshevik Revolution in Russia in 1917, saw the increasing penetration of the Third International, especially into China. If the two other changes were both successful in bringing about the enhancement of national economic strength, the course of action taken in response to this pressure was confrontation with the outside world through the use of force, denying the liberalist hope of successful 'cooperation diplomacy' pursued during the period of 'Taisho Democracy'. It resulted in defeat and occupation. An important feature of Japan's modernization lies in the fact that the two successful modernization drives were interrupted by this unhappy turn of events. In placing the history of Japanese economic history in the general context of Japan's economic and social development, we need to take all three changes into account, and trace how Japanese scholars perceived and responded to them.

Enlightenment, free trade and protectionism

During the first twenty years of the Meiji period (1868–1912), Yukichi Fukuzawa (1835–1901) and Ukichi Taguchi (1855–1905) exerted major influences in shaping modern economic thought. The two men had much in common. Both were committed to enlightenment and interested not just in economic thought but in a wide range of subjects relating to the humanities, social sciences and history. They were also heavily involved in the evolution of politics, economic affairs, education and publishing. Furthermore, both acquired a basic education during the Tokugawa period, and tried hard to absorb modern Western culture when they were exposed to its powerful impact. And they both became free traders. While their stance was liberal and individualistic overall, Fukuzawa tended to be receptive to nationalist and protectionist causes when it came to actual policy implementation, while Taguchi believed in the universal applicability of the principle of free trade, and retained a more fundamentalist approach. He argued that the study of political economy must be confined to the study of principles, and he sharply confronted the historical school which emphasized historical and policy-oriented research. Taguchi's stance is worth noting because Japanese political economy was generally inclined to leave theoretical study aside and concentrate on historical and policy-oriented research, a tendency common to late-developer countries.

If we put protectionists and state socialists in the same category, as against free traders, the majority of writers in the early Meiji period belonged to this group. They were responsible for the introduction of German historical and social policy schools to Japan. They contributed to the diffusion of German thought by learning the thought themselves from the lectures of invited German employees of the Japanese government, from studying abroad, and also by translating German books into Japanese. The German Studies Association (*Doitsugaku Kyokai*: founded 1881), the Nation Studies Association (*Kokka Gakkai*: founded 1887) and the National Economy Society (*Kokka Keizaikai*: founded 1890) were active in the 1880s and 1890s, serving those researchers interested in German-style studies and seeking the legal, political and economic basis of the state.

The study of social policy

As a result of these activities, interest in German-style economic policy, which was based on historicism and nationalism, grew into a strong enough force to counter the influence of the liberal economic thought of Britain and France. In the second half of the Meiji period the state promoted the policy of 'enriching the nation' through rapid industrialization and 'strengthening the military' for external expansion, without much concern for their effects on the lives of ordinary people. In order to deal with the resultant social problems (*shakai mondai*), the government attempted to enact various pieces of social legislation, modelled on German practices. It was out of this environment that a group of social scientists, consisting of bureaucrats, academics and independent intellectuals, emerged. Thus the Japanese Association for the Study of Social Policy (*Shakai Seisaku Gakkai*) was founded in 1896, with the hope of providing a viable intellectual framework for solving such problems.

The Association started as a study group led by those university professors who returned from Germany. By 1899 when the 'Goals of the Association' were published, however, it looked much more like a nationwide academic association. The 'Purposes' stated that the Association aimed at preserving the existing 'economic system based on private property rights', in opposition to the socialism led by Isoo Abe (1865–1949), while at the same time seeking social reform, in opposition to the idea of laissez-faire represented by Taguchi. Having formally become a full academic organization in 1907, the Association held its first meeting at the Imperial University of Tokyo at the end of that year. Heated debates took place between conservatives and progressives on the question of the legislation of the Factory Law, making it feel to the public as if the Association was rapidly becoming the core of social science circles in Japan. The 'opening speech' by Noburu Kanai (1865–1933), which appealed for a clear distinction between socialism and social policy in favour of the latter, gave a vivid impression of its political stance.

As for the main constituent forces of the Association, the standard perception put Noburu Kanai as leader of the right or reformist 'from above' wing, Kumazo Kuwata (1868–1932) as leader of the centre element, or reformist both 'from above' and 'from below', and Tokuzo Fukuda (1874–1930) as leader of the left group who were reformist 'from below'. By 1913 when the seventh meeting was held, taking up the theme of 'labour dispute', the difference of opinion between the right and the left had become so large that the discussion had to be made confidential to avoid open confrontation. With the advent of the Bolshevik Revolution, the Association came to a crisis point as to whether it could justify its existence as a unified force. In 1919 the right wing of the Association joined the Society for Harmony and Cooperation [between Capital and Labour] (*Kyochokai*), headed by Eiichi Shibusawa (1840–1931), which published *Shakai Seisaku Jiho* (the Journal of Social Policy). The left wing, on the other hand, came to base itself in the Ohara Institute for Social Research, which was also established in 1919 and headed by lwasaburo Takano (1871–1949). Among the members of this group were Hajime Kawakami (1879–1946) and Tatsuo Morito (1888–1984). Thus the Association, with nearly three hundred members at its peak and a reasonable record of promoting social reform including the implementation of legislation, was no longer able to hold a cohesive platform by the end of the Taisho period (1912–25) and disappeared in the midst of the second major turning point described above.

Tokuzo Fukuda and Hajime Kawakami represented the thought of a new generation of scholars. Liberally inclined Fukuda expressed his appreciation of the works of Baien Miura (1723–89), particularly his price theory, among the Tokugawa thinkers, while nationalistic Kawakami had a serious interest in Nobuhiro Sato (1769–1850) who was sometimes termed socialist. Within the Association, Fukuda represented a liberal (left-wing) camp, and Kawakami gradually joined forces with him. During the period of Taisho Democracy both men advocated the new liberalism from Britain and other reformist ideas, before receiving the full impact of Marxist–Leninist ideas. Yet their responses to the Bolshevik Revolution showed a stark contrast: Fukuda tried to observe the new development as calmly as he could and to understand the fate of the new regime and the ideology behind it, while Kawakami accepted it completely.

The birth of economic history

It was Ginzo Uchida (1872–1919), a historian who was taught by a German teacher at the Imperial University of Tokyo and studied at Oxford, who first lectured on Japanese economic history and was appointed professor of Japanese history at Kyoto Imperial University in 1906. Though given as a history subject, Uchida's lectures contained an attempt systematically to understand Japanese economic history. Eijiro Honjo (1888–1973), his student who became a professor of Japanese economic history at Kyoto, started the Japanese economic history seminar in 1926. *Keizaishi Kenkyu* (Studies in Economic History), a monthly journal, started in 1929, and the Institute for the Study of the Economic History of Japan was established in Kyoto in 1933. The Kyoto group of scholars was influenced by economic stage theory. They contributed to the establishment of academic research, by compiling dictionaries and a yearbook, which included an annual list of relevant publications, in addition to publishing their own empirical research.

Meanwhile, the Socio-economic History Society, a nationwide association, started *Shakai Keizai Shigaku* (Socio-economic History) in 1931, which became a monthly publication in 1932. Both journals continued publication as late as 1944. Although the Institute in Kyoto never quite recovered its strength postwar, the Socio-economic History Society restarted its activities in 1946, and expanded rapidly thereafter. Professors at Waseda and Keio, two private universities in Tokyo, took initiatives, and led the organization (Komatsu 1961).

The interwar debate on the nature of Japanese capitalism

During the period from 1927 to 1937 an intensive academic debate took place on the nature of Japanese capitalism.[3] It was carried out by a small group of Marxists, consisting primarily of left-wing activists, journalists and professors, and ended with their arrests as the government tightened its control over their political activities. The debate was strongly influenced by international and domestic socialist movements. The views of the Communist International (Comintern) on Japan, especially regarding the revolutionary strategy and tactics of the Japan Communist Party (JCP), had a profound influence in shaping the debate. In particular the question of whether the JCP should aim at a two-stage revolution – i.e. first, bourgeois–democratic revolution, followed by proletarian socialist revolution – or whether it should aim at a single-stage proletarian socialist revolution, occupied a central place in the minds of the participants in the debate.

Broadly speaking, the JCP supporters insisted on the two-stage revolution on the basis that Japan's bourgeois revolution had been incomplete and that her political and economic structure at that time was still deeply affected by feudal or semi-feudal remnants of society, particularly in the agrarian sector. Under the influence of Comintern's 1927 Theses and its 1932 Theses, they formulated a framework of analysis of Japanese capitalism, which was to highlight its militaristic and semi-feudalistic nature. In its complete form the framework suggested that the Meiji Restoration was not a bourgeois revolution but rather resulted in the emergence of an absolutist state which was neither bourgeois nor entirely feudal. The state, fully backed by the semi-feudal landlords of whom the Emperor was the most important, was to carry out the task of industrializing a country which did not yet have a strong indigenous bourgeoisie. Owing to the need to suppress the masses and to respond to external military pressures, the nature of this state-promoted capitalism was necessarily militaristic. The abolition of the Emperor system was an essential part of their political programme. In the early 1930s a seven-volume *Symposium on the History of the Development of Japanese Capitalism* (*Nihon Shihonshugi Hattatsushi Koza*, Iwanami Shoten 1932–33) was published, and the main framework became clear. The group of scholars who produced this framework was named the Koza school. Moritaro Yamada's *An Analysis of Japanese Capitalism* (*Nihon Shihonshugi Bunseki*) (1934) was the most influential work associated with this school.

In the meantime, a group of ex-JCP members, who had rejected the Comintern's depiction of Japan as too backward for an immediate socialist revolution, launched, in 1927, the Journal *Rono* (Labour Farmer), after which this other faction in the debate was named. The Rono school at a later stage included many writers who had no connection with the JCP. While acknowledging the ideological and institutional presence of absolutism, this school emphasized the hegemony of the financial bourgeoisie within the Japanese ruling class and its fully developed imperialism. By the 1920s Japanese capitalists were already forming powerful Zaibatsu groups, with all the major characteristics of a financial bourgeoisie. For the Rono school, the Koza school's emphasis on the absolutist elements of the state resulted in a failure to identify the real enemy. Thus, criticizing Yamada's *Analysis*, Rono scholars referred to the general tendency for capitalism to penetrate into all aspects of society, and urged the participants in the debate to acknowledge the dynamic shift from the feudal to the capitalist mode of production that had taken place as a result of Japan's industrialization. They sought to interpret the nature of a seemingly semi-feudal agrarian society as part of a predominantly capitalist Japan. Within the Rono school, however, there was some interesting divergence from this general stance. Some writers were willing to accept the notion of the continued existence of the semi-feudal nature of the agrarian sector and tried to interpret it in the context of the development of Japanese imperialism rather than consider it as merely a semi-feudal remnant.

The frame of reference

Three main issues emerged in the debate, all of which have shaped the frame of reference of later research. First, rural society was identified as a determinant of the nature of Japanese society. It was considered from the tripartite perspective of the landlords who owned about half of the arable land and exercised power in both rural society and national politics; the peasant household which typically managed a small plot of land through the absorption of family labour (rather than through the employment of agricultural labourers) and was involved in the market economy to some extent, be it as owner cultivator or as tenant farmer; and the village community which socially tied the peasant households to the land and appears to have restricted their movement in some regions. Whilst it was important for the Koza school to find evidence of feudal practices and to emphasize the fact that the ground rent was paid in kind, Rono school scholars suggested that agricultural production was completely commercialized and even the rent, paid in rice, was 'conceptually monetized' in the minds of the peasant farmer when he formulated his economic strategy.

Second, sources of the industrial strength of Japan were sought in the nature of the workforce. The rural society supplied young country girls to modern textile industries, for example. Modern industry paid them a low wage, which barely supported the worker's own livelihood. This meant that the cost of reproduction of workers was borne by the rural society. Since the land–labour ratio in Japan was so low, the landlord was able to extract a high ground rent, which suppressed the standard of living of the peasant household. Thus (in the absence of large-scale migration opportunities) the low wage persisted, and domestic demand remained stagnant, culminating in the impasse of Japanese capitalism. The Koza school used this logic to explain both the international competitiveness of Japanese industry and Japan's dependence on exports and overseas expansion, leading to aggression and war.

Third, the role of the state was interpreted in relation to both initial conditions and external pressures. An influential Koza school interpretation for the Meiji Restoration was that, under Western impact and the threat of colonization, the state tried, from above, to proceed with industrialization without a fully developed indigenous bourgeoisie. While this was a departure from the position of strict economic determinism, making political and institutional changes a vital agent of history and linking the framework to what was later termed the late-developer thesis (Gerschenkron 1962), it simultaneously acknowledged the significance of external pressures and the need to react to them as a fundamental force of change in modern Japanese history.

The assessment

These debates had relatively little influence on the general trend of Japanese political history. By the late 1920s, the liberalism that had featured prominently during the period of Taisho Democracy was losing ground and by the middle of the 1930s the government was in the process of smashing the labour movement altogether. It is true that, at a time when militarism, expansionism and imperial cosmology dominated the intellectual climate, these debates were almost the only systematic academic effort to produce an alternative view of society. They also served as a great stimulus to many liberal intellectuals. However, the participants in the debates did not find it easy to retain their political and ideological views. When arrested and tortured by the Special Thought Police, many of them agreed to change their views or abandon them. More importantly, a few became vocal advocates of the Greater East Asia Co-prosperity Sphere in the early 1940s.

The debate clearly posed the problem of reconciling the notion of the universality of capitalism with the need to differentiate Japanese capitalism. On the one hand, it was difficult enough to argue in favour of the universal applicability of Marxist theory, in view of the fact that it was formed primarily on the basis of Western historical experiences. On the other hand, there was a strong need to explain the differences between Japanese society and Western societies, in a more universal and coherent language than that which the imperial cosmology adopted. Thus the debates, in effect, focused on the issue of how to create an academic language that could deal with major problems of Japanese society whilst retaining its universal usage.

Postwar comparative economic history

After the defeat, the national sentiment favoured the modernization of Japan as thoroughly as possible, in order not to repeat the same mistake. For this purpose, the critical assessment of Japanese capitalism in the 1930s by Marxist scholars was deepened in several ways and, to some extent, they were successful in penetrating into universities and other branches of the public sphere under postwar democracy. First, some of the pre-war Marxist thinking was brought into academia, for example Moritaro Yamada became a professor at the Faculty of Economics of the University of Tokyo, and the framework of the debate became an important reference for empirical historians. Those scholars who broadly subscribed to left-wing movements or liberal democracy were given the opportunity to engage in serious empirical research. They often emphasized the feudal, militaristic and unequal nature of Japanese society to justify their claim for radical reforms. At the same time, empirically minded historians conducted more straightforward archival research, often ending up with critical comments on the ideologically framed or historically ungrounded assertions. The interactions between them raised the level of historical analysis.

More specifically, various Marxist theories and propositions exerted powerful influences in directing the attention of empirical historians in the early postwar period. Among the most influential was the orthodox Marxist perspective of historical materialism, which led some Japanese historians to identify the modes of production in specific periods (including the Asiatic mode) in Asian history. Tadashi Ishimoda (1912–86) argued for the early emergence of feudalism, and suggested that Japan was ahead of other Asian societies, using both the explicitly Eurocentric yardstick and the interpretation of some primary material available at the time (Ishimoda 1946; Yamanouchi 1979: 292). Meanwhile, Moriaki Araki (1927–93), using material relating to national cadastral surveys, argued that the emergence of the small peasant household in the sixteenth century was a major watershed of Japanese history (Araki 1959; Hall 1991: 7). The idea was that the dismantling of multilayered agrarian ownership and holding structures enabled the establishment of the household and the village as substantially 'autonomous' institutions, soon to be linked only to the centralized power through the appropriation of the land tax and other obligations. These notions have been fiercely debated but the attention to both early institutional developments and the independence of the peasant household has broadly been shared in the historiography, with a number of factual revisions and with the use of different vocabularies.

Second, there was an enthusiasm for the study of English and European economic and social history, which started pre-war, was interrupted during the war, and grew into an academic discipline postwar. An important characteristic of Japanese scholarship here is that the Marxist tradition merged with Weberian methodology, in the works of Hisao Otsuka (1907–96: see Otsuka 1982) and his colleagues and students, and exerted influence in the humanities and social sciences in general. In association with other specialists, for example of political thought (Masao Maruyama (1914–96)) and legal thought (Takeyoshi Kawashima (1909–92)), they discussed the nature of modernization and postwar reforms and their worth for Japanese society.

In his *Introduction to Modern European Economic History* (originally published in various forms in 1938–49: see Otsuka 1985), Otsuka described the process of European expansion and competition for hegemony among European states, and the eventual rise of England in the seventeenth century. As a person, Otsuka was a Christian who never visited Europe and a lay preacher whose mission was to see the diffusion of a thoroughly frugal, honest, faithful and hard-working ethic in Japanese society.[4] His central concepts included several contrasts between the actors in early modern European economic history: between Portugal and Spain on the one hand, and the Netherlands and England on the other; between the Netherlands, which remained as a country specialized in processing, and England, which developed woollen production; between merchant adventurers and merchant manufacturers; and between those merchants who would seek profits for their own sake and those who would represent the interests of rural industrial activities (and national wealth) with a good sense of decent business practice. His overall message was clear: social and economic development must include the full diffusion of an ethic that would withstand both short-term economic motivations and socially ungrounded state ambitions. In the introduction to his translation of Max Weber's *The Protestant Ethic and the Spirit of Capitalism* (1989), he detailed his understanding of the original spirit of capitalism in Europe, and how it was lost when modern capitalism, with the more explicit search for profit, came about. He was also sensitive to the assessment of fascism, which to him was not something that could be fully analysed, let alone prevented, by Marxism but needed a more comprehensive approach, including the analysis of societal values and their social careers.

It is important to note that postwar thinkers, including Otsuka, were by no means successful in securing a large number of followers of their theories. Rather, works of the Otsuka school were critically received from diverse perspectives and it is this (largely unintended) discourse that defined the 'domestic agenda' for European economic history in Japan. The discourse was very different from those in Europe, yet academics also pursued empirical research, often with the use of sophisticated methodology and primary material in European languages. As a result, Japanese economic historians were roughly grouped into those researching and writing 'Western economic history' and those pursuing 'Japanese economic history'. Since the former was regarded as a more established field of study and a normative value was attached to it to some extent, the subject was widely taught at the secondary and tertiary levels in an explicitly Eurocentric manner, that is, taking the Western experience as a norm and measuring the degree of Japanese development and characterizing Japanese society in that mirror. The growth of the study of the history of economic thought, especially classical political economy, was impressive too, which was also influenced by both Marxist and Weberian methodologies, and characterized by the German–Japanese emphasis on bibliographical details and historiography. Adam Smith's *The Theory of Moral Sentiments,* as well as *The Wealth of Nations*, was keenly read, studied and interpreted as a necessary reference point for Japan's modernization.

Third, one main opposition to the thinking of the Otsuka school was its relative lack of attention to connective history. Although Otsuka studied the activities of Dutch and English East India Companies, his overall methodological focus was on comparisons rather than connections. In the 1960s the notion of 'world capitalism' and Japan's position in its development (as against comparing Japan with several European nations) attracted attention, both among the Kyoto-based group of historians, who pioneered global connective history, and by the 'Uno school', which developed a sophisticated framework of Marxian economics under the leadership of Kozo Uno (1897–1977) at the University of Tokyo. Some of them were responsible for introducing the works of Gunder Frank and Immanuel Wallerstein, but the Japanese versions of world capitalism were independently developed, and here again academic interests were driven by the 'domestic agenda', and were different from the global intellectual currents. Japanese scholars of global history were less concerned with the Third

World and were more interested in writing a multicultural global history in which to locate Japanese culture (*The World History of Tea* (1980) by Sakae Tsunoyama (1921–2014) was a classic) or offering a broadly Marxist interpretation for assessing how powerful international economic and political connections were, and to what extent sovereignty of the less powerful nations was compromised. The latter questions had direct relevance to the issue of how 'autonomous' Japanese capitalism was against the American hegemony, a point fiercely debated among the participants of student movements in the late 1960s.

Quantitative economic history and beyond

Japanese high-speed growth in the 1950s and the 1960s was a totally unexpected event for all contemporary schools of economics, be it neoclassical, Keynesian or socialist, and for other social science disciplines. The attempt to explain it bore fruit largely afterwards, that is in the 1970s onwards. Economic history, with emphasis on quantitative methods, played a vital role in revising the perception of modern Japan, by offering a more proactive picture of peasants, entrepreneurs and leaders of society. Relying on the macro-accounting framework developed in the United States, the study of the history of Japanese economic growth began, almost as soon as the works of Simon Kuznets were introduced. A group of scholars at Hitotsubashi University, Tokyo, compiled long-term economic statistics (Ohkawa et al. 1965–88; Ohkawa et al. 1979), which provided the statistical basis for international discussion of the Japanese experience. Moreover, in an eight-volume *Economic History of Japan* (*Nihon Keizaishi*, Umemura et al. 1988–90),[5] the 'revisionist' scholars presented a coherent story that covered the entire period of early modern and modern Japanese economic history. What emerged was an elaborate account of the development of a modern market economy, making many major revisions to the prevailing view. Attempts were made to include demographic history, urban history, local history, business history, political economy of institution building and some social history.

In this period non-Japanese scholars began to play a visible role in Japanese academia. Thomas C. Smith (1916–2004) made important contributions, not just by introducing Japanese economic history, in a new light, to the English-language academy, but by directing Japanese research into the less ideological but sufficiently comparativist mode of scholarship (see Smith 1959, 1988). Works of Robert Bellah and Ronald Dore were among those that had profound influences on Japanese research (Bellah 1957; Dore 1973). The task of Japanese quantitative historians effectively involved discussion of the significance of institutional changes, as well as reasons for diverse patterns, and for the pace of industrialization and urbanization. They had to address these questions this time against the popularity of modernization theory and the new stage theory of economic growth by W. W. Rostow, rather than under the Marxist framework.

The argument of this chapter is that the new scholarship nevertheless inherited the frame of reference developed in Japan, by reducing the weight of econometric methods and by addressing issues relating to social structure. I summarize the revised frame of reference below, by taking into account more recent works and a degree of fusion between quantitative economic history and other branches of economic and business history.

The Tokugawa development

Perhaps the most remarkable revision came from the interpretation of Tokugawa history. A major contribution was made by Akira Hayami (1929–) at Keio University, who demonstrated the value of historical demography for economic and social history. Many of his views have been controversial and thought-provoking (see Hayami 2009). For example, his population estimates for 1600, which suggested a drastic downward revision (and thus a rapid population growth in the seventeenth century), have been seriously challenged. His concept of the 'industrious revolution' (the argument that Japan went through a labour-absorbing type of development before the industrial revolution, based on his interpretation of findings such as the decline of the number of horses) has been much debated inside and outside of Japan. It has been reinterpreted by many scholars, to suit different contexts, including by Jan de Vries, making Hayami's original thesis a very relevant, if partial one, in comparative global history (de Vries 2008; Sugihara and Wong 2015; but see also Hayami 2015). His characterization of the Tokugawa society as an 'economic society' (in which activities of the members of society were basically driven by economic motivations) became widely accepted and replaced the traditional picture of the dominance of a customary or command economy, heavy taxation and famine-stricken population trends.

Meanwhile, Matao Miyamoto (1943–), and others trained at Osaka University under Mataji Miyamoto (1907–1991), led an equally important revision of the understanding of market institutions (e.g. Miyamoto 1988). They studied merchant houses, the rice market, money supply, price movements, and Shogunal macroeconomic and domainal industrial policies. Their general conclusion of the overall growth of the domestic market and a gradual rise of per capita agricultural output replaced the traditional view of a stagnant society based on strict occupational division. Population stagnation after the eighteenth century as a result of relatively low fertility and relatively low mortality, and a gradual increase of population in the first half of the nineteenth century, were persuasively related to the picture of what is termed 'Smithian growth' today. Furthermore, Osamu Saito (1946–) (Keio and Hitotsubashi universities) made an analysis of the peasant family household, focusing its workings in the context of Smithian growth in the late Tokugawa period (Saito 1983) and related much of the new knowledge on Japanese economic and social history to international debates by adding his own research and insights. He remains influential in both Japanese academia and its English-language counterpart.

In my view, the most important comparative historical insight is that the peasant household was identified as the basic economic unit, which drove both the rise of land productivity and labour absorption, and influenced the decisions on consumption, savings and reproduction. This was further connected to the study of education, hygiene and cleanliness, upgrading our understanding of the standard of living in late Tokugawa Japan. These studies formed the content of the 'high initial conditions', upon which Meiji Japan was built. Works by revisionist scholars on Tokugawa Japan also influenced Kenneth Pomeranz's suggestion that the standard of living in the core regions of East Asia in the middle of the eighteenth century was roughly on a par with that in Western Europe, by offering relevant evidence and methodology to his global perspective (Pomeranz 2000).

Labour-intensive industrialization

If the birth of classical political economy and modern economic history is associated with the industrial revolution in England, the understanding of economic development outside the Western world has been influenced by Japanese industrialization since the late nineteenth century. With the diffusion of industrialization and economic development in Asia, Africa and Latin America in the postwar period, the explanation of why it was Japan, not elsewhere, that industrialized first in the non-Western world attracted renewed attention. The traditional methodological emphasis on external pressures and the advantage of the late-developer had to be supplemented by the story of how high initial conditions were transformed into industrialization.

In an earlier section of this chapter, I described the frame of reference for the interwar Marxist debate. Let me summarize the revised interpretation of the first two points, that is, the dominance of rural society and the sources of industrial strength. First, while the focus of research shifted from agriculture (and rural society) to industry (and entrepreneurship), the new understanding of Japanese industrialization nevertheless suggested a parallel development between a small, fast-growing, modern (largely urban–industrial) sector and a large, slow-growing, 'traditional' (both agricultural and proto-industrial) sector, in which linkages between the two sectors were successfully made. This was followed by the emergence of a 'dual structure' in the interwar period, in which the uneven development between the two sectors began to cause a strain (Nakamura 1983). Studies of traditional industries and their modernization pointed to the rural but dynamic orientation of Japanese industrialization (Abe 1989; Tanimoto 2006). The path of industrial development now included, in addition to the traditional focus on early government factories and the rise of zaibatsu, discussion on the development of the more labour-intensive industries, from proto-industrialization since the second half of the Tokugawa period through the Meiji modernization to the growth of small and medium-sized businesses in the interwar period and beyond. The latter path was an integral part of the persistence and development of the peasant household economy. In this revised picture, small-scale agriculture, while internationally uncompetitive, provided labour of a good quality, as well as a reasonable size of domestic market with distinct consumer tastes favouring domestic production and Japanese manufactures. Land productivity improved with partial mechanization such as the use of small irrigation pumps and the development of new seed varieties.

Second, while sources of industrial strength were traditionally sought in the use of cheap, abundant and disposable labour, studies of the labour market and factory management found evidence of incentive-inducing managerial and institutional arrangements, which contributed to securing efficiency and improving the quality of labour (Hazama 1997; Nakabayashi 2003). Although harsh working conditions, poor hygiene and low wages attracted contemporary attention, leading to heated debate on the implementation of the Factory Law, workers possessed the basic skills and the ethic that were required for labour-intensive work, and responded to economic incentives offered by the management. The successful retention of the rural work ethic on the factory floor must have mattered in the international competition of the production of cheap mass manufactured goods for Asian and other non-European markets.

I have argued that the Japanese experience can be termed labour-intensive industrialization, in the sense that the government strategy after the late 1880s clearly reflected the comparative advantage, and that technology and organizational arrangements were developed to reinforce that advantage (Sugihara 2013). Even in the rapid development of heavy and chemical industries in the 1930s where capital- and resource-intensive technology was vigorously adopted, one of Japan's relative strengths came from the organizational devices that ensured the effective absorption of competitive labour. In these industries the total wage bill was kept low, with the employment of relatively young workers, by a greater use of temporary workers and through cooperation with subcontracting firms (Hashimoto 1991).

Other major revisions include the interpretation of the strategy and structure of zaibatsu groups and other business organizations by business historians; the development of heavy industries and trading and shipping companies (industry-based histories achieved a high level of scholarship in Japan); and the history of technology and research and development (e.g. Sawai 2012). Furthermore, Tetsuji Okazaki (1958–) opened up a new field of comparative institutional analysis in Japanese economic history, which offers a more universal framework for analysing various institutions, such as merchant guilds, production organization and government policy, than had previously been attempted (Okazaki 2007).

It is also worth noting that a substantial amount of high quality research continued to be produced by those who were trained under the Marxist–empiricist tradition. The question of how capital was accumulated was particularly important (imports of foreign capital were not large). The well-respected works of Kanji Ishii (1938–), a Koza school figure with excellent empirical research skills, for example, remained engaged on this issue. He also trained such a diverse range of economic historians, including some who contributed to the eight-volume publication cited above, that the Marxist–revisionist dichotomy adopted in this chapter often looks unreal in practice. It is only useful to extract sea changes over a long period of time.

Postwar high-speed growth and beyond

During the occupation period (1945–51) the Supreme Commander of Allied Forces (SCAP), heavily influenced by the Koza school version of pre-war Japanese society, engaged in zaibatsu dissolution, land reform and labour reform, in addition to the more general agenda for democratization such as freedom of speech, rights to education and gender equality. Postwar economic policy concentrated on the modernization of the domestic economy, and the 'elimination of the dual structure' was vigorously attempted. That is, disparities between urban and rural areas, between big business and small and medium-sized business, and between white-collar workers and blue-collar workers had to be minimized (see the last two volumes of *The Economic History of Japan*, referred to above, for a revisionist synthesis of this interpretation). Against the international climate of free trade, cheap oil and American military support, Japanese industries quickly recovered international competitiveness, and, with technological advance, their comparative advantage shifted from light industries such as textiles and sundries to the relatively labour-intensive parts of heavy industries such as shipbuilding, consumer electronics, passenger cars and eventually to high-technology industries such as computer, telecommunications and medical equipment industries.

Even so, the egalitarian character of the economy and society was retained. The urban household replaced the rural household as the basic economic unit. The source of energy shifted from coal to oil, and the industrial complex was built along the Pacific coast, so that large tankers could access it. Exports now included manufactured goods, which were in direct competition with those produced in advanced Western countries and their destinations became worldwide. Japan's industrial competitiveness became a focus of international attention, with the factors contributing to it gradually shifting from cheap labour and state guidance to technological capabilities, the quality of labour, efficient management and 'market-enhancing' institutions.

Nevertheless, there were similarities between these observations and pre-war equivalents. The third feature of the pre-war frame of reference, outlined in the earlier section, was that the relationship between external pressures, initial conditions and the role of the state determined the nature of Japanese capitalism. While the Western impact made a critical contribution to the Meiji institutional changes, the state responded to the challenge by developing a strategy for industrialization, which however was largely executed 'from below', and high initial conditions made this possible. In the postwar period, external pressures (the occupation) forced drastic postwar institutional changes upon society, which until then had lacked the internal urge for democratization and economic modernization. The state responded to the challenge by implementing an industrial policy but this only offered administrative guidance and relatively minor incentives for the development of a stream of new, mainly machinery industries. It was these industries that exploited the competitiveness of an increasingly highly educated workforce, which in turn demanded a relatively egalitarian treatment between management and labour. Explanations based on such a sequence gave an impression that Japanese high-speed growth was basically an internal affair, with an occasional urge for exports and a strong resistance to free trade in agricultural products, lacking a sense of its position in the world economy.

Asian and global economic history

Japan became so proactive in the international economy from the 1970s that it became impossible to discuss the Japanese economy and the world economy as if they had no significant mutual influences. The pre-war frame of reference had to be reinterpreted to account for this development.

The most spectacular change was a surge of exports of Japanese manufactured goods, especially to advanced Western countries. After the oil crisis of 1973, Japan spent much of her trade surplus with them to purchase oil, especially from the Middle East. This led to the development of the 'oil triangle', the last link of which was made either by the flow of Japanese oil money from the Middle East to the international financial markets in the West, which formed a large part of the Eurodollar market, or by the Western export of arms to the Middle East. In spite of the trade dispute between the United States (and EC/EU) and Japan (and later other East Asian countries), the oil triangle became the largest multilateral settlement pattern in the world, and remained a central settlement mechanism between East Asia, the West and the Middle East for the next thirty-five years (Sugihara 2008).

At the same time, Japan began to be challenged by the rapid rise of Newly Industrialized Economies (NIEs), the Association of Southeast Asian Nations (ASEAN) and China as exporters of manufactured goods. Their high-speed growth with a certain sequence (named 'flying geese') was also quite unexpected. In fact many contemporaries had argued for Japanese 'exceptionalism', denying the potential of economic and social development in other Asian countries. Needless to say, however, neither high initial conditions nor any ethic or culture specific to Japan would explain the economic development of East and Southeast Asia on a regional scale.

In the last thirty years efforts were made to explore the origins of Asian economic development in its own light. A new field of 'Asian economic history' emerged, in addition to 'Western economic history' and 'Japanese economic history', although in practice it was a fresh reinterpretation of Japanese colonial, Chinese and other national histories with emphasis on wider regional dimensions, especially of intra-Asian trade. In more recent years, the origins and diffusion of labour-intensive industrialization were also traced back to the early modern period to establish an 'East Asian path' of economic development, while the paths of economic development in South and Southeast Asia are also being compared with the East Asian path. Implications of these developments are far-reaching, as themes on Japanese history are now treated as part of a larger unit of analysis much more freely, whenever necessary. The question we should pose is whether the pre-war frame of reference has fundamentally changed.

Intra-Asian trade and Japanese industrialization

In the mid-1980s Asian trading networks were identified as a regional force, which filtered the Western impact and connected various regions and countries of Asia across territorial boundaries. Takeshi Hamashita (1943–), Heita Kawakatsu (1948–) and myself (1948–) argued that there had been an Asian trading network since the sixteenth century that underpinned certain features common to the region, such as the material culture consisting of rice, cotton, silk and sugar, the circulation of silver, and regional commerce conducted by Chinese, Indian and other merchants. Under the Western impact this network was reorganized, rather than diminished. In fact, from the late nineteenth century to the 1930s, the rate of growth of intra-Asian trade was much faster than that of Asia's trade with the West or world trade. Furthermore, it was the growth of intra-Asian trade that provided the massive market for cheap manufactured goods for Japan's (and later China's) industrialization. In Africa or Latin America there was no such vigorous growth of regional trade (see Hamashita 2008; Kawakatsu 1991; Sugihara 2005).

In Japan the history of Japanese imperialism and colonialism has occupied a central place in modern Asian economic history. Understanding the road to the Second World War has also attracted serious scholarly attention. The literature on intra-Asian trade, by contrast, tried to study the depth of intra-regional trade that operated across various colonies and independent states, benefiting from the region's low tariff rates, as a result of colonialism, or the lack of tariff autonomy across the region. In the 1930s, however, the Yen bloc trade expanded so rapidly that it dominated intra-Asian trade and traditional Asian merchant networks were severely disrupted.

Nevertheless, intra-Asian trade recovered in the postwar period, especially after 1965. By 2010 the proportion of intra-regional trade in Asia's total exports was 73 per cent, a figure that exceeds most of intra-regional trade proportions that have ever been calculated in modern history. The trade-driven regional integration, which is also a source of transfer of technology, business management and other forms of knowledge, was a major feature of modern Asian economic development.

The Asian path and reciprocal comparison

The revisionist interpretation of Japanese economic history from the Tokugawa to the postwar period implied that there was a long-term path of economic development. Was this specific to Japan? Bin Wong argued that China's long-term path of economic (and political) development is comparable to Europe's, partially drawing on Japanese scholarship but suggesting a more fundamental rethinking of the methodology of comparative history (Wong 1997). If China had a long-term path that shared certain common features with Japan, in terms of the industrious revolution, Smithian growth and labour-intensive industrialization, it may be possible to think of an East Asian path, which has survived the Western impact, Japanese aggression and the Cold War divide, and has largely driven global economic development for the last half-century.

Moreover, there are common environmental features across different parts of Asia. In describing postwar economic development up to c.1980, Harry Oshima stressed the common socio-environmental characteristics of monsoon Asia, stretching from East and Southeast Asia to South Asia, in terms of seasonal rainfall patterns induced by monsoon winds, and the centrality of the large delta for the growth of rice farming and dense population. In some crucial respects the character of the Asian path originates from this unique environment (Oshima 1987). The rural capacity to hold a vast population for a long time has been a common feature of East Asia and South Asia. Although the timing and pace of industrialization were different in different areas, reflecting differences in resource endowments and policy reinforcement, regional trade and labour-intensive industrialization represented Asia's response to the Western impact from the 'long nineteenth century' on. Now the region has become the centre of the growth of the world economy and trade, if not of the development of technology and institutions.

A major implication of such a perspective is that it began to foster the notion of reciprocal comparison (Austin 2007), which the traditional Japanese comparative history with the West–Japan dichotomy had not been able to develop. Today most scholars accept the fundamental importance of the industrial revolution in England for global industrialization, but believe that the diffusion of industrialization was a result of negotiation with local and regional factor endowments and other conditions. They reject the view that other regions would eventually converge to the Western path of economic development. Appropriate relationships between economic development and the environment had to be established in each region, regardless of whether modern technology and institutions developed largely in that region, as in Europe, or came from outside.

Along with comparative history, the new scholarship also focused on connective history, with an explicit recognition of interdependence. Since industrialization began, different paths of economic development in major world regions (such as Western Europe, East Asia and South Asia) became much more closely connected with one another. Western impact was not a one-way process. Western traders, financiers and steamships developed long-distance trade routes, but local and regional merchants handled a corresponding growth of local and regional trade. In all likelihood, Asian merchants handled the majority of regional trade in 1840, measured globally. Local and regional entrepreneurs were also largely responsible for product and process innovations, which led, for example, to the introduction of modern manufacturing methods in the production of saris or kimonos and the invention of noodle-making machines. Western technology and institutions became a global influence, not because they were universally applicable, but because local and regional efforts neutralized their cultural and environmental specificity. The diffusion of industrialization was the result of multipolar agency (Sugihara 2015: 106–8).

Concluding remarks

In the postwar period, quantitative historians pushed a revisionist interpretation, by emphasizing the high 'initial conditions', culminating in the Tokugawa period, and the importance of traditional agriculture and proto-industry for Japan's industrialization. This negotiation between Western impact and initial conditions (through the 'developmental state') as a basic frame of reference has been observed in many historiographies of non-European countries, because of the similarity of their position in the world economy at the time of industrialization.

This chapter has argued that the same relationships between external pressures, the response of the state and the response of the local society have been central to the understanding of the more recent period of Japanese history, as well as parts of Asian economic history. Generally speaking, the themes running through all periods are remarkably similar, and conclusions have been revised, not necessarily as a direct result of changes in the social agenda, but also as a result of the introduction of new methodologies and evidence by economic historians.

This chapter also noted that recent Japanese scholarship engaged in the interpretation of Asian and global economic history. There the unit of analysis clearly changed, and the traditional (typically Euro-centred) yardstick has been challenged, but, in my view, these developments reflected the necessity of extending the coverage of historical analysis, rather than changing the basic intellectual agenda which is to locate Japan in a global context and to identify the indigenous strength to find its comparative advantage. Creating a culture-neutral, if not universal, language that would explain diverse paths of economic development remains a formidable task. The main message from the Japanese experience and historiography is that both comparative and connective economic histories are basic to the development of humanities and social sciences.

Today the discipline faces challenges such as the decline of interest in history among economists and the decline of interest in economic activities, as opposed to the cultural and social meanings of them, among intellectuals. However, these tendencies are common to international academia, and are arguably not as powerful in Japan as in the West. There are also signs of intellectual vitality in quantitative and institutional history, Asian and global history and in environmental history, all of which draw strength from Japan's peculiar trajectory of development and the historiographical traditions to which this has given rise.

Notes

1 I am grateful to Professors Kanji Ishii, Matao Miyamoto and Osamu Saito for their comments on the draft of this chapter. I have been able to respond to their critical comments and criticisms at a very superficial level. None of them should be accused of not pointing out the factual errors or missing references that remain.

2 This and the following sections on pre-First World War times draw extensively on Sugihara and Tanaka 1998.

3 This and the following two sections are based on Sugihara 1992.

4 This is an impression I gained from attending his lectures, and participating in the informal conversation sessions he held with young students after the lectures, at the International Christian University, Tokyo, in 1971–72.

5 Hayami et al. 2004 and Nakamura and Odaka 2003 contain translations of selected chapters of these volumes.

References

Abe, Takeshi (1989) *Nihon ni okeru Sanchi Menorimonogyo no Tenkai* (The Development of Local Cotton Weaving Centres in Japan), Tokyo: Tokyo Daigaku Shuppankai.

Araki, Moriaki (1959) *Bakuhan Taisei Shakai no Seiritsu to Kozo* (The Emergence and Structure of the Society under the Baku-han System), Tokyo: Ochanomizu Shobo.

Austin, Gareth (2007) 'Reciprocal Comparison and African History: Tackling Conceptual Euro-centrism in the Study of Africa's Economic Past', *African Studies Review*, 50(3): 1–28.

Bellah, Robert N. (1957) *Tokugawa Religion: The Values of Pre-industrial Japan*, Glencoe: Falcon's Wing Press.

de Vries, Jan (2008) *The Industrious Revolution: Consumer Behavior and the Household Economy, 1650 to the Present,* Cambridge: Cambridge University Press.

Dore, Ronald (1973) *British Factory, Japanese Factory: The Origins of National Diversity in Industrial Relations,* Berkeley: University of California Press.

Gerschenkron, Alexander (1962) *Economic Backwardness in Historical Perspective: A Book of Essays,* Cambridge, MA: Belknap Press.

Hall, John Whitney (1991) 'Introduction', in John Whitney Hall (ed.) *The Cambridge History of Japan, Volume 4: Early Modern Japan,* Cambridge: Cambridge University Press, 1–39.

Hamashita, Takeshi (2008) *China, East Asia and the Global Economy: Regional and Historical Perspectives,* edited by Linda Grove and Mark Selden, London: Routledge.

Hashimoto, Juro (1991) *Daikyoko-ki no Nihon Shihonshugi* (Japanese Capitalism during the Period of the Great Depression), Tokyo: Tokyo Daigaku Shuppankai.

Hayami, Akira (2009) *Population, Family and Society in Pre-Modern Japan,* Folkestone: Global Oriental.

Hayami, Akira (2015) *Japan's Industrious Revolution,* Tokyo: Springer.

Hayami, Akira, Osamu Saito and R. P. Toby, eds. (2004) *Emergence of Economic Society in Japan, 1600–1859 (The Economic History of Japan: 1600–1990, volume 1),* Oxford: Oxford University Press.

Hazama, Hiroshi (1997) *The History of Labour Management in Japan,* trans. Mari Sako and Eri Sako, Basingstoke: Macmillan.

Ishimoda, Tadashi (1946) *Chuseteki Sekai no Keisei* (The Emergence of a Medieval World), Tokyo: Ito Shoten.
Iwanami Shoten (1932–33) *Nihon Shihonshugi Hattatsushi Koza* (Symposium on the History of the Development of Japanese Capitalism), Tokyo: Iwanami Shoten.
Kawakatsu, Heita (1991) *Nihon Bunmei to Kindai Seiyo: Sakoku Saiko* (Japanese Civilization and Modern West: A Reappraisal of the Seclusion Policy), Tokyo: Enu-eichi-kei Hoso Shuppan Kyokai.
Komatsu, Yoshitaka (1961) 'The Study of Economic History in Japan', *Economic History Review*, 14(1): 115–21.
Miyamoto, Matao (1988) *Kinsei Nihon no Shijo Keizai: Osaka Komeshijo Bunseki* (The Market Economy of Early Modern Japan: An Analysis of the Osaka Rice Market), Tokyo: Yuhikaku.
Nakabayashi, Masaki (2003) *Kindai Shihonshugi no Soshiki: Seishigyo no Hatten ni okeru Torihiki no Tochi to Seisan no Kozo* (An Organization in Modern Capitalism: The Governance of Trade and the System of Production in the Development of the Silk Reeling Industry), Tokyo: Tokyo Daigaku Shuppankai.
Nakamura, Takafusa (1983) *Economic Growth in Prewar Japan*, trans. Robert A. Feldman, New Haven, CT: Yale University Press.
Nakamura, Takafusa, and Konosuke Odaka, eds. (2003) *Economic History of Japan, 1914–1955: A Dual Structure (The Economic History of Japan: 1600–1990, volume 3)*, trans. Noah S. Brannen, Oxford: Oxford University Press.
Ohkawa, Kazushi, Miyohei Shinohara and Mataji Umemura, eds. (1965–88) *Choki Keizai Tokei: Suikei to Bunseki* (Estimates of Long-term Economic Statistics of Japan since 1868), 14 volumes, Tokyo: Toyo Keizai Shinposha.
Ohkawa, Kazushi, and Miyohei Shinohara with Larry Meissner, eds. (1979) *Patterns of Japanese Economic Development: A Quantitative Appraisal,* New Haven, CT: Yale University Press.
Okazaki, Tetsuji ed. (2007) *Production Organizations in Japanese Economic Development,* London: Routledge.
Okazaki, Tetsuji, and Masahiro Okuno-Fujiwara, eds. (1999) *The Japanese Economic System and its Historical Origins*, trans. Susan Herbert, Oxford: Oxford University Press.
Oshima, Harry (1987) *Economic Development in Monsoon Asia: A Comparative Study,* Tokyo: University of Tokyo Press.
Otsuka, Hisao (1982) *The Spirit of Capitalism: The Max Weber Thesis in an Economic Historical Perspective,* Tokyo: Iwanami Shoten.
Otsuka, Hisao (1985) *Kindai Oshu Keizaishi Josetsu, Otsuka Hisao Chosakushu, Vol. 2* (Introduction to Modern European Economic History, Collected Works of Hisao Otsuka, Vol. 2), Tokyo: Iwanami Shoten.
Pomeranz, Kenneth (2000) *The Great Divergence: China, Europe, and the Making of the Modern World Economy,* Princeton, NJ: Princeton University Press.
Saito, Osamu (1983) 'Population and the Peasant Family Economy in Proto-industrial Japan', *Journal of Family History*, 8(1): 30–54.
Sawai, Munoru (2012) *Kindai Nihon no Kenkyu Kaihatsu Taisei* (The System of Research and Development in Modern Japan), Nagoya: Nagoya Daigaku Shuppankai.
Smith, Thomas C. (1959) *The Agrarian Origins of Modern Japan,* Stanford, CA: Stanford University Press.
Smith, Thomas C. (1988) *Native Sources of Japanese Industrialization, 1750–1920,* Berkeley: University of California Press.
Sugihara, Kaoru (1992) 'The Japanese Capitalism Debate, 1927–1937', in Peter Robb (ed.) *Agrarian Structure and Economic Development: Landed Property in Bengal and Theories of Capitalism in Japan,* Occasional Papers in Third-World Economic History, no. 4, School of Oriental and African Studies, London, 24–33.
Sugihara, Kaoru, ed. (2005) *Japan, China and the Growth of the Asian International Economy, 1850–1949,* Oxford: Oxford University Press.
Sugihara, Kaoru (2008) 'East Asia, Middle East and the World Economy: The Oil Triangle under Strain', in Y. Kawamura et al. eds, Proceedings of the Third Afrasian International Symposium 'Resources under Stress: Sustainability of the Local Community in Asia and Africa', Afrasian Centre for Peace and Development Studies, Ryukoku University and Center for Southeast Asian Studies, Kyoto University, Kyoto, 213–37.
Sugihara, Kaoru (2013) 'Labour-intensive Industrialization in Global History: An East Asian Perspective', in Gareth Austin and Kaoru Sugihara (eds.) *Labour-intensive Industrialization in Global History*, London: Routledge, 20–64.

Sugihara, Kaoru (2015) 'Global Industrialization: A Multipolar Perspective', in J.R. McNeill and Kenneth Pomeranz (eds.) *Cambridge World History Vol. 8: Production, Connection and Destruction, 1750–Present (1)*, Cambridge: Cambridge University Press, 106–35.

Sugihara, Shiro and Toshihiro Tanaka, eds. (1998) *Economic Thought and Modernization in Japan*, Cheltenham: Edward Elgar.

Sugihara, Kaoru, and Roy Bin Wong (2015) 'Industrious Revolutions in Early Modern World History', in Jerry H. Bentley and Sanjay Subrahmanyam (eds.) *Cambridge World History Vol. 7: The Construction of A Global World (2)*, Cambridge: Cambridge University Press, 283–309.

Tanimoto Masayuki, ed. (2006) *The Role of Tradition in Japan's Industrialization: Another Path to Industrialization*, Oxford: Oxford University Press.

Teranishi, Juro, and Yutaka Kosai, eds. (1993) *The Japanese Experience of Economic Reforms*, Basingstoke: Macmillan.

Tsunoyama, Sakae (1980) *Cha no Sekaishi: Ryokucha no Bunka to Kocha no Shakai* (The World History of Tea: Green-Tea-rooted Culture and (English-)Tea-rooted Society), Tokyo: Chuo Koronsha.

Umemura, Mataji, et al., eds. (1988–90) *Nihon Keizaishi* (The Economic History of Japan), 8 volumes, Tokyo: Iwanami Shoten.

Weber, Max (1989) *Purotesutantizumu no Rinri to Shihonshugi no Seishin* (The Protestant Ethic and the Spirit of Capitalism), revised translation by Hisao Otsuka, Tokyo: Iwanami Shoten: 'Yakusha Kaisetsu (The Translator's Introduction)', 373–412.

Wong, R. Bin (1997) *China Transformed: Historical Change and the Limits of European Experience*, Ithaca, NY: Cornell University Press.

Yamada, Moritaro (1934) *Nihon Shihonshugi Bunseki* (An Analysis of Japanese Capitalism), Tokyo: Iwanami Shoten.

Yamanouchi, Yasushi (1979) 'Japan', in Georg G. Iggers and Harold T. Parker (eds.) *International Handbook of Historical Studies: Contemporary Research and Theory*, Westport, CT: Greenwood Press, 253–76.

20

LATIN AMERICAN ECONOMIC HISTORY

Looking backwards for the future

Luis Bértola and Javier Rodríguez Weber

Latin America has experienced a long-term process of clear divergence from developed countries. At the same time, it has been a dynamic region, in the sense that it has been growing at world averages and has shown standards of living that are, on average, clearly above those of the poorer regions of the world (Bértola and Ocampo 2012).

These are some probable explanations why Latin America has a relatively strong tradition in economic history and why Latin Americans have searched for an explanation for the region's relative backwardness and for clues in order to find the path to development in its economic history. Compared to other regions, Latin American economic historiography has been interested as much in the future as in the past. Part of the reason is that the type of economic transformations that occurred in developed regions are current challenges in Latin America. To some extent, there is a tacit or explicit idea that developed countries are the mirror in which Latin America is looking for its future.

The 1960s and 1970s were the Golden Age of Latin American economic history. At that time, economists were mainly development economists. This means that they were focused on long-term performance and the main explanations were to be found in particular structures of production and institutional arrangements, both at the domestic and international levels. Historians in this period were mainly influenced by Annales-like and Marxist thinking, in which institutions, power and politics were always present, but mainly articulated through the economic determinants of social life. Even sociologists and the emerging political scientists were still very much concerned with the interaction between economics, social structures and politics, and they did not find a problem in letting economics play the determinant role. Within this historiography economic history became a field of convergence of the different social sciences. At the same time, Latin American economic history was very much influenced by different ideological points of view, especially concerning the question of whether the Western path of development was the one to be followed by Latin American countries, by necessity or desire, or if progress demanded alternative development patterns.

The 1980s and 1990s witnessed important changes. Most Latin American countries abandoned the developmentalist agenda and moved towards the structural reforms dominated by what was later known as the Washington Consensus. The decadence of the big theories of economic and social change and of the communist experiments, the almost complete dominance of neoclassical economics, the decreasing interest that economics had for historians, and the increasing autonomy of both sociology and political science, left economic history as a very marginal field in the social sciences, in clear contrast with the glorious 1960s and 1970s. The last two decades are showing a renaissance of economic history, in different directions. Some general trends are the clearly diminished role played by big theories and ideologies, a more professional approach to the construction of information and historical facts, and an increasing attempt to connect local with other national experiences. A positive outcome is the proliferation of research networks across countries and the increasing institutionalization of international forums.

This chapter will explore different trends in Latin American economic history written in different periods, relating them to contemporary academic, economic and political debates in Latin America and in the developed world. It will highlight the extent to which economic history in Latin America has shown similar development patterns to the Western canon, where particular and distinctive features can be found. We conclude with reflections on the future research agenda.

Up to the 'Golden Age'

In 1970, a group of economic historians met in Lima, Peru, in what was called the first Symposium of Latin American Economic History. The meeting had three goals: to make a critical review of the state of the art of economic history in the continent, to discuss the main problems and methods of the discipline, and to agree on a common research agenda for the future. In the introduction to the volume that comprised the papers from the conference, Heraclio Bonilla (1972: 10) wrote that the state of economic history in the different countries was 'embryonic'. Moreover, according to Tulio Halperin Donghi (1972), Latin American economic history was so recent that one could doubt its mere existence. In fact, the different papers dated the origins of the discipline not earlier than in the 1950s. It was in the mid-century when the first books on economic history began to be published, and this was no coincidence. As we will see later, the crisis of the export-led growth model, which occurred in the interwar period, had a catalyzing effect on the development of economic history.

Two main history writing traditions – often complementary – contributed to our knowledge of the economic past during what we can call the pre-history of economic history: a traditional nationalist tradition and Marxism. Latin American historiography, from its origins until well into the twentieth century, has been interested in the study of the political process of recently born republics, usually as an act of patriotism and with the explicit goal of contributing to the consolidation of the nation-state and the creation of a national identity. The study of the economic past was not totally absent in these studies, but it was clearly not more than a complement to the explanation of political processes. This is, for instance, the case with the work of the Argentine Bartolomé Mitre, who focused on the role of the economic expansion of the *Litoral* in the revolutionary process of his country; and of the Uruguayan Pablo Blanco Acevedo, who highlighted the role played by the rivalry between the harbors of Montevideo and Buenos Aires, as an important component of the creation of Uruguayan nationality. Nonetheless, the main objective was still to assess the political process: the criteria to analyze periods, and to find decisive benchmarks, were political. Therefore, Bonilla (1972) stressed the need to use different criteria to analyze the economic history of Latin America other than the political benchmarks.

The Marxist tradition is probably greatly responsible for the above-mentioned features of Latin American economic history writings, in the sense that understanding the past was a key element in understanding and changing the current situation. Luis Nieto Arteta's 1942

Economía y cultura en la Historia de Colombia, was one of the pioneering works in Colombian economic history (Meisel 2007: 586). In Chile, similar attempts were made by authors like Julio Cesar Jobet (*Ensayo crítico del desarrollo económico social de Chile*, 1951) or Luis Vitale. Broadly speaking, the Marxist tradition stressed the semi-feudal features of the Latin American societies and economies, and tended to assume that capitalist relations of production had to be reinforced in order to develop the productive forces than could make possible deeper transformations of social relations towards socialism in the future. Implicit in these analyses was the idea that economic development followed a universal pattern.

As we said, interest in economic history rose after 1930, a time when the old certainties were put into question. However, as a research field it was born two decades after the Second World War. Latin American economic history was the result of three traditions or sources: the economics developed at the Economic Commission for Latin America (ECLA), the Annales School and Marxism. The first one was a school deeply rooted in the continent and spread mainly among economists. The others had their origin in Europe and were mostly influenced by historians. However, these traditions tended to have an increasing interaction between them and also with contributions from other social sciences such as sociology and the emerging political science, but also from intellectuals participating in different political movements.

The 1930s were crucial in Latin American economic history and seriously impacted on intellectual production in Latin America. However, this was a very slow movement. The 1930s in almost all of Latin America were characterized by an increasing role played by the state, trying to counteract the huge balance of payments problems arising from the collapse of export prices and volumes. The first reactions were highly pragmatic. No alternative theory to the orthodox was presented yet (Bértola and Ocampo 2012).

Nevertheless, as time went by, different bodies of theories regarding Latin American long-run development appeared. They tried to find good explanations of the need for state engagement in policy making in order to overcome what was then called underdevelopment. This process was not totally endogenous. During the post-Second World War period, development economics arose as an alternative to both orthodox and Keynesian economic thinking. What happened in Latin America was closely related to the evolution of development economics. The Latin American Structuralist tradition developed what was later called the 'historical–structural' method of analysis (Sunkel and Paz 1970). It was assumed that economics could not rely on the hypothetic–deductive approach, but that it had to be combined with the study of the particular characteristics experienced by societies in a certain period of time. There were limits to general rules and it was vital to take into consideration the fact that Latin America is a peripheral region of a world dominated by industrialized countries. However, this approach is very common in the social sciences so it is not correct to claim that this is a distinctive feature only of Latin American Structuralism (Rodríguez 2005).

What is of particular interest for us is that this approach fueled a huge amount of economic research which departed from the assumption that development was a long-run process in which pure economic factors were strongly interacting with cultural, social and political ones. Thus, a large amount of work was dedicated to interpret long-term development in Latin America and important books were written about the continent as a whole. The more influential ones were Sunkel and Paz (1970), Cardoso and Faletto (1969), Celso Furtado (1969). These general works were paralleled by a large number of national studies, covering different periods and economic sectors.

A central component of this line of research was the creation of the Economic Commission for Latin America in 1948, which was dynamically led by the Argentine Raúl Prebisch during this period. The son of a German immigrant and a daughter of the decadent local aristocracy in Tucumán, Prebisch summarized the contradiction of the time between the promises of an industrial world and the reality of a poor periphery of settler economies. Facing the crisis of the 1930s as a distinguished civil servant stimulated his ideas about the need to introduce deep changes in the productive structure of a primary-based country experiencing drastic changes in demand and prices and with limited capacity to absorb the benefits of technical change. Prebisch transformed ECLA into a huge think tank that attracted the best Latin American scholars (such as Furtado and Sunkel) and promoted a research agenda that combined deep theoretical thinking, the creation of modern systems of information and statistics, and a profound engagement in current problems and policy making. The impact of the ECLA tradition on Latin American economic history writing, and more globally, is difficult to overestimate. It has gone far beyond the Latin American experience. One single example may suffice: the intensive debate on the tendency of the terms of trade of primary products vis-à-vis manufactures is based on the so-called Prebisch–Singer thesis and it is a debate that continues internationally to this day.

The Structuralist tradition had a particular interest in the study of center–periphery relations, i.e. the different forms of subordinate development, either under formal colonial rules or under informal forms of dependency (economic, commercial, financial, technological and even cultural). Nonetheless, already in the late 1950s the focus shifted more and more towards the study of domestic factors that blocked development: inequality in asset distribution (particularly land), concentration in the commercial sector, the cultural behavior of the elites (rent-seeking and luxurious consumption patterns), the weaknesses of the state, deficient educational system, among others.

In all of these fields, the Structuralist tradition promoted a great deal of studies. Even if they could hardly be labeled as economic history writings, they were, without any doubt, important contributions to the understanding of the economic history of the region. However, in doing that, this tradition did not constitute a break with what we can call the Western Canon of the time: Structuralism, even in focusing on the particular features of Latin American development, continued to see Latin America in the mirror of Western development.

While economists looked at the history of Latin American economies in search for answers to the difficulties of present economic development, historians were doing the same, but adopting the principles of the Annales-school and adapting Marxism to the reality of the continent. The French Historical Revolution[1] was welcomed by many young historians who were more interested in understanding the economic and social problems of the present than in the exaltation of the national heroes of the past. Many were also looking for answers which allowed them to contribute to changing their reality. They were *intelectuales comprometidos* (committed intellectuals). Besides highlighting the differences between Latin American countries, historians were interested in the Annales School for three main reasons. As an academic movement, the Annales historians fought against a historical tradition centered in the politics of the nation-state. Second, the long-run emphasis was considered particularly suited for Latin America, as many of the central problems of the present – such as the unequal distribution of land and its political and social consequences, or the problem of dependency upon foreign powers – had their origins in colonial times. Third, they were seduced by the goal of total history, which they considered essential to deal with the complexities of the development process of Latin America. Peru provides a good example of this. Manuel Burga (2005: 176–206) recounts the way in which, since 1960, different Peruvian historians went to Paris to study at the *Ecole Pratique des Hautes Etudes*. The first one was Pablo Macera. Many others followed – like Heraclio Bonilla and Manuel Burga himself. After his return, Pablo

Macera spread the ideas and works of the Annales School from his chair in Peruvian History and he gathered a group of young scholars who often met in his own house. Due to his studies in France, Macera gained an interest in economic history. On his return to Peru, he focused on the long-term study of the Andean hacienda. He was interested in prices, wages and commerce, conceived as the quantitative outcomes of social history (Burga 2005). Ruggiero Romano and Pierre Vilar were his favorite authors. Macera combined the lessons he learned from French historiography with local authors, who, like José Carlos Mariátegui (1928), had focused on the point of view of the indigenous population and culture. The synthesis was an interpretation of Peruvian history as a permanent defeat of this indigenous population, a story of continuous frustration and permanent degradation and exploitation. From his point of view, historical writings were important for revealing the exploitation of the Andean population. The Peruvian Revolution, he thought, would vindicate the indigenous people and their culture.

Between 1965 and 1975, a dozen young scholars traveled from Peru to Paris to study with the masters of the Annales School, especially with Ruggiero Romano.[2] The titles and themes of their books speak about their goal: to apply what they learned in Paris to Latin American development problems. Thus, in *Guano and Burguesía en el Perú,* Heraclio Bonilla studied the internal and external mechanisms that prevented the exploitation of a rich mineral resource – the guano – becoming a path to development. In his book *De la encomienda a la hacienda capitalista. El valle de Jequetepeque ss. XVI–XX,* Manuel Burga attempted to analyze the geography and economy of one region through centuries, from the very beginning of the conquest to the present. Both books, although different, are examples of the way in which the Annales School contributed to the renovation of Latin American historiography and, more specifically, economic history.

The influence of the Annales School went far beyond those who went to Paris. Historians like Mario Góngora and Rolando Mellafe in Chile, Enrique Tandeter and Jorge Gelman from Argentina, or José Pedro Barrán and Benjamín Nahúm from Uruguay, to cite just a few, approached history in the characteristic way of the Annales historians. Some of them studied in the *Ecole,* others not, but all of them applied the principles of the Annales School in a creative way trying to understand the evolution of Latin American institutions in the long run, especially in the rural sector.

Marxism was the other historiographical tradition that significantly influenced historians interested in the economic past. The first attempts to apply historical materialism to Latin American history were mostly interpretative and simplistic, in the vein of what Eric Hobsbawm called 'vulgar Marxism'. But things changed in the 1960s and 1970s, when Marxist economic historians combined erudition and deep knowledge of the sources with a non-dogmatic and creative use of Marxist theory. The analysis of the debate about the prevailing mode of production in Latin America between the sixteenth and nineteenth centuries will allow us to exemplify the characteristics of this approach to economic history.

The debate was triggered by the publication of *Capitalism and Underdevelopment in Latin America* in 1967 written by the German-born economist and sociologist Andre Gunder Frank, one of the fathers of dependency theory and the concept of the 'development of underdevelopment'. In his opinion, Latin American underdevelopment and Western development were the two sides of the same coin, an idea shared by all scholars who adopted the dependency approach. Much more controversial was his assertion that the capitalist mode of production became preeminent in Latin American economies from the very moment of the conquest. According to Gunder Frank, what differentiates feudalism from capitalism was that the former was a closed economy, and the latter was an open economy. As colonial Latin

America produced commodities for export from the sixteenth century, it was dominated by capitalism. A group of Latin American scholars reviewed the book in what became known as the 'Modes of Production Debate' (Assadourian 1975). Authors like Juan Carlos Garavaglia, Carlos Sempat Assadourian, Ernesto Laclau and Ciro Flamarion Santana Cardoso not only questioned the views of Gunder Frank, but also attempted to build a better model of Latin American colonial economies.

The debate was important because, although historical and theoretical in principle, its interest went far beyond the academic world. It affected the politics of leftist parties at a time of increasing social and political confrontation, as expressed by the Cuban Revolution. If colonial times could be assimilated to feudalism, then Latin America needed to go through a capitalist period before more advanced socialist goals could be achieved. On the contrary, if, as Gunder Frank argued, capitalism was the preeminent economic system in the continent since the sixteenth century, the revolution was feasible. As is usual in Latin American economic history, the study of the past was a path to change the present.

Many Latin American scholars taking part in the debate were critical of Frank's thesis, on theoretical and historical grounds. Theoretically, they questioned the definition of feudalism and capitalism. They argued that to consider feudalism as a closed system showed a great deal of ignorance about what was known about it. In the historical field, they claimed that Frank presented an oversimplified view of Latin American colonial history, which was refuted by historical evidence. Carlos Sempat Assadourian, who started his paper with a comment on the 'hard reality of underdevelopment which affected Latin America' in the 1960s, questioned the idea, sustained by Frank, that the crisis of the external sector – that linked the centers to the periphery – had positive impacts on the latter. Assadourian had shown, in his earlier works, the key role played by the mining sector and the big cities as centers of a much wider 'economic space' comprised of the regions that supplied many different inputs to the export sectors. Thus, the crisis of the external sector, rather than diminishing exploitation, produced a depression of the whole economic and social system.

Most Latin American historians agreed that talking about capitalism in the sixteenth century made no sense, but they disagreed on how to characterize the colonial economic system as feudal or something else. The most interesting view, in our opinion, was that of Ciro Cardoso, who, following Witold Kula, argued in favor of a theory of 'colonial modes of production'. These, not present in Marx's writings, included the 'colonial fact' – i.e. the reality of economic and political dependency – as its first and most important feature. Assuming that proposition as a starting point, the different colonial modes of production – for example the colonial slave mode of production – should take into account the differences in the labor regimes, demography and the characteristics of indigenous civilizations and cultures throughout the continent.

In sum, in the critique of Frank's thesis, Marxist Latin American historians vindicated an economic history that was theoretically informed and empirically grounded. This debate was, at the beginning, very much theoretical and political in character. However, it fueled a large amount of empirical research on the particular economic, environmental, social, demographic and political contexts of the different Latin American countries and regions. The changing political climate in different countries encouraged these writings: scholars were in many cases forced to move to other countries, thus increasing intellectual exchange and a more profound consciousness about Latin American diversity. At the same time, the process of industrialization had advanced in Latin America and the nation-states were playing a more active role in strengthening universities and academic life with the result that academic production increased significantly.

Tulio Halperín Donghi's *Contemporary History of Latin America* (1969) and Ciro Flamarión Santana Cardoso and Héctor Pérez Brignoli's *Historia Económica de América Latina* (1979) are two examples of the achievements and high standard of economic historiography in Latin America at this time. Halperín's book is a very good example of a work that clearly relies on the idea that economic forces play a decisive role in historical development: it is a 'total history' with an economic base. The book is subtle, very well informed, full of regional and national nuances and very well written. It sheds light on the interplay between the domestic determinants of historical events and the international sphere. Many editions of the book were published and it was translated into many different languages. Seen from today's perspective, the book has all the shortcomings expected from this kind of literature: lack of economic theory, lack of hard data, lack of crucial information on growth, accumulation and other critical variables. However, the book provided profound insights into Latin American economic history, by combining the different schools of thought prevailing at the time in a critical and creative manner.

Cardoso and Pérez Brignoli's book is an example of a non-orthodox Marxist approach to Latin American economic history. In short, their argument is as follows. Latin American colonial societies are based on three components: the European economy, African pre-colonial societies, and, obviously the pre-Columbian civilizations. These components combined in different ways in different parts of the region in response to local environmental and social conditions. Societies developed as part of or an extension of the European economy, but they also developed structures and dynamics of their own. The different regions are identified by four different criteria: (a) the colonial power (weak explanatory power); (b) the degree of connection to world markets (export centers, subsidiary economies and marginal regions often overlap in the same space); (c) the kind of products, highly dependent on geography (mining centers, tropical products, the production of foodstuffs and consumer goods for domestic markets), with big impacts on techniques and social organization; and (d) labor relations and the character of the colonization process.

Concerning the latter, the authors distinguish between different regions. First, the Euro-Indian regions, which were the core areas of the pre-Columbian civilizations and where colonization meant a redistribution of productive factors and the imposition of forced labor on reorganized peasant communities in many different and heterogeneous forms. Second, there were Euro-African societies, i.e. more homogeneous slave societies in regions suitable for tropical crops. Third, there were Euro-American societies in temperate regions with low native population densities and increasing European immigration. The various combinations of all these factors gave rise to a wide variety of transitions to peripheral capitalism, including those prompted by liberal reforms. The richness of this approach, the deep understanding of the interaction between international and domestic forces, the interwoven effect of geographical, social and cultural features, were unfortunately lost in the recent neo-institutional literature on Latin America. The latter has tended to oversimplify the Latin American pattern of development by searching for explanations that are too general.

Centrifugal forces and divorce, 1970–90

Contrary to what happened during what we called the Golden Age of economic history in Latin America, the following decades were characterized by centrifugal forces: the fragmentation of the Annales tradition, crisis within Marxism, weakening of development economics, hegemony of neoclassical economics and repression of academic life in many Latin American countries. As a result, economic history lost its central place among the social sciences and started a process of transformation that resulted in a new generation of more professional economic historians. However, they played a more marginal role in the social sciences.

The political atmosphere changed between the 1970s and 1990s. The collapse of real socialism, the crisis of Keynesianism and the hegemony of neoclassical and monetarist approaches impacted worldwide. In Latin America, this process went hand in hand with the crisis of state-led growth, and, in the countries with higher living standards where structural and social change had advanced the most, post-democratic military dictatorships had a very negative impact on the development of academic life, not to mention democracy and public debate.

As argued above, economic history in Latin America had always been very much involved in current debates on development strategies, and political involvement was not unusual in academia. The dictatorships had thus a huge negative impact on academic life in general, and particularly in the social sciences. The good side of the story, even if it weighs much less than the negative, was that many scholars and young students had to go into exile, thus favoring an increasing exchange with the international academic community. This is important as it counteracted propensities among Latin Americans to autonomous thinking and provincialism. Of course, academic life was not only weakened, but heterodox thinking was often repressed at the universities, although it varied between countries.

The Brazilian dictatorship, for instance, was the first of its kind and lasted for a long period (from 1964 to the early 1980s). Many scholars went into exile (to Chile before the state coup, then Mexico and many other countries in different continents). The Brazilian dictatorship was a pioneer in implementing ambitious national postgraduate and academic research programs. A combination of uncontested hegemony and rapid economic growth allowed for the expansion of research, even on heterodox lines. In Argentina, Chile and Uruguay, however, the damage done by the new political regimes went deeper. Mexico and Venezuela, on the contrary, were countries that attracted many refugees from other Latin American countries, and they became strongly internationalized academic milieus. After the state coup in Chile, ECLA survived as an island, with significantly reduced activity and influence.

Jointly with the adversities imposed by the political context dominated by authoritarian regimes, the crisis of macro-theories that linked historical research with development strategies, and the prevalence of neoclassical macroeconomic theory introduced all the elements for the divorce between history and economics, and even between economics and other social sciences. Economic historians of the Golden Age regarded the New Economic History (NEH) with a combination of interest and skepticism. The American school, and more broadly quantitative methods, were discussed by Ruggiero Romano (1972) and Marcello Carmagnani (1972), and later on by Cardoso and Pérez Brignoli (1976). They welcomed the systematic use of quantitative data,[3] but they were concerned about its perils, some of them especially important in the case of Latin American economic history.

First, the sources needed to make a rigorous use of quantitative methods were hardly available for Latin America. Second, not all of the central aspects which were relevant for the comprehension of historical reality – even in the reduced field of economic history – could be quantified. In their opinion, New Economic History had a tendency to ignore those aspects. Third, the use of standard economic theory and concepts were hardly useful for the analysis of the Latin American economic past.

The tensions involved in the transplantation of the methods of the NEH to Latin America were evident in the debate triggered by the publication of *An Economic History of Colombia, 1845–1930,* in 1971, a book written at the beginning of the 1960s by the economist William Paul McGreevey as his PhD dissertation in the Massachusetts Institute of Technology.

McGreevey's aim was to introduce cliometrics into Colombian history, but the result was exactly the opposite. In his book, McGreevey combined the use of sophisticated statistical methods, with a poor knowledge of Colombian sources and a simplistic theoretical approach grounded in neoclassical economics. The book led to a big controversy. Colombian historians of the Nueva Historia movement – a group close to the Annales School and to British Marxism, created in the 1960s and led by Jaime Jaramillo Uribe – considered that the book was flawed: false assumptions led to false conclusions. While some of the critics considered the author himself to be responsible for the errors, others considered that the problem lay in the assumption that cliometric methods and neoclassical theory could be applied to every historical context (Rodríguez and Arévalo 1994; Meisel 2007).[4]

In the decades that followed, the Annales School went through a process of splitting and combination with postmodern approaches, which left the study of economic issues looking completely old-fashioned. As economics became more and more formal, general, and less focused on historical changes, it became of less interest for historians, who tended to react negatively to formalization and abstract thinking. Among Marxists, confusion prevailed and historians, trying to understand more and more concrete cases, increasingly protected themselves behind the shelter of hard facts. Thus, a trend towards empirical research with weak theoretical, methodological and comparative reflection developed hand in hand with the increasing interest in local history, daily life, culture and related issues. These features did not need to go hand in hand, but this was the prevailing trend in Latin America.

In regard to economists, at least in Latin America, the new wave of neoclassical and monetary thinking did not stimulate the study of economic history. However, a new wave of studies tried to show that Latin American backwardness was a problem that first appeared due to import-substitution policies after the Great Depression, and that economic performance prior to that had been very good. However, the big picture is that economists, contrary to what happened during the Golden Age, became less interested in history and more focused on the short-run and contemporary problems.

Within this context, some cores of economic history writing persisted. In Brazil, one important research center was the Department of Economics of the State University of Campinas (Sao Paulo). Scholars such as Joâo Manuel Cardoso de Mello, Wilson Cano, Wilson Suzigan, Tamas Szmrecsányi, Fernando Novaes, Mario Posas and many others, made important contributions in the fields of 'late' capitalist development, 'early' (pre-1930) industrialization, slave economy and business history. Their research followed on the Structuralist tradition, but was rather precocious in developing it in interaction with new post-Keynesian, evolutionary and neo-Schumpeterian ideas, in line with what was later on called neo-Structuralism. In the 1990s a Master's program and a Doctoral program in Economic History were launched.

In Argentina the social sciences suffered a devastating attack during the 1970s. It was not until the early 1980s that the situation started to revert. The system of postgraduate studies developed first in the late 1990s. Postgraduate programs in social sciences evolved slowly and in a loosely articulated way. Even if some regional efforts were made, especially in Córdoba and Santa Fe, academic life was strongly concentrated in Buenos Aires. The divorce between history and economics in Argentina manifested a more profound ideological content. Mainstream economics had a much more powerful influence in Argentina than in Brazil, and the economic historiography written by economists had a strong neoclassical inspiration, as evidenced, for example, in the works of Díaz Alejandro, Roberto Cortés Conde and, more recently, Gerardo della Paolera and Alan Taylor. On the other hand, historians still working on economic history issues remained strongly committed to some type of Annales-like history writing, qualitatively oriented and highly concentrated on agricultural history, labor movements and state building. Dominated by left-wing thinking, this group tended to consider each attempt to quantify economic issues as ideologically suspicious. The Chilean and Uruguayan cases, even with subtle differences, developed similarly to the Argentine.

One important outcome of this period was that Latin American scholars hardly produced any books or general studies on the economic history of Latin America. This was in sharp contrast with previous developments. Although there were some exceptions, most projects on general Latin American economic history were led by anglophone scholars. The publication of the first *Cambridge History of Latin America* in the mid-1980s initiated a change in the way general works covering the whole Latin American region were written. From the mid-1980s, and until recently, the main general works on Latin America were written in English first. Rosemary Thorp and Victor Bulmer-Thomas came to be responsible for two of the most important comprehensive works which have been published since then. *The Economic History of Latin America since Independence* by Victor Bulmer-Thomas (1994) is analytically strong and penetrating, and uses a dualistic model to assess the performance of different Latin American countries in the export-led era. Rosemary Thorp's *Progress, Poverty and Exclusion: An Economic History of Latin America in the 20th Century* (1998) is the result of a research project financed by the Inter-American Development Bank, in which more than thirty outstanding scholars were involved. Finally, in 2006, the *Cambridge Economic History of Latin America* was edited by Victor Bulmer-Thomas, John Coastworth and Roberto Cortés Conde (still not translated into Spanish). In short, it seems that Latin American scholars were not, by themselves, producing as many comprehensive works on Latin American economic history and on history in general.

The renewal of economic history writing since the 1990s

After what we can call a downward phase in Latin American economic history during the 1980s, we can identify a phase of recovery in the late 1990s and a phase of expansion in the recent decades. This upward trend is the result of many different factors. Without any doubt, the comprehensive works on Latin American economic history edited outside Latin America had an important impact on the region, revealed the international interest in the topic and contributed with new lines of research. At the same time, they demanded new inputs from scholars of the region. Thus, these works had what we can call both backward and forward linkages. A second factor that contributed to the development of economic history was the changes in the political climate. Democratic consolidation in the region allowed for the recovery of plural academic life, the free circulation of ideas, the return of many scholars from exile, and the expansion of the educational system in general, with new research centers, networks and postgraduate programs. Furthermore, access to new technologies, as elsewhere, made it possible to process available data in different forms, stimulating historical research. Moreover, increasing opportunities for international exchange opened up new possibilities and stimulated research. In addition, radical changes in patterns of development due to the so-called structural reforms, the high volatility that still prevailed in the region and the combination of spasmodic growth and deepened social inequality, resulted in renewed interest in the study of long-term development patterns and, in particular, the study of the now-called first globalization boom.

While the neoclassical research agenda remained very active (relative prices, globalization, income inequality), economic history research was also fueled by the development of new institutional economics, which often used Latin America as the example of bad institutions and poor performance. Moreover, the development of neo-Structuralism and ECLA's recovery as an influential think tank in the region contributed to the theoretical renewal of economic history writings. The new phase of expansion is clearly noticed in scholarly production and in institutional success.

Scholarly production made progress along very varied lines. Without any doubt, one of the most dynamic fields was quantitative economic history. New generations of national accounts were produced, as well as important datasets on prices, wages, tariffs, taxes, state expenditure, energy production and consumption, inequality and more. On this basis, comparative research has increased and economic performance is being assessed. Institutional history made huge progress. Plenty of studies revisited old topics and opened new ones, both during the colonial and independency periods. Many national cases are clearly documented and the links to modern theoretical discussions on legal systems, property rights, liberal reforms and institutions (broadly speaking) are strong and fruitful. Many authors have tackled labor relations, legal frameworks for the operation of business, the creation of national states, the advance of the liberal reforms, the fiscal structures, institutional instability, the use of money and more. The programs of the Latin American Economic History Congresses (CLADHEs) are full of papers documenting these trends. A particular line of institutional research is the one linking institutions and technical change. This is particularly the case for the twentieth century. While institutions have been studied mainly within the Solowian framework, focusing on capital and human capital accumulation, the Structuralist tradition has focused more on Schumpeterian approaches to institutions.

Inequality was a central topic in the Structuralist and dependency approaches, both in terms of the international and the domestic economy: the outflow of resources and the concentration of property and income were considered to be permanent features of the export-led model, having a strong negative impact on development. Interest in this topic receded in the 1980s and 1990s. However, perhaps due to the intense political debate over who gains from the recent globalization experience, there has been a revival during the last few years of historical interest in income distribution, both theoretically and empirically. A special issue of the *Journal of Iberian and Latin American Economic History* was published, in which different approaches were noticeable. While mainstream approaches focus mainly on relative price movements as a result of market integration and disintegration (Williamson), Bértola and co-authors stress the role played by the different social structures, productive patterns and institutional frameworks (including international power relations) to explain the outcomes of market integration in terms of inequality. Bértola (2005) and Rodríguez Weber (2014) are examples of ambitious reconstruction of historical data in terms of long-run series, and interpretations that try to combine more conventional tools of analysis and socio-institutional approaches, that can be labeled as political economy approaches. These works, especially that of Rodríguez Weber, emphasize the role of colonial heritage in explaining structurally high inequality. Contrary to neo-institutional approaches, an important part of the Rodríguez Weber study aims to explain historical change, fluctuations in inequality trends, and the appearance of new actors and social relations with different outcomes. From a more quantitative point of view, Bértola et al. (2010, 2011) have enhanced the discussion of the application of the human development index to Latin America, particularly the weighting given to different components of the index. Latin American relative performance looks significantly worse when these considerations are taken into account.

Also within the Structuralist tradition, many studies have revisited classical topics, such as the features of the domestic productive structure, the constraints on the way in which Latin America relates to the world economy, the role of the state through regulation and through state-owned enterprises, the features of the agrarian sector and property concentration, the financial crisis and the patterns of international capital movements, the features of the national states and integration policies and so on. Moreover, entrepreneurial history has made important progress in trying to tackle the problem of lack of entrepreneurial capacities in Latin America and to assess the role of multinational enterprises.

Progress along these lines is evidenced in an important increase in publications. National compilations, such as the one edited by Sandra Kuntz Ficker in Mexico, the one edited by Jorge Gelman in Argentina, and the volumes edited by Banco de la República de Colombia (by Meisel and Ramírez, and by Robinson and Urrutia), are good examples. New reviews appeared, as *América Latina en la Historia Económica*, the *Revista Uruguaya de Historia Económica*, together with increased interest in Latin America shown, for example, by the Spanish *Revista de Historia Económica – Journal of Iberian and Latin American Economic History* and *Investigaciones en Historia Económica*. Finally, two books on Latin American economic history written by Latin American scholars were published during the last few years: *Institucionalidad y Desarrollo Económico,* edited by Luis Bértola and Pablo Gerchunoff (2011), and *The Economic Development of Latin America since Independence,* written by Luis Bértola and José Antonio Ocampo (2012). These two books reflect upon the collective efforts by many scholars working on Latin America (Latin Americans or not), in recent decades, that represent the recovery of old traditions mixed with new theoretical and methodological developments. They represent the development of Latin American capabilities to analyze the economic history of the region. From the point of view of the content of economic history in recent years, we can say that it closely followed the main trends in international economic history in its different versions. However, as happened during the Golden Age, the efforts to combine theory building at a meso-level with economic history analysis are also still vibrant.

Side by side with increasingly professionalized economic history production, we can notice a process of institution building. Economic history is cultivated in both departments of history and of economics, or development economics. There are more than a few postgraduate programs in economic history. Besides the already mentioned Universidad de Campinas, we have postgraduate programs in the University of San Paolo, University of Buenos Aires, in the Universidad Autónoma de México, and at the Universidad de la República, Uruguay. The latter, besides its Master's and PhD programs, has organized Southern Hemisphere Summer Schools annually, with the participation of students from different Latin American, European and even African countries. Very important to the academic training of young scholars have been also the Spanish universities, as well as American and the LSE.

We now have seven national economic history associations in the region (Argentina, Brazil, Chile, Colombia, Mexico, Peru and Uruguay), besides one in the Caribbean. The Argentine Economic History Association (Asociación Argentina de Historia Económica) is the oldest in the region and it is admirable that it has succeeded in organizing a National Congress every two years since the 1970s regardless of dramatic political and economic changes. These congresses, especially in the 1990s, have attracted a very wide range of scholars from different social sciences and have been held in many different cities of the Argentine interior, thus helping to strengthen local research groups. The Brazilian, Mexican and Uruguayan associations were created in the early 1990s, while the remaining four were created during the past couple of years, exemplifying the expansion phase we talked about.

However, probably the main institutional success in the region is the organization of the Latin American Economic History Congresses (CLADHE, for the Spanish acronym) every two or three years. The first one was organized in Montevideo in 2007 and the fifth is to be held in Sao Paulo in 2016. About 400 papers have been presented on average in these congresses, with participants from many Latin American countries and active participation of scholars from America and Europe. These congresses have promoted the creation of important international networks which in turn stimulated the development of comparative research. The congresses have attracted the participation of many young scholars, decisive for the future development of economic history. Another example of institutional progress was the move of the Latin American Economic History Database from Oxford to Montevideo. Hopefully, the now-named MOxLAD will continue to reflect and promote quantitative economic history in the region, and establish good interfaces with global databases.

Concluding remarks

In recent years economic history in Latin America has exhibited a new wave of expansion. It has not recovered the central role it had during the Golden Age of the 1960s and 1970s, but it is now an established field of research, with strong research centers and supportive institutions.

While economic history became more professional, it still seems to be very much engaged in current debates on development patterns and prospects in the region. In spite of the economic progress noticed during the last decade, as well as progress in many social indicators and democratic consolidation in the region, Latin America still faces the challenge to find a route to development. Economic history is still trying to shed light on the processes that have clear continuities in the present. Therefore, topics such as the origins and dynamics of inequality will remain on the agenda. The question about specialization in primary production connecting historical experience with future prospects, as well as the different attempts to produce changes in the productive structure will reemerge. Business history has still much to say about Latin American historical performance. Growth sustainability today is fueling more and more studies on energy consumption and environmental change from a historical perspective. Labor market studies, together with the challenges of the welfare states in different international environments, is another strong point of the agenda. And, last but not least, institutional research will continue to be a vibrant field of research with important debates that have contemporary implications. An active participation in international forums and networks will make sure that Latin American economic historiography will continue to be global and learn from developments abroad. If research is deeply rooted in domestic institutional environments and in an agenda for change in the region, it will surely continue in the good tradition of searching for answers to relevant questions for Latin America that might also be applied elsewhere.

Notes

1 This is also the title of a book written by Burke (1990).

2 Any analysis of the influence of Annales School in Latin American economic history would be incomplete without a specific reference to Ruggiero Romano. An Italian-born historian, Romano not only had a seminar on Latin American history, but also oriented the dissertations of most of the Latin American scholars who studied in the *Ecole* (Arcondo 2003).

3 The handbook written by Cardoso and Pérez Brignoli (1976) devoted many pages to teaching quantitative methods like index numbers, trend-cycle decomposition, and even had an appendix that introduced the reader to computers and punched cards. Also, in their view, not all kinds of quantitative history were the same. They distinguished between the French school of serial history, quantitative history *à la* Kuznets, and the 'new economic history'.

4 Even Meisel (2007), who lamented the slow diffusion of the NEH to Colombia, agreed that McGreevey's book had too many problems.

References

Arcondo, A. (2003) 'Ruggiero Romano y la historia económica colonial de América Latina', *Cuicuilco* 10 (29): 1–16.

Assadourian, C. S. (1975) *Modos de producción en América Latina*, Buenos Aires: Siglo Veintiuno Editores.

Bértola, L. (2005) 'A 50 años de la Curva de Kuznets: Crecimiento y distribución del ingreso en Uruguay y otras economías de nuevo asentamiento desde 1870', *Investigaciones de Historia Económica* 1 (3): 135–76.

Bértola, L. and P. Gerchunoff (2011) *Institucionalidad y desarrollo económico en América Latina*, Santiago de Chile: CEPAL.

Bértola, L. and J. A. Ocampo (2012) *The Economic Development of Latin America since Independence*, Oxford: Oxford University Press.

Bértola, L., M. Camou, S. Maubrigades and N. Melgar (2010) 'Human Development and Inequality in the Twentieth Century: The Mercosur Countries in a Comparative Perspective', in R. Salvatore, J. H. Coatsworth and A.E. Challú (eds.), *Living Standards in Latin American History: Height, Welfare and Development, 1750–2000*, Cambridge MA: Rockefeller Center for Latin American Studies.

Bértola, L., M. Hernandez, J. Rodríguez Weber and S. Siniscalchi (2011) 'Un siglo de desarrollo humano y desigualdad', paper presented at the 'V Jornadas de Historia Económica', Asociación Uruguaya de Historia Económica, Montevideo.

Bonilla, H. (1972) 'Introducción', in H. Bonilla (ed.), *La historia económica en América Latina. Situación y métodos*, Mexico City: Secretaría de Educación Pública.

Bulmer-Thomas, V. (1994) *The Economic History of Latin America since Independence*, Cambridge: Cambridge University Press.

Burga, M. (2005) *La historia y los historiadores en el Perú*, Lima: Fondo Editorial de la UNMSM.

Burke, P. (1990) *The French Historical Revolution: The Annales School, 1929–1989*, Stanford, CA: Stanford University Press.

Cardoso, F. E. and E. Faletto (1969) *Dependencia y desarrollo en América Latina. Ensayo de interpretación sociológica*, México: Siglo Veintiuno Editores.

Cardoso, C. F. S. and H. Pérez Brignoli (1976) *Los métodos de la historia: introducción a los problemas, métodos y técnicas de la historia demográfica, económica y social*, Barcelona: Editorial Crítica.

Cardoso, C. F. S. and H. Pérez Brignoli (1979) *Historia económica de América Latina*, Barcelona: Editorial Crítica.

Carmagnani, M. (1972) 'Metodología y técnicas para una historiografía económica latinoamericana', in H. Bonilla (ed.), *La historia económica en América Latina. Situación y métodos*, Mexico City: Secretaría de Educación Pública.

Furtado, C. (1969) *La economía latinoamericana: desde la conquista ibérica hasta la revolución cubana*, México: Siglo Veintiuno Editores.

Halperín Donghi, T. (1969) *Historia contemporánea de América Latina*, Madrid: Alianza.

Halperín Donghi, T. (1972) 'Situación de la historia económica en Argentina', in Bonilla, H. (ed.), *La historia económica en América Latina. Situación y métodos*, Mexico City: Secretaría de Educación Pública.

Mariátegui, J. C. (1928) *Siete ensayos de interpretación de la realidad peruana,* Lima: Biblioteca Amauta.

Meisel, A. (2007) 'Un balance de los estudios sobre historia económica de Colombia, 1942–2005', in M. Urrutia and J. Robinson (eds.), *Economía colombiana del siglo XX: un análisis cuantitativo*, Bogotá: Fondo de Cultura Económica – Banco de la República.

Rodríguez, O. (2005) *El estructuralismo latinoamericano,* Mexico City: Siglo Veintiuno Editores – CEPAL.

Rodríguez, O. and D. Arévalo (1994) 'La historiografía económica colombiana del siglo XIX', in B. Tovar Zambrano (ed.), *La historia al final del milenio: ensayos de historiografía colombiana y latinoamericana*, vol. I, Bogotá: Universidad Nacional de Colombia.

Rodríguez Weber, J. (2014) 'La economía política de la desigualdad de ingreso en Chile, 1850–2009', PhD thesis, Universidad de la República, Montevideo.

Romano, R. (1972) 'Conveniencias y peligros de aplicar los métodos de la "nueva história económica"', in H. Bonilla (ed.), *La historia económica en América Latina. Situación y métodos*, Mexico City: Secretaría de Educación Pública.

Sunkel, O. and P. Paz (1970) *El subdesarrollo latinoamericano y la teoría del desarrollo*, Mexico City: Siglo Veintiuno Editores.

Thorp, R. (1998) *Progress, Poverty and Exclusion: An Economic History of Latin America in the Twentieth Century*, Washington, DC: Inter-American Development Bank.

21

MEXICO'S ECONOMIC HISTORY

Much more than cliometrics and dependency theory

Sandra Kuntz Ficker[1]

As part of Latin America, Mexico's economic history shares some of the features described by Bértola and Rodríguez Weber (B&RW) in the previous chapter. The early interest in nation and state-building, the influence of European traditions such as Marxism and the *Annales* School, the engagement in the investigation of the origins of economic backwardness and the possible solutions to it are common features. However, it differs from B&RW's perception of what Latin American economic history has been in several respects. First, probably due to a long tradition of historical studies related to the colonial period, in Mexico a strong line of research on colonial economic history flourished, aiming at describing and understanding the main traits of the economy and society in New Spain. To a lesser extent, also the prehispanic society and later on the independent period became subjects of inquiry for their own sake. Those kinds of studies precede and probably outnumber the more recent interest in linking the past to current problems, as portrayed by B&RW. Second, in part for this reason, one cannot recognize as a preponderant feature of Mexico's economic historiography the somewhat reductionist attempts at instrumentalizing the past with the purpose of providing answers for the future, as seems to be the case for other parts of Latin America. Present issues have an impact, of course, in the questions posed to the past and in the ways to approach it, but the motivation in looking into history is not mainly informed by the urgency of finding solutions to current situations. This may also be a consequence of the fact that economic history in Mexico has been practiced by historians more than by economists. In this sense, one cannot say that in Mexico the discipline has been more interested in the future than in the past.

The specificities of Mexico's history conditioned early interests and subjects of academic endeavors also in the sense that political events unleashed exploration in some particular fields. The Mexican Revolution (1910–17) made historians wonder what kind of forces nurtured such a violent civil war, and the agrarian reform that followed fostered research on land-tenure systems, just to name a few notorious examples. In this sense, it fits the pattern that Pat Hudson describes for Great Britain, namely that it was from its inception "closely connected with the peculiarities of British socio-political and economic development, and with state formation and state policy" (Hudson, chapter 2 in this volume). On the other hand, in Mexico the development of the discipline has also been subject to the influence of external processes and currents of thought, as has been its own history as a country. Side by side with a traditional, historical school, which simply looked at economic aspects of the past in the same way as political or social aspects, since the mid-twentieth century economic historians in Mexico have been highly receptive to various stimuli from abroad that contributed to the professionalization of the discipline. The close and complex relationship with the United States has always represented a source of academic interaction and influence, to the extent that many scholars from that country have specialized in Mexico's history and many Mexican students have graduated in North American universities. Scholars from Europe and South America have frequently embraced the study of Mexico. European schools such as Marxism and the *Annales* also had an early presence in Mexico's economic historiography. To them was soon added the emergence of a Latin American current of thought, with strong influence in politics as well as in scholarship. At the same time, traditions stemming from growth economics (S. Kuznets) and development economics (A. Hirschman) with awareness of long-run perspectives began in the 1960s to have an impact on the practice of economists that cultivated an interest in Mexico's past. All these influences were reinforced by the work of scholars in the USA and Europe who were attracted to the study of Mexico's economic history because of its distinctive features or as a means to test particular theories, further enriching the discipline. A bit later than those stimuli, the New Economic History arrived in Mexico, with all of its variants of a neoclassical theoretical framework as well as the application of econometric tools to historical analysis; New Institutional Theory also found a place.

Of course, the type of economic history problems and periods embraced by scholars in Mexico depended largely on the sources available for their study at each point in time. The abundance of statistical material on some topics (like public finances) during the Spanish rule made it a more visited epoch than, say, the early nineteenth century, known for its proverbial lack of data. Strictly speaking, the statistical era started in Mexico only in the last decades of that century and, in some areas of the economy, only in 1938 when a national accounts system was formally established. For all periods and topics, new fields of study opened as unexplored sources of information became available, in Mexico or abroad. The study of regional banking, mining or industrial enterprises, and state and municipal finances developed as private and public regional archives became accessible to researchers. Scholars built innovative interpretive proposals thanks to the use of the Archivo de Indias in Seville that allowed tracing fiscal or commercial trends in the colonial period; explained foreign investment and entrepreneurial activities in the nineteenth century using private documentary resources in the USA or Great Britain; rebuilt trade series and reinterpreted the export era by taking advantage of the official publications kept at the US Library of Congress.

The last decades have witnessed contrasting phenomena. On the one hand, the confluence of many currents and approaches, the constant opening of new archival sources, and the increasing institutionalization of the discipline have facilitated research by old practitioners and attracted younger scholars to the field, both from history and economics. On the other, the emergence of new, competing areas of inquiry within history, and of alternative career options within economics, have dissuaded many students belonging to more recent generations from specializing in this field. Notwithstanding that, the discipline as such has consolidated, a fact that has its reflection in the establishment of formal graduate programs specializing in economic history, in the publication of long-term syntheses and textbooks, in the consolidation of an important journal (*América Latina en la Historia Económica*), and in the strengthening of an organization of practitioners (the Asociación Mexicana de Historia Económica, AMHE) which sponsors national and international events.

Precursors and traditionalists

In the prehispanic era, the area now covered by Mexico was occupied by an array of cultures, which together constituted the most populated conglomerate of America. Starting in 1521 this territory was progressively subjected to the Spanish crown forming the Viceroyalty of New Spain. Its rule was to last three centuries. After a ten-year war, in 1821 Mexico separated from Spain and started its life as an independent nation. What followed was a long and tortuous state-building process in which domestic turmoil and foreign threats left a durable mark in the loss of half of the territory to the United States (1848). In the last third of the nineteenth century, the defeat of the conservative parties and the progressive consolidation in power of a liberal-minded elite nurtured political stability – under an authoritarian rule – and created a legal framework favorable to investment and economic activity. Starting in the 1880s domestic and external conditions favoring globalization fostered a process of export-led growth, provided a stimulus for economic expansion and contributed to the onset of industrialization. An anti-authoritarian mobilization led to a change in power under a democratic leader in the early 1910s. However, the tensions and contradictions resulting from the dramatic social and economic transformations of the previous decades were hardly solved by this limited change and the elected president was overthrown by a military coup, triggering a revolutionary outbreak that was to last for most of the decade. Even though political and armed violence interfered with the dynamics of the domestic sector of the economy, export activities continued to some extent under the extraordinary stimulus provided by the First World War. The Mexican Revolution ended with the arrival in power of a new group of political leaders prone to nationalism and state-interventionism, eventually consolidating a new authoritarian rule that was to endure for the next seventy years.

As is the case everywhere, in Mexico the practice of economic history preceded its professionalization. It also preceded the separation of fields and the ensuing specialization that has created a clear-cut differentiation between political, social, and economic historians, even though that separation is not necessarily characteristic of some of the best fruits of the discipline. Not surprisingly, the first examples of historical analysis that dealt with economic issues appeared in the nineteenth century without explicit recognition of genre, as part of general histories or even as more specific assessments enriched by a historical perspective. This is the case with the famous Von Humboldt's *Political Essay on the Reign of New Spain* first published in 1803, of Mariano Otero's work on Mexico's situation, dated in 1847, or the collective enterprise of the three-volume *México and its Social Evolution*, an editorial hit in 1900.

However, the first conscious attempts at studying the past with particular focus on its economic features appeared in the 1930s. At that time one of the more celebrated early economic historians of Mexico (L. Chávez Orozco) dedicated himself to the publication of primary sources within a series titled *Documents for the economic history of Mexico*. Under the influence of historical materialism, he also carried out research in the field, bringing to light the first academic works on colonial institutions, workers and wages, artisans, and early industrialization. Silvio Zavala, a graduate from Law School, devoted his initial efforts to revealing the means – legal and material – whereby the conquerors managed to survive in the recently occupied territory of New Spain, and their implications in terms of economic organization (Zavala 1935). Later on, Zavala broadened the scope of his project to include other Spanish colonies, like Peru and Rio de la Plata, to undertake the endeavor of his life: collecting sources to write a history of work and working regimes in the colonial epoch.

Since those times, Mexico benefited from the interest of foreign scholars in its past. The early appeal of landownership regimes generated by the Mexican Revolution (as in the works of G. McBride and F. Tannenbaum in the 1920s), evolved to form a tradition on its own. Mexico's colonial institutions and economic organization also attracted early attention from abroad. In the late 1940s and early 1950s major studies published on Indian tribute (Miranda 1952), population in the sixteenth century, the seventeenth-century depression, and the formation of large estates, set the mainstream interpretations that dominated the field for many years. Works by S.F. Cook, L.B Simpson, and W. Borah assessed that as a result of war, economic and social distress, and new diseases, the population of central Mexico diminished by 90 percent within the first century of colonial rule. These studies had great impact on international historical demography. In turn, the French historian F. Chevalier stated that the land system established in colonial Mexico was an extension of European medieval agrarian structures (1952). The study of Mexico's legendary mineral richness also called the attention of foreign scholars, bringing to light publications that have become indispensable within the field, as exemplified by M. Bernstein's work on the mining industry between 1890 and 1940. Foreign "Mexicanists", as they are called, have enriched Mexico's economic history literature ever since.

The second generation of economic historians included among its practitioners some economists. As a result, since the 1950s economic history textbooks were written and the subject started to be taught in the formal training of the economics school at the National University. Research included topics like banking and financial history, foreign investment during the nineteenth century, international economic relations, and the history of economic thinking. A member of this group was later responsible for the first compendium approach to the economic history of Mexico, which in six volumes embraces (certainly in a fragmentary and rather rudimentary manner) the prehispanic period to the early decades of the twentieth century (López Rosado 1968).

This and the next generation of economic historians undertook empirical studies aimed at reconstructing pieces of a colorful and complex landscape. Many of them lacked a theoretical framework but found no sin in it; their purpose was, as one of them put it in response to a criticism that one of his books lacked "a discernible central thesis", that he intended to write "a monograph that sticks to facts and to reality" (Bazant 1976: 326). A significant part of the literature written on Mexico's economic history adopted this premise, aiming, in the purest positivistic tradition, at reconstructing the past. For a country with a long history and abundant and largely unexplored archival material this was not a shallow task. Furthermore, the absence of a theory did not necessarily mean lack of interpretation or even of an ideological stance. These authors lived amid the climax of Mexico's economic nationalism; it is no surprise that their concerns and reading of history were to some extent influenced by this reality. Just to provide an example, Chávez Orozco's portrayal of the past included a critique of liberalism (which in his view had been the cause of the Mexican Revolution) and a vindication of the role of the state in the promotion of economic activities, apparent in his emphasis on the early efforts at industrialization (Chávez Orozco 1938).

This was the way in which economic history was traditionally done in Mexico, a way that did not necessarily disappear with the arrival of new methodologies and analytical approaches.

Under the influence . . .

The period from the 1960s to the 1980s witnessed the arrival of new influences on Mexico's economic history, coming from Europe, Latin America, and the United States. It is very telling that this happened before the actual opening of the economy that started in the 1980s as part of the new wave of globalization. The phenomenon may be explained by several factors. Preceded by a few intense years of labor mobilization, the 1960s marked the beginning of the long demise of authoritarian rule in Mexico, signaled by the repression of the students' movement in 1968 and reaching a climax in the broadly challenged electoral process in 1988. Even though power-sharing was only to begin with the 2000 presidential election, the emergence of an opposition and active political participation created an environment favorable to the absorption of new and contesting theories. Ironically, the authoritarian regime had given a warm welcome to immigrants from all of the Latin American countries that were suffering from state coups and dictatorships. Mexican academic institutions embraced some of the more lucid minds from Central and South America, enriching the ongoing debates in the social sciences and broadening their scope to the entire region. It is likely that this circumstance had placed Mexico – despite its geographic situation neighboring the main economic power of the world, the USA – closer to the intellectual mood that prevailed within the Latin American region. Starting in the 1970s, the progressive deterioration and eventual exhaustion of import-substitution industrialization (ISI) and inward-looking development, which expressed itself in successive crises and spasmodic growth, fostered the search for answers to questions related to economic backwardness and development. All these factors stimulated the first boom in Mexico's economic history, which included a plethora of publications, ideas, and debates. Let us provide a more detailed picture of this fruitful age.

From the 1960s the appeal of development economics and structuralism from the Economic Commission for Latin America (ECLA) found a fertile ground amid the so-called revolutionary nationalism that dominated Mexico's politics. However, its influence was initially felt more among economists and policy makers than among economic historians. Their studies on economic development, public policies, and industrialization, even if adopting a historical perspective, had a distinct focus upon current situations. Authors like R. Vernon and R. Hansen, probably influenced by J.M. Keynes, were attracted by the active role of the state in Mexico's affairs and wondered whether this distinctive feature stemmed from history or from the recent legacy of the revolution. They concluded that it has been a constant in the evolution of the country, though they disagreed about the implications that this feature could have in terms of income distribution and future development.

For the most part, economic history continued to be practiced by historians and other social scientists, including economists who adopted Marxism as the key to understanding the world. The rather vague attraction felt by some Mexican scholars to Marxist-like approaches and language, which had been present since the 1930s in loose combination with the prevailing nationalist discourse, became more articulated in the 1960s, leading to the publication of a number of books that adopted a Marxist perspective and covered Mexico's economic history in the long run. Some embraced the long period from the prehispanic era to the twentieth century in an effort to make it fit in the historical scheme of the modes of production. In the more common view, it was suggested that the transit from (a particular form of) feudalism to capitalism began in the late eighteenth century, during the last decades of the colonial period, but was completed only in the twentieth century. The peasant struggles that made the core of the Mexican Revolution were an expression of the hindrances posed to this transit by feudal structures. Combining a Marxist approach with the nationalism in vogue, some of these accounts considered that the main obstacle was the "semifeudal and semicolonial regime" led by a liberal and outward-oriented elite, which impeded the development of a national bourgeoisie capable of consolidating a capitalist economy (López Gallo 1965: 345). Other authors, with a more pragmatic view, simply resorted to recent events (the Mexican Revolution in the 1910s, the agrarian reform and expropriation of foreign assets in the 1930s) to stress their potential for a deeper socio-economic transformation leading to socialism (A.F.

Shulgovskii). A debate ensued about the right way to characterize Mexico's modes of production, when capitalism really started, and whether a Marxist approach to Mexico's prehispanic and colonial period was pertinent at all. Of course, within this debate every stance had ideological and political implications, related to the kind of transformation that was to be pursued. The more sophisticated among Marxist economic historians drew from European contemporary scholars, like W. Kula and P. Vilar, to portray a nuanced picture of Mexico's long transition to capitalism (Semo 1973). Interestingly enough, beyond the construction of Marxian interpretations of Mexico's history, the influence of Marxism was even more pervasive in the use of language. Productive forces, infrastructure/superstructure, and class struggle became common jargon within the discipline.

As in the rest of Latin America, another influence felt in Mexico's economic historiography came from the *Annales* School, here introduced by Enrique Florescano in the late 1960s. His investigation of corn prices and agricultural crises between 1708 and 1810 was the first study in which quantitative information was systematically used to analyze economic phenomena from a *longue durée* perspective. In this particular case, changes in the price of the most important staple were found to be indicative of external shocks, like famines, loss of harvests, or social unrest. Serial, quantitative history was presented optimistically as the key to building a new, rigorous interpretation of Mexico's economic past (Florescano 1969: 36). Florescano's contribution to Mexico's economic historiography included the publication of massive volumes of sources and bibliography (as in Florescano and Gil 1973) and the promotion of numerous studies in economic and socio-demographic history, including those aiming at rebuilding trends in prices, population, and mining. However, there were limitations to a quantitative approach to Mexico's distant past. One of them was the scarcity of reliable statistical information for the period previous to the late nineteenth century, with some exceptions related to the late colonial era in areas like silver production and coinage or public finance. This may explain in part why further research under *Annales* influence had a more qualitative orientation, with emphasis on the history of agriculture and agrarian structures, frequently with a regional scope.

The first in-depth reconstructions of the economic history of particular periods also appeared in these years. This was the case with the volumes dedicated to the study of economic activities within the first massive work that covered Mexico's liberal era (Cosío Villegas 1955–72). Their authors (F. Calderón, F. Rosenzweig, and others) held no general theory, but provided a detached description of affairs (an "objective history", as R. Potash called it (1961: 395)), based upon extensive research in archival materials. By doing this, they took a healthy distance from the nationalist-oriented and official depictions that condemned nineteenth-century economic liberalism aimed at legitimizing the existing political order. At the same time, abundant monographs continued to be written within the well-established canons of Mexico's historical tradition. Topics included the economic life of prehispanic societies (Carrasco and Broda 1978), land and labor regimes (González Navarro 1970), and public finances. Using the scant quantitative information available from Mexican official sources, Inés Herrera provided the first approach to the study of Mexico's foreign trade in the decades after independence (1977).

An important field of inquiry – for nationals and foreigners alike – has been rural history, which is understandable for a country in which, up until the mid-twentieth century, two thirds of the population lived in the countryside. Studies in this area included, at first, the large estate or *hacienda* and, later on, the traditional peasant community as well. Scholars have tried to clarify their origins and features in terms of their organization, the relationship to and use of resources, and the rather conflictual interaction among them. With respect to the *hacienda*, the stereotype of a nearly feudal institution created by Chevalier (1952) was progressively modified as empirical case studies showed that there was a huge variation among them as to their size, specialization, technology, labor arrangements, and relationship with the market economy (J. Bazant, E. Semo). They were also found to have great malleability according to the circumstances (D. Brading, E. Van Young). Labor arrangements, previously seen as mainly exploitative and based on coercion (Katz 1976), were now perceived as very variable depending on time and place but frequently holding a "moral economy" component that had been overlooked by previous research (Nickel 1988).

Only starting in the 1970s did the once inaccurately called "Indian" community receive serious attention (D. Fraser, J. Meyer). Much of the inquiries were dedicated to the long and conflictual process of its dissolution and transformation as a consequence of both liberal attempts to create private property rights and the eroding forces of the market. At the same time, the study of rural structures grew in complexity by including the management of public lands by the liberal governments after the 1860s. The dominant view was that small landowners and peasant communities were deprived of their properties to benefit large companies and a small oligarchy, fostering land concentration on a formerly unknown scale (M. Mejía; M. Bellingeri and I. Gil).

Already in the 1980s researchers focused their attention on agriculture, taking as their initial goal the early colonial period (as in T. Rojas and W. Sanders). They addressed the way in which prehispanic crops were affected by the conquest and how the introduction of products, tools, and methods of cultivation by the new settlers transformed the rural landscape. Studies of agriculture soon broadened to include stockbreeding, an activity that gained in importance as the vast northern territories were progressively settled. Research privileged qualitative approaches and local or regional studies (R. Serrera, C. Esparza), a preference conditioned by the lack of statistical data on a sector that up until the late nineteenth century operated to a large extent outside the market sphere. This feature has also rendered its overall characteristics and trends in the long term difficult to grasp. Agricultural modernization starting in the 1940s also attracted the attention of researchers, who undertook the first studies on what would be known as the "green revolution" (C. Hewitt).

As in the past, research undertaken by foreign scholars – particularly from the USA, but also from Great Britain and Spain – contributed to enlarging understanding of some periods and areas of economic activity in Mexico. They addressed questions like the promotion and development of the textile industry (R. Potash, D. Keremitsis), public finances (B. Tenenbaum), railroads (J. Chapman, D. Pletcher), mining (D. Brading, R. Randall), the disentailment of Church and indigenous properties (M. Costeloe, D. Fraser, T.G. Powell), among many others. Some of them contributed to undermining dominant views on important issues. Just to mention one example, for many years the prevailing interpretation about the economic impact of the Mexican Revolution considered it to be devastating, to the extent that the decade that followed was officially titled the "Reconstruction" (A. Córdova, J.F. Leal). In this view, the civil war wiped out the former order and the pattern of development that it entailed, dominated by foreign interests and a diehard oligarchy. As a result, a new regime had emerged with the clear purpose of fostering national development under the lead of a strong state and a national – and nationalist – bourgeoisie. In 1978 John Womack published an article that challenged all these common assumptions about this crucial phase of Mexico's history (Womack 1978). Besides questioning the historical meaning of the revolution in general, he asked specifically about its significance in terms of the pattern of growth that Mexico had embraced since the 1880s and about the impact that the war itself might have had upon economic activities. Others nurtured this revisionist line by providing evidence that the revolution had a widely different impact between regions (Benjamin 1990; Joseph 1992).

These contributions were new in terms of Mexico's historiography but not necessarily with respect to the analytical approach employed. Influence from the new waves of US scholarship arrived in Mexico first in the form of growth economics and the interest in constructing national accounts *à la* Kuznets. In 1970 C. Reynolds inaugurated this line of inquiry gathering and analyzing macroeconomic indicators on the Mexican economy between 1910 and the late 1960s (Reynolds 1970). Mexican economists followed his lead, sometimes extending their interest to longer periods (Beltrán 1960; Solis 1970). A peculiar feature of Mexico's GDP accounts deserves mention. Up until the 1950s, the output of metallurgy was incorporated into that of the mining sector instead of the industrial (manufacturing) sector, thus underestimating the share of industry in GDP – and the significance of the industrialization process that took place before 1929 amid export-led growth (Kuntz Ficker 2010b: 144–5).

In the meantime, the impact of structuralism and dependency theory broadened to reach economic historians. It first arrived in the form of general texts on Latin American economic history that included Mexico. The key element within this tradition lay in the importance given to the external dimension in explaining the long-term process of economic development. The first historical studies within this current considered that the region's dependency and underdevelopment originated in the colonial period and was inherited in the independent era (O. Sunkel and P. Paz). However, they generally agreed that the current nature of Latin American underdevelopment consolidated during the late nineteenth century, when the transition to a modern, capitalist economy in Latin America coincided with its subordinate integration to the world division of labor as a provider of primary products (F.E. Cardoso and E. Faletto).

This time structuralism arrived in an environment that was exposed to many other influences, contributing to the generation of a handful of interesting debates. One of the more meaningful has taken place between those who sustain the thesis that Mexico's economic organization may be accounted for with the analytical tools already available for Europe and those who think that it has an originality stemming from its colonial status that requires a set of conceptual instruments of its own. The former line of thinking started with F. Chevalier and had subscribers among disciples of the *Annales* School as well as among orthodox Marxists. The latter developed with a variety of shades, from those that took inspiration in world-system (or core/periphery) approaches (as in I. Wallerstein), to those more closely associated with the emergence of Latin American schools of thought, be it within the structuralist/dependentist streams or in regional adaptations of Marxism.

Within core/periphery approaches, the most important aspect of the colonial situation was the external connection with Spain. By extracting precious metals from its colonies, the Spanish metropolis deprived the local economies of resources that were vital to start a process of capital accumulation. Thus the "colonial status" distorted their long-term possibilities for development. In turn, the "Europeists" within the *Annales* tradition focused on the internal dimension, and finding no need to create new concepts, they chose to define colonial Mexico (or Latin America in general) as an *ancien régime* economy (R. Romano, J.F. Guerra). An alternative to both of these interpretations was offered by S. Assadourian (1982), who proposed a new concept, the "system of the colonial economy", to explain the peculiarities of this situation. Even though everybody shared the idea that a large portion of colonial precious metals production went to the Spanish crown, Assadourian criticized core–periphery approaches by rejecting the primacy of the external dimension. He argued that even under conditions of a formal subjection to a foreign power, the dynamics of the domestic economies held a rationale of their own. In the case of colonial Mexico (and other parts of the Spanish empire), the production of a merchandise that had an immediate use as money exerted a direct impact upon local economic conditions by fostering economic activities and creating multiplier effects in the domestic sector, thus creating an incipient internal market. R. Romano (1984) disagreed with this interpretation on different grounds than those of core–periphery schemes. He stated that the colonial areas were characterized by the primacy of agriculture and a natural economy, one in which most of the population lived in a condition of self-sufficiency and resorted only marginally to the market. The proof of this was, in his view, the fact that almost all of the precious metals extracted from the mines were coined in high denomination currency, while smaller, fractional coins were practically nonexistent. The result was twofold: first, a very slow growth of the monetary sector of the economy; second, an early concentration of wealth in the hands of a small economic elite.

This intellectual melting pot of foreign and indigenous scholars also gave rise to original variants in which structuralism, dependency theory, Marxism, and New Economic History converged (or confronted with each other) to explain Mexico's underdevelopment. In the late 1970s the American scholar John Coatsworth (1990) introduced to the ongoing debate the thesis that its origins should be dated in the century previous to 1870. Economic decay would have started in the last decades of colonial rule, exacerbated by the independence wars (1810–21) and continued for half a century in what came to be called the *long* nineteenth-century depression. By saying this, he was challenging mainstream interpretations on the late colonial stage that thought it to be a thriving period (F. Rosenzweig), dependentist views that considered Latin American underdevelopment as intrinsically linked to the export era (1870–1929) (F.E. Cardoso and E. Faletto), as well as local variants with a Marxist touch that dated its origins in the class struggles that took place between 1854 and 1880 (Cardoso 1983). Research by other scholars (E. Van Young, C. Morin, R. Salvucci) on specific areas of the colonial economy supported Coatsworth's interpretation. It was also consistent with the state of political distress characteristic of the early independent period, in which centrifugal forces dominated the domestic scene while external powers threatened the integrity of the country.

Coatsworth's contribution to Mexico's economic historiography went further. He adopted New Institutional Economics – Douglass North's style – as a key to explaining the institutional constraints on Mexico's economic development resulting from the colonial setting. These came in the form of limitations to investment, occupation, and even geographic mobility under socio-ethnic criteria, as well as a system of regulations and monopolies that rendered inefficient the organization of the economy as a whole. Finally, Coatsworth is to be credited for the arrival of cliometrics in Mexico's economic history, with the publication, in the early 1980s, of his book on the economic impact of railroads in nineteenth-century Mexico. A disciple of R. Fogel, he applied the methodology created by his teacher to estimate the social savings generated by railroads between 1880 and 1910. In his assessment social savings were large, but were mostly concentrated in the export sector and thus, paradoxically, had a negative impact on the Mexican economy, by fostering dependency and underdevelopment.

The arrival of New Economic History (NEH) in its different kinds represented a breakpoint in Mexico's economic historiography not because of the scope of its impact upon domestic research but because, in an ambiance already nurtured by many currents and stances, it showed further possibilities to explore. In fact, Mexican scholars took rather long to adopt the theoretical and analytical framework of NEH, and even when that happened, they were a minority among those working within the field. In any event, New Institutional Theory had a larger impact on domestic scholarship than econometric approaches.

American scholars undertook research on Mexico without necessarily adopting a NEH approach. In 1981, Herbert Klein and John TePaske published a provocative article that questioned W. Borah's long-maintained thesis about the seventeenth-century depression in New Spain. They used original sources from Mexico and Spain to prove that fiscal incomes remained steady instead of declining throughout that century. They accepted a number of caveats that could nullify their point, like the use of nominal instead of real values, the assumption that fiscal incomes reflected economic performance, etc., starting a long-lasting debate on the subject. They also made an important contribution to the history of public finances of all of the Spanish empire in America (Klein and TePaske 1982). Moreover, the use of up to then unexplored archival sources fostered attempts at reconstructing GDP and other macroeconomic variables (R. Salvucci, R. Garner), and opened the door for a new branch of research and debate on the long-term economic performance of Mexico, from the colonial period to the late nineteenth century, that was to fill many pages of economic historiography.

Pluralism and revisionism

The last three decades have been characterized by profound changes in Mexico, both in the economic and political realms. The 1982 debt crisis, itself a reflection that the inward-looking pattern of growth was exhausted and that the excessive dependence on oil income was unsustainable, led to a harsh recovery followed by the transition to a new stage of liberalization and integration into the world economy. After only a few years of moderate economic expansion a new crisis hit the Mexican economy in 1994. Since then, the priorities of macroeconomic stability and price and deficit control have allowed only slow growth with a high social cost in terms of social spending and employment. On the other hand, increasing participation in the global economy probably contributed to accelerate political changes, leading to the end of the "one party era" in 2000. An imperfect democracy has been further challenged by social discontent and by the so-called "war against organized crime", which has had a widespread effect upon society. Structural reforms in areas like labor, taxes and public finances, energy, telecommunications, and others, which had been resisted by political parties for more than a decade, were introduced in 2014, generating high expectations that they will trigger investment and growth.

These changes were relevant to the development of the discipline. In the late 1980s a fistful of innovative works announced the boom in economic history research that was to follow. By the 1990s the discipline had taken roots in Mexico and could be considered a consolidated academic enterprise. It had a relatively large number of practitioners, most of them in history departments, particularly in Mexico City and a handful of states throughout the country. All the influences of past decades had created an environment that fostered heterodox stances and nuanced debates about issues related to the past, at times with implications for the present and future. Two features characterize the more recent period: on the one hand, a pluralism of approaches, topics, and sub-specialties; on the other, a wave of revisionism with respect to the interpretations that were developed in the previous decades and represented the dominant views in the field. The state of maturity of the discipline evidenced itself in the appearance of a specialized review in 1994, *America Latina en la Historia Económica* (which in 2004 changed its subtitle from *Sources' Bulletin* to *Research Review*), and the formation of the Mexican Economic History Association in 1998.

After early efforts by C. Reynolds, L. Solis, and others, Enrique Cárdenas (1987) opened an important line of research concerning Mexico's industrialization during and after the 1929 economic depression and the ensuing era of inward-looking growth. He provided substantial evidence that Mexico began to industrialize long before the post-Second World War era, when most economists usually dated the beginning of ISI. In the same years he edited a series of five volumes compiling readings on a variety of economic history themes (Cárdenas 1989–94). Scholars also paid attention to the history of particular products and economic activities: commodities like sugar (Crespo 1988) and cotton (Plana 1984), and modern fuels like oil (Meyer 1988) were the subject of research, as was the study of regions, in the colonial period (Van Young 1989) as much as in the nineteenth century (Sariego 1988). Following a long tradition, many scholars of younger generations continued the study of mining (I. Herrera, J.M. Romero Gil, E. Flores Clair) and monetary history (P. Pérez Herrero).

Within the current of so-called regional history, since the mid-1980s a particularly dynamic group was formed in Northern Mexico, under the leadership of Mario Cerutti, himself a prolific economic and business historian who revealed the virtuous dynamics generated at a macro-regional level by an intertwined entrepreneurial elite since the mid-nineteenth century (Cerutti 1992). Initially focused on the economic history of single Mexican states, their interests soon included entrepreneurial history and the study of economic sectors, like mining, agriculture, and industry, from a local/regional point of view (A. Carrillo, G. Aguilar, J.J. Gracida). Even though some of these studies continue to be rather descriptive, those that use theory draw from European rather than American scholarship and use concepts such as business fertility, business clusters, and agro-industrial cities to characterize the process by which the so-called "big eastern north" evolved from an infertile and scarcely populated area to the modern, fast-growing region that it is today. Also, from their initial focus on the nineteenth century, they have been able to adapt their research agendas in order to trace the evolution of some regions, products, lines of specialization, or business enterprises from their origins up until the present times (A. Almaraz, E. Rivas).

While some works on entrepreneurs or entrepreneurial families were published since the 1970s, business history only started to be a recognizable branch of economic history in Mexico from the late 1980s. Studies in this field showed the prevalence of family-owned enterprises with some common features, like their frequent links to political power or their inclination to diversify in order to reduce risk, but with large regional variants. Research in this field has also included the study of big business, such as railroads and banks, and of foreign corporations, especially in the mining–metallurgical sector (Gómez Serrano 1982). Special attention has been paid to Monterrey, the first pole of modern entrepreneurial activity, and other industrial cities such as Puebla and Orizaba (M. Cerutti, L. Gamboa). The history of entrepreneurs and industry has also been enriched by the contribution of foreign scholars (D. Walker, W. Bernecker, R. Liehr). As is to be expected, research on business and industrial activities has at times been accompanied by the socio-economic study of workers. The combination of business and labor history has somehow been made a field of inquiry of its own, in the search for a more balanced and comprehensive assessment of entrepreneurial activities in the transition to a modern economy (N. Cárdenas, C. Gutiérrez, A. Gómez).

Banking and financial history has benefited from work by another important research group, this one led by Carlos Marichal. In the late 1980s he published, in association with L. Ludlow, a number of works that started a line of study on Mexico's credit and banking institutions, with the aim of explaining their late birth and peculiarities in comparison to other Latin American countries (Ludlow and Marichal 1986). Simultaneously he undertook the study of Latin American foreign debt and debt crises (Marichal 1989) – a topic that he has recently revisited and broadened towards a global perspective (2010). Then he focused on the public finances of New Spain and their relationship to the Spanish treasury, providing a seminal contribution to our understanding of the dynamics and consequences of the colonial link at its later stage. In his award-winning book (Marichal 2007) he shows how dependent the Spanish treasury became on the reign of New Spain and to what extent the growing financial needs of the former were satisfied by its wealthiest colony. In order to do this, the reign had to bear a growing fiscal burden and resort to public indebtedness. Following his lead, many scholars have contributed to reveal important aspects of the structure and functioning of public – national and state – finances from the eighteenth to the twentieth centuries in Mexico (L. Jáuregui, J.A. Serrano, L. Aboites) and Latin America (Jáuregui 2006), of banking and monetary issues (L. Anaya, J.A. Batiz), and of public debt. Of special importance has been research on credit – or the lack of it – and the role of financing in development, which has been studied from its colonial origins (G. Del Valle) to its recent features (G. Del Angel, S. Haber), going through its troublesome evolution during the nineteenth century (P. Riguzzi, N. Maurer).

The study of rural structures has made considerable progress in recent decades. The traditional explanation that disentailment and the survey of public lands led to the dispossession of collective owners and the concentration of property in the hands of a small oligarchy unused to progress has changed. Even though the perception of a phenomenon of land concentration in the liberal period remains, fresher approaches confirm a variety of experiences and results that resist generalization. For a start, land was not the only resource undergoing dramatic changes of ownership and use, but also water, forests, and pastures (M. Sánchez, L. Aboites). There was a differentiated reaction to change on the part of landowners and farmers; some continued old practices of absenteeism and under-exploitation of resources, while others modernized, introducing new products and means of production, and a stronger relation with the market (A. Tortolero). Survey companies did not often target peasant communities, and public officers did not necessarily support their actions when that was the case (R. Holden). As for collective lands, changing property rights included experiences in which communities lost possession of their terrains, others in which they kept them, and some in which they transformed them into various modalities of individual or collective private ownership (E. Kouri, D. Marino). The renewed interest in the subject has created nuanced pictures about change in the countryside (Escobar and Butler 2013) and has weakened the widespread view of the agrarian question as the main cause and motive of the Mexican Revolution (R. Falcón).

Research topics multiplied since the 1990s. The relationship between the private and the public spheres (Carmagnani 1994; Collado 1995; Grunstein 2012), the economic dimension of public debates (Luna 2006), as well as the role of institutions (Beatty 2001; Riguzzi 2009) and public agencies in the promotion of development (Zuleta 2006) were the subject of inventive approaches. Several aspects of the external sector were addressed, such as foreign trade (S. Kuntz Ficker, I. Avella) and foreign economic relations (Riguzzi 2003), foreign finances (T. Passananti), commodity chains (C. Marichal), and the role of foreign entrepreneurs (P. Garner), frequently challenging previous interpretations. Economic thought (Romero Sotelo 2012), and economic biography (L. Ludlow, L.M. Uhthoff) also found a place in this broad mosaic of research endeavors. In the late 1990s several authors and institutions collaborated to publish, in nine volumes, a collection of papers on important themes of Mexico's economic history (money, banking, public debt, public finances, colonial credit, mining, railroads and public works, the textile industry, and the internal market) (Marichal and Ludlow 1998–99). This impulse continued in the 2000s. Old topics were studied in a new light, as was the case with regional markets (A. Ibarra, J. Silva), commodities (Aboites 2013), urban economies and demography (Miño 2006), at the same time that new topics were embraced by scholars, like environmental history (Boyer 2012) or anthropometric analysis

(López Alonso 2012). The combined study of economic and labor history (Gómez 2013) has yielded fruitful results, such as the construction of a price index and real wages in the long run (A. Gómez and A. Challú). After years of accumulation, in 2010 the first collective work, by economic historians and economists, aimed at synthesizing Mexico's economic history from the colonial period to the present was published (Kuntz Ficker 2010a).

The story of the Mexican economy in the twentieth century has been the subject of careful investigation by economists more than historians. Of particular relevance are the contributions made by Enrique Cárdenas to Mexico's macroeconomic history after 1929, and his in-depth studies of the nationalization of Mexican banks in the 1980s and their re-privatization in the 1990s (2010). In his works he reveals the hidden motives, the questionable methods and procedures, and the drastic consequences that those measures had upon confidence, the business environment, and the performance of the Mexican economy as a whole.

Scholars from the USA and other nationalities have continued to make significant contributions to these advances. In a series of works, Stephen Haber and other scholars under his lead have challenged some of the conventional interpretations about Mexico's economic history within the past hundred and fifty years. He studied the early outburst of industrialization in the 1890s and stressed the fact that it took place amid an export-led pattern of growth, something unthinkable within the typical reasoning of dependency theory. With N. Maurer and A. Razo (2003) he also outlined a model that explained the underlying continuity not only in the pattern of development but also in the institutional and political arrangements between 1880 and 1929 despite the partial rupture represented by the Mexican Revolution. Although including broader concerns, his interest on Mexico led him to coordinate several volumes on financial markets, industrial development, institutions and economic growth in the nineteenth and twentieth centuries (as in Haber and Bortz 2002). More recently, another American scholar published a well-researched book on Mexico's finances after independence (Salvucci 2009).

The last decades have witnessed revisionist voices in many areas in which one particular interpretation had dominated the scene. Let me provide some interesting examples. As we have seen, the once common view that the late colonial period had been a prosperous era was questioned in the late 1970s on several counts, giving way to a more pessimistic picture. According to this, some signs of decay appeared already in the late eighteenth century and only worsened as a result of the independence war and its aftermath, characterized by capital flight and the destruction of productive assets. The animosity generated by Spanish centralist rule and the lack of a unifying group and ideology among the Mexican nationals gave birth to a so-called Federal Pact, which granted extremely large powers – including in the fiscal realm – to the provincial governments at the expense of the national state. Factionalism thrived, provoking continuous changes in power and a state of despotic banditry – as S. Haber has called it. The political and fiscal fragmentation of the country was aggravated by its material fragmentation, as existing roads were deprived of maintenance and no new means of transportation were provided. The early default on two foreign loans left the country without resort to external sources of financing, and legal restrictions limited immigration and foreign investment. In the absence of formal credit institutions, the government relied on private lenders in order to survive, at the price of high interest rates and discretional privileges, further distorting economic activity.

Analysis of the economic dimension of this period faces the difficulty of scarce and fragmentary information. Some scholars (Coatsworth 1990; Cárdenas 2003), drawing on the scant indicators available and on economic reasoning, proposed since the 1980s that the fifty-year period after independence was one in which economic depression was followed by recession and intervals of slow recovery or stagnation. In the past fifteen years this thesis of the 'long nineteenth-century depression' has been challenged by a younger generation of scholars (e.g. Sánchez Santiró 2010). They rely on fragmentary data on population, sales of lands, agricultural production, and coinage, and alternative GDP estimates from contemporaries to change that view in two respects. First, they argue that within the period there may have been bad years, but there were also some years of economic recovery, even if they were eventually upset by a new depression. This pattern created the false impression that it was all recession or stagnation between the 1820s and the 1870s, and that it was only in the last third of the century that the economy experienced a real spurt. Second, they consider that as long as the Mexican economy was extremely fragmented and regionalized, it is likely that there were zones where the economic situation was better and improving even if this was not the case everywhere.

One aspect of this debate has not been put forward in an explicit manner, namely, the place and pertinence of economic reasoning. That is to say, to what extent is it sensible – from an economic logic – to talk of a good economic performance that does not leave traces in macroeconomic indicators, does not lead to the building of infrastructure, to the creation of credit institutions, or to the improvement of public finances? Another aspect has to do with the lack of information – something that might be considered in itself an indication of the extant situation. In sum, this dispute will probably not be reconciled until its theoretical terms are explicitly settled and more conclusive evidence is gathered at several levels (local, regional, national) and in diverse areas of research (economic sectors, public finances, international trade).

Revisionist interpretations of the liberal period and the Mexican Revolution continue to evolve, stressing the lines of continuity that suggest that both were part of the export era (1880–1929), and as such shared important traits. The somewhat simplifying and overall negative picture, provided by structuralism and dependency theory, of the export era as one in which foreign enclaves dominated the scene distorting economic structures and hindering the growth of industry and of an internal market, has been challenged on several counts. On the one hand, railroads, up until recently considered to be an instrument for the subordinated incorporation to the world economy, were proved to have a crucial role in the integration of the domestic market (S. Kuntz Ficker, P. Riguzzi). On the other, the export sector was shown to hold features (like productive and regional diversification, a meaningful participation of domestic entrepreneurs, increasing value added, and a relatively high return value) that had positive implications for the Mexican economy. In fact, its expansion provided the first surge of sustained economic growth since independence, which was to last for more than thirty years (Kuntz Ficker 2007). All in all, the shift in the perception of the liberal era has led to the idea that, against the conventional view, Mexico's industrialization actually took place as an endogenous process amid export-led growth (S. Haber, R. Salvucci). As for the impact of the Mexican Revolution, new approaches suggest that the nationalist rhetoric of the revolutionary regime was not accompanied by a change in the growth-model: far from it, various circumstances made the Mexican economy more outward-oriented and attached to the United States immediately after the civil war (Knight 2003). As part of this interpretive renewal a new consensus was established, placing the beginning of industrialization in the 1890s and drawing a subtle line of continuity between two eras that had been considered almost divorced conceptually: export-led growth and import-substitution industrialization (S. Haber, E. Cárdenas).

Comparative history has not been foreign to Mexico's economic historians. More recently this approach has yielded interesting results in terms of fruitful comparisons between Mexico and Spain (R. Dobado, A. Gómez, and G. Márquez), or Mexico and other Latin American countries. Comparisons have dealt with issues like factors of growth and backwardness (K. Sokoloff and S. Engerman; Acemoglu, Johnson, and Robinson) Spanish policies during the colonial period (A. Irigoin and R. Grafe), the economic consequences of independence (L. Prados de la Escosura, J. Coatsworth), and a fistful of other relevant topics. Global history approaches have also started to flourish, as exemplified by a recent work discussing the role and position of the Spanish colonies in the early world economy (Hausberger and Ibarra 2015).

Conclusion

If we consider the explicit attempts at studying the economic dimension of Mexico's history as the beginning of economic history as a discipline, then we shall conclude that it has enjoyed an existence of about 85 years. In contrast with other countries' experience, Mexico's economic history has benefited from a long and complex past, a deep historiographical tradition, and a variety of influences, all of which have insulated it against long-lasting dogmatism and theoretical reductionism. One of the more interesting developments of recent times is the increasing participation of its practitioners in international debates around subjects that are in essence transnational. This openness has contributed to enhance the quality of research and to create awareness about new approaches and interpretations, without necessarily depriving empirical studies of their originality.

Despite the growing professionalization of economic historians and the continuing appeal that the study of Mexico has among foreign scholars, it would be misleading to assert that the discipline is heading towards more cliometric approaches, or even towards the dominance of a neoclassical view. What the recent literature shows is a broader consciousness of the importance of a variety of analytical tools and conceptual frameworks in order to better understand the processes under study. This has benefited research in the field by making it more analytical and insightful. However, for good or bad, these conceptual tools are often taken from a variety of sources and do not necessarily compose a coherent theoretical body. Reminiscences from Marxism are to be found hand in hand with structuralism and new institutional theory; statistical analysis is often used without recourse to economic theory, and empirical studies with an ad hoc conceptual basis maintain an important presence within the field. Many scholars now possess a significant background in economics and make use of theory and even of sophisticated econometric techniques, but generally not such as to sweep away more qualitative approaches that provide contesting interpretations, or neglect evidence that may escape a purely economic rationale. In this sense, most scholars within the field have managed to live up to the principle that the classics established: a fine historical sense.

Note

1 I would like to thank Carlos Marichal and Paolo Riguzzi for their insightful comments on an earlier version of this text. Its content remains entirely my responsibility, of course.

References

Aboites, Luis (2013) *El norte entre algodones: población, trabajo agrícola y optimismo en México, 1930–1970*, México: El Colegio de México (ECM).

Assadourian, Carlos S. (1982) *El sistema de la economía colonial: mercado interno, regiones y espacio económico*, Lima: Instituto de Estudios Peruanos.

Bazant, Jan (1976) "A propósito de hacendados, niños y peones. Respuesta a una reseña de *Cinco haciendas mexicanas*", *Historia Mexicana*, 26 (2): 325–7.

Beatty, Edward (2001) *Institutions and Investment. The Political Basis of Industrialization in Mexico before 1911*, Stanford, CA: Stanford University Press.

Beltrán, Enrique et al. (1960) *México, cincuenta años de revolución*. Tomo I, *La economía*, México: FCE.

Benjamin, Thomas Louis (1990) *El camino a Leviatán. Chiapas y el Estado mexicano, 1891–1947*, México: Conaculta.

Boyer, Christopher R. (2012) *A Land between Waters: Environmental Histories of Modern Mexico*, Tucson: University of Arizona Press.

Cárdenas, Enrique (1987) *La industrialización mexicana durante la Gran Depresión*, México: ECM.

Cárdenas, Enrique (ed.) (1989–94) *Lecturas. Historia económica de México*, México: FCE.

Cárdenas, Enrique (2003) *Cuándo se originó el atraso económico de México. La economía mexicana en el largo siglo XIX, 1780–1920*, Madrid: Biblioteca Nueva.

Cárdenas, Enrique (2010) "La economía mexicana en el dilatado siglo XX", en Kuntz Ficker (ed.) (2010): 503–48.

Cardoso, Ciro (ed.) (1983) *México en el siglo XIX (1821–1910). Historia económica y de la estructura social*, México: Era.

Carmagnani, Marcello (1994) *Estado y mercado. La economía pública del liberalismo mexicano, 1850–1911*, México: FCE.

Carrasco, Pedro and Johanna Broda (eds.) (1978) *Economía política e ideología en el México prehispánico*, México: Nueva Imagen – INAH.

Cerutti, Mario (1992) *Burguesía, capitales e industria en el Norte de México: Monterrey y su ámbito regional*, México: UANL.

Chávez Orozco, Luis (1938) *Historia económica y social de México. Ensayo de interpretación*, México: Ed. Botas.

Chevalier, Francois (1952) *La formation des grands domaines au Mexique. Terre et société aux XVIe–XVIIe siècles*, Paris: Institut d'Ethnologie.

Escobar, Antonio and Matthew Butler (eds.) (2013) *México y sus transiciones: reconsideraciones sobre la historia agraria mexicana, siglos XIX y XX*, México: CIESAS.

Coatsworth, John (1990) *Los orígenes del atraso. Nueve ensayos de historia económica de México en los siglos XVIII y XIX*, México: Alianza Editorial Mexicana.

Collado, María del Carmen (1995) *Los empresarios mexicanos durante el gobierno del general Alvaro Obregón, 1920–1924*, México: Universidad Iberoamericana.

Cosío Villegas, Daniel (ed.) (1955–72) *Historia moderna de México*, México: Hermes.

Crespo, Horacio et al. (1988) *Historia del azúcar en México*, México: FCE.

Florescano, Enrique (1969) *Precios del maíz y crisis agrícolas en México, 1708–1810*, México: ECM.

Florescano, Enrique and Isabel Gil (eds.) (1973) *Fuentes para la historia económica de México*, 3 vols., México: INAH.

Gómez, Aurora (2013) *Industry and Revolution: Social and Economic Change in the Orizaba Valley, México*, Cambridge, MA: Harvard University Press.

González Navarro, Moisés (1970) *Raza y tierra: la guerra de castas y el henequén*, México: ECM.

Gómez Serrano, Jesús (1982) *Aguascalientes: imperio de los Guggenheim*, México: FCE.

Grunstein, Arturo (2012) *Consolidados: José Yves Limantour y la formación de los Ferrocarriles Nacionales de México*, México: CONACULTA.

Haber, Stephen and Jeffrey Bortz (eds.) (2002) *The Mexican Economy, 1870–1930: Essays on the Economic History of Institutions, Revolution, and Growth*, Stanford, CA: Stanford University Press.

Haber, Stephen, Armando Razo and Noel Maurer (2003) *The Politics of Property Rights. Political Instability, Credible Commitments, and Economic Growth in Mexico, 1876–1929*, Cambridge: Cambridge University Press.

Hausberger, Bernd and Antonio Ibarra (eds.) (2015) *Oro y plata en los inicios de la economía global: de las minas a la moneda*, México: ECM.

Herrera, Inés (1977) *El comercio exterior de México, 1821–1875*, México: ECM.

Jáuregui, Luis (ed.) (2006) *De riqueza e inequidad: el problema de las contribuciones directas en América Latina, siglo XIX*, México: Instituto Mora.

Joseph, Gilbert M. (1992) *Revolución desde afuera: Yucatán, México y los Estados Unidos, 1880–1924*, México: FCE.

Katz, Friedrich (1976) *La servidumbre agraria en México en la época porfiriana*, México: SepSetentas.

Klein, Herbert and John TePaske (1982) *The Royal Treasuries of the Spanish Empire in America*, Durham, NC: Duke University Press.

Knight, Alan (2003) "El estímulo mexicano de las exportaciones en el crecimiento económico mexicano, 1900–1930", in Enrique Cárdenas et al., *La era de las exportaciones latinoamericanas de fines del siglo XIX a principios del XX*, México: FCE: 165–202.

Kuntz Ficker, Sandra (2007) *El comercio exterior de México en la era del capitalismo liberal, 1870–1929*, México: ECM.

Kuntz Ficker, Sandra (ed.) (2010a) *Historia económica general de México. De la Colonia a nuestros días*, México: ECM-Secretaría de Economía.

Kuntz Ficker, Sandra (2010b) "Política comercial, importaciones e industrialización en México, 1880–1929", in J. Morilla et al., *Homenaje a Gabriel Tortella. Las claves del desarrollo económico y social*, Madrid: Universidad de Alcalá.

López Alonso, Moramay (2012) *Measuring Up: A History of Living Standards in Mexico, 1850–1950*, Stanford, CA: Stanford University Press.

López Gallo, Manuel (1965) *Economía y política en la historia de México*, México: El Caballito.

López Rosado, Diego (1968) *Historia y pensamiento económico de México*, 6 vols., México: UNAM.

Ludlow, Leonor and Carlos Marichal (eds.) (1986) *Banca y poder en México (1800–1925)*, México: Grijalbo.

Luna, María (2006) *El Congreso y la política mexicana (1857–1911)*, México: ECM–FCE.

Marichal, Carlos (1989) *A Century of Debt Crisis in Latin America: From Independence to the Great Depression, 1820–1930*, Princeton, NJ: Princeton University Press.

Marichal, Carlos (2007) *Bankruptcy of Empire. Mexican Silver and the Wars between Spain, Britain and France, 1870–1810*, Cambridge: Cambridge University Press.

Marichal, Carlos (2010) *Nueva historia de las grandes crisis financieras: una perspectiva global, 1873–1908*, Buenos Aires: Debate.

Marichal, Carlos and Leonor Ludlow (eds.) (1998–99) *Lecturas de Historia económica Mexicana*, México: Instituto Mora-El Colegio de Michoacán-ECM-IIH/UNAM.

Meyer, Lorenzo (1988) *México y Estados Unidos en el conflicto petrolero: 1917–1942*, México: Petróleos Mexicanos.

Miño, Manuel (ed.) (2006) *Núcleos urbanos mexicanos: siglos XVIII y XIX. Mercado, perfiles sociodemográficos y conflictos de autoridad*, México: ECM.

Miranda, José (1952) *El tributo indígena en la Nueva España durante el siglo XVI*, México: ECM.

Nickel, Herbert (1988) *Morfología social de la hacienda mexicana*, México: FCE.

Pérez Herrero, Pedro (1988) *Plata y libranzas. La articulación comercial del México borbónico*, México: ECM.

Plana, Manuel (1984) *Il regno del cotone in Messico: la struttura agraria de La Laguna, 1855–1910*, Milano: F. Angeli.

Potash, Robert A. (1961) "Historiografía del México Independiente", *Historia Mexicana*, 10 (3): 361–412.

Reynolds, Clark W. (1970) *The Mexican Economy. Twentieth-Century Structure and Growth*, New Haven, CT: Yale University Press.

Riguzzi, Paolo (2003) *¿Reciprocidad imposible? La política del comercio entre México y Estados Unidos, 1857–1938*, México: El Colegio Mexiquense/Instituto Mora.

Riguzzi, Paolo (2009) "From Globalisation to Revolution? The Porfirian Political Economy: An Essay on Issues and Interpretations", *Journal of Latin American Studies*, 41: 347–68.

Romano, Ruggiero (1984) "American Feudalism", *Hispanic American Historical Review*, 64 (1): 121–34.

Romero Sotelo, María Eugenia (ed.) (2012) *Fundamentos de la política económica en México, 1910–2010*, México: FE-UNAM.

Salvucci, Richard (2009) *Politics, Markets, and Mexico's 'London debt', 1823–1887*, New York: Cambridge University Press.

Sánchez Santiró, Ernest (2010) "El desempeño de la economía mexicana, 1810–1860: de la colonia al estado-nación", in Kuntz Ficker (ed.) (2010): 275–301.

Sariego, Juan Luis (1988) *Enclaves y minerales en el norte de México: historia social de los mineros de Cananea y Nueva Rosita, 1900–1970*, México: CIESAS.

Semo, Enrique (1973) *Historia del capitalismo en México: los orígenes, 1521–1763*, México: Era.

Solís, Leopoldo (1970) *La realidad económica mexicana. Retrovisión y perspectivas*, México: Siglo XXI.

Van Young, Eric (1989) *La ciudad y el campo en el México del siglo XVIII. La economía rural en la región de Guadalajara*, México: FCE.

Womack, John Jr. (1978) "The Mexican Economy during the Revolution, 1910–1920: Historiography & Analysis", *Marxist Perspectives*, 1 (4): 80–123.

Zavala, Silvio (1935) *Las instituciones jurídicas en la conquista de América*, Madrid: Helénica.

Zuleta, María Cecilia (2006) *De cultivos y contribuciones. Agricultura y hacienda estatal en México en la "época de la prosperidad". Morelos y Yucatán 1870–1910*, México: UAM-Iztapalapa.

22

THE FORMATION OF ECONOMIC HISTORY IN BRAZIL

From the South Atlantic to South America

Luiz Felipe de Alencastro

This chapter discusses economic history in and about Brazil focusing upon the issues and works that mark the two centuries of Brazil's emergence as an independent nation state. A sort of Brazilian exceptionalism could be suggested insofar as the country stands as the single colonial aggregate that was not fragmented after its Independence in 1822, as well as the only lusophone nation and long-standing constitutional monarchy in the Americas (1822–89). Encompassing the whole territory of Portugal's vice-kingdom, trading directly with Portuguese Africa slave ports until 1850 and chief destination of Portuguese immigration until 1950, Brazil maintains a long relationship with Portuguese overseas history and historiography. Because Lisbon's colonial policy tried to replicate in Angola the Brazilian plantation sector, economic debates during the nineteenth and twentieth centuries in the two countries were sometimes intermingled. Both Portuguese and Brazilian developmentalists, past and present, praised the Marquis of Pombal's enlightened despotism, which encouraged a protected manufacturing sector in eighteenth-century Portugal, but their liberal adversaries in the two countries criticized that view.[1]

The Lisbon Court's transfer to Rio de Janeiro (1808–21) embodied a Luso-Brazilian ruling class significantly experienced in European affairs and vested with a state-building project. Distinctive from the dominant class formed by landowners who handled regional and local powers, the central administration remained attentive to the world's changes. Edgy negotiations of commercial treaties, coupled with London's efforts to suppress the traffic of enslaved Africans, threatened the government's sovereignty. Brazil, alongside the United States, was one of the main independent exporters of slave-grown commodities and the only American nation to practise a large-scale Atlantic slave trade (1822–50). This was the distinctive feature of Anglo-Brazilian relations throughout the transition from informal to formal imperialism (Bethell 1970; Cain and Hopkins 2014, 260–7). The historical chasm separating Africa and Brazil caused international crises that bolstered the role of diplomats and the Foreign Affairs Ministry. From that time onwards, diplomats played a major role in the country's economic arrangements and agreements (Almeida 2001). Therefore, European and American overseas affairs were discussed among the ruling circles of Rio de Janeiro, a global maritime hub before the opening of the Panama Canal (1914). The end of slavery (1888) and the overthrow of the monarchy (1889) removed the two main disparities that singularized Brazil among the American nations.

Alongside earlier significant works, three recent books have covered the country's economic history. Paiva Abreu's (2014) collective book, mostly a survey of past and present economic policies, presents an updated and expanded edition of his 1989 publication used in many faculty courses. Economists who participated in the design and the implementation of the Real Plan during the Cardoso presidencies authored some of the chapters. Bresser Pereira's (2014) volume reviews the main moments of Brazil's economic and political history, emphasizing the last half-century in which he participated as a prominent development economist and policy maker. Luna and Klein's (2014) scholarly study covers the economic and social history of Brazil from 1889 onwards. In tracing the history of economic history in Brazil one should however start with the nineteenth century.

The slave trade and the endurance of slavery

Illustrative of the colonial elite's influence, the São Paulo-born José Bonifácio de Andrada had a career as a scientist and a high-ranking officer in Portugal. A follower of the Enlightenment and a Freemason, he joined the Court in Rio de Janeiro in 1819. Eventually, he became the first head of Brazil's national government (1822–23). Aware of the staunch British opposition to the Atlantic slave trade, he unsuccessfully proposed parliamentary measures for its suppression as well as complementary steps to peacefully incorporate the Amerindians into economic life. His writings inspired other economic and social reformers during the nineteenth century.

Brazil's slave traffic was bilateral, which explains its resilience in the national period. As is well known, around 95 per cent of the voyages disembarking Africans in Brazil had left the Brazilian ports loaded with locally produced or re-exported Asian and European goods.[2] The intensification of bilateral trade in the first half of the nineteenth century, along with the persistence of slavery until 1888, sustained the Brazilian elite's concern about Native American labour, slavery, plantation economics and immigration, past and present.

Edited and annotated in 1851 by Francisco Adolfo de Varnhagen, himself author of a commanding history of Brazil (Varnhagen 1854–57), Gabriel Soares de Souza's manuscript on the settlers' undertakings in 1587 disclosed the early stages of Portuguese America's merchant production.[3] In the same vein, André João Antonil's (1711) book on the cane sugar and tobacco plantations, and the gold rush in Minas Gerais, was reprinted in Rio de Janeiro in 1837. A Jesuit and missionary administrator in Bahia, Antonil's descriptions shed light on sugar mills, slave management and plantation administration. His work became the chief contemporary text on Brazil's colonial economy. Many annotated editions of Antonil's book followed, including more recent translations in French and English.

The government-funded *Instituto Histórico* (1838–) promoted research on economic history throughout the nineteenth and twentieth centuries. Likewise, the *Sociedade Auxiliadora da Indústria Nacional* published in its journal (1833–92) texts on industrial and plantation innovations. Entrepreneurial circles affiliated to the *Sociedade* formed associations that evolved into the National Industry Confederation (1938–). By themselves or associated with the government, those corporations stimulated research on the country's production and foreign exchanges.

Controversies over free trade (particularly about the 1844 Alves Branco Law instating the first protectionist tariff); over European and Asian immigration (related to the 1850 Law on Public Land); over companies' and plantation credit (regarding the Commercial Code of 1850 and the 1864 Mortgage Law); over bullion and paper money (at the 1853 re-foundation of the Banco do Brasil as a commercial and currency bank); and over the economic crises of

1857 and 1864 (the first to be fully felt in the country), generated surveys by Parliament and in the Rio de Janeiro press (da Silva Ferraz 1865). The reproduction of European and US publications that popularized science and contemporary issues also played a critical role in the propagation of the century's transformations. These included almanacs and papers, particularly the *Jornal do Commércio* (1827–), one of the oldest continuously circulating economic periodicals edited in the Americas. The essays of prominent economists, at times partially translated, were published in Rio (as happened to the writings of Tooke, Juglar and Leroy-Beaulieu). Moreover, debates on United States and Caribbean slavery offered updated references to Brazilian writers and policy makers. Among other authors, Wakefield's thesis was known and debated in relation to the 1850 Land Law, immigration policy and the rural economy.[4]

Plantation exports grew steadily in the 1840s and the country surpassed Java as the world's largest coffee exporter, a position that it would hold until today. This generated a surge in debates about railroads, canals and steamship navigation, and more generally on the transition from slavery to free labour. Employing Brazilian and Portuguese funds engaged in African exchanges that re-flowed into Rio de Janeiro at the end of the slave trade (1850), the Viscount of Mauá, a former British bank agent, emerged as a leading national entrepreneur. Later entitled 'Autobiography' and regularly re-edited and discussed, his creditors' report describes his mid-century industrial and banking undertakings in Brazil as well as in the Rio de la Plata (1878). Usually attributed to the government's interventionism, Mauá's bankruptcy fuels recurrent controversy among economic historians from Brazil and abroad (Marchant 1965; Renda Vitorino 2008).

In the 1840s and 1850s the central government subsidized the construction of a canal (lobbied for by sugar mill owners), a railroad (petitioned by coffee planters) around Rio de Janeiro, and the railroad Recife–São Francisco River (crossing plantations and cattle farms of the Northeast). Established in 1854, the Bureau of Public Land, later the Agriculture Ministry (1860) acted as a rural labour department. From that time onwards until 1960, when the Federal capital was transferred to Brasilia, Rio de Janeiro's economic and political circles retained dominance over the central government's decisions.

Overlooked by many historians, Ferreira Soares's (1860) survey of high food prices was most relevant in the mid-century transition, when Brazil's economy was decoupled from Africa's slave market.[5] Portuguese mass migration to Rio de Janeiro was in its early stages so the slave trade suppression constricted the labour market. Uncovering new statistics, Soares argued that agro-exports had nonetheless increased in the period, owing to the interprovincial slave trade and to migrant rural workers. Moreover, he aptly asserted that the high food prices, sparked by the coffee expansion around Rio de Janeiro, were a conjunctural trend that would not last. By doing so, he dismissed beliefs in a shortage of labour, which raised speculation about the reopening of the African slave trade.

The statistical age and the abolition of slavery

Given the fact that Parliament adopted gradual reforms to eliminate slavery from 1850 until 1885, most of the writing on economic history, including surveys on the Amerindian policy, refers to the labour question. Opinions on land and immigration policy were sharply divided. Planters and export merchants wanted rural workers and proletarians from any country. Chinese labourers were shipped to Rio de Janeiro in the 1850s, for example, to replace enslaved Africans on the plantations. By contrast, the central government preferred to sell public lands to European peasants and small farmers in order to 'civilize' and 'whiten' the country. Permeated by racial theories and social Darwinism, these policies revealed opposing views about the process of nation-building.

Perdigão Malheiro's (1864–67) historical and juridical study of African and Amerindian slavery in Brazil was central in the discussions about ending slavery and promoting immigration. Quoting Court judgements involving slaves, his record remains an authoritative reference for today's researchers. The economic and social coercion of freed and free workers, including immigrants, on the coffee frontier was denounced by European diplomats and by the press. Published in 1850 and later translated into Portuguese, with a penetrating comment by Sérgio Buarque de Holanda, the memoir of a Swiss immigrant exposed the hardship in a São Paulo plantation in the late 1840s (Holanda 1941). A topic further studied by Carvalho Franco (1964), Viotti da Costa (1966), Beiguelman (1968) and Lamounier (2012).

Notwithstanding substantial European immigration in the late nineteenth century, there was a widespread perception of Brazil as an Africanized country. The 'Scramble for Africa' spread stereotypes of Africa's wildness and this perennially troubled Brazilian elites and the middle classes. Recently updated data have shown that the number of Africans disembarked between 1550 and 1850 was six and half times larger than the number of Portuguese colonists and immigrants.[6] Concerns regarding the composition of the population and the labour question, as well as military recruitment problems during the War of the Triple Alliance (1864–70), drove the first national census (1872). Brazil was shown to have the largest slave system in the Americas at this time.[7] Disclosing data on sex, age, nationality, race, status, housing, professions and religions, the census portrayed the distribution of economic and social conditions of the nearly 10 million inhabitants.[8]

The census information transformed the ability to observe slavery, the national workforce and immigration. The data also supported the government report (1875) and Planters Society reports (1878) on rural work and export agriculture.[9] Furthermore, projections of the 1872 data revealed that slavery would survive everywhere in the country up to the twentieth century, notwithstanding the gradual effect of the emancipation laws. This discredited the gradualist policy and radicalized the abolitionist movement. Nabuco's *Abolitionism* (1883), considered by many as the country's foremost political writing, conveyed the new radicalism. Aiming for the end of slavery 'and of the evils that it engendered', he related Abolition to the agrarian reform proposed by the African–Brazilian engineer André Rebouças (1883).

In the view of the abolitionist and positivist thinkers who influenced the Republican leadership, social engineers appeared as better suited than the lawyers – prized by the Iberian tradition – to modernize the nation (Martins 1976, 83–7). Singled out from Rio de Janeiro's Military College, the Escola Politécnica included, from 1873, a Political Economy chair amongst other economic-driven disciplines. Similar establishments were created in São Paulo (1893) and Recife (1912) diversifying the economic debate conducted by lawyers or self-taught authors.

The rise of Latin Americanism

An abolitionist and the first Finance Minister of the Federal Republic (1889), Rui Barbosa helped to establish a Ministry of Industry and implemented a short-lived industrial policy. Considered by some authors as the first planned governmental action in this sector, Barbosa's policy ideas, albeit flimsily executed, foreshadowed development theories (Barbosa 1893; Dutra Fonseca 2004). New Republican governments also enhanced relations with neighbouring nations. Pan-Americanism and international law substantiated the new intellectual global context. Siting a Pan-American Conference (1906) and the First Congress of Americans Jurists (1912) in Rio de Janeiro reinforced ties with Washington. Thereafter, trade, banking and diplomatic negotiations led by the United States gained ascendancy in Brazil, to the detriment of France and England (Bethell 2010). In reaction to the new international order, the idea of Latin Americanism diffused by Public Law specialists and diplomats began to take root within Brazilian elites of the First Republic (1889–1930). Manoel Bonfim expressed a more radical view of Latin Americanism (1905). A well-travelled social scientist whose works have seen a resurgence of interest in Brazil, he denounced the tacit agreement between Europe and the United States to endorse the latter's economic and diplomatic 'protectorate' over Latin America. A promoter of technical education, he stated that the full political sovereignty of Brazil and Latin American countries would only be achieved with economic independence and industrialization (Bonfim 1993, 130).

Meanwhile, the 'governors' policy' emerged portraying the dominance of the regional oligarchies, especially from the Southeast coffee plantation states, over the Federal government. Henceforth, the distinction between the ruling classes and the dominant classes become less sharp. Bowing to the planters' oligarchies, the Federal government bought and stocked coffee in order to ensure a profit margin for the producers. From then onwards a subsidizing policy, to the agro-export sector's benefit, was established, reinforcing dominant ideas about the country's natural comparative advantage and 'agricultural vocation'.[10]

At the turn of the nineteenth century, the Argentinian boom gave rise to a rivalry between the two countries. Facing the emergence of Buenos Aires as a focus of South Atlantic investment and European immigration, the Federal and the São Paulo state governments undertook urban and economic reforms. Far-reaching sanitation and re-urbanization works transformed Rio de Janeiro and Santos into modern port cities. At the same time, the Ministry of Industry requested an economic inquiry in order to display updated data to investors and immigrants' agents. Ultimately, the work's six volumes of statistics and surveys formed the country's first economic and industrial census, which informs most research even today.[11] After the end of slavery, the wage-labour force and mass immigration expanded the consumer market. Textiles, amounting to a third of the imports during the second half of the nineteenth century, as well as shoes, beer and tobacco products were substituted by national production (Vilela and Suzigan 2001). The amount of small and middle-sized industries in the Southeast states revealed by the 1906 Census surprised some observers, giving rise to more consistent discussions about industrialization policies (Luz 1978, 142–7).

Federalism equally favoured regional research. Capistrano de Abreu, who authored the introductory essay for the 1906 economic census, extended his research in a work destined to become a major regionalist history reference (Capistrano de Abreu 1907). Arguably comparable to F. J. Turner's (1893) classic essay on the American Frontier, Capistrano's approach emphasized the ranching frontier in the Northeast backlands (*Sertões*) along the São Francisco valley and beyond, at the core of the settled Brazilian territory. Comprehending economic history and human geography, his work outlined a territorialized interpretation of the history that excluded the South Atlantic network. Followed then and now by most of Brazil's historians and by Brazilianist authors from Europe and America, such an approach confines Brazil's colonial past to the Portuguese America territory. The defining Atlantic slave trade and the three-century-long direct links with Portuguese Africa, particularly in the Gulf of Guinea and Central West Africa, still present in Varnhagen's *História*, are absent from Capistrano's work, which quotes a sole indirect reference to Angola.

Best known for his comprehensive research on mining history and legislation in Brazil (1904–05), João Pandiá Calogeras, a Finance Minister, wrote an important book on monetary policies (1910) and *Formação Histórica do Brasil* (1930) which contains chapters on economic subjects and brought in the notion of 'formation'. Refined by Caio Prado Junior (1942), Antonio Candido (1959) and Celso Furtado (1959), the concept of 'formation' involves critical analysis of the colonial past and of preceding Brazilian historians (Arantes and Arantes 1997).

From a wider perspective, the Portuguese historian J. L. de Azevedo (1929) studied Portuguese America and the scope of Lisbon's ultramarine economy. Versed in Brazil's history and close to Capistrano de Abreu, to whom he dedicated his book, Azevedo describes the central economic cycles of Portugal's overseas commodities (Asian pepper, African gold and Brazil's sugar – seventeenth century; gold and diamonds – eighteenth century). Most of the following Brazilian authors adopted that cycle scheme. Roberto Simonsen's *História econômica do Brasil* (1937), the first book to hold this title, adapted Azevedo's analysis, dismissing the Asian and African stages and incorporating the sixteenth-century Brazil wood trade as well as the nineteenth-century coffee exports, as the first and the last of Brazil's commodity cycles. Other authors, such as J. F. Normano (1935), added a rubber cycle at the turn of the nineteenth century and shorter cycles of tobacco, cotton, cacao. It is also currently suggested that from 1970 onwards Brazil initiated a soya bean cycle.

Later works demonstrated that the gold cycle changed Portuguese America substantially: it supplanted and reorganized other regional activities, nurturing an internal market, a 'dynamic centre' across the inland mining areas (Furtado 1959). By the same token, researchers showed that the sugar cane economy had a much larger range and remained profitable throughout the centuries, including during the period of the gold cycle (Schwartz 1986). Or else they argued that the 1550–1850 sugar, gold mining and coffee activities relied upon the flow of enslaved Africans provided by the Luso-Brazilian South Atlantic network. Therefore, a major three-century-long slave trade cycle yielded the development of all export products, which constitute sub-cycles, in Brazil's territory. Nevertheless, tellingly, and easily adaptable to lesson plans, the traditional cycle model is widely taught in Brazilian schools and faculties as well as in history classes abroad. Commodity and environmental studies emerged with Freyre's research on sugar cane monoculture and the devastation of the Northeast coastal forest (1937), along with Taunay's extensive work on coffee in Brazil (11 vols., 1929–41) and Alice Canabrava's book on the cotton plantation (1951). Partly inspired by those works and by concerns over the Amazon ecosystem, Warren Dean wrote his masterful book (1995) on the destruction of the Atlantic forest during the colonial and national periods.

The metabolization of the territorial labour market

The migration of rural workers from the Northeast states to São Paulo's coffee frontier surpassed the entry of immigrants around 1930 (Graham and Holanda Filho 1984). After the centuries of the Atlantic slave trade and the mass immigration, from the turn of the nineteenth century the Southeast plantations relied predominantly upon Brazilian workers, metabolizing the territorial labour market. In this context, the establishment of a Ministry of Labour handling official trade unions (1930), as much as the creation of a minimum wage for urban workers (1940) and a social insurance system, helped the authorities to cope with the emerging working class. The Vargas regime (1930–45) strengthened the Federal administration and promoted industrialization. One central achievement of Vargas's policy was the building of the heavily subsided Volta Redonda CSN steel mill (1941). Bringing state investment to basic inputs of production, a typical feature of the import-substitution process in Brazil, CNS turned into a symbol of the developmentalist policy, along with the state-owned mining company Vale do Rio Doce CVRD (1942), as well as the Petrobras (1953) hydrocarbon company and the Federal Development Bank BNDE, later BNDES (1952), created in the second Vargas administration, 1951–54 (Dinius 2011). The National Institute of Statistics (IBGE) established in 1938 and the organization of the 1940 Census launched a new age of demographic and economic data. Thanks to the economist and statistician Giorgio Mortara, a refugee from fascist Italy who joined the IBGE in 1939, data collection and analysis were enhanced and standardized. In addition to the updated statistics collected in systematic surveys, the 1940 Census revised data from the existing 1872, 1900, 1920 censuses.

At this crossroads in the 1930s, marked by the decline of the old regional oligarchies, the emergence of interregional migrations and a new centralized regime, the seminal books of Gilberto Freyre (1933), Caio Prado Júnior (1942) and Sérgio Buarque de Holanda (1936) came to light. Regularly republished and debated since, and translated in several languages, these works remain formative for Brazil's students and for foreign Brazilianists. Freyre's study of private life and societal relations in cane sugar plantations between the sixteenth and nineteenth centuries helped to understand slave life and sugar mill management. Moreover, his book emphasized the social viability of the Luso-Brazilian miscegenation. Obsessed with Afro-Brazilian demographic growth, Oliveira Vianna, a leading political thinker, commenting on the 1920 Census, had been concerned about the need for 'whitening' the nation (1923, 99–101). Opposing these dominant ideas, Freyre (1933) outdid the century-old debate on the unviability of the post-slave trade national society and the need for European immigration. By these means he also shaped the ideology of Brazil as a non-racist nation. Renewing connections with Portugal's historiography, his later works suggested features that were inherent to Portuguese colonization, thus revamping Lisbon's colonialist propaganda in Africa in the 1960s.

Writing on culture and social life, Sérgio Buarque de Holanda (1936) uncovered the historical traits that thwarted democracy in Brazil in the aftermath of the 1930 Revolution. Among other works, he wrote on river transportation in colonial times (1945) and on São Paulo's *Bandeirantes* and their enslaving raids and expeditions across the South American Lowlands (1957). More influential for economic historians and economists, Caio Prado Jr introduced a Marxist version of Brazil's history (1933) and broadened this in his best-known work analysing the colonial process (1942) and in his economic history book (1945), covering a larger period and including twentieth-century industrialization. It should be noted that Prado's economic history was first published in Mexico by the Fondo de Cultura Economica, which also issued Freyre's *Interpretación del Brasil* (1945), and Josué de Castro's work on food in the tropics, the first Brazilian book on global history (1946). In the same way, the Fondo translated into Spanish modern editions of Marx (1935), Max Weber (1944), Keynes (1945), Adam Smith (1958) and other classical authors. Intelligible for Portuguese speakers, these translations offered a broader spectrum of historical and economic knowledge to Brazilian readers. José Medina Echevarria, a Spanish republican refugee sociologist and a Fondo editor, was later the Social Science Director at the United Nations Economic Commission for Latin America and the Caribbean (CEPAL) where he worked with Celso Furtado and Fernando Henrique Cardoso.

Developmentalism and industrialization

Joining Raul Prebisch in Santiago in 1949, at CEPAL's beginnings, Furtado studied the development of the constituent countries. Whereas the Pan-Americanist writers of the early twentieth century had focused upon institution building and continental law, CEPAL's economists and sociologists did more policy-oriented research, planning the governance and, occasionally, the government of their own countries. Former CEPAL researchers such as Fernando Henrique Cardoso (twice the country's president), Celso Furtado, José Serra and Francisco Weffort (all leading ministers and high-ranking officials), had a critical role in economic and social policies, not to mention their support to the Mercosur (the sub-regional trading bloc of Argentina, Brazil, Paraguay, Uruguay and Venezuela).

Furtado's book on Brazil's economic formation (1959) gathered and analysed economic data on the colonial and national periods. He underscored the central role of eighteenth-century gold mining in the making of a continental Brazilian market, playing down explanations based on the ranching frontier (Capistrano), sugar mill communities (Freyre) or coffee plantations (Prado Junior). Examining the 1930s administration, Furtado introduced a Keynesian analysis of the Vargas expansionary fiscal policy and of the purchase, stock-piling and destruction of coffee. His book presented CEPAL's analysis of import-substitution industrialization, which became a dominant notion, especially after Conceição Tavares's extensive study on the subject (1972). Furtado's tight and engaging writing style added to his success with readers in Portuguese and in numerous translations.[12]

Gavin Kitching rightly observed that emphasis on the colonial past embodies a distinctive trait of Latin American dependency theory compared to Russian development ideas of the turn of the twentieth century. Still, the assessment of slavery's enduring consequences differentiates most of the Brazilian writings from corresponding development studies undertaken in other Latin American countries (1989, 152–60). To be sure, as much as Prado, Castro and Cardoso, Furtado underlies slavery's economic and social legacy in contemporary Brazil. In the same perspective, Francisco de Oliveira's 1972 seminal essay demonstrated the connection between the rural poverty subsequent to slavery and urban economic growth. Drawing on recent surveys on the topic, many authors of the new generation equally stress such historical parallels, as do Jesse Souza (2003) and Adalberto Cardoso (2010), in their significant books on the making of social citizenship and working society in contemporary Brazil.

It is not coincidental that Furtado's book, just as Candido's study of the formation of Brazilian literature, was published in 1959, in a period of democracy and economic growth that fortified optimism about the country's destiny.[13] Shifting from the previous economic pattern based on state or national entrepreneurship, the Kubitschek presidency (1956–61) encouraged American and European investments, especially in the automobile industry. The inauguration of Brasilia (1960) and the consolidation of industrial production seemed to confirm the country's positive views. Published in 1961 (2nd edn. 1978), the often-cited book of Vilela Luz reviewing economic policies from 1808 to 1930, is significantly entitled 'The Struggle for Brazil's industrialization', suggesting that the expansion of domestic industry was the main step towards progress.

In the 1950s and early 1960s, the reformist and Varguist platforms were based on three pillars designed to ensure national sovereignty and development: state-led industrialization associated with foreign investments; the 'Base Reforms', mainly the Land Reform, backed by the progressive movement and by organized labour; and the surge of a 'national bourgeoisie', supposedly supportive of such reforms. Cardoso (1964) questioned the significance of the national bourgeoisie's role in the reform movement, an interpretation that he expanded in a prominent book co-written with Faletto while they were at CEPAL (1969).[14] Another influential book of this period is Ignacio Rangel's work (1963) that set the basis of the inertial inflation interpretation in Brazil. Expanded in depth by other authors, such an analysis was put into practice by Edmar Bacha in the successful Real Plan enacted by Cardoso, then Finance Minister (1993).[15] This stabilized the economy and controlled the half-century-long inflationary process.

Foreign approaches and the expansion of research

As in other Latin American countries, French and American authors and theories considerably influenced Brazil's post-war historiography. Fernand Braudel taught at the University of São Paulo (1935–37, 1947) while his disciple Alice Canabrava was appointed in 1951 to the economic history chair as the first female professor. She authored pioneering works on the Atlantic world clearly affiliated with the *Annales* School. Moreover, Magalhães Godinho and Frédéric Mauro, who taught in São Paulo, as well as Pierre Chaunu, the *Annales*' authors whom Braudel had advised in their magisterial surveys on the Iberian empires, were generally read in Brazilian universities. As other economists and historians of the *Annales*' second generation, all three authors were followers of Earl J. Hamilton's writings and methods, a factor that accounted for the quantitative drive of many *Annales* essays and in contemporary monographs on Iberian and Latin American economic history. Vitorino Magalhães Godinho (1950, 1955, 1963) wrote critical surveys on the Portuguese American economy. Frédéric Mauro's (1960) book on the South Atlantic as well as his many works on economic history (e.g. Mauro 1970), introduced subjects subsequently developed by his numerous, mostly Brazilian, PhD candidates. His 1973 collective volume on Brazil's quantitative history inspired inquiries into prices conducted, among others, by Katia Mattoso, Yeda Linhares, Barbara Levy and Lahmeyer Lobo. The latter's two-volume book on Rio de Janeiro's nineteenth- and twentieth-century wages, prices and companies, represents one of the most accomplished works of the kind in Brazil (Lahmeyer Lobo 1978). An *Annales* special issue on Brazil's history (2006, n. 2) illustrated the new stage of French–Brazilian collaboration in history and economic history.

American economic history scholarship about Brazil was not new, as illustrated in the work of Alan Manchester (1933) and Alexander Marchant (1940).[16] However, it was Tannenbaum's (1946) endorsement of Freyre's ideas – when the Jim Crow Laws began to be more criticized – that enthused studies in American universities on slavery, labour and race relations in Brazil. In addition to the books of Stanley Stein and Warren Dean on coffee plantations, or Stuart Schwartz's works on sugar mills and the slave system, other surveys contributed to understanding of the labour market. These included essays on urban slavery by Mary Karash, Sandra Lauderdale Graham and A. J. R. Russell-Wood; the work of Herbert Klein and Dale Tomich on comparative slave systems; Herbert Klein and David Eltis on the slave trade, Colin MacLachlan, Barbara Sommer and John Monteiro on Indian slavery; Thomas Skidmore and Carl Degler on racial relations; and John French and Barbara Weinstein's researches on trade unions and the working class. Spurred by growing academic interest and, especially by research support for Latin American studies after the Cuban Revolution, surveys were also undertaken on Brazil's state enterprises and industrialization, (Steven C. Topik, Warren Dean, Albert Fishlow), long-term economic development (Nathaniel Leff, Werner Baer) and regional economies (A. J. R. Russell-Wood, Peter Eisenberg, Thomas Holloway, Robert Slenes, Robert Levine, Joseph Love, Richard Morse, Douglas Libby, Laird Bergad, Bert Barickman).[17]

Two generations of Brazilian historians such as João J. Reis, Junia Furtado, Marcus Carvalho, Sidney Chaloub, Rafael Marquese, Roquinaldo Ferreira, Mariana Cândido, Maria Helena Machado and many others, studied New World slavery or African economic history in North American universities. Economists who taught in Rio universities and later played a prominent role in the Cardoso government (Winston Fritsch, Gustavo Franco, Pedro Malan and Edmar Bacha) researched on economic history in Economics Departments of American institutions. Typically, the economic history works of Wilson Suzigan, Anibal Vilela, Flávio

Saes, Tamás Szmrecsányi, who founded in 1993 the Association of Economic History Researchers (ABPHE), rely on studies undertaken in both countries.

Werner Baer's (1979) survey of the Brazilian economy from the colonial period until today, regularly re-edited and updated with Brazilian collaborators in American and Brazilian editions, is often used as a textbook, illustrating academic cooperation between the two countries. The best example of American–Brazilian joint research however is the extensive Herbert Klein (UCLA) and Francisco Luna (USP) co-authorship that resulted, among other significant works, in their above-mentioned 2014 book on Brazil's social and economic history from 1889 to 2011.

Luso-Brazilian collaboration on colonial economic history also generated fruitful research as shown by Valentim Alexandre (1993) and Jorge Pedreira (1994), echoing the influential books of Fernando Novais (1979) and J. Jobson de Arruda (1980), and the ensuing discussion of the concept of 'colonial crisis' published in a special issue on Brazil in the *Hispanic American Historical Review* (2000, n. 4).

Broader sharing of data has improved economic history in recent years. The government-led and UNESCO-supported Projeto Resgate inventoried and digitized most of Portuguese archival documents on the colonial period. Other countries' archives, such as those of the Netherlands or Angola, are in process of digitalization. The same may be said of the Trans-Atlantic Slave Trade Database, which is being translated into Portuguese and has Brazilian historian Manolo Florentino as one of its main collaborators. Accessed by many researchers, such data has renewed colonial economic history, as evidenced by the works of Ângelo Alves Carrara on the Crown's Treasure in seventeenth- and eighteenth-century Portuguese America, A. C. Jucá de Sampaio on Rio de Janeiro's colonial merchants, Rafael Chambouleyron on the Amazon economic exploitation, and by Helen Osorio's surveys of South Brazil's ranching activities.

Likewise, National Household Surveys (PNADs), realized by the IBGE, enabled more detailed research on social data, especially from 1976 onwards, when the survey covered most of the country's regions and included data on income distribution and racial inequalities. Using the 1976 PNAD household sampling, the first to include skin colour among their criteria since the 1950s Census, Carlos Hasenbalg demonstrated that, despite two and half decades of economic growth and urbanization, ethnic inequality persisted. Along with Afro-Brazilian and progressive movements, other studies deepened these findings, launching a debate that led the government to pass, in August 2012, a law mandating quotas for entry of black, mixed-race and Amerindian students in Federal universities and technical schools.

Online data are much more frequently accessed these days especially since, as with many other Federal institutions, the IBGE, Central Bank and the Congress maintain sites with historical series. Above all, the required online presentation of all government-funded Master's and PhD theses greatly facilitates economic history research.

To some extent, regionalist novels enlarged Brazilians' knowledge of the country's ethnic and economic diversity. Representative of this literary movement are Lins do Rego's autobiography *Plantation Boy* (1932), on a sugar mill community; the social novel of Graciliano Ramos *Barren Lives* (1938), describing peasant migration caused by the Northeast droughts; the historical novel *Time and the Wind* (1949–51), by Erico Verissimo, narrating the *gaucho*'s life in the Rio Grande do Sul's past; or the best-selling novel by Jorge Amado, *Gabriela, Clove and Cinnamon* (1958), on a Bahia town transformed by the cacao crop expansion. Studied in secondary school, turned into movies or into telenovelas these novels have had long-standing repercussions. From a different perspective, generally highly popular telenovelas, or soap operas, have had a key impact on the country's demographic transition. Following Elza

Berquo's findings on the fall in fertility rates, Faria and Potter (1998) demonstrated that soap operas, favourably portraying small and less authoritarian families, have induced couples to choose fewer children.

Dictatorship, democracy, economic growth and income inequality

Across the dictatorship and the succeeding democratic regime, three main issues related to the country's past involved economic history research. The first was the Agrarian Reform and the agro-export sector. After the Varguist government's overthrow by a Washington-supported military dictatorship (1964–85), Prado Jr (1966) reinstated criticism of the Brazilian Communist Party (PCB) endorsement of the Komintern's thesis of an agrarian 'feudal' system in Brazil. Though affiliated to the PCB, Prado had his own view of the country's problems. In his perspective, the colonial economy, rooted in merchant capitalism and Atlantic slavery, was integrated in world trade from the sixteenth century. Therefore, programmes of land reform promoted by the PCB and its allies, seemed ineffective. The improvement of social conditions in the countryside, brought about by rural workers' organizations, would enlarge the internal market, favouring national industry. By contrast, other social activists and authors, galvanized by the impact of the Cuban Revolution, emphasized the major potential of land reforms. Historical and agrarian research by Marxist writers such as Alberto Passos Guimarães and Jacob Gorender was influential within that current, which included Catholic activists. Indeed, created in 1975 by the Catholic Bishops Conference (CNBB), the Pastoral Land Commission backed Land Reform organizations, later converted into the Landless Movement (MST). CNBB's opposition to the dictatorship – a distinctive characteristic of Brazil's Catholic hierarchy in 1970s authoritarian South America – evolved towards adoption of the developmentalist thesis. Meanwhile, peasants and rural workers' demonstrations, sometimes bloodily repressed by local police, posed the agenda of land reforms to the Federal government. Exposing the double feature of the post-slavery agrarian structure and the above debate, there are now two ministries of rural affairs. The traditional Agriculture Ministry (1860) supports the latifundia-based agribusiness, essential to the country's exports, but the new Ministry of Agrarian Development (1999) was designed to provide rural properties to landless families, a politically sensitive issue. As demonstrated by several authors, the coupling of the two agrarian policies has been one of the conflicting themes of the Workers' Party presidencies since 2003.[18]

Industrial policy was another key point of the economic history debates, as state entrepreneurship, mainly in Geisel's dictatorship (1974–79), expanded in many areas. Accordingly, state institutions increased investments in infrastructure, basic inputs and the capital goods sector, doubling the number of enterprises owned by the Federal government between 1964 and 1974. Subsequently, Antônio Barros de Castro (1985) and some other development economists assumed that the investments made by the Geisel administration would launch a new wave of industrialization and growth. However, the external debt crisis, initiated in 1982 in Mexico, struck also in Brazil, plunging the country into a political and economic crisis. The evolution of foreign debt, coincident with Brazil's history since independence, turned into a central research topic of the period.[19] Since 2005, when Brazil anticipated its reimbursements to the International Monetary Fund (IMF) and increased its foreign-exchange reserves, the subject has been less debated. Privatizations of state enterprises started in 1990 and expanded during the Cardoso presidencies (1995–2003). Some Vargas-era economic institutions such as CSN and CVRD integrated the privatizations achieved in 1990–2012. Considered by Luna and Klein (2014) as some of the largest in the world, the privatizations aroused controversies, even within the government. Thus, in his last book, L. C. Bresser, then Minister of Sciences (1999), argued that Cardoso policies were 'explicitly projected to close out the Vargas era', in order to globalize Brazil's economy under United States' hegemony (Bresser Pereira 2014, 318–19). Lula's presidencies (2003–11) partially reversed this trend, increasing infrastructure investments; Petrobras control over the pre-salt huge oil reserves; reinstating shipbuilding; and, above all, enlarging the domestic market through a dynamic policy of social welfare comprising increases in the minimum legal wage and the *bolsa família*, or family allowance (Barros et al. 2006). Nevertheless, the Real's overvaluation, and reliance upon commodity exports, reduced the external competitiveness of the industrial sector (IEDI 2007). Early twentieth-century ideas of planters and export merchants about the agricultural vocation of the country surfaced again.

The third main issue researched and debated during recent decades is income inequality, a chronic problem in Brazil. Despite repression from the dictatorship, Minas Gerais and São Paulo's metalworkers launched strikes in 1968 against low wages, originating a political and social movement that contributed to the founding of Lula's Workers Party PT (1979). Intermingling academic research with social engagement, research papers by Brazilian and American economists, one of them quoted by Robert MacNamara, then World Bank president, affirmed that economic growth provoked a substantial concentration of income, contradicting the dictatorship propaganda.[20] The Research Institute of the trade-unions (DIEESE) challenged official data on the 1973 inflation rate and the World Bank later corroborated its analysis. From then onwards government, academic and trade union research centres have debated the subject. Attaining its height from the late 1970s until the mid-1990s, the concentration of income declined after the Real Plan and experienced a steady fall after 2002 (Mendes 2014). Academic researchers, Federal government and non-governmental institutions studied anti-poverty policies in Brazil including *bolsa família*, the largest conditional cash transfer programme in the world.[21] The emergence of a 'new middle class' (Neri 2011) and the attachment of the votes of organized labour and the poor to the PT candidates, gives to 'Lulism' (Singer 2009) a broader and transforming dimension that outstrips the legacy of Vargas.

Conclusion

Economic history in Brazil is no longer a central research field, as it used to be in the post-war period up to the 1970s, the years of Prado Jr and Furtado. New disciplinary divisions and academic specialization have certainly contributed to this. Besides, in most Brazilian universities the discipline overlaps with, and is sometimes unduly absorbed by, the history of economic thought. There are, however, more substantial reasons. Drawing anachronistically on Leroy-Beaulieu's late nineteenth-century distinction between 'exploitation colonies' and 'settlement colonies', Brazil's historians have tended to ignore the European overseas factories or warehouses, thus leaving out significant elements of merchant capital expansion. In fact, it was the Atlantic slave trade and gold mining that turned Portuguese America's coastal factories and plantation enclaves into a single colony in the eighteenth century. Conceiving Brazil as a territorialized entity from the sixteenth century generates a tautological interpretation that overshadows Southern Atlantic history.[22] The bipolarity between South American slave production sectors and African slave reproduction areas sustained the colonial spatial matrix in the South Atlantic until 1850, well beyond Brazil's independence. Obliviousness to this is a dismaying tendency in a country where, according to the 2010 Census, more than half of its inhabitants are of African descent.

Along the same lines, while tens of Brazilian students wrote their PhDs on Brazilian history in American universities in the last decades, there is practically no research done by the Brazilians on North American history. Similarly, China has been Brazil's first trading partner since 2009, and yet Chinese history is not taught in secondary schools or, more seriously, in Brazilian universities, notwithstanding the four-century-long data and historiography in Portuguese engendered by Lisbon's dominion over Macau. Such a self-centred conception of history discourages comparative international studies and perspectives, hindering the economic history of Brazil itself and preventing the application of Brazilian ideas in other contexts.

Notes

1 As observed by Bairoch (1976, 269), Pombal's economic policies (1755–76) had a pioneering role insofar as they explicitly took into account the dependency relation between Portugal and England. On Pombal's policies see Pedreira (2011). For a liberal critique of Pombal's doctrinal influence in today's Brazil, Paim (1982).

2 Cf. Eltis and Richardson (2010), 120–2, 141–3, 151–3, 156.

3 Varnhagen's *História geral*, based on archival sources, disclosed significant data on economic activities. This valuable repository of information was integrated and enlarged in the 1907–28 edition of the work, annotated by Capistrano de Abreu and Rodolfo Garcia.

4 See, e.g., *O Auxiliador da Industria Nacional*, August 1850.

5 In 1841–50, around 400,000 enslaved Africans disembarked in Brazil, of whom 308,000 in the Rio de Janeiro area (the capital had 260,000 inhabitants, including 110,000 slaves, in 1849); not to mention the vast number of Africans imported in the previous decades. Trans-Atlantic Slave Trade Database TSTD http://www.slavevoyages.org/tast/index.faces (accessed January 2015).

6 For African deportees, see TSTD. Figures about Portuguese colonists and immigrants (after 1822) are from my estimates.

7 The War of the Triple Alliance (1864–70) was fought between the allied forces of Brazil, Argentina and Uruguay against Paraguay.

8 The census showed that Brazil's population living in 1440 parishes amounted to 9,930,478 inhabitants, including 1,510,806 slaves (15 per cent). Nevertheless, the 21 volumes of the census data published in 1873–76 contained inaccuracies due to addition and aggregation mistakes; Paiva et al. (2012).

9 Menezes e Souza (1875); 'Congresso Agrícola do Recife', Recife 1878; 'Congresso Agrícola do Rio de Janeiro', Rio de Janeiro 1878.

10 G. Maringoni, 'Simonsen versus Gudin, a controvérsia pioneira do desenvolvimento', *Desafios do desenvolvimento*, IPEA, 2012, 73 (9) http://ipea.gov.br/desafios/index.php?option=com_content&view=article&id=2801:catid=28&Itemid=23 (accessed February 2015).

11 *O Brasil, suas riquezas naturais, suas indústrias*, Rio de Janeiro 1907–09.

12 E.g. Furtado 1963. Cf. Dean (1965, 107): 'The tightness and compression of Furtado's style of writing is admirable. He eschews anecdote, and reduces description to the minimum necessary to his exposition of causal relationships.'

13 Candido's *Formação da literatura brasileira* (1959) is, arguably, the main work on Brazil's literary history.

14 Cardoso's later presidencies (1995–99 and 1999–2003), debatable as they are, should not overshadow his prominent role as sociologist and political scientist in Brazil.

15 See Nakano (1982); Bresser-Pereira and Nakano (1984); Lopes (1984); Arida and Lara-Resende (1984).

16 Manchester's survey inspired Graham (1968).

17 On the growth of funding for Latin American studies in the United States, in the aftermath of the Cuban Revolution, see Skidmore (1998).

18 See Nakatani et al. (2012); Motta and Zarth (2008).

19 Cf. Weller (2015); von Mettenheim (2015, forthcoming).

20 Fishlow (1972); Hoffmann and Duarte (1972); Leite Lopes (1975); Hoffmann (2001).

21 See http://www.worldbank.org/en/news/feature/2014/03/22/mundo-sin-pobreza-leccion-brasil-mundo-bolsa-familia (accessed January 2015).

22 Brazilian history books refer to Portuguese America as the *Colonia*, with capital C, as if it was a proper noun.

References

Alexandre, V. 1993. *Os sentidos do Império: questão nacional e questão colonial na crise do Antigo Regime português*, Porto.

Almeida, P. R. de. 2001. *Formação da diplomacia econômica no Brasil: as relações econômicas internacionais do Império*, São Paulo.

Antonil, A. J. 1711. *Cultura e opulencia do Brasil, por suas drogas e minas*. Critical edition and French translation by A. Mansuy, Paris 1968 (English trans., *Brazil at the Dawn of the Eighteenth Century*, prefaced by S. B. Schwartz, Dartmouth, MA, 2012).

Arantes, O. and P. E. Arantes. 1997. *Sentido da formação*, Rio de Janeiro.

Arida, P. and A. Lara-Resende. 1984. 'Inertial inflation and monetary reform in Brazil', paper prepared for the Conference 'Inflation and Indexation', Institute of International Economics, Washington, DC, December 6–8, 1–31.

Arruda, J. J. de. 1980. *O Brasil no comércio colonial*. São Paulo.

Azevedo, J. L. de. 1929. *Épocas de Portugal econômico*, Lisbon.

Baer, W. 1979. *The Brazilian Economy: Its Growth and Development*, Columbus, OH (3rd Brazilian edn., *A economia brasileira*, São Paulo, 2009).

Bairoch, P. 1976. *Commerce extérieur et développement économique de l'Europe au XIXe siècle*, Paris.

Barbosa, R. 1893. *Finanças e política da República: discursos e escritos*, Rio de Janeiro.

Barros, R. P. de, M. de Carvalho, S. Franco and R. Mendonça. 2006. 'Uma análise das principais causas da queda recente na desigualdade de renda brasileira', Texto 1203, IPEA, Brasília.

Beiguelman, P. 1968. *A Formação do povo no complexo cafeeiro: aspectos politicos*, São Paulo.

Bethell, L. 1970. *The Abolition of the Brazilian Slave Trade: Britain, Brazil and the Slave Trade Question, 1807–1869*, Cambridge.

Bethell, L. 2010. 'Brazil and Latin America', *Journal of Latin American Studies* 42 (3), 457–85.

Bonfim, M. 1993. *América Latina: males de origem*, Rio de Janeiro.

Bresser Pereira, L. C. 2014. *A construção política do Brasil*, São Paulo.

Bresser-Pereira, L. C. and Y. Nakano. 1984. 'Fatores aceleradores, mantenedores e sancionadores da inflação', *Revista de Economia Política* 4 (1), 5–21.

Cain, P. J. and A. G. Hopkins. 2014. *British Imperialism, 1688–2000*, London.

Calogeras, J. P. 1910. *La politique monétaire du Brésil*, Rio de Janeiro.

Calogeras, J. P. 1930. *Formação Histórica do Brasil*, Rio de Janeiro.

Canabrava, A. P. 1951. *O desenvolvimento da cultura do algodão na província de São Paulo, 1861–1875*, São Paulo.

Candido de Mello e Souza, A. 1959. *Formação da literatura brasileira: momentos decisivos*, São Paulo.

Capistrano de Abreu, J. 1907. *Capítulos da história colonial*, Rio de Janeiro (English trans., *Chapters of Brazil's Colonial History, 1500–1800*, New York, 1997).

Cardoso, A. 2010. *A construção da sociedade do trabalho no Brasil: uma investigação sobre a persistência secular das desigualdades*, Rio de Janeiro.

Cardoso, F. H. 1964. *Empresário industrial e desenvolvimento econômico no Brasil*, São Paulo.

Cardoso, F. H. and E. Faletto. 1969. *Dependency and Development in Latin America*, Berkeley, CA, 1979.

Carvalho Franco, M. S. de. 1964. *Homens livres na ordem escravocrata*, São Paulo.

Castro, J. de. 1946. *La alimentación en los Trópicos*, Mexico City.

da Silva Ferraz, A. M. 1865. *Relatório da Comissão encarregada pelo Governo Imperial de proceder a um inquérito sobre as causas principais e acidentes da crise de setembro, 1864*, Rio de Janeiro.

Dean, W. 1965. 'The Economic Growth of Brazil, by Celso Furtado', *Luso-Brazilian Review* 2 (2), 105–7.

Dean, W. 1995. *With Broadax and Firebrand: The Destruction of the Brazilian Atlantic Forest*, Los Angeles, CA.

Dinius, O. 2011. *Brazil's Steel City: Developmentalism, Strategic Power, and Industrial Relations in Volta Redonda, 1941–1964*, Stanford, CA.

Dutra Fonseca, P. C. 2004. 'Gênese e precursores do desenvolvimentismo no Brasil', *Pesquisa & Debate* 15 (26), 225–56.

Eltis, D. and D. Richardson. 2010. *Atlas of the Transatlantic Slave Trade*, London.

Faria, V. and J. Potter. 1998. 'Television, Telenovelas, and Fertility Change in North-East Brazil', in R. Leete, ed., *Dynamics of Values in Fertility Change*, Oxford.

Ferreira Soares, S. 1860. *Notas estatisticas sobre a produção agricola e carestia dos generos alimenticios no Imperio do Brasil*, Rio de Janeiro.

Fishlow, A. 1972. 'Brazilian Size Distribution of Income', *American Economic Review* 62 (2), 391–402.

Freyre, G. 1933. *The Masters and the Slaves*, New York 1946.

Freyre, G. 1937. *Nordeste: Aspectos da influência da cana sobre a vida e a paisagem do Nordeste do Brasil*, Rio de Janeiro.

Freyre, G. 1945. *Interpretación del Brasil*, Mexico City.

Furtado, C. 1959. *Formação econômica do Brasil*, Rio de Janeiro.

Furtado, C. 1963. *The Economic Growth of Brazil: A Survey from Colonial to Modern Times*, Westport, CT, 1984.

Graham, D. and S. B. de Holanda Filho. 1984. *Migrações internas no Brasil, 1872–1970*, Brasília.

Graham, R. 1968. *Britain and the Onset of Modernization in Brazil, 1850–1914*, Cambridge.

Hoffmann, R. 2001. 'Distribuição de renda e crescimento econômico', *Estudos Avançados* 15 (41), 67–76.

Hoffmann, R. and J. C. Duarte. 1972. 'A distribuição da renda no Brasil', *Revista de Administração de Empresas* 12 (2), 46–66.

Holanda, S. B. de. 1936. *Raízes do Brasil*, Rio de Janeiro (English trans., *Roots of Brazil*, Notre Dame, IN, 2012).

Holanda, S. B. de. 1941. *Memórias de um colono no Brasil – 1850*, São Paulo.

Holanda, S. B. de. 1945. *Monções*, Rio de Janeiro.

Holanda, S. B. de. 1957. *Caminhos e fronteiras*, Rio de Janeiro.

IEDI. 2007. *Desindustrialização e os dilemas do crescimento econômico recente*, São Paulo.

Kitching, G. 1989. *Development and Underdevelopment in Historical Perspective*, London.

Lahmeyer Lobo, E. 1978. *História do Rio de Janeiro: do capital comercial ao capital industrial e financeiro*, Rio de Janeiro.

Lamounier, M. L. 2012. *Ferrovias e mercado de trabalho no Brasil no século XIX*, São Paulo.

Leite Lopes, J. S. 1975. 'Sobre o debate da distribuição da renda: leitura crítica de um artigo de Fishlow', in R. Tolipan and A. C. Tinelli, eds., *A controvérsia sobre distribuição de renda e desenvolvimento*, Rio de Janeiro.

Lopes, F. 1984. 'Inflação inercial, hiperinflação e desinflação', *Revista da ANPEC* 7, 55–71.

Luna, F. V. and H. S. Klein. 2014. *The Economic and Social History of Brazil since 1889*, Cambridge.

Luz, N. V. 1978. *A luta pela industrialização do Brasil*, 2nd edn., São Paulo.

Magalhães Godinho, V. 1950. 'Problèmes d'économie atlantique. Le Portugal, flottes du sucre et flottes de l'or (1670–1770)', *Annales* 5 (2), 184–97.

Magalhães Godinho, V. 1955. *Prix et monnaies au Portugal, 1750–1850*, Paris.

Magalhães Godinho, V. 1963. *Os descobrimentos e a economia mundial*, Lisbon.

Manchester, A. K. 1933. *British Preeminence in Brazil*, Chapel Hill, NC.

Marchant, A. 1940. *The Economic Relations of Portuguese and Indians in the Settlement of Brazil, 1500–1580*, Baltimore, MD.

Marchant, A. 1965. *Viscount Maua and the Empire of Brazil: A Biography of Irineu Evangelista de Sousa, 1813–1889*, Berkeley, CA.

Martins, L. 1976. *Pouvoir et développement économique*, Paris.

Mauro, F. 1960. *Le Portugal et l'Atlantique au XVIIe siècle, 1570–1670: étude économique*, Paris.

Mauro, F. 1970. *Etudes économiques sur l'expansion portugaise, 1500–1900*, Paris.

Mauro, F., ed. 1973. *Histoire quantitative du Brésil, 1800–1930*, Paris.

Mendes, M. 2014. *Por que o Brasil cresce pouco?*, São Paulo.

Menezes e Souza, J. C. de. 1875. *Theses sobre a colonização do Brasil*, Rio de Janeiro.

Motta, M. and P. Zarth, eds. 2008. *Formas de resistência camponesa: visibilidade e diversidade de conflitos ao longo da história*, Brasília.

Nabuco, J. 1883. *Abolitionism: The Brazilian Antislavery Struggle*, Champaign, IL, 1977.

Nakano, Y. 1982. 'Recessão e inflação', *Revista de Economia Política* 2 (2), 133–7.

Nakatani, P., R. N. Faleiros and N. C. Vargas. 2012. 'Histórico e os limites da reforma agrária na contemporaneidade brasileira', *Serviço Social & Sociedade* 110, 213–40.

Neri, M. 2011. *A nova classe média*, Rio de Janeiro.

Normano, J. F. 1935. *Brazil, a Study of Economic Types*, Chapel Hill, NC.

Novais, F. A. 1979. *Portugal e Brasil na Crise do Antigo Sistema Colonial, 1777–1808*, São Paulo.

Oliveira Viana, F. J. de. 1923. *Evolução do povo brasileiro*, São Paulo.

Oliveira, F. de. 1972. *A Economia brasileira: crítica à razão dualista*, Petrópolis, RJ.

Paim, A., ed. 1982. *Pombal na cultura brasileira*, Rio de Janeiro.

Paiva Abreu, M. de. ed. 2014. *A ordem do progresso: dois séculos de política econômica no Brasil*, Rio de Janeiro.
Paiva, C. A. et al. 2012. *Publicação crítica do recenseamento geral do Império do Brasil de 1872*, Belo Horizonte.
Pedreira, J. M. 1994. *Estrutura industrial e mercado colonial. Portugal e Brasil, 1780–1830*, Lisbon.
Pedreira, J. M. 2011. 'A Indústria', in P. Lains and A. Ferreira da Silva, eds., *História económica de Portugal*, Lisbon, vol. 1.
Perdigão Malheiro, A. M. 1864–67. *A escravidão no Brasil: ensaio histórico, jurídico, social*, Rio de Janeiro.
Prado, C. Jr. 1933. *A evolução política do Brasil – Colôna e Império*, São Paulo.
Prado, C. Jr. 1942. *Formação do Brasil contemporâneo*, São Paulo (English trans., *Colonial Background of Modern Brazil*, Berkeley, CA, 1967).
Prado, C. Jr. 1945. *História econômica do Brasil*, São Paulo (enlarged edn., 1970).
Prado, C. Jr. 1966. *A Revolução brasileira*, São Paulo.
Rangel, I. 1963. *A inflação brasileira*, Rio de Janeiro.
Rebouças, A. 1883. *Agricultura nacional: estudos econômicos: propaganda abolicionista e democrática, 1874–1883*, Recife, 1988.
Renda Vitorino, A. J. 2008. 'Política, agricultura e a reconversão do capital do tráfico transatlântico de escravos para as finanças brasileiras na década de 1850', *Economia e sociedade* 17 (3), 461–92.
Schwartz, S. B. 1986. *Sugar Plantations in the Formation of Brazilian Society: Bahia 1550–1835*, Cambridge.
Simonsen, R. 1937. *História econômica do Brasil, 1500–1820*, São Paulo.
Singer, A. 2009. 'Raízes sociais e ideológicas do lulismo', *Novos Estudos* 85, 83–102.
Skidmore, T. E. 1998. 'Studying the History of Latin America: A Case of Hemispheric Convergence', *Latin American Research Review* 33 (1), 105–27.
Souza, J. 2003. *A construção social da subcidadania: para uma sociologia política da modernidade periférica*, Belo Horizonte.
Tannenbaum, F. 1946. *Slave and Citizen, the Negro in the Americas*, New York.
Taunay, A. de E. 1929–41. *História do café no Brasil*, Rio de Janeiro.
Tavares, M. da C. 1972. *Auge e declínio do processo de substituição de importações no Brasil*, Rio de Janeiro.
Turner, F. J. 1893. 'The Significance of the Frontier in American History', *Report of the American Historical Association*, Chicago, IL, 199–227.
Varnhagen, F. A. de. 1854–57. *História geral do Brasil*, Rio de Janeiro.
Vilela, A. V. and W. Suzigan. 2001. *Política do governo e crescimento da economia brasileira*, Brasília.
Viotti da Costa, E. 1966. *Da Senzala à Colônia*, São Paulo.
von Mettenheim, K. 2015. *Monetary Statecraft in Brazil*, London, forthcoming.
Weller, L. 2015. " 'Rothschilds' Delicate and Difficult Task": Reputation, Political Instability, and the Brazilian Rescue Loans of the 1890s', *Enterprise & Society* 16 (2), 381–412.

23

BEYOND A FOOTNOTE

Indigenous scholars and the writing of West African economic history

Ayodeji Olukoju[1]

Given the size and diversity of West Africa, charting the trends in, and the contours of, the historiography of its economic history, especially that written by indigenous scholars, is challenging.[2] The sub-region's fifteen sovereign countries vary in size and population, and have diverse historical experiences and intellectual traditions, partly because they have been under different European colonizers. Its peoples speak three European official languages – French, English and Portuguese – in addition to hundreds of indigenous languages. Tackling the multifaceted subject matter of economic history is further complicated by the range and diversity of the literature.

A striking feature of West African economic history is that the bulk of the literature has been contributed by scholars from the North. Contributions by indigenes of the sub-region – based at home and in various Western universities and research centres – have been largely focused on the important job of providing case studies and gap-filling in the historiography. While the bulk of this literature has been dependent on "thick descriptions and analytical narratives," there are notable exceptions of serious engagements at the individual and institutional levels with theory and concepts (Green and Nyambara 2015: 7; but compare Austin 2015).[3] The writings of indigenous economic historians of West Africa centre largely on the following themes – production, exchange (local and long distance trade), labour, population, transport, money and government policy – especially in the context of European colonialism. As West African colonies exported minerals and commodities – groundnuts, cocoa, palm produce and timber – much attention has been devoted to analysing their production and export.[4]

The scholarship of West African economic historians has been informed by received wisdom from the West ranging from classical and neoclassical economics through dependency theory to Marxism. As Saito (2015: 1) notes with reference to Japan, the "field took shape under Western influences and, as a history discipline." Yet, (as one of my West African colleagues stated in a private conversation) the publications of indigenous economic historians, even in mainstream Western outlets, are generally cited by their Western counterparts as *sources* rather than for the *arguments* advanced in them. This chapter attempts to rescue some of the contributions by West Africans themselves from the obscurity of footnotes. The task is frustrated by the absence of earlier reviews of the economic history of West Africa though numerous recent surveys of literature at the continental level provide some guidance.[5]

The profile of West African economic history

In general terms, West African economic history has been approached from two broad perspectives – the mainstream orthodox and the marginal radical. Most indigenous economic historians operate within the conventional domestic historical methodology, which is largely narrative and non-theoretical. As demonstrated in this chapter, the bulk of the literature on West African economic history follows the Western European tradition of historical scholarship, exemplified by A.G. Hopkins, the acknowledged leading authority on the subject. Conversely, a radical political economy streak runs through indigenous scholarship in the region. This is informed by the dependency and radical Marxist approaches. Walter Rodney's influential book (1972) set the tone for much of the radical scholarship of the 1970s and after. Apart from Rodney, Frantz Fanon was an ideological mentor of the radical scholars of West Africa.[6] An early centre of incubation for the radical political economy approach was the Department of History at the Ahmadu Bello University, Zaria, Nigeria. The Zaria School focused on history from below, labour and class struggles, and a radical reinterpretation of the nexus between the colonial state and colonial political economy. In opposition to colonial historiography, its forte was a methodology that encouraged the use of a wide range of sources, both written and non-written, in historical reconstruction. It denounced the fetish for, or overreliance upon, written sources and subjected all sources, especially archival material, to rigorous analysis. Zaria was noted for the radical historical scholarship of Yusufu Bala Usman and his disciples (such as Monday Mangvwat and Ibrahim Abdullah), and influenced by the Dar es Salaam School, two of whom, as resident members, authored a critique of African historiography (Temu and Swai 1981). Zaria was a hotbed of radical scholarship in the 1970s and 1980s, and Bala Usman, a blue blood turned radical, literally personified a new brand of historical scholarship. His writings (for example Usman 1981) applied interdisciplinarity (blending history, sociology, political science and economics) and historical materialism to the analysis of historical conditions and concrete social formations in his native Islamic Northern Nigeria and in Nigeria at large. Émigrés like the historian Bill Freund and the sociologist Patrick Wilmot added the American and Caribbean flavour to the intellectual ferment at Zaria in the 1970s and the 1980s. Non-radical scholars, such as Joseph Inikori, also contributed to the making of the Zaria brand of historical scholarship. An interdisciplinary journal, *Savannah*, was a respected outlet for the output of scholarship coming out of Zaria. The only drawback was, and remains, the insularity of this school: most of its publications, though generally of high quality, were published locally.

Nonetheless, the influence of the Zaria School extended to other parts of Nigeria. It was complemented by the mentorship of a younger group of economic historians at the University of Ife, notably Toyin Falola and Akanmu Adebayo, and by the Marxist historian, Segun Osoba (1969, 1978). But while both Falola (1984, 1987) and Adebayo (1993) adopted the radical political economy approach, they have also been eclectic in some of their other publications. As shown later in this chapter, the Zaria–Ife radical school was a riposte to the conventional approach at the University of Lagos and elsewhere.

The economic history of the West African sub-region, as elsewhere in Africa, has the following characteristics.[7] First, the field has been dominated by historians but a fair proportion of the literature is derived from studies carried out primarily in other fields, such as geography, anthropology, agricultural economics and political science. Second, most mainstream economic historians are not preoccupied with testing hypotheses or applying economic theory as such. This is assumed to be the province of economists and other social scientists.

This reflects an unwritten "cleavage in universities that divided history from economics and took the economic segment into technical complexities that escaped the interest, as well as the grasp, of most historians" (Hopkins 2009: 157). However, interdisciplinarity is widespread as economic historians cross disciplinary boundaries for data and analytical tools. Third, there is no sharp dichotomy between social and economic history. Histories of labour and urbanization, for example, straddle the divide between social and economic history. It is at this intersection that radical political economy has made notable scholarly interventions. Some of the outstanding publications on West African economic history have centred on pawnship, labour migrations, wages and the cost of living, strikes, labour unionization and urbanization. Fourth, research and publishing have been constrained by the linguistic and colonial boundaries within which scholars operate. With only a few exceptions (Adamu 1978; Olukoju 2000, 2010; Adebayo 2007), West African historians tend to focus on issues within their national boundaries. Only a handful of scholars are literate in more than one language.

Fifth, the bulk of the literature consists of microhistories or case studies, articles in learned journals and chapters in collections of essays and monographs, based upon original research and especially the work for postgraduate degrees. A few works of synthesis exist however, set within the mainstream conventional approach to economic history. The two best-known examples are Ekundare (1973) and Agbodeka (1992). The former, by a non-historian, enriched the synthesis of existing literature with primary source material in an attempt to highlight the economic impact of imperialism on a former British colony. In the Foreword to the book, Professor Peter Mathias of Oxford University hailed it as "the first systematic study of the general economic development of Nigeria, including its long pre-colonial story, and, with this, it stands as the first academic economic history of any black African country" (Ekundare 1973: xvii). Significantly, the feat has not been replicated by specialist economic historians.

Sixth, the spatial and gender distribution of practitioners is uneven. The field is male-dominated with only a handful of female practitioners. However, female scholars (Ekejiuba 1967; Awe 1973, 2001; Ikpe 1994; Apena 1997; Odotei 2002a, 2002b; Chuku 2005) have made significant contributions. Their publications highlight the often neglected gender dimension in the indigenous political economy, with emphasis on women's roles in warfare, entrepreneurship, artisanal fisheries and the food economy. Moreover, only a few departments (such as Lagos) have a cluster of economic (and social) historians. Otherwise, expertise is either thinly spread in Departments of History or non-existent. Finally, the vast bulk of the literature has been contributed by expatriate scholars based in Western countries, mainly France, the United Kingdom, Canada and the United States of America. This can be verified by the number of contributions in leading Africanist journals, publications by major publishing houses and major scholarly conferences – all domiciled in the North – and the citations in those scholarly works. Indigenous West Africans generally play a marginal role in these scholarly activities. This is largely a reflection of gaps in training and in the curriculum in West African universities, the balance of power and resources in the global economy, the brain drain from the sub-region to the West, and insufficient engagement of indigenous West African scholars with global narratives.

The rest of this chapter highlights the institutional framework for teaching and scholarship in West African economic history. It then discusses in more detail the contributions of indigenous scholars in both foreign and local outlets. Nigeria, which has more than half the overall population and tertiary institutions in West Africa, accounts for a preponderance of the literature considered.

Institutional structure for the study and teaching of economic history

Across West Africa, economic history as an academic discipline is domiciled in the Department of History at each of the major universities. It is taught in the Departments of Economics of some universities, but only as a marginal course and, in any case, differently from the approach in the History Departments. In Nigeria, for example, Olufemi Ekundare, Eno Usoro and Philip Elegalam taught the subject at the universities of Ife (now Obafemi Awolowo University), Ibadan and Lagos, respectively, in the 1970s–1990s. Until the 1980s, the discipline of History in West Africa was dominated by specialists in political, administrative and cultural history, mainly focused on the pre-colonial and colonial periods. Only a handful of specialists in social and economic history, both indigenous and expatriate, taught in those departments. A striking illustration of this marginality or non-existence of economic history as a speciality was the domination of the influential Ibadan History Series by studies of colonial conquest and administration, the spread and impact of Christian and Islamic missions, and the impact of colonialism and formal education on indigenous societies. The Ibadan History Series was grounded in the tradition of nationalist historiography and focused more on internal (as opposed to external) dynamics in explaining developments in African history but it did validate the use of oral sources.

In general, both indigenous and expatriate scholars of West African history focused largely on non-economic issues.The tendency was replicated at other sub-regional intellectual powerhouses: Legon (Ghana), Fourah Bay (Sierra Leone) and Dakar (Senegal). There were, of course, notable exceptions, such as Dike (1956), Aderibigbe (1962), Ikime (1968), Alagoa (1970) and Daaku (1970), all situated within the trade and politics genre of studies pioneered by Dike. Ikime's *Merchant Prince of the Niger Delta* (1968) centred on the career of Nana Olomu, an Itsekiri merchant, in the wider context of the international trade in palm produce, the dynamics of indigenous entrepreneurship and inter-group relations. The trade and politics studies might be described as an early form of orthodox or liberal political economy. Strands of economic history also appeared in other texts primarily devoted to warfare, political and administrative issues.

The late 1970s and early 1980s marked a major transition in the development of economic history in West Africa. Two contemporaneous internal developments took place – the rise of radical scholarship as explained above and the loss of status of the discipline of History as a privileged subject. The euphoria of independence having worn off, the passion for History, an ally in the decolonization process, waned. Indeed, in Nigeria, the subject was taken off the junior secondary school syllabus during the regime of General Ibrahim Babangida (1985–93). Social Studies soon proved a poor replacement, and both official and popular interest in History never recovered from that setback. University enrolment plummeted as History graduates were not as sought after for jobs in the bureaucracy and diplomatic service as they had been in previous decades. In effect, economic history was merely a branch of a marginal discipline in many West African universities.

Using Nigeria as a West African paradigm, it can be stated that the training of personnel in economic history in the sub-region has not been systematic. Until the 1980s, no institution had a notable reputation for teaching and producing specialists in the subject. The first generation of specialists obtained their higher degrees from the universities of Birmingham, UK, Wisconsin (Madison), USA, and Toronto, Canada, in the late 1960s and early 1970s. While Wale Oyemakinde obtained a Master's degree in Economics from Madison after a Doctorate in History at Ibadan, Babatunde Agiri (supervised by Philip Curtin), Walter Ofonagoro and Deji Ogunremi earned their Doctorates in History at the universities of

Wisconsin at Madison, Toronto and Birmingham, respectively, on such subjects as agriculture, trade, currency and transport. It is significant that those who studied at Birmingham were supervised by A.G. Hopkins, the well-known leading authority on West African economic history. This background in mainstream European scholarship explains why the approach to economic history in Nigeria and elsewhere in West Africa has been orthodox rather than radical, and without much grounding in theory. But, as indicated in the case of the Zaria School, external influences came from other directions – ideas from Marx, Fanon and Rodney – and personnel from the Dar es Salaam School.

As for the teaching of economic history in West African universities, the subject was for long subsumed in regional surveys or national topics. However, discrete courses on economic history were introduced into the curriculum from the mid-1970s. In this connection, the Department of History at the University of Lagos, noted for its specialization in applied or utilitarian history, was a trailblazer in many respects.[8] First, it employed a number of early specialists in the field – Oyemakinde (railway labour history), Ofonagoro (foreign trade and politics), Agiri (agricultural history) and Ogunremi (transport). These were later joined by a younger generation – Adebayo Lawal (financial history), Kehinde Faluyi (trade and agriculture) and Ayodeji Olukoju (maritime, transport and social history). These scholars were recruited primarily to teach general courses on Nigeria, Africa and its sub-regions, and the wider world, mainly Europe, the United States and Asia. However, there is no specific unifying theme in the scholarship produced by them beyond a common focus on Nigerian, African and comparative economic history. All have, however, utilized oral sources, newspapers, private papers and archival material (in English) in local and foreign repositories. The use and interpretation of multiple source material is the forte of this group of economic historians.

Second, the department at Lagos mounted several undergraduate and postgraduate courses in economic history. Most notable is the "Introduction to Economic History" course taken by students of the Faculties of Arts, Business Administration and Social Sciences. This has remained a compulsory and popular course for students of the Faculty of Business Administration. The importance attached to economic history in the department's undergraduate and postgraduate programmes is underscored by the fact that the subject is offered at every level and that specialist areas in economic history are taught as distinct courses. Among these are business history (final year), maritime history (a first for West Africa) at two levels, economic history of West Africa (before 1800, during the nineteenth century and since 1900), comparative history of developing economies and US economic history (colonial period to 1945). At the postgraduate level, ten courses are listed on the economic history of pre-colonial, colonial and contemporary Africa, economic history of Lagos, Latin America and Asia, and of the advanced economies.

Third, the department produced a course text on economic history (Olukoju et al. 2003), its chapters based on a synthesis of secondary literature and original research by individual contributors. Members of the department also contributed most of the chapters in a major textbook on West African economic history (Ogunremi and Faluyi 1996). Both textbooks are widely used in many Nigerian universities. Fourth, the economic history section has produced several notable doctoral theses, including one on national government budgets that was judged the best in the Humanities category in Nigerian universities (Ogunyemi 2008). On the basis of the foregoing, the Department of History, University of Lagos, prides itself as the leading centre of economic history in Nigeria. In addition to scholarly contributions by members of staff in the 1970s and 1980s (Oyemakinde,1975, 1977; Ofonagoro 1975, 1979a, 1979b; Ogunremi 1975, 1976, 1982; and Agiri 1974, 1977, 1983–84), a later generation

(Lawal, Faluyi, Olukoju and Iwuagwu), has produced significant publications on local and foreign themes in economic history. Activities in Lagos are complemented by work done elsewhere in Nigeria. Onwuka Njoku, Akinola Olorunfemi, Ben Naanen and Olutayo Adesina based at Nsukka, Ile-Ife, Port Harcourt and Ibadan, respectively, have taught courses and supervised doctoral theses in economic history. Only Naanen (1991, 1993) has been influenced by the radical political economy approach in his publications. Others have published important articles in mainstream Western journals and other outlets on agriculture, international trade and road transport (Njoku 1978, 1979; Olorunfemi 1981a, 1981b, 1984).

West African universities vary in terms of course offerings in economic history. Ahmadu Bello University, Zaria, offers eight undergraduate courses in economic history on West Africa; comparative history of industrialization; trade and politics in the Niger-Benue Valley; and on Africa and European imperialism. The University of Jos in northcentral Nigeria also has eight economic history courses on its history curriculum including comparative economic history; history of economic thought; Nigeria in the twentieth century; the African Union and African regional economic blocs; and land and labour in Africa. At the University of Nigeria, Nsukka, five courses are taught on economic history including West Africa in the twentieth century; comparative industrialization (USA, USSR, Japan and China); regional economic development in Africa; and economic history of Nigeria since 1800. Ibadan typifies the marginality of economic history by offering the fewest undergraduate courses, "Economic History of West Africa Since 1800" and "Development: Concepts and Realities in The Third World." "The Industrial Process and Economy of Colonial West Africa, 1885–1960" and "Economic Cooperation in West Africa since 1958" are taught at the postgraduate level.[9]

The foregoing survey indicates that generally, political/administrative history is dominant in the curriculum at the expense of economic and social history. Second, with the exception of the introductory or survey courses, economic history is offered only in the last two years at the undergraduate level. Third, there is a common interest in comparative industrialization and economic integration.

In terms of institution building in economic history, there is no pan-West African specialist journal or professional association. In Nigeria, however, Ogunremi spearheaded the founding of the Nigerian Economic History Society, which published several issues of the now rested *Nigerian Journal of Economic History*.[10] Edited by Tayo Adesina, it published 58 articles between 1998 and 2005, when it went into abeyance. The journal did cover wide-ranging and interesting topics stretching from the pre-colonial period to contemporary times. With the exception of a few articles on Latin America, Nigeria–Japanese trade relations, Sierra Leone and the Cameroun, the journal was essentially Nigerian. Though some non-Nigerians published in it, the journal does not appear to have had much impact beyond the country in terms of either the submission of articles or readership. That it has been suspended speaks volumes about the limits of the organizational capacity of economic historians in West Africa's biggest country.

Compared to Nigeria, much less appears to have been achieved elsewhere in West Africa. The University of Ghana at Legon, for example, offers only two undergraduate courses, while it has only just designed (but has not mounted) a postgraduate course on Global Economic History.[11] Undergraduate teaching material includes Hopkins's well-known *An Economic History of West Africa* (1973), and textbooks and articles written by both Western and indigenous scholars in learned journals. A Special Paper ("The Economic History of the Gold Coast") aims to "expose students to the main contours of the economic history of the Gold Coast from 1850 to 1957" and to train them in the use of material from the Public Records and Archives. History Departments at other Ghanaian universities also offer survey courses in economic history. A notable feature of the discipline in Ghana is that there are no major specialists in economic history in History Departments. Agbodeka, author of the aforementioned monograph on the economic history of Ghana, and Addo-Fening (1976), did not specialize in economic history.

Some of the most outstanding work on the domestic economy has been done by anthropologists with a bias for history. Those on trade and markets (Ukwu 1967; Arhin 1970, 1979, 1980) rank among the best in the entire region. The contribution of anthropologists was both theoretical and empirical. On the one hand, French anthropologists, notably Claude Meillassoux, influenced the analysis of indigenous social formations, applying the mode of production analysis. On the other, orthodox anthropologists, such as Arhin, Ukwu and Ekejiuba, made use of written and non-written sources, including oral sources, in their study of economic history.

The Department of History at the Cheikh Anta Diop University in Dakar, Senegal, is best known for its expertise in social history. Yet, its faculty has made significant contributions to the economic history of the Senegal basin. Perhaps the best-known historian in this regard is Boubacar Barry, who has produced some truly outstanding publications (Barry 1988a, 1988b,1998, 1985). His main monograph on Senegambia and the slave trade was also published in English by Cambridge University Press. He argued influentially that the slave trade resulted in economic regression, violence, the increased use of slave labour, loss of autonomy and the centralization of royal power in the region. The area lost population and those remaining were more vulnerable to poverty, violence and climate. Other scholars too have written on aspects of Senegalese and West African economic history (Thioub 1994, 2003; Thioub et al. 1998). Courses offered in the department include those (taught by Mamadou Fall) on "The Credit Market in West Africa during Colonial Days"; "Trade and Merchant Diaspora in Senegambia from the XVIIth to XXth centuries"; "The Labor Market and Informal Sector in Senegal"; "Random Capitalism or the Capitalist Experience of the Mourides of Senegal" and "Economic History of Mozambique in Modern World Economy XVth–XXth centuries."

Milestones in indigenous contributions to West African economic history

Contributions by some indigenous scholars represent milestones in the development of West African economic history. Most are national or sub-national in their coverage and there are also sub-regional collections of essays on a common subject, such as indigenous markets, currencies and trade. Kenneth Dike's seminal book (Dike 1956) is generally accepted as marking the birth of modern West African economic history. Its major contribution was the methodological innovation of using oral sources to interpret the history of trade, state formation and politics of the Lower Niger Delta and its hinterland. Reversing the focus on expatriate factors and actors as the subject of historical inquiry, it highlighted the importance of local actors and dynamics. The focus on trade and politics has also kindled the interest of historians and anthropologists in the indigenous commercial systems. Studies by the anthropologists Arhin in Ghana, and Ukwu and Ekejiuba in Nigeria shed light on market periodicity, capital formation, gender relations and indigenous entrepreneurship.

A complement to the engagement with indigenous systems of production and trade is the examination of transnational and continental issues including the trans-Atlantic slave trade and the external commodity trades during the colonial period. With regard to the former, there are several major case studies (Bathily 1986 and Barry 1988a, 1988b, 1998 for Senegambia) of the volume of the trans-Atlantic slave trade, its political, social and economic impact, resistance to slavery, and the process and consequences of Abolition. Inikori (1976a,

1976b, 1977, 1992) is a major contributor to the literature both in terms of quantifying the volume of slave exports and the linkage between gun imports and slave exports. He also linked the slave trade and West African history with British industrialization, partially rehabilitating the famous Williamson thesis (Inikori 2002).

West Africa's external trade in the context of colonial rule is a major theme in the literature. Most publications, including those influenced by dependency analysis (Olukoju 2003, 2004a, 2008), have focused on individual countries either in relation to the colonial power or the world market. They are useful for quantifying the volume and analysing the patterns of commercial relations in the contexts of world wars, trade cycles and colonialism. Economic historians of West Africa have examined aspects of colonial finances, including the demonetization of indigenous and non-imperial currencies, currency boards and colonial currencies, and financial administration (Ofonagoro 1979b; Lawal 1983/84, 1989, 1998; Naanen 1993). Related issues of the cultural and economic value of money, and the counterfeiting of colonial currencies also engaged scholarly attention (Falola 1997; Falola and Adebayo 2000; Olukoju 2002, 2010). These studies, and most of those by Western scholars, were produced within the conventional paradigm that is narrative and archive-based. Historians and financial experts with a bias for history have also made notable contributions in the study of banking and finance (Uche 1995, 2010).

Alongside preoccupation with the colonial economy, attention has been devoted to the workings of the indigenous economy. Capital and capital formation in the indigenous economy, especially indigenous entrepreneurship, the organization of trade (caravans) and trade diasporas have been examined in various studies (Adamu 1978; Dike and Ekejiuba 1990). Worth noting are Nwabughuogu's article (1984b), on *isusu* (thrift and rotating credit) among the Igbo, and Falola's essays (1989, 1991, 1993) on money-lending, the caravan system and tolls in Western Nigeria. Business biographies are an important dimension of indigenous entrepreneurship, a major topic. These cover various female and male entrepreneurs involved in colonial era export and import trade, money-lending, real estate development and agriculture (Ekejiuba 1967; Ikime 1968; Awe 2001; Njoku 2008).

Studies of external trade account for the bulk of the contributions by indigenous economic historians of West Africa (Olorunfemi 1980, 1981a, 1981b). The dependence of West African colonial economies on commodity exports is reflected in the volume of work done on such items as groundnuts (Senegal and Northern Nigeria), cotton (Sahelian West Africa), cocoa (Côte d'Ivoire, Ghana and Nigeria) and palm produce (Nigeria and Sierra Leone). Commodity imports too have attracted attention. Foreign liquors, for example, assumed great significance in the face of the prohibition policies of various colonial governments. Important studies on fiscal, cultural and social aspects of the imported liquor trade in Nigeria and Ghana have been undertaken by Olorunfemi (1984), Olukoju (1991, 1996, 1997), Korieh (2003) and Akyeampong (1996). The Nigerian studies have featured a lively debate between Olukoju and Simon Heap (1998, 1999) on aspects of the liquor traffic in colonial Nigeria. These studies employ the same sources (mainly archival) and ideas as their expatriate counterparts.

Next to trade, agricultural economic history appears to have attracted the widest interest. This genre is represented by single-crop studies of cotton, cocoa, cassava and the oil palm.[12] Much of this work emanated from postgraduate theses and dissertations completed in local and foreign universities. The introduction of cash crops (Agiri 1977) and exotic food crops to Africa, and the dynamics of the food crop economy and culture (Ikpe 1994; Korieh 2007) attracted some scholarly contributions. Ohadike (1981) established a linkage between the influenza pandemic of 1918/19 and the spread of cassava in South Central Nigeria. His conclusions have, however, been challenged (Iwuagwu 2012), in one of the intellectual skirmishes involving indigenous scholars in the field. These studies enjoy the leverage of insider knowledge of the cultural dimensions of the subject and milieu under consideration.

Allusion has been made to the conflation of economic and social history in West Africa. There is no compartmentalization between "core" economic history and "core" social history issues, such as labour (Osoba 1969; Thioub 1994; Abdullah 1997, 1998), criminality (Olukoju 2002), prostitution (Naanen 1991; Aderinto 2015) and urbanization. Labour was an early focus of scholarly research and publishing in West African economic history. Oyemakinde's pioneering study of indigenous labour on the Nigerian railway (Oyemakinde 1970) yielded several important articles on wages, cost of living, unionization and labour militancy in the *Journal of the Historical Society of Nigeria* during its heyday (Oyemakinde 1974, 1977). The pivotal role of transportation as the backbone of the local economy is duly acknowledged in the literature comprising studies in local and national contexts. In Nigeria, for example, scholarly articles have been published on human porterage, road, river and camel transport (Ogunremi 1982), bicycle transport (Nwabughuogu 1984a) and ports and shipping (Olukoju 1992a, 1992b, 1996). Railway transport was an early focus of interest in the context of colonial policy and labour (Oyemakinde 1974, 1975, 1977; Oshin 1991).

The study of seaports and port cities undertaken by economic historians straddle social and economic history. In Nigeria, aspects of port engineering, urbanization, trade, inter-group relations and social change in coastal West Africa, and the Lagos and Port Harcourt seaports have been examined in several publications (Olukoju 1992b, 1994, 1996). Fishing, migrations and coastal trade have been studied by some Nigerian and Ghanaian scholars (Olukoju 2000; Odotei 2002a, 2000b). Trade between the coastal outlets and the hinterland entailed conflict over tolls, terms of trade and embargoes. Sierra Leonian and Nigerian case studies have been produced by Aderibigbe (1962), Ijagbemi (1970) and Cole (2008).

During the 1970s and early 1980s, dependency theory influenced the analyses undertaken by indigenous scholars of the relationship between the metropolitan countries and their colonies. In addition to several microstudies, Falola (1987) produced a landmark collection of essays, mainly by indigenous West Africans. In the same vein, the role of expatriate firms in the colonial economy has received attention and this has generated debates on a "special relationship" between the colonial government and such firms in colonial Nigeria, argued by Olukoju (1992a, 1995, 2011), but disputed by Yearwood (1998). The role of British big business in Nigeria's decolonization has also received attention in the literature (Lawal 1994).

Most economic historians of West Africa tended to shy away from contemporary topics. Steeped in the orthodoxy of the parent Western European historical scholarship, they tended to avoid the post-independence period for which archival records did not open until the 1980s. As Morten Jerven et al. (2012: 16–17) noted, there has been "an informal division of labour between the disciplines whereby economists studied the post-1960 period, while historians were mainly occupied with the pre-1960 period." However, Falola (1987, 1991), Adebayo (1990, 1993), Dibua (2006, 2013), Ogunyemi (2008) and Iwuagwu (2009) are notable exceptions. They dealt with many contemporary issues, such as revenue allocation and budgeting in the context of nation building, devaluation, structural adjustment, development planning, industrial policy and agricultural modernization. Most engaged with radical theories and concepts in opposition to the dominant paradigms of modernization and patrimonialism/neo-patrimonialism in the explanation of Africa's development crisis.

The dominance of post-1960 scholarship by economists, in any case, added analytical depth to the study of West African economic history. This is epitomized by Bade Onimode, a Professor of Economics at Ibadan and a radical political economist, who, as early as 1982, scorned the use of GDP for measuring growth, arguing that it failed to capture "concrete realities on the ground."[13] He dismissed the use of GDP as a mere statistical exercise that did not capture how "development" affected the quality of life of the mass of the people. To be sure, the statistics themselves are not dependable: this is the lynchpin of Morten Jerven's more recent critiques (2012, 2013) of the statistics used for computing GDP in African countries. Such critiques of course have deeper antiquity: Phyllis Deane's (1953) study of East Africa of the 1940s highlighted the problems of applying the concept of GDP to regions where the subsistence sector dominated. And W.F. Stolper's work (1966), in an evocatively titled book on Nigeria's development planning in the 1960s, emphasized the inadequacy and unreliability of the statistics used in calculating GDP. Patrick Manning (chapter 25 in in this volume) highlights disquiet about contemporary measures of African growth where seemingly low rates of increase in GDP per capita are occurring at the same time as other indicators such as health, education and welfare are rising significantly in many regions.

Conclusion

This survey of contributions by indigenous scholars to the writing of West African economic history is by no means exhaustive. It has probably left out much more than it has covered. This is partly a consequence of the considerable volume and dispersion of the literature. Most of the literature focuses on themes of national significance. Nationalist history in some of these works is probably a consequence of the initial association of the discipline of History with the nationalist movements of the 1950s and 1960s, and the influence of dependency theory in the following two decades. The call for historians to embrace the "New Economic History" (Hopkins 2009) won very few converts, perhaps most notably Joseph Inikori, whose contributions to the quantification of the trans-Atlantic slave trade anticipated the new wave to some degree (Inikori 1977, 1992). In the same vein, Wariboko (1998) also demonstrated the possibilities of applying economic theory, this time to the analysis of indigenous politico-economic institutions.

While attempts have been made to challenge received wisdom, these have tended to be intellectual skirmishes rather than sustained challenges on the part of indigenous scholars of West African history. A major exception is Inikori's stellar role in the guns-for-slaves debate, described as "a great controversy in African history" (Whatley 2008: 17). Validating Inikori, Whatley (2008: 19) concluded that "[g]uns-for-slaves is an appropriate characterization of the 18th century British slave trade in Africa. Gunpowder shipments were a powerful determinant of the number of Africans entering the Middle Passage. This result is robust across a variety of econometric specifications." Second, Inikori's review of Phillip Curtin's *The Atlantic Slave Trade: A Census* (Inikori 1992) generated debates between him and Curtin's supporters (Eltis 1995; Richardson and Behrendt 1995) which contributed to the refinement and use of the historical statistics, and threw better light on the impact of the slave trade in Africa.

Much of the literature has in general focused on indigenous agency under colonial rule, utilizing insider knowledge and a rigorous engagement with diverse source material, particularly non-documentary. This is where the broad strength of indigenous scholarship lies, rather than in employing or debating received wisdom informed by econometrics or other similar analysis. In short, given the analytical quality of their work, the outlets of their publications, and the global recognition many of them have won, indigenous economic historians of West Africa deserve much more than occasional mention in footnotes as providers of sources or evidence.[14]

Notes

1 I thank Pat Hudson, Francesco Boldizzoni, Jeremiah Dibua and Ibrahim Abdullah for supplying useful references and for helpful comments on earlier versions of this chapter. The essay is dedicated to the loving memory of my wife, Abosede Omowumi Olukoju, née Olorunda (1961–2014) and my father, Israel Adeniyi Olukoju (1925–2015).

2 For similar recent efforts, see Roy (2014) and Saito (2015). Green and Nyambara (2015) offer illuminating perspectives that are equally applicable to West Africa. Austin (2015) has a more pessimistic view about the quality of African scholarship and has good coverage of West Africa. The inclusion of a wider range of studies (some perhaps strictly outside of economic history, more narrowly conceived), and of offshore-based indigenous West African economic historians allows one to paint a more optimistic picture than Austin.

3 The Zaria School examined in this chapter epitomizes the institutional adoption of a radical perspective while various individual scholars indicated in the text (Osoba, Usman, Onimode, Falola, Adebayo, Abdullah, Dibua and Naanen) have been influenced by radical political economy.

4 Green and Nyambara (2015: 8) summarized the preoccupation of African economic historians as follows: seeking "answers to a broad set of social, political and economic questions on how production is organized, exchanged and distributed as well as how factors of production are allocated."

5 See, for example, Alpers (1973), Hopkins (2009), Austin (2015), and Green and Nyambara (2015).

6 Yusufu Bala Usman, discussed at length below, was radicalized when he stumbled on a copy of Fanon's book at a London train station and stayed till he had finished reading it.

7 Details in Manning 1987: 53.

8 Details in Olukoju (2004b). As indicated in an earlier passage, Lagos had a counterpoise in the Zaria School of the 1970s–1980s.

9 Electronic communication from Professor Olutayo Adesina, Ibadan, Nigeria, March 2015.

10 It is accessible via http://www.africabib.org/query_p.php?pe=!227693256!&SR=3

11 Electronic communication from Dr. Kofi Baku, Legon, Ghana, November 2014.

12 One of the earliest studies, incidentally by a non-historian, is Agboola (1968).

13 I am grateful to Professor Jerry Dibua for this insight (electronic communication, March–May 2015). Onimode (1982) is a highly regarded radical treatise on Nigeria's political economy.

14 Books by Inikori (2002) and Nwokeji (2010), both published by Cambridge University Press, won the prestigious Melville J. Herskovits Book Prize in 2003 and 2011, respectively, while Toyin Falola alone has a catalogue of outstanding publications too numerous to cite here. Toyin Falola (in 2011) and Boubacar Barry (in 2014) won the prestigious Distinguished Africanist Awards of the African Studies Association.

Bibliography

Abdullah, Ibrahim. (1998) "Rethinking African Labour and Working-class History: The Artisan Origins of the Sierra Leonean Working Class," *Social History*, 23 (1): 80–96.

Abdullah, Ibrahim. (1997) "The Colonial State and Wage Labor in Postwar Sierra Leone, 1945–1960: Attempts at Remaking the Working Class," *International Labour and Working-Class History*, 52: 87–105.

Abdullah, Ibrahim. (1992) "Profit versus Social Reproduction: Labor Protests in the Sierra Leonian Iron-Ore Mines, 1933–38," *African Studies Review*, 35 (1): 13–41.

Adamu, Mahdi. (1978) *The Hausa Factor in West African History*, Zaria: Ahmadu Bello University Press.

Adebayo, Akanmu G. (2007) "Currency Devaluation and Rank: The Yoruba and Akan Experiences," *African Studies Review*, 50 (2): 87–109.

Adebayo, Akanmu G. (1994) "Money, Credit, and Banking in Precolonial Africa: The Yoruba Experience," *Anthropos*, 89 (4/6): 379–400.

Adebayo, Akanmu G. (1993) *Embattled Federalism: History of Revenue Allocation in Nigeria, 1946–1990*, London: Peter Lang.

Adebayo, Akanmu G. (1990) "The 'Ibadan School' and the Handling of Federal Finance in Nigeria," *Journal of Modern African Studies*, 28 (2): 245–64.

Aderibigbe, A.B. (1962) "Trade and British Expansion in the Lagos Area in the Second Half of the Nineteenth Century," *Nigerian Journal of Economic and Social Studies*, 4: 188–95.

Aderinto, Saheed. (2015) *When Sex Threatened the State: Illicit Sexuality, Nationalism, and Politics in Colonial Nigeria*, Chicago: University of Illinois Press.

Addo-Fening, Robert. (1976) "The Gold Mining Industry in Akyem-Abuakwa c.1850–1910," *Sankofa* 2: 33–9.

Afigbo, A.E. (1977) "Pre-colonial Trade Links between Southeastern Nigeria and the Benue Valley," *Journal of African Studies*, 4 (2): 119–39.

Agbodeka, Francis. (1992) *An Economic History of Ghana from the Earliest Times*, Accra: Ghana Universities Press.

Agboola, S.A. (1968) "The Introduction and Spread of Cassava in Western Nigeria," *Nigerian Journal of Economic and Social Studies*, 3: 369–86.

Agiri, B.A. (1983–84) "The Development of Wage Labour in Agriculture in Southern Yorubaland 1900–1940," *Journal of the Historical Society of Nigeria*, 12 (1&2): 95–107.

Agiri, B.A. (1977) "The Introduction of *Nitida Kola* (Gbanja Kola) into Nigerian Agriculture, 1880–1920," *African Economic History*, 3: 1–14.

Agiri, B.A. (1974) "Aspects of Socio-Economic Changes among the Awori, Egba and Ijebu Remo Communities during the Nineteenth Century," *Journal of the Historical Society of Nigeria*, 7 (3): 365–83.

Akeredolu-Ale, E.O. (1973) "A Sociohistorical Study of the Development of Entrepreneurship among the Ijebu of Western Nigeria," *African Studies Review*, 16 (3): 347–64.

Akintoye, S.A. (1968) "The Economic Background of the Ekitiparapo, 1978–1893," *Odu*, 4 (2): 30–52.

Akyeampong, Emmanuel. (1996) *Drink, Power, and Cultural Change: A Social History of Alcohol in Ghana, c.1800 to Recent Times*, Portsmouth: Heinemann.

Akyeampong, Emmanuel. (1994) "The State and Alcohol Revenues: Promoting 'Economic Development' in Gold Coast/Ghana, 1919 to the Present," *Histoire Sociale/Social History*, 27 (4): 393–411.

Alagoa, E.J. (1970) "Long-distance Trade and States in the Niger Delta," *Journal of African History*, 11 (3): 319–29.

Alpers, Edward A. (1973) "Rethinking African Economic History," *Ufahamu*, 3 (3): 97–129.

Apena, Adeline. (1997) *Colonization, Commerce and Entrepreneurship in Nigeria: The Western Delta, 1914–1960*, New York: Peter Lang.

Arhin, Kwame. (1980) "The Economic and Social Significance of Rubber Production and Exchange on the Gold and Ivory Coasts, 1880–1900," *Cahiers d'Etudes Africaines*, 20: 49–62.

Arhin, Kwame. (1979) *West African Traders in Ghana in the Nineteenth and Twentieth Centuries*, London: Longman.

Arhin, Kwame. (1970) "Aspects of Ashanti Northern Trade in the Nineteenth Century," *Africa*, 40: 363–73.

Austin, Gareth. (2015) "African Economic History in Africa," *Economic History of Developing Regions*: 1–18. http://dx.doi.org/10.1080/20780389.2015.1033686 (accessed 12 May 2015).

Awe, Bolanle. (2001) "Iyalode Efunsetan Aniwura (Owner of Gold)," in Bolanle Awe (ed.), *Nigerian Women: A Historical Perspective*, Ibadan: Sankore/Bookcraft: 63–82.

Awe, Bolanle. (1973) "Militarism and Economic Development in Nineteenth Century Yoruba Country: The Ibadan Example," *Journal of African History*, 14 (1): 65–77.

Barry, Boubacar. (1998) *Senegambia and the Atlantic Slave Trade*, Cambridge: Cambridge University Press.

Barry, Boubacar. (1988a) *La Sénégambie du XVe au XlXe siècle.Traite Négrière, Islam et Conquête Coloniale*, Paris: L'Harmattan.

Barry, Boubacar. (1988b) "L'esclavage Domestique en Sénégambie du XVe au XIX Siècle," in *Actes du Colloque International de Nantes sur la Traite des Noirs*. Centre de Recherche sur 1'Histoire du Monde Atlantique. Société Française d'Histoire d'Outre-Mer: 2213–22.

Barry, Boubacar. (1985) "La Sénégambie au XIXe Siècle: Commerce Légitime, Conquêtes et Résistances," in *Actes du Colloque de Bruxelles sur le Centenaire de la Conférence de Berlin*. Solidarité Sociale, Bruxelles: 45–66.

Barry, Boubacar and L. Harding (eds.). (1992) *Commerce et Commerçants en Afrique de l'Ouest – Le Sénégal avant la Conquête*, Paris: L'Harmattan.

Bathily, Abdoulaye. (1986) "La Traite Atlantique des Esclaves et ses Effets économiques et sociaux en Afrique: la Cas du Galam, Royaume de l'Hinterland Sénégambien au dix-huitième Siècle," *Journal of African History*, 27 (2): 269–91.

Chuku, Gloria. (2005) *Igbo Women and Economic Transformation in Southeastern Nigeria, 1900–1960*, London: Routledge.

Cole, Gibril R. (2008) "Religious Plurality and Economic Sustainability: Muslim Merchants in the Colonial Economy of Nineteenth Century Freetown," *African Economic History*, 26: 79–93.

Daaku, Kwame Yeboa. (1970) *Trade and Politics on the Gold Coast, 1600–1720: A Study of the African Reaction to European Trade*, Oxford: Clarendon Press.

Deane, Phyllis. (1953) *Colonial Social Accounting*, Cambridge: Cambridge University Press.

Dibua, J.I. (2013) *Development and Diffusionism: Looking beyond Neopatrimonialism in Nigeria, 1962–1985*, London: Palgrave Macmillan.

Dibua, J.I. (2006) *Modernization and the Crisis of Development: The Nigerian Experience*, London: Ashgate.

Dike, K. Onwuka. (1956) *Trade and Politics in the Niger Delta, 1830–1885: An Introduction to the Economic and Political History of Nigeria*, Oxford.

Dike, K. Onwuka and Felicia Ekejiuba. (1990) *The Aro of South-eastern Nigeria, 1650–1980: A Study of Socio-economic Formation and Transformation in Nigeria*, Ibadan: University Press.

Ekejiuba, Felicia. (1967) "Omu Okwei: Merchant Queen of Ossomari: A Biographical Sketch," *Journal of the Historical Society of Nigeria*, 3(3): 633–46.

Ekundare, Olufemi. (1973) *An Economic History of Nigeria, 1860–1960*, London: Methuen.

Eltis, David. (1995) "The Volume and African Origins of the British Slave Trade before 1714," *Cahiers d'Etudes Africaines*, 35 (2–3): 617–27.

Falola, Toyin. (2004) *Economic Reforms and Modernization in Nigeria, 1945–1965*, Kent, OH: Kent State University.

Falola, Toyin. (1997) " 'Manufacturing Trouble': Currency Forgery in Colonial Southwestern Nigeria," *African Economic History*, 25: 121–47.

Falola, Toyin. (1996) *Development Planning and Decolonization in Nigeria*, Gainesville: University of Florida Press.

Falola, Toyin. (1993) " 'My Friend the Shylock': Money Lenders and their Clients in South-western Nigeria," *Journal of African History*, 34 (3): 403–23.

Falola, Toyin. (1991) "The Yoruba Caravan System of the Nineteenth Century," *International Journal of African Historical Studies*, 24 (1): 111–32.

Falola, Toyin. (1989) "The Yoruba Toll System: Its Operation and Abolition," *Journal of African History*, 30 (1): 69–88.

Falola, Toyin (ed.). (1987) *Britain and Nigeria: Exploitation or Development?* London: Zed.

Falola, Toyin. (1984) *The Political Economy of a Pre-Colonial African State: Ibadan, 1830–1900*, Ile-Ife: University of Ife Press.

Falola, Toyin and A.G. Adebayo. (2000) *Culture and Politics of Money among the Yoruba*, New Brunswick, NJ: Transaction Publishers.

Faluyi, Kehinde. (1981) "The Impact of the Great Depression of 1929–33 on the Nigerian Economy," *Journal of Business and Social Studies*, n.s., 4 (2): 31–44.

Green, Erik and Pius Nyambara. (2015) "The Internationalization of Economic History: Perspectives from the African Frontier," *Economic History of Developing Regions*, 1–11. DOI: 10.1080/20780389.2015.1025744 (accessed 27 March 2015).

Heap, Simon. (1999) "The Quality of Liquor in Nigeria during the Colonial Period," *Itinerario: European Journal of Overseas History*, 23 (2): 29–47.

Heap, Simon. (1998) " 'We Think Prohibition Is a Farce': Drinking in the Alcohol-Prohibited Zone of Colonial Northern Nigeria," *International Journal of African Historical Studies*, 31 (1): 23–51.

Hopkins, A.G. (2009) "The New Economic History of Africa," *Journal of African History*, 50 (1): 155–77.

Hopkins, A.G. (1973) *An Economic History of West Africa*, London: Longman.

Ijagbemi, E.A. (1970) "The Freetown Colony and the Development of 'Legitimate' Commerce in the Adjoining Territories," *Journal of the Historical Society of Nigeria*, 5 (2): 243–56.

Ikime, Obaro. (1968) *Merchant Prince of the Niger Delta: The Rise and Fall of Nana Olomu, Last Governor of the Benin River*, London: Heinemann.

Ikpe, Eno Blankson. (1994) *Food and Society in Nigeria: A History of Food Customs, Food Economy and Cultural Change, 1900–1989*, Stuttgart: Frantz Steiner Verlag.

Inikori, J.E. (2007) "Africa and the Globalization Process: Western Africa, 1450–1850," *Journal of Global History*, 2 (1): 63–86.

Inikori, J.E. (2002) *Africans and the Industrial Revolution in England : A Study in International Trade and Economic Development*. Cambridge: Cambridge University Press.

Inikori, J.E. (1994) "Ideology versus the Tyranny of Paradigm: Historians and the Impact of the Atlantic Slave Trade on African Societies," *African Economic History*, 22: 37–58.

Inikori, J.E. (1992) "The Volume of the British Slave Trade, 1655–1807," *Cahiers d'Etudes Africaines*, 32 (4), 128: 643–88.

Inikori, J.E. (1977) "The Import of Firearms into West Africa 1750–1807: A Quantitative Analysis," *Journal of African History*, 18 (3): 339–68.

Inikori, J.E. (1976a) "Measuring the Atlantic Slave Trade: An Assessment of Curtin and Anstey," *Journal of African History*, 17 (2): 197–223.

Inikori, J.E. (1976b) "Measuring the Atlantic Slave Trade: A Rejoinder," *Journal of African History*, 17 (4): 607–27.

Iwuagwu, Obi. (2012) "The Spread of Cassava (*manioc*) in Igboland, Southeast Nigeria: A Reappraisal of the Evidence," *Agricultural History Review* 60: 60–76.

Iwuagwu, Obi. (2009) "Nigeria and the Challenge of Industrial Development: The New Cluster Strategy," *African Economic History*, 37: 151–80.

Jerven, Morten. (2013) *Poor Numbers: How We Are Misled by African Development Statistics and What to Do about It*, Ithaca, NY: New York University Press.

Jerven, Morten. (2012) "An Unlevel Playing Field: National Income Estimates and Reciprocal Comparison in Global Economic History," *Journal of Global History* 7: 107–28.

Korieh, Chima J. (2010) *The Land Has Changed: History, Society, and Gender in Colonial Eastern Nigeria*, Calgary: University of Calgary Press.

Korieh, Chima J. (2007) "Yam is King! But Cassava is the Mother of all Crops: Farming, Culture, and Identity in Igbo Agrarian Economy," *Dialectical Anthropology*, 31: 221–32.

Korieh, Chima J. (2003) "Alcohol and Empire: 'Illicit' Gin Prohibition and Control in Colonial Eastern Nigeria," *African Economic History*, 31: 111–34.

Lawal, A.A. (2003) "The Managerial and Financial Problems of the Railway in Colonial Nigeria," *Lagos Notes and Records*, 10: 1–20.

Lawal, A.A. (1998) "British Financial Administration in Nigeria, 1900–1960," *Nigerian Journal of Economic History*, 1: 104–28.

Lawal, A.A. (1989) "West African Currency Board Earnings and the Distribution of Its Income," *Odu: A Journal of West African Studies*, 35: 140–60.

Lawal, A.A. (1983/84) "The Politics of Revenue Allocation in Nigeria: The Early Phase, 1900–1935," *Journal of the Historical Society of Nigeria*, 12: 51–64.

Lawal, Olakunle. (1994) "British Commercial Interests and the Decolonization Process in Nigeria, 1950–1960," *African Economic History*, 22: 93–110.

Manning, Patrick. (1987) "The Prospects for African Economic History: Is Today included in the Long Run?" *African Studies Review*, 30 (2): 49–62.

Naanen, B. (1993) "Economy within an Economy: The Manilla Currency, Exchange Rate Instability and Social Conditions in South-Eastern Nigeria," *Journal of African History*, 34 (3): 425–46.

Naanen, B. (1991) " 'Itinerant Gold Mines': Prostitution in the Cross River Basin of Nigeria, 1930–1950," *African Studies Review*, 34 (2): 57–79.

Njoku, O.N. (1979) "Evolution of Produce Inspection in Nigeria before 1936," *Odu*, n.s. 19: 43–57.

Njoku, O.N. (1978) "Development of Road and Road Transport in Southeastern Nigeria, 1903–1939," *Journal of African Studies*, 4 (4): 471–97.

Njoku, Raphael Chijioke. (2008) "Ogaranya (Wealthy Men) in Late Nineteenth Century Igboland: Chief Igwebe Odum of Arondizuogu, c.1860–1940," *African Economic History*, 36: 27–52.

Nwabughuogu, Anthony I. (1984a) "The Role of Bicycle Transport in the Economic Development of Eastern Nigeria, 1930–45," *Journal of Transport History*, 5 (1): 91–8.

Nwabughuogu, Anthony I. (1984b) "The 'Isusu': An Institution for Capital Formation among the Ngwa Igbo; Its Origin and Development to 1951," *Africa*, 54 (4): 46–58.

Nwabughuogu, Anthony I. (1982) "From Wealthy Entrepreneurs to Petty Traders: The Decline of African Middlemen in Eastern Nigeria, 1900–1950," *Journal of African History*, 23 (3): 365–79.

Nwokeji, G. Ugo. (2010) *The Slave Trade and Culture in the Bight of Biafra: An African Society in the Atlantic World*, Cambridge: Cambridge University Press.

Ochonu, Moses. (2009) *Colonial Meltdown: Northern Nigeria in the Great Depression*, Athens: Ohio University Press.

Odotei, Irene. (2002a) *The Artisanal Marine Fishing Industry in Ghana: A Historical Overview*, Legon: Institute of African Studies.

Odotei, Irene. (2002b) *There is Money in the Sea: Ghanaian Migrant Fishermen and Women in the Ivory Coast*, Legon: Institute of African Studies.

Ofonagoro, W.I. (1979a) *Trade and Imperialism in Southern Nigeria, 1881–1929*, New York: Nok Publishers.

Ofonagoro, W.I. (1979b) "From Traditional to British Currency in Southern Nigeria: Analysis of a Currency Revolution, 1880–1948," *Journal of Economic History*, 39: 623–54.

Ofonagoro, W.I. (1975) "The Aro and Delta Middlemen of South-East Nigeria and the Challenge of the Colonial Economy," *Journal of African Studies*, 3 (2): 143–64.

Ogunremi, G.O. (1982) *Counting the Camels: The Economics of Transportation in Pre-Industrial Nigeria*, New York: Nok Publishers.

Ogunremi, G.O. (1976) "Characteristics of Trade Routes in Yorubaland in the Nineteenth Century," *Nigerian Geographical Journal*, 19 (2): 249–59.

Ogunremi, G.O. (1975) "Human Porterage in Nigeria in the Nineteenth Century – A Pillar in the Indigenous Economy," *Journal of the Historical Society of Nigeria*, 8 (1): 37–59.

Ogunremi, G.O. and E.K. Faluyi (eds.). (1996) *Economic History of West Africa since 1750*, Ibadan: Rex Charles.

Ogunyemi, Adetunji O. (2008) "Federal Budgets in Nigeria, 1954–1999: A History of the Processes, Policies and Problems," PhD Dissertation, University of Lagos.

Ohadike, Don C. (1981) "The Influenza Pandemic of 1918–1919 and the Spread of Cassava Cultivation on the Lower Niger: A Study in Historical Linkages," *Journal of African History*, 22 (3): 379–91.

Olorunfemi, A. (1984) "The Liquor Traffic in British West Africa: The Southern Nigerian Example, 1895–1918," *International Journal of African Historical Studies*, 7 (2): 220–42.

Olorunfemi, A. (1981a) "German Trade with British West African Colonies,1895–1918," *Journal of African Studies*, 8 (3): 111–20.

Olorunfemi, A. (1981b) "The Export Trade of South Western Nigeria,1918–36: Expansion and Instability in a Dependent Economy," *Odu*, n.s., 21: 149–67.

Olorunfemi, A. (1980) "Effects of War-Time Trade Controls on Nigerian Cocoa Traders and Producers, 1939–1945: A Case Study of the Hazards of a Dependent Economy," *International Journal of African Historical Studies*, 13 (4): 672–89.

Olukoju, Ayodeji. (2011) "Imperial Business Umpire: The Colonial Office, United Africa Company, Elder Dempster, and the 'Great Shipping War' of 1929–30," in Toyin Falola (ed.), *Africa, Empire and Globalization: Essays in Honor of A.G. Hopkins*, Durham: Carolina Academic Press: 167–89.

Olukoju, Ayodeji. (2010) "The Adisi Case: Currency Counterfeiting in Inter-War Colonial Gold Coast," in Catherine Eagleton and Harcourt Fuller (eds.), *Money in Africa*, London: The British Museum: 68–74.

Olukoju, Ayodeji. (2009) "The United Kingdom and the Political Economy of the Global Oils and Fats Business in the 1930s," *Journal of Global History*, 4 (1): 105–25.

Olukoju, Ayodeji. (2008) "Economic Relations between Nigeria and the United States of America in the Era of British Colonial Rule, ca.1900–1950," in Alusine Jalloh and Toyin Falola (eds.), *The United States and West Africa: Interactions and Relations*, Rochester, NY: Rochester University Press: 90–111.

Olukoju, Ayodeji. (2004a) *The Liverpool of West Africa: The Dynamics and Impact of Maritime Trade in Lagos, 1900–1950*, Trenton: Africa World Press.

Olukoju, Ayodeji. (2004b) "Economic History at the University of Lagos since the 1970s," *Lagos Historical Review*, 4: 77–94.

Olukoju, Ayodeji. (2003) "Nigeria and the World Market, 1890–1960: Local and Global Economic Dynamics in the Colonial Context," in K.S. Jomo and K. J. Khoo (eds.), *Globalization and Its Discontents, Revisited*, Delhi: Tulika Books: 141–56.

Olukoju, Ayodeji. (2002) "Self-Help Criminality as Resistance?: Currency Counterfeiting in Colonial Nigeria," *International Review of Social History*, 45 (3): 385–407.

Olukoju, Ayodeji. (2000) "Fishing, Migrations and Inter-Group Relations in the Gulf of Guinea (Atlantic Coast of West Africa) in the Nineteenth and Twentieth Centuries," *Itinerario: European Journal of Overseas History*, 24 (2): 69–85.

Olukoju, Ayodeji. (1997) "Rotgut and Revenue: Fiscal Aspects of the Liquor Trade in Southern Nigeria, 1890–1919," *Itinerario*, 21 (2): 66–81.

Olukoju, Ayodeji. (1996) "Playing the Second Fiddle: The Development of Port Harcourt and Its Role in the Nigerian Economy, 1917–1950," *International Journal of Maritime History*, 8 (1): 105–31.

Olukoju, Ayodeji. (1995) "Anatomy of Business–Government Relations: Fiscal Policy and Mercantile Pressure Group Activity in Nigeria, 1916–1933," *African Studies Review*, 38 (1): 23–50.

Olukoju, Ayodeji. (1994) "The Making of an 'Expensive Port': Shipping Lines, Government and Port Tariffs in Lagos, 1917–1949," *International Journal of Maritime History*, 6 (1): 141–59.

Olukoju, Ayodeji. (1992a) "Elder Dempster and the Shipping Trade of Nigeria during the First World War," *Journal of African History*, 33 (2): 255–71.

Olukoju, Ayodeji. (1992b) "The Development of the Port of Lagos, c.1892–1946," *Journal of Transport History*, 13 (1): 59–78.

Olukoju, Ayodeji. (1991) "Prohibition and Paternalism: The State and the Clandestine Liquor Traffic in Northern Nigeria, c. 1898–1918," *International Journal of African Historical Studies*, 24 (2): 349–68.

Olukoju, Ayodeji, Adebayo Lawal and Kehinde Faluyi (eds.). (2003) *Fundamentals of Economic History*, Lagos: First Academic Publishers.

Onimode, Bade. (1982) *Imperialism and Underdevelopment in Nigeria*, London: Zed Books.

Oshin, O. (1991) "Road Transport and the Declining Fortunes of the Nigeria Railway, 1901–1950," *Journal of Transport History*, 12 (2): 11–36.

Osoba, Segun. (1978) "The Deepening Crisis of the Nigeria National Bourgeoisie," *Review of African Political Economy*, 13: 63–77.

Osoba, Segun. (1969) "The Phenomenon of Labour Migration in the Era of British Colonial Rule: A Neglected Aspect of Nigerian Social History," *Journal of the Historical Society of Nigeria*, 4 (4): 515–38.

Oyemakinde, Wale. (1977) "The Impact of the Great Depression on the Nigerian Railway and Its Workers," *Journal of the Historical Society of Nigeria*, 8 (4): 143–60.

Oyemakinde, Wale. (1975) "The Nigerian General Strike of 1945," *Journal of the Historical Society of Nigeria*, 7 (4): 693–710.

Oyemakinde, Wale. (1974) "Railway Construction and Operation in Nigeria, 1895–1911: Labour Problems and Socio-Economic Impact," *Journal of the Historical Society of Nigeria*, 3 (3): 303–24.

Oyemakinde, Wale. (1970) "A History of Indigenous Labour on the Nigerian Railway, 1895–1945," PhD Dissertation, University of Ibadan.

Richardson, David and Stephen D. Behrendt. (1995) "Inikori's Odyssey: Measuring the British Slave Trade, 1655–1807," *Cahiers d'Etudes Africaines*, 35 (2–3): 138–9, 599–615.

Rodney, Walter. (1972) *How Europe Underdeveloped Africa*, London: Bogle-L'Ouverture Publications.

Roy, Tirthankar. (2014) "The Rise and Fall of Indian Economic History, 1920–2013," *Economic History of Developing Regions*, 29 (1): 15–41.

Saito, Osamu. (2015) "A Very Brief History of Japan's Economic and Social History Research," Paper for 17th World Economic History Congress, Kyoto, Japan, 3–7 August.

Stolper, W.F. (1966) *Planning without Facts: Lessons in Resource Allocation for Nigeria's Development*, Cambridge, MA: Harvard University Press.

Temu, A. and B. Swai. (1981) *Historians and African History: A Critique*, London: Zed Press.

Thioub, Ibrahima. (2003) "The Economic Foundation of the Nation-State in Senegal," in Alice Teichova and Herbert Matis (eds.), *Nation, State, and the Economy in History*, Cambridge: Cambridge University Press: 251–69.

Thioub, Ibrahima. (1994) " Economie coloniale et rémunération de la force de travail : le salaire du manoeuvre à Dakar de 1930 à 1954," *Revue Française d'Histoire d'Outre-Mer*, 305: 427–53.

Thioub, Ibrahima, Momar-Coumba Diop and Catherine Boone. (1998) "Economic Liberalization in Senegal : Shifting Politics of Indigenous Business Interests," *African Studies Review*, 41 (2): 63–89.

Uche, Chibuike Ugochukwu. (2010) "Indigenous Banks in Colonial Nigeria," *International Journal of African Historical Studies*, 43 (3): 467–87.

Uche, Chibuike Ugochukwu. (1999) "Foreign Banks, Africans and Credit in Colonial Nigeria, c. 1890–1912," *Economic History Review*, 52 (4): 669–91.

Uche, Chibuike Ugochukwu. (1995) "From Currency Board to Central Banking: The Gold Coast Experience," *South African Journal of Economic History*, 10 (2): 80–94.

Ukwu, U.I. (1967) "The Development of Trade and Marketing in Iboland," *Journal of the Historical Society of Nigeria*, 3 (3): 647–62.

Usman, Y.B. (1981) *The Transformation of Katsina, 1400–1883: The Emergence and Overthrow of the Sarauta System and the Establishment of the Emirate*, Zaria: Ahmadu Bello University Press.

Usoro, Eno J. (1977) "Colonial Economic Development Strategy in Nigeria, 1919–1939," *Nigerian Journal of Economic and Social Studies*, 19 (1): 121–41.

Usoro, Eno J. (1974) *The Nigerian Oil Palm Industry (Government Policy and Export Production, 1906–1965)*, Ibadan: Ibadan University Press.

Wariboko, Nimi. (1998) "A Theory of the Canoe House Corporation," *African Economic History*, 26: 141–72.

Whatley, Warren C. (2008) "Guns-for-Slaves: The 18th Century British Slave Trade in Africa," http://mpra.ub.uni-muenchen.de/58741/ (accessed 12 March 2015).

Yearwood, Peter J. (1998) "The Expatriate Firms and the Colonial Economy of Nigeria in the First World War," *Journal of Imperial and Commonwealth History*, 26 (1): 49–71.

24

REFLECTIONS ON THE ECONOMIC HISTORY OF SOUTH AFRICA

Bill Freund

In considering the study of economic history in and of South Africa, there is a need to make a distinction between the economic history of South Africa and economic history in South Africa. The peculiarities of capitalist development in the country and the glare of political light that this has attracted means that writers from outside have often generated important ideas as well as written studies set in South Africa, especially in the wake of the anti-apartheid movement. They have also extended debates beyond what South African academic life could or can hold. This will be the main focus of the following chapter.

However mention should be made of some other facts. A number of South African authors have written significant studies relevant to the economic history of other parts of Africa. It is striking that most of these contributions are about labour and focus on the hopes for the political development of the African labour movement that were prevalent for a time. They belong to a phase when African labour studies blossomed and were also typically generated from outside South Africa, whether as theses or research projects. Some but not all of these works considered activities in bordering countries (Cohen 1974; Cooper 1978; First et al. 1983; van Onselen 1980; Crush 1987). They had a clear relationship to simultaneous work discussed below researched inside the country.

A second point to be mentioned lies in comparative work that includes South African material. The most influential work of this kind really comes from political science and is particularly strong in looking at race as a concept but such work usually has only a marginal place for economic issues. An exception by an American social scientist is Greenberg 1980. Other comparisons that might be mentioned are in the early work of the geographer Alan Mabin (1984) who considered nineteenth-century Australian development with Cape history; and the comparative studies on Indian indentured workers using measurements such as physical height to test life conditions by the expatriate South African Ralph Shlomowitz independently or as part of Australian-based teams (Brennan et al. 1998). These have been quite peripheral however to South African debates. One should finally mention the group of South African economic historians who became significant writers on other parts of the world, notably the eminent mainstream Oxford scholar Charles Feinstein who wrote mainly about Europe but did return to his native country as a subject in his final posthumous work. Major theories of economic structure and development applied successfully to South Africa have been numerous and will emerge in this discussion but have not held the power of, for instance, resource and staple-based theories of development applied to a whole school of thought in Australia or Canada.

A further distinction needs to be made between political economy and economic history more narrowly construed. The significance of intellectual activity in the first category far outweighs the second. To concentrate on the South African application of economic propositions pure and simple would be to focus in overly loving detail on a small range of studies situated within a defined academic set of borders whereas the broader political economy issues have a much wider currency and influence. This may also reflect the author's view that narrow economic history alone is better understood as a special case of political economy with a historic perspective, a view that falls outside of any construction of economic history as a self-standing discipline. For instance, not only business history but labour history ought to be part of economic history's purview and descriptive as well as analytical material (qualitative as well as quantitative sources), should form part of it. The role of the state and the relationship of politics and economics deservedly loom large in a literature which has been consistently contentious. The promotion of academic writing has gone, as in other settler countries, together with a celebration of modernization in the form of economic achievement as an inherent part of progress. The struggles over apartheid that marked the second half of the twentieth century were echoed by arguments about the relationship of economic power and economic growth to the social system and the nature of the state. This is probably what gives particular interest to an investigation of economic history from a South African perspective. As the British economic historian Tom Kemp wrote on the eve of the political transition, '[economic history] is widely taught in South Africa, clearly a case where a society's development cannot be understood apart from its economic base. The considerable literature reflects wide ideological divisions as well as the considerations arising from the very conditions of existence of a white-dominated state in Southern Africa' (Kemp 1993: 208). Only South African material will be considered here although this implies a somewhat artificial divide. A regional perspective has an inherent logic, given that the boundaries of the country are hardly overwhelming natural divides. In the later pages of this chapter, there will be some consideration of economic history as a distinct university subject of study but this will be a secondary concern.

The development of a South African economic history

British economic history celebrated and commented on the emergence and institutional development of industrial capitalism and required a home which history and economics were at first reluctant to provide. South African economic history was its post-colonial stepchild. Following the British example, as early as 1923 a post was set aside within the University of Cape Town Economics Department specifically for the study of economic history. Out of this emerged an academic tradition of writing, broadly to be considered as liberal, with an orientation that was generally speaking pro-business and critical of state intervention in favour of economic development, intervention which big business, and notably mining interests, held in contempt.

Yet in fact economic questions loomed large within the corpus of early works of far greater influence on South African historiography. C. W de Kiewiet's monument – his was really the most significant synthesis of South African history of his time carried through by his impressive prose style – was entitled *A History of South Africa, Social and Economic* (1941). W. M. Macmillan, the most intellectually influential English-language historian of this period, put much of his emphasis in his earlier work on economic issues, looking at the impoverished Eastern Cape location of Keiskammahoek and considering the so-called poor white question, leading up to *Complex South Africa* (1930). De Kiewiet evocatively recreated the world of the assegai and the ox-wagon (particularly the latter) and the painful evolution out of these accompaniments to rural backwardness and agrarian stagnation, which dotted the terrain on which South African society stood. It is sobering to be reminded that this firm believer in progress, while recognizing the rapid growth of secondary industry in the years before the publication of his best-known work, was pessimistic about its prospects. Loyally adhering to the Smithian precepts of his contemporaries in the English-language academic world, he insisted on the role of gold, diamonds and wool as the foundational elements in which South Africa held a comparative advantage. Macmillan was more the pioneer who explored the world of poverty and social problems. A third classic work that deserves attention, where the influences were Continental, was the trilogy of P. J. van der Merwe (1995). This was the most impressive history written in Afrikaans quite outside the plodding political histories that were dominant in his time. The secretive van der Merwe, trained in the Netherlands, was closer in spirit to the *Annales* school and to meticulous social historians of his time such as Huizinga than any of the English-language historians. He expressed a far more nuanced view of the frontier world of which he held, as would most American historians, an often positive view. He made considerable use of economic phenomena and, when possible, documented facts.

In the days of the Union of South Africa, the outstanding political figure was Jan Christiaan Smuts, a Boer War general, who came to see the future of the country, and indeed of Africa as a whole, within a British penumbra. Unsympathetic to the fate of the white poor and unwilling to favour them legislatively, whether on the land or in the gold mines, he also held conventional racist views of the mass of black South Africans. However, he was an enthusiast for using the revenues from the mines to construct, in good part through state intervention, a modern society by diverting accumulation channels into the creation of heavy industry and sophisticated technology. In the inter-war period, the laissez-faire economists confronted a rising tide of protectionism. This in turn was followed by questions arising from the management of the war economy in the Second World War and the expansion and creation of parastatals. Only a few economists, largely on the Afrikaans side of the white language divide, supported this kind of nationalist approach (Schumann 1938; Norval 1962) and it cannot be said that South Africa supported any economic thinking of real power in this regard. Norval interestingly was not based at a university but at the Board of Trade and Industries which set the tone for South African protectionism. H. M. Robertson, an economic historian based at the University of Cape Town, signalled in a key article the importance of the Board as a lever of state intervention (Kooy and Robertson 1966).

Norval wrote at a time when the long South African boom years, that began when the country left the gold standard in 1933, were at a height. He produced a little paean of praise to progress and modernism. At a time when the so-called poor white problem, dominant as an economic issue in the inter-war years, was losing any political significance, he saw mass industrial employment as engaging the black majority as well. It is remarkable though that the achievements of H. J. van der Bijl, inventor and economic czar of the war years and his protégé, H. J. van Eck, key figure in the critical Industrial Development Corporation, did not find a supporting literature to sing their praises. Yet both of these men had much to say about the linkages between diversification, industrialization and social change at the heart of development.

By contrast, the mining interest, which dominated the business world, worried about what it saw as the diversion of resources from straightforward resource extraction to industry. Two academic figures of note in this regard were S. H. Frankel and C. S. Richards. Frankel was a much admired figure who was critical to the establishment of the economics profession at the University of the Witwatersrand, founded in the fulcrum of South African capital, Johannesburg. His monument was the key study of *Capital Investment in Africa,* widely circulated internationally (Frankel 1938). Frankel's attachment to laissez-faire economics was the main reason Smuts and van der Bijl froze him out of economic policy circles after the Second World War when he retreated to Oxford, a champion of mild imperial reform in the era of decolonization. Richards, also based at Wits, was closely associated with the great mining empire of the Anglo-American corporation and his best-known writing attacked state intervention in the steel industry, which effectively required state investment to be constructed (Richards 1940). Ironically, after the discovery of rich vanadium deposits on its property, Anglo-American turned itself to steel manufacture at the end of the 1950s. Richards too upheld the standard of traditional pre-war business-oriented and imperial-oriented economics with the main alternative voice being that of the eminent and very right-wing refugee Ludwig Lachmann, a prominent protagonist of the Austrian school of heterodox thought. Lachmann spent most of his career in South Africa and was probably its one internationally significant economic presence.

The intensity of debate about state intervention certainly weakened during what we might call the thirty fat years of South African capitalism. A writer, influenced by W. W. Rostow's *Stages of Economic Growth,* who is known for celebrating the successes of South African economic growth, was the Rhodes University based scholar D. Hobart Houghton. Houghton's importance can be signalled by his authoring the chapter on economic history in the important *Oxford History of South Africa* in 1969 as well as a first popular text for the growing number of South African university economics students. Houghton was certainly a more explicit liberal than Norval on social issues but his Pollyannaish views, predicting that South Africa would almost automatically attain a living standard, on average, that would seamlessly make the *apartheid* system irrelevant before the twentieth century ended, seems astonishing to a contemporary reader. 'On the more general question whether secondary industry will continue to grow towards a situation where it is fully self-supporting, past development and available resources give a confident answer that this goal can be reached' (Houghton 1967: 137).

Here was a completely naive understanding of the impact of industrial capital on South African society that failed to do justice to Houghton's critical insights in other contexts. Other liberal writers were however prepared to dissect the inequities and exclusions of the South African system and looked with a more critical eye at the exploitation and abuse of black labour, paid per capita a small fraction of what the beneficiaries of expanding South African capitalism could earn. At the University of the Witwatersrand, a particularly clear thinker in this regard was the law scholar Ellison Kahn (1943). Among University of Cape Town scholars, Sheila van der Horst and her standard study of African labour stood out (van der Horst 1971[1942]). Both were active in the 1940s when some thought the scale of urbanization and industrialization might indeed turn into shreds the racial segregation system agreed on by the white electorate. These two were steadfast opponents of the National Party in power after the defeat and death of Smuts and this political thrust became indistinguishable from a narrowly economic liberal critique. Simultaneously from outside the academy an industry emerged of corporate and entrepreneurial biographies and autobiographies, books which varied enormously in their perspicacity and frankness. Such works outnumber books directly on the economy, let alone economic history.

In academic circles and with reference to the all-important gold mining industry, a later contribution in the liberal vein, which ascribed the chief blame for racial inequities to the demands for exclusivity by white labour, was Francis Wilson's historical study of labour in the gold mines (1972). Wilson also wrote a pioneering agrarian history for the same *Oxford History* volume referred to above and in 1984 organized a massive research programme detailing poverty in South Africa. Some liberals continued to believe that while the main trajectory of South African capitalism could hardly be said to be benefiting black South Africans very substantially, this situation would inevitably change. A classic study of the 1980s by Merle Lipton, a historian by training rather than an economist, made the interesting distinction between farming and mining on the one hand, which she saw as indeed depending on harsh forms of exploitation for profitability with the more benevolent hand of secondary industry. Indeed a liberally inclined section of mining management was itself contesting the racial order in her view. Her interest in divergent sectoral capitalist perspectives continues to be of interest (Lipton 1985).

A parallel text of contemporary importance was *The South African Economy: Its Growth and Change* (1981) by Jill Nattrass of the University of Natal. Nattrass was considerably less optimistic in her views. She also saw manufacturing as a kind of road into a promised land of the good life for all but she had much more of a grasp of the realities of manufacturing in South Africa. She realized some of the intimate links between manufacturing and mining, especially heavy manufacturing, and was aware of the weaknesses of secondary industry: its poor skill base, the small domestic market, and the price and relative scarcity of investment capital. Despite the influence on her of W. Arthur Lewis, in accepting that manufacturing had the potential to soak up the vast army of impoverished peasants and informal sector participants in the third world, she was pessimistic about the rural poor of South Africa, her own particular research interest, ever being absorbed in this way. Moreover, whilst *apartheid* would place a high barrier to the advantages of industrialization flowing outside the white minority, its dissolution was likely to retain key divides, only deracializing them. Nattrass probably also deserves credit for introducing far more quantitative, mainly statistical, evidence, into her general assessment. A final difference between Lipton and Nattrass was contextual. If Nattrass's approach had been developmental, Lipton's work was in part ammunition in a shrill war strategy by pro-business economists and economic historians who, as we shall see, were still significant in the academic milieu. They saw themselves beleaguered by a new force of radicals, generally Marxists, inside and outside that milieu, who for a time felt that history was on their side.

In general the liberal critique of *apartheid* considered the economy as being shackled by racial legislation that was ultimately part of the rubric of undesirable and unwarranted state intervention in the market. The nature of the regime was such that this kind of critique had some purchase on policy in times and places and was accepted as legitimate. It represented a dominant view among English-speaking academics certainly by the 1960s but the Afrikaner business world, increasingly self-confident and inclined to model itself on its English comperes, also promoted a parallel critique especially once the good times gave way to an increasingly crisis-ridden era for the economy from the early 1970s onwards (Wassenaar 1977).

The radical school

At this point, we focus on a radical critique which may be seen as offering ideas worthy of international consideration in an understanding of modern capitalism. Here three foundational authors in particular will be discussed: Jack and Ray Simons, Harold Wolpe and Martin Legassick. All of them were South African university employees at one time or another, all can be linked to universities outside South Africa in Zambia and the United Kingdom, but also experienced long periods of exile and wrote outside normal university circuits to an important extent.

Jack and Ray Simons's *Class and Colour in South Africa* (1983[1969]), conceived in Cape Town in the late 1950s but finished and published only a decade later, was the work of the exiled political scientist and former leader of the South African Communist Party, Jack Simons and his trade unionist wife Ray Alexander. The contrast with previously discussed work is marked in terms of the use of class as an analytical category and the central importance given to labour history. However, in common with the liberals, these authors saw industrialization as a major stage in economic development with important progressive political consequences in tow. The malaise of mid-twentieth-century capitalist South Africa, taking this view further, 'stemmed from the impact of an advanced industrialism on an obsolete, degenerate colonial order' (Simons and Simons 1983: 610). This was a view not very different to that of Macmillan or de Kiewiet. In time, the Simons hoped that South African capitalism could be rescued from its racist trappings, through a democratic revolution, and inevitably then politics would revolve around a class struggle. Their lengthy study was critical for South African economic and social history.

Taking this work on board but with little or no continuation of the positive assessment of the modern that the Simons retained was the innovative writing of Wolpe and Legassick. Their ideas began to be broadcast at an iconic seminar series administered by Shula Marks, a South African lecturer at the School of African and Oriental Studies, London. Wolpe insisted that the racial order based on roots in colonial conquest was critical to the social context and accumulation form of South African capitalism and was not simply an accretion or degenerate aspect parasitizing dynamic growth. He stressed the importance of the migrant labour system, largely in place long before the National Party with its *apartheid* label took office (Wolpe 1972). It required intense cooperation between state and business despite occasional rifts. Indeed he believed that *apartheid* was itself distinctive as an attempt to shore up this system which was showing strains and problems, a Sisyphean task that Wolpe, also a Communist, thought could well bring down the government in time. He believed in the importance of studying development efforts in the so-called Bantustans and the state's creation, in the later *apartheid* period, of a black middle class as a subordinate layer to absorb pressure and prop up the system. In other words, capitalism (whatever the parallels internationally) had come to depend vitally in South Africa on its exploitative relationship with its primitive forebear. This made possible the continual re-emergence of a cheap labour force nurtured in a pre-capitalist framework towards which it was eventually thrown back.

It was Legassick, a trained historian with a flair for economic history but, like Wolpe, directing himself for a key period towards sociology, who did the most to nail the *apartheid* pin on the capitalist donkey. For Legassick, capitalism depended fundamentally on cheap labour, achieved its strength in large part and worked, not without contradiction, to bend the state to its purposes (Legassick 1977). The key lay in the gigantic gold-mining system of labour controls which operated so as to contradict the precepts liberals upheld about free labour under capitalism, as well as the very unequal partition of land and the emergence of 'tribal law' which structured residual and segregated land systems for blacks. Secondary industry, Legassick recognized, had diverse origins, but the key element was reinvestment from the forced labour economy. The manufacturing sector had failed to tear itself away from dependence there; the advantages of the system outweighed the disadvantages, despite the rather different needs of manufacturers who were sometimes at odds with the state. So there was in Legassick a notion of linkage between mining and manufacturing. Mining set the pace and tone, dominated as it was by a historically structured and intensely racialized labour hierarchy. It created a capitalism that was highly profitable but only partially functioning through a real free labour system. Yet the state, of the greatest importance as an agent of capitalist development, was becoming more and more effective at integrating and harmonizing capitalist interests. The modalities became clearer as secondary industrial interests too became dominated by a small number of oligopolistic firms after the middle of the twentieth century. Legassick went back earlier however, showing the roots of this system in an imperial policy, following the Anglo-Boer War, that was anxious to establish gold mining on a sound footing within a broader, stable social context.

These were critical interventions that also renewed the integration of ideas about the South African economy and its development with what at the time was the burgeoning sub-field of social history as well as other social sciences, notably sociology. They inspired a flood of creative work which really transformed the understanding of South Africa significantly. In an article published in 1996, I devoted some pages to itemizing what I saw as the highlights of that writing (Freund 1996: 135–41). Much of this writing is usually labelled as social history but perhaps most accurately it could be described as social history strongly reinforced or framed by economic history. Although the extensive references available in that article should be consulted, it might be worthwhile itemizing most of the categories that I created: (1) the reconsideration and historicization of the pre-colonial past influenced by the important Marxist idea of mode of production; (2) the interrelationship of expanding merchant capital under Dutch and British rule in particular to developing an understanding equally of slavery and the slave system and of frontier conflict (the latter allowed for transcending the older liberal idea of the frontier as a source of backwardness and archaic consciousness persisting and holding back modern capitalism); (3) the economic and social forces behind the consolidation of the Kimberley diamond fields and the development by stages of characteristic elements in the mining labour process; (4) the 'immensely complex economic and social structure of the gold mines developed in the [following] generation'; (5) the particular history of white workers, their distinctive struggles, and its relation to the socially and politically highly racialized overall development of South Africa; (6) the emergence of a wide-ranging and rich labour history of the twentieth century, surely the most massive category of all given the hopes that the Left expressed in a revived militant labour movement during the final two decades of *apartheid*; (7) an almost equally impressive urban history albeit with less purchase on economic forces; (8) so-called agrarian history that considered the stuttering rise of capitalist farming buttressed with state support and the gradual evisceration of both the older African way of life on the land and the marginalization of small-scale commercialized farming; and, finally, (9) the production of some fully fledged regional studies on particular sections of South Africa. A tenth category mentioned the beginnings of a study of health and medicine which indeed has critical implications for industrialization processes. However, these can perhaps now be considered in the light of a growing literature, to which I shall return, on social policy more generally.

It is hopefully forgivable on the part of this chapter not to reiterate the numerous outstanding works of historically governed political economy that belong to these categories which are available elsewhere and even then were quite selective. However, it might still be desirable to point to a very few highlights. These are works that must still be consulted as models and hypotheses today.

Class, Race and Gold, the British doctoral thesis of a Canadian sociologist Frederick Johnstone, was a seminal book (Johnstone 1976). It took into account the technology of gold mining and the conditions under which the industry quickly became highly concentrated and made possible its eventually steady, and in absolute terms huge, long-term profits. From this the racial hierarchy in the workplace, the regime under which the mass of migrant black workers were recruited over a very wide region, and the way lives were governed, including the structurally vulnerable position of white skilled and supervisory workers, emerged forcefully. This of course was the major destination of capital investment in South Africa, as Frankel's quantitative study had authoritatively demonstrated, the most important motor of technological innovation and the model of social control. Later studies have focused on changing facets of this regime over a long period of time, have brought out the role of individuals and given voice to workers more generally, but Johnstone must remain a cornerstone of South African economic history.

There is no single work that explains how African cultivators who measured wealth in cattle and could, when successful, harness the labour of youths and women on a significant scale, became migrant labourers within a rural economy that was residual at best. However, parts of this process can be discerned with particular insight in work by such writers as Jeff Guy (1987), William Beinart (1982), Colin Bundy (1988) and Colin Murray (1992). Bundy has been taken continually as revealing a nineteenth-century phase where such men may have flourished for a time with commercial impulses not yet accompanied by structural forms of discrimination imposed by the state. As such he is a liberal mainstay. Charles van Onselen's *The Seed is Mine* (1996) is a long biography of such a cultivator who lived into an increasingly impoverished old age as he lost the ability to accumulate and then survive as a tenant farmer and equally lost the capacity to govern the labour of his children. The classic summaries of how these processes affected the lives of women are by Belinda Bozzoli (1978) and Linzi Manicom (1992): foundational works to studies in feminist economics.

Two South African historians with strategically ideal placements in British academic institutions, Stanley Trapido and Shula Marks, played an inspirational role in the emergence and flourishing of this literature, organizing seminars and projects and supervising doctorates. However, they also attempted syntheses that considered how mining capital, agrarian interests and a state with a variety of interests came together in the course and the wake of the Anglo-Boer War, South Africa's most violent conflict, which paved the way for the creation of the Union in 1910 (Trapido 1971; Marks and Trapido 1979). Trapido suggested, on the analogy of Prussia, that South African capitalism was a [political more than economic] marriage of maize and gold. Marks and Trapido considered that the post-war regime under the guiding hand of Alfred Lord Milner began to fashion a state that could iron out some of the contradictions arising from such a marriage and link capital accumulation to racial exclusion and massive reliance on a cheap labour migrant system that kept the skeleton of an older form of material life standing in rural areas to which Africans were consigned. There was an initial hope that the *Cambridge History of South Africa*, which appeared after a very long gestation period in 2010–11, would represent a kind of definitive summing-up of this newer literature. However, in reality it revealed instead the increasingly eclectic and variable historiography dominant by the early twenty-first century.

From the economic perspective, however, a remarkable synthetic work, the only one of its kind, was produced posthumously by Charles Feinstein, an Oxford-based South African who began as a Communist and ultimately was a distinguished mainstream and quantitatively oriented economic historian of Europe. He was best known in Britain for his studies of historic national accounts on the Kuznets model. Feinstein succeeded in synthesizing liberal and left views of *apartheid*, focusing on what he considered a dead-end developmental model but with a full appreciation of the harsh exploitative conditions of labour and the effects of discrimination. Feinstein clearly absorbed and assimilated much of the radical literature in striking contrast to the mainstream economics writers within South Africa itself, as we shall see below (Feinstein 2005). Apart from Feinstein, one should probably also mention the work of another Oxford economist who for many years before 1990 focused on South Africa, John S. Knight (1988). Knight also took up the social and economic relations between *apartheid* and the economy from a liberal perspective and was much looked up to by liberal economists in the Republic.

Post-apartheid writings

Broadly speaking, this literature flourished between around 1970 and the transition to a democratic franchise in 1994, although a few key works did appear in the first few years subsequently. Several of these are significant enough to deserve particular mention. If Trapido had taken maize and gold as an analogy from international critical literature on political economy, the same process led to Ben Fine and Zavareh Rustomjee's mineral–energy complex, an adaptation of the well-known American paradigm of a military–industrial complex (Fine and Rustomjee 1996). Here we have perhaps the most significant economic thrust of the radical school in later years. Fine and Rustomjee define the complex or MEC as a series of linkages and agencies tied together through very well-developed institutional and financial structures which continue in post-*apartheid* times to have kneejerk state backing. The MEC lies at the heart of the economy; it is highly internationalized, particularly after 1996, with a strong export vocation but with exports consisting of more or less beneficiated raw materials and products rather than sophisticated fabricated products. Their work highlights the importance of the monographs by the American Nancy Clark on the rise of the great state industrial corporations and the South African Renfrew Christie, who tied the rise of heavy industry not merely to the parastatals but to the energy empire largely based on coal mining (Christie 1984, 1991; Clark 1994).

As mentioned above, studies of social policy and its history have flourished in South Africa. A key figure here has been the political sociologist Jeremy Seekings. Seekings has married this with important work examining poverty and the overall South African class structure written with his wife, the economist Nicoli Nattrass (Seekings and Nattrass 2005). Seekings addresses the internationally high levels of inequality as a fundamental theme in a present-centred but significantly historically structured synthesis that tries to merge liberal and radical paradigms. Inequality is also the focus of the work, relatively widely read in South Africa, by Sampie Terreblanche, an economist from the University of Stellenbosch. Terreblanche, more a successful polemicist than an original theorist, has addressed post-*apartheid* themes in terms of continuities from the *apartheid* period with a central focus on the state: 'Verwoerd's policies of creating a white or "European" economy at the southern tip of Africa had far-reaching effects on the South African economy. His policies for creating a capital-intensive first-world on a third-world economy not only weakened the employment capacity of that economy, but did so in a way that was highly detrimental to African workers' (Terreblanche 2002: 377).

These works reflect a strikingly different intellectual climate in the post-1994 era. They are all essentially works by social scientists, notably economists, rather than historians although their work has a historical dimension. Terreblanche is hardly an official figure but he is widely quoted as a source by those who fasten on the continued salience of inequality and above all racial inequality. Seekings and Nattrass contribute to a growing literature on social policy in the penumbra of a state that defines its post-*apartheid* legitimacy in terms not only of a struggle for racially defined economic equality and black economic power but in terms of social grants and infrastructure creation intended to benefit those excluded under the old regime.

By contrast, until recently, Fine and Rustomjee were more the preserve of a faithful but very small band of intellectuals interested in more significant structural and institutional change than was contemplated by the ANC government. The group of activists to which Fine belonged were pushed aside from the policy world by the end of the transition period in 1994. Some excellent studies of the economy were undertaken, notably by Rustomjee but including others with distinct perspectives on the most critical linkages in industrial South Africa (Crompton 1994, Marquard 2006). Most remained entirely unpublished and unknown even to the relevant academic public. Crompton's work belonged to a genre of industrial studies often of considerable quality produced at a time when former activists, some of whom had already contributed to the extant critical literature on the South African economy and with a good grasp of its history, hoped for salient changes in industrial policy. An outstanding individual here was David Kaplan (1990). Gelb's collection which provided an early summary that was not carried forth, was influenced by the discovery and influence of Michel Aglietta, Alain Lipietz and the French regulation school which did lend itself to historically driven economic assessment (Gelb 1991). This body of work was promoted through the good offices of the main trade union federation in its heyday.

Simultaneously, the writing of history also underwent what was at first a gradual but eventually a fairly drastic turn in accordance with the so-called cultural turn. Cultural analyses certainly provided important new historical insights but they did so while almost completely isolating History Departments in South African universities from economic ideas and political economy. Pens stopped writing or individuals reinvented themselves deciding that race or some other category was really far more important than any economic material reality. Institutionally, administrators favoured big units convenient for their purposes with little space for endeavours such as economic history. It became obvious with hindsight that the remarkable literature of the struggle years was itself a product of a finished historical phase.

This was powerfully underlined by changes in international historical writing which equally reflected the dramatic decline in radical critiques of contemporary capitalism, in the importance of labour movements and in the place of those who remained interested in deep systemic change. Instead new radical writers favoured a feminist or environmental discourse that often rejected modern economic forms out of hand. The radical writing of the late twentieth century had been strongly aligned to trends in British or perhaps North American intellectual life. The collapse of these struts, and the once powerful influence of writers such as E. P. Thompson and Eric Hobsbawm, had a major effect in South Africa. The concept of transformation in South Africa, in popular parlance, was largely reduced to racial empowerment and few if any black writers on economic history emerged either to continue with, or even to challenge, the radical tradition.

The institutional setting

At this point, having surveyed the intellectual past of modern economic history in South Africa, some comment needs to be made on its institutional history. Since the late 1920s and following the British model, the ground between history and economics found some institutional purchase at the South African English-language universities that were designated for whites. H. M. Robertson headed up a small distinct economic history unit at the University of Cape Town. Eventually this became a very dynamic and lively site of research and debate under the leadership of the Zimbabwean Ian Phimister during the 1980s. Equally a smaller but separate Economic History Department was created at the University of Natal, in both of its branches in Durban and Pietermaritzburg. The Cape Town department was particularly important as a home for the political economy school, even though its efflorescence occurred outside the South African universities, often outside the country and sometimes with key stimuli from works of foreign academics with no institutional connection to the country.[1] Both in Natal and Cape Town the affinities were far more to history than to economics.

Elsewhere Departments of Economics were sometimes entitled Departments of Economics and Economic History and as such employed individuals mainly focused on economic history. It should also be mentioned that after 1980 Economic History took off very successfully at the University of Zimbabwe as a large, popular self-standing department. Black students there enjoyed political economy and indeed often considered it their main interest in history by contrast with South Africa where few black students have felt attracted to the field.

The mainstream economic history specialists at the University of the Witwatersrand and elsewhere felt doubly threatened. For them, economic history was a space to defend the values of the English-language business community against state intervention, Afrikaner nationalism and any suspicion of socialism. Most of them disliked the new wave of radical critics on the one hand and feared the impact of sanctions, tied as they were intellectually to conservative voices in Britain. It was symptomatic that Helen Suzman, the doughty voice of the Progressive Party and its later incarnations, briefly lectured in economic history at Wits. She was herself a remarkable mixture of liberal constitutional ideals and very business-oriented and right-wing conceptions of the economy. The lack of a strong institutional home for this rump led to an alternative focus in regular annual meetings and the publication of a journal of South African economic history. The dearth of good locally generated material and the incapacity of South Africans of this school to keep up with the increasingly sophisticated mathematics that pinioned mainstream economics forced them to resort to republishing work, from foreign journals, by well-known scholars. A characteristic publication co-authored by Stuart Jones of the University of the Witwatersrand and Andre Muller of the University of Port Elizabeth was not much more than a commentary on the statistics easily available in the national collection, *Union Statistics Yearbook 1910–60* (Muller and Jones 1992). Meetings were celebrated by the invitation to an eminent foreign figure, inevitably from a developed country whose pleasurable trip could be accommodated through generous corporate funding, thus striking a little blow at those campaigning for boycotts of South African universities. The defence of the beleaguered liberal whites in their universities was strongly sustained by business and indeed vice versa. One might say that economic history as an academic subject was thus highly conflicted and contested in the 1970s and 1980s as Kemp picked up, on a visit, in our initial quote. However, after 1994, the right-wing path too proved to be largely a dead end that disintegrated as individuals retired and eventually the journal folded.

New trends

There is currently a new impetus in economic history that we can connect to mainstream economics primarily. This involves initiatives from the ambitious Economics Department of the University of Stellenbosch which has now created a new economic history unit with permanent posts. Stellenbosch hosted the World Economic History Congress in 2012 in which African material had some prominence and has been instrumental in initiating a new journal with a developmental focus and an international ambit, *Economic History of Developing Regions* (see Fourie and Schirmer 2012). A new regionally structured Economic History Society has emerged. At the same time, a global economic history especially associated with the far-reaching propositions on long-term development of Daron Acemoglu and James

Robinson has fastened its attention on Africa. Coupled with this is a Stellenbosch approach to economic history wedded to the discovery and unfolding of sources subject to quantitative manipulation and assessment. In the case of Stellenbosch, Johan Fourie has been a remarkably energetic researcher. With a colleague, he has found in the records of the Dutch East India Company considerable evidence for inequality within the colonist population, to take one area of interest (Fourie and von Fintel 2010). So far this new activity has not really taken on the big themes of nineteenth- and twentieth-century South African economic history, whether to support or critique particular hypotheses. It also is equally true, as A. G. Hopkins pointed out acutely, that an Acemoglu/Robinson approach that looks for very broad environmental or demographic causes as to why Africa has or has not developed more will remain fairly sterile unless it can take on itself the available political and social history, come to grips with the particular in history and take seriously concepts like class (Hopkins 2009). Too much reliance on counterfactuals may be acceptable fare for an entertaining conference performance but will not advance knowledge very far. This applies as much to South Africa as to the West Africa that Hopkins understands so well.

At the same time, a political economy approach has resurfaced to a certain extent after many years in the doldrums. This is not unrelated to the downfall of Thabo Mbeki as president with his assurance that South Africa's fundamental problems were all under control. One may note moreover that key figures in this revival are largely foreigners in part based in South Africa. One factor is the revival of the MEC approach. Ben Fine and colleagues such as Samantha Ashman and Seeraj Mohamed have added to the older concept the new literature on financialization which is of increasing importance in understanding contemporary Western capitalism. A recent issue of *Transformation* has re-examined and reapplied the MEC which is gaining more popular traction (*Transformation* 2009; Ashman et al. 2011). Another factor is the revival of Economic History as an undergraduate major and Honours course within History although thus far without much postgraduate activity at the University of Cape Town. A third would be the understanding that harsh forms of labour discipline and worker poverty have not gone away and indeed continue to fuel the most important sources of foreign exchange and economic specialization in South Africa (Capps 2012; Alexander et al. 2013; Pons-Vignon 2014). Mining, ignored for two decades, has come back as a crucial subject and not merely from an anthropological perspective. Fourth, perhaps should be added the impact of the Zimbabwean crisis which has driven many young Zimbabwean social scientists, who tend to have a political economy approach more generally, towards South African universities. At the moment, Ian Phimister, long active at Oxford and Sheffield, has returned to South Africa where he heads up a vibrant research unit at Free State University that attracts a number of them. If South African economic history was being written in Britain in large part at one time, Zimbabwean economic history is now being written to a considerable extent in South Africa. At the University of Pretoria, the Human Economy project, which has attracted the British anthropologist Keith Hart to South Africa, looks at, amongst other subjects, the growing importance of credit at every level of South African life. Consumerism and credit is a subject that did not much fit the anti-*apartheid* rubric but deservedly is finding increasing traction.

In conclusion, economic history has been and continues to be a subject with some institutional life in South Africa. Its greater interest is the political significance in which it has been held. South Africa has many of the economic characteristics of a European settler colony that industrialized successfully. But it also absorbed a range of indigenous societies, poorly equipped to assimilate capitalist norms and strategies, which consequently assumed very oppressive forms. South Africa has thus generated an impressive historical literature but the strongest features align the study of the country's particularities to political economy and to a more holistic historical project than to the narrowest confines of economic history. Contemplating this history, as with other countries where capitalism deviates from apparent Western norms, highlights the mix of internal development and outside forces at work here, as elsewhere.

Note

1 The Cape Town department has since closed although undergraduate and recently postgraduate programmes are still offered by Historical Studies.

Bibliography

Alexander, P., T. Lekgowa, B. Mmope, L. Sinwell and B. Xezwi (2013) *Marikana: A View from the Mountain and a Case to Answer*, Johannesburg: Jacana.

Ashman, S., B. Fine and S. Newman (2011) 'The Crisis in South Africa: Neoliberalism, Financialization, Uneven and Combined Development', *Socialist Register*, 47.

Beinart, W. (1982) *The Political Economy of Pondoland*, Cambridge: Cambridge University Press.

Bozzoli, B. (1978) 'Marxism, Feminism and South African Studies', *Journal of Southern African Studies*, 9(2): 139–71.

Brennan, L., J. McDonald and R. Shlomowitz (1998) 'The Geographic and Social Origins of Indian Indentured Labourers in Mauritius, Natal, Fiji, Guyana and Jamaica', *Journal of South Asian Studies*, 26 special issue, 39–71.

Bundy, C. (1988) *The Rise and Fall of the South African Peasantry*, 2nd edition, Cape Town: David Philip.

Capps, G. (2012) '"Victim of Its Own Success?", The Platinum Industry and the Apartheid Mineral Property System in South Africa's Political Transition', *Review of African Political Economy*, 131: 63–84.

Christie, R. (1984) *Electricity, Industry and Class in South Africa*, London: Macmillan.

Christie, R. (1991) '"Antiquated Industrialization": A Comment on William Martin's "The Making of an Industrial South Africa"', *International Journal of African Historical Studies*, 24(3): 589–608.

Clark, N. (1994) *Manufacturing Apartheid; State Corporations in South Africa*, New Haven, CT: Yale University Press.

Cohen, R. (1974) *Labour and Politics in Nigeria 1945–71*, London: Heinemann.

Cooper, D. (1978) 'The State, Mineworkers and Multinationals and the Selebi Pikwe Strike, Botswana', in P. Gutkind, R. Cohen and J. Copans (eds.), *African Labour History*, Beverly Hills, CA: Sage.

Crompton, R. (1994) 'The South African Plastics Commodity Filière: History and Future Strategy', PhD dissertation, University of Natal.

Crush, J. (1987) *The Struggle for Swazi Labour*, Montreal: McGill-Queens University Press.

de Kiewiet, C. W. (1941) *A History of South Africa: Social and Economic*, Oxford: Clarendon Press.

de Kock, M. H. (ed.) (1924) *Selected Subjects in the Economic History of South Africa*, Cape Town: Juta.

Feinstein, C. (2005) *An Economic History of South Africa: Conquest, Discrimination and Development*, Cambridge: Cambridge University Press.

Fine, B. and Z. Rustomjee (1996) *The Political Economy of South Africa: From Minerals–Energy Complex to Complex Industrialisation*, Boulder, CO: Westview Press.

First, R., R. Forjaz and A. Manghezi (1983) *Black Gold: The Mozambican Miner, Proletarian and Peasant*, Brighton: Harvester.

Fourie, J. and D. von Fintel (2010) 'The Dynamics of Inequality in a Newly Settled Pre-industrial Society', *Cliometrica*, 4: 229–67.

Fourie, J. and S. Schirmer (2012) 'The Future of South African Economic History', *Economic History of Developing Regions*, 27(1): 114–24.

Frankel, S. H. (1938) *Capital Investment in Africa*, London: Oxford University Press.

Freund, B. (2009) 'The Significance of the Minerals–Energy Complex in the Light of South African Historiography', *Transformation*, 71: 26–49.

Freund, B. (2011) 'The Union Years 1910–48', in A. K. Mager, B. Nasson and R. Ross (eds.), *Cambridge History of South Africa, II 1885–1994*, Cambridge: Cambridge University Press.

Freund, W. M. (1996) 'Economic History in South Africa; An Introductory Overview', *South African Historical Journal*, 34: 127–50.
Gelb, S. (ed.) (1991) *South Africa's Economic Crisis*, Cape Town: James Currey.
Glaser, D. (2001) *Politics and Society in South Africa*, London: Sage.
Goodfellow, D. M. (1931) *The Modern Economic History of South Africa*, London: Routledge.
Greenberg, S. (1980) *Race and State in Capitalist Development*, New Haven, CT: Yale University Press.
Guy, J. (1987) 'Analysing Pre-capitalist Societies in Southern Africa', *Journal of Southern African Studies*, 14(1): 18–37.
Hopkins, A. G. (2009) 'The New Economic History of Africa', *Journal of African History*, 50(2): 155–77.
Houghton, D. H. (1967) *The South African Economy*, Cape Town: Oxford University Press.
Johnstone, F. (1976) *Class, Race and Gold: A Study of Class Relations and Racial Discrimination in South Africa*, London: Routledge.
Kahn, E. (1943) 'The Right to Strike in South Africa: An Historical Analysis', *South African Journal of Economics*, 11(1): 24–47.
Kaplan, D. (1990) *The Crossed Line: Technological Change and Telecommunications in South Africa*, Johannesburg: Witwatersrand University Press.
Kemp, T. (1993) *Historical Patterns of Industrialization*, 2nd edition, Harlow: Macmillan.
Knight, J. S. (1988) 'A Comparative Analysis of South Africa as a Semi-Industrialised Developing Country', *Journal of Modern African Studies*, 26(3): 473–93.
Kooy, M. and H. M. Robertson (1966) 'The South African Board of Trade and Industries, the South African Customs Tariff and the Development of South African Industries', *South African Journal of Economics*, 34(3): 205–24.
Legassick, M. (1977) 'Gold, Agriculture and Secondary Industry in South Africa: From Periphery to Sub-metropole as a Forced Labour System', in R. Palmer and N. Parsons (eds.), *The Roots of Rural Poverty in Central and Southern Africa*, London: Heinemann.
Lipton, M. (1985) *Capitalism and Apartheid*, London: Gower.
Mabin, A. (1984) 'The Making of Colonial Capitalism: Intensification and Expansion in the Economic Geography of the Cape Colony 1854–99', PhD dissertation, Simon Fraser University.
Macmillan, W. M. (1930) *Complex South Africa*, London: Faber and Faber.
Manicom, L. (1992) 'Ruling Relations: Rethinking State and Gender in South African History', *Journal of African History*, 33(3): 441–65.
Marks, S. and S. Trapido (1979) 'Lord Milner and the South African State', *History Workshop Journal*, 8(1): 55–81.
Marquard, A. (2006) 'The Origins and Development of South African Energy Policy', PhD dissertation, University of Cape Town.
Muller, A. and S. Jones (1992) *The South African Economy 1910–90*, Basingstoke: Macmillan.
Murray, C. (1992) *Black Mountain: Land, Class and Power in the Eastern Orange Free State, 1880s–1980s*, Edinburgh: Edinburgh University Press.
Nattrass, J. (1981) *The South African Economy: Its Growth and Change*, Cape Town: Oxford University Press.
Norval, A. J. (1962) *Industrial Progress in South Africa*, Cape Town: Juta.
Pons-Vignon, Nicolas (2014) 'Tuer à la Tâche; économie politique de la sous-traitance dans le secteur forestier sud-africain', PhD dissertation, Ecole des Hautes Etudes en Sciences Sociales, Paris.
Richards, C. S. (1940) *The Iron and Steel Industry of South Africa*, Johannesburg: Witwatersrand University Press.
Schumann, C. G. W. (1938) *Structural Changes and Business Cycles in South Africa 1800–1936*, London: Staples Press.
Seekings, J. and N. Nattrass (2005) *Class, Race and Inequality in South Africa*, New Haven, CT: Yale University Press.
Simons, H. J. and R. Simons (1983[1969]) *Class and Colour in South Africa 1850–1950*, London: International Defence and Aid Fund.
Terreblanche, S. (2002) *A History of Inequality in South Africa 1652–2002*, Pietermaritzburg: University of Natal Press.
Trapido, S. (1971) 'South Africa in a Comparative Study of Industrialisation', *Journal of Development Studies*, 7(3): 309–20.
Transformation. (2009) Special issue on the Minerals–Energy Complex, 71.

van der Horst, S. (1971[1942]) *Native Labour in South Africa*, London: Frank Cass.
van der Merwe, P. J. (1995) *The Migrant Farmer in the History of the Cape Colony*, Athens: Ohio University Press.
van Onselen, C. (1980) *Chibaro: African Mine Labour in Southern Rhodesia 1900–33*, London: Pluto.
van Onselen, C. (1996) *The Seed is Mine: The Life of Kas Maine, a South African Sharecropper 1894–1985*, Cape Town: David Philip.
Wassenaar, A. D. (1977) *Assault on Private Enterprise: The Freeway to Communism*, Cape Town: Tafelberg.
Wilson, F. (1972) *Labour in the South African Gold Mines 1911–69*, Cambridge: Cambridge University Press.
Wolpe, H. (1972) 'Capitalism and Cheap Labour-Power in South Africa: From Segregation to Apartheid', *Economy and Society*, 1(4): 425–56.

25
AFRICAN ENCOUNTERS WITH GLOBAL NARRATIVES

Patrick Manning

In 1994, Paul Tiyambe Zeleza published *A Modern Economic History of Africa. Vol. 1: The Nineteenth Century*. Published by the Council for Development of Economic and Social Research in Africa (CODESRIA), the volume won the 1994 Noma Award for Publishing in Africa.[1] The work itself was the most substantial economic history yet published of nineteenth-century Africa, and appeared to open an era in which scholars born on the African continent would take leadership in the study of its economic history. The detailed synthesis of the literature made the case for the great diversity of African economic life, generated by African-led processes of growth emerging out of domestic economies and also by the undermining of African growth through the progressive impact of enslavement for overseas markets. CODESRIA had formed twenty years earlier as a collaborative body organized to link social scientists across the African continent; it appeared at this moment to be stepping forward in the field of economic history in addition to its established strength in policy studies.

In practice, the 1994 appearance of this book ended up as a significant but modest advance along an existing trajectory rather than as a real turning point. Zeleza, after the warm reception of his book, was drawn into other scholarly activities: he did not publish the projected second volume of his economic history.[2] His career paralleled that of several earlier writers on economic issues in Africa who began with key interventions in African economic history and then moved on to work in other fields.[3] Similarly CODESRIA, while it gradually gained in strength as a publisher, was not able to follow up Zeleza's volume with other studies in economic history.

Zeleza's work echoed and expanded that of earlier African-born scholars who published single volumes addressing economic history: Dike 1956; Ly 1958; Afana 1966; Daaku 1970; Ekundare 1973. One outstanding example of continuous intervention and evolution in economic analysis is Samir Amin, who published his first book in 1965 and continues to produce. Amin, born in Egypt, educated in economics in France, and based in Dakar for the majority of his long career, has been remarkable in writing on both historical and contemporary economic affairs in Africa and the world (Amin 1965; Amin 2009). With these and some other exceptions, the predominant writers in African economic history have lived and worked outside of Africa. The literature in African economic history has yielded some works of real excellence, written by both continental and overseas authors, but it has not thrived in any sense. Instead, African economic history has been marginal to the field of economic history generally and has been principally descriptive rather than analytical. While African history in general can be said to have developed with great success and achievement, economic history has remained marginal.

This chapter surveys the evolution of studies of African economic history and scrutinizes the debates within topical and especially temporal sub-fields of African economic history. The debates include whether the study of national-era (post-1960) African economies should incorporate data on the period before 1960 and, for earlier times, whether studies of Africa's overseas trade should be linked to socio-economic changes within Africa. To a remarkable extent, African economies have been analyzed through a variety of dualistic, two-sector models: domestic and international, traditional and modern, labor and capital, market and non-market, men's work and women's work.[4] African populations have been seen as dense or sparse, innovative or resistant to change, and able to generate surplus and investment or not. The tendency to analyze in dichotomous terms, compounded by the rudimentary skills in economic analysis of many contributors, has limited the clarity and value of the literature.

Despite these limits, much has been learned about African economic history during the past half-century. While neither datasets nor economic analysis have developed in much detail, African economic history benefits from historians' descriptions of economic life and from the multidisciplinary character of African studies, which has led to participation of adjoining disciplines in the analysis of African economic life – notably anthropology, demography, and agricultural economics. As a result, empirical evidence has accumulated and the inherited dualisms have been steadily nuanced. At least ten literature reviews have been composed for African economic history, though the unevenness of the reviews reflects the unevenness of research in the field.[5]

The task in this chapter is to analyze economic history at the continental rather than the national level; the chapter also treats Africa as part of a global economic system. Africa is the largest geographic unit analyzed in this book. Indeed, the African continent's surface area is well over half that of Eurasia, and Africa is nearly as large as North and South America combined. The Africa we analyze here has not one but over fifty national units, with a total population of over one billion – nearly matching that of India and China and exceeding the total population of Europe. African population density is best seen as *moderate* on a world scale rather than *sparse*. While only one-tenth that of India the density is more than one-third that of Eurasia as a whole and exceeds that of the Americas and Russia. In the eighteenth and nineteenth centuries, African population was stagnant while that of other regions grew substantially. Thus, the African proportion of Old World population declined from some 20 percent to 10 percent over two centuries, then regained most of its relative loss in the twentieth century (Manning 2014). In both population and economic activities, the African continent is best analyzed through its links with other regions and not only through its regional distinctiveness. Africa has often been presented as a distinct civilizational unit, but the idea of continental uniqueness tends to endorse belief in its backwardness and then to treating it as isolated from the world beyond its shores.

The topics addressed by economic historians of Africa stretch across the past five centuries. From 1500 to 1700 African continental trade fluctuated significantly, as did its maritime commerce and the extent of its large-scale polities. In coastal and in maritime zones, rising powers (Ottoman, Portuguese, Dutch, English, and French) gained hegemony, especially through a growing process of enslavement for overseas markets. The eighteenth century brought great expansion in the export slave trade resulting in population decline for West and Central Africa. In the nineteenth century slave exports peaked and then declined, after which enslavement on the mainland expanded to a peak, briefly setting up a new political economy that is not yet well understood.[6] African exports of agricultural commodities and minerals grew steadily as free-trade imperialism came to dominate maritime relations. From the late nineteenth century, European powers seized virtually the whole of African territory. They soon raised taxes and reoriented flows of labor, commodities, and money. Peasantries survived and even expanded during the colonial era – incorporating those who escaped slavery. After a half-century of integration into metropolitan economies, most African territories won national independence between 1960 and 1975. Independent governments focused initially on Keynesian policies of social welfare, thus extending the postwar era of economic growth. From about 1975 African economies stagnated, governments found themselves in debt and under the tutelage of the World Bank, urbanization accelerated, and the peasantry weakened. Meanwhile, the indices of health and education in African nations, having improved markedly from the 1950s in response to postcolonial state policies of social welfare, improved at a slower rate through the 1980s. The southern half of the continent has been hurt seriously in economic and demographic terms by the HIV/AIDS epidemic from the 1990s to the present. Nevertheless, continental GDP per capita and foreign direct investment have returned to growth in the twenty-first century.

Imperial and colonial studies of African economies, to 1960

The literature on African economic history, for the purposes of this chapter, is taken to begin with studies conducted during the colonial era. Colonial administrations developed and published records of revenue, expenditure, and overseas trade; official ethnologists studied African social life. European-style universities first arose in South Africa and Northern Africa among European settler groups; their policies and documents laid the groundwork for later academic study of economic history.

The colonial perspective focused on levels of tax revenue, the value of exports, and growth rates of these two variables. Programs of infrastructure in ports and railroads led to concern for public finance; loans were usually paid off rapidly through forced savings from African tax revenue. Monetary policies varied among the colonial powers, but generally consisted of imposing the metropolitan currency on the colonies, demonetizing prior currencies. Labor policies focused on selecting the degree of forced labor to be imposed. State-supported programs of agricultural development or experiment were given high visibility but entailed modest investment, mostly funds from local tax revenue. From the 1890s through the 1920s, the various colonial governments pursued this largely extractive economic policy: as a result, African trade came to be rerouted entirely through the colonial powers. Works of early-colonial enthusiasts show that the early twentieth century was an era of economic growth for much of Africa (Sarraut 1923; McPhee 1926). Further reflection suggests that the gradual movement of millions of slaves into peasant status may have been as significant in contributing to that era of growth as were the policies of colonial government.

From the 1930s, colonial regimes adopted greater concern for welfare within their territories, at once through advances of economic thinking in the colonial administrations and in response to the organization of social movements and political pressures from the governed (Hancock, Lord Hailey). Studies of African population became more detailed and anthropological analysis gave closer attention to the perspectives of those under study. In this era two publications by South African scholars arguably launched the formal study of economic history on the continent. S. H. Frankel's 1938 study of capital investment traced capital imports especially for southern Africa; C. W. de Kiewiet's 1941 overview of South

African socio-economic history emphasized a narrative of British colonial expansion. Soon thereafter, at the other extreme of the continent, Charles Issawi published a 1947 economic history of Egypt focusing especially on the nineteenth century (Frankel 1938; DeKiewiet 1941; Issawi 1947).

As the Second World War ended, Asian colonies gained immediate independence, so that African territories remained as the principal European colonies. Within those colonies, economic and social policies ranged widely. At one extreme, the 1948 elections in South Africa brought *apartheid* policies; in parallel, Portuguese and Belgian colonial rule remained highly restrictive. At another limit, France allowed establishment of some trade union rights and built new infrastructure with a combination of Marshall Plan funds and local taxation, while British colonies too emphasized conciliation across class and racial lines and began to apply Keynesian policies of economic growth and regulation. The St-Lucian-born economist W. A. Lewis consulted with the government of Gold Coast and completed a 1953 report on industrialization; out of it he developed his vision of "economic development with unlimited supplies of labour" a two-sector model (based on capitalist and subsistence sectors) that linked economic growth and international trade. This model has remained influential in the global literature to the present (Lewis 1954, 1963).

The issue of macroeconomic analysis and accompanying historical statistics arose in Africa as elsewhere from the 1940s. In an important innovation, Phyllis Deane began study of British colonial social accounting in 1941 and published a 1953 book on social accounting for Northern Rhodesia but her work was dropped in practice when Northern Rhodesia was incorporated into the Central African Federation.[7] Little effort was devoted to calculating retrospective national accounts and GDP for African territories, but two works demonstrated that the task was feasible if difficult. P. N. C. Okigbo created national accounts for the period 1950–57 in Nigeria (Okigbo 1962). Okigbo recognized the complexity and limitations of African national accounts, but strongly supported the creation of time series.[8] In parallel, Maldant and Haubert calculated national income estimates for the French territories of West and Central Africa from 1947 through to 1965 (Maldant and Haubert 1973). Their study was anachronistic in that the French colonial federations that they analyzed had been Balkanized into independent republics in 1956, yet they managed to show the feasibility of estimating national income back to 1947.[9] One might seek to argue that pre-independence African economies relied too heavily on non-market production and rural institutions for historical statistics and national income analysis to be of any value. However, historical analysis shows continuity rather than dramatic change in productive systems and institutions with the shift to the postcolonial era during which such statistics have been universally produced (Helleiner 1966; Manning 1982, 1990–91). Lack of estimation of time series for African national accounts was more a matter of lack of funding than of a sudden and sharp change from informal economies to modernity (Berry 1992).

Meanwhile, marketing boards for agricultural exports, first created in the 1930s, expanded as a device for appropriating revenue from peasants in order to invest it in infrastructure (Bauer 1954). Other areas of research and debate in African economic life included labor policy and labor migration, agricultural policy and peasant societies, and debates within economic anthropology on the nature of African rationality. Studies in economic anthropology, often with a historical dimension, developed substantially during the 1950s and 1960s (Herskovits 1952; Hill 1963; Meillassoux 1964). In the same era, historians began to publish studies of Africa's precolonial maritime and commercial history, including the works of Abdoulaye Ly on the Compagnie du Sénégal, K. G. Davies on the Royal Africa Company, and K. O. Dike on nineteenth-century trade and politics in the Niger Delta (Ly 1955; Dike 1956; Davies 1957).

Independence: the era of nationalism, growth, and Keynesianism, 1960–75

By the end of 1960 more than half of Africa's people and nations had gained political independence. Rapidly, a new national perspective replaced the colonial perspective in economic analysis and in social science generally. Multidisciplinary research in African Studies had begun in the last years of the colonial era, but accelerated greatly with the independence of African states: African Studies programs formed especially in the UK, France, and the USA, but also in Belgium, Italy, Germany, Portugal, Sweden, the Soviet Union, and Canada. Similarly, as African universities were established and gained strength, African Studies programs formed in Ghana, Nigeria, Kenya, Uganda, Senegal and, with a somewhat different dynamic, in South Africa. The innovation was that scholars in distinct disciplines worked relatively closely with one another. Thus economic studies of Africa have included, since this time, links among the disciplines of economics, history, anthropology, agricultural economics, and population studies.

International trade remained the principal focus in studies of African economies, both historical and contemporary. But the unit of analysis now became the nation state rather than the empire, and such macroeconomic variables as GDP began to be discussed; with time the discussion extended to levels of public debt. In international trade the focus changed as well: from the colonial concern with the value of exports to a national concern with trade balances. Microeconomic analysis also shifted in postcolonial times, adding firm-level studies of technology, finance, and output to the earlier institutional and policy-oriented studies of projects.

The shifts in perspective with independence were smaller in related fields where scholars had earlier established clear contact with African agriculturists and their perspectives. The works of agronomists thus provide substantial continuity in interpretive frameworks (Jones 1959; Miracle 1966, 1967; Boserup 1966, 1970). The outstanding exception was that of René Dumont, who provided a stinging critique of postcolonial agricultural policy for failing to break more fully with colonial policies (Dumont 1962). The study of economic anthropology flowered from the 1950s to the 1970s (Hill 1963; Meillassoux 1971). In addition, the literature exploring precolonial African trade and politics, written from a socio-political perspective, that emphasized the agency of African participants, continued up to the mid-1970s (Pankhurst 1961; Gray and Birmingham 1970; Daaku 1970; and Martin 1972).

Study of African economic history expanded first among scholars trained in economics, and somewhat later among scholars trained in history. Among economists, major publications appeared from the mid-1960s (Houghton 1964; Amin 1965, 1971; Afana 1966; Baldwin 1966; Helleiner 1966; Kay and Hymer 1972; Brett 1973; Berry 1975; Birnberg and Resnick 1975). For the French African colonies, a major effort at data collection and macroeconomic statistical analysis for the era 1947–60 had ended up as an anachronism. The federations of French West Africa and French Equatorial Africa, combined for analysis by Maldant and Haubert into the "African West" (l'Ouest africain), were dissolved by a 1956 act of the French government into nineteen separate units that became independent nations by 1960 (Maldant and Haubert 1973). During the transition to African independence, economic analysis included some further efforts to lay the groundwork for retrospective national accounts but these were not sustained (Okigbo 1965; Szereszewski 1965; Helleiner 1966). As a result, African countries initially had no time series on GDP. Only for South Africa has this distinction between colonial and national perspectives on the economy been resolved sufficiently to provide a continuous set of economic statistics going back as far as the early twentieth century (Houghton 1964).

Scholars trained in history soon joined the field and eventually became the principal contributors to the literature in African economic history. The initial wave of such works, appearing in the 1970s, came from historians with knowledge of economic principles (Coquery-Vidrovitch 1972; Latham 1973; Ekundare 1973; Hopkins 1973; Curtin 1975; Alpers 1975). In general, the outlook of these works focused on African social change. Subsequent postcolonial historiography was influenced by a number of external shocks. These included drought (in West, East, and Southern Africa), civil war (in the Congo and Nigeria), continuing struggles for national liberation (in Angola and South Africa), and growing Cold War confrontation in several African regions. In the 1970s, early programs in structural adjustment designed by the World Bank – to ensure that foreign debt would be repaid – led to cutbacks in Keynesian policies of social conciliation and reinforced the overall slowing in economic growth that had begun to take hold. These post-independence events of the 1960s and early 1970s brought substantial shifts in the emerging literature on African economic history.

One result was that radical nationalist and Black Power movements arose in the late 1960s, fueled by the insufficiencies of independence-era reform and a growing African critique of neocolonialism. These movements linked up with the concurrent global explosion in New Left, neo-Marxian, dependency-oriented studies.[10] Andre Gunder Frank's phrase, "the development of underdevelopment," while coined for the experience of colonial Latin America, had soon brought an impact to Africa with Walter Rodney's study of underdevelopment in Africa in somewhat later times (Rodney 1972).[11] Immanuel Wallerstein, a sociologist whose early work centered on the politics of newly independent states, turned in 1968 to focus on an analysis of the rise of Atlantic capitalism (Wallerstein 1974). Samir Amin and Giovanni Arrighi, each of whose early work focused on colonial African territories, found that Marxian and neo-Marxian economic paradigms offered a new potential for linking the national and colonial eras in economic studies that gradually expanded to a global scale (Amin 1973; Arrighi and Saul 1973). A literature on the creation of underdevelopment through colonialism arose particularly on Kenya, contesting earlier views of traditional societies being brought willingly or unwillingly to modernization. The analysis was reformulated to pose the question of the timing, the nature, and the causes of the African transition to capitalism (Brett 1973; Leys 1974; Wolff 1974; Kitching 1980; Langdon 1981).

Other scholars were working within the emerging framework of political economy specializing in various period studies of class formation focused on the national period (e.g. Bernstein and Campbell 1985); studies of underdevelopment focused on the colonial period (e.g. Brett 1973; but see Leys 1974); and studies of the articulation of modes of production centered on the precolonial era (e.g. Dupré and Rey 1973; but see Rey 1971). The same era of intellectual and political turmoil brought greater attention to studies of slavery – in the Americas, in Africa, and linking the two Atlantic shores. Expanding a literature that had emphasized studies of slavery in the Americas, Philip Curtin's 1969 book on the volume of the Atlantic slave trade opened up a huge area of study on linkages across the Atlantic: controversy began immediately and further research continued for decades. Eventually it became clear that these were studies of maritime African economic history.[12]

A wide-ranging field of African economic history appeared to be forming: it showed the potential of linkage to economics, social history, agronomy, and anthropology, with work on both continental and maritime history spanning neoclassical and Marxian outlooks and paradigms, and spanning several centuries of change (Herskovits and Harwitz 1964). On the African continent, CODESRIA took form in 1973 as an organization linking social science scholars of anglophone and francophone Africa; the Association of African Historians formed in the same year.[13] At the same time and overseas a Ford Foundation program provided research fellowships in Africa for roughly ten scholars in 1973, and brought the same scholars together for a workshop in Madison in the summer of 1974. The participants included several scholars of African birth who went on to publish their work.[14] Curtin's economic history of Senegambia appeared in print in the wake of this program (Curtin 1975). While the book was widely praised for its deep exploration of written and oral sources, differences arose between those who gave it full praise and those who argued that it underemphasized the negative influence of the slave trade and misstated the role of imported goods in the domestic economy. The skeptics included French academics who drew on work of Senegalese scholars and an American economist.[15]

Economic historians of both colonial and precolonial Africa showed increasing interest in firms, both African and European (Hopkins 1973; Berry 1975; Coquery-Vidrovitch 1975). Some writers breached the divide between precolonial and colonial economic history; their analyses focused on trade, government policies, and on studies of commercial firms (Hill 1963; Hopkins 1973). Connections to American-influenced cliometric history appeared in a few studies (Birnberg and Resnick 1975; Manning 1982). Overall, this era included initiatives in studies of African economies from a number of perspectives, with the possibility that they might have interacted productively. Such studies did much to open up discussion of long-term economic continuity and change and about the periodization of African economic history.

This first wave of studies in African economic history posed substantial challenges to the various sorts of dualism that had dominated colonial-era thinking. The scrutiny of African rationality no longer occupied great spaces in the literature. One of the major topics within that debate, the backward-sloping labor supply cure, died down after effective explication and refutation of the target-worker thesis (Miracle and Fetter). An anthropological dualism distinguishing market from non-market behavior declined after debate on the economic–historical terrain (Dalton, Hopkins). Other debates arose on African modes of production and on the relative contributions of the state and the private sector to African economic growth (Coquery-Vidrovitch 1969). More broadly, discussion continued on the question of whether economic change in Africa has resulted more from external (usually European) influences, from autonomous African developments, or from some interaction of the two. These discussions in African economic history, addressing various eras and topics, appeared to be expanding in scope and included a growing number of African-born scholars. Anthony Hopkins, whose *Economic History of West Africa* (1973) represented a bold step in synthesizing precolonial and colonial economic history, discerned among economists a rising interest in economic history, as a response to the failure of many short-range plans for rapid growth and development. Hopkins's judgment, however, turned out to have been premature.

Structural adjustment, neoliberalism, and new nations 1976–95

In the late 1970s and early 1980s, the modest momentum built up in African economic history continued to bring new studies. J. Forbes Munro published a skillful overview of Africa and the international economy in the nineteenth and early twentieth centuries, based on British Parliamentary Papers (Munro 1976). Bogumil Jewsiewicki led in publication of a collection of articles on the Great Depression in the Belgian Congo (Jewsiewicki 1977); Catherine Coquery-Vidrovitch led a parallel collection on the Great Depression in French colonies. Several monographs on African economic history appeared in this era: a study of the rise and persistence of groundnut exports from Northern Nigeria; a regional economic history of Central Niger focusing on the nineteenth century; a long-term study of Dahomey

(Benin Republic) combining cliometric and other quantitative economic history with long-term growth analysis and social history; a survey of Egyptian economic history focusing on the nineteenth century; and two studies of the South African economy from the late nineteenth century (Hogendorn 1977; Baier 1980; Natrass 1981; Manning 1982; Issawi 1982; Yudelman 1983; see also Cooper 1980 and Sheriff 1987). The US Social Science Research Council commissioned a review of Africa and the world economy and then a review of African agriculture (Cooper 1981; Berry 1984).

This expansion of studies in African economic history, however, clearly came to an end as the 1980s proceeded. A forceful campaign of the World Bank in the early 1980s, reducing African public expenditures, had the effect of undermining studies of African economic history. The campaign brought imposition of Structural Adjustment plans on African economies, privileging World Bank economists over national ministers of finance, and pressing for massive cuts in public services in order to ensure rapid repayment of huge debts that had grown up during the 1970s. In the 1981 Berg Report, named after its principal author, Harvard economist Elliott Berg, the World Bank generally condemned African governments for following mistaken, state-centered economic policy. In the same breath, Berg equally rejected the previous policies of colonial governments.[16] In practice, the World Bank showed no interest in the African past; policy was to start anew.

A new dualism became increasingly explicit: it divided Africa's past at the year 1960 and separated contemporary Africa (the national era) from historical Africa (the colonial and precolonial eras).[17] In this dualistic vision, the contemporary era was the preserve of economic development and economic policy experts, while the historical period was relegated to historians and anthropologists for antiquarian study. The successful imposition of this intellectual dichotomy cut African economic history off from the economic analysis of contemporary Africa, cut it off from the economic history of other world regions, and left studies of African economic history to atrophy.[18] Looking back to this era with today's terminology, one may say that an expanding neoliberal outlook conveyed the impression that African economic history was irrelevant.

The academic ostracism of African economic history was reinforced by shifts in global and African conditions that restricted resources for historical investigation. The field became further restricted in response to African economic difficulties, global conflicts, and widespread ideological change. The October 1973 war between Israel and its Arab neighbors led to a boycott in petroleum sales from nations of the Organization of the Petroleum Exporting Countries (OPEC) to Western powers. Petroleum prices remained at peak levels until 1984; in addition, interest rates (especially for African countries) rose in the 1970s and peaked in the early 1980s, so that most African nations ended up in severe international debt. Serious droughts affected West, Central, and East Africa. The Portuguese colonial empire ended with the revolution of 1975, but the aftermath brought expansion of Cold War struggles in various parts of Africa. The World Bank imposed increasingly stringent structural adjustment policies that cut back public expenditure throughout the continent. From the mid-1970s, one sort of austerity after another limited growth in African countries. The virtual halt to foreign investment, with the exception of investment in petroleum drilling, further limited growth. One result was that African universities, already restricted by governments as sites of potential political protest, were cut back for fiscal reasons.[19]

The Berg Report and Structural Adjustment Programs brought fragmentation as well as limits to the discourse on African economic history: scholars pursuing the various approaches to African economic life fell out of contact with one another. The potential collaborations among economists, historians, agronomists, and other scholars in the study of African economies gave way to isolated work by scholars in segregated fields. Studies of post-1960 economic change, directed by economists, advanced without reference to the preceding era. From this time, while many African students took up the study of economics, virtually none of these students took up economic history – nor even long-term approaches to economic policy. Economic historians of Africa met for a time in Britain through the Third World Economic History group and in Paris through the Laboratoire Connaissance du Tiers-Monde, but no regular meetings persisted. Attempts to link precolonial and colonial history, Marxian and neoclassical analysis, anthropological and historical data, or African maritime history and that of the continent, received even less attention than before.

Nor did African economic historians manage to establish and sustain a strong forum for publication and debate. A journal established in 1976, *African Economic History*,[20] gave primacy to social history, agricultural economics, and studies of colonial administrative policy; it privileged descriptive studies and economic anthropology rather than sharpened debates in economic history.[21] The articles, roughly equally divided between those covering colonial and precolonial Africa, tended to focus on trade, production, firm studies, and government policy. Slavery and slave trade, comprising a major issue in precolonial economic history, accounted for a small proportion of the articles in *African Economic History*. In sum, from this time most of the central contributions in African economic history were by scholars with little knowledge of economics. *Economic History Review* maintained some recognition of Africa especially during the 1980s when A. G. Hopkins served as the journal's co-editor. African articles published in the *Journal of Economic History* were mostly on the slave trade, an issue readily linked to the journal's extensive coverage of slavery in the American South.[22] The *Review of African Political Economy* (*ROAPE*), founded in 1973, had by the early 1980s turned its radical analysis away from historical issues to focus on contemporary issues.[23]

Scholars who had begun their work in African economic history moved to adjoining fields. A. G. Hopkins joined with P. J. Cain to propose an interpretation of the British Empire in general for the nineteenth and twentieth centuries (Cain and Hopkins 1980, 1993). Patrick Manning moved primarily to studies of African migration and demographic history, which enjoyed a period of productive activity under the leadership of Joel Gregory (Fetter 1983, 1990; Cordell and Gregory 1987; Manning 1990; Cordell et al. 1996). Nevertheless, a few historical studies of remarkable originality appeared in this era: a global study of the cowrie trade, encompassing the Indian Ocean and the Atlantic; a twentieth-century study of the subordination of peasant farmers to the urban, professional lives of their children; and a continental synthesis of African poverty in the nineteenth and twentieth centuries (Hogendorn and Johnson 1985; Berry 1985; Iliffe 1987). In some cases the turmoil of the time led to rapid responses in the scholarly literature: Gerald Helleiner focused his considerable energies on analysis of the contemporary African debt crisis (Helleiner 1981; see also Helleiner 1966). In another instance, several scholars responded to drought in the Saharan fringe and Central Africa with historical analyses tracing both the periodic episodes of drought and the social responses in earlier times (Lovejoy and Baier 1975; Dias 1981; Miller 1982; Becker 1985).

Additional studies appeared in fields allied to economic history. Thus, while the sustained discourse on economic history dissipated, works of relevance to economic history continued to appear. Jacques Marseille's critique of the ineffectiveness of French empire pursued this trend from a critical perspective (Marseille 1984). D. K. Fieldhouse defended the effectiveness of empire with the argument that economic decolonization brought arrested development. (Fieldhouse 1986). Labor history, both precolonial and colonial, developed a linkage to economic history, although it remains entirely separate from economic history for some regions (Gutkind et al. 1978; Van Onselen 1982; Freund 1984, 1988; Coquery-Vidrovitch and Lovejoy

1985; Phimister 1988). Studies in business history appeared in a brief flurry, focusing both on expatriate firms (Hopkins 1973; Coquery-Vidrovitch 1975; Fieldhouse 1978) and on African firms and enterprises (Berry 1975; Forest 1983). Social history analyses held clear relevance for economic history (Isaacman 1972; Gran 1979). And social scientists in adjoining disciplines published work that clearly reinforced contemporary study in economic history (Schatz 1977; Bates 1983). Among them, Keith Hart continued to develop a notion of informal economy that later gained wide currency (Hart 1982). In the compiling of data resources, Marion Johnson's work of coding all British trade with Africa from 1689 into the nineteenth century was the principal advance in this arena (Johnson 1990). Generally, these were continuing works by scholars who had entered the field earlier, rather than publications by junior scholars.[24]

The most impressive body of Africa-related data assembled from 1975 to 1995 that was relevant to African economic history in this period was that on the volume of Atlantic slave trade. From Curtin's initial synthetic census through Jean Mettas's complete listing of eighteenth-century French slave voyages to David Eltis's work on the nineteenth-century slave trade, this work demonstrates that a sustained and intensive effort can succeed in creating a historical database upon which a revealing historical analysis can be constructed (Curtin 1969; Mettas 1978, 1984; Eltis 1987). This work linked the issues of slavery, commerce, and migration for Africa, the Americas, Europe, and the Atlantic (Lovejoy 1983; Miller 1988, 1985; Manning 1990). However, this research remained an isolated field of study in that it did not become part of the literature on migration and only slowly became integrated into study of Africa's continental history.[25]

To return to the point at which this chapter began, Paul Tiyambe Zeleza's extensive 1994 economic history of nineteenth-century Africa brought a flurry of excitement and hopes for revival in the field, through its attention to shifting economic structures and the agency of merchants and producers within the continent. The book had the inherent capacity to reinvigorate the field, but interest and energy had simply expired. Previously and at a somewhat similar level, Ralph Austen's 1987 continental survey of African economic history, while it gave careful attention to the various schools and approaches within the field, and while it gave a long-term survey of the continent's economic change, did not succeed in launching debate or renewed research (Austen 1987).

Post-Cold War Africa, since 1995

For the last twenty years of the twentieth century, per capita GDP stagnated and commonly declined in Africa. In the 1990s the HIV/AIDS pandemic brought a collapse in life expectation in southern and eastern Africa, though lifespans rose again in the early twenty-first century. Remarkably, and despite the continent's recurring crisis and disaster, African societies had achieved striking overall advances in certain indices of social welfare by the early years of the twenty-first century. By 2010, the continent's land was able to support over four times as many people as it had in 1950, notwithstanding repeated food crises and famines, and the average lifespan had risen by one-third, from 35 to 50 years. Aggregate GDP had increased at rates roughly equal to those of population growth. In the same time period, adult literacy had risen from under 5 percent to near 50 percent (and most of the literacy was in second languages). Higher education too had advanced remarkably: by 2010, Nigeria was able to claim 100 universities within its borders. An extraordinary process of urbanization unfolded, bringing the African level of urbanization to some 40 percent, above that of Asia. In the virtual absence of public investment, communal facilities for health, education, and transportation were created and maintained.

How did this contradictory set of socio-economic changes emerge? The contrast of stagnation in GDP per capita, on the one hand, and African advance in social conditions and community development, on the other, is worthy of deeper study. A related question is whether GDP, in its standard calculations, is an adequate measure of African economic growth or social welfare.[26] Further, the apparent contrast between the nature of African economic change in the late twentieth century and that of other large regions of the world should call for study of African economies, both in their own contemporary terms and in terms of their trajectory over the past century or two. But the weakness of research institutions within Africa and the weakness of African-oriented economic history outside of the continent held back detailed documentation or analysis.

The era since 1995 has seen a gradual return of interest in the economic history of Africa. One may argue that, by 2010, the level of interest and activity had become roughly equal to that thirty years earlier when the field gained its first head of steam. The steps in academic advance, nevertheless, have been gradual. For instance, works published in the late 1990s addressing a range of historical and contemporary issues were valuable but small in number.[27] Meanwhile, the larger number of studies in African social history contributed to a revival of interest in economic history. David Eltis led in assembling a comprehensive dataset on Atlantic slave trade, published in 1999, which greatly facilitated research on the slave trade and its implications from the sixteenth century forward; a revised and expanded edition of this work appeared online in 2010 (Eltis et al. 1999, 2010). For West Africa, studies in the social history of enslavement and emancipation expanded (Diouf 2003; Scully and Paton 2005). For the Indian Ocean, Gwyn Campbell edited several conference volumes on slave trade, while other scholars published historical volumes focusing on East African labor history, identity, and consumption behavior (Allen 1999; Larson 2000; Campbell 2004, 2005a, 2005b; Alpers et al. 2005; Prestholdt 2008). More broadly, global studies in migration history, led by Jan and Leo Lucassen, accepted the arguments of Africanists that the African slave trade and other African migration should be explicitly incorporated into global migration history (Manning 2005; Lucassen et al. 2010).

An expanded number of economic history studies appeared in the new century. Joseph Inikori's study of the role of African trade in the British industrial revolution advanced the Atlantic dimension of economic history (Inikori 2002; see also Manning 2006). Gareth Austin's numerous studies of labor in Ghana culminated in a substantial work on the transition from slavery to free labor (Austin 2005). Gwyn Campbell's economic history of nineteenth-century Madagascar identified patterns of trade, production, and social structure that appeared to be relevant for other large African states (Campbell 2005b). Much new knowledge on African economic history was accumulating.[28] Promising trends appeared from several directions, suggesting that the scattered elements of research in African economic history might eventually be gathered into a program of sophisticated analysis. First, Master's theses and doctoral dissertations prepared in African universities over the years began to become more widely available, for instance through the process of digitization at the Université Cheikh-Anta Diop in Dakar.[29] Second, A. I. Asiwaju, working in association with the leadership of the Association of African Historians, developed a call for comparative studies within the African continent as a way of promoting scholarship on Africa to connect to studies in global history (Asiwaju 2003–4).[30]

A third trend arose from debates within neoclassical economic theory. Daron Acemoglu and colleagues took up the issue of the long-term causes of contemporary poverty, arguing that early deprivation could show up centuries later as slow economic growth (Acemoglu et al. 2001). Nathan Nunn offered an explicitly African application, arguing that early impoverishment through slave trade led across the centuries to slow growth in certain regions of modern Africa, and A. G. Hopkins responded that such research might indeed bring a revival of studies in African economic history (Nunn 2008; Hopkins 2009). In two further major advances, African-born scholars now became prominent in the revival of economic historical studies, and scholarship began to emphasize overlaps and interconnections of economic history (before 1960) and economic development (after 1960). Tetteh Kofi and Asayehgn Desta published a volume on agronomy linking history and policy (Kofi and Desta 2008). Ellen Hillborn and Erik Green published a Swedish-language continental survey of economic and social history (Hillborn and Green 2010). A 2010 conference in Accra, sponsored by Harvard University and including several African-born authors, addressed issues of African poverty, and resulted in an interdisciplinary volume (Akyeampong et al. 2014). A 2013 conference in Vancouver, organized by economist Morten Jerven, focused on African economic development but included several presentations by economic historians. A key innovation was the participation by several heads of statistical offices in African nations, who joined in the discussion of how to improve data on economic change in the postcolonial era.[31]

In another area of change, institutions providing support for study of African economic history began to emerge. Annual meetings of an African Economic History Workshop have taken place in Europe beginning 2005. Further, the African Economic History Network, founded in 2011, has maintained an initially high level of activity, including support for the annual workshops, working papers, newsletters, and a textbook.[32] In other institutional advances, the International Economic History Association chose to hold its sixteenth triennial congress at the University of Stellenbosch, in South Africa, in 2012, and a global historical organization of African-based scholars formed in Ilorin, Nigeria, in 2009.[33]

The numerous recent shifts in the study of African economic history can be summarized in three points. First is the growing recognition of the linkage of issues in contemporary economic development with pre-1960 economic patterns. Second is the recognition of the significance of African issues in understanding economic–historical dynamics more broadly. Third is the formation of institutions for study of the field linking the work of scholars on the continent and elsewhere. One may be optimistic about the future of African studies in economic history and their integration into economic studies generally. At the same time, it is prudent to give attention to intellectual and analytical costs that result from the three decades in which studies of African economic history were, in effect, actively discouraged by the economics profession. One must also recognize the work that remains to be done in data collection, data creation, and in drawing on the records of African communities, past and present, to understand their perspectives and their concerns on economic issues.

Notes

1 Zeleza, born in Harare of Malawian parents, studied in Rhodesia and London before completing his PhD at Dalhousie University. The Noma Award for Publishing in Africa has been supported by a major Japanese publishing firm since 1980.

2 Zeleza ultimately served a term as president of the African Studies Association of the USA.

3 Phyllis Deane, Giovanni Arrighi, and Immanuel Wallerstein, among others, fall into this category.

4 Further dualistic typologies include the dual economy, plural society, parallel or underground economy, monetary vs. non-monetary economy, and "traditional" vs. "modern" economy – as well as the notion that African and non-African ideas about economic life must be fundamentally different.

5 Cohen 1971; Alpers 1973; Hopkins 1975; Cooper 1981; Austen 1981; 1985; Freund 1984; Berry 1984; Manning 1987; Iliffe 1999; and Hopkins 2009.

6 These large-scale systems of slavery appeared to be disconnected from global commodity markets. For the best analyses of the political economy of large-scale, nineteenth-century slavery, see Meillassoux 1991; Lovejoy and Hogendorn 1993; Campbell 2005a; and Médard and Doyle 2007.

7 For a study including the early work of Phyllis Deane in the context of the development of British social accounting under Colin Clark, see Speich (2011). Speich is insightful in exploring the politics of social accounting in the UK and the United States, but took at face value and without further investigation certain colonial assertions of the backwardness of African economies. See also Deane 1948 and Deane 1953.

8 "In Nigeria, in the years immediately following World War II, the United Kingdom Colonial Office made limited efforts to determine the level of capital formation and to assess the balance of trade. After the first set of national accounts was prepared (for 1950–51), a few attempts were made to provide time series. When we came to work on a time series for 1950–57 it was clear from our discussion with Government officials that the potentialities of a fully articulated series of national accounts as a background to policy making were not fully appreciated. Our aim was therefore to provide a consistent time series for Nigeria to enable the user of the data to see the direction (if not the magnitude) of the changes over time in the economy as a whole as well as in the major sectors" (Okigbo 1962: 3). See also Prest and Stewart 1953 and Prest 1957.

9 As these authors argued (p. 15), "Les méthodes de la comptabilité économique sont utilisées depuis longtemps. . . . Mais on en voit souvent l'application refusée aux économies du Tiers-Monde. Ces économies, dit-on, du fait de leur dépendance vis-à-vis de l'Extérieur, et d'une certaine désarticulation du secteur moderne et du secteur traditionnel, n'auraient pas de personnalité nationale. Il serait donc vain d'en tenter la description organique et de leur supposer une quelconque stabilité de comportement. . . . Nous voudrions que notre étude contribue, dans son domaine, à écarter cette interprétation pessimiste et à montrer la possibilité d'une analyse quantifiée de l'économie des pays en voie de développement."

10 As another sign of the times, conflicts at the 1969 African Studies Association meeting in Montreal resulted in its split and the formation of the African Heritage Studies Association and the Canadian Association of African Studies.

11 Frank's interpretation of underdevelopment in Latin America focused in the sixteenth and seventeenth centuries; Rodney's vision of underdevelopment in Africa centered on the nineteenth century (Frank 1967; Rodney 1972).

12 For a list of major collective works on slave trade see Manning (1996). For a worldwide bibliography of studies on slavery see Miller (1985).

13 The Council for the Development of Economic and Social Research in Africa (CODESRIA) was formed with headquarters in Dakar and an office in Kampala. This organization, sustained by philanthropic support from Africa and the North Atlantic, served initially to encourage communication among English- and French-speaking African scholars.

14 Participants in the 1974 summer workshop, and their institutions at the time, included the director, Philip Curtin (University of Wisconsin), as well as Babatunde Agiri (University of Lagos), E. J. Alagoa (University of Port Harcourt), Ralph A. Austen (University of Chicago), Sara S. Berry (Boston University), Margaret Jean Hay (Wellesley College), A. G. Hopkins (University of Birmingham), Paul E. Lovejoy (York University), Patrick Manning (Cañada College), Abdul Sheriff (University of Dar es Salaam),

15 Reviews ranged from the full appreciation by B. Marie Perinbam in *American Historical Review* 81 (1976): 922–3, to the more critical views of Claude Meillassoux, in *Journal of African History* 18 (1977): 449–52; Jean Suret-Canale, in *Canadian Journal of African Studies* 11 (1977): 125–34; and Sara S. Berry, in *African Economic History*, No. 1 (1976), 114–18.

16 "Modern economic growth has a relatively brief history in Sub-Saharan Africa. Colonial administration established itself in most cases in the last two decades of the nineteenth century. Economic expansion came quickly in a few countries – Ghana, Senegal, Uganda, and Zaire, for example – and spread elsewhere later, with interruptions during World Wars I and II and the depression of the 1930s. However, general and sustained development came only after World War II in most of the countries of the region" (World Bank 1981: 11).

17 In fact the periodization of Africa's economic past was seen in more complex terms, in that the colonial era was treated as distinctive and the precolonial era was sometimes divided into sub-periods. But the divide at 1960 became primary in that it isolated post-1960 years as a period for short-term but serious economic analysis, cut off from longer-term patterns of apparently lesser relevance.

18 The Berg Report received sharp criticism from those who have argued that it erred by blaming the African victim of transnational structural constraints (Browne and Cummings 1984). Years later, an empirical response suggested that growth of African state sectors was not a post-independence

phenomenon but a twentieth-century phenomenon, initiated and sustained by colonial governments (Manning 1990–91).

19 Green and Nyambara (2015), in a useful and optimistic review of recent study in African economic history, acknowledge that African fiscal crises and neoliberal policies of global organizations during the 1980s restricted studies by African (and other) scholars in the field. I agree with their argument that African-based scholarship has grown significantly in recent years, though I think that this rebound came somewhat later than they argue.

20 *African Economic History Review*, edited by Margaret Jean Hay and Patrick Manning. Four issues of this publication appeared in 1974 and 1975.

21 *African Economic History*, edited by Margaret Jean Hay, appeared at the University of Wisconsin under the overall direction of Jan Vansina and Marvin Miracle. It was almost ten years before it began to be indexed in the *Journal of Economic Literature*.

22 The *Journal of Economic History* neglected, meanwhile, to review Philip Curtin's *Atlantic Slave Trade* (1969), though it remedied the omission by adding him to its editorial board in 1975; he stepped down after 1981 and was replaced by Ralph Austen in 1983.

23 Roughly 10 percent of the articles in *ROAPE* focused on the period before 1960; on the other hand, the extensive bibliographic coverage presented by Chris Allen gave close attention to articles and books in economic history.

24 Green and Nyambara (2015) emphasize the entry of African scholars in the late 1990s, but their account might also have taken into account the real shortage of new scholars – either Africans or others – in study of African economic history in the 1980s and early 1990s.

25 Otherwise, numerous articles relevant to economic history have appeared in *Journal of African History*, *International Journal of African Historical Studies*, and *Cahiers d'Etudes Africaines*.

26 The critique of GDP for Africa, however, has become conflated with the common skepticism among development economists about historical statistics for African economies. See Jerven 2013 and Manning 2014.

27 These included a study of nineteenth-century palm oil trade, microeconomic studies of rural saving, development policy, and globalization in Africa (Udry 1995; Yansane 1996; Lynn 1997; Edoho 1997).

28 Ironically, a chapter was included in the *Cambridge Economic History of Latin America* that compared and linked the economic histories of Latin America and Africa (Manning 2006).

29 The total number of institutions of higher education on the continent had risen to well over two hundred.

30 Asiwaju's argument was initially presented at the 2005 congress of the International Committee on Historical Sciences (CISH) in Sydney: this was the first CISH session devoted to the history of Africa.

31 "African Economic Development: Measuring Success and Failure," Vancouver, 17–21 April 2013. Jerven's critique of available African development statistics launched a lively discussion at the meeting (Jerven 2013).

32 The African Economic History Network (www.aehnetwork.org), co-founded by Morten Jerven and Erik Green, is funded by the Riksbankens Jubileumsfond, Sweden. Its textbook, edited by Ewout Frankema and Ellen Hillborn, is an online survey of major issues in African economic history aimed at secondary and university students in Africa.

33 The African Network in Global History/Réseau africain d'histoire mondiale (ANGH/RAHM) formed in July 2009, and affiliated with the Network of Global and World History Organizations and with the Association of African Historians. The World History Center at the University of Pittsburgh provided support for this founding meeting.

Bibliography

Acemoglu, Daron, Simon Johnson, and James A. Robinson, 2001. "The Colonial Origins of Comparative Development: An Empirical Investigation." *American Economic Review* 91: 1369–401.

Afana, Osendé. 1966. *L'Economie de l'Ouest-africain: Perspectives de développement*. Paris: François Maspero. (Revised edition 1977.)

Akyeampong, Emmanuel, Robert Bates, Nathan Nunn, and James Robinson, eds. 2014. *Africa's Development in Historical Perspective*. Cambridge: Cambridge University Press.

Allen, Richard B. 1999. *Slaves, Freedmen, and Indentured Laborers in Colonial Mauritius.* Cambridge: Cambridge University Press.

Alpers, Edward A. 1973. "Rethinking African Economic History." *Ufahamu* 3/3: 97–129.

Alpers, Edward A. 1975. *Ivory and Slaves: The Changing Pattern of International Trade in East Central Africa to the Later Nineteenth Century.* Berkeley: University of California Press.

Alpers, Edward A., Gwyn Campbell, and Michael Salman, eds. 2005. *Slavery and Resistance in Africa and Asia.* London: Routledge.

Amin, Samir. 1965. *Trois expériences africaines de développement, le Mali, le Ghana et la Guinée.* Paris: Presses Universitaires de France.

Amin, Samir. 1971. *L'Afrique de l'Ouest bloquée: L'Economie politique de la colonization, 1880–1970.* Paris: Editions de Minuit.

Amin, Samir. 1973. *Le développement inégal: essai sur les formes sociales du capitalism périphérique.* Paris: Editions de Minuit.

Amin, Samir. 2009. *La Crise: sortir de la crise du capitalism ou sortir du capitalism en crise.* Pantin: Temps des cerises.

Arrighi, Giovanni, and John S. Saul. 1973. *Essays on the Political Economy of Africa.* New York: Monthly Review Press.

Asiwaju, A. I. 2003–4. "African History in Comparative Perspective." *Afrika Zamani* 11–12: 1–17.

Austen, Ralph A. 1981. "Capitalism, Class, and African Colonial Agriculture: The Mating of Marxism and Empiricism." *Journal of Economic History* 41/3: 657–63.

Austen, Ralph A. 1985. "African Economies in Historical Perspective." *Business History Review* 59: 101–13.

Austen, Ralph A. 1987. *African Economic History.* London: James Currey.

Austin, Gareth. 2005. *Labour, Land and Capital in Ghana: From Slavery to Free Labour in Asante, 1807–1956.* Rochester, NY: University of Rochester Press.

Baier, Stephen. 1980. *An Economic History of Central Niger.* Oxford: Clarendon Press.

Baldwin, Robert E. 1966. *Economic Development and Export Growth: A Study of Northern Rhodesia, 1920–1960.* Berkeley: University of California Press.

Barry, Boubacar. 1988. *La Sénégambie du XVe au XIXe siècle: traite négrière, Islam et conquête coloniale.* Paris: L'Harmattan.

Bates, Robert H. 1983. *Essays on the Political Economy of Rural Africa.* Cambridge: Cambridge University Press.

Bauer, P. T. 1954. *West African Trade: A Study of Competition, Oligopoly and Monopoly in a Changing Economy.* Cambridge: Cambridge University Press.

Becker, Charles. 1985. "Notes sur les conditions écologiques en Sénégambie aux 17e et 18e siècles." *African Economic History* 14: 167–216.

Beinart, William. 1982. *The Political Economy of Pondoland, 1860–1930.* Cambridge: Cambridge University Press.

Bernstein, Henry, and Bonnie K. Campbell, eds. 1985. *Contradictions of Accumulation in Africa: Studies in Economy and State.* Beverly Hills, CA: Sage Publications.

Berry, Sara S. 1975. *Cocoa, Custom and Socio-Economic Change in Rural Western Nigeria.* Oxford: Clarendon Press.

Berry, Sara S. 1984. "The Food Crisis and Agrarian Change in Africa: A Review Essay." *African Studies Review* 27/2: 59–112.

Berry, Sara S. 1985. *Fathers Work for Their Sons: Accumulation, Mobility, and Class Formation in an Extended Yoruba Community.* Berkeley: University of California Press.

Berry, Sara S. 1992. "Hegemony on a Shoestring." *Africa: Journal of the International African Institute* 62: 327–55.

Birnberg, Thomas B., and Stephen A. Resnick. 1975. *Colonial Development: An Econometric Study.* New Haven, CT: Yale University Press.

Boserup, Ester. 1966. *The Conditions of Agricultural Growth: the Economics of Agrarian Change under Population Pressure.* Chicago, IL: Aldine Press.

Boserup, Ester. 1970. *Woman's Role in Economic Development.* New York: St. Martin's Press.

Brett, E. A. 1973. *Colonialism and Underdevelopment in East Africa: the Politics of Economic Change, 1919–1939.* New York: Nok Publications.

Browne, Robert S., and Robert J. Cummings. 1984. *The Lagos Plan of Action vs. the Berg Report: Contemporary Issues in African Economic Development.* Lawrenceville, VA: Brunswick Publishing.

Cain, P. J., and A. G. Hopkins. 1980. "The Political Economy of British Expansion Overseas, 1750–1914." *Economic History Review* n.s. 33/4: 463–90.

Cain, P. J., and A. G. Hopkins. 1993. *British Imperialism.* 2 vols. London: Longman.

Campbell, Gwyn, ed. 2004. *The Structure of Slavery in Indian Ocean Africa and Asia.* London: Frank Cass.

Campbell, Gwyn. 2005a. *An Economic History of Imperial Madagascar, 1750–1895: The Rise and Fall of an Island Empire.* Cambridge: Cambridge University Press.

Campbell, Gwyn, ed. 2005b. *Abolition and Its Aftermath in Indian Ocean Africa and Asia.* New York: Routledge.

Cohen, David W. 1971. "Agenda for African Economic History." *Journal of Economic History.* 31/1: 208–221.

Cooper, Frederick. 1980. *From Slaves to Squatters.* New Haven, CT: Yale University Press.

Cooper, Frederick. 1981. "Africa and the World Economy." *African Studies Review* 24/2–3: 1–86.

Coquery-Vidrovitch, Catherine. 1969. "Recherches sur un mode de production africain," *La Pensée,* 144. Paris: Editions Sociales.

Coquery-Vidrovitch, Catherine. 1972. *Le Congo au temps des grandes companies concessionnaires, 1898–1930.* Paris: Mouton.

Coquery-Vidrovitch, Catherine. 1975. "L'Impact des intérêts coloniaux: SCOA et CFAO dans l'Ouest africain, 1910–65." *Journal of African History* 16: 595–621.

Coquery-Vidrovitch, Catherine, and Paul E. Lovejoy, eds. 1985. *The Workers of African Trade.* Beverly Hills, CA: Sage Publishers.

Cordell, Dennis D., and Joel W. Gregory, eds. 1987. *African Population and Capitalism: Historical Perspectives.* Boulder, CO: Westview, 35–49.

Cordell, Dennis D., Joel W. Gregory, and Victor Piché. 1996. *Hoe and Wage: A Social History of a Circular Migration System in West Africa.* Boulder, CO: Westview Press.

Curtin, Philip D. 1969. *The Atlantic Slave Trade: A Census.* Madison: University of Wisconsin Press.

Curtin, Philip D. 1975. *Economic Change in Precolonial Africa: Senegambia in the Era of the Slave Trade.* 2 vols. Madison: University of Wisconsin Press.

Daaku, K.Y. 1970. *Trade and Politics on the Gold Coast 1600–1720.*

Davies, K.G. 1957. *The Royal African Company.* London: Longmans, Green.

Deane, Phyllis, 1948. *The Measurement of Colonial National Incomes: An Experiment.* Cambridge: Cambridge University Press.

Deane, Phyllis. 1953. *Colonial Social Accounting.* Cambridge: Cambridge University Press.

DeKiewiet, C.W. 1941. *A History of South Africa, Social and Economic.* Oxford: Clarendon Press.

Delage, Alain, and Alain Massiera. 1994. *Le Franc CFA: Bilan et Perspectives.* Paris: L'Harmattan.

Dias, Jill R. 1981. "Famine and Disease in the History of Angola c. 1830–1930." *Journal of African History* 22/3: 349–78.

Dike, K.O. 1956. *Trade and Politics in the Niger Delta, 1830–1895.* Oxford: Clarendon Press.

Diouf, Sylviane. 2003. *Fighting the Slave Trade: West African Strategies.* Athens: Ohio University Press.

Dumont, René. 1962. *L'Afrique noire est mal partie.* Paris: Editions du Seuil.

Dupré, Georges, and Pierre-Philippe Rey. 1973. "Reflections on the Pertinence of a Theory of the History of Exchange." *Economy and Society* 2/2: 131–63.

Edoho, Felix Moses, ed. 1997. *Globalization and the New World Order: Promises, Problems, and Prospects for Africa in the Twenty-first Century.* Westport, CT: Praeger.

Eicher, Carl, and Carl Liedhold, eds. 1970. *Growth and Development of the Nigerian Economy.* East Lansing: Michigan State University Press.

Ekundare, R. Olufemi. 1973. *An Economic History of Nigeria 1860–1960.* New York: Africana Publishers.

Eltis, David. 1987. *Economic Growth and Coercion: The Ending of the Atlantic Slave Trade.* New York: Oxford University Press.

Eltis, David, et al. 2009. "Voyages: The Transatlantic Slave Trade Database." http://www.slavevoyages.org/

Feinstein, Charles H. 2005. *An Economic History of South Africa: Conquest, Discrimination, and Development.* London: Oxford University Press.

Fetter, Bruce. 1983. *Colonial Rule and Regional Imbalance in Central Africa.* Boulder, CO: Westview Press.

Fetter, Bruce, ed. 1990. *Demography from Scanty Evidence: Central Africa in the Colonial Era.* Boulder, CO: Lynne Rienner.

Fieldhouse, David Kenneth. 1978. *Unilever Overseas: The Anatomy of a Multinational 1895–1965.* London: Croom Helm.

Fieldhouse, David Kenneth. 1986. *Black Africa, 1945–80: Economic Decolonization and Arrested Development*. London: Allen & Unwin.

Forest, Alain. 1983. *Entreprises et entrepreneurs en Afrique, XIXe et XXe siècles*. 2 vols. Paris: L'Harmattan.

Frank, Andre Gunder. 1967. *Capitalism and Underdevelopment in Latin America: Historical Studies of Chile and Brazil*. New York: Monthly Review Press.

Frankel, S. Herbert. 1938. *Capital Investment in Africa: Its Course and Effects*. London: Oxford University Press.

Freund, Bill. 1981. *Capital and Labour in the Nigerian Tin Mines*. Atlantic Highlands, NJ: Humanities Press.

Freund, Bill. 1984. "Labor and Labor History in Africa: A Review of the Literature." *African Studies Review* 27/2: 1–58.

Freund, Bill. 1988. *The African Worker*. New York: Cambridge University Press.

Freund, Bill. 2007. *The African City: A History*. Cambridge: Cambridge University Press.

Gann, L. H., and Peter Duignan. 1967. *Burden of Empire: An Appraisal of Western Colonialism in Africa South of the Sahara*. New York: Frederick A. Praeger.

Gran, Peter. 1979. *Islamic Roots of Capitalism: Egypt, 1760–1840*. Austin: University of Texas Press.

Gray, Richard, and David Birmingham, eds. 1970. *Pre-Colonial African Trade: Essays on Trade in Central and Eastern Africa before 1900*. London: Oxford University Press.

Green, Erik, and Pius Nyambara. 2015. "The Internationalization of Economic History: Perspectives from the African Frontier." *Economic History of Developing Regions*. DOI: 10.1080/20780389.2015.1025744

Gutkind, Peter C. W., Robin Cohen, and Jean Copans, eds. 1978. *African Labor History*. Beverly Hills, CA: Sage Publications.

Hart, Keith. 1982. *The Political Economy of West African Agriculture*. Cambridge: Cambridge University Press.

Helleiner, Gerald K. 1966. *Peasant Agriculture, Government, and Economic Growth in Nigeria*. Homewood, IL: Richard D. Irwin.

Helleiner, Gerald K. 1981. *International Economic Disorder: Essays in North–South Relations*. Toronto: University of Toronto Press.

Henry, Yves. 1912. *Le Mais africain, culture et production au Dahomey*. Paris.

Herskovits, Melville J. 1952. *Economic Anthropology: A Study in Comparative Economics*, 2nd ed. New York: Knopf.

Herskovits, Melville J., and Mitchell Harwitz. 1964. *Economic Transition in Africa*. Evanston, IL: Northwestern University Press.

Hill, Polly, 1963. *The Migrant Cocoa Farmers of Southern Ghana: A Study in Rural Capitalism*. Cambridge: Cambridge University Press.

Hill, Polly. 1970. *Studies in Rural Capitalism in West Africa*. Cambridge: Cambridge University Press.

Hill, Polly. 1977. *Population, Prosperity and Poverty: Rural Kano, 1900 and 1970*. Cambridge: Cambridge University Press.

Hillborn, Ellen, and Erik Green. 2010. *Afrika: en kontinents ekonomiska och sociala historia*. Stockholm: SNS förlag.

Hogendorn, Jan S. 1977. "The Economics of Slave Use on Two 'Plantations' in the Zaria Emirate of the Sokoto Caliphate." *International Journal of African Historical Studies* 10/3: 369–93.

Hogendorn, Jan S. and Marion Johnson. 1985. *Shell Money of the Slave Trade*. Cambridge: Cambridge University Press.

Hopkins, A. G. 1973. *An Economic History of West Africa*. London: Longman.

Hopkins, A. G. 1975. "Clio-Antics: A Horoscope for African Economic History," in C. Fyfe, ed. *African Studies since 1945*. Edinburgh: Centre for African Studies, 31–48.

Hopkins, A. G. 2009. "The New Economic History of Africa." *Journal of African History* 50: 155–77.

Houghton, D. Hobart. 1964. *The South African Economy*. Cape Town: Oxford University Press.

Iliffe, John. 1987. *The African Poor: A History*. Cambridge: Cambridge University Press.

Iliffe, John. 1999. "The South African Economy, 1652–1997." *Economic History Review*, 52, 87–103.

Inikori, Joseph E. 2002. *Africans and the Industrial Revolution in England: A Study in International Trade and Economic Development*. Cambridge: Cambridge University Press.

Isaacman, Allen F. 1972. *Mozambique: The Africanization of a European Institution: the Zambesi Prazos, 1750–1902*. Madison: University of Wisconsin Press.

Issawi, Charles. 1947. *Egypt, An Economic and Social Analysis*. London: Oxford University Press.

Issawi, Charles. 1982. *An Economic History of the Middle East and North Africa*. New York: Columbia University Press.

Jerven, Morten. 2013. *Poor Numbers: How We Are Misled by African Development Statistics and What to Do about It*. Ithaca, NY: Cornell University Press.

Jewsiewicki, Bogumil. 1977. "The Great Depression and the Making of the Economic System in the Belgian Congo." *African Economic History* 4: 153–76.

Johnson, Marion, eds. J. Thomas Lindblad and Robert Ross. 1990. *Anglo-African Trade in the Eighteenth Century: English Statistics on African Trade 1699–1808*. Leiden: Centre for the History of European Expansion.

Jones, William O. 1959. *Manioc in Africa*. Stanford, CA: Stanford University Press.

Kay, Geoffrey. 1975. *Development and Underdevelopment: A Marxist Analysis*. New York: St. Martin's Press.

Kay, Geoffrey B., with Stephen Hymer. 1972. *The Political Economy of Colonialism in Ghana; a Collection of Documents and Statistics, 1900–1960*. Cambridge: Cambridge University Press.

Kea, Ray A. 1982. *Settlements, Trade and Politics in the Seventeenth-Century Gold Coast*. Baltimore, MD: Johns Hopkins University Press.

Kitching, Gavin. 1980. *Class and Economic Change in Kenya: The Making of an African Petite-Bourgeoisie*. New Haven, CT: Yale University Press.

Kofi, Tetteh A., and Asayehgn Desta. 2008. *The Saga of African Underdevelopment: A Viable Approach for Africa's Sustainable Development in the 21st Century*. Trenton, NJ: Africa World Press

Langdon, Steven. 1981. *Multinational Corporations in the Political Economy of Kenya*. New York: St. Martin's Press.

Larson, Pier M. 2000. *History and Memory in the Age of Enslavement: Becoming Merina in Highland Madagascar, 1770–1822*. Portsmouth, NH: Heinemann

Latham, A.J.H. 1973. *Old Calabar, 1600–1891: The Impact of the International Economy upon a Traditional Society*. Oxford: Clarendon Press.

Lewis, W. A. 1954. "Economic Development with Unlimited Supplies Of Labour." Manchester School of Economic and Social Studies, Vol. 22, 139–91.

Lewis, W. A. 1963. *Report on Industrialisation and the Gold Coast*. Accra: Government Printing Department.

Leys, Colin. 1974. *Underdevelopment in Kenya: The Political Economy of Neo-colonialism, 1964–1971*. Berkeley: University of California Press.

Lovejoy, Paul E. 1980. *Caravans of Kola: The Hausa Kola Trade, 1700–1900*. Zaria: Ahmadu Bello University Press.

Lovejoy, Paul E. 1983. *Transformations in Slavery: A History of Slavery in Africa*. Cambridge: Cambridge University Press.

Lovejoy, Paul E., and Stephen Baier, 1975. "The Desert-Side Economy of the Central Sudan." *International Journal of African Historical Studies* 8/4: 551–81.

Lovejoy, Paul E., and Jan S. Hogendorn. 1993. *Slow Death for Slavery: The Course of Abolition in Northern Nigeria, 1897–1936*. Cambridge: Cambridge University Press.

Lucassen, Jan, Leo Lucassen, and Patrick Manning, eds. 2010. *Migration History in World History: Multidisciplinary Approaches*. Leiden: Brill.

Ly, Abdoulaye. 1958. *La Compagnie du Sénégal*. Paris: Présence africaine.

Lynn, Martin. 1997. *Commerce and Economic Change in West Africa: The Palm Oil Trade in the Nineteenth Century*. Cambridge: Cambridge University Press.

McPhee, Allan. 1926. *The Economic Revolution in British West Africa*. London: Routledge. (Reprinted 1970 by Negro Universities Press, New York.)

Maldant, Boris, and Maxim Haubert. 1973. *Crossance et conjoncture dans l'Ouest africain*. Paris: Presses Universitaires de France.

Manning, Patrick. 1982. *Slavery, Colonialism and Economic Growth in Dahomey, 1640–1960*. Cambridge: Cambridge University Press.

Manning, Patrick. 1987. "The Prospects for African Economic History: Is Today Included in the Long Run?" *African Studies Review* 30/2: 49–62.

Manning, Patrick. 1990–91. "African Economic Growth and the Public Sector: Lessons from Historical Statistics of Cameroon." *African Economic History* 19: 135–70.

Manning, Patrick. 1990. *Slavery and African Life: Occidental, Oriental, and African Slave Trades*. Cambridge: Cambridge University Press.

Manning, Patrick. 1996. *Slave Trades, 1500–1800: Globalization of Forced Labour.* Aldershot: Ashgate Variorum.

Manning, Patrick. 2005. *Migration in World History.* London: Routledge.

Manning, Patrick. 2006. "African Connections with American Colonization, 1400–1850." Victor Bulmer-Thomas and John Coatsworth, eds., *The Cambridge Economic History of Latin America.* Cambridge: Cambridge University Press, 43–71.

Manning, Patrick. 2014. "African Population, 1650–2000: Comparisons and Implications of New Estimates." Emmanuel Akyeampong, Robert Bates, Nathan Nunn, and James Robinson, eds., *Africa's Development in Historical Perspective.* Cambridge: Cambridge University Press, 131–52.

Marseille, Jacques. 1984. *Empire colonial et capitalisme français: histoire d'un divorce.* Paris: A. Michel.

Martin, Phyllis. 1972. *The External Trade of the Loango Coast, 1576–1870: The Effects of Changing Commercial Relations on the Vili Kingdom of Loango.* Oxford: Clarendon Press.

Médard, Henri, and Shane Doyle, eds. 2007. *Slavery in the Great Lakes Region of East Africa.* Oxford: James Currey.

Meillassoux, Claude, 1964. *Anthropologie économique des Gouro de Côte-d'Ivoire: de l'économie de subsistance à l'agriculture.* Paris: Mouton.

Meillassoux, Claude, ed. 1971. *The Development of Indigenous Trade & Markets in West Africa.* London: Oxford University Press.

Meillassoux, Claude, trans. Alide Dasnois. 1991. *The Anthropology of Slavery: The Womb of Iron and Gold.* Chicago, IL: University of Chicago Press.

Mettas, Jean. 1978, 1984. *Répertoire des expéditions négrières françaises au XVIIIe siècle.* 2 vols. Paris: Société française d'histoire d'outre-mer.

Miller, Joseph C. 1982. "The Significance of Drought, Disease and Famine in the Agriculturally Marginal Zones of West-Central Africa." *Journal of African History* 23/1: 17–62.

Miller, Joseph C. 1985. *Slavery: A Worldwide Bibliography, 1900–1982.* White Plains, NY: Kraus International.

Miller, Joseph C. 1988. *Way of Death.* Madison: University of Wisconsin Press.

Miracle, Marvin P. 1966. *Maize in Tropical Africa.* Madison: University of Wisconsin Press.

Miracle, Martin P. 1967. *Agriculture in the Congo Basin.* Madison: University of Wisconsin Press.

Miracle, Marvin P., and Bruce Fetter. 1970. "Backward-sloping Labor-Supply Functions and African Economic Behavior." *Economic Development and Cultural Change* 18/2: 240–51.

Munro, J. Forbes. 1976. *Africa and the International Economy 1800–1960.* Totowa, NJ: Rowman and Littlefield.

Natrass, Jill. 1981. *The South African Economy: Its Growth and Change.* Capetown: Oxford University Press.

Nunn, Nathan, 2008. "The Long Term Effects of Africa's Slave Trades." *Quarterly Journal of Economics* 123: 139–76.

Okigbo P.N.C. 1962. *Nigerian National Accounts, 1950–57.* Enugu: Government Printer.

Okigbo, P.N.C. 1965. *Nigerian Public Finance.* Evanston, IL: Northwestern University Press.

Pankhurst, Richard. 1961. *An Introduction to the Economic History of Ethiopia from Early Times to 1800.* London: Lalibela House.

Peemans, Jean-Philippe. 1968. *Diffusion du progrès économique et convergence des prix: le cas Congo-Belgique, 1900–1960. La formation du système des prix et salaires dans une économie dualiste.* Louvain: Nauwelaerts.

Phimister, Ian, 1988. *An Economic and Social History of Zimbabwe: 1890–1948: Capital Accumulation and Class Struggle.* London: Longman.

Prest, A. R. 1957. *The Investigation of National Income in British Tropical Dependencies.* London: University of London Press.

Prest, A. R., and I. G. Stewart. 1953. *The National Income of Nigeria, 1950–51.* London: HMSO.

Prestholdt, Jeremy. 2008. *Domesticating the World: African Consumerism and the Genealogies of Globalization.* Cambridge: Cambridge University Press.

Rey, Pierre-Philippe. 1971. *Colonialisme, néo-colonialisme et transition au capitalism; exemple de la Comilog au Congo-Brazzaville.* Paris: F. Maspero.

Roberts, Richard L. 1987. *Warriors, Merchants, and Slaves: The State and the Economy in the Middle Niger Valley, 1700–1914.* Stanford, CA: Stanford University Press.

Rodney, Walter. 1972. *How Europe Underdeveloped Africa.* London: Bogle-L'Ouverture Publications.

Sarraut, Albert. 1923. *La Mise en valeur des colonies françaises.* Paris: Payot.

Schatz, Sayre P. 1977. *Nigerian Capitalism.* Berkeley: University of California Press.

Scully, Pamela, and Diana Paton, eds. 2005. *Gender and Slave Emancipation in the Atlantic World*. Durham, NC: Duke University Press.

Sheriff, Abdul. 1987. *Slaves, Spices, and Ivory in Zanzibar: Integration of an East African Commercial Empire into The World Economy, 1770–1873*. London: James Currey.

Speich, Daniel. 2011. "The Use of Global Abstractions: National Income Accounting in the Period of Imperial Decline." *Journal of Global History* 6: 7–28.

Szereszewski, Robert. 1965. *Structural Changes in the Economy of Ghana, 1891–1911*. London: Weidenfeld and Nicholson.

Udry, Christopher. 1995. "Risk and Saving in Northern Nigeria." *American Economic Review* 85/5: 1287–300.

Van Onselen, Charles. 1982. *Studies in the Social and Economic History of the Witwatersrand, 1886–1914*. Harlow: Longman.

Wallerstein, Immanuel. 1974. *The Modern World-System*. New York: Academic Press.

Wolff, Richard D. 1974. *The Economics of Colonialism: Britain and Kenya, 1870–1930*. New Haven, CT: Yale University Press.

World Bank. 1981. *Accelerated Development in Sub-Saharan Africa: An Agenda for Action*. Washington, DC: World Bank.

Yansané, Aguibou Y, ed. 1996. *Prospects for Recovery and Sustainable Development in Africa*. Westport, CT: Greenwood Press.

Yudelman, David. 1983. *The Emergence of Modern South Africa: State, Capital, and the Incorporation of Organized Labor on the South African Gold Fields, 1902–1939*. Westport, CT: Greenwood Press.

PART V

Challenges and ways ahead

26

CULTURE, POWER AND CONTESTATION

Multiple roads from the past to the future

Francesco Boldizzoni and Pat Hudson

The historiographies we have gathered in this volume tell a multitude of stories about the development of economic history, in its various forms and guises, from its pre-history as an academic field, to the present. In some places and periods it has been conjoined with other disciplines or has even been defined in itself as a broadly based endeavour; in others it has been more narrowly delineated, largely to coincide with certain dominant forms of analysis or in engagement with regional political or policy imperatives, rather than with the subject matter of material history per se. The narratives highlight (by no means always congruent) periods of contraction and expansion, turning points in approaches and methods, the impact of varied ideas in broader social science, and the power of prejudice and ideology in limiting the influence of certain approaches and individuals, sometimes cutting short their careers and even their lives.[1] At the same time ideology and political favour have also, of course, been responsible for the elevation of certain individuals and ideas and for endorsing their influence over swathes of the subject, regardless of their shortcomings.

National, regional and trans-regional historiographical traditions can be seen to reflect the variety of ecological, socio-economic and political circumstances, and paths to development and modernization that have been experienced worldwide. History-writing is not necessarily determined by such factors but certainly they have proved a major influence upon particular preoccupations and approaches. Neither does the influence flow only in one direction. It is the case that national and regional traditions of writing, and the ideas and models that they promote, can become instruments of propaganda or policy and thus in turn reinforce the local trajectories and ideologies that they are also attempting, or purporting, to map. The influence of censorship and state control of ideas in altering the nature of economics and economic history, especially, but not solely, in command economies and authoritarian states, in turn reinforced the dominant ideology and the reality of the working of the economy. In freer societies, as Karl Polanyi argued more than half a century ago with respect to the transformation of Britain: 'there was nothing natural about *laissez-faire*', '*laissez-faire* was planned' and it was the power of the 'economistic prejudice' as expressed and reinforced by writers and by the political economy of the nineteenth century that persuaded people that the ideal of the free market should be at the heart of social action (1944: 139, 141, 161). The impulse to social reform that influenced the nature and evolution of economic history in many regions, in turn impacted upon government policy and economic outcomes just as the development of national accounting techniques, on the part of historians as well as economists, promoted the growth of the welfare state and macroeconomic management. Many chapters highlight the role played by government service in the careers of economic historians; this was particularly so in the United States where cliometricians often had executive positions and political power (see Lyons et al. 2008). The NBER was established in 1920 by Wesley C. Mitchell (soon joined by Edwin F. Gay) expressly to provide data as a foundation for economic policy making. In Latin America, especially Brazil, many historical economists became involved with state service and later with ECLA/CEPAL.[2] The close association between economic history and economic and social policy more widely is one reason why the nature of the subject has been so closely aligned with the trajectories of particular economies and societies, and even with particular regimes. The history profession played a central role in building national and nationalistic histories that are in turn deep rooted in associated historical orthodoxies. No less strong are colonial and post-colonial beliefs and understandings that have informed economic history, and many other disciplines, in all hemispheres. Ideologies, old and new, East and West, North and South, inspire historical research but also limit the potential for fresh approaches and thwart scholars' commitment to offer unbiased interpretations.

Our varied stories also demonstrate that the preoccupations of historians in different countries and world regions have, to a large degree, been governed by the economies, as well as the polities and cultures, within which they are placed: their dominant sectors, their level of development and speed of change, their positions in world trade or imperial relations, and the extent to which economies have been and are controlled by the state. The concentration, for many decades, of Polish and Russian historians on great estates and peasantries; of Indian historians on colonialism and subalterns; of Americans on the frontier, on slavery and big business; the Canadians and Australians on staples and natural resources; Latin American scholars on the primary sector and dependency; Brazil's writers on labour supply, land reform, commodity cycles and import substitution; African historians on cash crops and slave exports; South Africans on race, migrant labour and mining; the Dutch on maritime and financial enterprise; the British on the industrial revolution; Swedish scholars on the welfare state; French writers on regional issues, peasant mentalities and the role of the state; the Japanese on the nature and demise of feudalism and the rise of labour-intensive industrialization; are all understandable in these terms.

Such preoccupations also encouraged the transnational exchange of ideas where similar circumstances suggested the application of certain ideas and tools. Debates and theses about the variety and dynamics within a 'feudal mode of production' spread from Eastern Europe and Russia to Middle Eurasia, India and Latin America. Mexican historiography drew upon the works of Witold Kula and Pierre Vilar for example. Chinese historians, whilst drawing on Soviet theorizing in the 1950s, adapted the notion of 'precocious feudalism' to better suit Chinese conditions. Similarly staple theory travelled from Canada to Australia and in Latin America was dominated by preoccupation with the volatility of prices and the terms of trade of primary products. Analysis of development and social problems in South Africa has been aided by the adaptation of the US notion of the military–industrial complex to the idea of a mineral–energy complex. The analysis of slavery included borrowings from North America to South America and Africa; import-substitution studies grew to have a global reach; and studies of industrialization and economic growth have influenced one another transnationally. In most of these exchanges, ideas have been developed and adapted to suit different circumstances on the ground but global 'grand narratives' have also often been dismissed as outlandish, especially, but not always, when foreign scholars have brought in or imposed ideas from outside.

The degree to which economic history in a country or region has looked outward or has focused solely upon internal questions can also be related to wider histories of world trading relationships and experiences as colonizing or colonized entities. Concern with the histories of their imperial reach is deeply imbricated in the British and Dutch historiographies, for example, encouraged by the availability of trading company and colonial records. In some of our narratives the story of the development of economic history in a nation is largely confined to research on that nation. However, national, regional and local studies, in comparative context, can be globally informed and even pioneering examples of intellectual innovation. The regionally and locally focused studies in the *Annales* tradition and central European approaches to the study of large estates and late serfdom can be appreciated in this light, as we shall see. The complexities in, and contrasts between, the economies of sub-regions in France spawned much early work on the border between economic and cultural history: on birth control, literacy rates, local government that made French historical demography, in particular, peculiarly sophisticated from the outset. Showing sensitivity to the culture of time and place, such studies retain the ability to complement or indeed to undermine those conceived with a broader global sweep.

In this chapter we consider what the collective project overall can tell us about the past, the present and the possible future of our field.[3] We cover some of the general characteristics of economic history that have played themselves out differently in different contexts and we draw out some distinct ideas and concepts, often developed at the margins of the world system, that might usefully complement the tools currently employed by the international mainstream. We consider the way that various ideas and methodologies have been received, adapted or rejected in different environments. In the final section we seek to draw some methodological implications and conclusions for global history-writing.

The context of the emergence and development of social science

It many world regions the methodology of economic history has been closely associated with debates that accompanied the emergence of social science as well as the use of social science as a toolbox for state intervention, fiscal control and the amelioration of social distress caused by rapid economic change.

Practically all of the narratives in this volume refer to early struggles within social science over the degree to which human behaviour is universally predictable at the aggregate level and therefore amenable to general laws or to hypothetico–deductive or mechanical forms of analysis in the same way as natural science. Positions taken in the late nineteenth century and in continuing debates over the nature of political economy and economics have been vital in explaining different positions taken in economic history, within as well as between different world regions and intellectual cultures. In the Netherlands P. J. Blok, a major figure at the turn of the century, argued that the natural science approach could be 'equally successful in solving social questions as in clarifying the mysteries of the universe' (quoted in Bosma, section II of chapter 11). The role of the German Historical School in tempering such notions and in influencing the global development of our field is highlighted in many chapters, from Britain, across East and West Europe to Asia and Latin America. But the influence clearly played itself out differently in different contexts. In some places, as in Germany itself, it became a focus of reaction and partial rejection, in others it provided inspiration for the search beyond universalizing paradigms towards greater sensitivity to time, place and varying cultures. This can be seen, for example, in the emergence of British and continental historiographies such as the Belgian, the Italian, the Czech and the Hungarian; in a swathe of the early Polish historiography of Franciszek Bujak and Jan Rutkowski; or with the search in India for a political economy suitable for Indian circumstances on the part of Mahadev Govind Ranade and Romesh Chunder Dutt.

In France François Simiand had refused to accept economic laws detached from any historical or institutional context but French traditions in this respect emerged rather separately and differently from the German historiography. Marc Bloch and Lucien Febvre did not study Sombart and Weber closely and were careful to distinguish themselves from Marx. In Grenier's (chapter 7) words, 'they were interested in the economy because social relations were more dense and visible there than elsewhere, and not because it was the determining instance of the ensemble of social relations in Marx's sense'. These sorts of differences, similarly though not inevitably, have led to very different attitudes to the role of institutions, as well as culture, in economic life. In recent decades, for example, French research on institutions has adopted a contrasting approach to that found in the USA and associated with Douglass North. The accent is upon 'how economic systems with quite different institutional structures can achieve a comparative level of economic performance' (Grenier). Performance, however, does not occupy centre stage, nor is it seen as an explanation for the persistence of institutions.

Whereas economists generally focus upon institutions as potential constraints upon, or facilitators of, utility-maximizing activity, there is no such preconception with the approach to institutions from a socio-cultural history perspective which has been the one taken in many of the stories presented here. Indeed, one of the problems of the American institutional turn in economic history is the relatively limited departure from neoclassical orthodoxy and from a western-oriented modernization teleology that it has created despite celebrations to the contrary. For Fernand Braudel, whose ideas have been a key influence in many parts of the world, the rules of capitalism are the opposite to those conceived in the neoclassical schema. Free markets characterized by fair and efficient competition are not at the centre of capitalism as a concept but a privilege founded on the power of monopolies and their incorporation by the state. It is not surprising that the sort of institutional discourse employed in parts of the globe as various as China and Latin America in recent years has favoured the broader more historically oriented approach of Joseph Schumpeter and Albert O. Hirschman over that of North.

The social science context in different countries influences not only methodological leanings but also the boundaries of economic history: whether these are narrowly and firmly defined or, at the other pole, whether some sort of total history is pursued in the belief that economic history cannot extract the economy from the rest of life (for study), leaving the context and environment of stylized facts to other specialists. French historiography has had a preoccupation with *histoire totale*, articulated around relationships between the natural and human worlds, within which the economy has had no autonomous or independent role. Hence the pioneering French work on mental frameworks, feelings and beliefs but also on the human body, illness, climate and the environment. The necessary overlap between economic history and cultural analysis, if not 'total history', has been prominent elsewhere: in the early work of Rutkowski, for example, who favoured ethnography, and in attention to psychological factors in Italian approaches to microhistory. Elsewhere these topics and approaches would struggle to find a place within economic history.

As part of economics, economic history has been successively influenced by formalism, rational choice theory, the new institutional economics, the new home economics, and game theory amongst other things, and often professed its loyalty to neoliberalism. Its methodologies have become less and less useful for analysing long-term change even though this has become a major focus of global concern. As a part of history, economic history has been subject to a wider range of ideas, incorporating humanistic methods and non-documentary evidence. The potential strengths of both positions may seem obvious but so are their weaknesses, especially without dialogue between the two. The methodological bifurcation has undermined the subject and, in recent years, economic history in many regions has been in decline because it has been marginalized by both parent disciplines, albeit for different reasons.

Social science debates in the twentieth century polarized between *Erklären* and *Verstehen* or in relation to various versions of *Geistesgeschite,* and between logical–positivist and historicist positions, further fed variously into the field of economic history as did the force of Marxist and Marxian historical materialist models and controversies about modes of production. These figure prominently in the Russian, Indian, Latin American, Japanese and Middle Eurasian narratives and are not absent in others. Whether endorsed by authoritarian regimes or not these debates crossed continents, everywhere being reinterpreted in the light of different specificities of culture and environment. In East Germany the ideological climate spawned massive study of the history of the working class and labour movements. It informed the 'moral economy' and other work of the British Marxist historians, and research on capitalism and slavery by Caio Prado Jr, Eugene Genovese and others in the Americas. In Eastern Europe and Russia more rigid Marxist frameworks were imposed proving detrimental to the subject but despite this enforcement of uniformity, as our chapters on Czechoslovakia, Hungary and especially Poland demonstrate, many historians managed to produce major empirical and even analytical contributions.

The strength of different forms of historical materialism, and broader beliefs about the central role of the economy within social science, encouraged the expansion of economic history globally in the middle decades of the twentieth century. By contrast, since the 1980s the ideological taint of Marxism, the rise of neoliberalism and the general widening of the gulf between neopositivist and interpretive methodologies, has tended to leave economic history between a rock and a hard place. The subject is in decline in many regions, especially in its traditional forms. The present state of economic and social theory in the post-industrial West has left historians alienated from the economy and economists alienated from history. By contrast, it is in the more dynamic economies and societies of the developing world, in search of wide-ranging explanations for structural change, that the discipline seems to have maintained its appeal.

Relationship to statistical movements

The progress of political arithmetic and national statistical movements was closely related to the emergence and nature of nascent economic history in many regions but varied with the strength and stability of nation states.[4] State recording of vital events and indicators of production and trade provided the raw materials for the expansion of economic history and demographic history but differentially. Following the emergence of Belgium as an independent state in 1830 the Commission Centrale de Statistique was founded to provide instruments for policy making and social order, and soon developed an international reputation under the directorship of L. A. J. Quetelet, its first chairman who pioneered the application of statistics to social science. It is not surprising that quantitative methods and, later, national accounting geared to measuring the performance of the economy flourished earliest in those countries where reasonably good data at national level were available. This was generally the case in areas of the world with centralized states that promoted fact gathering and accounting for fiscal purposes as in Britain and France, and in Italy after unification. The accuracy, coverage and availability of statistical data on the economy were often pivotal to the emergence, nature and expansion of economic history. In Spain, parts of Latin America, India, Africa and elsewhere quantitative economic history was held back by the paucity of reliable figures.

Contributors to the volume have variously indicated, on the one hand, the historic appeal of statistical evidence and analysis in economic history but also the difficulties of applying similar quantitative measures and methods across time and space. Problems start with recognition of the poor quality of data in many regions. In Eastern Europe major historical discontinuities in political regimes coupled with wartime destructions of government records make it difficult to estimate output or national income figures for lengthy periods in the nineteenth and twentieth centuries, hence the reluctance of indigenous scholars to involve themselves in such exercises. Similarly in Africa time series are discontinuous and lack temporal comparability especially for the pre- and post-colonial periods. Elsewhere, political and economic conflicts, the desire for macroeconomic management and the needs of welfare states in the twentieth century drove innovation in statistical collection with knock-on effects upon the discipline. In Britain, Germany and the United States, for example, the needs of the war economy of 1939–45 created a turning point. And where national accounting developed, the methods and approaches of a significant branch of economic history soon followed.

The statistical approach to society, that became embedded in economic history, from the late nineteenth century in many countries, everywhere represents a very different quantitative tradition to that of the later, US-inspired 'new economic history', where deductive methods rather than induction were the touchstone. Most pioneers of the collection and use of historical statistics and those who developed national accounts shared a bias against deductive methods and equilibrium models and even seriously doubted whether market outcomes were optimal either in efficiency or welfare terms (Offer 2008). Part of their motivation was that time series of output, trade and income variables made it easier to address the most pressing issues of historical enquiry, regarding the long-term development of economies, levels of social welfare and the experience of fluctuations. It is no accident that national accounts were pioneered very early in Australia. Motives of social reform or tariff reform commonly lay behind historical statistical endeavour. Statistics were also pivotal, in different ways and using rather different methods, to the central planning of state socialism as in the Soviet bloc and China, and in absolutist regimes, as in Japan 1868–1940.

The so-called new economic history spreading from the USA from the 1970s as well as the current craze for generating global panel data to indicate relative levels and rates of development and growth have indeed had mixed receptions. In Britain the former was very much a minority taste, largely because quantitative analysis had already developed its own way (often associated with state intervention), free of any connection with neoclassical or other economic modelling. In France *histoire sérielle*, arising from the *Annales* School, was based upon the very different foundations of long-run time series rather than equilibrium or market-based frameworks. The same impulse encouraged quantitative approaches in other parts of continental Europe where stochastic elements, such as the impact of climatic fluctuations, wars, epidemics, fires and so on, were often a central concern. In Latin America, particularly Brazil, the approach of *histoire sérielle* was also influential. In the Netherlands historians felt pressured to develop a leading role in cross-national comparative quantitative history in order to regain a central place in analysing the precocious modernization of their own country in comparative perspective. Their specialization in this respect has recently developed outwards (in the CLIO-infra project) from GDP to a wide range of historical developmental indicators covering biological, institutional, environmental and human capital indices. However, doubts may be raised as to the reliability of such indices (often inadequately sourced) and the moral tales they seem to imply – by identifying democracy with western-style political competition for instance. In Belgium, by contrast, despite a strong tradition of quantitative social science, the influence of the *Annales* approach was too strong to allow the new economic history to displace it. Even in the USA itself the cliometric revolution created enormous controversy. As the cliometricians' claims became increasingly didactic the weight of disagreement grew over principles as well as practice. Most internal criticism of cliometrics concerned the quality of the data employed and the difficulties of reducing information to money values at one equilibrium point in time in order to effect social savings calculations that also frequently ignored the possible range of counterfactual responses (Lamoreaux, chapter 3; cf. Cain and Whaples 2013).

The association of US-style quantitative history with rational choice and other neoclassical approaches diminished its appeal in regions of the world with large subsistence and peasant sectors and where western-style market models and profit-maximizing assumptions were difficult to apply. Thus in India, in Japan, in Latin America and in Africa it had few converts. The Russian take-up of quantitative history in the heat of Cold War computer-aided scientific rivalry was marked, although the data and assumptions upon which quantitative exercises were based (state production, shadow pricing) were necessarily different before and even after 1989. Because of the common language of formal models and statistical enquiry, quantitative economic history provided a bridge between Soviet and western historians through exchanges and international conferences and via International Economic History Association networks, that the Russian and East European political authorities found harder than other fields to police. However, this did not prevent a gap emerging between indigenous measures of economic growth and those pursued, often for equally ideological reasons, by the CIA (Borodkin, chapter 12). Measures of growth or well-being have been applied transnationally only with great difficulty and much debate. Major controversy has surrounded the application of orthodox measures of GDP to Africa, for example.[5] And in Latin America the necessity of adjusting the weighted composition of the Human Development Index has been highlighted because in different cultural contexts elements of well-being take on different levels of importance (Bértola and Rodríguez Weber, chapter 20).

Nation state formation, nationalistic history, instrumentalism and ideology

In several countries the rise of economic history was closely related to nation building and associated political economy. In China much early analysis of agriculture, handicrafts, commerce, taxation, consumption and market management, money and prices took place during the process of unification and centralization of the imperial authority before the start of the first millennium. In most of the world such discussions, in different forms, started to take place between the sixteenth and the eighteenth centuries and intensified in the nineteenth and twentieth centuries when modern powerful mixed economy states evolved. State formation was also a main driver of the rise of economic history in twentieth-century command economies where it followed a distinctive path dictated by rigid adherence to a particular vision of the past and the future. In Sweden what Hasselberg (chapter 9) has termed 'the historic compromise' – a nationalistic master narrative of technological innovation, the achievement of social peace and the evolution of the welfare state – is the key event around which the story of economic history (its key preoccupations, its sources and its methods) unfolds.

In other cases, the relation between economic history and nation building appears to be retrospective. History is used rather to make sense of a civilization and contributes to a quest for identity. Nowhere is this more evident than in the Brazilian case, where the concept of 'formation' (*formação*), and the associated search for meaning (*sentido*), became paradigmatic in the period 1930–60 with the works of Caio Prado Jr and Celso Furtado in particular. 'Interpretations' of Brazil (Freyre) and a focus on deep 'roots' (Buarque de Holanda) were also part of what looks like a collective endeavour. By that time, it became clear to Brazilians that the roots of their national identity were in the South Atlantic, in an intermediate space between Africa and America (Alencastro 2000; chapter 22 in this volume). This space, more ideal than geographical, had come into being as an unintended consequence of European violence. Over the centuries, sugar, gold mining and coffee, which dominated the lives of slaves and free men, gradually shifted the country's centre of gravity towards the continental tropics. Braudel, who had taught in São Paulo and admired these works, observed that 'each part of the world mirrors the history of the entire world; it is subjected to it and adapts to it' (1948: 102). For him, who at that time was writing the *Mediterranean*, the South Atlantic became another Mediterranean. Here we can appreciate two different points of view: one internal, the other external. What they have in common is the perspective of a 'long duration' *ante litteram* whereby the past explains the present.

There has always been, and to a degree there remains, a driving need, felt universally, to document and to explain development in ways compatible with nationalist sentiments, with internal and external political changes, and with ideology. What is less predictable is the degree to which the imperative of explanation translates itself into particular methodological frameworks, intellectual traditions and theoretical approaches. Here politics, ideology and intellectual culture are important. Appreciation of the comparative history of economic thought is important for questioning temporal and cultural specificities and biases. In parts of continental Europe and Asia the history of political economy has been more prominent, and established in the educational system, than in the UK or the USA (cf. Backhouse 2004). This may help to account for the strength of universalizing modernization paradigms and free market models in the USA as well as major conflicts between imperialist and anti-imperialist/ nationalist interpretations as found in the historiographies of Southern Europe, including Greece (see Gazi 2012), Middle Eurasia, India, Japan and Latin America.

Taking the Indian historiography as an example, the strength of the nationalist impulse upon subject matter and interpretation in the discipline can be seen to be paramount from the search for an Indian political economy rooted in Indian conditions through colonial and post-colonial debates to subaltern studies and the rejection of new economic history and neoliberal impositions. One might cite the work of the Aligarh School in the 1980s, centred around Irfan Habib of the Aligarh Muslim University. In a controversial hard-hitting and detailed review of Volume II of the *Cambridge Economic History of India* (1983) which had just been published, Habib exposed the bias of a multitude of mostly western contributors, specifically the American Morris D. Morris. The authors had ignored much previous Indian, mostly nationalist but nevertheless serious scholarship, to produce a version of Indian history that entirely downplayed the negative aspects of British domination up to the 1940s. Using a rich array of statistics published by indigenous historians but ignored by Cambridge, Habib exposed the upbeat interpretation of the Tribute between 1757 and 1813; denial of de-industrialization and de-urbanization under the impact of western imports; and the dismissal of stalling per capita income growth and lowered life expectancy of the later nineteenth century. For his generation of Indian historians, the tendency of Anglo-Saxon historians to treat free trade and the munificence of the free market as an act of faith or ideology rather than reason was an important target to be attacked (Habib 1985; cf. Morris 1963).

Tirthankar Roy (2004) criticized the fact that the dominant paradigm guiding research in economic history in India during the second half of the twentieth century had stressed that the market-oriented policies of British colonial rule had led to underdevelopment and poverty. This idea appealed to economists, he argued, because 'it provided independent India's pursuit of socialist policies with an ideological basis'. But after the return to greater free market orientation in the 1990s, 'the compatibility between history and policy was undermined leading to a progressive irrelevance of [economic] history'. He thus urged the discipline to reinvent itself by moving from narratives centred on colonial power to a greater stress on resource-endowments and endogenous growth theory, but one could argue that he was advocating the replacement of one set of questionable tools with another. Not surprisingly, his work has become a target of harsh criticism in India, along with that of the Cambridge School of Eric Stokes (1978) and Christopher Bayly (2012). Their revisionist accounts emphasizing indigenous agency under British rule, highly respected in western academia, are often dubbed 'far-fetched' or even 'neo-colonial' by the current Indian historiographical mainstream. While it is understandable that such overtones cause Roy (2014: 30) considerable disappointment, it is hard to dismiss the historiography of an entire subcontinent as tendentious and unscientific.

Japanese economic historians in the early twentieth century focused much work on the so-called capitalism debate. This included discussion of economic development under feudalism in the late Tokugawa and the question of whether or not the Meiji Restoration could be seen as a bourgeois revolution, ushering in a specific form of Japanese capitalism, rather than marking the transition to a new sort of feudal regime within the absolutist monarchy (Yasuba 1975; Sugihara 1992). For a long time the western-inspired Marxist framework was central to these discussions. But Marxian models were generally applied flexibly with regard to the different environment of Asian culture and prior economic systems, particularly the late development of urbanization. Sensitivity to the specificities of Japanese culture in everyday life, particularly in village manufacturing, also promoted Weberian influence in Japanese economic history associated with the Otsuka School in particular. Following Weber, Hisao Otsuka stressed the embeddedness of economic life and decision-making in the social and cultural environment and emphasized the need for interdisciplinary understandings that took in the ideas and beliefs of actors, including their spiritual ethics and religious motivations.

As in India, western modernization paradigms and free trade/free market models were not seen as appropriate in Japanese economic history and were never popular. For the same reason econometric, as opposed to serial/quantitative, history has never been salient in Japan outside of the economics discipline. Also, as in India, Marxian interpretations appealed most strongly insofar as they could be harnessed to the nationalist view before the Second World War. Indeed some Japanese Marxist social scientists of the 1930s (dubbed turncoats by their peers) shifted neatly from Marxist models of economic subordination to the West, to varieties of nationalist history. As Marx had little to say about economic policy for and by developing nations, or for nations under the sway of more powerful economic actors, the ideas of Friedrich List were found attractive in Japan and elsewhere. List's views not only provided a model for Japanese policy for many years but also influenced the development of economic history (Metzler 2006).

List's framework for a national system of political economy with protectionism, where this was necessitated by unequal exchange, was also influential (partly because of fitting in with development needs) in National Socialist Germany, post-war Latin America, independent India and appealed to Den Xiaoping's post-Mao policies in China. The differential appeal of the model of industrialization via import substitution can be seen in a variety of lights but one is certainly ideological. As Ha-Joon Chang has recently argued, from a Korean perspective, 'the history of capitalism has been so totally re-written that many people in the rich world do not perceive the historical double standards involved in recommending free trade and free market to developing countries' (2007: 16).

The work of Braudel has been a pervasive influence upon the historiographies of large parts of Europe, Latin America and Middle Eurasia. Braudel's concept of total history to include taking account of ecosystems, mentalities and the environment, his rejection of Eurocentrism and the pioneering transnational framework embodied in his Mediterranean study, are all reflected far and wide in global historiographies where they often fitted neatly with anti-colonial and nationalist sentiments. These motives are prominent in the traditions of the Middle East where Braudel's concept of a unity amongst the connected economies of the Mediterranean world brought Ottoman scholarship a new legitimacy. It gave the regions of the former Ottoman Empire (and Qajar Iran) a common platform of analysis that did not depend on concepts of cultural sluggishness, obstructive religious obscurantism or failed states (Islamoglu, chapter 16).

For similar reasons, that is, because of the instrumental and ideological appeal, dependency theory emerged and was promoted in Latin America and had a major impact in Eastern Europe, Middle Eurasia and India during the 1970s to 1990s. Broader links between East and West, North and South are influenced by histories of imperialism, formal and informal, past and present. This has resulted in traditions of intellectual endeavour incorporating superiority/inferiority, dominance/resistance, imperial and anti-imperial stances which are central to the analyses of various chapters of this book.

Openness to external influences

There has been a surprising degree of cross-national and cross-ideological debate and borrowings in our subject. In Japan following the Meiji Restoration the intellectual environment was very open to western influence, and economic history first emerged from the late nineteenth century as a response to western classical economics and the ideal of moral as well as economic progress. The influence of the German Historical School in Japan was encouraged by Japanese scholars admiring and spending time at the great German universities. In China the 'Self-Strengthening Movement' of the early twentieth century deliberately explored and adopted western works starting with Adam Smith. What occurred was a westernization of tools rather than values but this had a profound impact in the absorption of Hegelian dialectics and Marxian historical materialism, although the Rankian School also flourished until China closed itself off from western influence during the Cultural Revolution.

Despite the similar closure of Russian scholarship from the West during the Soviet era, from at least the 1920s and throughout the Cold War many active international dialogues can be identified (see Berg 2015). These contacts owed a great deal to the international outlook and preoccupations of groups of economic historians in Britain and France in particular (Postan, Power, Pirenne, Braudel and others), and were encouraged partly by the migrations of intellectuals from East and Central Europe to the West between the 1880s and the 1940s. A degree of international cooperation arose through the activities of the early and later Annalistes in promoting their interdisciplinary concerns, zeal for statistical series, and regional and global vision beyond French borders. As the *Annales* School grew to become the most powerful force in French history by the 1950s and 1960s and with Braudel at the helm, not only was this internationalism reinforced on an intellectual front but also via active encouragement and funding of scholarships for many Eastern European and Asian historians to spend time at the Ecole des Hautes Etudes en Sciences Sociales (EHESS) and the Maison des Sciences de l'Homme (MSH) in Paris (Burke 1990: 44). A very influential transfer in the years of the Cold War was the influence of the *Annales* in Poland. Thanks to the nature of earlier traditions of Polish research in economic and social history, the French were pushing at an open door. As with most transfers however, the translation of a tradition or set of approaches into a new cultural and political environment did not see these unchanged. In Poland the *Annales* influence did not translate into serial history or into *longue durée* regional studies. Instead epoch-centred studies of estates or towns were the result.

In Latin America strong influences on the development of approaches to economic history arose from dominant traditions of training in either Western Europe or the USA. Many scholars trained in Paris in the 1960s and 1970s taking *Annales* ideas back to analyse Latin American conditions. In Chile the Pinochet Coup resulted in the exile of young intellectuals who were subsequently trained in Britain, Sweden, Cuba and the USA, often with the aid of World University Service awards. Similarly, many native African scholars have trained in France, Britain and Eastern Europe or in the Soviet Union taking dominant ideas from these cultures back with them into a different environment. In recent years, South African universities have attracted a number of Zimbabweans and the economic history of Zimbabwe is being increasingly written there. Such transplants of ideas via higher academic training have however had less impact than one might expect. In Brazil for example indigenous scholars, trained in recent decades in the USA have returned to careers in which they have continued to focus on the preoccupations of their predecessors favouring studies of aspects of Brazilian history over geographically more extensive research and few have adopted orthodox anglophone approaches. Mexico, by acting as an open magnet for scholars fleeing the regional coups and dictatorships of the 1960s to 1980s, drew itself closer to the intellectual mood of the rest of Latin America rather than to that of its nearer neighbour, the USA, from where a significant proportion of its scholars obtained higher degrees (Kuntz Ficker, chapter 21). Japanese scholars after training and or lengthy sojourns in the West have pursued distinctive lines of enquiry and developed research geared, in both methodology and concepts, to Asian conditions. Likewise African scholars have only rarely assimilated the ideas, source priorities and research methods of their western training, particularly when based back in Africa.

The long-term global intellectual impact of the Jewish diasporas of the late nineteenth century, and even more of the 1930s and 1940s, upon economics and history has yet to be fully explored. The chapters in this volume suggest disproportionately large influences throughout the major receiving regions, especially in the United States and illustrated in the personal biographies of many major scholars.[6]

State support and state policy

State socialism has been important in placing a premium on Marxist–Leninist and Maoist historical materialist analyses in which the role of the economy in the historical sciences is paramount. This gave a huge intellectual boost to economic history especially where incorporated into official views that accorded with state policy and perspectives. Economic history in the Soviet Union and in East European satellite states was encouraged by relatively generous state support and, in most countries, before the backlash of the late 1960s, scholars were relatively lightly policed. The fact that they were interested in economic history often gave them the status and the freedom to pursue their research unhindered and even to travel to the West to conferences and to take up scholarships. Furthermore, the advent of state socialism in countries like Poland resulted in the nationalization of archives previously in private hands, particularly those of the great landed estates which encouraged original research with such documents.

Degrees of relative freedom from authoritarianism coupled with existing national histories and intellectual cultures made for considerable variation within the Marxist approaches of the different satellites of the Soviet bloc. In Poland, for example, Malowist, Kula and Topolski all employed Marxist jargon in posing questions but do not seem to have been confined to straitjacket answers, particularly concerning the transition from feudalism to capitalism. This is partly explained by the strength of pre-existing traditions and of prevailing heretic Marxist approaches (including that of Oskar Lange). Kula produced a theory of specifically Eastern European late feudalism where the market sector played a marginal role and devoid of any internal dynamics leading to capitalism. He and Topolski stressed mechanisms locking Eastern Europe into structural reproduction. Economic history elsewhere in Eastern Europe particularly in the later Cold War years suffered greater repression as in the former Czechoslovakia where major figures in the subject lost their jobs in the 1960s and 1970s.

In other contexts ideology and state repression deliberately restricted the scope and approach of the subject as in Russia and China, where historians had to conform to a strict line under state socialism and Maoism. The persecution and imprisonment of Marxist historians by the Fascist regime in 1930s Japan left the field to be dominated by positivists and by the Otsuka school for a generation or so. Persecution and decimation of Jewish intellectuals and Communists in Europe in the 1930s and 1940s had a similar impact. In more subtle ways the ideology of the Cold War and McCarthyism influenced approaches in the United States. It is significant that the expansion of social history in the USA in the 1960s and 1970s was much less tied to Marxist frameworks than elsewhere.

State support for the social sciences and for economic history in particular has been vital in the progress of the subject in western mixed economy contexts, in Belgium after the Second World War for example and in Germany (with Marshall Aid). The 'catch-up' needed in late development of economic history in Spain could only occur with considerable state investment and the growth of cliometrics in the Netherlands has been heavily subsidized by the Dutch Science Foundation (NWO). The booming nature of the subject in Great Britain in the 1960s and 1970s accompanying the expansion of the university sector and investment in social science is also a good example. But in the current global economic crisis, public sector university education in West European neoliberal states is generally under strain, and instrumentalism is paramount. What cannot be justified in terms of direct contribution to economic growth and national income gets a low priority in funding. This biases research plans and research appointments in favour of those who can gain grant support most easily. In Australia the current precipitous decline in economic history can be associated with the priority given to vocational training within social science and business faculties and the consequent marginalization of history. Private sector universities in some countries, particularly in Japan, have been prominent in protecting the discipline from the excesses of state instrumentalism. In other cases (Britain, Germany, Norway and South Africa spring to mind), private financing of commissioned business histories has been important in boosting economic history but with mixed results because it encourages concentration on larger and more successful firms and often includes pressure (at worst censorship) to avoid a negative image.

Institutional factors

Institutional factors impacted strongly on the early history of the field. In some places legal or religious scholars, archivists or numismatists were among the first to analyse historical aspects of the economy bringing particular and enduring perspectives. In other places antiquarian commentators, folklorists, travellers, entrepreneurs and politicians have been prominent in producing formative influential works in the field, limited by their own perspectives and biases but free from the disciplinary boundaries that came to affect so much scholarship after the professionalization of academic life. The varied nature of economic history in different regions derives, to a large extent, from its relationship to economics and to history, as they themselves emerged as identifiable disciplines. A key factor is whether economic history evolved primarily within economics as a discipline and within economics departments, whether it has been allied more closely with business schools or, as is most common throughout Europe and many other parts of the world, whether the subject identifies itself as a branch of history. But these different affiliations are not accidental: they have arisen because of more fundamental elements in national histories and cultures, and hence in national methodological approaches. The spread of particular institutional influences and practices in academia from one part of the globe to another, partly but not solely through cultural hegemony and imperialism, is also relevant here.

At one end of the spectrum is economic history in the United States. The mailing addresses of the Economic History Association (EHA), the major professional organization of economic historians in the United States, suggest that two-thirds are in either economics departments or business schools. Only 8.5 per cent are based in economic history departments but all of these are accounted for by overseas membership. Likewise, three-quarters of those attending Economic History Association meetings in recent years are economists, only around 10 per cent are historians. Perhaps most tellingly, the overwhelming majority of authors publishing articles or notes in the *Journal of Economic History* in recent years are affiliated with departments of economics and/or trained as economists. It is not only that the field is dominated by economists; these economists rarely collaborate or seek advice from historians. Few historians are able to enter into debates with economists on the terms that the latter respect and vice versa. In sum, economic historians in the USA are primarily trained in economics by economists and have the culture of that profession (Whaples 2010).

Within Europe, by contrast, most economic history is sited in history or social science departments, more so now than at any time since the 1980s. It is predominantly pursued by the historical community and is defined by topic rather than by any particularly dominant methodological emphasis. The strongest affiliations institutionally between economic history and economics in Europe are in a restricted number of centres in Britain, Spain and the Netherlands. Elsewhere, modern and contemporary econometric history tends to be practised by economists within economics departments, separate from their colleagues in history, in an unfortunate bifurcation of the subject which allows for insufficient dialogue between economists and historians on particular topics. This notwithstanding, in Germany and Italy, but also in Japan and Latin America, economic history chairs are still found in faculties of economic and social sciences, even when occupied by historians. This reflects the importance that the discipline used to have in contexts once dominated by various forms of historicist or structuralist economics. In some of these countries, the progressive hegemony of the theoretical mainstream is posing a serious threat to the survival of economic history. Even in Australia, which was for a long time a stronghold of post-Keynesian economics, the marginalization of heterodox approaches has been a decisive factor in the recent decline of economic history (see King 2013).

Globalization

In his *Cosmopolitan Islanders* (2009), Richard Evans rebuked continental historians for being too focused on the history of their own countries contrary to their British counterparts whose research interests span across the globe. This objection is relatively common yet surprisingly naive. At the time of Thomas More, when England was still a peripheral country whose comparative advantage appeared to reside in sheep rearing, looking across the Channel was a practical need. The new interest in cosmopolitan matters that the British have developed over the past two centuries is largely a reflection of their changed geopolitical role, hence the founding of chairs in 'Imperial and Naval History' that survive to this day. By contrast, cultures evolving within well-delimited land borders, and in a context of continuous exchange with their neighbours, have tended to focus on regional specificities. This is why, for example, we find so much *Volkstumsgeschichte* or 'ethnic history' in Germany and Hungary. However, the fondness of 'the local' which many of the world's historiographies have in common, defined as a primary orientation to the problems and interests suggested by geographical proximity, by no means implies that this kind of research must have a provincial character. A comparative element is almost always implicit and in some cases is paramount. Thus, as Kochanowicz demonstrates, for example, key Polish works whilst focusing upon Polish evidence placed their analysis in a much broader European and global framework making it relevant to understanding geographically much wider processes of change.

If Japan's intellectual openness to external influences has had something of a chequered history, it is hard to imagine a more closed academic environment than that of the German Democratic Republic (GDR). Yet in both contexts, the need to reflect on the transition from feudalism to modernity arose from the encounter/clash with the West that had occurred one century earlier: an encounter affecting the social as much as the political spheres of late Tokugawa Japan and nineteenth-century Prussia. The idea of a 'Prussian way' (*preußische Weg*) to capitalism, which Jürgen Kuczynski borrowed from Lenin, became a model to explain the 'strange' alliance of interests between a landed aristocracy and the bourgeoisie in the 'Junker state' (Hobsbawm 1977: 182). Its characterization as 'Prussian' implicitly entails a comparison with the English or French way, whereby modernity emerged from the radical opposition between the two classes leading to the ultimate triumph of a liberal bourgeoisie. For the likes of Kuczynski, Emilio Sereni, and Gramsci before them, it was important to understand not only what were the prospects for socialism but also where Fascism had come from.

The age of global trade and finance, the internet and the transfer of information electronically, and the current era of global academic exchange and publications, might be expected to result in a convergence or consensus of thinking in particular disciplines concerning research priorities and methodologies. To a degree this is the case. Many scholars of the current generation in the southern hemisphere, Asia and even continental Europe receive degrees in Britain or the USA. The prestige of Anglo-American journals has attracted a subset of Spanish economic historians to high profile research on the growth process but this only accounts for a small part of the Spanish research. The continued global variation of perspectives and approaches in the humanities in general and in history, including much economic history, suggests the importance of long-embedded cultural and intellectual differences of perspective which we should explore and respect.

In economic history, contemporary globalization has given global history a high priority in research, particularly the need to understand the rise of the modern Asian economies, especially China, and the timing and nature of the Great Divergence, even when the usefulness of this concept might be questioned. The debate has called forth new estimates of long-run growth differentials between different European countries as well as between East and West. A major challenge from an Asian perspective has been mounted upon interpretations that are based upon acceptance of western precocity in finding the optimal route to long-term economic development. This challenge is indicative of the sorts of insights to be gained from alternative perspectives. In particular, Japanese scholarship has shown that much of the economic progress made during the later nineteenth century was not just based upon the adoption of foreign technology but upon the indigenous development of labour-intensive industries, labour-absorbing institutions and culturally specific technological adaptations and innovations. In Meiji Japan capital was substituted for labour but industrialization remained labour intensive in a way similar to the dominant patterns of industrialization in the contemporary world. In a challenge to western ideas about global development past and future, Sugihara maintains that East Asia would not have industrialized without western influence but 'it was the East Asian path of economic development that made it possible for the majority of the world's population to benefit from global industrialization' (2003: 81). New perspectives on Chinese and Korean development histories have similarly highlighted very different growth patterns and the need for different methodologies and approaches for understanding these together with the implications of contemporary high-speed growth for rethinking older and deeply ingrained assumptions about the superiority of western culture.

Methodological implications

As N. G. Butlin argued in 1964, Australia 'was not a footnote to the Industrial Revolution nor was [it] a sheep-walk for the benefit of British imperialism' (quoted in Meredith and Oxley, chapter 5). Australian history had suffered from such intellectual impositions. Similarly Spanish economic history has been shackled by the concepts of 'backwardness' and path dependency. It is not alone in this respect but recent sidelining of the concept in Spain has opened up research to alternative paths and the specifics of the Spanish developmental trajectory (Iriarte-Goñi, chapter 10). The emphasis upon path dependency and a unilinear perspective in the analysis of comparative economic growth by economic historians in the Netherlands is described by Bosma (section II of chapter 11) as more problematic for the subject there than the faith in cliometrics. Meanwhile in China economic history has currently stalled because 'scholars are not sure to what extent either the so far dominant Marxist scholarship or the newly introduced Western categories, concepts and tools can deal with Chinese experience' (Li Bozhong, chapter 18). A more genuine understanding of intellectual contexts may lead to greater caution in the lending and borrowing of historical categories and their application to distant world regions.

Problems have attended the application of the proto-industrialization thesis away from the household manufacture of consumer goods towards the very different context of the early modern producer goods sector, as with its use in relation to the iron industry of Sweden. Here the model was adapted to the Swedish master narrative that sited the source of dynamism of the economy in the entrepreneurship, skills and technological knowledge of eighteenth-century iron making. The framework of a theory first conceived as industrialization before industrialization also fits awkwardly in its application to village manufacture in Japan and to the sweated industries of industrialized Europe and America or modern East Asia. Likewise, the transposition of ideas about forced labour and 'market' exchanges, arising from earlier debates about the nature of serfdom and feudalism, to the world of slave plantations, indentured labour or the Gulag is profitable only with considerable sensitivity to time and place, without which such transpositions can be distorting or entirely misleading. This is the case especially when the natures of original concepts are adapted to cope with what one might term 'mission creep'.

For example, take the concept of 'industrious revolution', coined in 1976 by the Japanese historian and demographer Akira Hayami. It was intended as a tool to explain what would come to be known as the East Asian path of development. The transposition of the model to the seventeenth- and eighteenth-century Netherlands (De Vries 2008), has introduced elements, such as the response to market incentives and the household allocation of time according to Beckerian principles, that are quite alien to the original concept. In his recent reappraisal of the subject, Hayami observed that the term had 'started a journey of its own' and that the thesis of a particular kind of continuum between the industrious revolution and the industrial revolution 'differs from the author's original idea'. More importantly, he stressed that Japanese industriousness rested on neither utilitarian calculation nor religious drive but on a work ethic or 'mentalité' transmitted 'from parent to child, and from child to grandchild' (2015: 95–6, 103). This lay behind the very different pattern of labour-intensive rather than capital-intensive industrialization experienced in many parts of Asia in the twentieth century. Can we now think of reintroducing the 'westernized' version of the concept back to Asia and into the Great Divergence debate presenting it as a yardstick for 'reciprocal comparisons' (Saito 2010; De Vries 2011)? Of course not.

Ideas about the industrious revolution in the West, particularly in the work of De Vries, have been pivotal in creating debate and stimulating new research in the anglophone sphere but the extent to which these notions have diverged from their original conceptualization and the degree to which they have been put to different work is too little acknowledged. Transnational borrowings are vital to the task ahead but only with greater sensitivity to these elements. For example, the extent to which labour-intensive industrialization lay at the heart of industrialization in Britain and other parts of Western Europe has been hidden by stress in the master narrative upon the rise of energy and capital-intensive mass production. Yet the Factory was never the dominant form of manufacture even in Britain. Labour and skill-intensive activities expanded alongside centralized and mechanized work often though not always via subcontracting. Labour intensity was at the heart of the financial sector until the computer age and remains central to most of the service sector today. Much technological advance, during the industrial revolution and since, was not labour saving. These facts help to explain the slow growth of labour productivity in the British economy in the early nineteenth century. And partly because the labour-intensive sector was less well recorded and taxed, it also helps to explain the slow rise of GDP per capita, at the height of the classic industrial revolution, that has so puzzled scholars. Western historiography could thus learn much from ideas about labour-intensive industrialization in Asia and the capacity this creates past and present both for exploitation and sweating but also for reducing underemployment, increasing employment and thus for spreading the benefits of manufacturing advance across a broad swathe of the population.

The approaches of Latin American structuralism in the 1960s warned scholars from the northern hemisphere against the perils of applying western growth models to the Global South. Equally distant from both neoclassical and crude Marxist interpretations of underdevelopment – the opposite poles of what Albert O. Hirschman (1981) once termed the 'monoeconomics' – Latin American economists and historians challenged the principle of comparative advantage that is still at the root of mainstream textbooks on international trade. They also disproved the identification of economic growth with development posited by the neoclassical production function (a controversial model devised to describe mature economies, but of no use for analysing structural change). Their emphasis on long-term dynamics, which requires interdisciplinary rather than mechanistic approaches, has not yet exhausted its potential, despite being ostracized since the late 1970s, when the Southern Cone entered the dark age of military dictatorships, and subsequently by the Washington Consensus. The high level of sophistication with which Celso Furtado, Tulio Halperìn Donghi, Osvaldo Sunkel, and the two generations of scholars they inspired, addressed the interplay of international and domestic forces, of material elements and socio-cultural variables, represents an antidote to one-size-fits-all explanations of development.

Several chapters in the volume call into question interpretations of categories like 'capitalism' and 'market', as a result of the self-reflexive exercise carried out from the standpoint of national and regional experiences. The most striking example is probably China, but the historiography of Middle Eurasia, too, has much to say on this. Western scholarship is notoriously divided on the matter. Jack Goody (2004) argues that capitalism is not specifically European, but he does so at the cost of employing a definition so loose and diluted as to be of limited analytic significance. For Giovanni Arrighi (2007), on the contrary, China demonstrates that a market economy can exist independently of capitalism. This thesis rests on Braudel's idea (1977) that market and capitalism are different in nature and goals. Yet another view is associated with Polanyi (1957) who maintained that, while different allocation systems typically coexist in any socioeconomic formation, capitalism is characterized by a relative *prevalence* of markets over reciprocity and redistribution. What we have learned from the Chinese and Middle Eastern stories seems to confirm this view that markets can flourish even in contexts where a self-regulated market economy is absent, but only the latter is intrinsically tied to capitalism.

The historicization of capitalism and indeed of the terms, categories and language that 'modern economic growth' has generated (Grenier, chapter 7; see also Perrot 1992) brings us to the last fundamental lesson that we can draw from the chapters, which is one about rationality and economic behaviour. As usual, the 'margin', as epitomized by Witold Kula and Polish historiography, was at the vanguard in this respect. The classic alternative to the Anglo-Saxon rational choice model dates back to Weber and the German Historical School. They described economic activity carried out outside of capitalist contexts, including in early modern Europe, as 'less rational' compared to the modern West. Lucien Febvre (1942), one of the founders of *Annales*, qualified this hypothesis by arguing that the degree to which humans develop instrumental precision depends on the environment to which they need to adapt. Although the view that market societies stimulate 'calculative reason' has recently been reasserted in anthropology (Gudeman 2008), the relationship is neither automatic nor can it be generalized. Kula (1962), seeking to analyse non-capitalist systems, developed a historical model of what we might call 'contextual rationality'. He showed that, in societies where wealth acquisition is of secondary importance, actors express their rationality in pursuing goals like the achievement of status or free time. The conclusion is straightforward: economic behaviour can be rational without being utilitarian. Another equation of the 'monoeconomics' gets demolished. This is what global economic history at its best can achieve.

Notes

1 We are particularly pleased that so many persecuted writers and their ideas get attention in this volume, as a reminder of innovations and arguments that have too often been sidelined purely for ideological reasons. We hope that sections of the book bear some witness to their integrity.

2 United Nations Economic Commission for Latin America.

3 Unless otherwise indicated, all of the points and illustrations used in the following pages are drawn from the specific chapter presented in the volume.

4 See, for example, Cullen (1975), Mackenzie (1981), Desrosières (1993), Porter (1995), Patriarca (1996).

5 See discussion of the problem in chapter 1.

6 Among them, K. Polanyi, M. M. Postan, A. Gerschenkron, R. S. Lopez, A. O. Hirschman, W. W. Rostow and many others.

References

Alencastro, Luiz Felipe de. 2000. *O trato dos viventes. Formação do Brasil no Atlântico Sul, séculos XVI e XVII.* São Paulo: Companhia das Letras.

Arrighi, Giovanni. 2007. *Adam Smith in Beijing: Lineages of the Twenty-first Century.* London: Verso.

Backhouse, Roger E. 2004. 'History of Economics, Economics and Economic History in Britain, 1824–2000' *European Journal of the History of Economic Thought* 11.1, 107–27.

Bayly, C. A. 2012. *Rulers, Townsmen and Bazaars: North Indian Society in the Age of British Expansion, 1770–1870.* 3rd edn. Oxford: Oxford University Press.

Berg, Maxine. 2015. 'East–West Dialogues: Economic Historians, the Cold War, and Détente' *Journal of Modern History* 87.1, 36–71.

Braudel, Fernand. 1948. 'Au Brésil: deux livres de Caio Prado' *Annales ESC* 3.1, 99–103.

Braudel, Fernand. 1977. *Afterthoughts on Material Civilization and Capitalism.* Baltimore, MD: Johns Hopkins University Press.

Burke, Peter. 1990. *The French Historical Revolution: The Annales School, 1929–1989.* Cambridge: Polity.

Cain, Louis P. and Robert Whaples. 2013. 'Economic History and Cliometrics', in *Routledge Handbook of Modern Economic History*, ed. by Robert M. Whaples and Randall E. Parker. London: Routledge, 3–13.

Cambridge Economic History of India, vol. 2: *c. 1757–c. 1970*, ed. by Dharma Kumar and Meghnad Desai. Cambridge: Cambridge University Press, 1983.

Chang, Ha-Joon. 2007. *Bad Samaritans: Rich Nations, Poor Policies and the Threat to the Developing World.* London: Random House.

Cullen, M. J. 1975. *The Statistical Movement in Early Victorian Britain: The Foundations of Empirical Social Research.* Hassocks: Harvester Press.

Desrosières, Alain. 1993. *The Politics of Large Numbers: A History of Statistical Reasoning.* Cambridge, MA: Harvard University Press, 1998.

De Vries, Jan. 2008. *The Industrious Revolution: Consumer Behavior and the Household Economy, 1650 to the Present.* Cambridge: Cambridge University Press.

De Vries, Jan. 2011 'Industrious Peasants in East and West: Markets, Technology, and Family Structure in Japanese and Western European Agriculture' *Australian Economic History Review* 51.2, 107–19.

Evans, Richard J. 2009. *Cosmopolitan Islanders: British Historians and the European Continent.* Cambridge: Cambridge University Press.

Febvre, Lucien. 1942. *The Problem of Unbelief in the Sixteenth Century: The Religion of Rabelais.* Cambridge, MA: Harvard University Press, 1982.

Gazi, Effi. 2012. 'Reflections on Marxist Historiography in the Eastern Mediterranean: Examples from Greece, Italy and Turkey' *Storia della Storiografia* 62.2, 95–103.

Goody, Jack. 2004. *Capitalism and Modernity: The Great Debate.* Cambridge: Polity.

Gudeman, Stephen. 2008. *Economy's Tension: The Dialectics of Community and Market.* Oxford: Berghahn.

Habib, Irfan. 1985. 'Studying a Colonial Economy – Without Perceiving Colonialism' *Modern Asian Studies* 19.3, 355–81.

Hayami, Akira. 2015. *Japan's Industrious Revolution: Economic and Social Transformations in the Early Modern Period.* Tokyo: Springer.

Hirschman, Albert O. 1981. 'The Rise and Decline of Development Economics', in *Essays in Trespassing: Economics to Politics and Beyond.* Cambridge: Cambridge University Press, 1–24.

Hobsbawm, Eric J. 1977. *The Age of Capital, 1848–1875.* London: Abacus.

King, J. E. 2013. 'A Case for Pluralism in Economics' *Economic and Labour Relations Review* 24.1, 17–31.

Kula, Witold. 1962. *An Economic Theory of the Feudal System: Towards a Model of the Polish Economy, 1500–1800.* London: NLB, 1976.

Lyons, John S., Louis P. Cain and Samuel H. Williamson, eds. 2008. *Reflections on the Cliometrics Revolution: Conversations with Economic Historians.* London: Routledge.

Mackenzie, Donald A. 1981. *Statistics in Britain, 1865–1930: The Social Construction of Scientific Knowledge.* Edinburgh: Edinburgh University Press.

Metzler, Mark. 2006. 'The Cosmopolitanism of National Economics: Friedrich List in a Japanese Mirror', in *Global History: Interactions between the Universal and the Local*, ed. by A. G. Hopkins. Basingstoke: Palgrave Macmillan, 98–130.

Morris, Morris D. 1963. 'Towards a Reinterpretation of Nineteenth-Century Indian Economic History' *Journal of Economic History* 23.4, 606–18.

Offer, Avner. 2008. 'Charles Feinstein, 1932–2004', in *Proceedings of the British Academy*, vol. 153 (Biographical Memoirs of Fellows, VII), 189–212.

Patriarca, Silvana. 1996. *Numbers and Nationhood: Writing Statistics in Nineteenth-Century Italy*. Cambridge: Cambridge University Press.

Perrot, Jean-Claude. 1992. *Une histoire intellectuelle de l'économie politique, XVIIe–XVIIIe siècle*. Paris: Editions de l'EHESS.

Polanyi, Karl. 1944. *The Great Transformation: The Political and Economic Origins of Our Time*. Boston, MA: Beacon Press, 1957.

Polanyi, Karl. 1957. 'The Economy as Instituted Process', in *Trade and Market in the Early Empires: Economies in History and Theory*, ed. by Karl Polanyi, Conrad M. Arensberg and Harry W. Pearson. Glencoe, IL: Free Press, 243–70.

Porter, Theodore M. 1995. *Trust in Numbers: The Pursuit of Objectivity in Science and Public Life*. Princeton, NJ: Princeton University Press.

Roy, Tirthankar. 2004. 'Economic History: An Endangered Discipline' *Economic and Political Weekly* 39.29, 3238–43.

Roy, Tirthankar. 2014. 'The Rise and Fall of Indian Economic History, 1920–2013' *Economic History of Developing Regions* 29.1, 15–41.

Saito, Osamu. 2010. 'An Industrious Revolution in an East Asian Market Economy? Tokugawa Japan and Implications for the Great Divergence' *Australian Economic History Review* 50.3, 240–61.

Stokes, Eric. 1978. *The Peasant and the Raj: Studies in Agrarian Society and Peasant Rebellion in Colonial India*. Cambridge: Cambridge University Press.

Sugihara, Kaoru. 1992. 'The Japanese Capitalism Debate, 1927–1937', in *Agrarian Structure and Economic Development: Landed Property in Bengal and Theories of Capitalism in Japan*, ed. by Peter Robb (Occasional Papers in Third-World Economic History, no. 4). London: SOAS, 24–33.

Sugihara, Kaoru. 2003. 'The East Asian Path of Economic Development: A Long-Term Perspective' in *The Resurgence of East Asia: 500, 150 and 50 Year Perspectives*, ed. by Giovanni Arrighi, Takeshi Hamashita and Mark Selden. London: Routledge, 78–123.

Whaples, Robert. 2010. 'Is Economic History a Neglected Field of Study?' *Historically Speaking* 11.2, 17–20.

Yasuba, Yasukichi. 1975. 'Anatomy of the Debate on Japanese Capitalism' *Journal of Japanese Studies* 2.1, 63–82.

INDEX

Locators in *italics* indicate figures and tables